Chapter-wise
Topical Objective
Study Package *for*

CBSE 2022 Class 12 Term I

Mathematics

www.dishapublication.com

Books & ebooks for School & Competitive Exams

www.mylearninggraph.com

Etests for Competitive Exams

Write to us at **feedback_disha@aiets.co.in**

Contents

1. RELATIONS AND FUNCTIONS — 1-30

2. INVERSE TRIGONOMETRIC FUNCTIONS — 31-44

3. MATRICES — 45-84

4. DETERMINANTS — 85-123

5. CONTINUITY AND DIFFERENTIABILITY — 124-183

6. APPLICATION OF DERIVATIVES — 184-233

7. LINEAR PROGRAMMING — 234-248

Concept Map

RELATIONS AND FUNCTIONS

① Relation

A relation from a non-empty set A to itself is a subset of cartesian product $A \times A$.

Relation from a set A to set B is a subset of cartesian product $A \times B$.

② Types of Relations

Empty relation is the relation R in a set A, in which no element of A is related to any element of A, i.e., $R = \phi \subset A \times A$.

Universal relation is the relation R in a set A, in which each element of A is related to every element of A, i.e., $R = A \times A$.

Reflexive relation : $(a, a) \in R$, for every $a \in A$

Symmetric relation : $(a_1, a_2) \in R$ implies that $(a_2, a_1) \in R$, for all $a_1, a_2 \in A$

Transitive relation : $(a_1, a_2) \in R$ & $(a_2, a_3) \in R$ implies that $(a_1, a_3) \in R$, for all $a_1, a_2, a_3 \in A$

Equivalence relation : A relation R in a set A is said to be an equivalence relation if R is reflexive, symmetric & transitive.

Equivalence class {a} containing $a \in A$ for an equivalence relation R in A is a subset of A containing all elements b related to a.

③ Function

For any two non-empty sets X & Y, a function f is a rule or mapping which associates each element of set X to a unique element in set Y.

④ Types of Functions

One-one function : A function $f : X \to Y$ is one-one (or injective) if
$f(x_1) = f(x_2) \Rightarrow x_1 = x_2, \forall\, x_1, x_2 \in X$.
Otherwise, f is called many-one.

Onto function : A function is onto (or surjective) if for every $y \in Y$, there exists an element x in X such that $f(x) = y$

Into function : A function $f : X \to Y$ is into if there exists atleast one element in Y which has no pre-image in A.

One-one & onto function : A function $f : X \to Y$ is said to be one-one & onto (or bijective) if f is both one-one & onto.

Topic 1   Relations and Types of Relations

RECAPITULATION

In this section, we will recall some definitions which have been discussed in earlier class.

ORDERED PAIR

A pair of objects (elements) taken (listed) in a definite (specific) order is known as an ordered pair. In the ordered pair (a_i, b_i), a_i is known as first element and b_i is known as second element.

EQUALITY OF ORDERED PAIRS

Two ordered pairs (a_1, b_1) and (a_2, b_2) are equal iff $a_1 = a_2$ and $b_1 = b_2$

CARTESIAN PRODUCT

Let A and B be two non-empty sets, then the set of all distinct ordered pair of the form (a_i, b_i) is called cartesian product of A and B and is denoted by $A \times B$. i.e. $A \times B = \{(a_i, b_i) : a_i \in A \text{ and } b_i \in B\}$

Note that If $A = \phi$, $B = \phi$ then $A \times B = \phi$.

Example : If $A = \{1, 2, 3\}$ and $B = \{a, b\}$, then $A \times B = \{1, 2, 3\} \times \{a, b\} = \{(1, a), (1, b), (2, a), (2, b), (3, a), (3, b)\}$.

RELATIONS

Let A and B denote the sets of all male and female members in the Royal family of Dasrath's Kingdom. Clearly, A = {Dasrath, Ram, Laxman, Shatrughan, Bharat} and B = {Kaushaliya, Kaikai, Sumitra, Sita, Urmila, Shrutkriti, Mandvi}

If we wrote R for the relation "was husband of" then the fact that Dasrath was husband of Kaushalya, Kaikai and Sumitra, Ram was husband of Sita and so on. It can be represented as: Dasrath R Kaushalya, Dasrath R Kaikai, Dasrath R Sumitra, Ram R Sita, ..., ...

Now, if we omit the letter 'R' between the pairs of names and wrote them as ordered pairs, then the above fact can also be written as a set R of ordered pairs where

R = {(Dasrath, Kaushaliya), (Dasrath, Kaikai), (Dasrath, Sumitra), (Ram, Sita), ...}

Clearly, $R \subseteq A \times B$ i.e. $(a, b) \in R$ iff a R b. Keeping this example in mind we may define a **relation** as follows:

Relations: Let A and B be two non-empty sets then every subset of $A \times B$ defines a relation from A to B and every relation from A to B is a subset of $A \times B$.

Let $R \subseteq A \times B$ and $(a, b) \in R$, then we say that a is related to b by the relation R and written as aRb. $(a, b) \notin R$ as a $\cancel{R}$ b.

Domain (D) and Range (R) of a Relation

If R be a relation from A to B then the set of first entries of all ordered pairs in R is called **domain**. Set of all second entries in R is called Range of R. Finally we say $D \subseteq A$ and $R \subseteq B$.

Example: If $A = \{1, 3, 5, 7\}$, $B = \{2, 4, 6, 8, 10\}$ and let $R = \{(1, 8), (3, 6), (5, 2), (1, 4)\}$ be a relation from A to B then, Dom (R) = $\{1, 3, 5\}$ and Range (R) = $\{8, 6, 2, 4\}$.

Relation on a Set Itself

Let A be a non-void set, then a relation from a set A to itself i.e. a subset of $A \times A$ is called a relation on set A.

NUMBER OF RELATION

Let A and B be two non-empty finite sets having m and n elements respectively then no. of ordered pair in $A \times B$ are $m \times n$.

So, no. of subset of $A \times B = 2^{m \times n}$

i.e. no. of Relation from A to B $= 2^{mn}$

Note that no. of non-empty relation $= 2^{mn} - 1$

TYPES OF RELATION

(i)   **Universal Relation:** A relation R in a set A is called **universal** relation if $R = A \times A$

     i.e. if $A = \{1, 2\}$, then universal relation in A = $\{(1, 1), (1, 2), (2, 1), (2, 2)\}$.

(ii)   **Void Relation or Empty Relation :** A relation R in a set A is called **empty** relation, if no element of A is related to any element of A. i.e. $R = \phi \subset A \times A$

     Note that empty relation and universal relation are some times called **trivial** relations.

SPECIAL TYPES OF RELATIONS

(i) **Reflexive Relation:** A relation R in a set A is called a reflexive relation if each element of set A is related to itself we denote it as a R a $\forall$ a $\in$ A

i.e. A = $\{2, 7, 8\}$ then a relation R = $\{(2, 2), (2, 7), (2, 8), (7, 7), (8, 8)\}$ is reflexive on set A

But $R_1 = \{(2, 2), (7, 8), (7, 2), (8, 2)\}$ is not reflexive on set A because $7 \in A$ but $(7, 7) \notin R_1$.

(ii) **Symmetric Relation:** A relation R is said to be symmetric if a R b $\Rightarrow$ b R a.

The necessary and sufficient condition that a relation R in set A be symmetric is that $R = R^{-1}$.

As for example : Let L be the set of all lines in a plane and let R be a relation defined on L by the rule $(a, b) \in R \Leftrightarrow$ a is $\perp$r to b then R is symmetric relation on L, because $L_1 \perp r \, L_2 \Rightarrow L_2 \perp r \, L_1$

i.e. $(L_1, L_2) \in R \Rightarrow (L_2, L_1) \in R$.

(iii) **Transitive Relation :** R is called a transitive relation if $(a, b) \in R$ and $(b, c) \in R \Rightarrow (a, c) \in R$

(iv) **Equivalence Relation :** Any relation on a set A which is 'reflexive', 'symmetric' and 'transitive' is called an equivalence relation.

Illustration :

Show that the relation R in the set Z of integers given by R = $\{(a, b) : 2$ divides $a - b\}$ is equivalence relation.

Sol. Let a, b, c $\in$ Z

Reflexivity : $\because$ $a - a = 0$ is divisible by 2

$\therefore$ $(a, a) \in R$

So, R is reflexive

Symmetry : Let $(a, b) \in R$

$\Rightarrow$ $a - b$ is divisible by 2

$\Rightarrow$ $-(b - a)$ is divisible by 2

$\Rightarrow$ $b - a$ is divisible by 2

$\Rightarrow$ $(b, a) \in R$

So, R is symmetric

Transitivity : Let $(a, b) \in R$

$\Rightarrow$ $a - b$ is divisible by 2

$\Rightarrow$ $a - b = 2 k_1$ ..... (i)

and $(b, c) \in R$

$\Rightarrow$ $b - c$ is divisible by 2

$\Rightarrow$ $b - c = 2 k_2$ ..... (ii)

On adding eqns. (i) and (ii), we get

$a - c = 2(k_1 + k_2)$ is divisible by 2

$\therefore$ $(a, c) \in R$

So, R is transitive

Hence, R is equivalence relation.

Illustration :

Check whether the relation R on R defined by R = $\{(a, b) : 1 + ab > 0\}$ is reflexive, symmetric or transitive.

Sol. Since $1 + a^2 > 0$

$\therefore$ $(a, a) \in R$

so, R is reflexive

Let $(a, b) \in R \Rightarrow 1 + ab > 0$

$\Rightarrow$ $1 + ba > 0$ $[\because ab = ba]$

$\Rightarrow$ $(b, a) \in R$

so, R is symmetric.

$\because$ $1 + 2 \times \left(-\dfrac{1}{4}\right) > 0 \Rightarrow \left(2, -\dfrac{1}{4}\right) \in R$

and $1 + \left(-\dfrac{1}{4}\right)(-4) > 0 \Rightarrow \left(-\dfrac{1}{4}, -4\right) \in R$

But $1 + 2 \times (-4) \not> 0 \Rightarrow (2, -4) \notin R$

Practice Exercise-1

Multiple Choice Questions

1. Let $P = \{(x, y) \mid x^2 + y^2 = 1, x, y \in R\}$. Then, P is
   (a) Reflexive　　　　(b) Symmetric
   (c) Transitive　　　　(d) Anti-symmetric

2. For real numbers x and y, we write $x\,R\,y \Leftrightarrow x - y + \sqrt{2}$ is an irrational number. Then, the relation R is
   (a) Reflexive　　　　(b) Symmetric
   (c) Transitive　　　　(d) None of these

3. Let L denote the set of all straight lines in a plane. Let a relation R be defined by $\alpha\,R\,\beta \Leftrightarrow \alpha \perp \beta, \alpha, \beta \in L$. Then, R is
   (a) Reflexive　　　　(b) Symmetric
   (c) Transitive　　　　(d) None of these

4. Let S be the set of all real numbers. Then, the relation $R = \{(a, b) : 1 + ab > 0\}$ on S is
   (a) Reflexive and symmetric but not transitive
   (b) Reflexive and transitive but not symmetric
   (c) Symmetric, transitive but not reflexive
   (d) Reflexive, transitive and symmetric

5. The relation $R = \{(1, 1), (2, 2), (3, 3)\}$ on the set $\{1, 2, 3\}$ is :
   (a) symmetric only　　　(b) reflexive only
   (c) an equivalence relation　(d) transitive only

Case/Passage Based Question

DIRECTIONS (Q. 6) : *has 5 subparts based on Case/Passage given, attempt any 4 out of 5 questions.*

6. For sport day activity the class teacher of class-XII measures the weight of students. The set of their weight is given as $W = \{40, 41, 42, 43, 44, 45, 46, 47, 48, 49, 50\}$.

Based on the above information answer the following:

(i) If the relation R in set W define as
   $R = \{(x, y) : |x - y| = 1\}$ then R is
   (a) Reflexive　　　　(b) Symmetric
   (c) Transitive　　　　(d) Equivalence

(ii) If the relation R in set W define as
   $R = \{(x, y): x > y\}$ then R is
   (a) Reflexive　　　　(b) Symmetric
   (c) Transitive　　　　(d) Equivalence

(iii) The number of relations from W to W are
   (a) 100　　　　　　(b) 20
   (c) 2^{100}　　　　　(d) 2^{121}

(iv) The number of non-empty relation from W to W are
   (a) 2^{10}　　　　　(b) 2^{100}
   (c) $2^{121} - 1$　　　(d) 99

(v) If set A have m and set B have n elements then number of ordered pair $A \times B$ is
   (a) $m + n$　　　　　(b) mn
   (c) 2^{mn}　　　　　(d) m^n

One Word Questions

7. For the set $A = \{1, 2, 3\}$, define a relation R in the set A as follows $R = \{(1, 1), (2, 2), (3, 3), (1, 3)\}$. Then, find the ordered pair to be added to R to make it the smallest equivalence relation.

8. Let $A = \{1, 2, 3\}$ and $R = \{(1, 2), (2, 3)\}$ be a relation in A. Then, find the minimum number of ordered pairs may be added, so that R becomes an equivalence relation

9. Let $A = \{1, 2, 3\}$. Then find the number of relations containing $(1, 2)$ and $(1, 3)$, which are reflexive and symmetric but not transitive.

Very Short Answer Questions

10. Let R be a relation on the set N be defined by $\{(x, y) : x, y \in N, 2x + y = 41\}$. Then define R.

11. Consider the relation ϕ on a non-empty set A then define ϕ.

12. For the set $A = \{1, 2, 3\}$, define a relation R in the set A as follows :

    $R = \{(1, 1), (2, 2), (3, 3), (1, 3)\}$

    Write the ordered pairs to be added to R to make it the smallest equivalence relation.

13. Let R be the equivalence relation in the set Z of integers given by

    $R = \{(a, b) : 2 \text{ divides } a - b\}$. Write the equivalence class [0]

14. If $R = \{(1, 3), (4, 2), (2, 4), (2, 3), (3, 1)\}$ be a relation in set $A = \{1, 2, 3, 4\}$. Is the relation R symmetric?

Short Answer Questions

15. Show that the relation R in the set $\{1, 2, 3, 4\}$ given by $R = \{(1, 1), (2, 2), (3, 3), (4, 4), (1, 2), (2, 1), (1, 4), (4, 1), (3, 4), (4, 3)\}$ is reflexive, symmetric but not transitive.

16. Show that the relation R is a set of members of a family is defined by $R = \{(a, b): a \text{ and } b \text{ live in the same building}\}$.

17. Show that the relation R in the set z of integers defined by $R = \{(a, b): 3 \text{ divides } a - b\}$ is an equivalence relation.

18. Give example of a relation which are
    (i) symmetric but neither reflexive nor transitive.
    (ii) reflexive and transitive but not symmetric.

19. Determine whether R in the set $A = \{1, 2, 3, 4\}$ defined by $R = \{(a, b) : |a - b| \text{ is odd}\}$ is an equivalence relation. Justify your answer.

20. Let A = set of workers in a publication house. Let $a\,R\,b$, if and only if a and b tell lie ; $a, b \in A$
    (i) Is R symmetric relation ?
    (ii) Is this relation an equivalence relation?

21. Let A = a set of people.

Let a R b if and only if a and b are brothers.

(i) Is the relation reflexive?

(ii) Is the relation symmetric ?

(iii) Is the relation an equivalence relation ?

22. Let A = set of boys of class XII in some school. Let a R b, if and only if a and b use unfair means in the exam; a, b ∈ A.

Is R a transitive relation?

NCERT Exercise-1

1. Determine whether each of the following relations are reflexive, symmetric and transitive:

(i) Relation R in the set A = {1, 2, 3, ..., 13, 14} defined as R = {(x, y) : 3x − y = 0}

(ii) Relation R in the set N of natural numbers defined as R = {(x, y) : y = x + 5 and x < 4}

(iii) Relation R in the set A = {1, 2, 3, 4, 5, 6} as R = {(x, y) : y is divisible by x}

(iv) Relation R in the set Z of all integers defined as R = {(x, y) : x − y is an integer}

(v) Relation R in the set A of human beings in a town at a particular time given by

(a) R = {(x, y) : x and y work at the same place}

(b) R = {(x, y) : x and y live in the same locality}

(c) R = {(x, y) : x is exactly 7 cm taller than y}

(d) R = {(x, y) : x is wife of y}

(e) R = {(x, y) : x is father of y}

2. Show that the relation R in the set R of real numbers, defined as

R = {(a, b) : a ≤ b²} is neither reflexive nor symmetric nor transitive.

3. Check whether the relation R defined in the set {1, 2, 3, 4, 5, 6} as

R = {(a, b) : b = a + 1} is reflexive, symmetric or transitive.

4. Show that the relation R in R defined as R = {(a, b) : a ≤ b}, is reflexive and transitive but not symmetric.

5. Check whether the relation R in R defined by R = {(a, b) : a ≤ b³} is reflexive, symmetric or transitive.

6. Show that the relation R in the set {1, 2, 3} given by R = {(1, 2), (2, 1)} is symmetric but neither reflexive nor transitive.

7. Show that the relation R in the set A of all the books in a library of a college, given by R = {(x, y) : x and y have same number of pages} is an equivalence relation.

8. Show that the relation R in the set A = {1, 2, 3, 4, 5} given by R = {(a, b) : |a − b| is even}, is an equivalance relation. Show that all the elements of {1, 3, 5} are related to each other and all the elements of {2, 4} are related to each other. But no element of {1, 3, 5} is related to any element of {2, 4}.

9. Show that each of the relation R in the set A = {x ∈ Z : 0 ≤ x ≤ 12}, given by

(i) R = {(a, b) : |a − b| is a multiple of 4}

(ii) R = {(a, b) : a = b}

is an equivalence relation. Find the set of all elements related to 1 in each case.

10. Give an example of a relation which is

(i) Symmetric but neither reflexive nor transitive.

(ii) Transitive but neither reflexive nor symmetric.

(iii) Reflexive and symmetric but not transitive.

(iv) Reflexive and transitive but not symmetric.

(v) Symmetric and transitive but not reflexive.

11. Show that the relation R in the set A of points in a plane given by R = {(P, Q) : distance of the point P from the origin is same as the distance of the point Q from the origin}, is an equivalence relation. Further, show that the set of all points related to a point P ≠ (0, 0) is the circle passing through P with origin as centre.

12. Show that the relation R defined in the set A of all triangles as R = {(T₁, T₂) : T₁ is similar to T₂}, is equivalence relation. Consider three right angle triangles T₁ with sides 3, 4, 5, T₂ with sides 5, 12, 13 and T₃ with sides 6, 8, 10. Which triangles among T₁, T₂ and T₃ are related?

13. Show that the relation R defined in the set A of all polygons as R = {(P₁, P₂) : P₁ and P₂ have same number of sides}, is an equivalence relation. What is the set of all elements in A related to the right angle triangle T with sides 3, 4 and 5?

14. Let L be the set of all lines in XY plane and R be the relation in L defined as R = {(L₁, L₂) : L₁ is parallel to L₂}. Show that R is an equivalence relation. Find the set of all lines related to the line y = 2x + 4.

15. Let R be the relation in the set {1, 2, 3, 4} given by R = {(1, 2), (2, 2), (1, 1), (4, 4), (1, 3), (3, 3), (3, 2)}. Choose the correct answer.

(a) R is reflexive and symmetric but not transitive.

(b) R is reflexive and transitive but not symmetric.

(c) R is symmetric and transitive but not reflexive.

(d) R is an equivalence relation.

16. Let R be the relation in the set N given by R = {(a, b) : a = b − 2, b > 6}. Choose the correct answer.

(a) (2, 4) ∈ R   (b) (3, 8) ∈ R

(c) (6, 8) ∈ R   (d) (8, 7) ∈ R

Topic 2 — Functions and Types of Functions

FUNCTIONS

Let A and B be two non-empty set, then a function 'f' from A to B is a rule or method or correspondence which Associates elements of set A to element of set B such that

(i)   all element of set A are associated to elements in set B.

(ii) an element of set A is associated to a unique element in set B.

In other words - A function 'f' from set A to set B associates to each element x in A, a unique element $f(x)$ is B and is written as

e.g. If $x \in A$, $y = (f(x)) \in B$ then $(x, y) \in f$

e.g. If $(x_1, y_1) \in f$ and $(x_1, y_2) \in f$ then $y_1 = y_2$

$$f : A \to B \quad \text{or} \quad A \xrightarrow{f} B$$

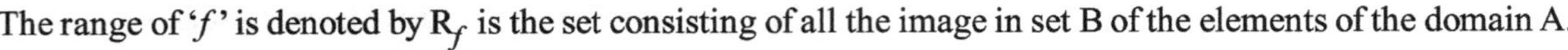

Domain, Co-domain and Range of the Function

The set A is called the domain of 'f' (denoted by D_f)

The set B is called the co-domain of 'f' (denoted by C_f)

The range of 'f' is denoted by R_f is the set consisting of all the image in set B of the elements of the domain A.

Range of $f = \{ f(x) : x \in A \}$

Note that every function is a relation but converse is not always true.

TYPES OF MAPPING OR FUNCTIONS

(i)   **One-One Function (Injective):** Let $f : A \to B$ then f is called a one-one function if no two different elements in A have the same image i.e. different elements in A have different elements in B.

Symbolically : f is one-one if

$f(a) = f(a') \Rightarrow a = a'$ i.e. $a \neq a' \Rightarrow f(a) \neq f(a')$

A mapping which is not one-one is called many one function.

Let $f : A \to B$ function represented by diagram

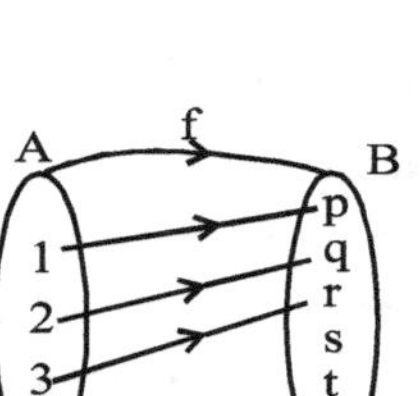

(i) (one-one)

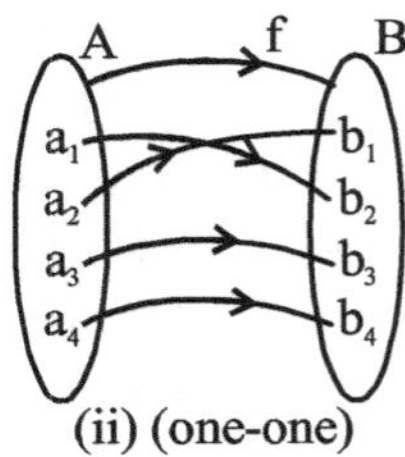

(ii) (one-one)

(ii) **Onto Function (Surjective) :** A function $f : A \to B$ is said to be onto function, if every element of B is the image of some element of A under f.

i.e. for every $b \in B$, there exists an element $a \in A$ such that $f(a) = b$.

Note that $f : A \to B$ is onto iff Range of f = B.

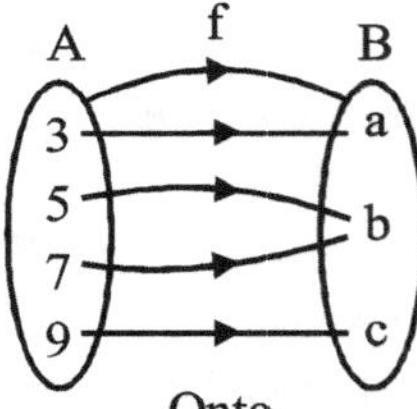

Onto

(iii) **One-One Onto Function (Bijective) :** A function $f : A \to B$ is said to be bijective if f is both one-one and onto.

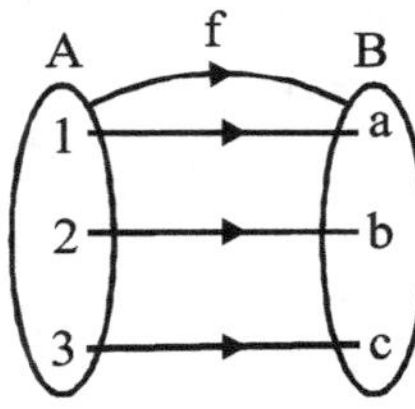

Bijective function

(iv) **Many-One Function :** A map $f : A \to B$ is said to be many-one if two or more elements of set A have the same image in B.

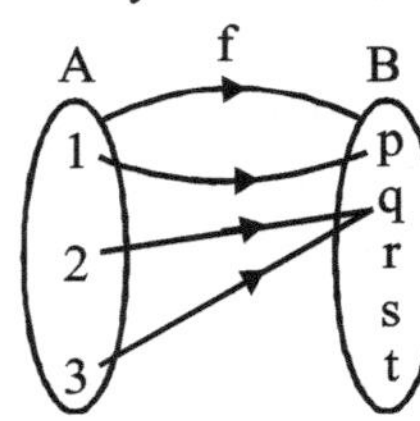

Many one function

(v) **Into Function:** A function $f : A \to B$ is into, if there exists at least one element in B which is not the f - image of any element in A. Therefore, at least one element of B such that $f^{-1}(y) = \phi$, then function is into. In other words, range of $f \neq$ co-domain of f

The following arrow-diagrams show into function.

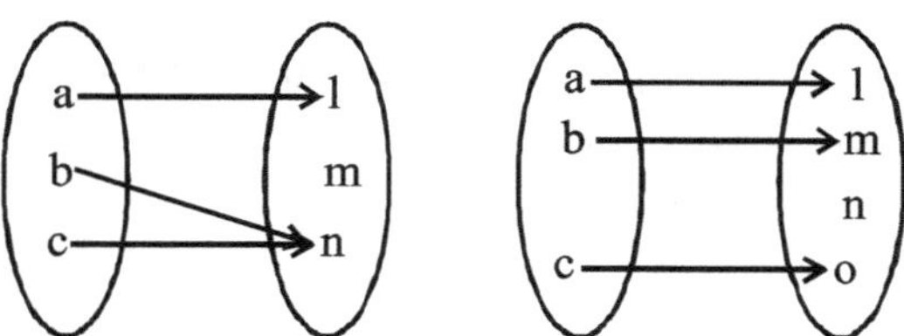

(vi) **One-One Into Function :** A function is said to be one-one into,

if f is one-one but not onto

Ex. (i) If $f : [-\pi/2, \pi/2] \to R$, $f(x) = \sin x$ (ii) $f : R^+ \to R$, $f(x) = |x|$

($\because$ co-domain and range are not equal, so function is not onto)

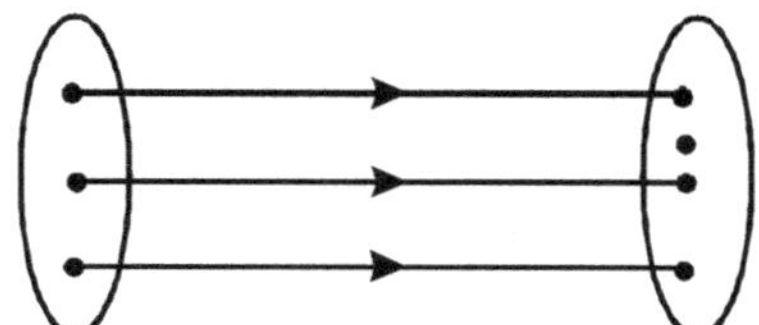

(vii) Many One-Onto Function: A function f is said to be many one- onto,

if f is onto but not one-one.

Ex. (i) $f : R \to R^+ \cup \{0\}$, $f(x) = x^2$

(ii) $f : R \to [0, \infty)$, $f(x) = |x|$

(iii) $f : R \to [-1, 1]$, $f(x) = \sin x$

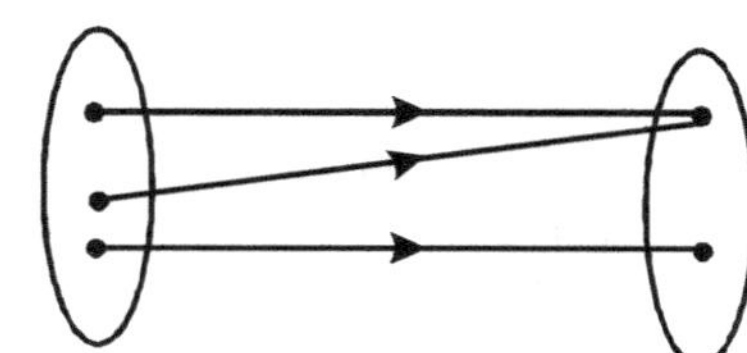

(viii)   **Many One-Into Function:** A function is said to be many one-into if it is neither one-one nor onto.

Ex. (i) $f : R \to R$, $f(x) = \sin x$

(ii) $f : R \to R$, $f(x) = |x|$

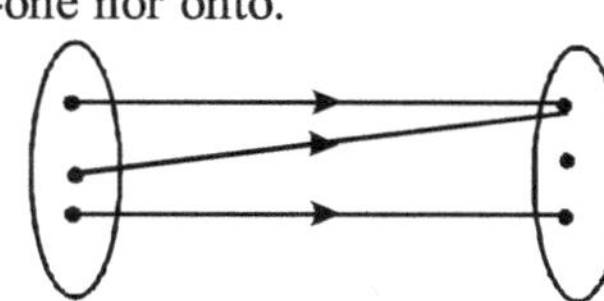

TYPES OF FUNCTIONS

(i)   **Even and Odd Function:** A function $f(x)$ is said to be even function iff $f(-x) = + f(x)$ and A function $f(x)$ is said to be odd function iff $f(-x) = -f(x)$.

(ii)   **Explicit & Implicit Function:** A function is said to be explicit function if its variable x, y can be easily separated.

A function is said to be implicit function if the variable x, y cannot be separated easily.

(iii)   **Constant Function ($y = k$):** It is a many-one function where domain is $x \in R$ and range $y \in (k)$.

(iv)   **Identity Function ($y = x$):** It is a one-one function whose domain is $x \in R$ and range $y \in R$.

(v)   **Linear Function ($y = ax + b$):** It is a one-one function where domain is $x \in R$ and Range is $y \in R$.

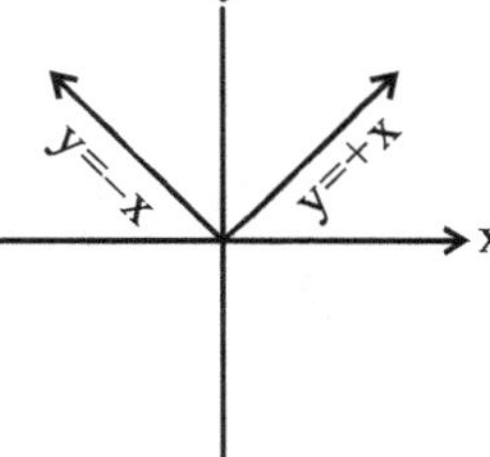

(vi)   **Modulus Function:** ($y = |x|$) is defined as $|x| = +x$ if $x > 0 = -x$ if $x < 0$

It is Many-one function where domain is $x \in R$ and Range $y \in [0, \infty)$

(vii) Logarithmic Function ($y = \log_a x$) : It is defined as $y = \log_a x \Rightarrow x = a^y$.

Thus $\log_a x$ is the inverse of a^x.

RULE FOR FINDING DOMAIN

(i)   Expression under even root (i.e. sq. root, forth root etc.) ≥ 0.

(ii) $D^r \neq 0$.

(iii)   If dom of $y = f(x)$ and $y = g(x)$ are D_1 & D_2 respectively then dom $\{(f(x) \pm g(x)\}$ and dom $(f(x)\, g(x))$ is $D_1 \cap D_2$

(iv)   While Dom $\left(\dfrac{f(x)}{g(x)}\right)$ is $D_1 \cap D_2 - [g(x) = 0]$.

RULES FOR FINDING RANGE

First of all find the domain of $y = f(x)$

(i)   if dom $\in$ finite number of points $\Rightarrow$ Range $\in$ set of corresponding $f(x)$.

(ii)   if domain $\in$ a finite interval, find the least and greatest value for Range using monotonicity.

Illustration :

Show that $f : R^+ \to R^+$ be define by $f(x) = x^2 + x$ is bijection. Where R^+ is positive real number.

Sol. **Injectivity :** Let $x_1, x_2 \in R^+$

Such that $f(x_1) = f(x_2)$

$$\Rightarrow x_1^2 + x_1 = x_2^2 + x_2$$

$$\Rightarrow x_1^2 - x_2^2 + x_1 - x_2 = 0$$

$$\Rightarrow (x_1 - x_2)(x_1 + x_2) + (x_1 - x_2) = 0$$

$$\Rightarrow (x_1 - x_2)(x_1 + x_2 + 1) = 0$$

$$\Rightarrow x_1 - x_2 = 0 \qquad [\because x_1 + x_2 + 1 \neq 0 \text{ for } x_1, x_2 \in R^+]$$

$$\Rightarrow x_1 = x_2$$

So, $f(x)$ is injective.

Surjectivity : Let $y = x^2 + x$

$$\Rightarrow x^2 + x - y = 0$$

$$\Rightarrow x = \frac{-1 \pm \sqrt{1 + 4y}}{2}$$

$$1 + 4y \geq 0 \qquad \Rightarrow y \geq -\frac{1}{4} \qquad \ldots (i)$$

By $x > 0$

$$\Rightarrow \frac{-1 \pm \sqrt{1 + 4y}}{2} > 0$$

$$\Rightarrow y > 0 \qquad \ldots (ii)$$

From (i) and (ii)

$y > 0$ i.e $y \in R^+$

$\therefore$ Range $= R^+ =$ Codomain

So, $f(x)$ is surjective

Hence, $f : R^+ \to R^+$ is bijective

Practice Exercise-2

Multiple Choice Questions

1. Let $f : R \to R$ be defined as $f(x) = x^4$, then
   (a) f is one-one onto
   (b) f is many-one onto
   (c) f is one-one but not onto
   (d) f is neither one-one nor onto

2. Let $A = \{1, 2, 3\}$ and $B = \{a, b, c\}$, and let $f = \{(1, a), (2, b), (P, c)\}$ be a function from A to B. For the function f to be one-one and onto, the value of $P =$
   (a) 1　　(b) 2　　(c) 3　　(d) 4

3. If $f : R \to R$, $f(x) = \begin{cases} x|x| - 4, & x \in Q \\ x|x| - \sqrt{3} & x \notin Q \end{cases}$, then $f(x)$ is
   (a) one to one and onto　　(b) many to one and onto
   (c) one to one and into　　(d) many to one and into

4. A function $f : R \to [-1, 1]$ defined by $f(x) = \sin x, \forall x \in R$, where R is the subset of real numbers is one-one and onto if R is the interval:
   (a) $[0, 2\pi]$　　(b) $\left[-\dfrac{\pi}{2}, \dfrac{\pi}{2}\right]$
   (c) $[-\pi, \pi]$　　(d) $[0, \pi]$

5. Let $f : R \to R$ be a function defined by $f(x) = x^3 + 4$, then f is
   (a) injective　　(b) surjective
   (c) bijective　　(d) None of these

Assertion & Reason Questions

DIRECTIONS : *Each of these questions contains an assertion followed by reason. Read them carefully and answer the question on the basis of following options. You have to select the one that best describes the two statements.*

(a) If both Assertion and Reason are correct and the Reason is the correct explanation of the Assertion.

(b) If both Assertion and Reason are correct but Reason is not the correct explanation of the Assertion.

(c) If the Assertion is correct but Reason is incorrect.

(d) If the Assertion is incorrect but the Reason is correct.

6. **Assertion :** Let $A = \{-1, 1, 2, 3\}$ and $B = \{1, 4, 9\}$, where $f : A \to B$ given by $f(x) = x^2$, then f is a many-one function.
Reason : If $x_1 \neq x_2 \Rightarrow f(x_1) \neq f(x_2)$, for every $x_1, x_2 \in$ domain, then f is one-one or else many-one.

7. Consider the following statements
Assertion : An onto function $f : \{1, 2, 3\} \to \{1, 2, 3\}$ is always one-one.
Reason : A one-one function $f : \{1, 2, 3\} \to \{1, 2, 3\}$ must be onto.

Case/Passage Based Question

DIRECTIONS (Q. 8) : *has 5 subparts based on Case/Passage given, attempt any 4 out of 5 questions.*

8. The total cost of producing x T.V. sets per day is ₹ $(x^2 - 5x + 4)$ and the price per set at which they may be sold is ₹ $(2x - 5)$. Based on the above information answer the following.

(i) The profit function is
(a) $48x + 4$ (b) $x^2 - 4$
(c) $x^2 - 3x + 54$ (d) $-x^2 + 7x - 9$

(ii) The profit function is
(a) one-one   (b) one-many
(c) many-one   (d) many-many

(iii) If 20 units T.V. produced in one day then profit is
(a) ₹ 400   (b) ₹ 35
(c) ₹ 396   (d) None of these

(iv) The number of T.V. produced in a day such that profit is zero are
(a) 2 units   (b) ± 2 units   (c) 5 units   (d) ± 5 units

(v) The minimum number of T.V. produced in a day to make loss are
(a) 2 units   (b) 1 unit   (c) 5 units   (d) 10 units

One Word Questions

9. Let $A = \{1, 2, 3\}$ and $B = \{a, b, c\}$, then find the number of bijective functions from A to B.

10. Find the number of all one-one functions from set $A = \{1, 2, 3\}$ to itself .

11. Find the number of surjection from
$A = \{1, 2, ..., n\}$, $n \geq 2$ onto $B = \{a, b\}$

12. If $f : R \to S$, defined by $f(x) = \sin x - \sqrt{3} \cos x + 1$, is onto, then find the interval of S

Very Short Answer Questions

13. Let $A = \{x, y, z\}$, $B = \{u, v, w\}$ and $f : A \to B$ be defined by $f(x) = u$, $f(y) = v$, $f(z) = v$, then define f.

14. Determine the range of $f(x) = \cos x + \sin x + \sqrt{2}$

15. Find the number of one-one onto mapping from A to B, where $n(A) = 5$, $n(B) = 6$.

16. Find the number of surjections from
$A = \{1, 2, ..., n\}$ $n \geq 2$, onto $B = \{a, b\}$

17. Let $f : R \to R$, $f(x) = \dfrac{1}{x}$, then define f.

18. Let $f : R \to R$ such that $f(x) = \log_e x$, then define f.

19. Show that the modulus function $f : R \to R$, given by $f(x) = |x|$ is neither one-one nor onto.

Short Answer Questions

20. Find the domain of the function
$$\Psi(x) = \frac{1}{x} + 2^{\sin^{-1} x} + \frac{1}{\sqrt{x-2}}$$

21. Show that the function $f : R \to R$ defined by $f(x) = x^2 - 1$ is neither one-one nor onto.

22. Let $A = R - \{2\}$ and $B = R - \{1\}$, consider the function $f : A \to B$ defined by $f(x) = \dfrac{x-1}{x-2}$. Is f one-one and onto?

23. Prove that the function $f : R \to R$ given by $f(x) = x^3$ is bijective.

24. Consider the following sets $R = \{(x, y) \mid x, y, \in R, x^2 + y^2 \leq 25\}$ and $R' = \{(x, y) \mid x, y \in R, y \geq 4x^2/9\}$ Is $R \cap R'$ a function? If so find its domain and range?

25. Prove that the greatest integer function $f : R \to R$, given by $f(x) = [x]$, is neither one-one nor onto, where [x] denotes the greatest integer less than or equal to x.

NCERT Exercise-2

1. Show that the function $f : R \to R$ defined by $f(x) = \dfrac{1}{x}$ is one-one onto, where R is the set of all non-zero real numbers. Is the result true, if the domain R is replaced by N with co-domain being same as R ?

2. Check the injectivity and surjectivity of the following functions:
(i) $f : N \to N$ given by $f(x) = x^2$
(ii) $f : Z \to Z$ given by $f(x) = x^2$
(iii) $f : R \to R$ given by $f(x) = x^2$
(iv) $f : N \to N$ given by $f(x) = x^3$
(v) $f : Z \to Z$ given by $f(x) = x^3$

3. Prove that the Greatest Integer Function $f : R \to R$ given by $f(x) = [x]$, is neither one-one nor onto, where [x] denotes the greatest integer less than or equal to x.

4. Show that the Modulus Function $f : R \to R$ given by $f(x) = |x|$, is neither one-one nor onto, where |x| is x, if x is positive or 0 and |x| is – x, if x is negative.

5. Show that the Signum Function $f : R \to R$ given by $f(x)$
$$= \begin{cases} 1, & \text{if } x > 0 \\ 0, & \text{if } x = 0 \\ -1, & \text{if } x < 0 \end{cases} \text{ is neither one-one nor onto.}$$

6. Let $A = \{1, 2, 3\}$, $B = \{4, 5, 6, 7\}$ and let $f = \{(1, 4), (2, 5), (3, 6)\}$ be a function from A to B. Show that f is one-one.

7. In each of the following cases, state whether the function is one-one, onto or bijective. Justify your answer.

    (i) $f : R \to R$ defined by $f(x) = 3 - 4x$

    (ii) $f : R \to R$ defined by $f(x) = 1 + x^2$

8. Let A and B be sets. Show that $f : A \times B \to B \times A$ such that $f(a, b) = (b, a)$ is bijective function.

9. Let $f : N \to N$ be defined by $f(n)$

$$= \begin{cases} \dfrac{n+1}{2}, & \text{if n is odd} \\[2mm] \dfrac{n}{2}, & \text{if n is even} \end{cases} \quad \text{for all } n \in N.$$

    State whether the function f is bijective. Justify your answer.

10. Let $A = R - \{3\}$ and $B = R - \{1\}$. consider the function $f : A \to B$ defined by $f(x) = \left(\dfrac{x-2}{x-3}\right)$. Is f one-one and onto? Justify your answer.

11. Let $f : R \to R$ be defined as $f(x) = x^4$. Choose the correct answer.

    (a) f is one-one onto

    (b) f is many-one onto

    (c) f is one-one but not onto

    (d) f is neither one-one nor onto

12. Let $f : R \to R$ be defined as $f(x) = 3x$. Choose the correct answer.

    (a) f is one-one onto

    (b) f is many-one onto

    (c) f is one-one but not onto

    (d) f is neither one-one nor onto

Important Tips & Formulae

- **Identity relation :** Let X be a set. Then the relation $I_x = \{(x, x) : x \in X\}$, on X is called the identity relation on X i.e. a relation I_x on X is identity relation if every element of X is related to itself only.

- **Reflexive relation :** A relation R on set X is said to be reflexive if every element in set X, must be a related to itself.

- **Anti-symmetric relation :** A relation R on set A is said to be an anti symmetric relation iff $(a, b) \in R$ and $(b, a) \in R$
$\Rightarrow a = b$ for all $a, b \in A$

- **One-one into function :** A function is said to be one-one into, if f is one-one but not onto

- **Many one-onto function:** A function f is said to be many one-onto, if f is onto but not one-one.

- **Many one-into function:** A function is said to be many one-into if it is neither one-one nor onto.

- All identity relations are reflexive but all reflexive relations are not identity.

- Indentity relation on a non-void set A is always reflexive on A. However, the converse need not be true.

- Universal relation on a non-void set A is reflexive

- In null set ϕ, every relation is reflexive.

- Let X be a non-void set, then a relation R on P(X), the power set of X such that $(A, B) \in R \Leftrightarrow A \subseteq B$ is reflexive for $A \subseteq A \ \forall \ A$ [every set is subset by itself]

- Identity relation and universal relation on a non-void set are symmetric.

- In the null set every relation is symmetric.

- The relation R on P(X) for a non-empty set X, defined by $ARB \Leftrightarrow A \subseteq B$ is not symmetric.

- A reflexive relation on the set A is not necessarily symmetric.

- Identity and Universal relations on a non-empty set are transitive.

- Every relation defined on the null set ϕ is transitive

- Identity relation on a non-empty set is antisymmetric

- Universal relation on a set A containing at least two distinct elements connot be anti-symmetric.

- If f is both injective and surjective, then it is called a bijective mapping. The bijective functions are also named as invertible, or non singular functions.

- Every polynomial function $f : R \to R$ of degree odd is **ONTO.**

- If A and B are two finite sets having m and n elements respectively, then
(a) Total number of functions from the set A to the set $B = n^m$
(b) The number of one-one (injective) functions from A

$$\text{to } B = \begin{cases} {}^n P_m = \dfrac{n!}{(n-m)!} & \text{If } n \geq m \\[2mm] 0, & \text{If } n < m \end{cases}$$

(c) If $n = m$, then every one-one function is a bijective function, thus, the number of bijective functions from A to B, provided $n = m$ is $n! = m!$
(d) The number of onto (surjective) functions from A to

$$B = \sum_{r=1}^{n} (-1)^r \ {}^n C_r \ (n-r)^m, \text{ where } 1 \leq n \leq m$$

MISCELLANEOUS NCERT EXERCISE

1. Let $f : W \to W$ be defined as $f(n) = n - 1$, if n is odd and $f(n) = n + 1$, if n is even. Show that f is invertible. Find the inverse of f. Here, W is the set of all whole numbers.

Sol. We are given $f : W \to W$, defined as $f(n)$

$$= \begin{cases} n - 1, & n \text{ is odd} \\ n + 1, & n \text{ is even} \end{cases}$$

Let $f(n_1) = f(n_2)$. If n_1 is odd and n_2 is even then $n_1 - 1 = n_2 + 1$, i.e. $n_1 - n_2 = 2$

Which is not possible as n_1 is odd and n_2 is even. When n_1 and n_2 both are odd.

then $f(n_1) = f(n_2) \Rightarrow n_1 - 1 = n_2 - 1 \Rightarrow n_1 = n_2$

When n_1 and n_2 both are even $f(n_1) = f(n_2) = n_1 + 1 = n_2 + 1 = n_1 = n_2$

This shows f is one-one. Any odd number $2r + 1$ in co-domain is the image of 2r and any even number 2r in the codomain W in the image of $2r + 1$.

$\Rightarrow$ f is one-one and onto $\quad \therefore$ f is invertible

Further, when n is odd, $y = n - 1$, $n = y + 1$ y is even.

When n is even, $y = n + 1$, $n = y - 1$, y is odd. Hence $f^{-1}(y) = g(y)$ is defined as

$g : W \to W$, such that

$$g(y) = \begin{cases} y - 1, & \text{if y is odd} \\ y + 1, & \text{if y is even} \end{cases}$$

$\Rightarrow$ The inverse of f is itself.

2. Show that the function $f : R \to \{x \in R : -1 < x < 1\}$ defined by $f(x) = \dfrac{x}{1 + |x|}$, $x \in R$ is one one and onto function.

Sol. (i) Let $x \geq 0$, $f(x) = \dfrac{x}{1 + x}$, $f(x_1) = f(x_2)$

$$\Rightarrow \frac{x_1}{1 + x_1} = \frac{x_2}{1 + x_2}$$

or $x_1 (1 + x_2) = x_2 (1 + x_1)$

or $x_1 + x_1 x_2 = x_2 + x_2 x_1 \Rightarrow x_1 = x_2$,

when $x < 0$, $f(x) = \dfrac{x}{1 - x}$

$$f(x_1) = f(x_2) \Rightarrow \frac{x_1}{1 - x_1} = \frac{x_2}{1 - x_2}$$

or $x_1 (1 - x_2) = x_2 (1 - x_1)$ or $x_1 - x_1 x_2 = x_2 - x_2 x_1$

$\Rightarrow x_1 = x_2 \Rightarrow$ f is one one

(ii) As $-1 < x < 1$, $f(x) = \dfrac{x}{1 + |x|}$ lies between $-\dfrac{1}{2}$ and

$\dfrac{1}{2}$ when $x \geq 0$,

let $y = \dfrac{x}{1 + x}$ $\therefore$ $(1 + x) y = x \quad$ or $\quad xy - x = y$

$$\therefore x(y - 1) = y \quad \Rightarrow \quad x = \frac{y}{y - 1}$$

when $x < 0$, $f(x) = \dfrac{x}{1 - x} = y$

$$\therefore x = y - xy \therefore x = \frac{y}{1 + y}$$

In both cases such value of y in codomain of has a unique value in its domain. Hence f is onto.

Thus, f is one one and onto.

3. Show that the function $f : R \to R$ given by $f(x) = x^3$ is injective.

Sol. $f(x) = x^3 \quad f(x_1) = f(x_2) \Rightarrow x_1^3 = x_2^3$

$\Rightarrow x_1 = x_2 \Rightarrow$ f is one-one i.e. f is injective.

4. Give examples of two functions $f : N \to Z$ and $g : Z \to Z$ such that g o f is injective but g is not injective. **Hint – Consider $f(x) = x$ and $g(x) = |x|$).**

Sol. (i) Let $f(x) = x$, $g(x) = |x|$

Consider $g(x) = |x| \Rightarrow$ g is not injective

Since -1, 1 have the same image 1.

But $(gof)(x) = g(f(x)) = g(x) = |x|$

But domain of gof is N. For every natural number n, $|n| = n$, $n \in N$ gof has a unique image.

$\therefore$ gof is injective.

(ii) $f(x) = 2x$, $g(x) = x^2$.

5. Given a non empty set X, consider P (X) which is the set of all subsets of X. Define the relation R in P (X) as follows: For subsets A, B in P (X), ARB if and only if $A \subset B$, Is R an equivalence relation on P (X)? Justify your answer.

Sol. (i) $A \subset B \Rightarrow$ R is reflexive

(ii) $A \subset B, B \not\subset A \quad \therefore$ R is not commutative

(iii) If $A \subset B, B \subset C$, then $A \subset C$

$\therefore$ R is transitive. $\therefore$ R is not equivalence relation.

6. Let $A = \{-1, 0, 1, 2\}$, $B = \{-4, -2, 0, 2\}$ and $f, g : A \to B$ be functions defined by $f(x) = x^2 - x$, $x \in A$ and $g(x) = 2\left|x - \dfrac{1}{2}\right| - 1$, $x \in A$. Are f and g equal? Justify your answer.

Hint : One may not that two functions $f : A \to B$ and $g : A \to B$ such that $f(a) = g(a) \; \forall \; a \in A$, are called equal functions).

Sol. At $x = -1$, $f(x) = 1^2 + 1 = 2$ and $g(x) = 2\left|-1 - \dfrac{1}{2}\right| - 1 = 2 \times \dfrac{3}{2} - 1 = 2$

At $x = 0$, $f(0) = 0$ and $g(0) = 2\left|-\dfrac{1}{2}\right| - 1 = 2 \times \dfrac{1}{2} - 1 = 0$,

At $x = 1$, $f(1) = 1^2 - 1 = 0$

$$g(1) = 2\left|1 - \frac{1}{2}\right| - 1 = 2 \times \frac{1}{2} - 1 = 0 \quad \text{At } x = 2, f(2) = 2^2 - 2 = 2,$$

$$g(2) = 2\left|2 - \frac{1}{2}\right| - 1 = 3 - 1 = 2$$

Thus, for each $a \in A$, $f(a) = g(x) \Rightarrow f$ and g are equal function.

7. Let A = {1, 2, 3}. The number of relations containing (1, 2) and (1, 3) which are reflexive and symmetric but not transitive is

(a) 1   (b) 2   (c) 3   (d) 4

Sol. There is only one relation containing (1, 2) and (1, 3) which are reflexive and symmetric but not transitive option (a) is correct.

i.e. R = {(1, 2), (1, 3), (1, 1), (2, 2), (3, 3), (2, 1) (3, 1)}

8. Let A = {1, 2, 3}. The number of equivalence relations containing (1, 2) is

(a) 1   (b) 2   (c) 3   (d) 4

Sol. There are two equivalence relations containing (1, 2).

i.e. R_1 = {(1, 2), (1, 1), (2, 2), (3, 3), (2, 1)} and

R_2 = {(1, 2), (1, 1), (2, 2), (3, 3), (2, 1), (1, 3), (3, 1), (2, 3), (3, 2)}

Past year Exercise

Very Short Answer Question

1. If R = {(x, y) : x + 2y = 8} is a relation on N, write the range of R.

Short Answer Questions

2. Show that f : N → N, given by $f(x) = \begin{cases} x+1, & \text{if } x \text{ is odd} \\ x-1, & \text{if } x \text{ is even} \end{cases}$

is bijective (both one-one and onto).

3. Let A = {1, 2, 3, ..., 9} and R be the relation in $A \times A$ defined by $(a, b)\, R\, (c, d)$ if $a + d = b + c$ for (a, b), (c, d) in $A \times A$. Prove that R is an equivalence relation. Also obtain the equivalence class [(2, 5)].

4. Let N denote the set of all natural numbers and R be the relation on N × N defined by (a, b) R (c, d) if ad (b + c) = bc (a + d). Show that R is an equivalence relation.

5. Let A = {$x \in Z : 0 \le x \le 12$}. Show that R = {$(a, b) : a, b \in A, |a - b|$ is divisible by 4} is an equivalence relation. Find the set of all elements related to 1. Also write the equivalence class [2].

6. Let A = R − {2} and B = R − {1}. If f : A → B is a function

defined by $f(x) = \dfrac{x-1}{x-2}$, show that f is one-one and onto.

Hence, find f^{-1}.

OR

Show that the relation S in the set A = {$x \in Z : 0 \le x \le 12$} given by S = {$(a, b) : a, b \in Z, |a - b|$ is divisible by 3} is an equivalence relation.

7. Let N be the set of natural numbers and R be the relation on N × N defined by $(a, b)\, R\, (c, d)$ if $ad = bc$ for all $a, b, c, d \in N$. Show that R is an equivalence relation.

NCERT Exemplar

Multiple Choice Questions

1. Let T be the set of all triangles in the Euclidean planen and let a relation R on T be defined as aRb, if a is congruent to b, $\forall\, a, b \in T$. Then, R is

(a) reflexive but not transitive

(b) transitive but not symmetric

(c) equivalence

(d) None of these

2. Consider the non-empty set consisting of children in a family and a relation R defined as $a\,R\,b$ if a is brother of b. Then R is

(a) symmetric but not transitive

(b) transitive but not symmetric

(c) neither symmetric nor transitive

(d) both symmetric and transitive

3. Let f : R → R be defined by $f(x) = \dfrac{1}{x} \forall x \in R$. Then f is

(a) one-one   (b) onto

(c) bijective   (d) f is not defined

4. Which of the following functions from Z into Z are bijective?

(a) $f(x) = x^3$ (b) $f(x) = x + 2$

(c) $f(x) = 2x + 1$ (d) $f(x) = x^2 + 1$

Short Answer Questions

5. Is g = {(1, 1), (2, 3), (3, 5), (4, 7)} a function ? If this is described by the formula $g(x) = \alpha x + \beta$, then what values should be assigned to α and β ?

Objective Practice Exercise

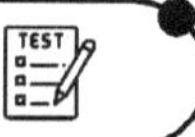

1. Let W denote the words in the English dictionary. Define the relation R by: $R = \{(x, y) \in W \times W |$ the words x and y have at least one letter in common$\}$
   (a) Not reflexive, symmetric and transitive
   (b) Reflexive, symmetric and not transitive
   (c) Reflexive, symmetric and transitive
   (d) Reflexive, not symmetric and transitive

2. Let $R = \{(3, 3), (6, 6), (9, 9), (12, 12), (6, 12), (3, 9), (3, 12), (3, 6)\}$ be a relation on the set $A = \{3, 6, 9, 12\}$. The relation is
   (a) reflexive and transitive only
   (b) reflexive only
   (c) an equivalence relation
   (d) reflexive and symmetric only

3. The number of reflexive relations of a set with four elements is equal to
   (a) 2^{16}
   (b) 2^{12}
   (c) 2^8
   (d) 2^4

4. $aRb \Leftrightarrow |a| \leq b$. Then R is
   (a) Reflexive
   (b) Symmetric
   (c) Transitive
   (d) Equivalence

5. Let $P = \{(x, y) : |x^2 + y^2| = 1, x, y \in R\}$. Then P is
   (a) Reflexive
   (b) Symmetric
   (c) Transitive
   (d) Anti-symmetric

6. For any two real numbers a and b, we define $a\,R\,b$ if and only if $\sin^2 a + \cos^2 b = 1$. The relation R is
   (a) Reflexive but not symmetric
   (b) Symmetric but not transitive
   (c) Transitive but not reflexive
   (d) An equivalence relation

7. On the set N of all natural numbers define the relation R by $a\,R\,b$ if and only if the G.C.D. of a and b is 2. then R is
   (a) Reflexive, but not symmetric
   (b) Symmetric only
   (c) Reflexive and transitive
   (d) Reflexive, symmetric and transitive

8. Let R be an equivalence relation on a finite set A having n elements. Then the number of ordered pairs in R is
   (a) Less than n
   (b) Greater than or equal to n
   (c) Less than or equal to n
   (d) None of these

9. $x^2 = xy$ is a relation which is
   (a) Symmetric
   (b) Reflexive
   (c) Transitive
   (d) None of these

10. Let $A = \{1, 2, 3, 4\}$ and let $R = \{(2, 2), (3, 3), (4, 4), (1, 2)\}$ be a relation on A. Then R is
    (a) Reflexive
    (b) Symmetric
    (c) Transitive
    (d) None of these

11. Let A be the non-void set of the children in a family. The relation 'x is a brother of y' on A is
    (a) Reflexive
    (b) Symmetric
    (c) Transitive
    (d) None of these

12. Let R be a reflexive relation on a set A and I be the identity relation on A. Then
    (a) $R \subset I$
    (b) $I \subset R$
    (c) $R = I$
    (d) None of these

13. The relation "is subset of" on the power set $P(A)$ of a set A is
    (a) Symmetric
    (b) Anti-symmetric
    (c) Equivalency relation
    (d) None of these

14. Given the relation $R = \{(1, 2), (2, 3)\}$ on the set $A = \{1, 2, 3\}$, the minimum number of ordered pairs which when added to R make it an equivalence relation is
    (a) 5
    (b) 6
    (c) 7
    (d) 8

15. Let R be a reflexive relation on a finite set A having n-elements, and let there be m ordered pairs in R. Then
    (a) $m \geq n$
    (b) $m \leq n$
    (c) $m = n$
    (d) None of these

16. The function $f : R \to R$ defined by $f(x) = (x - 1)(x - 2)(x - 3)$ is
    (a) one-one but not onto
    (b) onto but not one-one
    (c) both one-one and onto
    (d) neither one-one nor onto

17. For real x, let $f(x) = x^3 + 5x + 1$, then
    (a) f is one-one but not onto R
    (b) f is onto R but not one-one
    (c) f is one-one and onto R
    (d) f is neither one-one nor onto R

18. Let $E = \{1, 2, 3, 4\}$ and $F = \{1, 2\}$. Then the number of onto functions from E to F is
    (a) 14
    (b) 16
    (c) 12
    (d) 8

19. Set A has 3 elements and set B has 4 elements. The number of injection that can be defined from A to B is
    (a) 144
    (b) 12
    (c) 24
    (d) 64

20. Let $f(x) = [x]^2 + [x + 1] - 3$ where $[x] = $ the greatest integer function. Then
    (a) $f(x)$ is a many-one and into function
    (b) $f(x) = 0$ for infinite number of values of x
    (c) $f(x) = 0$ for only two real values
    (d) Both (a) and (b)

21. Which one of the following is a bijective function on the set of real numbers

    (a) $2x - 5$ (b) $|x|$

    (c) x^2 (d) $x^2 + 1$

22. Set of all values of p for which the function $f(x) = px + \sin x$ is bijective is

    (a) $[-2, \infty)$ (b) $(-\infty, -1] \cup [1, \infty)$

    (c) $(-\infty, -2] \cup [2/3, \infty)$ (d) $[-2, 2/3]$

23. The function $f : R \to R$ defined by $f(x) = e^x$ is

    (a) Onto

    (b) Many-one

    (c) One-one and into

    (d) Many one and onto

24. If $f : R \to C$ is defined by $f(x) = e^{2ix}$ for $x \in R$, then f is (where C denotes the set of all complex numbers)

    (a) One-one

    (b) Onto

    (c) One-one and onto

    (d) Neither one-one nor onto

25. Which of the following is one-one function ?

    (a) e^x (b) e^{x^2}

    (c) $\sin x$ (d) None of these

26. A mapping from N to N is defined as follows:
    $f : N \to N,\quad f(n) = (n+5)^2, n \in N$

    (N is the set of natural numbers). Then

    (a) f is not one to one

    (b) f is onto

    (c) f is both one to one and onto

    (d) f is one to one but not onto

27. Let A and B be two finite sets having m and n elements respectively. Then, the total number of mappings from A to B is :

    (a) mn   (b) 2^{mn}

    (c) m^n (d) n^m

28. $f(x) = x + \sqrt{x^2}$ is a function from $R \to R$, then $f(x)$ is

    (a) Injective   (b) Surjective

    (c) Bijective   (d) None of these

29. Which of the function defined below is one–one?

    (a) $f : (0, \infty) \to R$, $f(x) = x^2 - 4x + 3$

    (b) $f : [0, \infty) \to R$, $f(x) = x^2 + 4x - 5$

    (c) $f : R \to R$, $f(x) = e^x + \dfrac{1}{e^x}$

    (d) $f : R \to R$, $f(x) = \ell n(x^2 + x + 1)$

30. $A = \{1, 2, 3, 4\}$, $B = \{1, 2, 3, 4, 5, 6\}$ are two sets and function $f : A \to B$ is defined by $f(x) = x + 2; \forall x \in A$, then the function f is

    (a) Bijective   (b) Onto

    (c) One-one   (d) Many-one

31. If $f : R \to R$, $f(x) = \begin{cases} x|x| - 4, & x \in Q \\ x|x| - \sqrt{3} & x \notin Q \end{cases}$, then $f(x)$ is

    (a) one to one and onto   (b) many to one and onto

    (c) one to one and into   (d) many to one and into

32. If $f : R \to S$, defined by $f(x) = \sin x - \sqrt{3}\cos x + 1$, is onto, then the interval of S is

    (a) $[-1, 3]$ (b) $[-1, 1]$

    (c) $[0, 1]$ (d) $[0, 3]$

33. If the functions f(x) and g(x) are defined on $R \to R$ such that $f(x) = \begin{cases} 0, & x \in \text{rational} \\ x, & x \in \text{irrational} \end{cases}$; $g(x) = \begin{cases} 0, & x \in \text{irrational} \\ x, & x \in \text{rational} \end{cases}$

    then $(f - g)(x)$ is

    (a) one-one and onto

    (b) neither one-one nor onto

    (c) one-one but not onto

    (d) onto but not one-one

34. A function f from the set of natural numbers to integers defined by

    $$f(n) = \begin{cases} \dfrac{n-1}{2}, & \text{when n is odd} \\ -\dfrac{n}{2}, & \text{when n is even} \end{cases} \quad \text{is}$$

    (a) neither one -one nor onto

    (b) one-one but not onto

    (c) onto but not one-one

    (d) one-one and onto both.

35. Which one of the following relations on R is an equivalence relation

    (a) $a R_1 b \Leftrightarrow |a| = |b|$ (b) $a R_2 b \Leftrightarrow a \geq b$

    (c) $a R_3 b \Leftrightarrow a$ divides b (d) $a R_4 b \Leftrightarrow a < b$

36. Let R be a relation on the set N of natural numbers defined by $nRm \Leftrightarrow n$ is a factor of m (i.e., n/m). Then R is

    (a) Reflexive and symmetric

    (b) Transitive and symmetric

    (c) Equivalence

    (d) Reflexive, transitive but not symmetric

37. Let N denote the set of all natural numbers and R be the relation on $N \times N$ defined by $(a, b) R (c, d)$ if $ad(b + c) = bc(a + d)$, then R is

    (a) Symmetric only   (b) Reflexive only

    (c) Transitive only   (d) An equivalence relation

38. Let $f : R \to R$ be a function defined by $f(x) = \dfrac{x-m}{x-n}$, where $m \neq n$, then

(a) f is one-one onto   (b) f is one-one into

(c) f is many-one onto   (d) f is many-one into

39. Let R be the relation on the set R of all real numbers defined by $a\,R\,b$ if $|a-b| \leq 1$. Then R is

(a) Reflexive and symmetric

(b) Symmetric only

(c) Transitive only

(d) Anti-symmetric only

40. Let a relation R in the set N of natural numbers be defined as

$(x, y) \Leftrightarrow x^2 - 4xy + 3y^2 = 0 \, \forall x, y \in N$. The relation R is

(a) Reflexive   (b) Symmetric

(c) Transitive   (d) An equivalence relation

DIRECTIONS : *Study the given Case/Passage and answer the following questions.*

Case/Passage-I

A general election of Lok Sabha is a gigantic exercise. About 911 million people were eligible to vote and voter turnout was about 67%, the highest ever

Let I be the set of all citizens of India who were eligible to exercise their voting right in general election held in 2019. A relation 'R' is defined on I as follows:

$R = \{V_1, V_2\} : V_1, V_2 \in I$ and both use their voting right in general election-2019}   **[From CBSE Question Bank-2021]**

41. Two neighbors X and Y $\in$ I. X exercised his voting right while Y did not cast her vote in general election-2019. Which of the following is true?

(a) $(X,Y) \in R$ (b) $(Y,X) \in R$

(c) $(X,X) \notin R$ (d) $(X,Y) \notin R$

42. Mr. 'X' and his wife 'W' both exercised their voting right in general election-2019. Which of the following is true?

(a) both (X,W) and $(W,X) \in R$

(b) $(X,W) \in R$ but $(W,X) \notin R$

(c) both (X,W) and $(W,X) \notin R$

(d) $(W,X) \in R$ but $(X,W) \notin R$

43. Three friends F_1, F_2 and F_3 exercised their voting right in general election-2019, then which of the following is true?

(a) $(F_1, F_2) \in R, (F_2, F_3) \in R$ and $(F_1, F_3) \in R$

(b) $(F_1, F_2) \in R, (F_2, F_3) \in R$ and $(F_1, F_3) \notin R$

(c) $(F_1, F_2) \in R, (F_2, F_2) \in R$ but $(F_3, F_3) \notin R$

(d) $(F_1, F_2) \notin R, (F_2, F_3) \notin R$ and $(F_1, F_3) \notin R$

44. The above defined relation R is __________.

(a) symmetric and transitive but not reflexive

(b) universal relation

(c) equivalence relation

(d) reflexive but not symmetric and transitive

45. Mr. Shyam exercised his voting right in General Election-2019, then Mr. Shyam is related to which of the following?

(a) All those eligible voters who cast their votes

(b) Family members of Mr.Shyam

(c) All citizens of India

(d) Eligible voters of India

Case/Passage-II

Sherlin and Danju are playing Ludo at home during Covid-19. While rolling the dice, Sherlin's sister Raji observed and noted the possible outcomes of the throw every time belongs to set {1,2,3,4,5,6}. Let A be the set of players while B be the set of all possible outcomes.

$A = \{S, D\}, B = \{1,2,3,4,5,6\}$

[From CBSE Question Bank-2021]

46. Let $R : B \to B$ be defined by $R = \{(x, y) : y$ is divisible by} is

(a) Reflexive and transitive but not symmetric

(b) Reflexive and symmetric and not transitive

(c) Not reflexive but symmetric and transitive

(d) Equivalence

47. Raji wants to know the number of functions from A to B. How many number of functions are possible?

(a) 6^2 (b) 2^6 (c) $6!$ (d) 2^{12}

48. Let R be a relation on B defined by R = {(1,2), (2,2), (1,3), (3,4), (3,1), (4,3), (5,5)}. Then R is

(a) Symmetric   (b) Reflexive

(c) Transitive   (d) None of these

49. Raji wants to know the number of relations possible from A to B. How many numbers of relations are possible?

(a) 6^2 (b) 2^6 (c) 6!   (d) 2^{12}

50. Let $R : B \to B$ be defined by R={(1,1),(1,2), (2,2), (3,3), (4,4), (5,5),(6,6)}, then R is

(a) Symmetric   (b) Reflexive and Transitive

(c) Transitive and symmetric   (d) Equivalence

Case/Passage-III

An organization conducted bike race under 2 different categories-boys and girls. Totally there were 250 participants. Among all of them finally three from Category 1 and two from Category 2 were selected for the final race. Ravi forms two sets B and G with these participants for his college project.

Let B = {b_1, b_2, b_3} G={g_1, g_2} where B represents the set of boys selected and G the set of girls who were selected for the final race.

[From CBSE Question Bank-2021]

Ravi decides to explore these sets for various types of relations and functions

51. Ravi wishes to form all the relations possible from B to G. How many such relations are possible?

(a) 2^6 (b) 2^5 (c) 0   (d) 2^3

52. Let $R : B \to B$ be defined by R = {(x, y): x and y are students of same sex}, then this relation R is__________.

(a) equivalence

(b) reflexive only

(c) reflexive and symmetric but not transitive

(d) reflexive and transitive but not symmetric

53. Ravi wants to know among those relations, how many functions can be formed from B to G?

(a) 2^2 (b) 2^{12} (c) 3^2 (d) 2^3

54. Let $R : B \to G$ be defined by R ={(b_1, g_1), (b_2, g_2), (b_3, g_1)}, then R is__________.

(a) injective

(b) surjective

(c) neither surjective nor injective

(d) surjective and injective

55. Ravi wants to find the number of injective functions from B to G. How many numbers of injective functions are possible?

(a) 0   (b) 2!

(c) 3!   (d) 0!

Case/Passage-IV

Students of Grade 9, planned to plant saplings along straight lines, parallel to each other to one side of the playground ensuring that they had enough play area. Let us assume that they planted one of the rows of the saplings along the line $y = x - 4$. Let L be the set of all lines which are parallel on the ground and R be a relation on L.

[From CBSE Question Bank-2021]

Answer the following using the above information.

56. Let relation R be defined by R = {(L_1, L_2) : $L_1 \parallel L_2$ where L_1, $L_2 \in L$} then R is________relation

(a) equivalence

(b) only reflexive

(c) not reflexive

(d) symmetric but not transitive

57. Let R = {(L_1, L_2) : $L_1 \perp L_2$ where L_1, $L_2 \in L$ } which of the following is true?

(a) R is symmetric but neither reflexive nor transitive

(b) R is reflexive and transitive but not symmetric

(c) R is reflexive but neither symmetric nor transitive

(d) R is an equivalence relation

58. The function $f : R \to R$ defined by $f(x) = x - 4$ is______.

(a) bijective

(b) surjective but not injective

(c) injective but not surjective

(d) neither surjective nor injective

59. Let $f : R \to R$ be defined by $(x) = x - 4$. Then the range of $f(x)$ is__________.

  (a) R   (b) Z

  (c) W   (d) Q

60. Let $R = \{(L_1, L_2) : L_1$ is parallel to L_2 and $L_1 : y = x - 4\}$ then which of the following can be taken as L_2?

  (a) $2x - 2y + 5 = 0$ (b) $2x + y = 5$

  (c) $2x + 2y + 7 = 0$ (d) $x + y = 7$

Case/Passage-V

Raji visited the exhibition along with her family. The exhibition had a huge swing, which attracted many children. Raji found that the swing traced the path of a parabola as given by $y = x^2$.

[From CBSE Question Bank-2021]

Answer the following questions using the above information.

61. Let $f : R \to R$ be defined by $f(x) = x^2$ is__________.

  (a) neither surjective nor injective

  (b) surjective

  (c) injective

  (d) bijective

62. Let $f : N \to N$ be defined by $f(x) = x^2$ is__________.

  (a) surjective but not injective

  (b) surjective

  (c) injective

  (d) bijective

63. Let $f : \{1,2,3,....\} \to \{1,4,9,....\}$ be defined by $f(x) = x^2$ is__________.

  (a) bijective

  (b) surjective but not injective

  (c) injective but surjective

  (d) neither surjective nor injective

64. Let $f : N \to R$ be defined by $f(x) = x^2$. Range of the function among the following is__________.

  (a) $\{1, 4, 9, 16, ...\}$

  (b) $\{1, 4, 8, 9, 10, ...\}$

  (c) $\{1, 4, 9, 15, 16, ...\}$

  (d) $\{1, 4, 8, 16, ...\}$

65. The function $f : Z \to Z$ defined by $f(x) = x^2$ is__________.

  (a) neither injective nor surjective

  (b) injective

  (c) surjective

  (d) bijective

Chapter Test

Time : *45 Minutes*   **Max. Marks : 20**

Directions :

(i)   **Questions number 1-8 carry** 1 mark **each.**

(ii)   **Question number** 9 **carry** 4 marks.

(iii)   **Questions number 10-13 are** Very Short Answer Questions **and carry** 2 marks **each.**

Multiple Choice Questions

1. The maximum number of equivalence relations on the set A = {1, 2, 3} are

   (a)   1   (b)   2   (c)   3   (d)   5

2. If the set A contains 5 elements and the set B contains 6 elements, then the number of one-one and onto mapping from A to B is

   (a)   720   (b)   120

   (c)   0   (d)   None of these

3. The number of all one-one functions from set A = {1, 2, 3} to itself is

   (a)   2   (b)   6   (c)   3   (d)   1

4. The number of equivalence relations in the set {1, 2, 3} containing (1, 2) and (2, 1) is

   (a)   2   (b)   3   (c)   1   (d)   4

One Word Answer Questions

5. Given two finite sets A and B such that n (A) = 2, n (B) = 3. Determine the total number of relation from A to B.

6. Let A = {1, 2, 3} and R = {(1, 2), (2, 3)} be a relation in A. Then, find the minimum number of ordered pairs may be added, so that R becomes an equivalence relation.

Assertion & Reason Questions

DIRECTIONS : *Each of these questions contains an assertion followed by reason. Read them carefully and answer the question on the basis of following options. You have to select the one that best describes the two statements.*

(a) If both Assertion and Reason are correct and the Reason is a correct explanation of the Assertion.

(b) If both Assertion and Reason are correct but Reason is not a correct explanation of the Assertion.

(c) If the Assertion is correct but Reason is incorrect.

(d) If the Assertion is incorrect but the Reason is correct.

7. **Assertion:** $f(x) = \dfrac{x-1}{x+1}$ be define on R–{–1}.

   Reason: $f(x)$ is a bijective function.

8. **Assertion:** If $f(x)$ is even function and $g(x)$ is odd function then f.g is an odd function.

   Reason: If $f(-x) = f(x)$ then $f(x)$ is called even function.

Case/Passage Based Question

DIRECTIONS (Q. 9): *has 5 subparts based on Case/Passage given, attempt any 4 out of 5 questions.*

9. If h denotes the number of honest people and p denotes the number of punctual people and a relation between honest people and punctual people is given as h = p + 5.

   Using the information given above answer the folowing.

(i) If number of honest people is 17 then number of punctual people is

   (a)   22   (b)   12

   (c)   10   (d)   11

(ii) The *h* is

   (a)   only one-one   (b)   only onto

   (c)   bijective   (d)   None of these

(iii) The *h* is

   (a)   reflexive   (b)   symmetric

   (c)   transitive   (d)   None of these

(iv) The equivalence class of [0] is ________.

   (a)   5   (b)   0

   (c)   1   (d)   None of these

(v) The value of h (–2) is equal to

   (a)   3   (b)   5

   (c)   7   (d)   None of these

Very Short Answer Questions

10. If the function f: $[1, \infty) \to [1, \infty)$ is defined by $f(x) = 2^{x(x-1)}$ then determine f^{-1}.

11. Let n be a fixed positive integer. Define a relation R on Z (set of integers) by a R b iff n divides (a – b), then what is R.

12. For real numbers x and y, we write x R y iff $x - y + \sqrt{2}$ is an irrational number, then what is the relation R.

13. If f : R → R is defined by f(x) = 2x – 3 then find fof.

Solutions

Practice Exercise-1

1. (b) 2. (a) 3. (b) 4. (a) 5. (b)

6. (i) (b) (ii) (c) (iii) (d) (iv) (c) (v) (c)

7. 3, 1

8. 7

9. 1

10. On the set N of natural numbers

    $R = \{(x, y) : x, y \in N, 2x + y = 41\}$

    Since $(1, 1) \notin R$ as $2 \cdot 1 + 1 = 3 \neq 41$. So, R is not reflexive.

    $(1, 39) \in R$ but $(39, 1) \notin R$. So, R is not symmetric $(20, 1)$, $(1, 39) \in R$ but $(20, 39) \notin R$. So, R is not transitive.

11. On $A \neq \phi$, consider the relation $\phi \leq A \times A$ let $a \in A$, $(a, a) \notin \phi$. So ϕ is not reflexive. Trivially ϕ is symmetric as well as transitive.

12. $(3, 1)$ is the single ordered pair which needs to be added to R to make it the smallest equivalence relation.

13. $[0] = \{0, \pm2, \pm4, \pm6, ...\}$

14. Since, $(2, 3) \in R$ but $(3, 2) \notin R$

    Therefore, R is not symmetric.

18. (i) Let $A = \{1, 2, 3\}$, then $R = \{(1, 2), (2, 1), (1, 3), (3, 1)\}$

    (ii) Let $A = \{1, 2, 3\}$, then $R = \{(1, 1), (2, 2), (3, 3), (1, 2), (2, 3), (1, 3)\}$

19. R is not equivalence relation.

20. (i) Yes, R is symmetric relation

    $\because$ $a\,R\,b \Rightarrow b\,R\,a \; \forall\, a, b \in A$

    (ii) Yes $\because$ Given relation is reflexive as

    $a\,R\,a \; \forall\, a \in A$. Also, relation is symmetric as

    $a\,R\,b \Rightarrow b\,R\,a \; \forall\, a, b \in A$

    and Given relation R is transitive as

    $a\,R\,b, b\,R\,c \Rightarrow a\,R\,c \; \forall\, a, b, c \in A$

21. A = set of people

    $R = \{(a, b) : a$ and b are brothers $a, b \in A\}$

    (i) Clearly, R is reflexive $\because$ $a\,R\,a$

    (ii) Also, R is symmetric $\because$ if $a\,R\,b$ then $b\,R\,a$

    (iii) Also, if $a\,R\,b, b\,R\,c$ then $a\,R\,c$

    $\therefore$ Relation R is transitive.

    $\therefore$ Relation R is an equivalence relation.

22. Yes, R is a transitive relation

    $a\,R\,b, b\,R\,c \Rightarrow a\,R\,c.$

NCERT Exercise-1

1. (i) Relation R in the set $A = \{1, 2, ..., 14\}$ defined as $R = \{(x, y) : 3x - y = 0\}$

    (a) Put $y = x$, $3x - x \neq 0 \Rightarrow R$ is not reflexive.

    (b) If $3x - y = 0$, then $3y - x \neq 0$, R is not symmetric

    (c) If $3x - y = 0$, $3y - z = 0$, then $3x - z \neq 0$, R is not transitive.

    (ii) Relations in the set N of natural numbers in defined by $R = \{(x, y): y = x + 5$ and $x < 4\}$

    (a) Putting $y = x$, $x \neq x + 5$, R is not reflexive

    (b) Putting $y = x + 5$, then $x \neq y + 5$, R is not symmetric.

    (c) If $y = x + 5$, $z = y + 5$, then $z \neq x + 5$ $\Rightarrow R$ is not transitive.

    (iii) Relation R in the set $A = \{1, 2, 3, 4, 5, 6\}$ as $R = \{(x, y) : y$ is divisible by $x\}$

    (a) Putting $y = x$, x is divisible by $x \Rightarrow R$ is reflexive.

    (b) If y is divisible by x, then x is not divisible by y when $x \neq y \Rightarrow R$ is not symmetric.

    (c) If y is divisible by x and z is divisible by y then z is divisible by x e.g., 2 is divisible by 1, 4 is divisible by 2.

    $\Rightarrow$ 4 is divisible by $1 \Rightarrow R$ is transitive.

    (iv) Relation R in Z of all integers defined as $R = \{(x, y) : x - y$ is an integer$\}$

    (a) $x - x = 0$ is an integer $\Rightarrow R$ is reflexive

    (b) $x - y$ is an integer so is $y - x \Rightarrow R$ is transitive.

    (c) $x - y$ is an integer, $y - z$ is an integer and $x - z$ is also an integer $\Rightarrow R$ is transitive.

    (v) R is a set of human beings in a town at a particular time.

    (a) $R = \{(x, y)\} : x$ and y work at the same place. It is reflexive as x works at the same place. It is symmetric since x and y or y and x work at same place.

    It is transitive since x, y work at the same place and if y, z work at the same place, then x and z also work at the same place.

    (b) $R : \{(x, y) : x$ and y line in the same locality$\}$

    With similar reasoning as in part (a), R is reflexive, symmetrical and transitive.

    (c) $R : \{(x, y)\} : x$ is exactly 7 cm taller than y it is not reflexive : x cannot 7 cm taller than x. It is not symmetric : x is exactly 7 cm taller than y, y cannot be exactly 7 cm taller than x. It is not transitive : If x is exactly 7 cm taller than y and if y is exactly taller than z, then x is not exactly 7 cm taller than z.

(d) $R = \{(x, y) : x \text{ is wife of } y\}$

R is not reflexive : x cannot be wife of x. R is not symmetric : x is wife of y but y is not wife of x.

R is not transitive : if x is a wife of y then y cannot be the wife of anybody else.

(e) $R = \{(x, y) : x \text{ is a father of } y\}$

It is not reflexive : x cannot be father of himself. It is not symmetric : x is a father of y but y cannot be the father of x.

It is not transitive : x is a father of y and y is a father of z then x cannot be the father of z.

2. (i) R is not reflexive, $\because$ a is not less than or equal to a^2 for all $a \in R$, e.g., $\dfrac{1}{2}$ is not less than $\dfrac{1}{4}$.

(ii) R is not symmetric since if $a \leq b^2$ then b is not less than or equal to a^2 e.g. $2 < 5^2$ but 5 is not less than 2^2.

(iii) R is not transitive : If $a \leq b^2$, $b \leq c^2$, then a is not less than c^2, e.g. $2 < (-2)^2$, $-2 < (-1)^2$, but 2 is not less than $(-1)^2$.

3. (i) R is not reflexive $a \neq a + 1$.

(ii) R is not symmetric if $b = a + 1$, then $a \neq b + 1$

(iii) R is not transitive if $b = a + 1$, $c = b + 1$ then $c \neq a + 1$.

4. $R = \{(a, b) : a \leq b\}$

(i) R is reflexive, replacing b by a, $a \leq a \Rightarrow a = a$ is true.

(ii) R is not symmetric, $a \leq b$, and $b \leq a$ which is not true $2 < 3$, but 3 is not less than 2.

(iii) R is transitive, if $a \leq b$ and $b \leq c$, then $a \leq c$, e.g. $2 < 3, 3 < 4 \Rightarrow 2 < 4$.

5. (i) R is not reflexive.

(ii) R is not symmetric.

(iii) R is not transitive.

6. (i) $(1, 1), (2, 2), (3, 3)$ do not belong to relation R $\therefore$ R is not reflexive.

(ii) It is symmetric $(1, 2)$ and $(2, 1)$ belong to R.

(iii) there are only two element 1 and 2 in this relation and there is no third element c in it $\Rightarrow$ R is not transitive.

7. (i) The number of pages in a book remain the same $\Rightarrow$ Relation R is reflexive.

(ii) The book x has the same number of pages as the book y.

$\Rightarrow$ Book y has the same number of pages as the book x.

$\Rightarrow$ The relation R is symmetric.

(iii) Book x and y have the same number of pages. Also book y and z have the same number of pages.

$\Rightarrow$ Books x and z also have the same number of pages.

$\Rightarrow$ R is transitive also

Thus, R is an equivalence relation.

8. $A = \{1, 2, 3, 4, 5\}$ and $R = \{(a, b) : |a - b| \text{ is even}\}$

$R = \{(1, 3), (1, 5), (3, 5), (2, 4)\}$

(a) (i) Let us take any element of a set A.

then $|a - a| = 0$ which is even.

$\Rightarrow$ R is reflexive.

(ii) If $|a - b|$ is even, then $|b - a|$ is also even, where,

$R = \{(a, b) : |a - b| \text{ is even}\} \Rightarrow$ R is symmetric.

(iii) Further $a - c = a - b + b - c$

If $|a - b|$ and $|b - c|$ are even, then their sum $|a - b + b - c|$ is also even.

$\Rightarrow |a - c|$ is even, $\therefore$ R is transitive.

Hence R is an equivalence relation.

(b) Elements of $\{1, 3, 5\}$ are related to each other.

Since $|1 - 3| = 2$, $|3 - 5| = 2$, $|1 - 5| = 4$. All are even numbers.

= Elements of $\{1, 3, 5\}$ are related to each other. Similarly elements of $\{2, 4\}$ are related to each other. Since $|2 - 4| = 2$ an even number. No element of set $\{1, 3, 5\}$ is related to any element of $\{2, 4\}$.

9. The set A $\therefore \{x \in Z : 0 \leq x \leq 12\} = \{0, 1, 2, \ldots\ldots\ldots, 12\}$

(i) $R = \{(a, b) : |a - b| \text{ is a multiple of } 4\}$

$|a - b| = 4k$ on $b = a + 4k$.

$\therefore$ R = $\{(1, 5), (1, 9), (2, 6), (2, 10), (3, 7), (3, 11), (4, 8), (4, 12), (5, 9), (6, 10), (7, 11), (8, 12), (0, 0), (1, 1), (2, 2), \ldots\ldots (12, 12)\}$

(a) $(a - a) = 0 = 4k$, where $k = 0 \Rightarrow (a, a) \in R$

$\therefore$ R is reflexive.

(b) If $|a - b| = 4k$, then $|b - a| = 4k$ i.e. (a, b) and (b, a) both belong to R. R is symmetric.

(c) $a - c = a - b + b - c$

when $a - b$ and $b - c$ are both multiples of 4 then $a - c$ is also a multiple of 4. This shows if (a, b) $(b, c) \in R$ then $a - c$ also $\in R$

$\therefore$ R is an equivalence relation. The sets related 1 are $\{(1, 5), (1, 9)\}$.

(ii) $R = \{(a, b) : a = b\}$

$\therefore \{(0, 0), (1, 1), (2, 2) \ldots\ldots (12, 12)\}$

(a) $a = a \Rightarrow (a, a) \in R$ $\therefore$ R is reflexive.

(b) Again if $(a, b) \in R$, then (b, a) also $\in R$

Since $a = b$ and $(a, b) \in R \Rightarrow$ R is symmetric.

(c) If $(a, b) \in R$, then $(b, c) \in R \Rightarrow a = b = c$

$\therefore a = c \Rightarrow (a, c) \in R$, Hence, R is transitive set related is $\{1\}$.

10. (i) Let A = set of straight lines in a plane

R : $\{(a, b) : a \text{ is perpendicular to } b\}$ let a, b be two perpendicular lines.

(ii) Let A = set of real numbers $R = \{(a, b) : a > b\}$

(a) An element is not greater than itself

$\therefore$ R is not reflexive.

(b) If $a > b$ than b is not greater than a
$\Rightarrow$ R is not symmetric

(c) If $a > b$ also $b > c$, then $a > c$ thus R is transitive

Hence, R is transitive but neither reflexive nor symmetric.

(iii) The relation R in the set $\{1, 2, 3\}$ is given by
$R = \{(a, b) : a + b \leq 4\}$
$R = \{(1, 1), (1, 2), (2, 1), (1, 3), (3, 1), (2, 2)\}$ $(1, 1), (2, 2)$
$\in R \Rightarrow R$ is reflexive
$(1, 2), (2, 1), (1, 3), (3, 1) \Rightarrow R$ is symmetric

But it is not transitive, since $(2, 1) \in R$, $(1, 3) \in R$ but $(2, 3) \notin R$.

(iv) The relation R in the set $\{1, 2, 3\}$ given by $R = \{(a, b) : a \leq b\} = \{(1, 2), (2, 2), (3, 3), (2, 3), (1, 3)\}$

(a) $(1, 1), (2, 2), (3, 3) \in R \Rightarrow R$ is reflexive

(b) $(1, 2) \in R$, but $(2, 1) \notin R \Rightarrow R$ is not symmetric

(c) $(1, 2) \in R, (2, 3) \in R$, Also $(1, 3) \in R \Rightarrow R$ is transitive.

(v) The relation R in the set $\{1, 2, 3\}$ given by
$R = \{(a, b) : 0 < |a - b| \leq 2\} = \{(1, 2), (2, 1), (1, 3), (3, 1), (2, 3), (3, 2)\}$

(a) R is not reflexive
$\because$ $(1, 1), (2, 2), (3, 3)$ do not belong to R.

(b) R is symmetric
$\because$ $(1, 2), (2, 1), (1, 3), (3, 1), (2, 3), (3, 2) \in R$

(c) R is transitive $(1, 2) \in R, (2, 3) \in R$, Also $(1, 3) \in R$

11. Let O be the origin then the relation
$R = \{(P, Q) : OP = OQ\}$

(i) R is reflexive. Take any distance OP,
$\therefore$ $OP = OP \Rightarrow R$ is reflexive.

(ii) R is symmetric, if $OP = OQ$ then $OQ = OP$

(iii) R is transitive, let $OP = OQ$ and $OQ = OR$
$\Rightarrow OP = OR$

Hence, R is an equivalence relation.

Since $OP = K$ (constant) $\Rightarrow$ P lies on a circle with centre at the origin.

12. (i) In a set of triangles $R = \{(T_1, T_2) : T_1$ is similar $T_2\}$

(a) Since A triangle T is similar to itself. Therefore $(T, T) \in R$ for all $T \in A$.

Since R is reflexive

(b) If triangle T_1 is similar to triangle T_2 then T_2 is similar triangle T_1
$\therefore$ R is symmetric.

(c) Let T_1 is similar to triangle T_2 and T_2 to T_3 then triangle T_1 is similar to triangle T_3, $\therefore$ R is transitive.

Hence, R is an equivalence relation.

(ii) Two triangles are similar if their sides are proportional now sides 3, 4, 5 of triangle T_1 are proportional to the sides 6, 8, 10 of triangle T_3.

$\therefore$ T_1 is related to T_3.

13. Let n be the number of sides of polygon P_1.
$R = \{(P_1, P_2) : P_1$ and P_2 are n sides polygons$\}$

(i) (a) Any polygon P_1 has n sides $\Rightarrow$ R is reflexive

(b) If P_1 has n sides, P_2 also has n sides then if P_2 has n sides P_1 also has n sides.
$\Rightarrow$ R is symmetric.

(c) Let P_1, P_2 ; P_2, P_3 are n sided polygons. P_1 and P_3 are also n sided polygons.
$\Rightarrow$ R is transitive. Hence R is an equivalence relation.

(ii) The set A = set of all the triangles in a plane.

14. L = set of all the lines in XY plane, $R = \{(L_1, L_2) : L_1$ is parallel to $L_2\}$

(i) (a) L_1 is parallel to itself $\Rightarrow$ R is reflexive.

(b) L_1 is parallel to L_2 $\Rightarrow L_2$ is parallel to L_1 $\Rightarrow$ R is symmetric.

(c) Let L_1 is parallel to L_2 and L_2 is parallel to L_3 and L_1 is parallel to L_3 $\Rightarrow$ R is transitive.

Hence, R is an equivalence relation.

(ii) Set of parallel lines related to $y = 2x + 4$ is $y = 2x + c$, where c is an arbitrary constant.

15. **(b)**

16. **(c)** Option (c) satisfies the condition that $a = b - 2$
i.e. $6 = 8 - 2$ and $b > 6$, i.e. $b = 8$

Practice Exercise-2 

1. **(d)** **2.** **(c)** **3.** **(d)** **4.** **(b)** **5.** **(c)** **6.** **(a)**

7. **(c)**

8. **(i)** **(b)** **(ii)** **(a)** **(iii)** **(c)** **(iv)** **(a)** **(v)** **(b)**

9. 6 **10.** 6

11. $2^n - 2$

12. $[-1, 3] = S$

13. $f = \{(x, u), (y, v), (z, v)\}$ is the given mapping from $A = \{x, y, z\}$ to $B = \{u, v, w\}$

Since $f(y) = f(z) = v$, f is many one and range $f = \{u, v\} \neq B$ so it is into.

14. $-\sqrt{2} \leq \cos x + \sin x \leq \sqrt{2}$

$\Rightarrow 0 \leq \cos x + \sin x + \sqrt{2} \leq 2\sqrt{2}$ $\therefore$ Range $f = \left[0, 2\sqrt{2}\right]$

15. Since $n(A) \neq n(B)$, there cannot exist any one-one onto mapping from A to B. Hence number of one-one onto mapping from A to B is zero.

16. Total number of mappings from A to B is 2^n of which the 2 mappings are not surjective i.e. not onto. Thus the number of surjective mapping is $2^n - 2$.

17. It is not a mapping as $f(0) = \dfrac{1}{0} \notin R$. Hence no questions of it to be one-one or onto.

18. Since $f: R \to R$, $f(x) = \log_e x$ is not a mapping as far $x < 0$, $\log_e x \notin R$ $[\because \log_e(-2)$ is imaginary$]$

Thus, there is no question of being one-one onto.

19. We observe that $f(-2) = f(2)$. So, f is not one-one.

Also, $f(x) = |x|$ assumes only non-negative values. So, negative real numbers in R (co-domain) do not have their pre-images in R (domain).

Hence, f is neither one-one nor onto.

20. $R - \{0\} \cap [-1, 1] \cap (2, \infty) = \phi$ (null set)

Hint: Let $\Psi(x) = f(x) + g(x) + h(x)$, $f(x) = \dfrac{1}{x}$, $g(x)$

$= 2 \sin^{-1} x$ and $h(x) = \dfrac{1}{\sqrt{x-2}}$

domain $(f) = R - \{0\}$, domain $(g) = [-1, 1]$ and domain $h = (2, \infty)$

$\therefore$ Domain $(\Psi) = R - \{0\} \cap [-1, 1] \cap (2, \infty) = \phi$ (null set).

22. Bijective

24. Domain of $R \cap R' = [-5, 5]$ and Range of $R \cap R' = [0, 5]$

Hint: $R \cap R'$ is a function is clear from fig. that $R \cap R'$ is defined when $25 - x^2 \geq 0$ i.e. when $-5 \leq x \leq 5$

So, the domain of $R \cap R'$ is $[-5, 5]$.

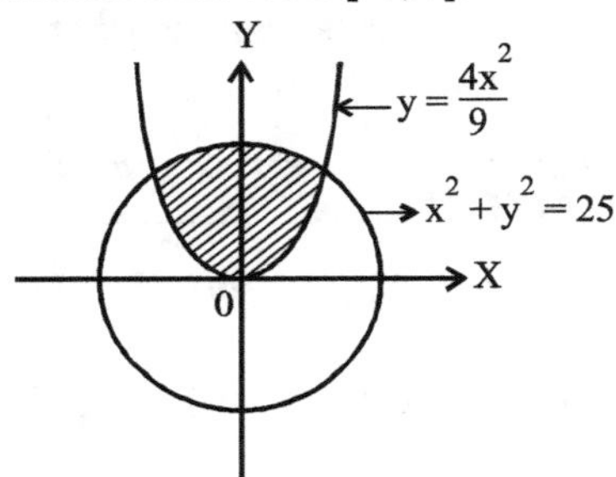

The range of R is also $[-5, 5]$ and the range of R' is R^+. Hence the range of $R \cap R'$ is $[0, 5]$.

25. We observe that $f(x) = 0$ for all $x \in [0, 1)$

So, $f: R \to R$ is not one-one.

Also, $f: R \to R$, does not attain non-integral values. Therefore, non-integer points in R do not have their pre-images in the domain. So, $f: R \to R$ is not onto.

Hence, $f: R \to R$ is neither one-one nor onto.

NCERT Exercise-2

1. (a)   We observe the following properties of f:

(i) $f(x) = \dfrac{1}{x}$, if $f(x_1) = f(x_2)$

$\Rightarrow \dfrac{1}{x_1} = \dfrac{1}{x_2} \Rightarrow x_1 = x_2$

Each $x \in R$ has a unique image in codomain $\Rightarrow f$ is one-one.

(ii) For each y belonging codomain then $y = \dfrac{1}{x}$ or

$x = \dfrac{1}{y}$ there is a unique pre-image of y.

$\Rightarrow f$ is onto.

(b)   When domain R is replaced by N. codomain remaining the same, then $f: N \to R$ If $f(x_1) = f(x_2)$

$\Rightarrow \dfrac{1}{n_1} = \dfrac{1}{n_2} \Rightarrow n_1 = n_2$ where $n_1, n_2 \in N$

$\Rightarrow f$ is one-one.

But for every real number belonging to codomain may not have a pre-image in N.

e.g. $\dfrac{1}{2}, \dfrac{3}{2}, N$ $\therefore$ f is not onto.

2.   (i) $f: N \to N$ given by $f(x) = x^2$

(a) $f(x_1) \Rightarrow f(x_2) \Rightarrow x_1^2 = x_2^2 \Rightarrow x_1 = x_2$

$\therefore$ f is one-one i.e. it is injective.

(b)   There are such member of codomain which have no image in domain N. e.g. $3 \in$ codomain N. But there is no pre-image in domain of f.

$\Rightarrow f$ is not onto i.e. not surjective.

(ii) $f: z \to z$ given by $f(x) = x^2$

(a) $f(-1) = f(1) = 1 \Rightarrow -1$ and 1 have the same image.

$\therefore$ f is not one-one i.e. not injective.

(b)   There are many such elements belonging to codomain have no pre-image in its codomain z.

e.g. $3 \in$ codomain z but $\sqrt{3} \notin$ domain z of f,

$\therefore$ f is not onto i.e. not surjective

(iii) $f: R \to R$, given by $f(x) = x^2$

(a) f is not one-one since $f(-1) = f(1) = 1$

-1 and 1 have the same image i.e., f is not injective

(b) $-2 \in$ codomain R of f but $\sqrt{-2}$ does not belong to domain R of f.

$\Rightarrow f$ is not onto i.e. f is not surjective.

(iv) Injective but not surjective.

(v) Injective but not surjective.

3. $f: R \to R$ given by $f(x) = [x]$

(a) $f(1.2) = 1$, $f(1.5) = 1 \Rightarrow f$ is not one-one

(b)   All the images of $x \in R$ belonging to its domain have integers as the images in codomain. But no fraction proper or improper belonging to codomain of f has any pre-image in its domain.

$\Rightarrow f$ is not onto.

4. $f: R \to R$ given by $f(x) = |x|$

(a) $f(-1) = |-1| = 1$, $f(1) = |1| = 1$

$\Rightarrow -1$ and 1 have the same image

$\therefore$ f is not one-one

(b)   No negative value belonging to codomain of f has any pre-image in its domain

$\therefore$ f is not onto. Hence, f is neither one-one nor onto.

5. $f: R \to R$ given by $f(x) = \begin{cases} 1, & \text{if } x > 0 \\ 0, & \text{if } x = 0 \\ -1, & \text{if } x < 0 \end{cases}$

(a) $f(1) = f(2) = 1$

∴ 1 and 2 have the same image i.e.

$f(x_1) = f(x_2) = 1$ for $x > 0 \Rightarrow x_1 \neq x_2$

Similarly $f(x_1) = f(x_2) = -1$, for $x < 0$ where $x_1 \neq x_2$

$\Rightarrow f$ is not one-one.

(b) Except $-1, 0, 1$ no other member of codomain of f has any pre-image in its domain.

∴ f is not onto. $\Rightarrow f$ is neither into nor onto.

6. $A = \{1, 2, 3\}, B = \{4, 5, 6, 7\}$ $f = \{(1, 4), (2, 5), (3, 6)\}$.

Every member of A has a unique image in B

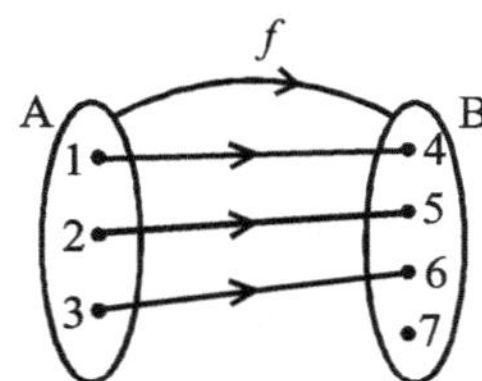

∴ f is one-one

7. (i) $f: R \to R$ defined by $3 - 4x$,

$f(x_1) = 3 - 4x_1, f(x_2) = 3 - 4x_2$

(a) $f(x_1) = f(x_2) \Rightarrow 3 - 4x_1 = 3 - 4x_2$

$\Rightarrow x_1 = x_2$. This shows that f is one-one

(b) $f(x) = y = 3 - 4x$ ∴ $x = \dfrac{3 - y}{4}$

For every value of y belonging to its codomain. There is a pre-image in its domain $\Rightarrow f$ is onto.

Hence, f is one-one onto

(ii) $f: R \to R$ given by $f(x) = 1 + x^2$

(a) $f(1) = 1 + 1 = 2, f(-1) = 1 + 1 = 2$

∴ $f(-1) = f(1) = 2$ i.e. -1 and 1 have the same image 2.

$\Rightarrow f$ is not one-one.

(b) No negative number belonging to its codomain has its pre-image in its domain

$\Rightarrow f$ is not onto. Thus f is neither one-one nor onto.

8. We have $f: (A \times B) \to B \times A$ such that $f(a, b) = b, a$

(a) ∴ $f(a_1, b_1) = (b_1, a_1)$ $f(a_2, b_2) = (b_2, a_2)$

$f(a_1, b_1) = f(a_2, b_2) \Rightarrow (b_1, a_1) = (b_2, a_2)$

$\Rightarrow b_1 = b_2$ and $a_1 = a_2$ ∴ f is one-one

(b) Every member (p, q) belonging to its codomain has its pre-image in its domain as (q, p)

f is onto. Thus, f is one-one and onto

i.e. it is bijective.

9. $f: N \to N$, defined by

$$f(n) = \begin{cases} \dfrac{n+1}{2}, & \text{if } n \text{ is odd} \\ \dfrac{n}{2}, & \text{if } n \text{ is even} \end{cases}$$

(a) $f(1) = \dfrac{n+1}{2} = \dfrac{1+1}{2} = \dfrac{2}{2} = 1, f(2) = \dfrac{n}{2} = \dfrac{2}{2} = 1$

The elements 1, 2 belonging to domain of f have the same image 1 in its codomain

$\Rightarrow f$ is not one-one. ∴ it is not injective.

(b) Every member of codomain has pre-image in its domain e.g. 1 has two pre-images 1 and 2

$\Rightarrow f$ is onto. Thus f is not one-one but it is onto

$\Rightarrow f$ is not bijective.

10. $f: A \to B$ where $A = R - \{3\}, B = R - \{1\}$ f is defined by $f(x) = \dfrac{x-2}{x-3}$

(a) $f(x_1) = \dfrac{x_1 - 2}{x_1 - 3}, f(x_2) = \dfrac{x_2 - 2}{x_2 - 3}$

$f(x_1) = f(x_2) = \dfrac{x_1 - 2}{x_1 - 3} = \dfrac{x_2 - 2}{x_2 - 3}$

or $(x_1 - 2)(x_2 - 3) = (x_2 - 2)(x_1 - 3)$

or $x_1 x_2 - 3x_1 - 2x_2 + 6 = x_1 x_2 - 2x_1 - 3x_2 + 6$

i.e. $-3x_1 - 2x_2 = -2x_1 - 3x_2$

or $-x_1 = -x_2$

$\Rightarrow x_1 = x_2$ ∴ f is one-one

(b) Let $y = \dfrac{x-2}{x-3}, xy - 3y = x - 2$

or $x(y - 1) = 3y - 2 \Rightarrow x = \dfrac{3y - 2}{y - 1}$

For every value of y except $y = 1$, there is a pre-image.

$x = \dfrac{3y - 2}{y - 1} \Rightarrow f$ is onto. Thus, f is one-one and onto.

11. $f(-1) = (-1)^4 = 1, f(1) = 1^4 = 1$

∴ $-1, 1$ have the same image $1 \Rightarrow f$ is not one-one

Further -2 in the codomain of f has no pre-image in its domain.

∴ f is not onto i.e. f is neither one-one nor onto

Option (d) is correct.

12. $f: R \to R$ is defined by $f(x) = 3x$

(a) $f(x_1) = 3x_1, f(x_2) = 3x_2 \Rightarrow f(x_1) = f(x_2)$

$\Rightarrow 3x_1 = 3x_2 \Rightarrow x_1 = x_2 \Rightarrow f$ is one-one

(b) for every member y belonging to co-domain has pre-image x in domain of f.

∵ $y = 3x \Rightarrow x = \dfrac{y}{3}$, ∴ f is onto

∴ f is one-one and onto. Option (a) is correct.

1. $R = \{(x, y) : x + 2y = 8\}$

$x = 1,\ y = \dfrac{7}{2} \notin N,\ x = 5,\ y = \dfrac{3}{2} \notin N$

$x = 2,\ y = 3 \in N,\ x = 6,\ y = 1 \in N$

$x = 3,\ y = \dfrac{5}{2} \notin N,\ x = 7,\ y = \dfrac{1}{2} \notin N$

$x = 4, y = 2,\ \in N, x = 8,\ y = 0 \notin N$

$\therefore$ Range $(R) = \{1, 2, 3\}$

2. Given function is $f : N \to N$ such that

$$f(x) = \begin{cases} x + 1, & \text{if x is odd} \\ x - 1, & \text{if x is even} \end{cases}$$

One-one From the given function, we observe that

Case I : When x is odd

Let $f(x_1) = f(x_2) \Rightarrow x_1 + 1 = x_2 + 1 \Rightarrow x_1 = x_2$

$\because f(x_1) = f(x_2) \Rightarrow x_1 = x_2,\ \forall\ x_1, x_2 \in N$. So, $f(x)$ is one-one.

Case II : When x is even

Let $f(x_1) = f(x_2) \Rightarrow x_1 - 1 = x_2 - 1 \Rightarrow x_1 = x_2$

$\because f(x_1) = f(x_2) \Rightarrow x_1 = x_2,\ \forall\ x_1, x_2 \in N$. So, $f(x)$ is one-one.

Hence, from case I and case II, we observe that $f(x_1) = f(x_2)$

$\Rightarrow x_1 = x_2 \forall x_1, x_2 \in N$

$\because f(x)$ is a one-one function.

Onto: To show $f(x)$ is onto, we show that its range and co-domain are same.

From the definition of given function, we observe that

$f(1) = 2, f(2) = 1, f(3) = 4, f(4) = 3$ and so on.

So, we get set of natural numbers as the set of values of $f(x)$.

$\Rightarrow$ Range of $f(x) = N$. Also, given that co-domain $= N$

$$\left[\because f: \underset{\text{domain}}{N} \to \underset{\text{co-domain}}{N} \right]$$

$\because$ Range $=$ Co-domain $\therefore f(x)$ is an onto function.

Hence, the function $f(x)$ is bijective.

3. $A = \{1, 2, 3, \ldots\ldots, 9\} \subset \mathbb{N}$, the set of natural numbers.

Let R be the relation in $A \times A$ defined by $(a, b) R (c, d)$ if $a + d = b + c$ for $(a, b), (c, d)$ in $A \times A$. We have to show that R is an equivalence relation.

Reflexivity:

Let (a, b) be an arbitrary element of $A \times A$.

Then, we have: $(a, b) \in A \times A$

$\Rightarrow a, b \in A$

$\Rightarrow a + b = b + a$ (by commutativity of addition on $A \subset \mathbb{N}$)

$\Rightarrow (a, b) R (a, b)$

Thus, $(a, b) R (a, b)$ for all $(a, b) \in A \times A$

So, R is reflexive.

Symmetry:

Let $(a, b), (c, d) \in A \times A$ such that $(a, b) R (c, d)$.

$a + d = b + c \Rightarrow b + c = a + d$

$\Rightarrow c + b = d + a$ (by commutativity of addition on $A \subset N$)

$\Rightarrow (c, d) R (a, b)$. Thus, $(a, b) R (c, d) \Rightarrow (c, d) R (a, b)$

for all $(a, b), (c, d) \in A \times A$

So, R is symmetric.

Transitivity:

Let $(a, b), (c, d), (e, f) \in A \times A$ such that $(a, b) R (c, d)$ and $(c, d) R (e, f)$. Then, we have:

$(a, b) R (c, d)$

$\Rightarrow a + d = b + c$ ...(i)

$(c, d) R (e, f) \Rightarrow c + f = d + e$ ...(ii)

Adding equations (i) and (ii), we get:

$(a + d) + (c + f) = (b + c) + (d + e)$

$\Rightarrow a + f = b + e \Rightarrow (a, b) R (e, f)$

Thus, $(a, b) R (c, d)$ and $(c, d) R (e, f)$

$\Rightarrow (a, b) R (e, f)$ for all $(a, b), (c, d), (e, f) \in A \times A$.

So, R is transitive on $A \times A$.

Thus, R is reflexive, symmetric and transitive.

$\therefore$ R is an equivalence relation.

To write the equivalence class of $[(2, 5)]$, we need to search all the elements of the type (a, b) such that $2 + b = 5 + a$. $\therefore$ Equivalence class of

$[(2, 5)] = \{(1, 4), (2, 5), (3, 6), (4, 7), (5, 8), (6, 9)\}$

4. To prove a relation R is an equivalence relation, it will be suffient to prove it as a reflexive, symmetric and transitive relation.

(i) Reflexivity :

Let (a, b) be an arbitrary element of $N \times N$.

Now,

$a, b \in N$

$\Rightarrow ab(a + b) = ba (a + b) \Rightarrow (a, b) R (a, b)$

$\therefore$ $(a, b) R (a, b)$ for all $(a, b) \in N \times N$

Hence, R is reflexive.

(ii) Symmetry :

Let (a, b), (c, d) be an arbitrary element of $N \times N$ such that (a, b) R (c, d).

$\therefore \quad ad(b + c) = bc \ (a + d)$

$\Rightarrow \quad cb(d + a) = da \ (c + b) \Rightarrow (c, d)$ R (a, b)

$\therefore \quad (a, b)$ R (c , d)

$\Rightarrow \quad (c, d)$ R (a, b) for all (a, b) , $(c, d) \in N \times N$

Hence, R is symmetric.

(iii) Transitivity :

Let (a, b), (c, d), (e, f) be an arbitrary element of $N \times N$ such that (a, b) R (c, d) and (c, d) R (e, f).

$\Rightarrow \quad a f \ (b + e) = be \ (a + f)$

$\Rightarrow \quad (a, b)$ R (e, f)

$\therefore \quad (a, b)$ R (c, d) and (c, d) R (e, f)

$\Rightarrow \quad (a, b)$ R (e , f) for all (a, b), (c, d), $(e, f) \in N \times N$

Hence, R is transitive.

Thus, R being reflexive, symmetric and transitive, is an equivalence relation on $N \times N$.

5. Let $A = \{x \in z : 0 \leq x \leq 12\}$

$\therefore \quad A = \{0, 1, 2, 3, 4, 5, 6, 7, 8, 9, 10, 11, 12\}$

Now $R = \{(a, b): a, b \in A, |a - b| \text{ is divisible by } 4\}$

$\therefore \quad R = \{(0, 4), (0, 8), (0, 12), (1, 5), (1, 9), (2, 6), (2, 10), (3, 7), (3, 11), (4, 8), (4, 12), (9, 1), (9, 5), (10, 2), (10, 6), (11, 7), (11, 3), (12, 4)(12, 8), (0, 0), (1, 1), (2, 2), (3, 3), (4, 4), (5, 5), (6, 6), (7, 7), (8, 8), (9, 9), (10, 10), (11, 11), (12, 12), (4, 0), (8, 0), (12, 0)\}$

Now we see is that

(i) $(a, a) \in R$ as $|a - a| = 0$ which is divisible by 4

$\qquad \therefore \quad R$ is reflexive

(ii) If $(a, b) \in R$, then $(b, a) \in R$ as if $|a - b|$ is divisible by 4, then $|b - a|$ is also divisible by 4.

$\qquad \therefore \quad R$ is symmetric

(iii) If $(a, b) \in R$ and $(b, c) \in R$, then $(a, c) \in R$

Because if $|a - b|$ is divisible by 4 and $|b - c|$ is divisible by 4 then $|a - b + b - c| = |a - c|$ is divisible by 4

$\qquad \therefore \quad R$ is transitive

Hence R is Reflexive Symmetric and Transitive

$\qquad \Rightarrow \quad R$ is equivalence relation

All elements related to 1

$\{(1, 1), (1, 5), (5, 1), (1, 9), (9, 1)\}$

$\qquad \therefore \quad \{1, 5, 9\}$ is set of elements related to 1.

Equivalence class [2]

$= \{(2, 6), (2, 10), (10, 2), (6, 2), (2, 2)\}$

6. Let x_1, x_2 be any two elements of set A, such that $f(x_1) = f(x_2)$

$\Rightarrow \quad \dfrac{x_1 - 1}{x_1 - 2} = \dfrac{x_2 - 1}{x_2 - 2}$

$\Rightarrow x_1 x_2 - 2x_1 - x_2 + 2 = x_1 x_2 - x_1 - 2x_2 + 2$

$\Rightarrow -2x_1 + x_1 = -2x_2 + x_2 \Rightarrow x_1 = x_2$

Thus, f is one-one, for all $x_1, x_2 \in A$.

Let y be an arbitrary element of B, then $f(x) = y$

$\Rightarrow \quad \dfrac{x - 1}{x - 2} = y, x \neq 2 \quad \Rightarrow \quad x = \dfrac{1 - 2y}{1 - y}$

Clearly, $x = \dfrac{1 - 2y}{1 - y}$ is a real number for all $y \neq 1$.

$\Rightarrow$ Corresponding to each $y \in B$, there exists

$\dfrac{1 - 2y}{1 - y} \in A$, such that $f\left(\dfrac{1 - 2y}{1 - y}\right) = y$

Thus, f is onto $\Rightarrow$ f is invertible.

$x = \dfrac{1 - 2y}{1 - y} \quad \Rightarrow \quad f^{-1}(y) = \dfrac{1 - 2y}{1 - y}$

Hence, $f^{-1}(x) = \dfrac{1 - 2x}{1 - x}$ for all $x \in R - \{1\}$

OR

Given set A = $\{ 0, 1, 2, 3, 4, 5, 6, 7, 8, 9, 10, 11, 12\}$.

and S = $\{(a, b) : a, b \in Z, |a - b| \text{ is divisible by } 3\}$.

(i) For all $a \in A$, $(a, a) \in S$ $\quad (\because a - a = 0 \text{ is divisible by } 3)$.

$\qquad \therefore$ S is reflexive in A.

(ii) For all $a, b \in A$,

If $(a, b) \in S$, i.e, $|a - b|$ is divisible by 3.

$\Rightarrow |b - a|$ is also divisible by 3.

$\qquad \therefore$ S is symmetric in A.

(iii) For all a, b, c $\in$ A.

Let $(a, b) \in S$ and $(b, c) \in S$.

i.e; $|a - b|$ is divisible by 3 and $|b - c|$ is divisible by 3.

and let $(a - b) = \pm 3q, (b - c) = \pm 3p$.

Adding we get :

$a - c = \pm 3(p + q) = \pm 3m$ (say)

$\Rightarrow |a - c| = 3m$ (divisible by 3).

$\qquad \therefore$ S is transitive in A.

Hence, S is an equivalence relation in A.

7. $(a, b) R(c, d) \Leftrightarrow ad = bc$ \hfill (given relation)

(i) Reflexivity

Since $ab = ba$ $\qquad \because ab \in N$

(a, b) R (a, b) is true

Relation R is reflexive.

(ii) Symmetry

Let (a, b) R (c, d)

$ad = bc$

But $bc = cb$ and $ad = da$

$\because \quad cb = da \Rightarrow cb = ad$

$(c, d)\ R\ (a, b)$

$\therefore (a, b)\ R\ (c, d) \Leftrightarrow (c, d)\ R\ (a, b)$

Relation is symmetric.

(iii) Transitivity

Let $(a, b)\ R\ (c, d)$ and $(c, d)\ R\ (e, f)$

$ad = bc$ and $cf = de$

$(ad)\ (cf) = (bc)\ (de)$

$(af)\ (dc) = (be)\ (dc)$

$af = be$

$\Rightarrow (a, b)\ R\ (e, f)$

$\therefore (a, b)\ R\ (c, d)$ and $(c, d)\ R\ (e, f)$

$\Rightarrow (a, b)\ R\ (e, f)$

$\Rightarrow$ Relation is transitive

Relation is symmetric, equivalence and transitive.

$\therefore$ Relation is equivalence relation.

1. **(c)** Since, aRb is defined as, if a is congruent to $b, \forall\ a, b \in T$.

As, $a \cong a$, so aRa So, R is reflexive,

Suppose, $aRb \Rightarrow a \cong b$

Then, $b \cong a \Rightarrow b \cong a \Rightarrow bRa$

So, R is symmetric

Suppose, aRb and bRc

$\Rightarrow a \cong b$ and $b \cong c$ Then, $a \cong c \Rightarrow aRc$

So, R is transitive. Hence, R is equivalence relation.

2. **(b)** Given aRb $\in$ R $\Rightarrow$ a is brother of b.

But bRa $\notin$ R $\because$ b may or may not be brother of a.

$\therefore$ R is not symmetric.

Let aRb $\in$ R and bRc $\in$ R

$\Rightarrow$ a is brother of b and b is brother of c.

$\therefore$ a is brother of c $\Rightarrow$ (a, c) $\in$ R. $\therefore$ It is transitive.

3. **(d)** Since, $\dfrac{1}{x}$ is not defined for $x = 0$

$\therefore$ f: R $\to$ R can not be defined.

4. **(b)** The function f(x) = x + 2 is one-one as for $x_1, x_2 \in$ Z.

Consider, $f(x_1) = f(x_2)$

$\Rightarrow x_1 + 2 = x_2 + 2 \Rightarrow x_1 = x_2$

Also, let y $\in$ codomain of f = Z such that y = f(x)

$\Rightarrow$ y = x + 2 $\Rightarrow$ x = y − 2 $\in$ Z for all y $\in$ Z

$\therefore$ f is onto. Hence, f(x) = x + 2 is bijective.

5. As $\alpha = 2, \beta = -1$

Domain A = {1, 2, 3, 4}. Range B = {1, 3, 5, 7}

Every element of domain has a unique image in B and hence g is a function. Now $g(x) = \alpha x + \beta$ but $g(2) = 3, g(3) = 5$

$\therefore \quad 2 = 2\alpha + \beta$ and $5 = 3\alpha + \beta$. $\alpha = 2, \beta = -1$

1. **(b)** Relation $R = \{(x, y) \in W \times W \mid$ the words x and y have at least one letter in common$\}$

   R is reflexive as every word has the same letters with itself, R is symmetric also

   But R is not transitive

   For example, BOLD is related BALL

   BALL is related to APE

   But BOLD has no letter in common with APE.

2. **(a)** Reflexive and transitive only.

   e.g. $(3, 3), (6, 6), (9, 9), (12, 12)$ [Reflexive]

   $(3, 6), (6, 12), (3, 12)$ [Transitive].

3. **(b)** Total number of elements in a set = 4

   Total number of relations = $2^{4 \times 4} = 2^{16}$

   In cartesian product we have 16 ordered pairs in which 4 are compulsory for reflexive relation, out of 12 ordered pairs.

   We can take $^{12}C_0 + ^{12}C_1 + \ldots + ^{12}C_{12} = 2^{12}$.

4. **(c)** **Reflexive:** R is not reflexive $\because |a| \geq a$

   Symmetric: R is not symmetric

   $aRb \Rightarrow |a| \leq b$ but for all a & b it is not necessary

   $|b| \leq a$

   Transitive: R is transitive

   $\because aRb \Rightarrow |a| \leq b$ ...(i)

   $bRc \Rightarrow |b| \leq c$ ...(ii)

   From (i) and (ii), we get

   $|a| \leq b \leq |b| \leq c \Rightarrow |a| \leq c \Rightarrow aRc$.

5. **(b)** Obviously, the relation is not reflexive and transitive but it is symmetric, because $x^2 + y^2 = 1 \Rightarrow y^2 + x^2 = 1$

6. **(d)** $\sin^2 a + \cos^2 b = 1$

   Reflexive: $\sin^2 a + \cos^2 a = 1 \Rightarrow aRa$

   $\sin^2 a + \cos^2 b = 1, 1 - \cos^2 a + 1 - \sin^2 b = 1$

   $\sin^2 b + \cos^2 a = 1 \Rightarrow bRa$

   Hence symmetric

   Let aRb, bRc

$$\sin^2 a + \cos^2 b = 1 \qquad \text{...(i)}$$

$$\sin^2 b + \cos^2 c = 1 \qquad \text{...(ii)}$$

(i) + (ii)

$$\sin^2 a + \cos^2 c = 1$$

7. (b) For any $a \in N$, GCD of a and $a = a$

So, R is not reflexive.

Let $(a,b) \in R$, Then, $a \, R \, b$

$\Rightarrow$ GCD of a and b is 2

$\Rightarrow$ GCD of b and a is also 2 $\Rightarrow$ $b \, R \, a$

So, R is symmetric.

Now, GCD of 6 and 4 is 2 and GCD of 4 and 18 is also 2.

But, GCD of 6 and 18 is 6.

i.e. $6 \, R \, 4$ and $4 \, R \, 18$ but $6 \, \cancel{R} \, 18$.

So, R is not transitive.

8. (b) Since R is an equivalence relation on set A.

$(a,a) \in R$ for all $a \in A$.

Hence, R has at least n ordered pairs.

9. (b) It is obvious.

10. (c) Since $(1, 1) \notin R$ So, R is not reflexive

Now $(1, 2) \in R$ but $(2, 1) \notin R$, therefore R is not symmetric.

Clearly R is transitive.

11. (c) x is a brother of y, but y is not necessarily of x it may be a sister so it is not symmetric. It is only transitive.

12. (b) It is obvious.

13. (b) The relation is not symmetric, because $A \subset B$ does not imply that $B \subset A$.

But it is anti-symmetric because

$$A \subset B \text{ and } B \subset A \Rightarrow A = B.$$

14. (c) R is reflexive if it contains $(1,1), (2,2), (3,3)$

$$\because (1,2) \in R, (2,3) \in R$$

$\because R$ is symmetric if $(2,1), (3,2) \in R.$

Now, $R = \{(1,1),(2,2),(3,3),(2,1),(3,2),(2,3),(1,2)\}$

R will be transitive if $(3,1), (1,3) \in R.$

Thus, R becomes an equivalence relation by adding $(1,1)(2,2)(3,3)(2,1)(3,2)(1,3)(3,1)$.

Hence, the total number of ordered pairs is 7.

15. (a) Since R is reflexive relation on A, therefore $(a,a) \in$ R for all a $\in$A.

The minimum number of ordered pairs in R is n.

Hence, $m \geq n$.

16. (b) In the function $f(x) = (x-1)(x-2)(x-3)$ for more than one value of x, i.e. $x = 1$, $x = 2$ and $x = 3$, value of the function is zero.

So, the function is not one-one.

Range of the function is the set of all real number i.e. R.

Since Range = Co-domain = R the function is onto.

Thus the given function f(x) is onto but not one-one.

17. (c) $f(x) = x^3 + 5x + 1 \Rightarrow f'(x) = 3x^2 + 5 > 0, \ \forall \, x \notin R$

Therefore, $f(x)$ is a strictly increasing function and so it is one-one.

Clearly, $f(x)$ is a continuous function and also increasing on R.

$$\lim_{x \to -\infty} f(x) = -\infty \text{ and } \lim_{x \to \infty} f(x) = \infty$$

Hence, $f(x)$ takes every value between $-\infty$ and ∞.

Thus, $f(x)$ is an onto function.

18. (a) If set A has m elements and set B has n elements then number of onto functions from A to B is

$$\sum_{r=1}^{n} (-1)^{n-r} \, {}^{n}C_r \, r^m \text{ where } 1 \leq n \leq m$$

Here $E = \{1,2,3,4\}$, $F = \{1,2\}$; $m = 4, n = 2$

$\therefore$ no. of onto functions from E to F

$$= \sum_{r=1}^{2} (-1)^{2-r} \, {}^{2}C_r (r)^4 = (-1) \, {}^{2}C_1 + {}^{2}C_2 (2)^4$$

$$= -2 + 16 = 14$$

19. (c) The total number of injective functions from a set A containing 3 elements to a set B containing 4 elements is equal to the total number of arrangement of 4 by taking 3 at a time i.e., ${}^{4}P_3 = 24$.

20. (d) $f(x) = [x]^2 + [x+1] - 3 = \{[x]+2\}\{[x]-1\}$

So, $x = 1, 1.1, 1.2, \ldots\ldots$ for $f(x) = 0$

$\therefore$ $f(x)$ is many one.

Only integral values will be attained.

$\therefore$ $f(x)$ is into.

21. (a) $|x|$ is not one-one; x^2 is not one-one;

$x^2 + 1$ is not one-one.

$2x - 5$ is one-one because

$$f(x) = f(y) \Rightarrow 2x - 5 = 2y - 5 \Rightarrow x = y$$

and $f(x) = 2x - 5$ is onto.

$\therefore f(x) = 2x - 5$ is bijective.

Every linear function is bijective.

22. (b) $f(x) = px + \sin x$

$f'(x) = p + \cos x$

either $f'(x) \leq 0$ or $f'(x) \geq 0$

$p + \cos x \leq 0$ or $p + \cos x \geq 0$

$p \leq -1$ or $p \geq 1$

$p \in (-\infty, -1] \cup [1, \infty)$

23. (c) Function $f : R \to R$ is defined by $f(x) = e^x$. Let x_1, x_2

$\in R$ and $f(x_1) = f(x_2)$ or $e^{x_1} = e^{x_2}$ or $x_1 = x_2$.

Therefore f is one-one. Let $f(x) = e^x = y$. We know that negative real numbers have no pre-image or the function is not onto and zero is not the image of any real number. Therefore function f is into.

24. (d) Given function, $f(x) = e^{2ix}$ and $f : R \to C$.

Function $f(x)$ is not one-one, because after some values

of $x (i.e., \pi)$ it will give the same values.

And, $f(x)$ is not onto, because it has minimum and

maximum values $-1 - i$ and $1 + i$ respectively.

25. (a) Function $f(x) = e^x$ is one-one function

$\therefore$ $f(x_1) = f(x_2) \Rightarrow e^{x_1} = e^{x_2} \Rightarrow$ $x_1 = x_2$

26. (d) $f(n) = (n+5)^2$

Let $n = n_1, n_2 \in N$ such that $n_1 \neq n_2$

$\Rightarrow n_1 + 5 \neq n_2 + 5 \Rightarrow (n_1 + 5)^2 \neq (n_2 + 5)^2$

$\Rightarrow f(n_1) \neq f(n_2)$

$\therefore f$ is one-one

$\because n \in N, i.e., n = 1, 2, 3, ...$

$\therefore f(1) = 36, f(2) = 49, ...$

$\therefore$ range $= \{f(1), f(2), f(3), ...\}$

$= \{36, 49, ...\} \neq N$ [Co-domain]

$\therefore f$ is one to one but not onto.

27. (d) The image of any given element in A can be any one of the image of n element in B.

$\therefore$ The m elements in A can be assigned images

$n \times n....... \times n$ (m times) $= n^m$ ways

$\therefore$ Total mapping from A to B $= n^m$

28. (d) We have, $f(x) = x + \sqrt{x^2} = x + |x|$

f is not one-one as $f(-1) = f(-2) = 0$ but $-1 \neq 2$.

$\because f(x) \geq 0, \forall x \in R, \therefore f$ is not onto

And range of $f = (0, \infty) \subset R$.

29. (b) By definition only $f(x) = x^2 + 4x - 5$ with domain $[0, \infty)$ is one to one.

30. (c) $f(x) = f(y) \Rightarrow x + 2 = y + 2 \Rightarrow x = y$

$\therefore$ function f is one-one.

31. (d) $f(2) = f\left(3^{1/4}\right)$ $\Rightarrow$ many to one function

and $f(x) \neq -\sqrt{3}$ $\forall$ x $\in$ R $\Rightarrow$ into function

32. (a) $f(x)$ is onto $\therefore S =$ range of $f(x)$

Now $f(x) = \sin x - \sqrt{3} \cos x + 1 = 2 \sin\left(x - \dfrac{\pi}{3}\right) + 1$

$\because -1 \leq \sin\left(x - \dfrac{\pi}{3}\right) \leq 1$

$-1 \leq 2 \sin\left(x - \dfrac{\pi}{3}\right) + 1 \leq 3$

$\therefore f(x) \in [-1, 3] = S$

33. (a) We are given that

$$f : R \to R \text{ such that } f(x) = \begin{cases} 0, & x \in \text{rational} \\ x, & x \in \text{irrational} \end{cases}$$

$$g : R \to R \text{ such that } g(x) = \begin{cases} 0, & x \in \text{irrational} \\ x, & x \in \text{rational} \end{cases}$$

$\therefore (f - g) : R \to R$ such that

$$(f - g)(x) = \begin{cases} -x, if & x \in \text{rational} \\ x, if & x \in \text{irrational} \end{cases}$$

Since $f - g : R \to R$ for any x there is only one value of $(f(x) - g(x))$ whether x is rational or irrational. Moreover as $x \in R, f(x) - g(x)$ also belongs to R. Therefore, $(f - g)$ is one-one onto.

34. (d) We have $f : N \to I$

If x and y are two even natural numbers, then

$$f(x) = f(y) \Rightarrow \frac{-x}{2} = \frac{-y}{2} \Rightarrow x = y$$

Again if x and y are two odd natural numbers then

$$f(x) = f(y) \Rightarrow \frac{x-1}{2} = \frac{y-1}{2} \Rightarrow x = y$$

$\therefore f$ is onto.

Also each negative integer is an image of even natural number and each positive integer is an image of odd natural number.

$\therefore f$ is onto.

Hence f is one one and onto both.

35. (a) It is obvious.

36. (d) Since $n \mid n$ for all $n \in N$.

Therefore R is reflexive.

Since $2 \mid 6$ but $6 \nmid 2$, therefore R is not symmetric.

Let $n \, R \, m$ and $m \, R \, p \Rightarrow n|m$ and $m|p \Rightarrow n|p \Rightarrow nRp$.

Hence, R is transitive.

37. (d) For $(a,b),(c,d) \in N \times N$

$(a,b) R(c,d) \Rightarrow ad(b+c) = bc(a+d)$

Reflexive : Since $ab(b+a) = ba(a+b) \forall ab \in N$,

$\therefore (a,b) R(a,b) \Rightarrow R$ is reflexive.

Symmetric : For $(a,b),(c,d) \in N \times N$,

let $(a,b) R(c,d)$

$\therefore ad(b+c) = bc(a+d) \Rightarrow bc(a+d) = ad(b+c)$

$\Rightarrow cb(d+a) = da(c+b) \Rightarrow (c,d) R(a,b)$

$\Rightarrow R$ is symmetric

Transitive : For $(a,b),(c,d),(e,f) \in N \times N$,

Let $(a,b) R(c,d),(c,d) R(e,f)$

$\therefore \ ad(b+c) = bc(a+d), cf(d+e) = de(c+f)$

$\Rightarrow \ adb + adc = bca + bcd \qquad \text{...(i)}$

and $cfd + cfe = dec + def \qquad \text{...(ii)}$

$(i) \times ef + (ii) \times ab$ gives,

$adbef + adcef + cfdab + cfeab$

$= bcaef + bcdef + decab + defab$

$\Rightarrow adcf(b+e) = bcde(a+f) \Rightarrow af(b+e) = be(a+f)$

$\Rightarrow (a,b) R(e,f) \Rightarrow R$ is transitive.

Hence R is an equivalence relation.

38. (b) Let $f : R \to R$ be a function defined by

$f(x) = \dfrac{x-m}{x-n}$

For any $(x, y) \in R$

Let $f(x) = f(y)$

$\Rightarrow \dfrac{x-m}{x-n} = \dfrac{y-m}{y-n} \Rightarrow x = y$

$\therefore$ f is one – one

Let $\alpha \in R$ such that $f(x) = \alpha$

$\Rightarrow \alpha = \dfrac{x-m}{x-n} \Rightarrow (x-n)\alpha = x-m$

$\Rightarrow x\alpha - n\alpha = x-m \Rightarrow x\alpha - x = n\alpha - m$

$\Rightarrow x(\alpha - 1) = n\alpha - m$

$\Rightarrow x = \dfrac{n\alpha - m}{\alpha - 1}$. for $\alpha = 1$, $x \notin R$

So, f is not onto.

39. (a) $|a - a| = 0 < 1$

$\therefore a \, R \, a \ \forall a \in R$

$\therefore R$ is reflexive.

Again $a \, R \, b \Rightarrow |a-b| \le 1 \Rightarrow |b-a| \le 1 \Rightarrow b \, R \, a$

$\therefore R$ is symmetric.

Now, $1 R \dfrac{1}{2}$ and $\dfrac{1}{2} R 1$ but $\dfrac{1}{2} \ne 1$

$\therefore R$ is not anti-symmetric.

Further, $1 \, R \, 2$ and $2 \, R \, 3$ but $1 \not{R} \, 3$, $\left[\because |1-3| = 2 > 1\right]$

$\therefore R$ is not transitive.

40. (a) $x^2 - 4x^2 + 3x^2 = 0$

$\therefore x \, R \, x \Rightarrow$ Reflexive

41. (d) $(X,Y) \notin R$

42. (a) Both (X,W) and $(W,X) \in R$

43. (a) $(F_1, F_2) \in R, (F_2, F_3) \in R$ and $(F_1, F_3) \in R$

44. (c) Equivalence relation

45. (a) All those eligible voters who cast their votes.

46. (a) Since, y is divisible by x but x may not be divisible by y. So, reflexive and transitive but not symmetric.

47. (a) Number of possible functions from A to B

= (Number of elements in B)$^{\text{(number of elements in A)}}$

= $(n(B))^{n(A)} = 6^2$

48. (d)

49. (d) Number of possible relations from A to B

$= 2^{n(A) \cdot n(B)} = 2^{12}$

50. (b) Reflexive and transitive

51. (a) Number of possible relations from B to G

$2^{n(B) \times n(G)} = 2^{2 \times 3} = 2^6$

52. (a) Equivalence

53. (d) Number of possible function from B to G

$(n(G))^{n(B)} = 2^3$

54. (b) Since, b_1 and b_3 both are related to same element g_1. So, R is surjective.

55. (a) Since, n(B) > n(G)

So, no injective function from B to G.

56. (a) Equivalence

57. (a) Since, no line is perpendicular to itself and perpendicular relation is not transitive. So, R is symmetric but neither reflexive nor transitive.

58. (a) Since, $f: R \to R$ is one-one and onto. So, f is bijective.

59. (a) Since, f attains all the values of set of real numbers. So, range of $f(x)$ is R.

60. (a) $2x - 2y + 5 = 0$

61. (a) Since, $f(-1) = 1 = f(1)$

$\Rightarrow f$ is not injective and $f(x) \geq 0$ for all $x \in R$

$\Rightarrow f$ is not onto

$\therefore$ Neither surjective nor injective.

62. (c) Since, there is no pre image of all prime number and composite number which do not have perfect square root. So, f is not onto, but f is injective.

63. (a) Since, f is one-one and onto. So, f is bijective.

64. (a) $\{1, 4, 9, 16, ...\}$

65. (a) Since, $f(-1) = 1 = f(1) \Rightarrow f$ is not one-one

and $f(x) \geq 0$ for all $x \in Z \Rightarrow f$ is not onto

$\therefore$ Neither injective nor surjective.

Chapter Test

1. (d)   2. (b)

3. (b) One-one function from $\{1, 2, 3\}$ to itself is simply a permutation on three symbols 1, 2, 3. Therefore, total number of one-one maps from $\{1, 2, 3\}$ to itself is same as total number of permutations on symbols 1, 2, 3, which is $3! = 6$.

4. (a) The smallest equivalence relation R_1 containing $(1, 2)$ and $(2, 1)$ is $\{(1, 1), (2, 2), (3, 3), (1, 2), (2, 1)\}$. Now, we are left with only 4 pairs namely $(2, 3)$, $(3, 2)$, $(1, 3)$ and $(3, 1)$. If we add any one, say $(2, 3)$ to R_1, then for symmetry we must add $(3, 2)$ also and now for transitivity we are forced to add $(1, 3)$ and $(3, 1)$. Thus, the only equivalence relation bigger than R_1 is the universal relation. This shows that the total number of equivalence relations containing $(1, 2)$ and $(2, 1)$ is two.

5. (64)

6. (7) The given relation is R = $\{(1, 2), (2, 3)\}$ in the set A = $\{1, 2, 3\}$.

Now, R is reflexive, if $(1, 1), (2, 2), (3, 3) \in R$.

R is symmetric, if $(2, 1), (3, 2) \in R$.

R is transitive, if $(1, 3)$ and $(3, 1) \in R$.

Thus, the minimum number of ordered pairs which are to be added, so that R becomes an equivalence relation, is 7.

7. (b)

8. (b)

9. (i) (b) (ii) (c) (iii) (d) (iv) (a) (v) (a)

10. $f^{-1}(x) = \dfrac{1}{2}[1 + \sqrt{(1 + 4\log_2 x)}]$

11. Equivalence relation

12. R is reflexive but not symmetric and not transitive.

13. $4x - 9$

2

Inverse Trigonometric Functions

Inverse Function	Domain	Principal Value Branch
$y = \sin^{-1} x$	$[-1, 1]$	$\left[\dfrac{-\pi}{2}, \dfrac{\pi}{2}\right]$
$y = \cos^{-1} x$	$[-1, 1]$	$[0, \pi]$
$y = \operatorname{cosec}^{-1} x$	$R - (-1, 1)$	$\left[\dfrac{-\pi}{2}, \dfrac{\pi}{2}\right] - \{0\}$
$y = \sec^{-1} x$	$R - (-1, 1)$	$[0, \pi] - \left\{\dfrac{\pi}{2}\right\}$
$y = \tan^{-1} x$	R	$\left(\dfrac{-\pi}{2}, \dfrac{\pi}{2}\right)$
$y = \cot^{-1} x$	R	$(0, \pi)$

Topic 1 — Principal Value Branch of Inverse Trigonometric Functions 

DOMAIN AND RANGE OF TRIGONOMETRIC FUNCTION

	Functions	Domain	Range
(i)	$\sin x$	R	$[-1, 1]$
(ii)	$\cos x$	R	$[-1, 1]$
(iii)	$\tan x$	$R - \{x : x = (2n+1)\dfrac{\pi}{2}, n \in Z\}$	R
(iv)	$\cot x$	$R - \{x : x = n\pi, n \in Z\}$	R
(v)	$\sec x$	$R - \{x : x = (2n+1)\dfrac{\pi}{2}\}, n \in Z$	$R - (-1, 1)$
(vi)	$\operatorname{cosec} x$	$R - \{x : x = n\pi, n \in Z\}$	$R - (-1, 1)$

INVERSE FUNCTION

If $f : X \to Y$ such that $y = f(x)$ is one-one and onto, then we define another function $g : Y \to X$ such that $x = g(y)$, where $x \in X$ and $y \in Y$ which is also one-one and onto. In such a case domain of $g = $ Range of f and Range of $g = $ domain of f, then g is called inverse of f or $g = f^{-1}$
Inverse of $g = g^{-1} = (f^{-1})^{-1} = f$.

PRINCIPAL VALUE BRANCH OF FUNCTION $\sin^{-1}x$

Domain of the function is $[-1, 1]$. Its range is one of the intervals - - -,

$$\left[-\frac{3\pi}{2}, \frac{-\pi}{2}\right], \left[\frac{-\pi}{2}, \frac{\pi}{2}\right], \left[\frac{\pi}{2}, \frac{3\pi}{2}\right], \text{- - -,}$$ Corresponding to each interval we get a branch

of the function $\sin^{-1}x$. The branch with range $\left[\dfrac{-\pi}{2}, \dfrac{\pi}{2}\right]$ is called the principal value

branch, because in the branch $\left[-\dfrac{\pi}{2}, \dfrac{\pi}{2}\right]$, the numerical value (i.e., the value without

sign) of $\sin^{-1}x$ is smallest. Thus $\sin^{-1}x : [-1, 1] \to \left[\dfrac{-\pi}{2}, \dfrac{\pi}{2}\right]$

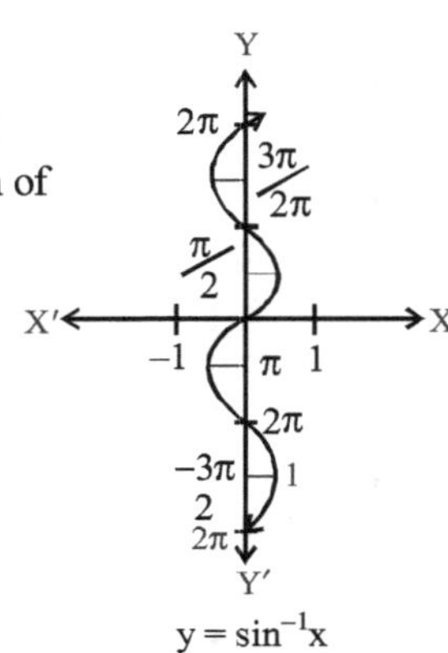

$y = \sin^{-1}x$

PRINCIPAL VALUE BRANCH OF FUNCTION $\cos^{-1}x$

Domain of the function $\cos^{-1}x$ is $[-1, 1]$. Its range is one of the intervals - - -, $[-\pi, 0], [0, \pi]$, $[\pi, 2\pi]$, - - -. The branch with range $[0, \pi]$ is called the principal value branch of the function $\cos^{-1}x$, because in the branch $[0, \pi]$, the numerical value (i.e. the value without sign) of $\cos^{-1}x$ is smallest. Thus $\cos^{-1}x : [-1, 1] \to [0, \pi]$

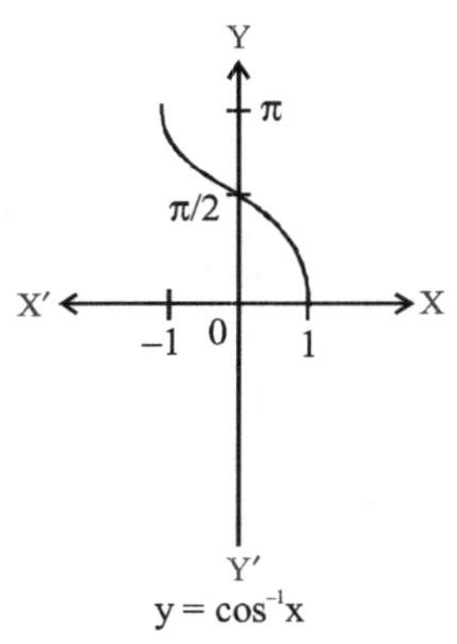

$y = \cos^{-1}x$

PRINCIPAL VALUE BRANCH OF FUNCTION $\tan^{-1}x$

The domain of the function $\tan^{-1}x$ is the set of real numbers and range is one of the

intervals ---, $\left(\dfrac{-3\pi}{2}, \dfrac{-\pi}{2}\right), \left(\dfrac{-\pi}{2}, \dfrac{\pi}{2}\right), \left(\dfrac{\pi}{2}, \dfrac{3\pi}{2}\right), \ldots,$

The branch $\left(\dfrac{-\pi}{2}, \dfrac{\pi}{2}\right)$ is called the pricnipal value branch of function $\tan^{-1}x$, because in

the branch $\left[\dfrac{-\pi}{2}, \dfrac{\pi}{2}\right]$, the numerical vlaue (i.e., value without sign) of $\tan^{-1}x$ is

smallest. Thus $\tan^{-1}x : R \to \left(\dfrac{-\pi}{2}, \dfrac{\pi}{2}\right)$.

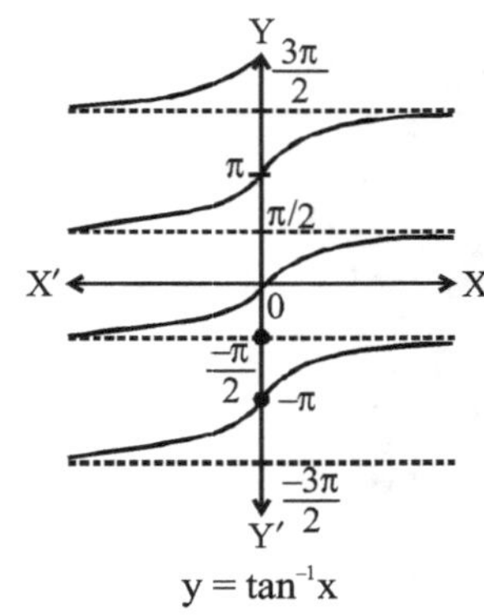

$y = \tan^{-1}x$

PRINCIPAL VALUE BRANCH OF FUNCTION cosec⁻¹x

The domain of the function $\text{cosec}^{-1}x$ is $R - (-1, 1)$ and the range is any one of the interval ...., $\left[\dfrac{-3\pi}{2}, \dfrac{-\pi}{2}\right] - \{-\pi\}, \left[\dfrac{-\pi}{2}, \dfrac{\pi}{2}\right] - \{0\}, \left[\dfrac{\pi}{2}, \dfrac{3\pi}{2}\right] - \{\pi\}, ...$ The branch $\left[-\dfrac{\pi}{2}, \dfrac{\pi}{2}\right] - \{0\}$ is called the principal value branch of $\text{cosec}^{-1}x$, because in the branch $\left[-\dfrac{\pi}{2}, \dfrac{\pi}{2}\right]$, the numerical value (i.e. value without sign) of $\text{cosec}^{-1}x$ is smallest.

Thus, $\text{cosec}^{-1}x : R - (-1, 1) \rightarrow \left[-\dfrac{\pi}{2}, \dfrac{\pi}{2}\right] - \{0\}$

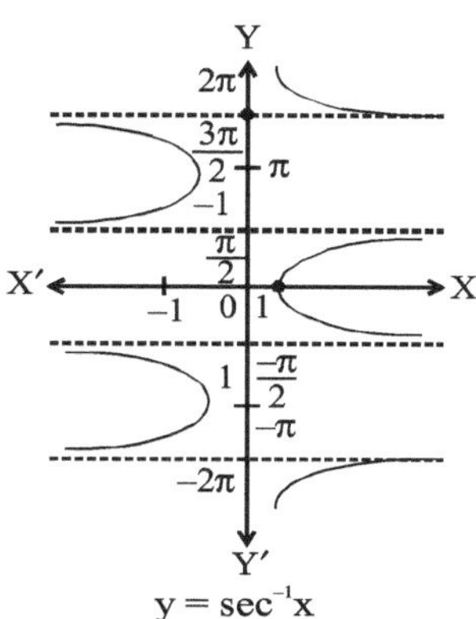

$y = \text{cosec}^{-1}x$

PRINCIPAL VALUE BRANCH OF FUNCTION sec⁻¹x

The domain of the function $\sec^{-1}x$ is $R - (-1, 1)$ and the range could be any of the intervals is ...., $[-\pi, 0] - \left\{\dfrac{-\pi}{2}\right\}, [0, \pi] - \left\{\dfrac{\pi}{2}\right\}, [\pi, 2\pi] - \left\{\dfrac{3\pi}{2}\right\}, ...$

The branch $[0, \pi] - \left\{\dfrac{\pi}{2}\right\}$ is known as the principal value branch of $\sec^{-1}x$, because in the branch $[0, \pi] - \left\{\dfrac{\pi}{2}\right\}$, the numerical value (i.e. value without sign) of $\sec^{-1}x$ is smallest. Thus $\sec^{-1}x : R - (-1, 1) \rightarrow [0, \pi] - \left\{\dfrac{\pi}{2}\right\}$.

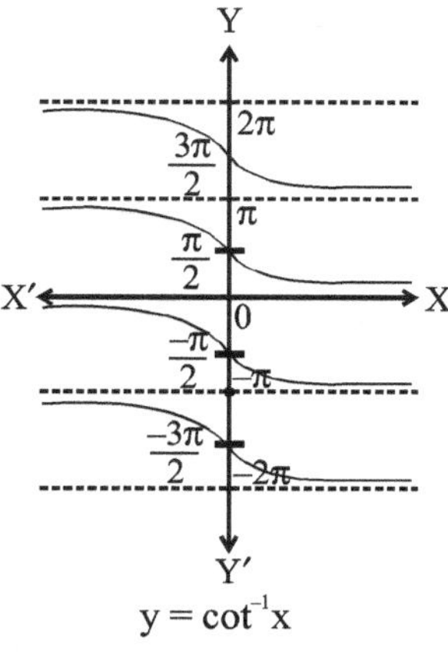

$y = \sec^{-1}x$

PRINCIPAL VALUE BRANCH OF FUNCTION cot⁻¹x

The domain of the function $\cot^{-1}x$ is R and the range is any of the intervals....., $(-\pi, 0)\ (0, \pi), (\pi, 2\pi), ...$. The branch $(0, \pi)$ is called the principal value branch of the function $\cot^{-1}x$ because in the branch $(0, \pi)$, the numerical value (i.e. value without sign) of $\cot^{-1}x$ is smallest. Thus $\cot^{-1}x : R \rightarrow (0, \pi)$

$y = \cot^{-1}x$

Inverse function	Domain	Principal Value Branch
$\sin^{-1}x$	$[-1, 1]$	$\left[\dfrac{-\pi}{2}, \dfrac{\pi}{2}\right]$
$\cos^{-1}x$	$[-1, 1]$	$[0, \pi]$
$\text{cosec}^{-1}x$	$R - (-1, 1)$	$\left[\dfrac{-\pi}{2}, \dfrac{\pi}{2}\right] - \{0\}$
$\sec^{-1}x$	$R - (-1, 1)$	$[0, \pi] - \left\{\dfrac{\pi}{2}\right\}$
$\tan^{-1}x$	R	$\left(\dfrac{-\pi}{2}, \dfrac{\pi}{2}\right)$
$\cot^{-1}x$	R	$(0, \pi)$

Illustration :

Find the principal values of $\sin^{-1}\left(\dfrac{1}{2}\right)$ and $\cos^{-1}\left(\dfrac{-1}{\sqrt{2}}\right)$.

Sol. We know that $\sin^{-1}x$ gives an angle in the interval $\left[\dfrac{-\pi}{2}, \dfrac{\pi}{2}\right]$ and $x \in [-1, 1]$ $\therefore$ $\sin^{-1}\left(\dfrac{1}{2}\right) = \dfrac{\pi}{6}$

Similarly $\cos^{-1}x$ gives an angle in the interval $[0, \pi]$ and $x \in [-1, 1]$ $\therefore$ $\cos^{-1}\left(\dfrac{-1}{\sqrt{2}}\right) = \pi - \dfrac{\pi}{4} = \dfrac{3\pi}{4}$.

Practice Exercise-1

Multiple Choice Questions

1. Principal value of $\cosec^{-1}\left(\dfrac{-2}{\sqrt{3}}\right)$ is equal to

(a) $-\dfrac{\pi}{3}$ (b) $\dfrac{\pi}{3}$ (c) $\dfrac{\pi}{2}$ (d) $-\dfrac{\pi}{2}$

2. Principal value of $\sec^{-1}(2)$ is equal to

(a) $\dfrac{\pi}{6}$ (b) $\dfrac{\pi}{3}$ (c) $\dfrac{2\pi}{3}$ (d) $\dfrac{5\pi}{3}$

3. Prinicpal value of $\tan^{-1}\left(\sqrt{3}\right)$ is equal to

(a) $\dfrac{\pi}{6}$ (b) $\dfrac{\pi}{3}$ (c) $\dfrac{2\pi}{3}$ (d) $\dfrac{5\pi}{3}$

4. $-\dfrac{2\pi}{5}$ is the principal value of

(a) $\cos^{-1}\left(\cos\dfrac{7\pi}{5}\right)$ (b) $\sin^{-1}\left(\sin\dfrac{7\pi}{5}\right)$

(c) $\sec^{-1}\left(\sec\dfrac{7\pi}{5}\right)$ (d) None of these

5. The principal value of $\sin^{-1}\left(\sin\dfrac{5\pi}{3}\right)$ is

(a) $-\dfrac{5\pi}{3}$ (b) $\dfrac{5\pi}{3}$ (c) $-\dfrac{\pi}{3}$ (d) $\dfrac{4\pi}{3}$

Assertion & Reason Questions

DIRECTIONS : *Each of these questions contains an assertion followed by reason. Read them carefully and answer the question on the basis of following options. You have to select the one that best describes the two statements.*
(a) If both Assertion and Reason are correct and the Reason is a correct explanation of the Assertion.
(b) If both Assertion and Reason are correct but Reason is not a correct explanation of the Assertion.
(c) If the Assertion is correct but Reason is incorrect.
(d) If the Assertion is incorrect but the Reason is correct.

6. **Assertion:** The domain of the function $\sec^{-1}x$ is the set of all real numbers.
Reason: For the function $\sec^{-1}x$, x can take all real values except in the interval $(-1, 1)$.

7. **Assertion :** The value of $\tan^{-1}\left(\dfrac{3}{4}\right)+\tan^{-1}\left(\dfrac{1}{7}\right)$ is $\dfrac{\pi}{4}$

Reason : If $x>0, y>0$ then $\tan^{-1}\left(\dfrac{x}{y}\right)+\tan^{-1}\left(\dfrac{y-x}{y+x}\right)=\dfrac{\pi}{4}$

One Word Answer Questions

8. The value of $\cos^{-1}\left(\cos\dfrac{5\pi}{3}\right)+\sin^{-1}\left(\sin\dfrac{5\pi}{3}\right)$ is ______.

9. $\cos\left[\cos^{-1}\left(\dfrac{-1}{7}\right)+\sin^{-1}\left(\dfrac{-1}{7}\right)\right]= ?$

10. The value of
$$\cos\left[\dfrac{1}{2}\cos^{-1}\left(\cos\left(\sin^{-1}\dfrac{\sqrt{63}}{8}\right)\right)\right] \text{ is } -$$

11. Given that $\sin^{-1}\left(\sin\dfrac{3\pi}{4}\right)=\dfrac{2\pi}{k}$, then $k=?$

12. The value of $\cos\left[\tan^{-1}\left\{\tan\left(\dfrac{15\pi}{4}\right)\right\}\right]$ is ______.

Very Short Answer Questions

13. Find principal value of $\tan^{-1}1+\cos^{-1}\left(\dfrac{-1}{2}\right)+\sin^{-1}\left(\dfrac{-1}{2}\right)$.

14. Solve : $\cos^{-1}\left(\dfrac{1}{2}\right)+\sin^{-1}\left(\dfrac{1}{2}\right)+\tan^{-1}\dfrac{1}{\sqrt{3}}$.

15. Find the principal value of $\sin^{-1}\left(-\dfrac{\sqrt{3}}{2}\right)$.

16. Find the value of $\cos\left(\dfrac{1}{2}\cos^{-1}\dfrac{1}{8}\right)$.

17. Find the value of $\cos^{-1}\left(\cos\dfrac{5\pi}{3}\right)+\sin^{-1}\left(\sin\dfrac{5\pi}{3}\right)$.

Short Answer Questions

18. If $\sin^{-1}\left(\dfrac{1}{\sqrt{2}}\right)+\cosec^{-1}(2)$ has the value $k\dfrac{\pi}{12}$, then find value of k.

19. Find the principal value of $\sin^{-1}\left(-\dfrac{1}{2}\right)+2\cos^{-1}\left(-\dfrac{\sqrt{3}}{2}\right)$.

20. Find the principal value of $\tan^{-1}(-1)+\cos\left(-\dfrac{1}{\sqrt{2}}\right)$.

21. If $\cos^{-1}x+\cos^{-1}y+\cos^{-1}z=3\pi$ then find $xy+yz+zx$.

22. Find value of $\sin^{-1}\left(-\dfrac{\sqrt{2}}{2}\right)+\cos^{-1}\left(-\dfrac{1}{2}\right)$

$-\tan^{-1}\left(-\sqrt{3}\right)+\cot^{-1}\left(-\dfrac{1}{\sqrt{3}}\right)$.

23. Find the principal value of $\cos^{-1}(\cos 7\pi/6)$

NCERT Exercise-1

Find the principal values of the following :

1. $\sin^{-1}\left(-\dfrac{1}{2}\right)$

2. $\cos^{-1}\left(\dfrac{\sqrt{3}}{2}\right)$

3. $\text{cosec}^{-1}(2)$

4. $\tan^{-1}(-\sqrt{3})$

5. $\cos^{-1}\left(-\dfrac{1}{2}\right)$

6. $\tan^{-1}(-1)$

7. $\sec^{-1}\left(\dfrac{2}{\sqrt{3}}\right)$

8. $\cot^{-1}(\sqrt{3})$

9. $\cos^{-1}\left(-\dfrac{1}{\sqrt{2}}\right)$

10. $\text{cosec}^{-1}(-\sqrt{2})$

Find the values of the following :

11. $\tan^{-1}(1)+\cos^{-1}\left(-\dfrac{1}{2}\right)+\sin^{-1}\left(-\dfrac{1}{2}\right)$

12. $\cos^{-1}\left(\dfrac{1}{2}\right)+2\sin^{-1}\left(\dfrac{1}{2}\right)$

13. If $\sin^{-1}x=y$, then

  (a) $0\le y\le\pi$ (b) $-\dfrac{\pi}{2}\le y\le\dfrac{\pi}{2}$

  (c) $0<y<\pi$ (d) $-\dfrac{\pi}{2}<y<\dfrac{\pi}{2}$

14. $\tan^{-1}\sqrt{3}-\sec^{-1}(-2)$ is equal to

  (a) π (b) $-\dfrac{\pi}{3}$ (c) $\dfrac{\pi}{3}$ (d) $\dfrac{2\pi}{3}$

Important Tips & Formulae

- If for any other inverse trigonometric function, the numerical value of y is smallest in two branch, then we consider those branch as principal value branch in which there is no negative value.

- I quadrant is common to all the inverse functions.

- III quadrant is not used in inverse function.

- IV quadrant is used in the clockwise direction.

- If no branch of a inverse trigonometric function is mentioned, then the principal value branch is taken for the inverse trigonometric function.

MISCELLANEOUS NCERT EXERCISE

Find the value of the following:

1. $\cos^{-1}\left(\cos\dfrac{13\pi}{6}\right)$

Sol. $\cos^{-1}\left(\cos\dfrac{13\pi}{6}\right)=\cos^{-1}\cos\left(2\pi+\dfrac{\pi}{6}\right)$

$\qquad =\cos^{-1}\left(\cos\dfrac{\pi}{6}\right)=\dfrac{\pi}{6}$

2. $\tan^{-1}\left(\tan\dfrac{7\pi}{6}\right)$

Sol. $\tan^{-1}\left(\tan\dfrac{7\pi}{6}\right)=\tan^{-1}\tan\left(\pi+\dfrac{\pi}{6}\right)=\tan^{-1}\left(\tan\dfrac{\pi}{6}\right)=\dfrac{\pi}{6}$

3. **Prove that** $\cos^{-1}\dfrac{4}{5}+\cos^{-1}\dfrac{12}{13}=\cos^{-1}\dfrac{33}{65}$

Sol. Let $\cos^{-1}\dfrac{4}{5}=\alpha$

$\qquad\therefore\ \cos\alpha=\dfrac{4}{5},\ \sin\alpha=\dfrac{3}{5},\ \cos^{-1}\dfrac{12}{13}=\beta$

$\qquad\therefore\ \cos\beta=\dfrac{12}{13},\ \sin\beta=\dfrac{5}{13}$

$\qquad\cos(\alpha+\beta)=\cos\alpha\cos\beta-\sin\alpha\sin\beta$

$\qquad\qquad =\dfrac{4}{5}\times\dfrac{12}{13}-\dfrac{3}{5}\times\dfrac{5}{13}=\dfrac{48-15}{65}=\dfrac{33}{65}$

$\qquad\therefore\ \alpha+\beta=\cos^{-1}\dfrac{33}{65}$

$\qquad\therefore\ \alpha+\beta=\cos^{-1}\dfrac{4}{5}+\cos^{-1}\dfrac{12}{13}=\cos^{-1}\dfrac{33}{65}.$

4. **Prove that** $\cos^{-1}\dfrac{12}{13}+\sin^{-1}\dfrac{3}{5}=\sin^{-1}\dfrac{56}{65}$

Sol. Let $\cos^{-1}\dfrac{12}{13}=\alpha,$

$\qquad\therefore\ \cos\alpha=\dfrac{12}{13},\ \sin\alpha=\dfrac{5}{13},\ \sin^{-1}\dfrac{3}{5}=\beta$

$\qquad\therefore\ \sin\beta=\dfrac{3}{5},\ \cos\beta=\dfrac{4}{5}$

$\qquad\sin(\alpha+\beta)=\sin\alpha\cos\beta+\cos\alpha\sin\beta$

$\qquad\qquad =\dfrac{5}{13}\times\dfrac{4}{5}+\dfrac{12}{13}\times\dfrac{3}{5}=\dfrac{20+36}{65}=\dfrac{56}{65}$

Mathematics

$$\therefore \quad \alpha + \beta = \sin^{-1}\frac{56}{65}$$

$$\Rightarrow \cos^{-1}\frac{12}{13} + \sin^{-1}\frac{3}{5} = \sin^{-1}\frac{56}{65}.$$

5. Prove that $\cos\tan^{-1}\frac{63}{16} = \sin^{-1}\frac{5}{13} + \cos^{-1}\frac{3}{5}$

Sol. Let $\sin^{-1}\frac{5}{13} = \alpha$, $\sin\alpha = \frac{5}{13}$, $\tan\alpha = \frac{5}{12}$

$$\cos^{-1}\frac{3}{5} = \beta, \quad \cos\beta = \frac{3}{5}, \quad \tan\beta = \frac{4}{3}$$

$$\tan(\alpha + \beta) = \frac{\tan\alpha + \tan\beta}{1 - \tan\alpha\tan\beta} = \frac{\frac{5}{12} + \frac{4}{3}}{1 - \frac{5}{12} \times \frac{4}{3}} = \frac{63}{16}$$

$$\therefore \quad \alpha + \beta = \tan^{-1}\frac{63}{16}$$

Thus, $\tan^{-1}\frac{63}{16} = \sin^{-1}\frac{5}{13} + \cos^{-1}\frac{3}{5}.$

6. $\sin(\tan^{-1}x)$, $|x| < 1$ is equal to

(a) $\dfrac{x}{\sqrt{1-x^2}}$ (b) $\dfrac{1}{\sqrt{1-x^2}}$

(c) $\dfrac{1}{\sqrt{1+x^2}}$ (d) $\dfrac{x}{\sqrt{1+x^2}}.$

Sol. (d) Let $\tan^{-1}x = \alpha$ $\therefore \tan\alpha = x$

$$\sin\alpha = \sqrt{1 - \cos^2\alpha}$$

$$= \sqrt{1 - \frac{1}{\sec^2\alpha}} = \sqrt{1 - \frac{1}{\tan^2\alpha + 1}} = \sqrt{1 - \frac{1}{x^2 + 1}}$$

$$\sin\alpha = \frac{x}{\sqrt{1+x^2}} \Rightarrow \alpha = \sin^{-1}\left(\frac{x}{\sqrt{1+x^2}}\right)$$

$$\Rightarrow \tan^{-1}x = \sin^{-1}\left(\frac{x}{\sqrt{1+x^2}}\right)$$

Now, $\sin\left(\tan^{-1}x\right) = \sin\left(\sin^{-1}\frac{x}{\sqrt{1+x^2}}\right) = \frac{x}{\sqrt{1+x^2}}$

Past year Exercise

Very Short Answer Questions

1. Write the value of $\cos^{-1}\left(\frac{1}{2}\right) - 2\sin^{-1}\left(\frac{1}{2}\right)$.

2. Find principal value of $\tan^{-1}\sqrt{3} - \sec^{-1}(-2)$.

3. Prove that $\sin^{-1}\left(\frac{8}{17}\right) + \sin^{-1}\left(\frac{3}{5}\right) = \cos^{-1}\left(\frac{36}{85}\right)$

4. Write the value of $\tan\left(2\tan^{-1}\frac{1}{5}\right)$

5. Write the principal value of $\tan^{-1}(1) + \cos^{-1}\left(-\frac{1}{2}\right)$.

6. Write the principal value of $\left[\cos^{-1}\frac{\sqrt{3}}{2} + \cos^{-1}\left(-\frac{1}{2}\right)\right]$

7. Write the principal value of $\tan^{-1}\left(\sqrt{3}\right) - \cot^{-1}\left(-\sqrt{3}\right)$

8. Write the value of $\tan^{-1}\left[2\sin\left(2\cos^{-1}\frac{\sqrt{3}}{2}\right)\right]$

9. Evaluate : $\sin^{-1}\left(\sin\frac{3\pi}{5}\right)$

10. Write the principal value of $\left[\tan^{-1}\left(-\sqrt{3}\right) + \tan^{-1}(1)\right]$.

11. Prove that $\sin^{-1}(2x\sqrt{1-x^2}) = 2\cos^{-1}x$, $\frac{1}{\sqrt{2}} \le x \le 1$.

NCERT Exemplar

Short Answer Questions

1. Find the value of $\tan^{-1}\left(\tan\frac{5\pi}{6}\right) + \cos^{-1}\left(\cos\frac{13\pi}{6}\right)$.

2. Evaluate $\cos\left[\cos^{-1}\left(\frac{-\sqrt{3}}{2}\right) + \frac{\pi}{6}\right]$.

3. Find the value of $\tan^{-1}\left(-\frac{1}{\sqrt{3}}\right) + \cot^{-1}\left(\frac{1}{\sqrt{3}}\right) + \tan^{-1}\left[\sin\left(\frac{-\pi}{2}\right)\right].$

4. Find the value of $\tan^{-1}\left(\tan\frac{2\pi}{3}\right)$.

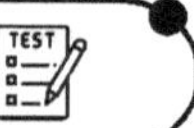

Objective Practice Exercise

Multiple Choice Question

1. The domain of the function

$$f(x) = \sin^{-1}\left\{\log_2\left(\frac{1}{2}\,x^2\right)\right\} \text{ is}$$

(a) $[-2, -1) \cup [1, 2]$ (b) $(-2, -1] \cup [1, 2]$

(c) $[-2, -1] \cup [1, 2]$ (d) $(-2, -1) \cup (1, 2)$

Case/Passage Based Questions

DIRECTIONS : *Study the given case/passage and answer the following questions.*

Case/Passage-I

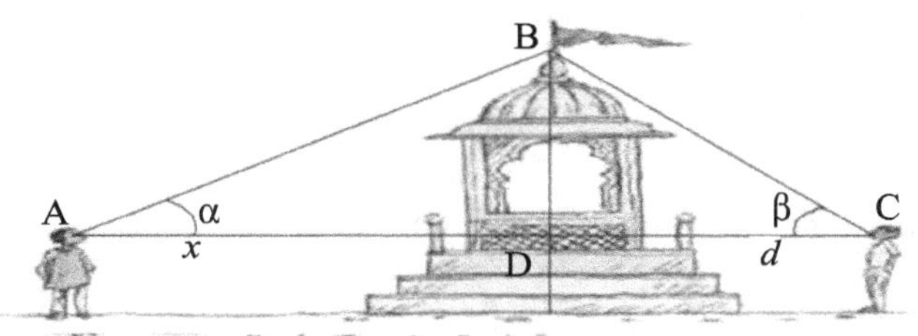

Two men on either side of a temple of 30 meters high observe its top at the angles of elevation α and β respectively. (as shown in the figure above). The distance between the two men is $40\sqrt{3}$ meters and the distance between the first person A and the temple is $30\sqrt{3}$ meters. Based on the above information answer the following: **[From CBSE Question Bank-2021]**

2. $\angle CAB = \alpha =$

(a) $\sin^{-1}\left(\dfrac{2}{\sqrt{3}}\right)$ (b) $\sin^{-1}\left(\dfrac{1}{2}\right)$

(c) $\sin^{-1}(2)$ (d) $\sin^{-1}\left(\dfrac{\sqrt{3}}{2}\right)$

3. $\angle CAB = \alpha =$

(a) $\cos^{-1}\left(\dfrac{1}{5}\right)$ (b) $\cos^{-1}\left(\dfrac{2}{5}\right)$

(c) $\cos^{-1}\left(\dfrac{\sqrt{3}}{2}\right)$ (d) $\cos^{-1}\left(\dfrac{4}{5}\right)$

4. $\angle BCA = \beta =$

(a) $\tan^{-1}\left(\dfrac{1}{2}\right)$ (b) $\tan^{-1}(2)$

(c) $\tan^{-1}\left(\dfrac{1}{\sqrt{3}}\right)$ (d) $\tan^{-1}(\sqrt{3})$

5. $\angle ABC =$

(a) $\dfrac{\pi}{4}$ (b) $\dfrac{\pi}{6}$

(c) $\dfrac{\pi}{2}$ (d) $\dfrac{\pi}{3}$

6. Domain and range of $\cos^{-1} x =$

(a) $(-1, 1), (0, \pi)$ (b) $[-1, 1], (0, \pi)$

(c) $[-1, 1], [0, \pi]$ (d) $(-1, 1), \left[-\dfrac{\pi}{2}, \dfrac{\pi}{2}\right]$

Case/Passage-II

The Government of India is planning to fix a hoarding board at the face of a building on the road of a busy market for awareness on COVID-19 protocol. Ram, Robert and Rahim are the three engineers who are working on this project. "A" is considered to be a person viewing the hoarding board 20 metres away from the building, standing at the edge of a pathway nearby. Ram, Robert and Rahim suggested to the firm to place the hoarding board at three different locations namely C, D and E. "C" is at the height of 10 metres from the ground level. For the viewer A, the angle of elevation of "D" is double the angle of elevation of "C" The angle of elevation of "E" is triple the angle of elevation of "C" for the same viewer. Look at the figure given and based on the above information answer the following:

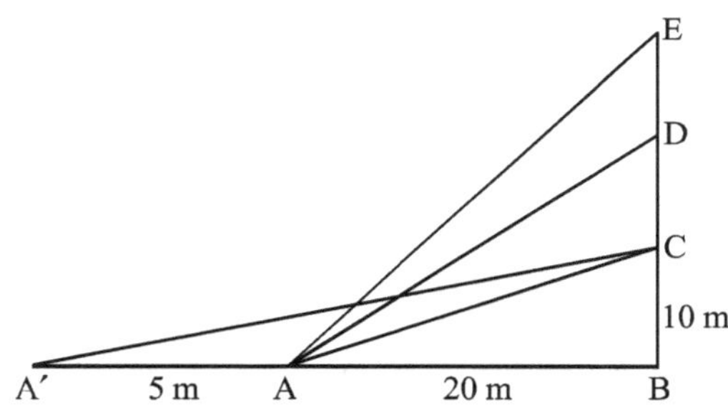

[From CBSE Question Bank-2021]

7. Measure of $\angle CAB =$

(a) $\tan^{-1}(2)$ (b) $\tan^{-1}\left(\dfrac{1}{2}\right)$

(c) $\tan^{-1}(1)$ (d) $\tan^{-1}(3)$

8. Measure of $\angle DAB =$

(a) $\tan^{-1}\left(\dfrac{3}{4}\right)$ (b) $\tan^{-1}(3)$

(c) $\tan^{-1}\left(\dfrac{4}{3}\right)$ (d) $\tan^{-1}(4)$

9. Measure of $\angle EAB =$
    (a) $\tan^{-1}(11)$
    (b) $\tan^{-1} 3$
    (c) $\tan^{-1}\left(\dfrac{2}{11}\right)$
    (d) $\tan^{-1}\left(\dfrac{11}{2}\right)$

10. A′ is another viewer standing on the same line of observation across the road. If the width of the road is 5 meters, then the difference between $\angle CAB$ and $\angle CA'B$ is
    (a) $\tan^{-1}(1/2)$
    (b) $\tan^{-1}(1/12)$
    (c) $\tan^{-1}\left(\dfrac{2}{5}\right)$
    (d) $\tan^{-1}\left(\dfrac{11}{21}\right)$

11. Domain and range of $\tan^{-1} x =$
    (a) $R^+, \left(-\dfrac{\pi}{2}, \dfrac{\pi}{2}\right)$
    (b) $R^-, \left(-\dfrac{\pi}{2}, \dfrac{\pi}{2}\right)$
    (c) $R, \left(-\dfrac{\pi}{2}, \dfrac{\pi}{2}\right)$
    (d) $R, \left(0, \dfrac{\pi}{2}\right)$

Chapter Test

Time : *45 minutes* **Max. Marks : *20***

Directions :

(i)   Questions number **1-8** carry **1 mark** each.
(ii) Question number **9** carry **4 marks.**
(iii) Questions number **10-13** are **Very Short Answer Questions** and carry **2 marks** each.

Multiple Choice Questions

1. Which of the following is the principal value branch of $\cos^{-1} x$?
    (a) $\left[\dfrac{-\pi}{2}, \dfrac{\pi}{2}\right]$
    (b) $(0, \pi)$
    (c) $[0, \pi]$
    (d) $(0, \pi) - \left\{\dfrac{\pi}{2}\right\}$

2. The value of $\cos^{-1}\left(\cos\dfrac{3\pi}{2}\right)$ is equal to
    (a) $\dfrac{\pi}{2}$
    (b) $\dfrac{3\pi}{2}$
    (c) $\dfrac{5\pi}{2}$
    (d) $\dfrac{7\pi}{2}$

3. The value of the expression $2\sec^{-1}2 + \sin^{-1}\left(\dfrac{1}{2}\right)$ is
    (a) $\dfrac{\pi}{6}$
    (b) $\dfrac{5\pi}{6}$
    (c) $\dfrac{7\pi}{6}$
    (d) 1

4. The principle value of $\sin^{-1}\left(-\dfrac{\sqrt{3}}{2}\right)$ is
    (a) $-\dfrac{\pi}{3}$
    (b) $\dfrac{\pi}{3}$
    (c) $-\dfrac{\pi}{6}$
    (d) $\dfrac{\pi}{6}$

One Word Answer Questions

5. Find the principal value branch of $\operatorname{cosec}^{-1} x$.

6. Evaluate $\tan^{-1}\left(\sin\left(\dfrac{-\pi}{2}\right)\right)$.

Assertion & Reason Questions

DIRECTIONS : *Each of these questions contains an assertion followed by reason. Read them carefully and answer the question on the basis of following options. You have to select the one that best describes the two statements.*

(a) If both Assertion and Reason are correct and the Reason is the correct explanation of the Assertion.
(b) If both Assertion and Reason are correct but Reason is not the correct explanation of the Assertion.
(c) If the Assertion is correct but Reason is incorrect.
(d) If the Assertion is incorrect but the Reason is correct.

7. **Assertion:** The domain of $\cos^{-1}\log_2\left(x^2 + 5x + 8\right)$ is
    $\pi - \dfrac{x}{2}[-3, -2]$
    Reason: Domain of $\cos^{-1}$ is $[-\pi, \pi]$

8. **Assertion:** To define the inverse of the function $f(x) = \tan x$ any of the intervals $\left(-\dfrac{3\pi}{2}, \dfrac{-\pi}{2}\right), \left(-\dfrac{\pi}{2}, \dfrac{\pi}{2}\right), \left(\dfrac{\pi}{2}, \dfrac{3\pi}{2}\right)$ etc. can be chosen.

    Reason: The branch having range $\left(-\dfrac{\pi}{2}, \dfrac{\pi}{2}\right)$ is called principal value branch of the function $g(x) = \tan^{-1} x$.

Case/Passage Based Questions

DIRECTIONS (Q. 9): *has 5 subparts based on case/passage given, attempt any 4 out of 5 questions.*

9. An observer views a rocket of firecracker that takes off from a distance of the launch pad and he tracks the elevation. If the height h of the rocket B from the ground O, horizontal distance x between observer A and the initial point on the ground O, oblique distance y from observer to the rocket and the angle θ of elevation are in the inverse trigonometric equations as shown in the figure.

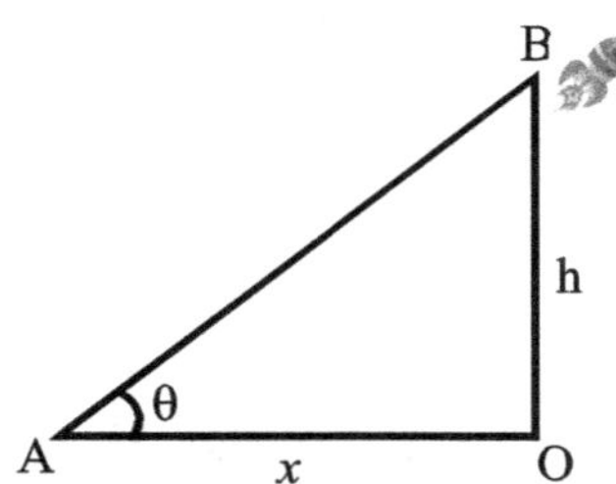

where h, x, y and θ are

$$AB = y = \tan\left\{\frac{\pi}{4} + \frac{1}{2}\cos^{-1}\frac{\sqrt{2}}{25}\right\} + \tan\left\{\frac{\pi}{4} - \frac{1}{2}\cos^{-1}\frac{\sqrt{2}}{25}\right\}$$

$$OA \equiv \tan^{-1}\left(\frac{5}{x}\right) + \tan^{-1}\left(\frac{125}{x}\right) = \frac{\pi}{2}$$

$$OB = h = \tan\left\{\frac{\pi}{4} + \frac{1}{2}\cos^{-1}\frac{2}{25}\right\} + \tan\left\{\frac{\pi}{4} - \frac{1}{2}\cos^{-1}\frac{2}{25}\right\}$$

$$\theta = \sin^{-1}\left(\frac{1}{\sqrt{5}}\right) + \cot^{-1}(3)$$

Then, answer the following questions:

(i) Find the height of the rocket from the ground.
(a) 25　　　　　(b) 30
(c) 35　　　　　(d) 45

(ii) Find the shortest distance y between observer and rocket.
(a) 25　　　　　(b) $25\sqrt{2}$
(c) 35　　　　　(d) $35\sqrt{2}$

(iii) Find the angle of elevation of the observer to the rocket.

(a) $\dfrac{\pi}{3}$　　　　　(b) $\dfrac{\pi}{4}$

(c) $\dfrac{\pi}{6}$　　　　　(d) $\dfrac{\pi}{2}$

(iv) Find the horizontal distance x between observer and the initial position of the rocket.
(a) 15　　　　　(b) 20
(c) 25　　　　　(d) 30

(v) If the angle of elevation gets changed by $\phi = \dfrac{1}{2}\tan^{-1}(\cot\phi)$ after sometime, then what is the angle of elevation now?

(a) $\dfrac{\pi}{3}$　　　　　(b) $\dfrac{\pi}{4}$

(c) $\dfrac{\pi}{6}$　　　　　(d) $\dfrac{\pi}{2}$

Very Short Answer Questions

10. Find the domain of the function $\cos^{-1}(2x-1)$

11. Find the domain of the function defined by $f(x) = \sin^{-1}\sqrt{x-1}$.

12. Let $\cos(2\tan^{-1}x) = \dfrac{1}{2}$, then find the value of x.

13. Find the value of $\cos^{-1}\dfrac{1}{2} + 2\sin^{-1}\dfrac{1}{2}$.

Solutions

Practice Exercise-1 

1. (a) 2. (b) 3. (b) 4. (b) 5. (c) 6. (d)

7. (a) 8. 0 9. 0 10. 0.75 11. 8 12. $\dfrac{1}{\sqrt{2}}$

13. Principal value of $\tan^{-1}(1) + \cos^{-1}\left(\dfrac{-1}{2}\right) + \sin^{-1}\left(\dfrac{-1}{2}\right)$

$$= \frac{\pi}{4} + \frac{2\pi}{3} - \frac{\pi}{6} = \frac{3\pi}{4}$$

14. $\cos^{-1}\left(\dfrac{1}{2}\right) + \sin^{-1}\left(\dfrac{1}{2}\right) + \tan^{-1}\dfrac{1}{\sqrt{3}}$

$$= \frac{\pi}{3} + \frac{\pi}{2} + \frac{\pi}{6} = \frac{6\pi}{6} = \pi$$

15. $\sin^{-1}\left(-\dfrac{\sqrt{3}}{2}\right) = \left[\sin^{-1}\sin\left(-\dfrac{\pi}{3}\right)\right] = -\dfrac{\pi}{3}$

16. Let $\cos^{-1}\dfrac{1}{8} = \theta$, where $0 < \theta < \dfrac{\pi}{2}$. Then

$$\frac{1}{2}\cos^{-1}\frac{1}{8} = \frac{1}{2}\theta \Rightarrow \cos\left(\frac{1}{2}\cos^{-1}\frac{1}{8}\right) = \cos\frac{1}{2}\theta$$

Now, $\cos^{-1}\dfrac{1}{8} = \theta$

$$\Rightarrow \cos\theta = \frac{1}{8} \Rightarrow 2\cos^2\frac{\theta}{2} - 1 = \frac{1}{8} \Rightarrow \cos^2\frac{\theta}{2} = \frac{9}{16}$$

$$\Rightarrow \cos\frac{\theta}{2} = \frac{3}{4} \qquad \left[\because 0 < \frac{\theta}{2} < \frac{\pi}{4}, \text{ so } \cos\frac{\theta}{2} \neq -\frac{3}{4}\right]$$

17. $\cos^{-1}\left[\cos\left(\dfrac{5\pi}{3}\right)\right] + \sin^{-1}\left(\sin\dfrac{5\pi}{3}\right) = \dfrac{\pi}{3} - \dfrac{\pi}{3} = 0$

18. $\sin^{-1}\left(\dfrac{1}{\sqrt{2}}\right) + \operatorname{cosec}^{-1}(2) = k\dfrac{\pi}{12}$

$$\Rightarrow \frac{\pi}{4} + \frac{\pi}{6} = \frac{k\pi}{12} \Rightarrow \frac{5\pi}{12} = \frac{k\pi}{12} \quad \therefore \quad k = 5$$

19. $\sin^{-1}\left(-\dfrac{1}{2}\right) + 2\cos^{-1}\left(-\dfrac{\sqrt{3}}{2}\right)$

$$= -\frac{\pi}{6} + 2\left(\frac{5\pi}{6}\right) = \frac{9}{6}\pi = \frac{3}{2}\pi$$

20. $\tan^{-1}(-1) + \cos^{-1}\left(-\dfrac{1}{\sqrt{2}}\right)$

$$= -\frac{\pi}{4} + \frac{3\pi}{4} = \frac{\pi}{2}$$

21. As given: $\cos^{-1}x + \cos^{-1}y + \cos^{-1}z = 3\pi$

and we know that $0 \leq \cos^{-1}x \leq \pi$

$\therefore \cos^{-1}x = \pi$, $\cos^{-1}y = \pi$, $\cos^{-1}z = \pi$

$\therefore x = y = z = \cos\pi = -1$.

$\therefore xy + yz + zx = (-1)(-1) + (-1)(-1) + (-1)(-1)$
$$= 1 + 1 + 1 = 3$$

22. The given expression is equal to

$$-\frac{\pi}{4} + \frac{2\pi}{3} + \frac{\pi}{3} + \frac{2\pi}{3} = \frac{5\pi}{3} - \frac{\pi}{4} = \frac{7\pi}{12}$$

23. $\cos^{-1}[\cos(2\pi - 5\pi/6)] = \cos^{-1}(\cos 5\pi/6) = 5\pi/6$

NCERT Exercise-1

1. Principal value of $\sin^{-1}\left(-\dfrac{1}{2}\right)$ is $-\left(\dfrac{\pi}{6}\right)$

2. Principal value of $\cos^{-1}\left(\dfrac{\sqrt{3}}{2}\right)$ is $\dfrac{\pi}{6}$

3. Principal value of $\operatorname{cosec}^{-1}(2)$ is $\dfrac{\pi}{6}$

4. Principal value of $\tan^{-1}\left(-\sqrt{3}\right)$ is $-\dfrac{\pi}{3}$.

5. Principal value is $\dfrac{2\pi}{3}$

6. Principal value of $\tan^{-1}(-1)$ is $\dfrac{-\pi}{4}$

7. The principal value of $\sec^{-1}\left(\dfrac{2}{\sqrt{3}}\right)$ is $\dfrac{\pi}{6}$.

8. The principal value of $\cot^{-1}\sqrt{3}$ is $\dfrac{\pi}{6}$

9. Principal value of $\cos^{-1}\left(\dfrac{-1}{\sqrt{2}}\right) = \dfrac{3\pi}{4}$.

10. Principal value of $\operatorname{cosec}^{-1}\left(-\sqrt{2}\right) = -\dfrac{\pi}{4}$

11. $\tan^{-1}(1) + \cos^{-1}\left(\dfrac{1}{2}\right) + \sin^{-1}\left(-\dfrac{1}{2}\right)$

$$= \frac{\pi}{4} + \frac{2\pi}{3} - \frac{\pi}{6} = \frac{3\pi + 8\pi - 2\pi}{12} = \frac{9\pi}{12} = \frac{3\pi}{4}$$

12. $\cos^{-1}\left(\dfrac{1}{2}\right) + 2\sin^{-1}\left(\dfrac{1}{2}\right)$

$\dfrac{\pi}{3} + 2 \times \dfrac{\pi}{6} = \dfrac{2\pi}{3}$

13. **(b)**   **14.** **(b)**

Past year Exercise

1. $\cos^{-1}\left(\dfrac{1}{2}\right) - 2\sin^{-1}\left(-\dfrac{1}{2}\right)$

$= \dfrac{\pi}{3} - 2\left(-\dfrac{\pi}{6}\right) = \dfrac{\pi}{3} + \dfrac{\pi}{3} = \dfrac{2\pi}{3}$

2. We know that, principal value for $\tan^{-1}x$ is $\left(-\dfrac{\pi}{2}, \dfrac{\pi}{2}\right)$ and

that of $\sec^{-1}x$ is $[0, \pi] - \left\{\dfrac{\pi}{2}\right\}$

So, $\tan^{-1}(\sqrt{3}) - \sec^{-1}(-2)$

$= \tan^{-1}\left(\tan\dfrac{\pi}{3}\right) - \sec^{-1}\left(\sec\dfrac{2\pi}{3}\right)$

$$\left[\because\ \tan\dfrac{\pi}{3} = \sqrt{3}\ \text{and}\ \sec\dfrac{2\pi}{3} = -2\right]$$

$= \dfrac{\pi}{3} - \dfrac{2\pi}{3} = \dfrac{-\pi}{3}$

3. **To prove :** $\sin^{-1}\dfrac{8}{17} + \sin^{-1}\dfrac{3}{5} = \cos^{-1}\left(\dfrac{36}{85}\right)$

Let $\sin^{-1}\dfrac{8}{17} = x$ and $\sin^{-1}\dfrac{3}{5} = y$

$\Rightarrow \quad \sin x = \dfrac{8}{17}$ and $\sin y = \dfrac{3}{5}$

$\because \quad \cos^2 x = 1 - \sin^2 x = 1 - \dfrac{64}{289}$

$\Rightarrow \quad \cos x = \dfrac{15}{17}$

Also, $\cos^2 y = 1 - \sin^2 y = 1 - \dfrac{9}{25} = \dfrac{16}{25}$

$\therefore \quad \cos y = \dfrac{4}{5}$

Now, $\cos(x + y) = \cos x \cos y - \sin x \sin y$

$\therefore \quad \cos(x + y) = \dfrac{15}{17} \times \dfrac{4}{5} - \dfrac{8}{17} \times \dfrac{3}{5}$

$\Rightarrow \quad \cos(x + y) = \dfrac{60}{85} - \dfrac{24}{85} = \dfrac{36}{85}$

$\therefore \quad x + y = \cos^{-1}\left(\dfrac{36}{85}\right)$

$\Rightarrow \quad \sin^{-1}\dfrac{8}{17} + \sin^{-1}\dfrac{3}{5} = \cos^{-1}\dfrac{36}{85}$

4. Consider $\tan\left(2\tan^{-1}\dfrac{1}{5}\right)$

$= \tan\left(\tan^{-1}\left\{\dfrac{2 \times \dfrac{1}{5}}{1 - \left(\dfrac{1}{5}\right)^2}\right\}\right) = \dfrac{\dfrac{2}{5}}{\dfrac{24}{25}} = \dfrac{5}{12}$

5. Consider $\tan^{-1}(1) + \cos^{-1}\left(-\dfrac{1}{2}\right)$

$= \tan^{-1}\left(\tan\dfrac{\pi}{4}\right) + \cos^{-1}\left(\cos\left(\pi - \dfrac{\pi}{3}\right)\right)$

$= \dfrac{\pi}{4} + \dfrac{2\pi}{3} = \dfrac{11\pi}{12}$

6. Let $\cos^{-1}\left(\dfrac{\sqrt{3}}{2}\right) = \theta$, where $\theta \in [0, \pi]$

$\Rightarrow \quad \cos\theta = \dfrac{\sqrt{3}}{2} = \cos\dfrac{\pi}{6} \Rightarrow \theta = \dfrac{\pi}{6}$

$\Rightarrow \quad \cos^{-1}\left(\dfrac{\sqrt{3}}{2}\right) = \dfrac{\pi}{6}$

Also, let $\cos^{-1}\left(-\dfrac{1}{2}\right) = \phi$ where $\phi \in [0, \pi]$

$\Rightarrow \quad \cos\phi = -\dfrac{1}{2} = -\cos\dfrac{\pi}{3} = \cos\left(\pi - \dfrac{\pi}{3}\right) = \cos\dfrac{2\pi}{3}$

$\Rightarrow \quad \phi = \dfrac{2\pi}{3} \Rightarrow \cos^{-1}\left(-\dfrac{1}{2}\right) = \dfrac{2\pi}{3}$

Now, $\cos^{-1}\left(\dfrac{\sqrt{3}}{2}\right) + \cos^{-1}\left(-\dfrac{1}{2}\right) = \dfrac{\pi}{6} + \dfrac{2\pi}{3} = \dfrac{5\pi}{6}$

7. Consider $\tan^{-1}\sqrt{3} - \cot^{-1}\left(-\sqrt{3}\right)$

$= \tan^{-1}\left(\tan\dfrac{\pi}{3}\right) - \cot^{-1}\left(-\cot\dfrac{\pi}{6}\right)$

$= \dfrac{\pi}{3} - \cot^{-1}\left(\cot\left(\pi - \dfrac{\pi}{6}\right)\right)$

$= \dfrac{\pi}{3} - \dfrac{5\pi}{6} = -\dfrac{\pi}{2}$

8. Consider $\tan^{-1}\left[2\sin\left(2\cos^{-1}\dfrac{\sqrt{3}}{2}\right)\right]$

$$= \tan^{-1}\left[2\sin\left(2\cos^{-1}\left(\cos\dfrac{\pi}{6}\right)\right)\right]$$

$$= \tan^{-1}\left[2\sin\left(2\times\dfrac{\pi}{6}\right)\right]$$

$$= \tan^{-1}\left[2\sin\dfrac{\pi}{3}\right] = \tan^{-1}\left[2.\dfrac{\sqrt{3}}{2}\right]$$

$$= \tan^{-1}\sqrt{3} = \tan^{-1}\left(\tan\dfrac{\pi}{3}\right) = \dfrac{\pi}{3}$$

9. $\sin^{-1}\left(\sin\dfrac{3\pi}{5}\right) = \sin^{-1}\left(\sin\left(\pi - \dfrac{2\pi}{5}\right)\right)$

$$= \sin^{-1}\left(\sin\dfrac{2\pi}{5}\right) = \dfrac{2\pi}{5}$$

10. Let $\tan^{-1}\left(-\sqrt{3}\right) = \theta, \theta \in \left(-\dfrac{\pi}{2}, \dfrac{\pi}{2}\right)$

$\Rightarrow \quad \tan\theta = -\sqrt{3} \qquad \Rightarrow \quad \tan\theta = -\tan\dfrac{\pi}{3}$

$\Rightarrow \quad \tan\theta = \tan\left(\dfrac{-\pi}{3}\right) \quad \Rightarrow \quad \theta = \dfrac{-\pi}{3}$

$\Rightarrow \quad \tan^{-1}\left(-\sqrt{3}\right) = \dfrac{-\pi}{3}$

and $\tan^{-1}(1) = \tan^{-1}\left(\tan\dfrac{\pi}{4}\right) = \dfrac{\pi}{4}$

$\therefore \quad \tan^{-1}\left(-\sqrt{3}\right) + \tan^{-1}(1) = \dfrac{-\pi}{3} + \dfrac{\pi}{4}$

$$= \dfrac{-4\pi + 3\pi}{12} = \dfrac{-\pi}{12}$$

11. L.H.S. $= \sin^{-1}\left(2x\sqrt{1-x^2}\right), \dfrac{1}{\sqrt{2}} \le x \le 1$

Let $x = \cos\theta \Rightarrow \theta = \cos^{-1}x,\ 0 \le \theta \le \dfrac{\pi}{4}$

$\therefore \quad$ L.H.S. $= \sin^{-1}\left(2\sin\theta\sqrt{1-\sin^2\theta}\right)$

$\quad = \sin^{-1}(2\sin\theta\cos\theta) \qquad [\because \sin^2\theta + \cos^2\theta = 1]$

$\quad = \sin^{-1}(\sin2\theta) \qquad\qquad [\because \sin2\theta = 2\sin\theta.\cos\theta]$

$\quad = 2\theta$

$\quad = 2\cos^{-1}x = $ R.H.S.

1. $\therefore \tan^{-1}\left(\tan\dfrac{5\pi}{6}\right) + \cos^{-1}\left(\cos\dfrac{13\pi}{6}\right)$

$$= \tan^{-1}\left[\tan\left(\pi - \dfrac{\pi}{6}\right)\right] + \cos^{-1}\left[\cos\left(\pi + \dfrac{7\pi}{6}\right)\right]$$

$$= \tan^{-1}\left(-\tan\dfrac{\pi}{6}\right) + \cos^{-1}\left(-\cos\dfrac{7\pi}{6}\right)$$

$$[\because \cos(\pi + \theta) = -\cos\theta]$$

$$= -\tan^{-1}\left(\tan\dfrac{\pi}{6}\right) + \pi - \left[\cos^{-1}\cos\left(\dfrac{7\pi}{6}\right)\right]$$

$\{\because \tan^{-1}(-x) = -\tan^{-1}x,\ x \in$ R and $\cos^{-1}(-x) - \pi - \cos^{-1}$ x; x $\in [-1, 1]\}$

$$= -\tan^{-1}\left(\tan\dfrac{\pi}{6}\right) + \pi - \cos^{-1}\left[\cos\left(\pi + \dfrac{\pi}{6}\right)\right]$$

$$= -\tan^{-1}\left(\tan\dfrac{\pi}{6}\right) + \pi - \left[\cos^{-1}\left(-\cos\dfrac{\pi}{6}\right)\right]$$

$$[\because \cos(\pi + \theta) = -\cos\theta]$$

$$= -\tan^{-1}\left(\tan\dfrac{\pi}{6}\right) + \pi - \pi + \cos^{-1}\left(\cos\dfrac{\pi}{6}\right)$$

$$[\because \cos^{-1}(-x) = \pi - \cos^{-1} x]$$

$$= -\dfrac{\pi}{6} + 0 + \dfrac{\pi}{6} = 0$$

$\left(\because \tan^{-1}\tan x = x,\ x \in \left(-\dfrac{\pi}{2}, \dfrac{\pi}{2}\right)$ and $\cos^{-1}\cos x = x; x \in [0, \pi]\right)$

2. Let A $= \cos\left[\cos^{-1}\left(\dfrac{-\sqrt{3}}{2}\right) + \dfrac{\pi}{6}\right]$

$\Rightarrow \quad$ A $= \cos\left[\cos^{-1}\left(\cos\dfrac{5\pi}{6}\right) + \dfrac{\pi}{6}\right]\left[\because \cos\dfrac{5\pi}{6} = \dfrac{-\sqrt{3}}{2}\right]$

$$= \cos\left(\dfrac{5\pi}{6} + \dfrac{\pi}{6}\right)$$

$$\{\because \cos^{-1}(\cos x) = x;\ x \in [0, \pi]\}$$

$$= \cos(\pi) = -1$$

3. We have, $\tan^{-1}\left(-\dfrac{1}{\sqrt{3}}\right) + \cot^{-1}\left(\dfrac{1}{\sqrt{3}}\right)$

$$+ \tan^{-1}\left[\sin\left(\dfrac{-\pi}{2}\right)\right]$$

$$= \tan^{-1}\left(\tan\dfrac{5\pi}{6}\right) + \cot^{-1}\left(\cot\dfrac{\pi}{3}\right) + \tan^{-1}(-1)$$

$$= \tan^{-1}\left[\tan\left(\pi - \dfrac{\pi}{6}\right)\right] + \cot^{-1}\left[\cot\left(\dfrac{\pi}{3}\right)\right]$$

$$+ \tan^{-1}\left[\tan\left(\pi - \dfrac{\pi}{4}\right)\right]$$

$$= \tan^{-1}\left(-\tan\frac{\pi}{6}\right) + \cot^{-1}\left(\cot\frac{\pi}{3}\right) + \tan^{-1}\left(-\tan\frac{\pi}{4}\right)$$

$$\left[\begin{array}{l} \because \tan^{-1}(\tan x) = x, x \in \left(-\frac{\pi}{2}, \frac{\pi}{2}\right), \\ \cot^{-1}(\cot x) = x, x \in (0, \pi) \\ \text{and } \tan^{-1}(-x) = -\tan^{-1} x \end{array}\right]$$

$$= -\frac{\pi}{6} + \frac{\pi}{3} - \frac{\pi}{4}$$

$$= -\frac{\pi}{12}$$

4. We have, $\tan^{-1}\left(\tan\frac{2\pi}{3}\right)$

$$= \tan^{-1}\tan\left(\pi - \frac{\pi}{3}\right)$$

$$= \tan^{-1}\left(-\tan\frac{\pi}{3}\right)$$

$$[\because \tan^{-1}(-x) = -\tan^{-1} x]$$

$$= -\tan^{-1}\tan\frac{\pi}{3} = -\frac{\pi}{3}$$

$$\left[\because \tan^{-1}(\tan x) = x, x \in \left(\frac{-\pi}{2}, \frac{\pi}{2}\right)\right]$$

Objective Practice Exercise

1. **(c)** For $f(x)$ to be defined, we must have

$$-1 \le \log_2\left(\frac{1}{2} x^2\right) \le 1$$

$$\Rightarrow 2^{-1} \le \frac{1}{2} x^2 \le 2^1 \ [\because \text{ the base} = 2 > 1]$$

$$\Rightarrow 1 \le x^2 \le 4 \qquad \qquad \qquad ...(i)$$

Now, $1 \le x^2$

$$\Rightarrow x^2 - 1 \ge 0 \text{ i.e. } (x-1)(x+1) \ge 0$$

$$\Rightarrow x \le -1 \text{ or } x \ge 1 \qquad \qquad ...(ii)$$

Also, $x^2 \le 4$

$$\Rightarrow x^2 - 4 \le 0 \text{ i.e. } (x-2)(x+2) \le 0$$

$$\Rightarrow -2 \le x \le 2 \qquad \qquad \qquad ...(iii)$$

Form (ii) and (iii), we get the domain of f

$$= \{(-\infty, -1] \cup [1, \infty)\} \cap [-2, 2]$$

$$= [-2, -1] \cup [1, 2]$$

2. **(b)** $\angle CAB = \angle DAB = \alpha$

Hypotenuse $(AB) = \sqrt{(30)^2 + (30\sqrt{3})^2} = 60$

$$\therefore \ \sin\alpha = \frac{BD}{AB} = \frac{30}{60} = \frac{1}{2} \Rightarrow \alpha = \sin^{-1}\left(\frac{1}{2}\right)$$

$$\therefore \ \angle CAB = \alpha = \sin^{-1}\left(\frac{1}{2}\right)$$

3. **(c)** $\because \cos\alpha = \frac{AD}{AB} = \frac{30\sqrt{3}}{60} = \frac{\sqrt{3}}{2} \Rightarrow \alpha = \cos^{-1}\left(\frac{\sqrt{3}}{2}\right)$

$$\therefore \ \angle CAB = \alpha = \cos^{-1}\left(\frac{\sqrt{3}}{2}\right)$$

4. **(d)** $\tan\beta = \frac{BD}{CD} = \frac{30}{10\sqrt{3}} = \sqrt{3}$

$$\Rightarrow \beta = \tan^{-1}\left(\sqrt{3}\right)$$

$$\therefore \angle BCA = \beta = \tan^{-1}\left(\sqrt{3}\right)$$

5. **(c)** $\dfrac{\pi}{2}$

6. **(c)** $[-1, 1], [0, \pi]$

7. **(b)** $\tan(\angle CAB) = \frac{BC}{AB} = \frac{10}{20} \Rightarrow \angle CAB = \tan^{-1}\left(\frac{1}{2}\right)$

8. **(c)** $\because \angle DAB = 2\angle CAB$

$$\therefore \tan(\angle DAB) = \tan(2\angle CAB)$$

$$= \frac{2\tan(\angle CAB)}{1 - \tan^2(\angle CAB)} = \frac{2 \cdot \frac{1}{2}}{1 - \left(\frac{1}{2}\right)^2} = \frac{4}{3}$$

$$\Rightarrow \angle DAB = \tan^{-1}\left(\frac{4}{3}\right)$$

9. **(d)** $\because \angle EAB = 3\angle CAB$

$$\therefore \tan(\angle EAB) = \tan(3\angle CAB)$$

$$= \frac{3\tan(\angle CAB) - \tan^3(\angle CAB)}{1 - 3\tan^2(\angle CAB)} = \frac{\frac{3}{2} - \frac{1}{8}}{1 - \frac{3}{4}} = \frac{11}{2}$$

$$\Rightarrow \angle EAB = \tan^{-1}\left(\frac{11}{2}\right)$$

10. (b) $\tan\left(\angle CA'B\right) = \dfrac{BC}{A'B} = \dfrac{10}{25} = \dfrac{2}{5}$

$\Rightarrow \angle CA'B = \tan^{-1}\left(\dfrac{2}{5}\right)$

Now, $\angle CAB - \angle CA'B = \tan^{-1}\left(\dfrac{1}{2}\right) - \tan^{-1}\left(\dfrac{2}{5}\right)$.

$= \tan^{-1}\left(\dfrac{\dfrac{1}{2} - \dfrac{2}{5}}{1 + \dfrac{1}{2} \times \dfrac{2}{5}}\right) = \tan^{-1}\left(\dfrac{1}{12}\right)$

11. (c) $R, \left(-\dfrac{\pi}{2}, \dfrac{\pi}{2}\right)$

Chapter Test

1. (c) Principal value branch of $\cos^{-1}x = [0, \pi]$

2. (a)   **3. (b)**   **4. (a)**

5. $\left[\dfrac{-\pi}{2}, \dfrac{\pi}{2}\right] - \{0\}$

6. $-\dfrac{\pi}{4}$

7. (c)   **8. (b)**

9. (i) (a) ; (ii) (b); (iii) (b); (iv) (c); (v) (c)

10. Here, $-1 \le 2x - 1 \le 1$ $[\because -1 \le \cos\theta \le 1]$

$\Rightarrow \quad 0 \le 2x \le 2 \Rightarrow 0 \le x \le 1$. So, $x \in [0, 1]$

Hence, domain of $\cos^{-1}(2x - 1)$ is $[0, 1]$.

11. $\dfrac{-\pi}{2} \le \sin^{-1}\sqrt{x - 1} \le \dfrac{\pi}{2} \Rightarrow -1 \le \sqrt{x - 1} \le 1$

$\Rightarrow \quad 0 \le x - 1 < 1 \Rightarrow 1 \le x \le 2$

$\therefore$ Domain of $f(x)$ is $[1, 2]$

12. $\because \cos\left(2\tan^{-1}x\right) = \dfrac{1}{2}$

$\therefore \cos\left(2\tan^{-1}x\right) = \cos\dfrac{\pi}{3}$

$\Rightarrow \tan^{-1}x = \dfrac{\pi}{6} \Rightarrow x = \tan\dfrac{\pi}{6} = \dfrac{1}{\sqrt{3}}$

13. $\cos^{-1}\dfrac{1}{2} + 2\sin^{-1}\dfrac{1}{2} = \dfrac{\pi}{3} + \dfrac{2\pi}{6} = \dfrac{2\pi}{3}$

3

Matrices

MATRICES

(1) Multiplication of a Matrix by a Scalar

Let $A = [a_{ij}]_{m \times n}$ be a matrix & k be a number. Then, $kA = Ak = [ka_{ij}]_{m \times n}$

(2) Multiplication of Matrices

If A & B are any two matrices, then their product AB will be defined only when the number of columns in A is equal to the number of rows in B. If $A = [a_{ij}]_{m \times n}$ & $B = [b_{ij}]_{n \times p}$, then their product $AB = C = [C_{ij}]$, is a matrix of order $m \times p$, where $(ij)^{th}$ element of $AB = C_{ij} = \sum_{r=1}^{n} a_{ir} b_{rj}$

(5) Symmetric & Skew Symmetric Matrices

Symmetric Matrix

A square matrix $A = [a_{ij}]$ is called a symmetric matrix, if $a_{ij} = a_{ji}$ for all i, j or $A^T = A$

Skew Symmetric Matrix

A square matrix $A = [a_{ij}]$ is called a skew-symmetric matrix, if $a_{ij} = -a_{ji}$ for all i, j or $A^T = -A$

Properties of Symmetric & Skew Symmetric Matrices

(i) For any square matrix A with real number entries, $(A + A^T)$ is a symmetric matrix & $(A - A^T)$ is a skew symmetric matrix.

(ii) Any square matrix A can be expressed as the sum of a symmetric & a skew symmetric matrix as

$$A = \left[\frac{1}{2}(A + A^T)\right] + \left[\frac{1}{2}(A - A^T)\right]$$

(3) Properties of Matrix Multiplication

(i) **Associative Law for Multiplication :** If A, B & C are three matrices of order $m \times n$, $n \times p$ & $p \times q$ respectively, then $(AB)C = A(BC)$

(ii) **Distributive Law :** For three matrices A, B & C

(a) $A(B + C) = AB + AC$

(b) $(A + B)C = AC + BC$, whenever both sides of equality are defined.

(iii) **Matrix Multiplication** is not commutative in general, i.e., $AB \neq BA$ (in general).

(iv) **Existence of Multiplicative Identity :** For every square matrix A, there exists an identity matrix I of same order such that $IA = AI = A$.

(4) Properties of Transpose of the Matrices

For any matrices A & B of suitable orders, we have

(i) $(A^T)^T = A$ (ii) $(kA)^T = k(A)^T$

(iii) $(A \pm B)^T = A^T \pm B^T$ (iv) $(AB)^T = B^T A^T$

Topic 1 — Matrix, Order and Types of Matrices

MATRIX

A matrix is an ordered rectangular array of numbers or functions. The numbers or functions are called the elements or the entries of the matrix.

ORDER OF MATRIX

A matrix having m rows and n columns is called the matrix of order m × n.

TYPES OF MATRICES

In this section we shall discuss different types of matrices.

(a) **Row Matrix :** A matrix is said to be row matrix if it has only one row.

   Ex. $A = [1\ 2\ 3]_{1 \times 3}$

(b) **Column Matrix :** A matrix is said to be column matrix if it has only one column.

   Ex. $A = \begin{bmatrix} 1 \\ 2 \\ 3 \end{bmatrix}_{3 \times 1}$

(c) **Square Matrix :** A matrix in which the number of rows are equal to number of columns, is said to be square matrix. Thus m × n matrix is said to be square matrix if m = n

(d) **Null or (Zero) Matrix :** A matrix having all the elements zero is called zero matrix.

(e) **Diagonal Matrix :** A square matrix is called diagonal matrix if all its non-diagonal elements are zero. The diagonal elements may or may not be zero.

   Ex. $\begin{bmatrix} K_1 & 0 \\ 0 & K_2 \end{bmatrix}, \begin{bmatrix} K_1 & 0 & 0 \\ 0 & K_2 & 0 \\ 0 & 0 & K_3 \end{bmatrix}$

(f) **Scalar Matrix :** A diagonal matrix in which all the diagonal element are equal and all other elements equal to zero is called a scalar matrix.

   i.e. In a scalar matrix $a_{ij} = k$ for $i = j$ and $a_{ij} = 0$ for $i \neq j$. Hence $\begin{bmatrix} K & 0 & 0 \\ 0 & K & 0 \\ 0 & 0 & K \end{bmatrix}$ is a scalar matrix.

(g) **Unit Matrix or Identity Matrix :** A diagonal matrix in which all its diagonal elements are equal to 1 and all other elements equal to zero is called a unit matrix or an identity matrix. It is denoted by I.

   E.g. a unit or identity matrix of order 2 and 3 are $\begin{bmatrix} 1 & 0 \\ 0 & 1 \end{bmatrix}$ and $\begin{bmatrix} 1 & 0 & 0 \\ 0 & 1 & 0 \\ 0 & 0 & 1 \end{bmatrix}$ respectively.

(h) **Upper Triangular Matrix :** A square matrix $A = [a_{ij}]$ is called an upper triangular matrix if $a_{ij} = 0$ for all $i > j$. Thus in an upper triangular matrix, all elements below the main diagonal are zero.

   e.g. $\begin{bmatrix} 1 & 2 & 4 & 3 \\ 0 & 5 & 1 & 3 \\ 0 & 0 & 2 & 9 \\ 0 & 0 & 0 & 5 \end{bmatrix}$ is an upper triangular matrix.

(i) **Lower Triangular Matrix :** A square matrix $A = [a_{ij}]$ is called a lower triangular matrix if $a_{ij} = 0$ for all $i < j$

Thus in a lower triangular matrix, all elements above the main diagonal are zero.

e.g. $A = \begin{bmatrix} 2 & 0 & 0 \\ 3 & 2 & 0 \\ 4 & 5 & 3 \end{bmatrix}$ is a lower triangular matrix.

Note that in triangular matrices (both upper and lower) non-zero elements can also be zero.

EQUALITY OF MATRICES

Two matrices A and B are said to be equal, written as $A = B$ if

(i) they are of the same order i.e. have the same number of rows and columns, and

(ii) each element of A is equal to the corresponding element of B that is $a_{ij} = b_{ij}$ for all i & j

e.g. if $A = \begin{bmatrix} 1 & 2 \\ 3 & 4 \end{bmatrix}$, $B = \begin{bmatrix} 1 & 2 \\ 3 & 4 \end{bmatrix}$ then, we say $A = B$

Practice Exercise-1

Multiple Choice Questions

1. Choose the incorrect statement.
(a) A matrix $A = [3]$ is a scalar matrix of order 1
(b) A matrix $B = \begin{bmatrix} -1 & 0 \\ 0 & -1 \end{bmatrix}$ is a scalar matrix of order 2
(c) A matrix $C = \begin{bmatrix} \sqrt{3} & 0 & 0 \\ 0 & \sqrt{3} & 0 \\ 0 & 0 & \sqrt{3} \end{bmatrix}$ of order 3 is not a scalar matrix
(d) None of the above

2. Which of the following is correct statement?
(a) Diagonal matrix is also a scalar matrix
(b) Identity matrix is a particular case of scalar matrix
(c) Scalar matrix is not a diagonal matrix
(d) Null matrix cannot be a square matrix

3. If $A = [a_{ij}]$ is a matrix of order 4×5, then the diagonal elements of A are
(a) $a_{11}, a_{22}, a_{33}, a_{44}$
(b) $a_{55}, a_{44}, a_{33}, a_{22}, a_{11}$
(c) a_{11}, a_{22}, a_{33}
(d) do not exist

4. If the matrices $A = [a_{ij}]$ and $B = [b_{ij}]$ and $C = [c_{ij}]$ are of the same order, say $m \times n$, satisfy Associative law, then
(a) $(A + B) + C = A + (B + C)$
(b) $A + B = B + C$
(c) $A + C = B + C$
(d) $A + B + C = A - B - C$

5. If a matrix has 8 elements, then which of the following will not be a possible order of the matrix?
(a) 1×8 (b) 2×4
(c) 4×2 (d) 4×4

Assertion & Reason Questions

DIRECTIONS : *Each of these questions contains an assertion followed by reason. Read them carefully and answer the question on the basis of following options. You have to select the one that best describes the two statements.*

(a) If both Assertion and Reason are correct and the Reason is a correct explanation of the Assertion.
(b) If both Assertion and Reason are correct but Reason is not a correct explanation of the Assertion.
(c) If the Assertion is correct but Reason is incorrect.
(d) If the Assertion is incorrect but the Reason is correct.

6. **Assertion :** The possible dimensions of a matrix containing 32 elements is 6.
Reason : The no. of ways of expressing 32 as a product of two positive integers is 6.

7. **Assertion :** Scalar matrix $A = [a_{ij}] = \begin{cases} k; & i = j \\ 0; & i \neq j \end{cases}$ where k is a scalar, in an identity matrix when $k = 1$.
Reason : Every identity matrix is not a scalar matrix.

One Word Questions

8. A square matrix $B = [b_{ij}]_{n \times n}$ is said to be a scalar matrix, if _____________.

9. If the diagonal elements of a diagonal matrix are all equal, then the matrix is called _____________.

10. Find the number of all possible matrices of order 3×3 with each entry 0 or 1.

Very Short Answer Questions

11. Construct a 2×3 matrix A, whose elements are given by

$$a_{ij} = \frac{(i - 2j)^2}{2}.$$

12. If A is a 3×2 matrix, B is a 3×3 matrix and C is a 2×3 matrix, then find the elements in A, B and C.

Short Answer Questions

13. If $\begin{bmatrix} x-y & 2x+z \\ 2x-y & 3z+w \end{bmatrix} = \begin{bmatrix} -1 & 5 \\ 0 & 13 \end{bmatrix}$, find x, y, z, w.

14. If $\begin{bmatrix} x+y & 2x+z \\ x-y & 2z+w \end{bmatrix} = \begin{bmatrix} 4 & 7 \\ 0 & 10 \end{bmatrix}$, then find the values of x, y, z and w

15. For what values of x and y are the following matrices equal $A = \begin{bmatrix} 2x+1 & 3y \\ 0 & y^2-5y \end{bmatrix}$, $B = \begin{bmatrix} x+3 & y^2+2 \\ 0 & -6 \end{bmatrix}$

NCERT Exercise-1

1. (i)   The order of the matrix.

(ii)   The number of elements.

(iii) Write the elements a_{13}, a_{21}, a_{33}, a_{24}, a_{23} for the

matrix $A = \begin{bmatrix} 2 & 5 & 19 & -7 \\ 35 & -2 & \dfrac{5}{2} & 12 \\ \sqrt{3} & 1 & -5 & 17 \end{bmatrix}$

2. If a matrix has 24 elements, what are the possible orders it can have? What, if it has 13 elements?

3. If a matrix has 18 elements, what are the possible orders it can have ? What, if it has 5 elements .

4. Construct a 2×2 matrix, $A = [a_{ij}]$ whose elements are given by :

(i) $a_{ij} = \dfrac{(i+j)^2}{2}$ (ii) $a_{ij} = \dfrac{i}{j}$

(iii) $a_{ij} = \dfrac{(i+2j)^2}{2}$

5. Construct a 3×4 matrix, whose element are given by:

(i) $a_{ij} = \dfrac{1}{2}\left| -3i + j \right|$ (ii) $a_{ij} = 2i - j$

6. Find the values of x, y, z from the following equations :

(i) $\begin{bmatrix} 4 & 3 \\ x & 5 \end{bmatrix} = \begin{bmatrix} y & z \\ 1 & 5 \end{bmatrix}$ (ii) $\begin{bmatrix} x+y & 2 \\ 5+z & xy \end{bmatrix} = \begin{bmatrix} 6 & 2 \\ 5 & 8 \end{bmatrix}$

(iii) $\begin{bmatrix} x+y+z \\ x+z \\ y+z \end{bmatrix} = \begin{bmatrix} 9 \\ 5 \\ 7 \end{bmatrix}$

7. Find the values of a, b, c and d from the equation:

$\begin{bmatrix} a-b & 2a+c \\ 2a-b & 3c+d \end{bmatrix} = \begin{bmatrix} -1 & 5 \\ 0 & 13 \end{bmatrix}$.

8. $A = [a_{ij}]_{m \times n}$ is a square matrix, if

(a) $m < n$ (b) $n > n$

(c) $m = n$ (d)   none of these

9. Which of the given values of x and y make the following pairs of matrices equal:

$\begin{bmatrix} 3x+7 & 5 \\ y+1 & 2-3x \end{bmatrix}, \begin{bmatrix} 0 & y-2 \\ 8 & 4 \end{bmatrix}$

(a) $x = \dfrac{-1}{3}, y = 7$ (b)   Not possible to find

(c) $y = 7, x = \dfrac{-2}{3}$ (d) $x = \dfrac{-1}{3}, y = \dfrac{-2}{3}$.

10. The number of all possible matrices of order 3×3 with each entry 0 or 1 is

(a)   27   (b)   18

(c)   81   (d)   512

Topic 2 — Operations on Matrices

OPERATION ON MATRICES

(a) Addition of Matrices

Let there be two matrices A and B of the same order m × n. then the sum denoted by A + B is defined to be the matrix of order m × n obtained by adding the corresponding elements of A and B.

Thus if $A = [a_{ij}]_{m \times n}$ and $B = [b_{ij}]_{m \times n}$, then $A + B = [a_{ij} + b_{ij}]_{m \times n}$

(i) Matrix Addition is Commutative : If A and B be two matrices of the same order, then A + B = B + A i.e. matrix addition is commutative.

(ii) Matrix Addition is Associative : If A, B and C be three matrices of the same order, then

(A + B) + C = A + (B + C)   i.e. matrix addition is associative.

(iii) Existence of Identity: The null matrix is the identity element for matrix addition, i.e., A + 0 = 0 + A = A

(iv) Existence of Inverse: For every matrix $A = [a_{ij}]_{m \times n}$ there exists a matrix $[-a_{ij}]_{m \times n}$, denoted by − A such that A + (−A) = 0 = (−A) + A

(b) Differences of Matrices

If $A = [a_{ij}]$ and $B = [b_{ij}]$ are two matrices of the same order m × n, then $A - B = [a_{ij} - b_{ij}]$ for all values of i and j.

(c) Scalar Multiplication of Matrices

Let $A = [a_{ij}]_{m \times n}$ be a matrix and k be a number then the matrix which is obtained by multiplying every element of A by any scalar k is called scalar multiple of A and it is denoted by

kA thus if A $= [a_{ij}]_{m \times n}$ then

$$kA = Ak = [ka_{ij}]_{m \times n}$$

Ex.   If $A = \begin{bmatrix} 1 & 3 & 5 \\ 2 & 4 & 6 \end{bmatrix}$, then $3A = \begin{bmatrix} 3 & 9 & 15 \\ 6 & 12 & 18 \end{bmatrix}$

(d) Multiplication of Matrices

Product of two matrices exists only if number of column of first matrix is equal to the number of rows of the second. Let A be m × n and B be n × p matrices. Then the product of matrices A and B denated by A × B is the matrix of order m × p whose (i, j) th element is obtained by adding the products of corresponding elements of ith row of matrix A and jth column of B.

$A = [a_{ij}]_{m \times n}$ and $B = [b_{ij}]_{n \times p}$ then their product $AB = C = [c_{ij}]$, will be matrix of order m × p, where,

$$(ij)^{\text{th}} \text{ element of } AB = c_{ij} = \sum_{r=1}^{n} a_{ir} b_{rj}$$

Ex.   If $A = \begin{bmatrix} 1 & 4 & 2 \\ 2 & 3 & 1 \end{bmatrix}$ and $B = \begin{bmatrix} 1 & 2 \\ 2 & 2 \\ 1 & 3 \end{bmatrix}$

then $AB = \begin{bmatrix} 1.1 + 4.2 + 2.1 & 1.2 + 4.2 + 2.3 \\ 2.1 + 3.2 + 1.1 & 2.2 + 3.2 + 1.3 \end{bmatrix}$

$AB = \begin{bmatrix} 11 & 16 \\ 9 & 13 \end{bmatrix}$

(i) Associative Law for Multiplication : If A, B and C be three matrices of order m × n and n × p and p × q, respectively, then (AB) C = A (BC).

(ii) Distributive Law : If A, B, C be three matrices of order m × n, n × p and n × q respectively. then A (B + C) = AB + AC

(iii) Matrix multiplication is not commutative.

i.e. AB ≠ BA   (in general)

(iv) Existence of Identity : For every square matrix A, there exist an identity matrix (I) of same order such that IA = AI = A.

Practice Exercise-2

Multiple Choice Questions

1. If p, q, r are 3 real numbers satisfying the matrix equation,
$$[p\,q\,r]\begin{bmatrix} 3 & 4 & 1 \\ 3 & 2 & 3 \\ 2 & 0 & 2 \end{bmatrix} = [3\,0\,1], \text{ then } 2p + q - r \text{ equals :}$$

   (a) -3 (b) -1 (c) 4   (d) 2

2. If matrix $A = [a_{ij}]_{2 \times 2}$, where $a_{ij} = \begin{cases} 1 & \text{if } i \neq j \\ 0 & \text{if } i = j \end{cases}$, then A^2 is equal to

   (a) I   (b) A
   (c) O   (d) None of these

3. Let A, B and C are three matrices of same order. Now, consider the following statements

   I.   If $A = B$, then $AC = BC$
   II.   If $AC = BC$, then $A = B$

   Choose the correct option

   (a) Only I is true   (b) Only II is true
   (c) Both I and II are true   (d) Neither I nor II is true

4. If A and B are 2×2 matrices, then which of the following is true?

   (a) $(A + B)^2 = A^2 + B^2 + 2AB$
   (b) $(A - B)^2 = A^2 + B^2 - 2AB$
   (c) $(A - B)(A + B) = A^2 + AB - BA - B^2$
   (d) $(A + B)(A - B) = A^2 - B^2$

5. If A and B are two matrices such that $A + B$ and AB are both defined, then

   (a) A and B are two matrices not necessarily of same order.
   (b) A and B are square matrices of same order.
   (c) Number of columns of A = Number of rows of B.
   (d) None of these.

Assertion & Reason Questions

DIRECTIONS : *Each of these questions contains an assertion followed by reason. Read them carefully and answer the question on the basis of following options. You have to select the one that best describes the two statements.*

   (a) If both Assertion and Reason are correct and the Reason is a correct explanation of the Assertion.

   (b) If both Assertion and Reason are correct but Reason is not a correct explanation of the Assertion.

   (c) If the Assertion is correct but Reason is incorrect.

   (d) If the Assertion is incorrect but the Reason is correct.

6. **Assertion :** If AB and BA are both defined, then they must be equal i.e., $AB = BA$.

   Reason : If AB and BA are both defined, it is not necessary that $AB = BA$.

7. **Assertion :** The order of the matrix A is 3×5 and that of B is 2×3. Then the matrix AB is not possible.

   Reason : The order of the matrix is $m \times n$ and that of B is $n \times p$. Then the order of the matrix AB is $m \times p$.

Case/Passage Based Question

DIRECTIONS (Q. 8) : *has 5 subparts based on case/passage given, attempt any 4 out of 5 questions.*

8. On a Diwali day Niharika Singh went to bazaar to purchase fireworks at the rates given as:

   10 hangers at ₹ 3 each, 8 fountains at ₹ 2 each, 6 atom bombs at ₹ 12 and 18 rockets at ₹ 8 each.

Based on the above information answer the following questions.

(i) Representation of the prices in column matrix is

   (a) [3 2 12 8]   (b) [3 2 8 12]

   (c) $\begin{bmatrix} 3 \\ 2 \\ 8 \\ 12 \end{bmatrix}$ (d) $\begin{bmatrix} 3 \\ 2 \\ 12 \\ 8 \end{bmatrix}$

(ii) Find the individual total cost of each item

   (a) [30 16 72 144]   (b) [3 2 12 8]
   (c) [10 8 6 18]   (d) [30 16 144 72]

(iii) Find how much Niharika Singh paid for the fireworks.

   (a) ₹ 262   (b) ₹ 42
   (c) ₹ 25   (d) ₹ 1050

(iv) If each price hike by 2%, then how much Niharika Singh paid for the fireworks.

   (a) ₹ 264   (b) ₹ 267
   (c) ₹ 1052   (d) ₹ 1071

(v) If Niharika purchase only 10 rockets, then how much she paid for the fireworks.

   (a) ₹ 850   (b) ₹ 198   (c) ₹ 34   (d) ₹ 25

One Word Questions

9. If A is matrix of order m × n and B is a matrix such that AB' and $B'A$ are both defined, then find order of matrix B.

10. If $A^2 = \begin{bmatrix} \alpha & 0 \\ 1 & 1 \end{bmatrix}^2 = \begin{bmatrix} 1 & 0 \\ 5 & 1 \end{bmatrix}$, how many values of α exist which satisfy the condition.

11. If $A = \begin{bmatrix} \alpha & \beta \\ \gamma & \delta \end{bmatrix}$ such that A^2 is a two-rowed unit matrix, then find value of δ.

12. If $A = \begin{bmatrix} \alpha & 0 \\ 1 & 1 \end{bmatrix}$ and $B = \begin{bmatrix} 9 & a \\ b & c \end{bmatrix}$ and $A^2 = B$, then find the value of $a + b + c$

Very Short Answer Questions

13. If $A = \begin{bmatrix} \alpha & \beta \\ \gamma & -\alpha \end{bmatrix}$ is such that $A^2 = I$, then what is the relation between α, β, γ ?

14. Find the product of the matrix $\begin{bmatrix} 1 \\ 2 \\ -1 \end{bmatrix} [1 \ -2 \ -1]$

15. If $A = \begin{bmatrix} 4 & 2 \\ -1 & 1 \end{bmatrix}$ and I is the identity matrix of order 2, then prove that $(A - 2I)(A - 3I) = O$.

16. A, B are two matrices such that AB and $(A + B)$ both are defined; show that A and B are square matrices of the same order.

17. If A and B are 3×3 matrices such that $AB = A$ and $BA = B$, then find the value of $A^3 - B^3$.

Short Answer Questions

18. If ω is complex cube root of unity, and $A = \begin{bmatrix} \omega & 0 \\ 0 & \omega \end{bmatrix}$, then determine A^{100}.

19. Find the value of x for which the matrix product
$$\begin{bmatrix} 2 & 0 & 7 \\ 0 & 1 & 0 \\ 1 & -2 & 1 \end{bmatrix} \begin{bmatrix} -x & 14x & 7x \\ 0 & 1 & 0 \\ x & -4x & -2x \end{bmatrix}$$ equals an identity matrix.

20. Find the value of x, if $[1 \ x \ 1] \begin{bmatrix} 1 & 2 & 3 \\ 4 & 5 & 6 \\ 3 & 2 & 5 \end{bmatrix} \begin{bmatrix} 1 \\ -2 \\ 3 \end{bmatrix} = 0$

21. There are two families P and Q. There are 3 men, 3 women and 12 children in family P and 2 men, 2 women and 4 children in family Q. The recommended daily allowance for calories is:
Man : 2400, woman : 2000, child : 1400 and for proteins is : man : 60 g; woman : 40 g and child : 35 g.
Represent the above information by matrices. Using matrix multiplication, calculate the total requirement of calories and proteins of each of the two families.

22. If $A = \begin{bmatrix} 1 & 0 & 0 \\ 0 & 1 & 0 \\ a & b & -1 \end{bmatrix}$ and I is the unit matrix of order 3, then find $A^2 + 2A^4 + 4A^6$.

NCERT Exercise-2

1. $A = \begin{bmatrix} 2 & 4 \\ 3 & 2 \end{bmatrix}$, $B = \begin{bmatrix} 1 & 3 \\ -2 & 5 \end{bmatrix}$ and $C = \begin{bmatrix} -2 & 5 \\ 3 & 4 \end{bmatrix}$

Find each of the following :
(i) $A + B$ (ii) $A - B$
(iii) $3A - C$ (iv) AB
(v) BA

2. Compute the following :

(i) $\begin{bmatrix} a & b \\ -b & a \end{bmatrix} + \begin{bmatrix} a & b \\ b & a \end{bmatrix}$

(ii) $\begin{bmatrix} a^2 + b^2 & b^2 + c^2 \\ a^2 + c^2 & a^2 + b^2 \end{bmatrix} + \begin{bmatrix} 2ab & 2bc \\ -2ac & -2ab \end{bmatrix}$

(iii) $\begin{bmatrix} -1 & 4 & -6 \\ 8 & 5 & 16 \\ 2 & 8 & 5 \end{bmatrix} + \begin{bmatrix} 12 & 7 & 6 \\ 8 & 0 & 5 \\ 3 & 2 & 4 \end{bmatrix}$

(iv) $\begin{bmatrix} \cos^2 x & \sin^2 x \\ \sin^2 x & \cos^2 x \end{bmatrix} + \begin{bmatrix} \sin^2 x & \cos^2 x \\ \cos^2 x & \sin^2 x \end{bmatrix}$

3. Compute the indicated products.

(i) $\begin{bmatrix} a & b \\ -b & a \end{bmatrix} \begin{bmatrix} a & -b \\ b & a \end{bmatrix}$

(ii) $\begin{bmatrix} 1 \\ 2 \\ 3 \end{bmatrix} [2 \ 3 \ 4]$

(iii) $\begin{bmatrix} 1 & -2 \\ 2 & 3 \end{bmatrix} \begin{bmatrix} 1 & 2 & 3 \\ 2 & 3 & 1 \end{bmatrix}$

(iv) $\begin{bmatrix} 2 & 3 & 4 \\ 3 & 4 & 5 \\ 4 & 5 & 6 \end{bmatrix} \begin{bmatrix} 1 & -3 & 5 \\ 0 & 2 & 4 \\ 3 & 0 & 5 \end{bmatrix}$

(v) $\begin{bmatrix} 2 & 1 \\ 3 & 2 \\ -1 & 1 \end{bmatrix} \begin{bmatrix} 1 & 0 & 1 \\ -1 & 2 & 1 \end{bmatrix}$

(vi) $\begin{bmatrix} 3 & -1 & 3 \\ -1 & 0 & 2 \end{bmatrix} \begin{bmatrix} 2 & -3 \\ 1 & 0 \\ 3 & 1 \end{bmatrix}$.

4. If $A = \begin{bmatrix} 1 & 2 & -3 \\ 5 & 0 & 2 \\ 1 & -1 & 1 \end{bmatrix}$, $B = \begin{bmatrix} 3 & -1 & 2 \\ 4 & 2 & 5 \\ 2 & 0 & 3 \end{bmatrix}$,

$C = \begin{bmatrix} 4 & 1 & 2 \\ 0 & 3 & 2 \\ 1 & -2 & 3 \end{bmatrix}$

then compute $(A + B)$ and $(B - C)$. Also verify that
$A + (B - C) = (A + B) - C$.

5. If $A = \begin{bmatrix} \dfrac{2}{3} & 1 & \dfrac{5}{3} \\ \dfrac{1}{3} & \dfrac{2}{3} & \dfrac{4}{3} \\ \dfrac{7}{3} & 2 & \dfrac{2}{3} \end{bmatrix}$ and $B = \begin{bmatrix} \dfrac{2}{5} & \dfrac{3}{5} & 1 \\ \dfrac{1}{5} & \dfrac{2}{5} & \dfrac{4}{5} \\ \dfrac{7}{5} & \dfrac{6}{5} & \dfrac{2}{5} \end{bmatrix}$, then compute

$3A - 5B$.

6. Simplify : $\cos\theta \begin{bmatrix} \cos\theta & \sin\theta \\ -\sin\theta & \cos\theta \end{bmatrix} + \sin\theta \begin{bmatrix} \sin\theta & -\cos\theta \\ \cos\theta & \sin\theta \end{bmatrix}$.

7. Find X and Y if

(i) $X + Y = \begin{bmatrix} 7 & 0 \\ 2 & 5 \end{bmatrix}$ and $X - Y = \begin{bmatrix} 3 & 0 \\ 0 & 3 \end{bmatrix}$

(ii) $2X + 3Y = \begin{bmatrix} 2 & 3 \\ 4 & 0 \end{bmatrix}$ and $3X + 2Y = \begin{bmatrix} 2 & -2 \\ -1 & 5 \end{bmatrix}$

8. Find X if $Y = \begin{bmatrix} 3 & 2 \\ 1 & 4 \end{bmatrix}$ and $2X + Y = \begin{bmatrix} 1 & 0 \\ -3 & 2 \end{bmatrix}$.

9. Find x and y, if $2\begin{bmatrix} 1 & 3 \\ 0 & x \end{bmatrix} + \begin{bmatrix} y & 0 \\ 1 & 2 \end{bmatrix} = \begin{bmatrix} 5 & 6 \\ 1 & 8 \end{bmatrix}$.

10. Solve the equation for x, y, z and t, if

$$2\begin{bmatrix} x & z \\ y & t \end{bmatrix} + 3\begin{bmatrix} 1 & -1 \\ 0 & 2 \end{bmatrix} = 3\begin{bmatrix} 3 & 5 \\ 4 & 6 \end{bmatrix}.$$

11. If $x\begin{bmatrix} 2 \\ 3 \end{bmatrix} + y\begin{bmatrix} -1 \\ 1 \end{bmatrix} = \begin{bmatrix} 10 \\ 5 \end{bmatrix}$ then find the values of x and y.

12. Given $3\begin{bmatrix} x & y \\ z & w \end{bmatrix} = \begin{bmatrix} x & 6 \\ -1 & 2w \end{bmatrix} + \begin{bmatrix} 4 & x+y \\ z+w & 3 \end{bmatrix}$ find the

values of x, y, z and w.

13. $F(x) = \begin{bmatrix} \cos x & -\sin x & 0 \\ \sin x & \cos x & 0 \\ 0 & 0 & 1 \end{bmatrix}$, then show

that $F(x) . F(y) = F(x + y)$.

14. Show that

(i) $\begin{bmatrix} 5 & -1 \\ 6 & 7 \end{bmatrix}\begin{bmatrix} 2 & 1 \\ 3 & 4 \end{bmatrix} \neq \begin{bmatrix} 2 & 1 \\ 3 & 4 \end{bmatrix}\begin{bmatrix} 5 & -1 \\ 6 & 7 \end{bmatrix}$

(ii) $\begin{bmatrix} 1 & 2 & 3 \\ 0 & 1 & 0 \\ 1 & 1 & 0 \end{bmatrix}\begin{bmatrix} -1 & 1 & 0 \\ 0 & -1 & 1 \\ 2 & 3 & 4 \end{bmatrix}$

$\neq \begin{bmatrix} -1 & 1 & 0 \\ 0 & -1 & 1 \\ 2 & 3 & 4 \end{bmatrix}\begin{bmatrix} 1 & 2 & 3 \\ 0 & 1 & 0 \\ 1 & 1 & 0 \end{bmatrix}$

15. Find $A^2 - 5A + 6I$, if $A = \begin{bmatrix} 2 & 0 & 1 \\ 2 & 1 & 3 \\ 1 & -1 & 0 \end{bmatrix}$

16. If $A = \begin{bmatrix} 1 & 0 & 2 \\ 0 & 2 & 1 \\ 2 & 0 & 3 \end{bmatrix}$, prove that

$A^3 - 6A^2 + 7A + 2I = 0$

17. If $A = \begin{bmatrix} 3 & -2 \\ 4 & -2 \end{bmatrix}$ and $I = \begin{bmatrix} 1 & 0 \\ 0 & 1 \end{bmatrix}$, then find k so that
$A^2 = kA - 2I$

18. If $A = \begin{bmatrix} 0 & -\tan\dfrac{\alpha}{2} \\ \tan\dfrac{\alpha}{2} & 0 \end{bmatrix}$ and I is the identity matrix of

order 2, show that $I + A = I - A\begin{bmatrix} \cos\alpha & -\sin\alpha \\ \sin\alpha & \cos\alpha \end{bmatrix}$

19. A trust has ₹ 30,000 that must be invested in two different types of bonds. The first bond pays 5% interest per year and second bond pays 7% interest per year. Using matrix multiplication, determine how to divide ₹ 30,000 among the two types of bond if the trust fund obtains an annual total interest of

(a) ₹ 1800 (b) ₹ 2000

20. The book-shop of a particular school has 10 dozen Chemistry books, 8 dozen Physics books, 10 dozen Economics books. Their selling price are ₹ 80, ₹ 60 and ₹ 40 each respectively. Find the total amount the book-shop will receive from selling all the books using matrix algebra.

21. The restrictions on n, k and p so that $PY + WY$ will be defined are

(a) $k = 3, p = n$

(b) k is arbitrary, $p = 2$

(c) p is arbitrary, $k = 3$

(d) $k = 2, p = 3$

22. If $n = p$, then the order of the matrix $7X - 5Z$ is :

(a) $p \times 2$ (b) $2 \times n$

(c) $n \times 3$ (d) $p \times n$

Topic 3 — Transpose of a Matrix, Symmetric and Skew Symmetric Matrices

TRANSPOSE OF A MATRIX

If $A = [a_{ij}]$ be an $m \times n$ matrix, then the matrix obtained by interchanging the rows and columns of A is called the transpose of A. It is denoted by A' or A^T.

Properties of transpose of the matrices-

(i) $(A + B)' = A' + B'$

(ii) $(KA)' = KA'$, where K is scalar multiple

(iii) $(AB)' = B'A'$

(iv) $(A')' = A$

(v)   **Symmetric Matrix :** A square matrix A is said to be symmetric if $A' = A$ where $A' =$ Transpose of matrix A

(vi)   **Skew-symmetric Matrix :** A square matrix A is said to be skew-symmetric if $A' = -A$

ANY SQUARE MATRIX CAN BE EXPRESSED AS THE SUM OF A SYMMETRIC AND A SKEW SYMMETRIC MATRIX

If A be a square matrix, then we can write $A = \dfrac{1}{2}(A + A') + \dfrac{1}{2}(A - A')$, here $\dfrac{1}{2}(A + A')$ is symmetric matrix and $\dfrac{1}{2}(A - A')$ is skew symmetric matrix.

Illustration :

Express the matrix $\begin{bmatrix} 2 & 3 & 1 \\ 1 & -1 & 2 \\ 4 & 1 & 2 \end{bmatrix}$ **as the sum of a symmetric and a skew-symmetric matrix.**

Sol. We have, $A = \begin{bmatrix} 2 & 3 & 1 \\ 1 & -1 & 2 \\ 4 & 1 & 2 \end{bmatrix}$

$\therefore \quad A' = \begin{bmatrix} 2 & 1 & 4 \\ 3 & -1 & 1 \\ 1 & 2 & 2 \end{bmatrix}$

Now, $\dfrac{A + A'}{2} = \begin{bmatrix} 2 & 2 & \dfrac{5}{2} \\ 2 & -1 & \dfrac{3}{2} \\ \dfrac{5}{2} & \dfrac{3}{2} & 2 \end{bmatrix}$

and $\dfrac{A - A'}{2} = \begin{bmatrix} 0 & 1 & \dfrac{-3}{2} \\ -1 & 0 & \dfrac{1}{2} \\ \dfrac{3}{2} & \dfrac{-1}{2} & 0 \end{bmatrix}$

$\therefore \dfrac{A + A'}{2} + \dfrac{A - A'}{2} = \begin{bmatrix} 2 & 2 & \dfrac{5}{2} \\ 2 & -1 & \dfrac{3}{2} \\ \dfrac{5}{2} & \dfrac{3}{2} & 2 \end{bmatrix} + \begin{bmatrix} 0 & 1 & \dfrac{-3}{2} \\ -1 & 0 & \dfrac{1}{2} \\ \dfrac{3}{2} & \dfrac{-1}{2} & 0 \end{bmatrix}$ which is the required answer.

Practice Exercise-3

Multiple Choice Questions

1. If $A = \begin{pmatrix} 2 & -1 \\ -7 & 4 \end{pmatrix}$ and $B = \begin{pmatrix} 4 & 1 \\ 7 & 2 \end{pmatrix}$ then which statement is true ?

   (a) $AA^T = I$ (b) $BB^T = I$

   (c) $AB \neq BA$ (d) $(AB)^T = I$

2. If A is any square matrix, then which of the following is skew-symmetric?

   (a) $A + A^T$ (b) $A - A^T$

   (c) AA^T (d) $A^T A$

3. If A is symmetric as well as skew-symmetric matrix, then A is

   (a) Diagonal

   (b) Null

   (c) Triangular

   (d) None of these

Assertion & Reason Questions

DIRECTIONS : *Each of these questions contains an assertion followed by reason. Read them carefully and answer the question on the basis of following options. You have to select the one that best describes the two statements.*

(a) If both Assertion and Reason are correct and the Reason is the correct explanation of the Assertion.

(b) If both Assertion and Reason are correct but Reason is not the correct explanation of the Assertion.

(c) If the Assertion is correct but Reason is incorrect.

(d) If the Assertion is incorrect but the Reason is correct.

4. **Assertion :** The matrix $A = \begin{bmatrix} 0 & -1 & -2 \\ 1 & 0 & -3 \\ 2 & 3 & 0 \end{bmatrix}$ is a skew symmetric matrix.

   Reason : For the given matrix A we have $A' = A$.

5. **Assertion :** $A + A'$ is a symmetric matrix.

   Reason: $A - A'$ is a skew-symmetric matrix.

One Word Questions

6. If $A = [a_{ij}]_{m \times n}$, then find A'

7. If $A = \begin{bmatrix} 2x & 0 \\ x & x \end{bmatrix}$ and $A^{-1} = \begin{bmatrix} 1 & 0 \\ -1 & 2 \end{bmatrix}$, then find value of x.

Very Short Answer Questions

8. If $A = \begin{bmatrix} 1 \\ -4 \\ 3 \end{bmatrix}$ and $B = \begin{bmatrix} -1 & 2 & 1 \end{bmatrix}$, then find $(AB)'$

9. If $\begin{bmatrix} 3 & -4 \\ 1 & -1 \end{bmatrix}$ is the sum of a symmetric matrix B and a skew-symmetric matrix C, then find C

10. If C is skew-symmetric matrix of order n and X is $n \times 1$ column matrix, then find X'CX.

11. If A is a square matrix, then find $A + A^T$

Short Answer Question

12. Find the values of x, y, z if the matrix $A = \begin{bmatrix} 0 & 2y & z \\ x & y & -z \\ x & -y & z \end{bmatrix}$ satisfy the equation $A^T A = I_3$.

NCERT Exercise-3

1. Find the transpose of each of the following matrices :

   (i) $\begin{bmatrix} 5 \\ \frac{1}{2} \\ -1 \end{bmatrix}$ (ii) $\begin{bmatrix} 1 & -1 \\ 2 & 3 \end{bmatrix}$ (iii) $\begin{bmatrix} -1 & 5 & 6 \\ \sqrt{3} & 5 & 6 \\ 2 & 3 & -1 \end{bmatrix}$

2. If $A = \begin{bmatrix} -1 & 2 & 3 \\ 5 & 7 & 9 \\ -2 & 1 & 1 \end{bmatrix}$ and $B = \begin{bmatrix} -4 & 1 & -5 \\ 1 & 2 & 0 \\ 1 & 3 & 1 \end{bmatrix}$, then verify that:

   (i) $(A + B)' = A' + B'$

   (ii) $(A - B)' = A' - B'$

3. If $A' = \begin{bmatrix} 3 & 4 \\ -1 & 2 \\ 0 & 1 \end{bmatrix}$ and $B = \begin{bmatrix} -1 & 2 & 1 \\ 1 & 2 & 3 \end{bmatrix}$ then verify that

   (i) $(A + B)' = A' + B'$ (ii) $(A - B)' = A' - B'$

4. If $A' = \begin{bmatrix} -2 & 3 \\ 1 & 2 \end{bmatrix}$ and $B = \begin{bmatrix} -1 & 0 \\ 1 & 2 \end{bmatrix}$, then find $(A + 2B)'$.

5. For the matrices A and B, verify that $(AB)' = B'A'$, where

   (i) $A = \begin{bmatrix} 1 \\ -4 \\ 3 \end{bmatrix}, B = [-1\ 2\ 1]$ (ii) $A = \begin{bmatrix} 0 \\ 1 \\ 2 \end{bmatrix}, B = [1\ 5\ 7]$.

6. If (i) $A = \begin{bmatrix} \cos\alpha & \sin\alpha \\ -\sin\alpha & \cos\alpha \end{bmatrix}$, then verify that $A'A = I$.

   (ii) If $A = \begin{bmatrix} \sin\alpha & \cos\alpha \\ -\cos\alpha & \sin\alpha \end{bmatrix}$, then verify that $A'A = I$.

7. (i) Show that the matrix $A = \begin{bmatrix} 1 & -1 & 5 \\ -1 & 2 & 1 \\ 5 & 1 & 3 \end{bmatrix}$ is a symmetric matrix.

(ii) Show that the matrix $A = \begin{bmatrix} 0 & 1 & -1 \\ -1 & 0 & 1 \\ 1 & -1 & 0 \end{bmatrix}$ is a skew-symmetric matrix.

8. For the matrix, $A = \begin{bmatrix} 1 & 5 \\ 6 & 7 \end{bmatrix}$, verify that

(i) $(A + A')$ is a symmetric matrix.

(ii) $(A - A')$ is a skew-symmetric matrix.

9. Find $\dfrac{1}{2}(A + A')$ and $\dfrac{1}{2}(A - A')$, when

$$A = \begin{bmatrix} 0 & a & b \\ -a & 0 & c \\ -b & -c & 0 \end{bmatrix}$$

10. Express the following matrices as the sum of a symmetric and a skew-symmetric matrix.

(i) $\begin{bmatrix} 3 & 5 \\ 1 & -1 \end{bmatrix}$

(ii) $\begin{bmatrix} 6 & -2 & 2 \\ -2 & 3 & -1 \\ 2 & -1 & 3 \end{bmatrix}$

(iii) $\begin{bmatrix} 3 & 3 & -1 \\ -2 & -2 & 1 \\ -4 & -5 & 2 \end{bmatrix}$

(iv) $\begin{bmatrix} 1 & 5 \\ -1 & 2 \end{bmatrix}$

11. Choose the correct answer in the following questions :

If A, B are symmetric matrices of same order then $AB - BA$ is a

(a) Skew-symmetric matrix

(b) Symmetric matrix

(c) Zero matrix

(d) Identity matrix

12. If $A = \begin{bmatrix} \cos\alpha & -\sin\alpha \\ \sin\alpha & \cos\alpha \end{bmatrix}$, then $A + A' = I$, if the value of α is

(a) $\dfrac{\pi}{6}$

(b) $\dfrac{\pi}{3}$

(c) π

(d) $\dfrac{3\pi}{2}$

Important Tips & Formulae

- **Singleton matrix:** If in a matrix there is only one element then it is called singleton matrix. Thus $A = [a_{ij}]_{m \times n}$ is a singleton matrix if $m = n = 1$

- **Trace of a matrix:** The sum of diagonal elements of a square matrix A is called the trace of matrix A which is denoted by tr A.

$$\text{tr } A = \sum_{i=1}^{n} a_{ii} = a_{11} + a_{22} + \dots a_{nn}$$

- **Triangular matrix:** A Square Matrix $[a_{ij}]$ is said to be triangular matrix if each element above or below the principal diagonal is zero it is of two types –

  (a) **Upper triangular matrix :** A square matrix $[a_{ij}]$ is called the upper triangular matrix, if $a_{ij} = 0$ when $i > j$.

  (b) **Lower triangular matrix :** A square matrix $[a_{ij}]$ is called the lower triangular matrix, if $a_{ij} = 0$ when $i < j$

- **Properties of matrix multiplication:** If A, B and C are three matrices such that their product is defined, then

  (a) If $AB = AC$ this not implies that $B = C$ (Cancellation Law is not applicable for matrix multiplication)

  (b) If $AB = O$

  It does not mean that $A = O$ or $B = O$, i.e. product of two non-zero matrix may be zero matrix.

  (c) $tr(AB) = tr(BA)$

- **Positive integral powers of a matrix:** The positive integral powers of a matrix A are defined only when A is a square matrix. Also

  $A^2 = A. A, A^3 = A.A.A = A^2 A$

  For any positive integers m, n

  (a) $A^m A^n = A^{m+n}$

  (b) $(A^m)^n = A^{mn} = (A^n)^m$

  (c) $I^n = I, I^m = I$

  (d) $A^\circ = I_n$ where A is a square matrices of order n.

- **Nilpotent matrix :** A square matrix A is said to be nilpotent matrix if there exists a positive integer m such that $A^m = 0$. If m is the least positive integer such that $A^m = 0$, then m is called the index of the nilpotent matrix A.

- **Idempotent matrix :** A square matrix A is called an idempotent matrix if $A^2 = A$.

- **Involutory matrix :** A square matrix A is said to be involutory matrix if $A^2 = 1$.

- **Properties of transpose**

  (a) $I^T = I$

  (b) $(KA)^T = KA^T$.

  (c) $(A_1 A_2 A_3 \dots A_{n-1} A_n)^T$
  $= A_n^T A_{n-1}^T \dots A_3^T A_2^T A_1^T$

- **Properties of symmetric and skew-symmetric matrices**

  (a) If A is a square matrix, then $A + A^T, AA^T, A^TA$ are symmetric matrices while $A - A^T$ is Skew - Symmetric Matrix.

  (b) If A is a Symmetric Matrix, then $-A, kA, A^T, A^n, A^{-1}$, B^TAB are also symmetric matrices where $n \in N, k \in R$ and B is a square matrix of order that of A

  (c) If A is a skew symmetric matrix, then
  - (i) A^{2n} is a symmetric matrix for $n \in N$
  - (ii) A^{2n+1} is a skew-symmetric matrices for $n \in N$
  - (iii) kA is also skew -symmetric matrix where $k \in R$
  - (iv) B^TAB is also skew - symmetric matrix where B is a square matrix of order that of A.

  (d) If A, B are two symmetric matrices, then –
  - (i) $A \pm B, AB + BA$ are also symmetric matrices.
  - (ii) $AB - BA$ is a skew-symmetric matrix
  - (iii) AB is a symmetric matrix when $AB = BA$.

  (e) If A, B are two skew-symmetric matrices, then
  - (i) $A \pm B, AB - BA$ are skew-symmetric matrices
  - (ii) $AB + BA$ is a symmetric matrix

  (f) If A is a skew-symmetric matrix and C is a column matrix, then C^TAC is a zero matrix.

- No element of principal diagonal in diagonal matrix is zero.
- Number of zero in a diagonal matrix is given by $n^2 - n$ where n is a order of the matrix.
- Minimum number of zero in a triangular matrix is given by $\dfrac{n(n-1)}{2}$, where n is order of matrix.
- The multiplication of two diagonal matrices is again a diagonal matrix.
- The multiplication of two triangular matrices is again a triangular matrix.
- The multiplication of two scalar matrices is also a scalar matrix.
- All Principal diagonal elements of a skew-symmetric matrix are always zero because for any diagonal element $a_{ii} = - a_{ii} \Rightarrow a_{ii} = 0$
- Trace of a skew symmetric matrix is always 0.

MISCELLANEOUS NCERT EXERCISE

1. Let $A = \begin{bmatrix} 0 & 1 \\ 0 & 0 \end{bmatrix}$, show that $(aI + bA)^n = a^n I + na^{n-1}bA$, where I is the identity matrix of order 2 and $n \in N$.

Sol. L.H.S. $= [aI + bA]^n = \left[a\begin{pmatrix} 1 & 0 \\ 0 & 1 \end{pmatrix} + b\begin{pmatrix} 0 & 1 \\ 0 & 0 \end{pmatrix} \right]^n$

$$= \left[\begin{pmatrix} a & 0 \\ 0 & a \end{pmatrix} + \begin{pmatrix} 0 & b \\ 0 & 0 \end{pmatrix} \right]^n = \begin{pmatrix} a & b \\ 0 & a \end{pmatrix}^n$$

R.H.S. $= a^n I + na^{n-1} bA$

$$= a^n \begin{pmatrix} 1 & 0 \\ 0 & 1 \end{pmatrix} + na^{n-1} b \begin{pmatrix} 0 & 1 \\ 0 & 0 \end{pmatrix}$$

$$= \begin{pmatrix} a^n & 0 \\ 0 & a^n \end{pmatrix} + \begin{pmatrix} 0 & na^{n-1}b \\ 0 & 0 \end{pmatrix} = \begin{pmatrix} a^n & na^{n-1}b \\ 0 & a^n \end{pmatrix}$$

We have to prove that

$$\begin{bmatrix} a & b \\ 0 & a \end{bmatrix}^n = \begin{bmatrix} a^n & na^{n-1}b \\ 0 & a^n \end{bmatrix}$$

Applying the principle of Mathematical Induction

Put $P(n): \begin{bmatrix} a & b \\ 0 & a \end{bmatrix}^n = \begin{bmatrix} a^n & na^{n-1}b \\ 0 & a^n \end{bmatrix}$ for $n = 1$,

$$P(1): \begin{bmatrix} a & b \\ 0 & a \end{bmatrix} = \begin{bmatrix} a & b \\ 0 & a \end{bmatrix}$$

$\therefore$ P (n) is true for n = 1, Let P (n) be true for n = k

$$\therefore \ P(k): \begin{bmatrix} a & b \\ 0 & a \end{bmatrix}^k = \begin{bmatrix} a^k & ka^{k-1}b \\ 0 & a^k \end{bmatrix}$$

Multiplying both sides by $\begin{bmatrix} a & b \\ 0 & a \end{bmatrix}$

$$\text{L.H.S.} = \begin{bmatrix} a & b \\ 0 & a \end{bmatrix}^k \begin{bmatrix} a & b \\ 0 & a \end{bmatrix} = \begin{bmatrix} a & b \\ 0 & a \end{bmatrix}^{n+1}$$

$$\text{R.H.S.} = \begin{bmatrix} a^k & ka^{k-1}b \\ 0 & a^k \end{bmatrix} \begin{bmatrix} a & b \\ 0 & a \end{bmatrix}$$

$$= \begin{bmatrix} a^{k+1} & ba^k + ka^kb \\ 0 & a^{k+1} \end{bmatrix} = \begin{bmatrix} a^{k+1} & (k+1)a^kb \\ 0 & a^{k+1} \end{bmatrix}$$

This shows P (n) is true for n = k + 1 then by principle of mathematical induction, P (n) is true for all positive integral values of n.

2. If $A = \begin{bmatrix} 1 & 1 & 1 \\ 1 & 1 & 1 \\ 1 & 1 & 1 \end{bmatrix}$, prove that

$$A^n = \begin{bmatrix} 3^{n-1} & 3^{n-1} & 3^{n-1} \\ 3^{n-1} & 3^{n-1} & 3^{n-1} \\ 3^{n-1} & 3^{n-1} & 3^{n-1} \end{bmatrix}, \ n \in N.$$

Sol. Let $P(n) : A^n = \begin{bmatrix} 3^{n-1} & 3^{n-1} & 3^{n-1} \\ 3^{n-1} & 3^{n-1} & 3^{n-1} \\ 3^{n-1} & 3^{n-1} & 3^{n-1} \end{bmatrix}$,

where $A = \begin{bmatrix} 1 & 1 & 1 \\ 1 & 1 & 1 \\ 1 & 1 & 1 \end{bmatrix}$

For $n = 1$ L.H.S. $= A^n = A = \begin{bmatrix} 1 & 1 & 1 \\ 1 & 1 & 1 \\ 1 & 1 & 1 \end{bmatrix}$

R.H.S. $= A^n = \begin{bmatrix} 3^o & 3^o & 3^o \\ 3^o & 3^o & 3^o \\ 3^o & 3^o & 3^o \end{bmatrix} = \begin{bmatrix} 1 & 1 & 1 \\ 1 & 1 & 1 \\ 1 & 1 & 1 \end{bmatrix}$

$\therefore$ P (n) is true for $n = 1$

Let it be true for $n = k$

$\therefore \ A^k = \begin{bmatrix} 3^{k-1} & 3^{k-1} & 3^{k-1} \\ 3^{k-1} & 3^{k-1} & 3^{k-1} \\ 3^{k-1} & 3^{k-1} & 3^{k-1} \end{bmatrix}$

Multiplying both sides by A

L.H.S. $= A^k A = A^{k+1}$

R.H.S. $= \begin{bmatrix} 3^{k-1} & 3^{k-1} & 3^{k-1} \\ 3^{k-1} & 3^{k-1} & 3^{k-1} \\ 3^{k-1} & 3^{k-1} & 3^{k-1} \end{bmatrix} A$

$A^{k+1} = \begin{bmatrix} 3^{k-1} & 3^{k-1} & 3^{k-1} \\ 3^{k-1} & 3^{k-1} & 3^{k-1} \\ 3^{k-1} & 3^{k-1} & 3^{k-1} \end{bmatrix} \begin{bmatrix} 1 & 1 & 1 \\ 1 & 1 & 1 \\ 1 & 1 & 1 \end{bmatrix}$

$= \begin{bmatrix} 3^k & 3^k & 3^k \\ 3^k & 3^k & 3^k \\ 3^k & 3^k & 3^k \end{bmatrix} = \begin{bmatrix} 3^{(k+1)-1} & 3^{(k+1)-1} & 3^{(k+1)-1} \\ 3^{(k+1)-1} & 3^{(k+1)-1} & 3^{(k+1)-1} \\ 3^{(k+1)-1} & 3^{(k+1)-1} & 3^{(k+1)-1} \end{bmatrix}$

$\therefore$ P (n) is true for $n = k + 1$

By principle of mathematical induction that P (n) is true for all n, $n \in N$.

3. If $A = \begin{bmatrix} 3 & -4 \\ 1 & -1 \end{bmatrix}$, then prove that $A^n = \begin{bmatrix} 1+2n & -4n \\ n & 1-2n \end{bmatrix}$, where n is any positive integer.

Sol. Let $P(n) : A^n = \begin{bmatrix} 1+2n & -4n \\ n & 1-2n \end{bmatrix}$, where $A = \begin{bmatrix} 3 & -4 \\ 1 & -1 \end{bmatrix}$

Put $n = 1$ $A = \begin{bmatrix} 1+2 & -4 \\ 1 & 1-2 \end{bmatrix} = \begin{bmatrix} 3 & -4 \\ 1 & -1 \end{bmatrix}$

$\therefore$ P (n) is true for $n = 1$

Let P (n) be true for $n = K$

$\therefore \ A^K = \begin{bmatrix} 1+2K & -4K \\ K & 1-2K \end{bmatrix}$

Multiplying both sides by A

$A^K A = A^{K+1} = \begin{bmatrix} 1+2K & -4K \\ K & 1-2K \end{bmatrix} A$

$= \begin{bmatrix} 1+2K & -4K \\ K & 1-2K \end{bmatrix} \begin{bmatrix} 3 & -4 \\ 1 & -1 \end{bmatrix}$

$= \begin{bmatrix} 3+2K & -4-4K \\ 1+K & -1-2K \end{bmatrix} = \begin{bmatrix} 1+2(K+1) & -4(K+1) \\ K+1 & 1-2(K+1) \end{bmatrix}$

This proves that P(n) is true for $n = K + 1$. Hence, P(n) is true for all $n \in N$.

4. **If A and B are symmetric matrices, prove that $AB - BA$ is a skew symmetric matrix.**

Sol. A and B are symmetric matrix is $A' = A$ and $B' = B$ Also $(AB)' = B'A'$. Now, $(AB - BA)'$
$= (AB)' - (BA)' = B'A' - A'B' = BA - AB$
$= -(AB - BA)$
Hence $AB - BA$ is skew symmetric matrix.

5. **Show that the matrix $B'AB$ is symmetric or skew symmetric according as A is symmetric or skew symmetric.**

Sol. (i) Let A be symmetric matrix
$\Rightarrow A' = A$ $\therefore$ $(B'AB)' = (B'(AB))' = (AB)'(B)'$
$= (B'A')B = B'(AB)$ $\because A' = A$
$\Rightarrow B'AB$ is skew symmetric matrix.
(ii) Let A be skew symmetric matrix
$\Rightarrow A' = -A$ $\therefore$ $(B'AB)' = B'A'B = -B'AB$
$\Rightarrow B'AB$ is skew symmetric matrix.

6. **Find the values of x, y, z if the matrix A**

$= \begin{bmatrix} 0 & 2y & z \\ x & y & -z \\ x & -y & z \end{bmatrix}$ **satisfy the equation $A'A = I$.**

Sol. $A = \begin{bmatrix} 0 & 2y & z \\ x & y & -z \\ x & -y & z \end{bmatrix}$ $\therefore A' = \begin{bmatrix} 0 & x & x \\ 2y & y & -y \\ z & -z & z \end{bmatrix}$

$A'A = \begin{bmatrix} 0 & x & x \\ 2y & y & -y \\ z & -z & z \end{bmatrix} \begin{bmatrix} 0 & 2y & z \\ x & y & -z \\ x & -y & z \end{bmatrix}$

$$= \begin{bmatrix} 2x^2 & 0 & 0 \\ 0 & 6y^2 & 0 \\ 0 & 0 & 3z^2 \end{bmatrix} = \begin{bmatrix} 1 & 0 & 0 \\ 0 & 1 & 0 \\ 0 & 0 & 1 \end{bmatrix} \quad A'A = I_3$$

Equating corresponding elements, we get

$$2x^2 = 1, \quad x = \pm \frac{1}{\sqrt{2}} \qquad 6y^2 = 1, \quad y = \pm \frac{1}{\sqrt{6}}$$

$$3z^2 = 1, \quad z = \pm \frac{1}{\sqrt{3}}$$

7. For what values of x : $[1\ 2\ 1] \begin{bmatrix} 1 & 2 & 0 \\ 2 & 0 & 1 \\ 1 & 0 & 2 \end{bmatrix} \begin{bmatrix} 0 \\ 2 \\ x \end{bmatrix} = 0$?

Sol. L.H.S. $= [1\ 2\ 1] \begin{bmatrix} 1 & & 0 \\ 2 & 0 & 1 \\ 1 & 0 & 2 \end{bmatrix} \begin{bmatrix} 0 \\ 2 \\ x \end{bmatrix} = [1\ 2\ 1] \begin{bmatrix} 4 \\ x \\ 2x \end{bmatrix}$

$$= [4 + 2x + 2x] = [4x + 4] = [0]$$
$$\Rightarrow 4x + 4 = 0 \ \therefore x = -1$$

8. If $A = \begin{bmatrix} 3 & 1 \\ -1 & 2 \end{bmatrix}$, show that $A^2 - 5A + 7I = 0$.

Sol. $A^2 = \begin{bmatrix} 3 & 1 \\ 1 & 2 \end{bmatrix}\begin{bmatrix} 3 & 1 \\ -1 & 2 \end{bmatrix} = \begin{bmatrix} 8 & 5 \\ -5 & 3 \end{bmatrix}$

L.H.S. $= A^2 - 5A + 7I$

$$= \begin{bmatrix} 8 & 5 \\ -5 & 3 \end{bmatrix} - 5\begin{bmatrix} 3 & 1 \\ -1 & 2 \end{bmatrix} + 7\begin{bmatrix} 1 & 0 \\ 0 & 1 \end{bmatrix}$$

$$= \begin{bmatrix} 0 & 0 \\ 0 & 0 \end{bmatrix} = \text{R.H.S.}$$

Hence $A^2 - 5A + 7I = 0$

9. Find x, if $[x\ -5\ -1] \begin{bmatrix} 1 & 0 & 2 \\ 0 & 2 & 1 \\ 2 & 0 & 3 \end{bmatrix} \begin{bmatrix} x \\ 4 \\ 1 \end{bmatrix} = 0$

Sol. L.H.S. $= [x\ -5\ -1] \begin{bmatrix} 1 & 0 & 2 \\ 0 & 2 & 1 \\ 2 & 0 & 3 \end{bmatrix}\begin{bmatrix} x \\ 4 \\ 1 \end{bmatrix} = [x-5-1]\begin{bmatrix} x+2 \\ 9 \\ 2x+3 \end{bmatrix}$

$$= [x(x+2) - 45 - (2x+3)] = [x^2 + 2x - 45 - 2x - 3]$$
$$= [x^2 - 48]$$

R.H.S. $= [0] \Rightarrow x^2 - 48 = 0, x = \pm 4\sqrt{3}$.

10. A manufacturer produces three products x, y, z which he sells in two markets. Annual sales are indicated below :

Market	Products		
I	10,000	2,000	18,000
II	6,000	20,000	8,000

(a) If unit sale prices of x, y and z are ₹ 2.50, ₹ 1.50 and ₹ 1.00, respectively, find the total revenue in each market with the help of matrix algebra.

(b) If the unit costs of the above three commodities are ₹ 2.00, ₹1.00 and 50 paise respectively. Find the gross profit.

Sol. **(a)** Matrix for the products x, y, z is

$$\begin{array}{ccc} x & y & z \\ \downarrow & \downarrow & \downarrow \end{array}$$
$$\begin{array}{c} I \to \\ II \to \end{array} \begin{bmatrix} 10000 & 2000 & 18000 \\ 6,000 & 20,000 & 8,000 \end{bmatrix}$$

Matrix corresponding to sale price of each product

$$\begin{array}{c} x \to \\ y \to \\ z \to \end{array} \begin{bmatrix} 2 \cdot 50 \\ 1 \cdot 50 \\ 1 \cdot 00 \end{bmatrix}$$

$\therefore$ The revenue collected by market is given by

$$\begin{bmatrix} 10,000 & 2,000 & 18,000 \\ 6,000 & 20,000 & 8,000 \end{bmatrix}\begin{bmatrix} 2 \cdot 50 \\ 1 \cdot 50 \\ 1 \cdot 00 \end{bmatrix} = \begin{bmatrix} 46,000 \\ 53,000 \end{bmatrix}$$

Revenue in each market ₹ 46,000 and ₹ 53,000
Total revenue $= ₹ (46,000 + 53,000) = ₹ 99,000$

(b) The cost price of commodities x, y and z are respectively. ₹ 2·00, ₹ 1·00 and 0.50 cost price of each market is given below.

$$\begin{bmatrix} 10,000 & 2000 & 18,000 \\ 6,000 & 20,000 & 8,000 \end{bmatrix}\begin{bmatrix} 2 \cdot 00 \\ 1 \cdot 00 \\ 0 \cdot 50 \end{bmatrix}$$

$$= \begin{bmatrix} 20,000 & 2000 & 9000 \\ 12000 & 20000 & 4000 \end{bmatrix} = \begin{bmatrix} 31,000 \\ 36,000 \end{bmatrix}$$

Total cost price of the commodities each market I and II are ₹ 31,000, ₹ 36,000
Total cost price $= ₹ (31,000 + 36,000) = ₹ 67,000$
Gross profit = Revenue – Cost price
$$= 99,000 - 67,000 = ₹ 32,000.$$

11. Find the matrix X so that

$$X\begin{bmatrix} 1 & 2 & 3 \\ 4 & 5 & 6 \end{bmatrix} = \begin{bmatrix} -7 & -8 & -9 \\ 2 & 4 & 6 \end{bmatrix}$$

Sol. $\therefore$ Let $X = \begin{bmatrix} a & b \\ c & d \end{bmatrix}$,

$$X\begin{bmatrix} 1 & 2 & 3 \\ 4 & 5 & 6 \end{bmatrix} = \begin{bmatrix} -7 & -8 & -9 \\ 2 & 4 & -6 \end{bmatrix}$$

$$\therefore \ \begin{bmatrix} a & b \\ c & d \end{bmatrix}\begin{bmatrix} 1 & 2 & 3 \\ 4 & 5 & 6 \end{bmatrix} = \begin{bmatrix} a+4b & 2a+5b & 3a+6b \\ c+4d & 2c+5d & 3c+6d \end{bmatrix}$$

$$= \begin{bmatrix} -7 & -8 & -9 \\ 2 & 4 & -6 \end{bmatrix}$$

Equating the corresponding elements

$$a + 4b = -7 \qquad \ldots(i)$$
$$2a + 5b = -8 \qquad \ldots(ii)$$
$$3a + 6b = -9 \qquad \ldots(iii)$$

Multiplying (i) by 2

$$2a + 8b = -14 \qquad \ldots(iv)$$

and $\qquad 2a + 5b = -8$

Subtracting (ii) from (iv)

$$3b = -6 \qquad \therefore \ b = -2$$

Putting the value of b in (i)

$$a - 8 = -7, \qquad \therefore \ a = 8 - 7 = 1$$

$a = 1, b = -2$ satisfy eqn. (iii) also equating the element of second row

$$c + 4d = 2 \qquad \ldots(v)$$
$$2c + 5d = 4 \qquad \ldots(vi)$$
$$3c + 6d = 6 \qquad \ldots(vii)$$

Multiplying equ. (v) by 2

$$2c + 8d = 4 \qquad \ldots(viii)$$

Subtracting (vi) from (viii)

$$3d = 4 - 4 = 0 \quad \therefore \quad d = 0$$
$$\therefore \text{ from } c + 4d = 2 \qquad \therefore \quad c = 2$$

$c = 2, d = 0$, satisfy equ. (vii) also

Thus $a = 1, b = -2, c = 2, d = 0$

Hence, $X = \begin{bmatrix} 1 & -2 \\ 2 & 0 \end{bmatrix}$

12. If A and B are square matrices of the same order such that AB = BA, then prove by induction that $AB^n = B^n A$. Further, prove that $(AB)^n = A^n B^n$ for all $n \in N$.

Sol. Let $P(n) : AB^n = B^n A$,

But $n = 1, AB = BA$ $\qquad$ (Given)

$\therefore$ P(n) is true for $n = 1$ Let P(n) be true for $n = K$

$$AB^K = B^K A$$

Multiplying both side by B

L.H.S. $= AB^K B = A(B^K B) = AB^{K+1}$

R.H.S. $= (B^K A) B = B^K (AB)$

$$= B^K (BA) \qquad \because AB = BA$$
$$= (B^K B) A$$
$$= B^{K+1} A \text{ is P(n) is true for } n = K + 1$$

By principle of mathematical induction. P(n) is true for all $n \in N$.

Choose the correct answer in the following questions (ii)

$P(n) : (AB)^n = A^n B^n$

For $n = 1$, L.H.S. $= AB$ and R.H.S. $= AB$

$\therefore$ P(n) is true for $n = 1$ Let P(n) be true for $n = k$

$$(AB)^K = A^K B^K$$

Multiply both sides by AB

L.H.S. $= (AB)^K (AB) = (AB)^{K+1}$

R.H.S. $= A^K B^K (AB) = A^K B^K (BA)$

$\because AB = BA = A^K (B^K \cdot B) A = A^K (B^{K+1} A)$

$$\qquad\qquad\qquad\qquad [\because AB^n = B^n A]$$
$$= A^K (AB^{K+1}) = A^{K+1} B^{K+1}$$

$\Rightarrow$ P(n) is true for $n = K + 1$

By principal of mathematical induction P(n) is true for all $n \in N$.

13. If $A = \begin{bmatrix} \alpha & \beta \\ \gamma & -\alpha \end{bmatrix}$ is such that $A^2 = I$, then

(a) $1 + \alpha^2 + \beta\gamma = 0$ $\qquad$ (b) $1 - \alpha^2 + \beta\gamma = 0$

(c) $1 - \alpha^2 - \beta\gamma = 0$ $\qquad$ (d) $1 + \alpha^2 - \beta\gamma = 0$

Sol. $A^2 = \begin{bmatrix} \alpha & \beta \\ \gamma & -\alpha \end{bmatrix} \begin{bmatrix} \alpha & \beta \\ \gamma & -\alpha \end{bmatrix}$

$$= \begin{bmatrix} \alpha^2 + \beta\gamma & \alpha\beta - \alpha\beta \\ \alpha\gamma - \alpha\gamma & \beta\gamma + \alpha^2 \end{bmatrix} = \begin{bmatrix} 1 & 0 \\ 0 & 1 \end{bmatrix}$$

$\therefore A^2 = I \qquad \alpha^2 + \beta\gamma = 1 \quad$ or $\quad 1 - \alpha^2 - \beta\gamma = 0$

Option (c) is correct.

14. If the matrix A is both symmetric and skew symmetric, then

(a) A is a diagonal matrix

(b) A is a zero matrix

(c) A is a square matrix

(d) None of these

Sol. A is a symmetric matrix if $a_{ij} = a_{ji}$ A is a skew symmetric matrix if $a_{ij} = -a_{ji}$

If $a_{ij} = a_{ji} = -a_{ji} \ \Rightarrow \ a_{ij} = 0$

$\Rightarrow$ A is a zero matrix. Option (b) is correct.

15. If A is square matrix such that $A^2 = A$, then $(I + A)^3 - 7A$ is equal to

(a) A $\qquad\qquad\qquad\qquad$ (b) I – A

(c) I $\qquad\qquad\qquad\qquad$ (d) 3A

Sol. $A^3 = A^2 \cdot A \qquad$ But $A^2 = A$

$$= A \cdot A = A^2 = A$$
$$(1 + A)^3 - 7A = (1 + 3A + 3A^2 + A^3) - 7A$$
$$= (1 + 3A + 3A + A) - 7A$$
$$= (1 + 7A) - 7A = 1$$

Option (c) is correct.

Past year Exercise

Multiple Choice Question

1. If A is a square matrix such that $A^2 = A$, then $(I - A)^3 + A$ is equal to

(a) I $\qquad\qquad\qquad\qquad$ (b) 0

(c) I – A $\qquad\qquad\qquad\qquad$ (d) I + A

Very Short Answer Questions

2. Find the value of $y - x$ from following equation

$$2 \begin{bmatrix} x & 5 \\ 7 & y-3 \end{bmatrix} + \begin{bmatrix} 3 & -4 \\ 1 & 2 \end{bmatrix} = \begin{bmatrix} 7 & 6 \\ 15 & 14 \end{bmatrix}$$

3. If $\begin{bmatrix} 9 & -1 & 4 \\ -2 & 1 & 3 \end{bmatrix} = A + \begin{bmatrix} 1 & 2 & -1 \\ 0 & 4 & 9 \end{bmatrix}$ then find the matrix A.

4. Find the value of b if

$$\begin{bmatrix} a-b & 2a+c \\ 2a-b & 3c+d \end{bmatrix} = \begin{bmatrix} -1 & 5 \\ 0 & 13 \end{bmatrix}$$

5. If A is a square matrix such that $A^2 = A$, then write the value of $7A - (I + A)^3$, where I is an identity matrix.

6. If $\begin{bmatrix} x-y & z \\ 2x-y & w \end{bmatrix} = \begin{bmatrix} -1 & 4 \\ 0 & 5 \end{bmatrix}$, find the value of $x + y$.

7. If matrix $A = \begin{bmatrix} 3 & -3 \\ -3 & 3 \end{bmatrix}$, and $A^2 = \lambda A$, then write the value of λ.

8. If $2\begin{bmatrix} 1 & 3 \\ 0 & x \end{bmatrix} + \begin{bmatrix} y & 0 \\ 1 & 2 \end{bmatrix} = \begin{bmatrix} 5 & 6 \\ 1 & 8 \end{bmatrix}$, then write the value of $(x + y)$.

9. For what value of x, is the matrix $A = \begin{bmatrix} 0 & 1 & -2 \\ -1 & 0 & 3 \\ x & -3 & 0 \end{bmatrix}$ a skew-symmetric matrix?

10. If $\begin{bmatrix} x-y & 2y \\ 2y+z & x+y \end{bmatrix} = \begin{bmatrix} 1 & 4 \\ 9 & 5 \end{bmatrix}$, then write the value of $(x+y+z)$.

11. Solve the following matrix equation for x :

$$[x \ 1]\begin{bmatrix} 1 & 0 \\ -2 & 0 \end{bmatrix} = O$$

12. If $2\begin{bmatrix} 3 & 4 \\ 5 & x \end{bmatrix} + \begin{bmatrix} 1 & y \\ 0 & 1 \end{bmatrix} = \begin{bmatrix} 7 & 0 \\ 10 & 5 \end{bmatrix}$, find $(x - y)$.

13. If A is a square matrix such that $A^2 = I$, then find the simplified value of $(A - I)^3 + (A + I)^3 - 7A$.

14. Matrix $A = \begin{bmatrix} 0 & 2b & -2 \\ 3 & 1 & 3 \\ 3a & 3 & -1 \end{bmatrix}$ is given to be symmetric, find values of a and b.

15. If the matrix $A = \begin{bmatrix} 0 & a & -3 \\ 2 & 0 & -1 \\ b & 1 & 0 \end{bmatrix}$ is skew symmetric, find the values of 'a' and 'b'.

16. To raise money for an orphanage, students of three schools A, B and C organised an exhibition in their locality, where they sold paper bags, scrap-books and pastel sheets made by them using recycled paper, at the rate of ₹ 20, ₹15 and ₹ 5 per unit respectively. School A sold 25 paper bags, 12 scrap-books and 34 pastel sheets. School B sold 22 paper bags, 15 scrap-books and 28 pastel sheets while school C sold 26 paper bags, 18 scrap-books and 36 pastel sheets. Using matrix, find the total amount raised by each school.

17. If $A = \begin{pmatrix} 2 & 0 & 1 \\ 2 & 1 & 3 \\ 1 & -1 & 0 \end{pmatrix}$, find $A^2 - 5A + 16I$.

18. If $A = \begin{pmatrix} 2 & 0 & 1 \\ 2 & 1 & 3 \\ 1 & -1 & 0 \end{pmatrix}$ find $A^2 - 5A + 4I$ and a matrix X such that $A^2 - 5A + 4I + X = 0$

19. Three schools A, B and C organized a mela for collecting funds for helping the rehabilitation of flood victims. They sold hand made fans, mats and plates from recycled material at a cost of ₹ 25, ₹ 100 and ₹ 50 each. The number of articles sold are given below:

School Article	A	B	C
Hand-fans	40	25	35
Mats	50	40	50
Plates	20	30	40

Find the funds collected by each school separately by selling the above articles. Also find the total funds collected for the purpose.

NCERT Exemplar

1. If $A = \dfrac{1}{\pi}\begin{bmatrix} \sin^{-1}(x\pi) & \tan^{-1}\left(\dfrac{x}{\pi}\right) \\ \sin^{-1}\left(\dfrac{x}{\pi}\right) & \cot^{-1}(\pi x) \end{bmatrix}$ and

$B = \dfrac{1}{\pi}\begin{bmatrix} -\cos^{-1}(x\pi) & \tan^{-1}\left(\dfrac{x}{\pi}\right) \\ \sin^{-1}\left(\dfrac{x}{\pi}\right) & -\tan^{-1}(\pi x) \end{bmatrix}$ then $A - B$ is equal to

(a) I (b) 0   (c) $2I$ (d) $\dfrac{1}{2}I$

2. If A and B are two matrices of the order $3 \times m$ and $3 \times n$, respectively and $m = n$, then order of mamtrix $(5A - 2B)$ is

(a) $m \times 3$ (b) 3×3
(c) $m \times n$ (d) $3 \times n$

3. If matrix $A = [a_{ij}]_{2 \times 2}$, where $a_{ij} = 1$, if $i \neq j$ and 0 if $i = j$, then A^2 is equal to

(a) I (b) A
(c) 0   (d) None of these

4. If A and B are matrices of same order, then $\left(AB' - BA' \right)$ is a

(a) skew symmetric matrix (b) null matrix
(c) symmetric matrix (d) unit matrix

6. Find non-zero values of x satisfying the matrix equation

$$x\begin{bmatrix} 2x & 2 \\ 3 & x \end{bmatrix} + 2\begin{bmatrix} 8 & 5x \\ 4 & 4x \end{bmatrix} = 2\begin{bmatrix} (x^2+8) & 24 \\ (10) & 6x \end{bmatrix}.$$

Very Short Answer Questions

5. Construct a matrix A = $[a_{ij}]_{2 \times 2}$ Whose elements a_{ij} are given by $a_{ij} = e^{2ix} \sin jx$.

Short Answer Questions

7. Give an example of two non zero 2×2 matrices A, B such that AB = O.

8. Show that a matrix which is both symmetric and skew symmetric is a zero matrix.

Objective Practice Exercise

Multiple Choice Questions

DIRECTIONS : *This section contains multiple choice questions. Each question has four choices (a), (b), (c) and (d) out of which only one is correct.*

1. If A = $\begin{bmatrix} 1 & 0 & 0 \\ 0 & 1 & 0 \\ a & b & -1 \end{bmatrix}$, then $A^2 =$

(a) Unit matrix (b) Null matrix
(c) A (d) −A

2. If A = $\begin{bmatrix} 2 & 0 & 0 \\ 0 & 2 & 0 \\ 0 & 0 & 2 \end{bmatrix}$, then $A^5 =$

(a) 5A (b) 10A (c) 16A (d) 32A

3. If $A = \begin{bmatrix} \alpha & 0 \\ 1 & 1 \end{bmatrix}$ and $B = \begin{bmatrix} 1 & 0 \\ 5 & 1 \end{bmatrix}$, then value of α for which $A^2 = B$, is

(a) 1 (b) −1
(c) 4 (d) no real values

4. If $\begin{bmatrix} 2 & 1 \\ 3 & 2 \end{bmatrix} A \begin{bmatrix} -3 & 2 \\ 5 & -3 \end{bmatrix} = \begin{bmatrix} 1 & 0 \\ 0 & 1 \end{bmatrix}$, then A is equal to

(a) $\begin{bmatrix} 1 & 1 \\ 1 & 0 \end{bmatrix}$ (b) $\begin{bmatrix} 1 & 1 \\ 0 & 1 \end{bmatrix}$

(c) $\begin{bmatrix} 1 & 0 \\ 1 & 1 \end{bmatrix}$ (d) $\begin{bmatrix} 0 & 1 \\ 1 & 1 \end{bmatrix}$

5. If $2A + 3B = \begin{bmatrix} 2 & -1 & 4 \\ 3 & 2 & 5 \end{bmatrix}$ and $A + 2B = \begin{bmatrix} 5 & 0 & 3 \\ 1 & 6 & 2 \end{bmatrix}$, then B =

(a) $\begin{bmatrix} 8 & -1 & 2 \\ -1 & 10 & -1 \end{bmatrix}$ (b) $\begin{bmatrix} 8 & 1 & 2 \\ -1 & 10 & -1 \end{bmatrix}$

(c) $\begin{bmatrix} 8 & 1 & -2 \\ -1 & 10 & -1 \end{bmatrix}$ (d) $\begin{bmatrix} 8 & 1 & 2 \\ 1 & 10 & 1 \end{bmatrix}$

6. If A = $\begin{bmatrix} \cos \alpha & \sin \alpha \\ -\sin \alpha & \cos \alpha \end{bmatrix}$, then A^2 is equal to

(a) $\begin{bmatrix} \sin 2\alpha & \cos 2\alpha \\ \cos 2\alpha & -\sin 2\alpha \end{bmatrix}$ (b) $\begin{bmatrix} \cos 2\alpha & -\sin \alpha \\ -\sin \alpha & \cos 2\alpha \end{bmatrix}$

(c) $\begin{bmatrix} \cos 2\alpha & \sin 2\alpha \\ -\sin 2\alpha & \cos 2\alpha \end{bmatrix}$ (d) $\begin{bmatrix} 1 & 0 \\ 0 & 1 \end{bmatrix}$

7. If A = $[a \quad b]$, B = $[-b \quad -a]$ and C = $\begin{bmatrix} a \\ -a \end{bmatrix}$, then the correct statement is

(a) A = −B (b) A + B = A − B
(c) AC = BC (d) CA = CB

8. If $e\begin{bmatrix} e^x & e^y \\ e^y & e^x \end{bmatrix} = \begin{bmatrix} 1 & 1 \\ 1 & 1 \end{bmatrix}$, then the values of x and y are respectively

(a) −1, −1 (b) 1, 1 (c) 0, 1 (d) 1, 0

9. If $A = \begin{bmatrix} 0 & 1 \\ 0 & 0 \end{bmatrix}$, I is the unit matrix of order 2 and a, b are arbitrary constants, then $(aI + bA)^2$ is equal to

(a) $a^2I + abA$ (b) $a^2I + 2abA$
(c) $a^2I + b^2 A$ (d) None of these

10. If X = $\begin{bmatrix} 3 & -4 \\ 1 & -1 \end{bmatrix}$, then the value of X^n is

(a) $\begin{bmatrix} 3n & -4n \\ n & -n \end{bmatrix}$ (b) $\begin{bmatrix} 2+n & 5-n \\ n & -n \end{bmatrix}$

(c) $\begin{bmatrix} 3^n & (-4)^n \\ 1^n & (-1)^n \end{bmatrix}$ (d) None of these

11. If $A = \begin{bmatrix} 0 & 2 \\ 3 & -4 \end{bmatrix}$ and $kA = \begin{bmatrix} 0 & 3a \\ 2b & 24 \end{bmatrix}$, then the values of k, a, b are respectively

(a) −6, −12, −18 (b) −6, 4, 9
(c) −6, −4, −9 (d) −6, 12, 18

12. If $\begin{bmatrix} \alpha & \beta \\ \gamma & -\alpha \end{bmatrix}$ is square root of identity matrix of order 2 then,

(a) $1 + \alpha^2 + \beta\gamma = 0$ (b) $1 + \alpha^2 - \beta\gamma = 0$

(c) $1 - \alpha^2 + \beta\gamma = 0$ (d) $\alpha^2 + \beta\gamma = 1$

13. Given $A = \begin{bmatrix} 3 & 5 \\ 4 & 2 \end{bmatrix}$, then $A^2 - 5A - 11\,I$ is equal to

(a) $3\,I$ (b) I (c) O (d) $2\,I$

14. If $A = \begin{bmatrix} 1 & 2 \\ -3 & 0 \end{bmatrix}$ and $B = \begin{bmatrix} -1 & 0 \\ 2 & 3 \end{bmatrix}$, then

(a) $A^2 = A$ (b) $B^2 = B$

(c) $AB \neq BA$ (d) $AB = BA$

15. If I is a unit matrix, then 3I will be

(a) A unit matrix   (b) A triangular matrix

(c) A scalar matrix   (d) None of these

16. If $A = \begin{bmatrix} ab & b^2 \\ -a^2 & -ab \end{bmatrix}$ and $A^n = O$, then the minimum value of n is

(a) 2   (b) 3   (c) 4   (d) 5

17. If A and B are 3×3 matrices such that $AB = A$ and $BA = B$, then

(a) $A^2 = A$ and $B^2 \neq B$ (b) $A^2 \neq A$ and $B^2 = B$

(c) $A^2 = A$ and $B^2 = B$ (d) $A^2 \neq A$ and $B^2 \neq B$

18. If $A = \begin{bmatrix} 1 & 1 \\ 1 & 1 \end{bmatrix}$ then A^{100} :

(a) $2^{100}A$ (b) $2^{99}A$

(c) $2^{101}A$ (d) None of these

19. If $A = \begin{pmatrix} 2 & -1 \\ -1 & 2 \end{pmatrix}$ and I is the unit matrix of order 2, then A^2 equals

(a) $4A - 3I$ (b) $3A - AI$

(c) $A - I$ (d) $A + I$

20. If $A = \begin{bmatrix} 1 & 0 & 0 \\ 0 & 1 & 0 \\ a & b & -1 \end{bmatrix}$ and I is the unit matrix of order 3, then $A^2 + 2A^4 + 4A^6$ is equal to

(a) $7A^8$ (b) $7A^7$

(c) $8\,I$ (d) $6\,I$

21. Which is true about matrix multiplication ?

(a) It is commutative   (b) It is associative

(c) Both of the above   (d) None of these

22. If A is a square matrix such that $A^2 = A$, then $(I - A)^3 + A$ is equal to

(a) A (b) $I - S$ (c) I (d) $3A$

23. If $A = \begin{bmatrix} 4 & 2 \\ -1 & 1 \end{bmatrix}$ and I is the identity matrix of order 2, then $(A - 2I)(A - 3I) =$

24. If $A = \begin{bmatrix} 1 & -2 \\ 3 & 0 \end{bmatrix}$, $B = \begin{bmatrix} -1 & 4 \\ 2 & 3 \end{bmatrix}$ and $C = \begin{bmatrix} 0 & 1 \\ -1 & 0 \end{bmatrix}$, then $5A - 3B + 2C$ is equal to

(a) $\begin{bmatrix} 8 & 20 \\ 7 & 9 \end{bmatrix}$ (b) $\begin{bmatrix} 8 & -20 \\ 7 & -9 \end{bmatrix}$

(c) $\begin{bmatrix} -8 & 20 \\ -7 & 9 \end{bmatrix}$ (d) $\begin{bmatrix} 8 & 7 \\ -20 & -9 \end{bmatrix}$

25. If $A = \begin{bmatrix} 1 & 0 & 0 \\ 0 & 1 & 0 \\ 0 & 0 & 1 \end{bmatrix}$, then $A^2 + 2A$ is equal to

(a) A (b) $2A$ (c) $3A$ (d) $4A$

26. If $3X + 2Y = I$ and $2X - Y = O$, where I and O are unit and null matrices of order 3 respectively, then

(a) $X = \left(\dfrac{1}{7}\right), Y = \left(\dfrac{2}{7}\right)$ (b) $X = \left(\dfrac{2}{7}\right), Y = \left(\dfrac{1}{7}\right)$

(c) $X = \left(\dfrac{1}{7}\right)I, Y = \left(\dfrac{2}{7}\right)I$ (d) $X = \left(\dfrac{2}{7}\right)I, Y = \left(\dfrac{1}{7}\right)I$

27. If A and B are 2×2 matrices, then which of the following is true ?

(a) $(A + B)^2 = A^2 + B^2 + 2AB$

(b) $(A - B)^2 = A^2 + B^2 - 2AB$

(c) $(A - B)(A + B) = A^2 + AB - BA - B^2$

(d) $(A - B)(A + B) = A^2 - B^2$

28. If $A = \begin{bmatrix} 0 & 1 \\ 0 & 0 \end{bmatrix}$ and $AB = O$, then $B =$

(a) $\begin{bmatrix} 1 & 1 \\ 1 & 1 \end{bmatrix}$ (b) $\begin{bmatrix} 0 & 1 \\ -1 & 0 \end{bmatrix}$

(c) $\begin{bmatrix} 0 & -1 \\ 1 & 0 \end{bmatrix}$ (d) $\begin{bmatrix} -1 & 0 \\ 0 & 0 \end{bmatrix}$

29. If $A = \begin{bmatrix} 6 & 8 & 5 \\ 4 & 2 & 3 \\ 9 & 7 & 1 \end{bmatrix}$ is the sum of a symmetric matrix B and skew-symmetric matrix C, then B is

(a) $\begin{bmatrix} 6 & 6 & 7 \\ 6 & 2 & 5 \\ 7 & 5 & 1 \end{bmatrix}$ (b) $\begin{bmatrix} 0 & 2 & -2 \\ -2 & 5 & -2 \\ 2 & 2 & 0 \end{bmatrix}$

(c) $\begin{bmatrix} 6 & 6 & 7 \\ -6 & 2 & -5 \\ -7 & 5 & 1 \end{bmatrix}$ (d) $\begin{bmatrix} 0 & 6 & -2 \\ 2 & 0 & -2 \\ -2 & -2 & 0 \end{bmatrix}$

30. If A is 3×4 matrix and B is a matrix such that A'B and BA' are both defined. Then B is of the type
    (a) 3×4 (b) 3×3
    (c) 4×4 (d) 4×3

31. If $O(A) = 2 \times 3$, $O(B) = 3 \times 2$, and $O(C) = 3 \times 3$, which one of the following is not defined
    (a) $CB + A'$ (b) BAC
    (c) $C(A + B')'$ (d) $C(A + B')$

32. If A and B are symmetric matrices of the same order, then which one of the following is not true
    (a) $A + B$ is symmetric   (b) $A - B$ is symmetric
    (c) $AB + BA$ is symmetric   (d) $AB - BA$ is symmetric

33. If A is a square matrix for which $a_{ij} = i^2 - j^2$, then A is
    (a) Zero matrix   (b) Unit matrix
    (c) Symmetric matrix   (d) Skew symmetric matrix

34. If $A = \begin{bmatrix} 4 & x+2 \\ 2x-3 & x+1 \end{bmatrix}$ is symmetric, then $x =$
    (a) 3   (b) 5   (c) 2   (d) 4

35. Which one of the following is correct?
    (a) Skew-symmetric matrix of odd order is non-singular
    (b) Skew-symmetric matrix of odd order is singular
    (c) Skew-symmetric matrix of evern order is always singular
    (d) None of these

36. If A is a square matrix $A + A^T$ is symmetric matrix, then $A - A^T =$
    (a) Unit matrix   (b) Symmetrix matrix
    (c) Skew symmetrix matrix   (d) Zero matrix

37. If A is a symmetric matrix, then matrix M'AM is
    (a) Symmetric   (b) Skew-symmetric
    (c) Hermitian   (d) Skew-Hermitian

38. If $A = \begin{bmatrix} 0 & 1 & -2 \\ -1 & 0 & 5 \\ 2 & -5 & 0 \end{bmatrix}$, then
    (a) $A' = A$ (b) $A' = -A$
    (c) $A' = 2A$ (d) None of these

39. If $A = \begin{bmatrix} \cos\theta & \sin\theta \\ -\sin\theta & \cos\theta \end{bmatrix}$ then A. A' is
    (a) I (b) A (c) $-A$ (d) A^2

40. If A is a skew symmetric matrix and n is a positive integer, then A^n is
    (a) A symmetric matrix   (b) Skew-symmetric matrix
    (c) Diagonal matrix   (d) None of these

41. If A is a square matrix, then which of the following matrices is not symmetric
    (a) $A + A'$ (b) AA' (c) $A'A$ (d) $A - A'$

42. Which of the following is correct?
    (a) $B'AB$ is symmetric if A is symmetric
    (b) $B'AB$ is skew-symmetric if A is symmetric
    (c) $B'AB$ is symmetric if A is skew-symmetric
    (d) None of these

43. Let $A = \begin{pmatrix} 1 & -1 & 1 \\ 2 & 1 & -3 \\ 1 & 1 & 1 \end{pmatrix}$ and $10B = \begin{pmatrix} 4 & 2 & 2 \\ -5 & 0 & \alpha \\ 1 & -2 & 3 \end{pmatrix}$. If B is the inverse of matrix A, then α is
    (a) 5   (b) -1 (c) 2   (d) -2

44. If $A = \begin{bmatrix} \cos\theta & \sin\theta \\ -\sin\theta & \cos\theta \end{bmatrix}$ then $\lim\limits_{n\to\infty} \dfrac{1}{n} A^n$ is
    (a) a null matrix   (b) an identity matrix
    (c) $\begin{bmatrix} 0 & 1 \\ -1 & 0 \end{bmatrix}$ (d) None of these

45. For the matrix $A = \begin{bmatrix} 1 & 1 & 0 \\ 1 & 2 & 1 \\ 2 & 1 & 0 \end{bmatrix}$, which of the following is correct ?
    (a) $A^3 + 3A^2 - I = O$ (b) $A^3 - 3A^2 - I = O$
    (c) $A^3 + 2A^2 - I = O$ (d) $A^3 - A^2 + I = O$

46. If $[1 \quad x \quad 1]\begin{bmatrix} 1 & 2 & 3 \\ 0 & 5 & 1 \\ 0 & 3 & 2 \end{bmatrix}\begin{bmatrix} x \\ 1 \\ -2 \end{bmatrix} = O$, then $x =$
    (a) $\dfrac{3}{4}$ (b) 1   (c) $\dfrac{5}{4}$ (d) $\dfrac{1}{4}$

47. $M = \begin{pmatrix} 1 & 1 & 1 \\ 1 & 1 & 1 \\ 1 & 1 & 1 \end{pmatrix}$, $M^{50} =$
    (a) $3^{49} M$ (b) 0   (c) -1 (d) 1

48. If $f(x) = x^2 + 4x - 5$ and $A = \begin{bmatrix} 1 & 2 \\ 4 & -3 \end{bmatrix}$, then $f(A)$ is equal to
    (a) $\begin{bmatrix} 0 & -4 \\ 8 & 8 \end{bmatrix}$ (b) $\begin{bmatrix} 2 & 1 \\ 2 & 0 \end{bmatrix}$
    (c) $\begin{bmatrix} 1 & 1 \\ 1 & 0 \end{bmatrix}$ (d) $\begin{bmatrix} 8 & 4 \\ 8 & 0 \end{bmatrix}$

49. If $A = \begin{bmatrix} 1 & -1 \\ 2 & -1 \end{bmatrix}$, $B = \begin{bmatrix} a & 1 \\ b & -1 \end{bmatrix}$ and $(A + B)^2 = A^2 + B^2$, then the values of a and b are
    (a) $a = 4, b = 1$ (b) $a = 1, b = 4$
    (c) $a = 0, b = 4$ (d) $a = 2, b = 4$

50. If $A = \begin{bmatrix} 1 & -2 \\ 4 & 5 \end{bmatrix}$ and $f(t) = t^2 - 3t + 7$, then $f(A) + \begin{bmatrix} 3 & 6 \\ -12 & -9 \end{bmatrix}$ is equal to
    (a) $\begin{bmatrix} 1 & 1 \\ 0 & 1 \end{bmatrix}$ (b) $\begin{bmatrix} 0 & 0 \\ 0 & 0 \end{bmatrix}$
    (c) $\begin{bmatrix} 1 & 0 \\ 0 & 1 \end{bmatrix}$ (d) $\begin{bmatrix} 1 & 1 \\ 0 & 0 \end{bmatrix}$

Case/Passage Based Questions

DIRECTIONS : *Study the given Case/Passage and answer the following questions.*

Case/Passage-I

A manufacture produces three stationery products pencil, eraser and sharpener which he sells in two markets. Annual sales are indicated below

Market	Products (in numbers)		
	Pencil	Eraser	Sharpener
A	10,000	2000	18,000
B	6000	20,000	8,000

If the unit Sale price of Pencil, Eraser and Sharpener are ₹ 2.50, ₹ 1.50 and ₹ 1.00 respectively, and unit cost of the above three commodities are ₹ 2.00, ₹ 1.00 and ₹ 0.50 respectively, then,

Based on the above information answer the following:

[From CBSE Question Bank-2021]

51. Total revenue of market A
  - (a) ₹ 64,000
  - (b) ₹ 60,400
  - (c) ₹ 46,000
  - (d) ₹ 40600

52. Total revenue of market B
  - (a) ₹ 35,000
  - (b) ₹ 53,000
  - (c) ₹ 50,300
  - (d) ₹ 30,500

53. Cost incurred in market A
  - (a) ₹ 13,000
  - (b) ₹ 30,100
  - (c) ₹ 10,300
  - (d) ₹ 31,000

54. Profit in market A and B respectively are
  - (a) (₹ 15,000, ₹ 17,000)
  - (b) (₹ 17,000, ₹ 15,000)
  - (c) (₹ 51,000, ₹ 71,000)
  - (d) (₹ 10,000, ₹ 20,000)

55. Gross profit in both market
  - (a) ₹ 23,000
  - (b) ₹ 20,300
  - (c) ₹ 32,000
  - (d) ₹ 30,200

Case/Passage-II

Amit, Biraj and Chirag were given the task of creating a square matrux of order 2.

Below are the matrices created by them. A, B , C are the matrices created by Amit, Biraj and Chirag respectively.

$$A = \begin{bmatrix} 1 & 2 \\ -1 & 3 \end{bmatrix} \quad B = \begin{bmatrix} 4 & 0 \\ 1 & 5 \end{bmatrix} \quad C = \begin{bmatrix} 2 & 0 \\ 1 & -2 \end{bmatrix}$$

If a = 4 and b = – 2, based on the above information answer the following: **[From CBSE Question Bank-2021]**

56. Sum of the matrices A, B and C, A + (B + C) is
  - (a) $\begin{bmatrix} 1 & 6 \\ 2 & 7 \end{bmatrix}$
  - (b) $\begin{bmatrix} 6 & 1 \\ 7 & 2 \end{bmatrix}$
  - (c) $\begin{bmatrix} 7 & 2 \\ 1 & 6 \end{bmatrix}$
  - (d) $\begin{bmatrix} 2 & 1 \\ 7 & 6 \end{bmatrix}$

57. $(A^T)^T$ is equal to
  - (a) $\begin{bmatrix} 1 & 2 \\ -1 & 3 \end{bmatrix}$
  - (b) $\begin{bmatrix} 2 & 1 \\ 3 & -1 \end{bmatrix}$
  - (c) $\begin{bmatrix} 1 & -1 \\ 2 & 3 \end{bmatrix}$
  - (d) $\begin{bmatrix} 2 & 3 \\ -1 & 1 \end{bmatrix}$

58. $(bA)^T$ is equal to
  - (a) $\begin{bmatrix} -2 & -4 \\ 2 & -6 \end{bmatrix}$
  - (b) $\begin{bmatrix} -2 & 2 \\ -4 & -6 \end{bmatrix}$
  - (c) $\begin{bmatrix} -2 & 2 \\ -6 & -4 \end{bmatrix}$
  - (d) $\begin{bmatrix} -6 & -2 \\ 2 & 4 \end{bmatrix}$

59. AC – BC is equal to
  - (a) $\begin{bmatrix} -4 & -6 \\ -4 & 4 \end{bmatrix}$
  - (b) $\begin{bmatrix} -4 & -4 \\ 4 & -6 \end{bmatrix}$
  - (c) $\begin{bmatrix} -4 & -4 \\ -6 & 4 \end{bmatrix}$
  - (d) $\begin{bmatrix} -6 & 4 \\ -4 & -4 \end{bmatrix}$

60. (a + b) B is equal to
  - (a) $\begin{bmatrix} 0 & 8 \\ 10 & 2 \end{bmatrix}$
  - (b) $\begin{bmatrix} 2 & 10 \\ 8 & 0 \end{bmatrix}$
  - (c) $\begin{bmatrix} 8 & 0 \\ 2 & 10 \end{bmatrix}$
  - (d) $\begin{bmatrix} 2 & 0 \\ 8 & 10 \end{bmatrix}$

Case/Passage-III

Three schools DPS, CVC and KVS decided to organize a fair for collecting money for helping the flood victims. They sold handmade fans, mats and plates from recycled material at a cost of ₹ 25, ₹ 100 and ₹ 50 each respectively. The numbers of articles sold are given as

School/Article	DPS	CVC	KVS
Handmade fans	40	25	35
Mats	50	40	50
Plates	20	30	40

Based on the information given above, answer the following questions: **[From CBSE Question Bank-2021]**

61. What is the total money (in ₹) collected by the school DPS?
    (a) 700   (b) 7,000   (c) 6,125   (d) 7,875

62. What is the total amount of money (in ₹) collected by schools CVC and KVS?
    (a) 14,000   (b) 15,725
    (c) 21,000   (d) 13,125

63. What is the total amount of money collected by all three schools DPS, CVC and KVS?
    (a) ₹ 15,775   (b) ₹ 14,000
    (c) ₹ 21,000   (d) ₹ 17,125

64. If the number of handmade fans and plates are interchanged for all the schools, then what is the total money collected by all schools?
    (a) ₹ 18,000   (b) ₹ 6,750
    (c) ₹ 5,000   (d) ₹ 21,250

65. How many articles (in total) are sold by three schools?
    (a) 230   (b) 130
    (c) 430   (d) 330

Case/Passage-IV

On her birth day, Seema decided to donate some money to children of an orphanage home. If there were 8 children less, everyone would have got ₹ 10 more. However, if there were 16 children more, everyone would have got ₹ 10 less. Let the number of children be x and the amount distributed by Seema for one child be y (in ₹).

Based on the information given above, answer the following questions: **[From CBSE Question Bank-2021]**

66. The equations in terms x and y are
    (a) $5x - 4y = 40$
    $5x - 8y = -80$
    (b) $5x - 4y = 40$
    $5x - 8y = 80$
    (c) $5x - 4y = 40$
    $5x + 8y = -80$
    (d) $5x + 4y = 40$
    $5x - 8y = -80$

67. Which of the following matrix equations represent the information given above?

    (a) $\begin{bmatrix} 5 & 4 \\ 5 & 8 \end{bmatrix}\begin{bmatrix} x \\ y \end{bmatrix} = \begin{bmatrix} 40 \\ -80 \end{bmatrix}$
    (b) $\begin{bmatrix} 5 & -4 \\ 5 & -8 \end{bmatrix}\begin{bmatrix} x \\ y \end{bmatrix} = \begin{bmatrix} 40 \\ 80 \end{bmatrix}$

    (c) $\begin{bmatrix} 5 & -4 \\ 5 & -8 \end{bmatrix}\begin{bmatrix} x \\ y \end{bmatrix} = \begin{bmatrix} 40 \\ -80 \end{bmatrix}$
    (d) $\begin{bmatrix} 5 & 4 \\ 5 & -8 \end{bmatrix}\begin{bmatrix} x \\ y \end{bmatrix} = \begin{bmatrix} 40 \\ -80 \end{bmatrix}$

68. The number of children who were given some money by Seema, is
   (a) 30   (b) 40
   (c) 23   (d) 32

69. How much amount is given to each child by Seema?
   (a) ₹ 32   (b) ₹ 30
   (c) ₹ 62   (d) ₹ 26

70. How much amount Seema spends in distributing the money to all the students of the Orphanage?
   (a) ₹ 609   (b) ₹ 960
   (c) ₹ 906   (d) ₹ 690

Case/Passage-V

Two farmers Ramakishan and Gurucharan Singh cultivate only three varieties of rice namely Basmati, Permal and Naura. The sale (in rupees) of these varieties of rice by both the farmers in the month of September and October are given by the following matrices A and B

September sales (in ₹)

$$A = \begin{bmatrix} 10,000 & 20,000 & 30,000 \\ 50,000 & 30,000 & 10,000 \end{bmatrix} \begin{matrix} \text{Ramakishan} \\ \text{Gurucharan} \end{matrix}$$

October sales (in ₹)

$$B = \begin{bmatrix} 5,000 & 10,000 & 6,000 \\ 20,000 & 10,000 & 10,000 \end{bmatrix} \begin{matrix} \text{Ramakishan} \\ \text{Gurucharan} \end{matrix}$$

[From CBSE Question Bank-2021]

71. The total sales in September and October for each farmer in each variety can be represented as _______..
   (a) A + B   (b) A − B
   (c) A > B   (d) A < B

72. What is the value of A_{23}?
   (a) 10000   (b) 20000
   (c) 30000   (d) 40000

73. The decrease in sales from September to October is given by _______.
   (a) A+B   (b) A − B
   (c) A > B   (d) A < B

74. If Ramkishan receives 2% profit on gross sales, compute his profit for each variety sold in October.
   (a) ₹ 100, ₹ 200 and ₹ 120
   (b) ₹ 100, ₹ 200 and ₹ 130
   (c) ₹ 100, ₹ 220 and ₹ 120
   (d) ₹ 110, ₹ 200 and ₹ 120

75. If Gurucharan receives 2% profit on gross sales, compute his profit for each variety sold in September.
   (a) ₹ 100, ₹ 200, ₹ 120   (b) ₹ 1000 , ₹ 600, ₹ 200
   (c) ₹ 400, ₹ 200, ₹ 120   (d) ₹ 1200, ₹ 200, ₹ 120

Chapter Test

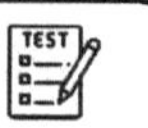

Time : 45 Minutes **Max. Marks : 20**

Directions :

(i) Questions number **1-8** carry **1 mark** each.

(ii) Question number **9** carry **4 marks**.

(iii) Questions number **10-13** are **Very Short Answer Questions** and carry **2 marks** each.

Multiple Choice Questions

1. If $A = \begin{bmatrix} \alpha & 0 \\ 1 & 1 \end{bmatrix}$ and $B = \begin{bmatrix} 1 & 0 \\ 5 & 1 \end{bmatrix}$, then value of α for which $A^2 = B$, is

   (a) 1
   (b) –1
   (c) 4
   (d) no real values

2. If $A = \begin{bmatrix} \cos x & -\sin x \\ \sin x & \cos x \end{bmatrix}$, then AA^T is

   (a) Zero matrix
   (b) I_2
   (c) $\begin{bmatrix} 1 & 1 \\ 1 & 1 \end{bmatrix}$
   (d) None of these

3. The order of $[x\ y\ z]\begin{bmatrix} a & h & g \\ h & b & f \\ g & f & c \end{bmatrix}\begin{bmatrix} x \\ y \\ z \end{bmatrix}$ is

   (a) 3×1
   (b) 1×1
   (c) 1×3
   (d) 3×3

4. If $A = \begin{bmatrix} a & b \\ b & a \end{bmatrix}$ and $A^2 = \begin{bmatrix} \alpha & \beta \\ \beta & \alpha \end{bmatrix}$, then

   (a) $\alpha = 2ab, \beta = a^2 + b^2$
   (b) $\alpha = a^2 + b^2, \beta = ab$
   (c) $\alpha = a^2 + b^2, \beta = 2ab$
   (d) $\alpha = a^2 + b^2, \beta = a^2 - b^2$

One Word Answer Questions

5. If $A = [a_{ij}] = \begin{bmatrix} 4 & -2 & 1 & 3 \\ 5 & 7 & 9 & 6 \\ 21 & 15 & 18 & -25 \end{bmatrix}$

   write the order of A and find the elements a_{24}, a_{34}. Also, show that $a_{32} = a_{23} + a_{24}$.

6. If $A = \begin{bmatrix} 2 & -1 \\ 3 & 1 \end{bmatrix}$ and $B = \begin{bmatrix} 1 & 4 \\ 7 & 2 \end{bmatrix}$, find $3A - 2B$.

Assertion & Reason Questions

DIRECTIONS : *Each of these questions contains an assertion followed by reason. Read them carefully and answer the question on the basis of following options. You have to select the one that best describes the two statements.*

(a) If both Assertion and Reason are correct and the Reason is the correct explanation of the Assertion.

(b) If both Assertion and Reason are correct but Reason is not the correct explanation of the Assertion.

(c) If the Assertion is correct but Reason is incorrect.

(d) If the Assertion is incorrect but the Reason is correct.

7. **Assertion :** If the matrix $\begin{bmatrix} a & b \\ c & d \end{bmatrix}$ is commutative with the matrix $\begin{bmatrix} 1 & 1 \\ 0 & 1 \end{bmatrix}$ then $c = 0$ and $d = a$.

   Reason : If A and B are two matrices such that $A \cdot B = B \cdot A$ then A and B are square matrices.

8. **Assertion :** The possible dimensions of a matrix containing 16 elements is 6.

   Reason : The number of ways of expressing 16 as a product of two positive integers is 6.

Case/Passage Based Question

DIRECTIONS (Q. 9) : *has 5 subparts based on case/passage given, attempt any 4 out of 5 questions.*

9. Kartik is a student of class 12, whose father has two factories at Jalandhar and Ludhiana. Each factory maufactures three types of shoes numbers 5, 6 and 7 with different costs for boys as well as girls. The production items in each factory has been given in the form of matrices as:

	Jalandhar Factory		Ludhiana Factory		Shoe No.
	Boys	Girls	Boys	Girls	
$A =$	105	65	70	60	5
	85	60	95	55	6
	90	85	80	75	7

with $A = \begin{bmatrix} 105 & 65 \\ 85 & 60 \\ 90 & 85 \end{bmatrix}$ and $B = \begin{bmatrix} 70 & 60 \\ 95 & 55 \\ 80 & 75 \end{bmatrix}$

   Then, Kartik have to answer the follwoing questions using matrices.

(i) Find the total number of shoes for boys as well as for girls.

    (a) $325, 375$ (b) $425, 400$

    (c) $500, 400$ (d) $525, 400$

(ii) The difference in the number of shoes prepared for boys and girls.

    (a) 50 (b) 100

    (c) 125 (d) 150

(iii) Find the sex ratio of girls to boys.

    (a) $16 : 21$ (b) $21 : 25$

    (c) $25 : 21$ (d) $21 : 38$

(iv) If the cost of shoes for a boy is ₹500, then total cost of shoes for all the boys.

    (a) ₹262500   (b) ₹200500

    (c) ₹260500   (d) ₹262000

(v) If the total cost invested for all types of shoes is ₹382500 and cost of a shoe for a boy is ₹500, then find the cost of a shoe for a girl.

    (a) ₹250   (b) ₹300

    (c) ₹350   (d) ₹400

Very Short Answer Questions

10. Find the values of x, y, z and a which satisfy the matrix equation

$$\begin{bmatrix} x+3 & 2y+x \\ z-1 & 4a-6 \end{bmatrix} = \begin{bmatrix} 0 & -7 \\ 3 & 2a \end{bmatrix}$$

11. If $A = \begin{bmatrix} ab & b^2 \\ -a^2 & -ab \end{bmatrix}$ and $A^n = O$, then find the minimum value of n

12. If $\begin{bmatrix} x+y & 2x+z \\ x-y & 2z+w \end{bmatrix} = \begin{bmatrix} 4 & 7 \\ 0 & 10 \end{bmatrix}$, then find the values of x, y, z, w

13. Find the number of 3×3 matrices M with entries from $\{0, 1, 2\}$ for which the sum of the diagonal entries of $M^T M$ is 5

Solutions

Practice Exercise-1

1. (c) **2.** (b) **3.** (d) **4.** (a) **5.** (d)
6. (c) **7.** (c)
8. $b_{ij} = 0$ when $i \neq j$
$b_{ij} = k$ when $i = j$, for some constant k
9. A diagonal matrix is said to be a scalar matrix, if its diagonal elements are equal.
10. There are in total 9 entries and each entry can be selected in exactly 2 ways. Hence, the total number of all possible matrices of the given type is 2^9.

11. $\begin{bmatrix} \dfrac{1}{2} & \dfrac{9}{2} & \dfrac{25}{2} \\ 0 & 2 & 8 \end{bmatrix}$

12. $6, 9, 6$
13. $x = 1, y = 2, z = 3, w = 4$
Hint : $\Rightarrow x - y = -1, 2x + z = 5, 2x - y = 0,$
$3z + w = 13$ and solve find the value of x, y, z, w.

14. Since, $\begin{bmatrix} x+y & 2x+z \\ x-y & 2z+w \end{bmatrix} = \begin{bmatrix} 4 & 7 \\ 0 & 10 \end{bmatrix}$
$\Rightarrow x + y = 4$ ...(i)
$x - y = 0$ ...(ii)
$2x + z = 7$ ...(iii)
and $2z + w = 10$ ...(iv)
On solving these equations, we get
$x = 2, y = 2, z = 3, w = 4$

15. Since the corresponding elements of two equal matrices are equal, therefore
$A = B \Rightarrow 2x + 1 = x + 3, 3y = y^2 + 2$ and $y^2 - 5y = -6$
Now, $2x + 1 = x + 3 \Rightarrow x = 2,$
$3y = y^2 + 2 \Rightarrow y^2 - 3y + 2 = 0 \Rightarrow y = 1, 2$
and $y^2 - 5y = -6 \Rightarrow y^2 - 5y + 6 = 0 \Rightarrow y = 2, 3$
since, $3y = y^2 + 2$ and $y^2 - 5y = -6$
must hold good simultaneously so, we take the common solution of these two equations. Therefore $y = 2$.
Hence, $A = B$ if $x = 2, y = 2$

NCERT Exercise-1

1. (i) The matrix A has 3 rows and 4 columns. The order of the matrix is 3×4.
(ii) There are $3 \times 4 = 12$ elements in the matrix A
(iii) $a_{13} = 19, a_{21} = 35, a_{33} = -5, a_{24} = 12, a_{23} = \dfrac{5}{2}$.

2. (i) $24 = 1 \times 24 = 2 \times 12 = 3 \times 8 = 4 \times 6$
Thus there are 8 matrices having 24 elements their order are $(1 \times 24), (24 \times 1), (2 \times 12), (12 \times 2), (3 \times 8),$
$(8 \times 3), (4 \times 6), (6 \times 4)$.
(ii) $13 = 1 \times 13$
There are 2 matrices of 13 elements of order (1×13) and (13×1).

3. We know that if a matrix is of order m×n, it has mn elements.
$\Rightarrow 18 = 1 \times 18 = 2 \times 9 = 3 \times 6$
Thus, all possible ordered pairs of the matrix having 18 elements are:
$(1, 18), (18, 1), (2, 9), (9, 2), (3, 6), (6, 3)$
If it has 5 elements, then possible order are: $(1, 5), (5, 1)$

4. $A = [a_{ij}]_{2\times 2} = \begin{bmatrix} a_{11} & a_{12} \\ a_{21} & a_{22} \end{bmatrix}$

(i) $a_{ij} = \dfrac{(i+j)^2}{2}$

$\therefore \quad a_{11} = \dfrac{(1+1)^2}{2} = 2 \; ; \; a_{12} = \dfrac{9}{2}$
Similarly,
$a_{21} = \dfrac{9}{2} \; ; \; a_{22} = 8$

$\therefore \quad A = \begin{bmatrix} 2 & \dfrac{9}{2} \\ \dfrac{9}{2} & 8 \end{bmatrix}$

(ii) $a_{ij} = \dfrac{i}{j}$

$\therefore \quad a_{11} = \dfrac{1}{1} = 1 \; ; \; a_{12} = \dfrac{1}{2}$
$a_{21} = \dfrac{2}{2} = 1 \; ; \; a_{22} = \dfrac{2}{2} = 1$

$\therefore \quad A = \begin{bmatrix} 1 & \dfrac{1}{2} \\ 2 & 1 \end{bmatrix}$.

(iii) We have $a_{ij} = \dfrac{(i+2j)^2}{2}$

$i = 1, j = 1, \quad a_{11} = \dfrac{(1+2)^2}{2} = \dfrac{9}{2}$
Similarly,
$a_{12} = \dfrac{25}{2} \; ; \; a_{21} = \dfrac{16}{2} = 8 \; ; \; a_{22} = \dfrac{36}{2} = 18$

$\therefore \quad A = \begin{bmatrix} \dfrac{9}{2} & \dfrac{25}{2} \\ 8 & 18 \end{bmatrix}$.

5. $A = [a_{ij}]_{3\times 4} = \begin{bmatrix} a_{11} & a_{12} & a_{13} & a_{14} \\ a_{21} & a_{22} & a_{23} & a_{24} \\ a_{31} & a_{32} & a_{33} & a_{34} \end{bmatrix}$

(i) $a_{ij} = \dfrac{1}{2}|-3i + j|$

$a_{11} = \dfrac{1}{2}|-3 \times 1 + 1| = \dfrac{1}{2}|-2| = 1$

$$a_{12} = \frac{1}{2}|-3 \times 1 + 2| = \frac{1}{2}|-1| = \frac{1}{2}$$

Similarly,

$$a_{13} = 0, \quad a_{14} = \frac{1}{2}$$

$$a_{21} = \frac{5}{2}, \quad a_{22} = 2$$

$$a_{23} = \frac{3}{2}, \quad a_{24} = 1$$

$$a_{31} = 4, \quad a_{32} = \frac{7}{2}$$

$$a_{33} = 3, \quad a_{34} = \frac{5}{2}$$

$$\therefore \quad A = \begin{bmatrix} 1 & \frac{1}{2} & 0 & \frac{1}{2} \\ \frac{5}{2} & 2 & \frac{3}{2} & 1 \\ 4 & \frac{7}{2} & 3 & \frac{5}{2} \end{bmatrix}$$

(ii) $a_{ij} = 2i - j$

$$a_{11} = 2 \times 1 - 1 = 1$$
$$a_{12} = 2 \times 1 - 2 = 0$$

Similarly,

$$a_{13} = -1, \quad a_{14} = -2$$
$$a_{21} = 3, \quad a_{22} = 2$$
$$a_{23} = 1, \quad a_{24} = 0$$
$$a_{31} = 5, \quad a_{32} = 4$$
$$a_{33} = 3, \quad a_{34} = 2$$

Hence $A = \begin{bmatrix} 1 & 0 & -1 & -2 \\ 3 & 2 & 1 & 0 \\ 5 & 4 & 3 & 2 \end{bmatrix}$.

6. (i) $\begin{bmatrix} 4 & 3 \\ x & 5 \end{bmatrix} = \begin{bmatrix} y & z \\ 1 & 5 \end{bmatrix}$

Clearly $x = 1, y = 4, z = 3$.

(ii) $\begin{bmatrix} x+y & 2 \\ 5+z & xy \end{bmatrix} = \begin{bmatrix} 6 & 2 \\ 5 & 8 \end{bmatrix}$

Now $5 + z = 5 \Rightarrow z = 0$

Now $x + y = 6$ and $xy = 8$

$$\therefore \quad y = 6 - x \text{ and } x(6-x) = 8$$
$$6x - x^2 = 8$$
$$x^2 - 6x + 8 = 0$$
$$(x-4)(x-2) = 0 \Rightarrow x = 2, 4$$

When $x = 2, \therefore y = 6 - 2 = 4$

and when $x = 4, y = 6 - 4 = 2$

Hence $x = 2, y = 4, z = 0$ or $x = 4, y = 2, z = 0$.

(iii) Equating the corresponding elements.

$$\Rightarrow \quad x + y + z = 9 \qquad \text{...(i)}$$
$$x + z = 5 \qquad \text{...(ii)}$$
$$y + z = 7 \qquad \text{...(iii)}$$

Adding eqs. (ii) & (iii)

$$x + y + 2z = 12$$
$$\Rightarrow (x + y + z) + z = 12,$$
$$9 + z = 12 \qquad \text{(from equ (i))}$$
$$z = 3 \quad x + z = 5 \Rightarrow x + 3 = 5 \Rightarrow x = 2$$

and $y + z = 7 \Rightarrow y + 3 = 7 \Rightarrow y = 4$

$$\Rightarrow \quad x = 2, y = 4 \text{ and } z = 3$$

7. $\begin{bmatrix} a-b & 2a+c \\ 2a-b & 3c+d \end{bmatrix} = \begin{bmatrix} -1 & 5 \\ 0 & 13 \end{bmatrix}$

Now $a - b = -1$

$$\begin{array}{r} 2a - b = 0 \\ \underline{-\quad+\quad-} \\ -a = -1 \end{array} \qquad \text{(On subtraction)}$$

$$\Rightarrow a = 1$$
$$\therefore a - b = -1$$
$$\Rightarrow 1 - b = -1 \Rightarrow b = 2$$

Again $2a + c = 5$

$$\Rightarrow c = 3$$

Also $3c + d = 13 \Rightarrow d = 4$

Hence, $a = 1, b = 2, c = 3, d = 4$.

8. For a square matrix $m = n$.

Thus option (c) $m = n$, is correct.

9. Let $A = \begin{bmatrix} 3x+7 & 5 \\ y+1 & 2-3x \end{bmatrix} = \begin{bmatrix} 0 & y-2 \\ 8 & 4 \end{bmatrix}$

On comparing, $3x + 7 = 0 \Rightarrow x = -7/3$

and $2 - 3x = 4 \Rightarrow x = -2/3$

Since value of x is not unique, so it is not possible to find.

10. There are 3×3 matrix or 9 entries in matrix each place can be filled with 0 or 1

$$\therefore \quad 9 \text{ places can be filled in } 2^9 = 512 \text{ ways}$$

Number of such matrices $= 512$

Option (d) is correct.

Practice Exercise-2 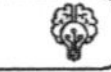

1.	(a)	2.	(a)	3.	(a)	4.	(c)

5. (b)   6. (d)   7. (b)

8. (i) (d)   (ii) (a)   (iii) (a)

(iv) (b) $262 \times (1 + 0.02) = 267.24$ (v) (b)

9. $m \times n$

10. No value of α satisfies this.

11. $\delta = \alpha$

12. We have

$$A^2 = \begin{bmatrix} \alpha & 0 \\ 1 & 1 \end{bmatrix}\begin{bmatrix} \alpha & 0 \\ 1 & 1 \end{bmatrix} = \begin{bmatrix} \alpha^2 & 0 \\ \alpha+1 & 1 \end{bmatrix} = \begin{bmatrix} 9 & a \\ b & c \end{bmatrix}$$

$\Rightarrow$ we get $\alpha^2 = 9 \Rightarrow \alpha = \pm 3$
and $a = 0, c = 1, b = \alpha + 1 = 3 + 1 = 4$ or $b = -3 + 1 = -2$
So $a + b + c = (0 + 4 + 1) = 5$ or $(0 - 2 + 1) = -1$

13. We have

$$A^2 = \begin{bmatrix} \alpha & \beta \\ \gamma & -\alpha \end{bmatrix}\begin{bmatrix} \alpha & \beta \\ \gamma & -\alpha \end{bmatrix} = \begin{bmatrix} \alpha^2 + \beta\gamma & \alpha\beta - \alpha\beta \\ \alpha\gamma - \alpha\gamma & \beta\gamma + \alpha^2 \end{bmatrix}$$

Thus $A^2 = I \Rightarrow \alpha^2 + \beta\gamma = 1$ or $1 - \alpha^2 - \beta\gamma = 0$.

14. We have $\begin{bmatrix} 1 \\ 2 \\ -1 \end{bmatrix}[1 \ -2 \ -1] = \begin{bmatrix} 1 & -2 & -1 \\ 2 & -4 & -2 \\ -1 & 2 & 1 \end{bmatrix}$

15. $\because \quad I = \begin{bmatrix} 1 & 0 \\ 0 & 1 \end{bmatrix}$

$\therefore \quad (A - 2I) = \begin{bmatrix} 2 & 2 \\ -1 & -1 \end{bmatrix}$; and $(A - 3I) = \begin{bmatrix} 1 & 2 \\ -1 & -2 \end{bmatrix}$

Consequently, $(A - 2I)(A - 3I)$

$$= \begin{bmatrix} 2 & 2 \\ -1 & -1 \end{bmatrix}\begin{bmatrix} 1 & 2 \\ -1 & -2 \end{bmatrix} = \begin{bmatrix} 0 & 0 \\ 0 & 0 \end{bmatrix} = O$$

16. Le A be an $m \times n$ matrix. Since $A + B$ is defined, therefore B is also an $m \times n$ matrix. Further since AB exists, therefore the number of columns in A is same as the number of rows in B i.e. $n = m$.
Hence, A and B are square matrices of the same order.

17. Given $AB = A$, $\therefore$ $B = I$
$BA = B$, $\therefore A = I$
Now, $A^3 - B^3 = (I)^3 - (I)^3 = O$.

18. We have

$$A^2 = \begin{bmatrix} \omega & 0 \\ 0 & \omega \end{bmatrix}\begin{bmatrix} \omega & 0 \\ 0 & \omega \end{bmatrix} = \begin{bmatrix} \omega^2 & 0 \\ 0 & \omega^2 \end{bmatrix} \text{ and}$$

$$A^3 = A^2 A = \begin{bmatrix} \omega^2 & 0 \\ 0 & \omega^2 \end{bmatrix}\begin{bmatrix} \omega & 0 \\ 0 & \omega^2 \end{bmatrix} = \begin{bmatrix} \omega^3 & 0 \\ 0 & \omega^3 \end{bmatrix}$$

$$= \begin{bmatrix} 1 & 0 \\ 0 & 1 \end{bmatrix} = I [\because \omega^3 = 1]$$

Now, $A^{100} = A^{99} A = (A^3)^{33} A = I^{33} A = A$.

19. Product of the two given matrices is

$$\begin{bmatrix} 5x & 0 & 0 \\ 0 & 1 & 0 \\ 0 & 10x-2 & 5x \end{bmatrix} = \begin{bmatrix} 1 & 0 & 0 \\ 0 & 1 & 0 \\ 0 & 0 & 1 \end{bmatrix}$$

if and only if $x = 1/5$.

20. **Hint:** $[1 \ \ x \ \ 1]\begin{bmatrix} 1 & 2 & 3 \\ 4 & 5 & 6 \\ 3 & 2 & 5 \end{bmatrix}\begin{bmatrix} 1 \\ -2 \\ 3 \end{bmatrix} = 0$

$\Rightarrow [1 \ \ x \ \ 1]\begin{bmatrix} 1-4+9 \\ 4-10+18 \\ 3-4+15 \end{bmatrix} = 0$

$\Rightarrow [1 \ \ x \ \ 1]\begin{bmatrix} 6 \\ 12 \\ 14 \end{bmatrix} = 0$

$\Rightarrow [1.6 + x.12 + 1.14] = 0$
$\Rightarrow [6 + 12x + 14] = 0$
$\Rightarrow 12x + 20 = 0$
$\Rightarrow x = \dfrac{-20}{12} = \dfrac{-5}{3}$

21. Here, we have

$$A = \begin{array}{c} P \\ Q \end{array}\begin{bmatrix} 3 & 3 & 12 \\ 2 & 2 & 4 \end{bmatrix} , B = \begin{bmatrix} 2400 & 60 \\ 2000 & 40 \\ 1400 & 35 \end{bmatrix}$$

(columns of A labelled Men, Women, Children; columns of B labelled Calories, Proteins)

$$AB = \begin{bmatrix} 3 & 3 & 12 \\ 2 & 2 & 4 \end{bmatrix}\begin{bmatrix} 2400 & 60 \\ 2000 & 40 \\ 1400 & 35 \end{bmatrix}$$

$$= \begin{bmatrix} 3 \times 2400 + 3 \times 2000 + 12 \times 1400 & 3 \times 60 + 3 \times 40 + 12 \times 35 \\ 2 \times 2400 + 2 \times 2000 + 4 \times 1400 & 2 \times 60 + 2 \times 40 + 4 \times 35 \end{bmatrix}$$

$$= \begin{bmatrix} 7200+6000+16800 & 180+120+420 \\ 4800+4000+5600 & 120+80+140 \end{bmatrix}$$

$$= \begin{array}{c} P \\ Q \end{array}\begin{bmatrix} 30000 & 720 \\ 14400 & 340 \end{bmatrix}$$

(columns labelled Calories, Proteins)

Thus, the total requirement of calories and proteins for family P are 30000 calories and 720 g respectively and for family Q are 14400 calories and 340 g respectively.

22. $A^2 = \begin{bmatrix} 1 & 0 & 0 \\ 0 & 1 & 0 \\ a & b & -1 \end{bmatrix}\begin{bmatrix} 1 & 0 & 0 \\ 0 & 1 & 0 \\ a & b & -1 \end{bmatrix} = \begin{bmatrix} 1 & 0 & 0 \\ 0 & 1 & 0 \\ 0 & 0 & 1 \end{bmatrix}$

$A^2 = A^4 = A^6 = I_3 \Rightarrow A^2 + 2A^4 + 4A^6$

$$= \begin{bmatrix} 1 & 0 & 0 \\ 0 & 1 & 0 \\ 0 & 0 & 1 \end{bmatrix} + \begin{bmatrix} 2 & 0 & 0 \\ 0 & 2 & 0 \\ 0 & 0 & 2 \end{bmatrix} + \begin{bmatrix} 4 & 0 & 0 \\ 0 & 4 & 0 \\ 0 & 0 & 4 \end{bmatrix}$$

$$= \begin{bmatrix} 7 & 0 & 0 \\ 0 & 7 & 0 \\ 0 & 0 & 7 \end{bmatrix}$$

NCERT Exercise-2

1. (i) $A + B = \begin{bmatrix} 2 & 4 \\ 3 & 2 \end{bmatrix} + \begin{bmatrix} 1 & 3 \\ -2 & 5 \end{bmatrix} = \begin{bmatrix} 3 & 7 \\ 1 & 7 \end{bmatrix}$

(ii) $A - B = \begin{bmatrix} 2 & 4 \\ 3 & 2 \end{bmatrix} - \begin{bmatrix} 1 & 3 \\ -2 & 5 \end{bmatrix} = \begin{bmatrix} 1 & 1 \\ 5 & -3 \end{bmatrix}$

(iii) $3A - C = 3\begin{bmatrix} 2 & 4 \\ 3 & 2 \end{bmatrix} - \begin{bmatrix} -2 & 5 \\ 3 & 4 \end{bmatrix} = \begin{bmatrix} 8 & 7 \\ 6 & 2 \end{bmatrix}$

(iv) $AB = \begin{bmatrix} 2 & 4 \\ 3 & 2 \end{bmatrix}\begin{bmatrix} 1 & 3 \\ -2 & 5 \end{bmatrix}$

$= \begin{bmatrix} 2-8 & 6+20 \\ 3-4 & 9+10 \end{bmatrix} = \begin{bmatrix} -6 & 26 \\ -1 & 19 \end{bmatrix}$

(v) $BA = \begin{bmatrix} 1 & 3 \\ -2 & 5 \end{bmatrix}\begin{bmatrix} 2 & 4 \\ 3 & 2 \end{bmatrix} = \begin{bmatrix} 11 & 10 \\ 11 & 2 \end{bmatrix}$

2. (i) $\begin{bmatrix} a & b \\ -b & a \end{bmatrix} + \begin{bmatrix} a & b \\ b & a \end{bmatrix} = \begin{bmatrix} 2a & 2b \\ 0 & 2a \end{bmatrix}$

(ii) $\begin{bmatrix} a^2+b^2 & b^2+c^2 \\ a^2+c^2 & a^2+b^2 \end{bmatrix} + \begin{bmatrix} 2ab & 2bc \\ -2ac & -2ab \end{bmatrix}$

$= \begin{bmatrix} a^2+b^2+2ab & b^2+c^2+2bc \\ a^2+c^2-2ac & a^2+b^2-2ab \end{bmatrix}$

$= \begin{bmatrix} (a+b)^2 & (b+c)^2 \\ (a-c)^2 & (a-b)^2 \end{bmatrix}$

(iii) We have

$\begin{bmatrix} -1+12 & 4+7 & -6+6 \\ 8+8 & 5+0 & 16+5 \\ 2+3 & 8+2 & 5+4 \end{bmatrix} = \begin{bmatrix} 11 & 11 & 0 \\ 16 & 5 & 21 \\ 5 & 10 & 9 \end{bmatrix}$

(iv) $\begin{bmatrix} \cos^2 x & \sin^2 x \\ \sin^2 x & \cos^2 x \end{bmatrix} + \begin{bmatrix} \sin^2 x & \cos^2 x \\ \cos^2 x & \sin^2 x \end{bmatrix}$

$= \begin{bmatrix} \cos^2 x + \sin^2 x & \sin^2 x + \cos^2 x \\ \sin^2 x + \cos^2 x & \cos^2 x + \sin^2 x \end{bmatrix} = \begin{bmatrix} 1 & 1 \\ 1 & 1 \end{bmatrix}$

3. (i) $\begin{bmatrix} a & b \\ -b & a \end{bmatrix}\begin{bmatrix} a & -b \\ b & a \end{bmatrix} = \begin{bmatrix} a^2+b^2 & 0 \\ 0 & b^2+a^2 \end{bmatrix}.$

(ii) $\begin{bmatrix} 1 \\ 2 \\ 3 \end{bmatrix}\begin{bmatrix} 2 & 3 & 4 \end{bmatrix} = \begin{bmatrix} 1\times2 & 1\times3 & 1\times4 \\ 2\times2 & 2\times3 & 2\times4 \\ 3\times2 & 3\times3 & 3\times4 \end{bmatrix}$

$= \begin{bmatrix} 2 & 3 & 4 \\ 4 & 6 & 8 \\ 6 & 9 & 12 \end{bmatrix}$

(iii) $\begin{bmatrix} 1 & -2 \\ 2 & 3 \end{bmatrix}\begin{bmatrix} 1 & 2 & 3 \\ 2 & 3 & 1 \end{bmatrix} = \begin{bmatrix} -3 & -4 & 1 \\ 8 & 13 & 9 \end{bmatrix}$

(iv) $\begin{bmatrix} 2 & 3 & 4 \\ 3 & 4 & 5 \\ 4 & 5 & 6 \end{bmatrix}\begin{bmatrix} 1 & -3 & 5 \\ 0 & 2 & 4 \\ 3 & 0 & 5 \end{bmatrix} = \begin{bmatrix} 14 & 0 & 42 \\ 18 & -1 & 56 \\ 22 & -2 & 70 \end{bmatrix}$

(v) $\begin{bmatrix} 2 & 1 \\ 3 & 2 \\ -1 & 1 \end{bmatrix}\begin{bmatrix} 1 & 0 & 1 \\ -1 & 2 & 1 \end{bmatrix}$

$= \begin{bmatrix} 2\times1+1\times(-1) & 2\times0+1\times2 & 2\times1+1\times1 \\ 3\times1+2\times(-1) & 3\times0+2\times2 & 3\times1+2\times1 \\ -1\times1+1\times(-1) & -1\times0+1\times(2) & -1\times1+1\times1 \end{bmatrix}$

$= \begin{bmatrix} 2-1 & 2 & 2+1 \\ 3-2 & 4 & 3+2 \\ -1-1 & 2 & -1+2 \end{bmatrix} = \begin{bmatrix} 1 & 2 & 3 \\ 1 & 4 & 5 \\ -2 & 2 & 0 \end{bmatrix}$

(vi) $\begin{bmatrix} 3 & -1 & 3 \\ -1 & 0 & 2 \end{bmatrix}\begin{bmatrix} 2 & -3 \\ 1 & 0 \\ 3 & 1 \end{bmatrix}$

$= \begin{bmatrix} 3\times2+(-1)\times1+3\times3 & 3\times(-3)+(-1)\times0+3\times1 \\ -1\times2+0\times1+2\times3 & -1\times(-3)+0\times0+2\times1 \end{bmatrix}$

$= \begin{bmatrix} 14 & -6 \\ 4 & 5 \end{bmatrix}.$

4. $A+B = \begin{bmatrix} 4 & 1 & -1 \\ 9 & 2 & 7 \\ 3 & -1 & 4 \end{bmatrix}$ ...(i)

$B-C = \begin{bmatrix} -1 & -2 & 0 \\ 4 & -1 & 3 \\ 1 & 2 & 0 \end{bmatrix}$ ...(ii)

L.H.S. $A+(B-C)$ putting the value of $(B-C)$ from (ii)

$\begin{bmatrix} 1 & 2 & -3 \\ 5 & 0 & 2 \\ 1 & -1 & 1 \end{bmatrix} + \begin{bmatrix} -1 & -2 & 0 \\ 4 & -1 & 3 \\ 1 & 2 & 0 \end{bmatrix} = \begin{bmatrix} 0 & 0 & -3 \\ 9 & -1 & 5 \\ 2 & 1 & 1 \end{bmatrix}$ ...(iii)

R.H.S : $(A+B)-C$ putting the value of $(A+B)$ from (i)

$\begin{bmatrix} 4 & 1 & -1 \\ 9 & 2 & 7 \\ 3 & -1 & 4 \end{bmatrix} - \begin{bmatrix} 4 & 1 & 2 \\ 0 & 3 & 2 \\ 1 & -2 & 3 \end{bmatrix} = \begin{bmatrix} 0 & 0 & -3 \\ 9 & -1 & 5 \\ 2 & 1 & 1 \end{bmatrix}$ ...(iv)

from equ (iii) & (iv) L.H.S. = R.H.S.

$\Rightarrow \quad A+(B-C)=(A+B)-C.$

5. $3A-5B = 3\begin{bmatrix} \dfrac{2}{3} & 1 & \dfrac{5}{3} \\ \dfrac{1}{3} & \dfrac{2}{3} & \dfrac{4}{3} \\ \dfrac{7}{3} & 2 & \dfrac{2}{3} \end{bmatrix} - 5\begin{bmatrix} \dfrac{2}{5} & \dfrac{3}{5} & 1 \\ \dfrac{1}{5} & \dfrac{2}{5} & \dfrac{4}{5} \\ \dfrac{7}{5} & \dfrac{6}{5} & \dfrac{2}{5} \end{bmatrix}$

$= \begin{bmatrix} 2 & 3 & 5 \\ 1 & 2 & 4 \\ 7 & 6 & 2 \end{bmatrix} - \begin{bmatrix} 2 & 3 & 5 \\ 1 & 2 & 4 \\ 7 & 6 & 2 \end{bmatrix} = \begin{bmatrix} 0 & 0 & 0 \\ 0 & 0 & 0 \\ 0 & 0 & 0 \end{bmatrix}.$

6. $\cos\theta \begin{bmatrix} \cos\theta & \sin\theta \\ -\sin\theta & \cos\theta \end{bmatrix} + \sin\theta \begin{bmatrix} \sin\theta & -\cos\theta \\ \cos\theta & \sin\theta \end{bmatrix}.$

$= \begin{bmatrix} \cos^2\theta & \sin\theta\cos\theta \\ -\sin\theta\cos\theta & \cos^2\theta \end{bmatrix} + \begin{bmatrix} \sin^2\theta & -\cos\theta\sin\theta \\ \cos\theta\sin\theta & \sin^2\theta \end{bmatrix}$

$= \begin{bmatrix} \cos^2\theta+\sin^2\theta & \sin\theta\cos\theta-\sin\theta\cos\theta \\ -\sin\theta\cos\theta+\sin\theta\cos\theta & \cos^2\theta+\sin^2\theta \end{bmatrix}$

$= \begin{bmatrix} 1 & 0 \\ 0 & 1 \end{bmatrix}.$

7. (i) $X+Y = \begin{bmatrix} 7 & 0 \\ 2 & 5 \end{bmatrix}, \; X-Y = \begin{bmatrix} 3 & 0 \\ 0 & 3 \end{bmatrix}$

$\therefore \quad (X+Y)+(X-Y) = \begin{bmatrix} 7 & 0 \\ 2 & 5 \end{bmatrix} + \begin{bmatrix} 3 & 0 \\ 0 & 3 \end{bmatrix}$

$\Rightarrow 2X = \begin{bmatrix} 10 & 0 \\ 2 & 8 \end{bmatrix} \Rightarrow X = \begin{bmatrix} 5 & 0 \\ 1 & 4 \end{bmatrix}$

Now as $X+Y = \begin{bmatrix} 7 & 0 \\ 2 & 5 \end{bmatrix} \Rightarrow Y = \begin{bmatrix} 2 & 0 \\ 1 & 1 \end{bmatrix}$

Hence, $X = \begin{bmatrix} 5 & 0 \\ 1 & 4 \end{bmatrix}$ and $Y = \begin{bmatrix} 2 & 0 \\ 1 & 1 \end{bmatrix}.$

(ii) $2X+3Y = \begin{bmatrix} 2 & 3 \\ 4 & 0 \end{bmatrix}$ ......(i)

and $3X+2Y = \begin{bmatrix} 2 & -2 \\ 1 & 5 \end{bmatrix}$ ......(ii)

From (i) and (ii) and on addition,

$X+Y = \dfrac{1}{5}\begin{bmatrix} 4 & 1 \\ 3 & 5 \end{bmatrix}$ ......(iii)

Again on subtraction from (i) and (ii)

$(3X+2Y)-(2X+3Y) = -\begin{bmatrix} 2 & 3 \\ 4 & 0 \end{bmatrix} + \begin{bmatrix} 2 & -2 \\ -1 & 5 \end{bmatrix}$

$X-Y = \begin{bmatrix} 0 & 3 \\ -5 & 5 \end{bmatrix}$ ......(iv)

Adding (iii) and (iv), we get

$2X = \dfrac{1}{5}\begin{bmatrix} 4 & 1 \\ 3 & 5 \end{bmatrix} + \begin{bmatrix} 0 & -5 \\ -5 & 5 \end{bmatrix}$

$X = \begin{bmatrix} \dfrac{2}{5} & -\dfrac{12}{5} \\ \dfrac{-11}{5} & 3 \end{bmatrix}$

Now $X+Y = \dfrac{1}{5}\begin{bmatrix} 4 & 1 \\ 3 & 5 \end{bmatrix}$

$\Rightarrow Y = \begin{bmatrix} \dfrac{2}{5} & \dfrac{13}{5} \\ \dfrac{14}{5} & -2 \end{bmatrix}$

Hence, $X = \begin{bmatrix} \dfrac{2}{5} & -\dfrac{12}{5} \\ \dfrac{-11}{5} & 3 \end{bmatrix}, Y = \begin{bmatrix} \dfrac{2}{5} & \dfrac{13}{5} \\ \dfrac{14}{5} & -2 \end{bmatrix}$

8. $Y = \begin{bmatrix} 3 & 2 \\ 1 & 4 \end{bmatrix}$

We are given that

$2X+Y = \begin{bmatrix} 1 & 0 \\ -3 & 2 \end{bmatrix} \therefore \; 2X + \begin{bmatrix} 3 & 2 \\ 1 & 4 \end{bmatrix} = \begin{bmatrix} 1 & 0 \\ -3 & 2 \end{bmatrix}$

$\Rightarrow 2X = \begin{bmatrix} -2 & -2 \\ -4 & -2 \end{bmatrix}$

$\Rightarrow X = \dfrac{1}{2}\begin{bmatrix} -2 & -2 \\ -4 & -2 \end{bmatrix}.$ Hence, $X = \begin{bmatrix} -1 & -1 \\ -2 & -1 \end{bmatrix}.$

9. $2\begin{bmatrix} 1 & 3 \\ 0 & x \end{bmatrix} + \begin{bmatrix} y & 0 \\ 1 & 2 \end{bmatrix} = \begin{bmatrix} 5 & 6 \\ 1 & 8 \end{bmatrix}.$

$\Rightarrow \begin{bmatrix} 2+y & 6 \\ 1 & 2x+2 \end{bmatrix} = \begin{bmatrix} 5 & 6 \\ 1 & 8 \end{bmatrix}$

$\Rightarrow 2+y = 5$ and $2x+2 = 8$

$\Rightarrow y = 3$ and $x = 3$

Hence, $x = 3$ and $y = 3$.

10. $2\begin{bmatrix} x & z \\ y & t \end{bmatrix} + 3\begin{bmatrix} 1 & -1 \\ 0 & 2 \end{bmatrix} = 3\begin{bmatrix} 3 & 5 \\ 4 & 6 \end{bmatrix}.$

$\Rightarrow \begin{bmatrix} 2x+3 & 2z-3 \\ 2y+0 & 2t+6 \end{bmatrix} = \begin{bmatrix} 9 & 15 \\ 12 & 18 \end{bmatrix}$

$\Rightarrow 2x+3 = 9 \qquad\qquad 2y = 12$

$\Rightarrow 2x = 6 \Rightarrow x = 3 \qquad y = 6$

$\Rightarrow 2z-3 = 15 \qquad\qquad 2t+6 = 18$

$\Rightarrow 2z = 18 \Rightarrow z = 9 \qquad 2t = 12 \Rightarrow t = 6$

Hence, $x = 3, y = 6, z = 9, t = 6$.

11. $x\begin{bmatrix} 2 \\ 3 \end{bmatrix} + y\begin{bmatrix} -1 \\ 1 \end{bmatrix} = \begin{bmatrix} 10 \\ 5 \end{bmatrix}$

$\Rightarrow \begin{bmatrix} 2x-y \\ 3x+y \end{bmatrix} = \begin{bmatrix} 10 \\ 5 \end{bmatrix}$

$\Rightarrow 2x-y = 10$

$\quad\;\; 3x+y = 5$

$\rule{3cm}{0.4pt}$

$\qquad 5x = 15 \qquad\qquad$ on addition,

$\qquad\; x = 3$

$\therefore \quad 3\times 3+y = 5$

$\Rightarrow \qquad\qquad y = -4$

Hence, $x = 3$ and $y = -4$.

12. $3\begin{bmatrix} x & y \\ z & w \end{bmatrix} = \begin{bmatrix} x & 6 \\ -1 & 2w \end{bmatrix} + \begin{bmatrix} 4 & x+y \\ z+w & 3 \end{bmatrix}$

$\Rightarrow \begin{bmatrix} 3x & 3y \\ 3z & 3w \end{bmatrix} = \begin{bmatrix} x+4 & 6+x+y \\ -1+z+w & 2w+3 \end{bmatrix}$

$\Rightarrow 3x = x+4 \Rightarrow x = 2$

and $3y = 6+x+y \Rightarrow y = 4$

Also, $\quad 3w = 2w+3 \Rightarrow w = 3$

Again, $\quad 3z = -1 + z + w$

$\Rightarrow \quad 2z = -1 + 3 \Rightarrow 2z = 2 \Rightarrow z = 1$

Hence $x = 2, y = 4, z = 1, w = 3$.

13. $F(x) = \begin{bmatrix} \cos x & -\sin x & 0 \\ \sin x & \cos x & 0 \\ 0 & 0 & 1 \end{bmatrix}$

$\therefore \quad F(y) = \begin{bmatrix} \cos y & -\sin y & 0 \\ \sin y & \cos y & 0 \\ 0 & 0 & 1 \end{bmatrix}$

L.H.S. = $F(x) \cdot F(y)$

$= \begin{bmatrix} \cos x & -\sin x & 0 \\ \sin x & \cos x & 0 \\ 0 & 0 & 1 \end{bmatrix} \cdot \begin{bmatrix} \cos y & -\sin y & 0 \\ \sin y & \cos y & 0 \\ 0 & 0 & 1 \end{bmatrix}$

$= \begin{bmatrix} \cos x \cos y - \sin x \sin y & -\sin y \cos x - \sin x \cos y & 0 \\ \sin x \cos y + \cos x \sin y & -\sin x \sin y + \cos x \cos y & 0 \\ 0 & 0 & 1 \end{bmatrix}$

$= \begin{bmatrix} \cos(x+y) & -\sin(x+y) & 0 \\ \sin(x+y) & \cos(x+y) & 0 \\ 0 & 0 & 1 \end{bmatrix}$

$= F(x+y) = $ R.H.S.

Hence, the result.

14. (i) $\quad$ L.H.S. $= \begin{bmatrix} 5 & -1 \\ 6 & 7 \end{bmatrix}\begin{bmatrix} 2 & 1 \\ 3 & 4 \end{bmatrix} = \begin{bmatrix} 7 & 1 \\ 33 & 34 \end{bmatrix}$

$\quad$ R.H.S. $= \begin{bmatrix} 2 & 1 \\ 3 & 4 \end{bmatrix}\begin{bmatrix} 5 & -1 \\ 6 & 7 \end{bmatrix} = \begin{bmatrix} 16 & 5 \\ 39 & 25 \end{bmatrix}$

Hence, $\quad$ L.H.S. $\ne$ R.H.S.

(ii) $\quad$ L.H.S. $= \begin{bmatrix} 1 & 2 & 3 \\ 0 & 1 & 0 \\ 1 & 1 & 0 \end{bmatrix}\begin{bmatrix} -1 & 1 & 0 \\ 0 & -1 & 1 \\ 2 & 3 & 4 \end{bmatrix}$

$= \begin{bmatrix} 5 & 8 & 14 \\ 0 & -1 & 1 \\ -1 & 0 & 1 \end{bmatrix}$

R.H.S. $= \begin{bmatrix} -1 & 1 & 0 \\ 0 & -1 & 1 \\ 2 & 3 & 4 \end{bmatrix}\begin{bmatrix} 1 & 2 & 3 \\ 0 & 1 & 0 \\ 1 & 1 & 0 \end{bmatrix}$

$= \begin{bmatrix} -1+0+0 & -2+1+0 & -3+0+0 \\ 0-0+1 & 0-1+1 & 0-0+0 \\ 2+0+4 & 4+3+4 & 6+0+0 \end{bmatrix} = \begin{bmatrix} -1 & -1 & -3 \\ 1 & 0 & 0 \\ 6 & 11 & 6 \end{bmatrix}$

Hence, $\quad$ L.H.S. $\ne$ R.H.S.

15. $A^2 - 5A + 6I = \begin{bmatrix} 2 & 0 & 1 \\ 2 & 1 & 3 \\ 1 & -1 & 0 \end{bmatrix}\begin{bmatrix} 2 & 0 & 1 \\ 2 & 1 & 3 \\ 1 & -1 & 0 \end{bmatrix}$

$-5\begin{bmatrix} 2 & 0 & 1 \\ 2 & 1 & 3 \\ 1 & -1 & 0 \end{bmatrix} + 6\begin{bmatrix} 1 & 0 & 0 \\ 0 & 1 & 0 \\ 0 & 0 & 1 \end{bmatrix}$

$= \begin{bmatrix} 5 & -1 & 2 \\ 9 & -2 & 5 \\ 0 & -1 & -2 \end{bmatrix} - \begin{bmatrix} 10 & 0 & 5 \\ 10 & 5 & 15 \\ 5 & -5 & 0 \end{bmatrix} + \begin{bmatrix} 6 & 0 & 0 \\ 0 & 6 & 0 \\ 0 & 0 & 6 \end{bmatrix}$

$= \begin{bmatrix} 1 & -1 & -3 \\ -1 & -1 & -10 \\ -5 & 4 & 4 \end{bmatrix}$ Hence, the result.

16. We have

$A^2 = A \times A = \begin{bmatrix} 1 & 0 & 2 \\ 0 & 2 & 1 \\ 2 & 0 & 3 \end{bmatrix} \times \begin{bmatrix} 1 & 0 & 2 \\ 0 & 2 & 1 \\ 2 & 0 & 3 \end{bmatrix} = \begin{bmatrix} 5 & 0 & 8 \\ 2 & 4 & 5 \\ 8 & 0 & 13 \end{bmatrix}$

$A^3 = A^2 \times A = \begin{bmatrix} 5 & 0 & 8 \\ 2 & 4 & 5 \\ 8 & 0 & 13 \end{bmatrix} \times \begin{bmatrix} 1 & 0 & 2 \\ 0 & 2 & 1 \\ 2 & 0 & 3 \end{bmatrix} = \begin{bmatrix} 21 & 0 & 34 \\ 12 & 8 & 23 \\ 34 & 0 & 55 \end{bmatrix}$

i.e. $A^3 - 6A^2 + 7A + 2I$

$= \begin{bmatrix} 21 & 0 & 34 \\ 12 & 8 & 23 \\ 34 & 0 & 55 \end{bmatrix} - 6\begin{bmatrix} 5 & 0 & 8 \\ 2 & 4 & 5 \\ 8 & 0 & 13 \end{bmatrix} + 7\begin{bmatrix} 1 & 0 & 2 \\ 0 & 2 & 1 \\ 2 & 0 & 3 \end{bmatrix} + \begin{bmatrix} 2 & 0 & 0 \\ 0 & 2 & 0 \\ 0 & 0 & 2 \end{bmatrix}$

$= \begin{bmatrix} 21-30+7+2 & 0-0+0+0 & 34-48+14+0 \\ 12-12+0+0 & 8+24+14+2 & 23-30+7+0 \\ 34-48+14+0 & 0-0+0+0 & 55-78+21+2 \end{bmatrix}$

$= \begin{bmatrix} 0 & 0 & 0 \\ 0 & 0 & 0 \\ 0 & 0 & 0 \end{bmatrix} = 0.$

17. Given : $A = \begin{bmatrix} 3 & -2 \\ 4 & -2 \end{bmatrix}, I = \begin{bmatrix} 1 & 0 \\ 0 & 1 \end{bmatrix}$

Required : To find the value of k.

Now, $\quad A^2 = kA - 2I$

$\Rightarrow \begin{bmatrix} 3 & -2 \\ 4 & -2 \end{bmatrix}\begin{bmatrix} 3 & -2 \\ 4 & -2 \end{bmatrix} = k\begin{bmatrix} 3 & -2 \\ 4 & -2 \end{bmatrix} - 2\begin{bmatrix} 1 & 0 \\ 0 & 1 \end{bmatrix}$

$\Rightarrow \begin{bmatrix} 1 & -2 \\ 4 & -4 \end{bmatrix} = \begin{bmatrix} 3k-2 & -2k \\ 4k & -2k-2 \end{bmatrix}$

$\Rightarrow 3k - 2 = 1 \Rightarrow k = 1$

Hence, $k = 1$.

18. L.H.S. $= I + A = \begin{bmatrix} 1 & 0 \\ 0 & 1 \end{bmatrix} + \begin{bmatrix} 0 & -\tan\dfrac{\alpha}{2} \\ \tan\dfrac{\alpha}{2} & 0 \end{bmatrix}$

$$= \begin{bmatrix} 1 & -\tan\dfrac{\alpha}{2} \\[2mm] \tan\dfrac{\alpha}{2} & 1 \end{bmatrix}$$

Putting $\tan\dfrac{\alpha}{2} = t$, $\cos\alpha = \dfrac{1-\tan^2\dfrac{\alpha}{2}}{1+\tan^2\dfrac{\alpha}{2}}$,

$$\sin\alpha = \dfrac{2\tan\dfrac{\alpha}{2}}{1+\tan^2\dfrac{\alpha}{2}}$$

$$\text{L.H.S.} = (I+A) = \begin{bmatrix} 1 & -t \\ t & 1 \end{bmatrix},$$

$$\text{R.H.S.} = (I-A)\begin{bmatrix} \cos\alpha & -\sin\alpha \\ \sin\alpha & \cos\alpha \end{bmatrix}$$

$$= \left(\begin{bmatrix} 1 & 0 \\ 0 & 1 \end{bmatrix} - \begin{bmatrix} 0 & -\tan\dfrac{\alpha}{2} \\[2mm] \tan\dfrac{\alpha}{2} & 0 \end{bmatrix} \right)$$

$$\begin{bmatrix} \dfrac{1-\tan^2\dfrac{\alpha}{2}}{1+\tan^2\dfrac{\alpha}{2}} & \dfrac{-2\tan\dfrac{\alpha}{2}}{1+\tan^2\dfrac{\alpha}{2}} \\[4mm] \dfrac{2\tan\dfrac{\alpha}{2}}{1+\tan\dfrac{\alpha}{2}} & \dfrac{1-\tan^2\dfrac{\alpha}{2}}{1+\tan^2\dfrac{\alpha}{2}} \end{bmatrix}$$

Since $\begin{bmatrix} 1 & 0 \\ 0 & 1 \end{bmatrix} - \begin{bmatrix} 0 & -t \\ t & 0 \end{bmatrix} = \begin{bmatrix} 1 & t \\ -t & 1 \end{bmatrix}$

$$= \begin{bmatrix} 1 & t \\ -t & 1 \end{bmatrix}\begin{bmatrix} \dfrac{1-t^2}{1+t^2} & \dfrac{-2t}{1+t^2} \\[3mm] \dfrac{2t}{1+t^2} & \dfrac{1-t^2}{1+t^2} \end{bmatrix}$$

$$= \begin{bmatrix} \dfrac{1+t^2}{1+t^2} & \dfrac{-2t+t-t^3}{1+t^2} \\[3mm] \dfrac{-t+t^3+2t}{1+t^2} & \dfrac{1+t^2}{1+t^2} \end{bmatrix}$$

$$= \begin{bmatrix} 1 & \dfrac{-t(1+t^2)}{1+t^2} \\[3mm] \dfrac{t(1+t^2)}{1+t^2} & 1 \end{bmatrix} = \begin{bmatrix} 1 & -t \\ t & 1 \end{bmatrix}$$

$$= \begin{bmatrix} 1 & -\tan\dfrac{\alpha}{2} \\[2mm] \tan\dfrac{\alpha}{2} & 1 \end{bmatrix} = \text{L.H.S.}$$

19. Let ₹ 30,000 be divided into two parts and ₹ x and ₹ (30,000−x)

Let it be represented by 1×2 matrix

[x (30,000−x)]

Rate of interest is 0·05 and 0·07 per rupee.

It is denoted by the matrix R of order 2×1.

$$R = \begin{bmatrix} 0\cdot05 \\ 0\cdot07 \end{bmatrix}$$

(a) $AR = 1800$ $[x\ (30,000-x)]\begin{bmatrix} 0\cdot05 \\ 0\cdot07 \end{bmatrix}$,

$[x \times 0\cdot05 + (30,000-x) \times 0\cdot07] = [1800]$

Multiplying by 100

$$\begin{aligned}
\text{or} \quad 5x + 21,0000 - 7x &= 180000 \\
2x &= 21,0000 - 180000 \\
x &= 15,000 \\
\therefore \quad 30,000 - x &= 30,000 - 15,000 \\
&= 15,000
\end{aligned}$$

Thus the two parts are 15,000 each.

(b) Then the total interest is ₹ 2000

$$[x\ (30,000-x)]\begin{bmatrix} 0\cdot05 \\ 0\cdot07 \end{bmatrix} = [2000]$$

$\Rightarrow [x \times 0\cdot05 + (30,000-x) \times 0\cdot07] = [2000]$

or $\dfrac{5x}{100} + \dfrac{7}{100}(30,000-x) = 2000$

Multiplying by 100

$$\begin{aligned}
5x + 21,000 - 7x &= 200000 \\
2x &= 210000 - 200000 \\
x &= 5000 \\
\therefore \quad 30,000 - x &= 30,000 - 5000 \\
&= 25,000
\end{aligned}$$

∴ Two parts are ₹ 5000 and 25,000.

20. Number of Chemistry books = 10 dozen books
  = 120 books
Number of Physics books = 8 dozen books = 96 books
Number of Economics books = 10 dozen books
  = 120 books

Now $[120\ \ 96\ \ 120]\begin{bmatrix} 80 \\ 60 \\ 40 \end{bmatrix}$

$= 120 \times 80 + 96 \times 60 + 120 \times 40$

$= 9,600 + 5,760 + 4800 = ₹ 20,160$

Hence, total amount received = ₹ 20,160.

Assuming X, Y, Z, W and P are the matrices of order $2 \times n$, $3 \times k$, $2 \times p$, $n \times 3$ and $p \times k$ respectively. Choose the correct answer in exercises 21 and 22.

21. Given : $x_{2 \times n}, y_{3 \times k}, z_{2 \times p}, w_{n \times 3}, P_{p \times k}$

Now $py + wy = P_{p \times k} \times y_{3+k} \times w_{n \times 3} \times y_{3 \times k}$

Clearly, $k = 3$ and $p = n$

Hence, option (a) is correct $p \times 2$.

22. $7X - 5Z = 7X_{2 \times n} - 5X_{2 \times p}$

We can add two matrices if their order is same

∴ $n = p$

∴ Order of $7X - 5Z$ is $2 \times n$.

Hence, option (b) is correct $2 \times n$.

Practice Exercise-3

1. (d)   2. (b)   3. (b)   4. (c)

5. (b)   6. $A' = [a_{ji}]_{n \times m}$ 7. $x = \dfrac{1}{2}$

8. $AB = \begin{bmatrix} 1 \\ -4 \\ 3 \end{bmatrix} \begin{bmatrix} -1 & 2 & 1 \end{bmatrix} = \begin{bmatrix} -1 & 2 & 1 \\ 4 & -8 & -4 \\ -3 & 6 & 3 \end{bmatrix}$

$\therefore (AB)' = \begin{bmatrix} -1 & 4 & -3 \\ 2 & -8 & 6 \\ 1 & -4 & 3 \end{bmatrix}$

9. Now, $C = \dfrac{A - A'}{2} = \dfrac{1}{2}\left\{ \begin{bmatrix} 3 & -4 \\ 1 & -1 \end{bmatrix} \begin{bmatrix} 3 & 1 \\ -4 & -1 \end{bmatrix} \right\}$

$= \dfrac{1}{2}\begin{bmatrix} 0 & -5 \\ 5 & 0 \end{bmatrix} = \begin{bmatrix} 0 & -5/2 \\ 5/2 & 0 \end{bmatrix}$

10. $(X'CX)' = X'CX'' = X'(-C)X = -X'CX$ $[\because C' = -C]$
$\Rightarrow X'CX$ is null matrix.

11. $(A + A^T)^T = A^T + (A^T)^T = A^T + A$
Hence, A is a symmetric matrix.

12. We have,
$A = \begin{bmatrix} 0 & 2y & z \\ x & y & -z \\ x & -y & z \end{bmatrix} \Rightarrow A^T = \begin{bmatrix} 0 & x & x \\ 2y & y & -y \\ z & -z & z \end{bmatrix}$

$\therefore \quad A^T A = I_3$

$\Rightarrow \begin{bmatrix} 0 & x & x \\ 2y & y & -y \\ z & -z & z \end{bmatrix} \begin{bmatrix} 0 & 2y & z \\ x & y & -z \\ x & -y & z \end{bmatrix} = \begin{bmatrix} 1 & 0 & 0 \\ 0 & 1 & 0 \\ 0 & 0 & 1 \end{bmatrix}$

$\Rightarrow \begin{bmatrix} 2x^2 & 0 & 0 \\ 0 & 6y^2 & 0 \\ 0 & 0 & 3z^2 \end{bmatrix} = \begin{bmatrix} 1 & 0 & 0 \\ 0 & 1 & 0 \\ 0 & 0 & 1 \end{bmatrix}$

$\Rightarrow \quad 2x^2 = 1, 6y^2 = 1, 3z^2 = 1$

$\Rightarrow \quad x = \pm\dfrac{1}{\sqrt{2}}, y = \pm\dfrac{1}{\sqrt{6}}, z = \pm\dfrac{1}{\sqrt{3}}$

NCERT Exercise-3

1. (i) Let $A = \begin{bmatrix} 5 \\ \frac{1}{2} \\ -1 \end{bmatrix}$

$\therefore$ Transpose of $A = A' = \begin{bmatrix} 5 & \frac{1}{2} & -1 \end{bmatrix}$

(ii) Let $A = \begin{bmatrix} 1 & -1 \\ 2 & 3 \end{bmatrix}$

$\therefore$ Transpose of $A = A' = \begin{bmatrix} 1 & 2 \\ -1 & 3 \end{bmatrix}$

(iii) Let $A = \begin{bmatrix} -1 & 5 & 6 \\ \sqrt{3} & 5 & 6 \\ 2 & 3 & -1 \end{bmatrix}$

$\therefore$ Transpose of $A = A' = \begin{bmatrix} -1 & \sqrt{3} & 2 \\ 5 & 5 & 3 \\ 6 & 6 & -1 \end{bmatrix}$

2. (i) $A + B = \begin{bmatrix} -1 & 2 & 3 \\ 5 & 7 & 9 \\ -2 & 1 & 1 \end{bmatrix} + \begin{bmatrix} -4 & 1 & -5 \\ 1 & 2 & 0 \\ 1 & 3 & 1 \end{bmatrix}$

$= \begin{bmatrix} -5 & 3 & -2 \\ 6 & 9 & 9 \\ -1 & 4 & 2 \end{bmatrix}$

Now $A' = \begin{bmatrix} -1 & 5 & -2 \\ 2 & 7 & 1 \\ 3 & 9 & 1 \end{bmatrix}$ and $B' = \begin{bmatrix} -4 & 1 & 1 \\ 1 & 2 & 3 \\ -5 & 0 & 1 \end{bmatrix}$

L.H.S. $= (A + B)' = \begin{bmatrix} -5 & 6 & 1 \\ 3 & 9 & 4 \\ -2 & 9 & 2 \end{bmatrix}$

R.H.S. $= A' + B'$

$= \begin{bmatrix} -1 & 5 & -2 \\ 2 & 7 & 1 \\ 3 & 9 & 1 \end{bmatrix} + \begin{bmatrix} -4 & 1 & 1 \\ 1 & 2 & 3 \\ -5 & 0 & 1 \end{bmatrix} = \begin{bmatrix} -5 & 6 & -1 \\ 3 & 9 & 4 \\ -2 & 9 & 2 \end{bmatrix}$

Hence, $(A + B)' = A' + B'$.

(ii) $A - B = \begin{bmatrix} -1 & 2 & 3 \\ 5 & 7 & 9 \\ -2 & 1 & 1 \end{bmatrix} - \begin{bmatrix} -4 & 1 & -5 \\ 1 & 2 & 0 \\ 1 & 3 & 1 \end{bmatrix}$

$= \begin{bmatrix} 3 & 1 & 8 \\ 4 & 5 & 9 \\ -3 & -2 & 0 \end{bmatrix}$

L.H.S. $= (A - B)' = \begin{bmatrix} 3 & 4 & -3 \\ 1 & 5 & -2 \\ 8 & 9 & 0 \end{bmatrix}$

R.H.S. $= A' - B'$

$= \begin{bmatrix} -1 & 5 & -2 \\ 2 & 7 & 1 \\ 3 & 9 & 1 \end{bmatrix} - \begin{bmatrix} -4 & 1 & 1 \\ 1 & 2 & 3 \\ -5 & 0 & 1 \end{bmatrix}$

$= \begin{bmatrix} -1+4 & 5-1 & -2-1 \\ 2-1 & 7-2 & 1-3 \\ 3+5 & 9-0 & 1-1 \end{bmatrix} = \begin{bmatrix} 3 & 4 & -3 \\ 1 & 5 & -2 \\ 8 & 9 & 0 \end{bmatrix}$

Hence, $(A - B)' = A' - B'$.

3. (i) $A' = \begin{bmatrix} 3 & 4 \\ -1 & 1 \\ 0 & 2 \end{bmatrix} \Rightarrow A = \begin{bmatrix} 3 & -1 & 0 \\ 4 & 2 & 1 \end{bmatrix}$

$$A+B=\begin{bmatrix} 3 & -1 & 0 \\ 4 & 2 & 1 \end{bmatrix}+\begin{bmatrix} -1 & 2 & 1 \\ 1 & 2 & 3 \end{bmatrix}$$

$$=\begin{bmatrix} 2 & 1 & 1 \\ 5 & 4 & 4 \end{bmatrix}$$

$$\therefore (A+B)'=\begin{bmatrix} 2 & 1 & 1 \\ 5 & 4 & 4 \end{bmatrix}'=\begin{bmatrix} 2 & 5 \\ 1 & 4 \\ 1 & 4 \end{bmatrix}$$

$$R.H.S=A'+B'=\begin{bmatrix} 3 & 4 \\ -1 & 2 \\ 0 & 1 \end{bmatrix}+\begin{bmatrix} -1 & 2 & 1 \\ 1 & 2 & 3 \end{bmatrix}$$

$$=\begin{bmatrix} 2 & 5 \\ 1 & 4 \\ 1 & 4 \end{bmatrix}=L.H.S.$$

Hence, $(A+B)'=A'+B'$.

(ii) $A'=\begin{bmatrix} 3 & 4 \\ -1 & 2 \\ 0 & 1 \end{bmatrix}$

$$\therefore A=\begin{bmatrix} 3 & -1 & 0 \\ 4 & 2 & 1 \end{bmatrix}; A-B=\begin{bmatrix} 4 & -3 & -1 \\ 3 & 0 & -2 \end{bmatrix}$$

$$L.H.S.=(A-B)'=\begin{bmatrix} 4 & -3 & -1 \\ 3 & 0 & -2 \end{bmatrix}=\begin{bmatrix} 4 & 3 \\ -3 & 0 \\ -1 & -2 \end{bmatrix}$$

$$R.H.S.=A'-B'=\begin{bmatrix} 3 & 4 \\ -1 & 2 \\ 0 & 1 \end{bmatrix}-\begin{bmatrix} -1 & 2 & 1 \\ 1 & 2 & 3 \end{bmatrix}'$$

$$=\begin{bmatrix} 3 & 4 \\ -1 & 2 \\ 0 & 1 \end{bmatrix}-\begin{bmatrix} -1 & 1 \\ 2 & 2 \\ 1 & 3 \end{bmatrix}=\begin{bmatrix} 4 & 3 \\ -3 & 0 \\ -1 & -2 \end{bmatrix}$$

Hence, $(A-B)'=A'-B'$.

4. $A'=\begin{bmatrix} -2 & 3 \\ 1 & 2 \end{bmatrix}\Rightarrow A=\begin{bmatrix} -2 & 1 \\ 3 & 2 \end{bmatrix}$

Also $B=\begin{bmatrix} -1 & 0 \\ 1 & 2 \end{bmatrix}$

Now $A+2B=\begin{bmatrix} -2 & 1 \\ 3 & 2 \end{bmatrix}+2\begin{bmatrix} -1 & 0 \\ 1 & 2 \end{bmatrix}$

$$=\begin{bmatrix} -2 & 1 \\ 3 & 2 \end{bmatrix}+\begin{bmatrix} -2 & 0 \\ 2 & 4 \end{bmatrix}=\begin{bmatrix} 4 & 1 \\ 5 & 6 \end{bmatrix}$$

Hence, $(A+2B)'=\begin{bmatrix} -4 & 5 \\ 1 & 6 \end{bmatrix}$.

5. (i) $A=\begin{bmatrix} 1 \\ -4 \\ 3 \end{bmatrix}\Rightarrow A'=[1 \ -4 \ 3]$

and $B=[-1 \ 2 \ 1]\Rightarrow B'=\begin{bmatrix} -1 \\ 2 \\ 1 \end{bmatrix}$

$$AB=\begin{bmatrix} 1 \\ -4 \\ 3 \end{bmatrix}[-1 \ 2 \ 1]$$

$$=\begin{bmatrix} 1\times(-1) & 1(2) & 1(1) \\ -4(-1) & (-4)(2) & (-4)(1) \\ 3(-1) & 3(2) & +3\times1 \end{bmatrix}=\begin{bmatrix} -1 & 2 & 1 \\ 4 & -8 & -4 \\ -3 & 6 & 3 \end{bmatrix}$$

$$L.H.S.=(AB)'=\begin{bmatrix} -1 & 4 & -3 \\ 2 & -8 & 6 \\ 1 & -4 & 3 \end{bmatrix}$$

$$R.H.S.=B'A'=\begin{bmatrix} -1 \\ 2 \\ 1 \end{bmatrix}[1 \ -4 \ 3]$$

$$=\begin{bmatrix} -1\times1 & -1\times(-4) & -1\times3 \\ 2\times1 & 2\times(-4) & 2\times3 \\ 1\times1 & 1\times(-4) & 1\times3 \end{bmatrix}=\begin{bmatrix} -1 & 4 & -3 \\ 2 & -8 & 6 \\ 1 & -4 & 3 \end{bmatrix}$$

Hence, $(AB)'=B'A'$.

(ii) $A=\begin{bmatrix} 0 \\ 1 \\ 2 \end{bmatrix}, B=[1 \ 5 \ 7]$

$\Rightarrow A'=[0 \ 1 \ 2]$ and $B'=\begin{bmatrix} 1 \\ 5 \\ 7 \end{bmatrix}$

Now $AB=\begin{bmatrix} 0 \\ 1 \\ 2 \end{bmatrix}[1 \ 5 \ 7]=\begin{bmatrix} 0 & 0 & 0 \\ 1 & 5 & 7 \\ 2 & 10 & 14 \end{bmatrix}$

$$\therefore L.H.S.=(AB)'=\begin{bmatrix} 0 & 1 & 2 \\ 0 & 5 & 10 \\ 0 & 7 & 14 \end{bmatrix}$$

$$R.H.S=B'A'=\begin{bmatrix} 1 \\ 5 \\ 7 \end{bmatrix}[0 \ 1 \ 2]$$

$$=\begin{bmatrix} 1\times0 & 1\times1 & 1\times2 \\ 5\times0 & 5\times1 & 5\times2 \\ 7\times0 & 7\times1 & 7\times2 \end{bmatrix}=\begin{bmatrix} 0 & 1 & 2 \\ 0 & 5 & 10 \\ 0 & 7 & 14 \end{bmatrix}$$

Hence, $(AB)'=B'A'$

6. (i) $A=\begin{bmatrix} \sin\alpha & \cos\alpha \\ -\sin\alpha & \cos\alpha \end{bmatrix}\Rightarrow A'=\begin{bmatrix} \cos\alpha & -\sin\alpha \\ \sin\alpha & \cos\alpha \end{bmatrix}$

$$L.H.S.=A'A=\begin{bmatrix} \cos\alpha & -\sin\alpha \\ \sin\alpha & \cos\alpha \end{bmatrix}\begin{bmatrix} \cos\alpha & \sin\alpha \\ -\sin\alpha & \cos\alpha \end{bmatrix}$$

$$=\begin{bmatrix} \cos^2\alpha+\sin^2\alpha & \cos\alpha\sin\alpha-\sin\alpha\cos\alpha \\ \sin\alpha\cos\alpha-\cos\alpha\sin\alpha & \sin^2\alpha+\cos^2\alpha \end{bmatrix}$$

$$= \begin{bmatrix} 1 & 0 \\ 0 & 1 \end{bmatrix} = 1$$

Hence, A'A = I.

(ii) $A' = \begin{bmatrix} \sin\alpha & -\cos\alpha \\ \cos\alpha & \sin\alpha \end{bmatrix}$

LHS = A'A

$$= \begin{bmatrix} \sin^2\alpha + \cos^2\alpha & \sin\alpha\cos\alpha - \cos\alpha\sin\alpha \\ \cos\alpha\sin\alpha - \sin\alpha\cos\alpha & \cos^2\alpha + \sin^2\alpha \end{bmatrix}$$

$$= \begin{bmatrix} 1 & 0 \\ 0 & 1 \end{bmatrix} = I$$

7. (i) For a symmetric matrix $a_{ij} = a_{ji}$

$$\text{Now, } A = \begin{bmatrix} 1 & -1 & 5 \\ -1 & 2 & 1 \\ 5 & 1 & 3 \end{bmatrix}$$

$a_{21} = -1 = a_{12}, \ a_{31} = 5 = a_{13}$

$a_{32} = 1\ a_{23}, \ a_{11}, a_{22}, a_{33}$, are 1, 2, 3 respectively.

Hence, $a_{ji} = a_{ij} \ \therefore$ A is a symmetric matrix.

(ii) For a skew symmetric matrix $a_{ji} = -a_{ij}$

$$\text{Now, } A = \begin{bmatrix} 0 & -1 & -1 \\ -1 & 0 & 1 \\ 1 & -1 & 0 \end{bmatrix}$$

$a_{21} = -1, \ a_{12} = 1,$

$\therefore \ -a_{12} = -1 \quad$ or $\quad a_{21} = -a_{12}$

$a_{31} = 1, \ a_{13} = -1,$

$\therefore \ -a_{13} = 1 \quad$ or $\quad a_{31} = -a_{13}$

$a_{32} = -1, \ a_{23} = 1,$

$\therefore \ -a_{23} = -1 \quad$ or $\quad a_{32} = -a_{23}$

$a_{11} = 0, \quad a_{22} = 0, \quad\quad a_{33} = 0$

Hence, A skew-symmetric matrix.

8. $A = \begin{bmatrix} 1 & 5 \\ 6 & 7 \end{bmatrix} \Rightarrow A' = \begin{bmatrix} 1 & 6 \\ 5 & 7 \end{bmatrix}$

(i) $A + A' = \begin{bmatrix} 1 & 5 \\ 6 & 7 \end{bmatrix} + \begin{bmatrix} 1 & 6 \\ 5 & 7 \end{bmatrix} = \begin{bmatrix} 2 & 11 \\ 11 & 14 \end{bmatrix}$

Let $Z = \begin{bmatrix} 2 & 11 \\ 11 & 14 \end{bmatrix} \Rightarrow Z' = \begin{bmatrix} 2 & 11 \\ 11 & 14 \end{bmatrix}$

$\therefore \ Z' = Z$

Hence, Z or $A + A'$ is a symmetric matrix.

(ii) $A - A' = \begin{bmatrix} 1 & 5 \\ 6 & 7 \end{bmatrix} - \begin{bmatrix} 1 & 6 \\ 5 & 7 \end{bmatrix} = \begin{bmatrix} 0 & -1 \\ 1 & 0 \end{bmatrix}$

Let $Z = \begin{bmatrix} 0 & -1 \\ 1 & 0 \end{bmatrix} \Rightarrow Z' = \begin{bmatrix} 0 & 1 \\ -1 & 0 \end{bmatrix}$

$\Rightarrow Z' = -\begin{bmatrix} 0 & -1 \\ 1 & 0 \end{bmatrix} = -Z$

Hence, Z or $A - A'$ is a skew-symmetric matrix.

9. $A = \begin{bmatrix} 0 & a & b \\ -a & 0 & c \\ -b & -c & 0 \end{bmatrix}, A' = \begin{bmatrix} 0 & -a & -b \\ a & 0 & -c \\ b & c & 0 \end{bmatrix}$

$$A + A' = \begin{bmatrix} 0 & a & b \\ -a & 0 & c \\ -b & -c & 0 \end{bmatrix} + \begin{bmatrix} 0 & -a & -b \\ a & 0 & -c \\ b & c & 0 \end{bmatrix} = \begin{bmatrix} 0 & 0 & 0 \\ 0 & 0 & 0 \\ 0 & 0 & 0 \end{bmatrix}$$

$$\Rightarrow \ \frac{1}{2}(A + A') = \frac{1}{2}\begin{bmatrix} 0 & 0 & 0 \\ 0 & 0 & 0 \\ 0 & 0 & 0 \end{bmatrix} = \begin{bmatrix} 0 & 0 & 0 \\ 0 & 0 & 0 \\ 0 & 0 & 0 \end{bmatrix}$$

$$\text{Again } (A - A') = \begin{bmatrix} 0 & a & b \\ -a & 0 & c \\ -b & -c & 0 \end{bmatrix} - \begin{bmatrix} 0 & -a & -b \\ a & 0 & -c \\ b & c & 0 \end{bmatrix}$$

$$= \begin{bmatrix} 0 & 2a & 2b \\ -2a & 0 & 2c \\ -2b & -2c & 0 \end{bmatrix}$$

$$\text{Thus, } \frac{1}{2}(A - A') = \frac{1}{2}\begin{bmatrix} 0 & 2a & 2b \\ -2a & 0 & 2c \\ -2b & -2c & 0 \end{bmatrix}$$

$$= \begin{bmatrix} 0 & a & b \\ -a & 0 & c \\ -b & -c & 0 \end{bmatrix}$$

10. (i) Let $A = \begin{bmatrix} 3 & 5 \\ 1 & -1 \end{bmatrix} \Rightarrow A' = \begin{bmatrix} 3 & 1 \\ 5 & -1 \end{bmatrix}$

We know that $A = \frac{1}{2}(A + A') + \frac{1}{2}(A - A')$

where $\frac{1}{2}(A + A')$ is symmetric and $\frac{1}{2}(A - A')$ is skew-symmetric.

$$(A + A') = \begin{bmatrix} 3 & 5 \\ 1 & -1 \end{bmatrix} + \begin{bmatrix} 3 & 1 \\ 5 & -1 \end{bmatrix} = \begin{bmatrix} 6 & 6 \\ 6 & -2 \end{bmatrix}$$

$$\therefore \ \frac{1}{2}(A + A') = \frac{1}{2}\begin{bmatrix} 6 & 6 \\ 6 & -2 \end{bmatrix} = \begin{bmatrix} 3 & 3 \\ 3 & -1 \end{bmatrix}$$

$$\text{Again, } (A - A') = \begin{bmatrix} 3 & 5 \\ 1 & -1 \end{bmatrix} - \begin{bmatrix} 3 & 1 \\ 5 & -1 \end{bmatrix} = \begin{bmatrix} 0 & 4 \\ -4 & 0 \end{bmatrix}$$

$$\therefore \ \frac{1}{2}(A - A') = \frac{1}{2}\begin{bmatrix} 0 & 4 \\ -4 & 0 \end{bmatrix} = \begin{bmatrix} 0 & 2 \\ -2 & 0 \end{bmatrix}$$

$$\text{Hence, } A = \begin{bmatrix} 3 & 3 \\ 3 & -1 \end{bmatrix} + \begin{bmatrix} 0 & 2 \\ -2 & 0 \end{bmatrix}$$

(ii) Let $A = \begin{bmatrix} 6 & -2 & 2 \\ -2 & 3 & -1 \\ 2 & -1 & 3 \end{bmatrix} \Rightarrow A' = \begin{bmatrix} 6 & -2 & 2 \\ -2 & 3 & -1 \\ 2 & -1 & 3 \end{bmatrix}$

We know that $A = \frac{1}{2}(A + A') + \frac{1}{2}(A - A')$

where $\frac{1}{2}(A + A')$ is a symmetric matrix and $\frac{1}{2}(A - A')$ is a skew-symmetric matrix.

$$\therefore \ A + A' = \begin{bmatrix} 6 & -2 & 2 \\ -2 & 3 & -1 \\ 2 & -1 & 3 \end{bmatrix} + \begin{bmatrix} 6 & -2 & 2 \\ -2 & 3 & -1 \\ 2 & -1 & 3 \end{bmatrix}$$

$$= \begin{bmatrix} 12 & -4 & 4 \\ -4 & 6 & -2 \\ 4 & -2 & 6 \end{bmatrix}$$

$$\therefore \ \frac{1}{2}(A+A') = \frac{1}{2}\begin{bmatrix} 12 & -4 & 4 \\ -4 & 6 & -2 \\ 4 & -2 & 6 \end{bmatrix} = \begin{bmatrix} 6 & -2 & 2 \\ -2 & 3 & -1 \\ 2 & -1 & 3 \end{bmatrix}$$

Now, $(A-A') = \begin{bmatrix} 6 & -2 & 2 \\ -2 & 3 & -1 \\ 2 & -1 & 3 \end{bmatrix} - \begin{bmatrix} 6 & -2 & 2 \\ -2 & 3 & -1 \\ 2 & -1 & 3 \end{bmatrix}$

$$= \begin{bmatrix} 0 & 0 & 0 \\ 0 & 0 & 0 \\ 0 & 0 & 0 \end{bmatrix}$$

$$\therefore \ \frac{1}{2}(A-A') = \frac{1}{2}\begin{bmatrix} 0 & 0 & 0 \\ 0 & 0 & 0 \\ 0 & 0 & 0 \end{bmatrix} = \begin{bmatrix} 0 & 0 & 0 \\ 0 & 0 & 0 \\ 0 & 0 & 0 \end{bmatrix}$$

Hence, $A = \begin{bmatrix} 6 & -2 & 2 \\ -2 & 3 & -1 \\ 2 & -1 & 3 \end{bmatrix} + \begin{bmatrix} 0 & 0 & 0 \\ 0 & 0 & 0 \\ 0 & 0 & 0 \end{bmatrix}$

(iii) Let $A = \begin{bmatrix} 3 & 3 & -1 \\ -2 & -2 & 1 \\ -4 & -5 & 2 \end{bmatrix}$

$$\Rightarrow \ A' = \begin{bmatrix} 3 & -2 & -4 \\ 3 & -2 & -5 \\ -1 & 1 & 2 \end{bmatrix}$$

$(A+A') = \begin{bmatrix} 3 & 3 & -1 \\ -2 & -2 & 1 \\ -4 & -5 & 2 \end{bmatrix} + \begin{bmatrix} 3 & -2 & -4 \\ 3 & -2 & -5 \\ -1 & 1 & 2 \end{bmatrix}$

$$= \begin{bmatrix} 6 & 1 & -5 \\ 1 & -4 & -4 \\ -5 & -4 & 4 \end{bmatrix}$$

$$\therefore \ \frac{1}{2}(A+A') = \frac{1}{2}\begin{bmatrix} 6 & 1 & -5 \\ 1 & -4 & -4 \\ -5 & -4 & 4 \end{bmatrix}$$

Again $(A-A') = \begin{bmatrix} 0 & 5 & 3 \\ -5 & 0 & 6 \\ -3 & -6 & 0 \end{bmatrix}$

$$\therefore \ \frac{1}{2}(A-A') = \frac{1}{2}\begin{bmatrix} 0 & 5 & 3 \\ -5 & 0 & 6 \\ -3 & -6 & 0 \end{bmatrix}$$

Hence, $A = \frac{1}{2}\begin{bmatrix} 6 & 1 & -5 \\ 1 & -4 & -4 \\ -5 & -4 & 4 \end{bmatrix} + \frac{1}{2}\begin{bmatrix} 0 & 5 & 3 \\ -5 & 0 & 6 \\ -3 & -6 & 0 \end{bmatrix}$

or $A = \begin{bmatrix} 3 & \frac{1}{2} & \frac{-5}{2} \\ \frac{1}{2} & -2 & -2 \\ \frac{-5}{2} & -2 & 2 \end{bmatrix} + \begin{bmatrix} 0 & \frac{5}{2} & \frac{3}{2} \\ \frac{-5}{2} & 0 & 3 \\ \frac{-3}{2} & -3 & 0 \end{bmatrix}$

(iv) Let $A = \begin{bmatrix} 1 & 5 \\ -1 & 2 \end{bmatrix}$

$$\Rightarrow \ A' = \begin{bmatrix} 1 & -1 \\ 5 & 2 \end{bmatrix}$$

We know that $A = \frac{1}{2}(A+A') + \frac{1}{2}(A-A')$

where $\frac{1}{2}(A + A')$ is symmetric and $\frac{1}{2}(A - A')$ is skew-symmetric.

$$A+A' = \begin{bmatrix} 1 & 5 \\ -1 & 2 \end{bmatrix} + \begin{bmatrix} 1 & -1 \\ 5 & 2 \end{bmatrix} = \begin{bmatrix} 2 & 4 \\ 4 & 4 \end{bmatrix}$$

$$\therefore \ \frac{1}{2}(A+A') = \frac{1}{2}\begin{bmatrix} 2 & 4 \\ 4 & 4 \end{bmatrix} = \begin{bmatrix} 1 & 2 \\ 2 & 2 \end{bmatrix}$$

Again $(A-A') = \begin{bmatrix} 0 & 6 \\ -6 & 0 \end{bmatrix}$

$$\therefore \ \frac{1}{2}(A-A') = \frac{1}{2}\begin{bmatrix} 0 & 6 \\ -6 & 0 \end{bmatrix} = \begin{bmatrix} 0 & 3 \\ -3 & 0 \end{bmatrix}$$

Hence, $A = \begin{bmatrix} 1 & 2 \\ 2 & 2 \end{bmatrix} + \begin{bmatrix} 0 & 3 \\ -3 & 0 \end{bmatrix}$

11. Now $A' = B, B' = B$

$$(AB-BA)' = (AB)' - (BA)'$$
$$= B'A' - A'B' = BA - AB$$
$$= -(AB-BA)$$

$AB - BA$ is a skew-symmetric matrix

Hence, option (a) is correct.

12. Now

$$A+A' = \begin{bmatrix} \cos\alpha & -\sin\alpha \\ \sin\alpha & \cos\alpha \end{bmatrix} + \begin{bmatrix} \cos\alpha & \sin\alpha \\ -\sin\alpha & \cos\alpha \end{bmatrix}$$

$$= \begin{bmatrix} 2\cos\alpha & 0 \\ 0 & 2\cos\alpha \end{bmatrix} = I = \begin{bmatrix} 1 & 0 \\ 0 & 1 \end{bmatrix}$$

$$\therefore \ 2\cos\alpha = 1 \Rightarrow \cos\alpha = \frac{1}{2} \Rightarrow \alpha = \frac{\pi}{3}$$

Thus option (b) is correct.

Past year Exercise 

1. **(a)**

2.
$$\begin{bmatrix} 2x & 10 \\ 14 & 2y-6 \end{bmatrix} = \begin{bmatrix} 7 & 6 \\ 15 & 14 \end{bmatrix} - \begin{bmatrix} 3 & -4 \\ 1 & 2 \end{bmatrix}$$

$$\Rightarrow \begin{bmatrix} 2x & 10 \\ 14 & 2y-6 \end{bmatrix} = \begin{bmatrix} 4 & 10 \\ 14 & 12 \end{bmatrix}$$

On equating the corresponding elements, we get

$2x = 4$ and $2y - 6 = 12$

$\therefore \quad x = 2$ and $y = 9$

$\therefore \quad y - x = 9 - 2 = 7$

3. $A = \begin{bmatrix} 9 & -1 & 4 \\ -2 & 1 & 3 \end{bmatrix} - \begin{bmatrix} 1 & 2 & -1 \\ 0 & 4 & 9 \end{bmatrix} = \begin{bmatrix} 8 & -3 & 5 \\ -2 & -3 & -6 \end{bmatrix}$

4. Let $\begin{bmatrix} a-b & 2a+c \\ 2a-b & 3c+d \end{bmatrix} = \begin{bmatrix} -1 & 5 \\ 0 & 13 \end{bmatrix}$

$\Rightarrow \quad a - b = -1, \, 2a - b = 0$

$\Rightarrow \quad a - b = -1, \, a = \dfrac{b}{2}$

$\Rightarrow \quad \dfrac{b}{2} - b = -1 \Rightarrow b = 2$

5. $A^2 = A$ $\qquad\qquad$ (Given)

We have,

$7A - (I + A)^3$

$= 7A - (I^3 + A^3 + 3I^2A + 3IA^2)$

$= 7A - (I + A^2 \cdot A + 3IA + 3IA)$

$= 7A - (I + A^2 + 3A + 3A)$

$= 7A - (I + A + 6A)$

$= 7A - I - 7A$

$7A - (I + A)^3 = -I$

6. We have

$\begin{bmatrix} x-y & z \\ 2x-y & w \end{bmatrix} = \begin{bmatrix} -1 & 4 \\ 0 & 5 \end{bmatrix}$

By the equality of matrices, we have

$\quad x - y = -1, \, 2x - y = 0$

On subtracting, we get

$\quad 2x - y = 0$
$\quad x - y = -1$
$\quad \underline{- \quad + \quad +}$
$\qquad\quad x = 1$

$\Rightarrow \quad y = 2$

$\therefore \quad x + y = 3$

7. $A^2 = A.A = \begin{bmatrix} 3 & -3 \\ -3 & 3 \end{bmatrix}\begin{bmatrix} 3 & -3 \\ -3 & 3 \end{bmatrix}$

$= \begin{bmatrix} 9+9 & -9-9 \\ -9-9 & 9+9 \end{bmatrix} = \begin{bmatrix} 18 & -18 \\ -18 & 18 \end{bmatrix} = 6\begin{bmatrix} 3 & -3 \\ -3 & 3 \end{bmatrix}$

Given, $A^2 = \lambda A \Rightarrow \lambda = 6$

8. Let $2\begin{bmatrix} 1 & 3 \\ 0 & x \end{bmatrix} + \begin{bmatrix} y & 0 \\ 1 & 2 \end{bmatrix} = \begin{bmatrix} 5 & 6 \\ 1 & 8 \end{bmatrix}$

$\Rightarrow \begin{bmatrix} 2+y & 6 \\ 1 & 2x+2 \end{bmatrix} = \begin{bmatrix} 5 & 6 \\ 1 & 8 \end{bmatrix}$

Equating the corresponding elements of two matrices, we obtain

$\quad 2 + y = 5 \Rightarrow y = 3$ and

$\quad 2x + 2 = 8 \Rightarrow x = 3$

Thus, $x + y = 3 + 3 = 6$

9. $A = \begin{bmatrix} 0 & 1 & -2 \\ -1 & 0 & 3 \\ x & -3 & 0 \end{bmatrix}$, $A' = \begin{bmatrix} 0 & -1 & x \\ 1 & 0 & -3 \\ -2 & 3 & 0 \end{bmatrix}$

We know that A is skew-symmetric, if $A' = -A$

$\Rightarrow \quad -x = -2 \Rightarrow x = 2$

10. On comparing the corresponding elements, we have

$\quad x - y = 1$ $\qquad\qquad\qquad$ ...(i)
$\quad 2y + z = 9$ $\qquad\qquad\quad$ ...(ii)
$\quad 2y = 4$ $\qquad\qquad\qquad$ ...(iii)
$\quad x + y = 5$ $\qquad\qquad\quad$ ...(iv)

Adding (i) and (ii), we obtain

$\therefore \quad x + y + z = 1 + 9 = 10$

11. Let $\begin{bmatrix} x & 1 \end{bmatrix}\begin{bmatrix} 1 & 0 \\ -2 & 0 \end{bmatrix} = O$

$\Rightarrow \quad [x - 2 \quad 0] = [0 \quad 0]$

$\Rightarrow \quad x - 2 = 0 \Rightarrow x = 2$

12. Let $2\begin{bmatrix} 3 & 4 \\ 5 & x \end{bmatrix} + \begin{bmatrix} 1 & y \\ 0 & 1 \end{bmatrix} = \begin{bmatrix} 7 & 0 \\ 10 & 5 \end{bmatrix}$

$\Rightarrow \begin{bmatrix} 6 & 8 \\ 10 & 2x \end{bmatrix} + \begin{bmatrix} 1 & y \\ 0 & 1 \end{bmatrix} = \begin{bmatrix} 7 & 0 \\ 10 & 5 \end{bmatrix}$

$\Rightarrow \quad 8 + y = 0 \Rightarrow y = -8$

and $2x + 1 = 5 \Rightarrow x = 2$

Hence $x - y = 2 - (-8) = 10$

13. $(A - I)^3 + (A + I)^3 - 7A$

$= A^3 - I^3 - 3A^2I + 3AI^2 + A^3 + I^3 + 3A^2I + 3AI^2 - 7A$

$= 2A^3 + 6AI^2 - 7A$

$= 2A.A^2 + 6AI^2 - 7A$ $\qquad$ (Given : $A^2 = I$)

$= 8A - 7A$

$= A$

14. Given : $A = \begin{bmatrix} 0 & 2b & -2 \\ 3 & 1 & 3 \\ 3a & 3 & -1 \end{bmatrix}$

$\Rightarrow A^T = \begin{bmatrix} 0 & 3 & 3a \\ 2b & 1 & 3 \\ -2 & 3 & -1 \end{bmatrix}$

A matrix is symmetric if $A = A^T$.

Therefore, $a = \dfrac{-2}{3}$ and $b = \dfrac{3}{2}$

15. $A = \begin{bmatrix} 0 & a & -3 \\ 2 & 0 & -1 \\ b & 1 & 0 \end{bmatrix}$ is skew symmetric.

$\begin{bmatrix} 0 & 2 & b \\ a & 0 & 1 \\ -3 & -1 & 0 \end{bmatrix} = \begin{bmatrix} 0 & -a & 3 \\ -2 & 0 & 1 \\ -b & -1 & 0 \end{bmatrix} \quad (\because A^T = -A)$

$\therefore \quad a = -2, \, b = 3$

16. School

Article	A	B	C
Paper bags	25	22	26
Scrap-books	12	15	18
Pastel sheets	34	28	36

The number of articles sold by each school can be written in the matrix form as follows:

$X = \begin{bmatrix} 25 & 22 & 26 \\ 12 & 15 & 18 \\ 34 & 28 & 36 \end{bmatrix}$

The rate of each article can be written in the matrix form as follows:

$Y = \begin{bmatrix} 20 & 15 & 5 \end{bmatrix}$

The amount collected by each school is given by

$YX = \begin{bmatrix} 20 & 15 & 5 \end{bmatrix} \begin{bmatrix} 25 & 22 & 269 \\ 12 & 15 & 18 \\ 34 & 28 & 36 \end{bmatrix}$

$YX = \begin{bmatrix} 850 & 805 & 970 \end{bmatrix}$

Thus, the amount collected by schools A, B and C are ₹ 850, ₹ 805 and ₹ 970. respectively

$\therefore$ Total amount collected = ₹ (850 + 805 + 970)

$\qquad\qquad\qquad\qquad = ₹ \, 2,625$

17. $A = \begin{bmatrix} 2 & 0 & 1 \\ 2 & 1 & 3 \\ 1 & -1 & 0 \end{bmatrix}$

$\therefore A^2 = A.A = \begin{bmatrix} 2 & 0 & 1 \\ 2 & 1 & 3 \\ 1 & -1 & 0 \end{bmatrix} \begin{bmatrix} 2 & 0 & 1 \\ 2 & 1 & 3 \\ 1 & -1 & 0 \end{bmatrix}$

$\Rightarrow A^2 = \begin{bmatrix} 4+0+1 & 0+0-1 & 2+0+0 \\ 4+2+3 & 0+1-3 & 2+3+0 \\ 2-2+0 & 0-1+0 & 1-3+0 \end{bmatrix} = \begin{bmatrix} 5 & -1 & 2 \\ 9 & -2 & 5 \\ 0 & -1 & -2 \end{bmatrix}$

Thus,

$A^2 - 5A + 16I = \begin{bmatrix} 5 & -1 & 2 \\ 9 & -2 & 5 \\ 0 & -1 & -2 \end{bmatrix} - 5 \begin{bmatrix} 2 & 0 & 1 \\ 2 & 1 & 3 \\ 1 & -1 & 0 \end{bmatrix} + 16 \begin{bmatrix} 1 & 0 & 0 \\ 0 & 1 & 0 \\ 0 & 0 & 1 \end{bmatrix}$

$= \begin{bmatrix} 5-10+16 & -1-0+0 & 2-1+0 \\ 9-10+0 & -2-5+16 & 5-15+0 \\ 0-5+0 & -1+5+0 & -2-0+16 \end{bmatrix}$

$= \begin{bmatrix} 11 & -1 & -3 \\ -1 & 9 & -10 \\ -5 & 4 & 14 \end{bmatrix}$

18. We have $A = \begin{bmatrix} 2 & 0 & 1 \\ 2 & 1 & 3 \\ 1 & -1 & 0 \end{bmatrix}$

$\Rightarrow \quad A^2 = AA$

$= \begin{bmatrix} 2 & 0 & 1 \\ 2 & 1 & 3 \\ 1 & -1 & 0 \end{bmatrix} \begin{bmatrix} 2 & 0 & 1 \\ 2 & 1 & 3 \\ 1 & -1 & 0 \end{bmatrix} = \begin{bmatrix} 5 & -1 & 2 \\ 9 & -2 & 5 \\ 0 & -1 & -2 \end{bmatrix}$

$\therefore \quad A^2 - 5A + 4I = \begin{bmatrix} 5 & -1 & 2 \\ 9 & -2 & 5 \\ 0 & -1 & -2 \end{bmatrix} + \begin{bmatrix} -10 & 0 & -5 \\ -10 & -5 & -15 \\ -5 & 5 & 0 \end{bmatrix}$

$+ \begin{bmatrix} 4 & 0 & 0 \\ 0 & 4 & 0 \\ 0 & 0 & 4 \end{bmatrix} = \begin{bmatrix} -1 & -1 & -3 \\ -1 & -3 & -10 \\ -5 & 4 & 2 \end{bmatrix}$

Now, $A^2 - 5A + 4I + X = 0$

$\Rightarrow \quad X = -(A^2 - 5A + 4I)$

$\Rightarrow \quad X = -(1) \begin{bmatrix} -1 & -1 & -3 \\ -1 & -3 & -10 \\ -5 & 4 & 2 \end{bmatrix} = \begin{bmatrix} 1 & 1 & 3 \\ 1 & 3 & 10 \\ 5 & -4 & -2 \end{bmatrix}$

19. The number of articles sold by each school can be written in the matrix form as follows :

$X = \begin{bmatrix} 40 & 25 & 35 \\ 50 & 40 & 50 \\ 20 & 30 & 40 \end{bmatrix}$

The cost of each article can be written in the matrix form as follows:

$Y = [25 \quad 100 \quad 50]$

The fund collected by each school is given by

$YX = [25 \quad 100 \quad 50] \begin{bmatrix} 40 & 25 & 35 \\ 50 & 40 & 50 \\ 20 & 30 & 40 \end{bmatrix}$

$YX = [7000 \quad 6125 \quad 7875]$

Thus, the funds collected by schools A, B and C are ₹ 7,000, ₹ 6,125 and ₹ 7,875, respectively.

The total fund collected = ₹ (7000 + 6125 + 7875)

$\qquad\qquad\qquad\qquad = ₹ \, 21,000$

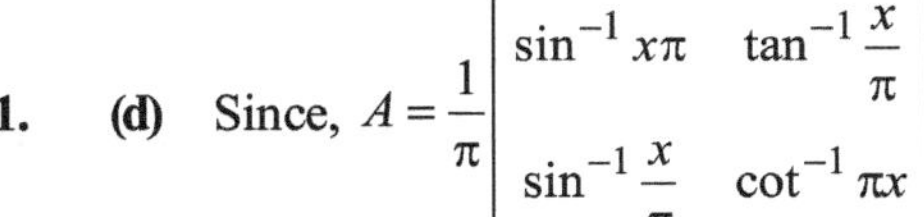

NCERT Exemplar

1. **(d)** Since, $A = \dfrac{1}{\pi} \begin{bmatrix} \sin^{-1} x\pi & \tan^{-1} \dfrac{x}{\pi} \\ \sin^{-1} \dfrac{x}{\pi} & \cot^{-1} \pi x \end{bmatrix}$

and $B = \dfrac{1}{\pi}\begin{bmatrix} -\cos^{-1} x\pi & \tan^{-1}\dfrac{x}{\pi} \\ \sin^{-1}\dfrac{x}{\pi} & -\tan^{-1}\pi x \end{bmatrix}$

So,

$A - B = \dfrac{1}{\pi}\begin{bmatrix} \sin^{-1} x\pi + \cos^{-1} x\pi & \tan^{-1}\dfrac{x}{\pi} - \tan^{-1}\dfrac{x}{\pi} \\ \sin^{-1}\dfrac{x}{\pi} - \sin^{-1}\dfrac{x}{\pi} & \cot^{-1}\pi x + \tan^{-1}\pi x \end{bmatrix}$

$= \dfrac{1}{\pi}\begin{bmatrix} \dfrac{\pi}{2} & 0 \\ 0 & \dfrac{\pi}{2} \end{bmatrix} = \dfrac{1}{2}\begin{bmatrix} 1 & 0 \\ 0 & 1 \end{bmatrix} = \dfrac{1}{2} I$

2. (d) As, $m = n$, so A and B are of same orders $3 \times n$
Hence, the order of matrix $(5A - 2B)$ is same as $3 \times n$

3. (a) Since, $A = [a_{ij}]_{2\times 2}$, where $a_{ij} = 1$, if $i \neq j$ and 0 if $i = j$

So, $A = \begin{bmatrix} 0 & 1 \\ 1 & 0 \end{bmatrix}$. Hence $A^2 = \begin{bmatrix} 0 & 1 \\ 1 & 0 \end{bmatrix}\begin{bmatrix} 0 & 1 \\ 1 & 0 \end{bmatrix} = \begin{bmatrix} 1 & 0 \\ 0 & 1 \end{bmatrix} = I$

4. (a) $(AB' - BA')' = (AB')' - (BA')'$

$= (B')'A' - (A')'B' = BA' - AB' = -(AB' - BA')$

Hence, $(AB' - BA')$ is a skew-symmetric matrix.

5. $a_{11} = e^{2x}\sin x$
$a_{12} = e^{2x}\sin 2x$
$a_{21} = e^{4x}\sin x$
$a_{22} = e^{4x}\sin 2x$

Thus $A = \begin{bmatrix} e^{2x}\sin x & e^{2x}\sin 2x \\ e^{4x}\sin x & e^{4x}\sin 2x \end{bmatrix}$

6. $\because\ x\begin{bmatrix} 2x & 2 \\ 3 & x \end{bmatrix} + 2\begin{bmatrix} 8 & 5x \\ 4 & 4x \end{bmatrix} = 2\begin{bmatrix} (x^2+8) & 24 \\ (10) & 6x \end{bmatrix}$

$\Rightarrow \begin{bmatrix} 2x^2+16 & 2x+10x \\ 3x+8 & x^2+8x \end{bmatrix} = \begin{bmatrix} 2x^2+16 & 48 \\ 20 & 12x \end{bmatrix}$

$\Rightarrow 2x + 10x = 48 \ \therefore\ x = \dfrac{48}{12} = 4$

7. Let $A = \begin{bmatrix} 1 & 0 \\ 2 & 0 \end{bmatrix}$ and $B = \begin{bmatrix} 0 & 0 \\ 0 & 3 \end{bmatrix}$ be two non-zero 2×2 matrices such that

$\therefore\quad AB = \begin{bmatrix} 1 & 0 \\ 2 & 0 \end{bmatrix}\begin{bmatrix} 0 & 0 \\ 0 & 3 \end{bmatrix}$

$= \begin{bmatrix} 0+0 & 0+0 \\ 0+0 & 0+0 \end{bmatrix} = \begin{bmatrix} 0 & 0 \\ 0 & 0 \end{bmatrix} = O$

Thus, $AB = O$
Hence, an example of two such non-zero 2×2 matrices is

$\begin{bmatrix} 1 & 0 \\ 2 & 0 \end{bmatrix}, \begin{bmatrix} 0 & 0 \\ 0 & 3 \end{bmatrix}.$

8. Let $A = [a_{ij}]$ be a matrix which is both symmetric and skew symmetric.

Since A is a skew symmetric matrix, so $A' = -A$.
Thus, for all i and j, we have $a_{ij} = -a_{ji}$ ...(i)
Again, since A is a symmetric matrix, so $A' = A$.
Thus, for all i and j, we have
$\quad a_{ji} = a_{ij}$ ...(ii)
Therefore, from (i) and (ii), we get
$\quad a_{ij} = -a_{ij}$ for all i and j
or $\quad 2a_{ij} = 0$,
i.e., $\quad a_{ij} = 0$ for all i and j. Hence A is a zero matrix.

Objective Practice Exercise

1. (a)   2. (c)   3. (d)   4. (a)   5. (b)

6. (c) $A^2 = \begin{bmatrix} \cos\alpha & \sin\alpha \\ -\sin\alpha & \cos\alpha \end{bmatrix}\begin{bmatrix} \cos\alpha & \sin\alpha \\ -\sin\alpha & \cos\alpha \end{bmatrix}$

$= \begin{bmatrix} \cos^2\alpha - \sin^2\alpha & \sin\alpha\cos\alpha + \sin\alpha\cos\alpha \\ -\sin\alpha\cos\alpha - \sin\alpha\cos\alpha & -\sin^2\alpha + \cos^2\alpha \end{bmatrix}$

$= \begin{bmatrix} \cos 2\alpha & \sin 2\alpha \\ -\sin 2\alpha & \cos 2\alpha \end{bmatrix}$

7. (c) $AC = [a \ \ b]\begin{bmatrix} a \\ -a \end{bmatrix} = [a^2 - ab]$

and $BC = [-b \ \ -a]\begin{bmatrix} a \\ -a \end{bmatrix} = [-ab + a^2]$

$\Rightarrow AC = BC.$

8. (a) $e\begin{bmatrix} e^x & e^y \\ e^y & e^x \end{bmatrix} = \begin{bmatrix} 1 & 1 \\ 1 & 1 \end{bmatrix} \Rightarrow \begin{bmatrix} e^{x+1} & e^{y+1} \\ e^{y+1} & e^{x+1} \end{bmatrix} = \begin{bmatrix} e^0 & e^0 \\ e^0 & e^0 \end{bmatrix}$

$e^{x+1} = e^0$ and $e^{y+1} = e^0 \Rightarrow x = -1$ and $y = -1$

9. (b) $(aI + bA)^2 = a^2I^2 + b^2A^2 + 2ab\,AI$

$= a^2I^2 + b^2A^2 + 2abA$

But $A^2 = \begin{bmatrix} 0 & 0 \\ 0 & 0 \end{bmatrix} \ \therefore\ (aI + bA)^2 = a^2I + 2abA.$

10. (d) $X = \begin{bmatrix} 3 & -4 \\ 1 & -1 \end{bmatrix} \Rightarrow X^2 = \begin{bmatrix} 5 & -8 \\ 2 & -3 \end{bmatrix}$

Clearly for $n = 2$, the matrices in (a), (b), (c) do not tally with

$\begin{bmatrix} 5 & -8 \\ 2 & -3 \end{bmatrix}.$

11. (c) Given that $kA = \begin{bmatrix} 0 & 3a \\ 2b & 24 \end{bmatrix}$ and $A = \begin{bmatrix} 0 & 2 \\ 3 & -4 \end{bmatrix}$

$\Rightarrow k\begin{bmatrix} 0 & 2 \\ 3 & -4 \end{bmatrix} = \begin{bmatrix} 0 & 3a \\ 2b & 24 \end{bmatrix}$

$\Rightarrow 2k = 3a,\ 3k = 2b,\ -4k = 24$

$\Rightarrow a = \dfrac{2k}{3},\ b = \dfrac{3k}{2},\ k = -6 \Rightarrow k = -6,\ a = -4,\ b = -9.$

12. (d) $\begin{bmatrix} \alpha & \beta \\ \gamma & -\alpha \end{bmatrix} = \sqrt{I_2}\ ;\ \begin{bmatrix} \alpha & \beta \\ \gamma & -\alpha \end{bmatrix}\begin{bmatrix} \alpha & \beta \\ \gamma & -\alpha \end{bmatrix} = \begin{bmatrix} 1 & 0 \\ 0 & 1 \end{bmatrix}$

$\Rightarrow \alpha^2 + \beta\gamma = 1$

13. **(a)** **14.** **(c)**

15. **(c)** It is based on fundamental concept.

16. **(a)** $A^2 = A.\ A = \begin{bmatrix} ab & b^2 \\ -a^2 & -ab \end{bmatrix} \begin{bmatrix} ab & b^2 \\ -a^2 & -ab \end{bmatrix}$

$$= \begin{bmatrix} a^2b^2 - a^2b^2 & ab^3 - ab^3 \\ -a^3b + a^3b & -a^2b^2 + a^2b^2 \end{bmatrix} = O$$

Now, $A^3 = A.\ A^2 = O$ and $A^n = O$, for all $n \geq 2$.

17. **(c)** Given $AB = A,\ \therefore B = I \Rightarrow BA = B,\ \therefore A = I$.

Hence, $A^2 = A$ and $B^2 = B$

18. **(b)** **19.** **(a)** **20.** **(a)**

21. **(b)** Matrix multiplication is not commutative i.e. $AB \neq BA$
But it is associative i.e. $(AB)C = A(BC)$

22. **(c)** A is a square matrix such that $A^2 = A$.
Now, $(I - A)^3 + A = (I - A)^2 (I - A) + A$
$= (I^2 - 2AI + A^2)(I - A) + A$
$= (I - 2A + A)(I - A) + A$ $[\therefore A^2 = A]$
$= (I - A)(I - A) + A = (I^2 - 2AI + A^2) + A$
$= (I - 2A + A) + A = I - A + A = I$ $[\therefore A^2 = A]$

23. **(b)** $(A - 2I)(A - 3I) = \begin{bmatrix} 2 & 2 \\ -1 & -1 \end{bmatrix} \begin{bmatrix} 1 & 2 \\ -1 & -2 \end{bmatrix} = \begin{bmatrix} 0 & 0 \\ 0 & 0 \end{bmatrix} = O$

24. **(b)** **25.** **(c)**

26. **(c)** $\left.\begin{array}{r} 3X + 2Y = I \\ 2X - Y = O \end{array}\right\} \Rightarrow \left.\begin{array}{r} 3X + 2Y = I \\ 4X - 2Y = O \end{array}\right\} \Rightarrow 7X = I \Rightarrow X = \dfrac{1}{7}I$

[Solving simultaneously]

$\therefore \qquad 2Y = I - \dfrac{3}{7}I = \dfrac{4}{7}I \Rightarrow Y = \dfrac{2}{7}I$

27. **(c)** For two 2×2 matrices, A & B
$(A - B) \times (A + B)$
$= A \times A + A \times B - B \times A - B \times B = A^2 - B^2 + AB - BA$
Hence, $(A - B)(A + B) = A^2 + AB - BA - B^2$

28. **(d)** $\because \begin{bmatrix} 0 & 1 \\ 0 & 0 \end{bmatrix} \begin{bmatrix} -1 & 0 \\ 0 & 0 \end{bmatrix} = \begin{bmatrix} 0 & 0 \\ 0 & 0 \end{bmatrix} = O = AB$

$\Rightarrow B = \begin{bmatrix} -1 & 0 \\ 0 & 0 \end{bmatrix}$

29. **(a)**

30. **(a)** $A_{3 \times 4} \Rightarrow A'_{4 \times 3}$; Now $A'B$ is defined.
$\Rightarrow B$ is of order $3 \times p$

And $B_{3 \times p} A'_{4 \times 3}$ is defined $\Rightarrow p = 4$.

$\therefore$ Order of B is 3×4.

31. **(d)** $O(A) = 2 \times 3, O(B) = 3 \times 2, O(C) = 3 \times 3$
$\Rightarrow O(B') = 2 \times 3 \Rightarrow O(A + B') = 2 \times 3$
$\Rightarrow C(A + B')$ is not defined
($\because$ number of rows of C $\neq$ number of columns of $(A + B')$)

32. **(d)** $\because$ A and B are symmetric matrices.
$\therefore A^T = A$ and $B^T = B$

Now, $(A + B)^T = A^T + B^T = A + B$

Also, $(A - B)^T = A^T - B^T = A - B$

$(AB + BA)^T = (AB)^T + (BA)^T = BA + AB = AB + BA$

$(AB - BA)^T = (AB)^T - (BA)^T$
$= B^T A^T - A^T B^T = BA - AB.$

33. **(d)** $a_{ij} = i^2 - j^2$ is a square matrix.
For a skew symmetric matrix $a_{ij} = -a_{ji}$
$\Rightarrow a_{ij} = i^2 - j^2$ and $a_{ji} = j^2 - i^2$
$\Rightarrow a_{ij} + a_{ji} = 0 \Rightarrow a_{ij} = -a_{ji}.$
$\therefore a_{ij}$ is a skew symmetric matrix.

34. **(b)** $\because$ the given matrix is symmetric
$\therefore a_{12} = a_{21} \Rightarrow x + 2 = 2x - 3 \Rightarrow x = 5.$

35. **(b)** It is a concept.

36. **(c)** If A is a square matrix, then $A + A^T, AA^T, A^TA$ are
symmetric matrices, while $A - A^T$ is skew-symmetric matrix.

37. **(a)** $(M'AM)' = M'A'M = M'AM$ ($\because$ A is symmetrix.)
Hence $M'AM$ is a symmetric matrix

38. **(b)** **39.** **(a)**

40. **(d)** $\because$ A is a skew-symmetrix matrix, therefore
$$A^T = -A \Rightarrow (A^T)^n = (-A)^n$$
$$\Rightarrow \quad (A^n)^T = \begin{cases} A^n, & \text{if } n \text{ is even} \\ -A^n, & \text{if } n \text{ is odd} \end{cases}$$

41. **(d)** **42.** **(a)** **43.** **(a)**

44. **(a)** $A^n = \begin{bmatrix} \cos n\theta & \sin n\theta \\ -\sin n\theta & \cos n\theta \end{bmatrix}$

$\dfrac{1}{n} A^n = \begin{bmatrix} \dfrac{\cos n\theta}{n} & \dfrac{\sin n\theta}{n} \\ -\dfrac{\sin n\theta}{n} & \dfrac{\cos n\theta}{n} \end{bmatrix}$

But $-1 \leq \cos n\theta \leq 1$ and $-1 \leq \sin n\theta \leq 1$

$\lim\limits_{n \to \infty} \dfrac{\sin n\theta}{n} = 0,\ \lim\limits_{n \to \infty} \dfrac{\cos n\theta}{n} = 0$

$\lim\limits_{n \to \infty} \dfrac{1}{n} A^n = \begin{bmatrix} 0 & 0 \\ 0 & 0 \end{bmatrix}$

45. **(b)** **46.** **(c)** **47.** **(a)** **48.** **(d)** **49.** **(b)**

50. **(b)**

51. **(c)** Total revenue of market A
$$= [10,000\ \ 2000\ \ 18000] \begin{bmatrix} 2.50 \\ 1.50 \\ 1.00 \end{bmatrix} = ₹\,46,000$$

52. **(b)** Total revenue of market B
$$= [6,000\ \ 20000\ \ 8000] \begin{bmatrix} 2.50 \\ 1.50 \\ 1 \end{bmatrix} = ₹\,53,000$$

53. **(d)** Total cost incurred in market A

$$= \begin{bmatrix} 10000 & 2000 & 18000 \end{bmatrix} \begin{bmatrix} 2.00 \\ 1.00 \\ 0.50 \end{bmatrix} = ₹\,31{,}000$$

54. **(a)** $(₹\,15{,}000, ₹\,17{,}000)$

55. **(c)** $₹\,32{,}000$

56. **(c)** $\begin{bmatrix} 7 & 2 \\ 1 & 6 \end{bmatrix}$

57. **(a)** $(A^T)^T = A = \begin{bmatrix} 1 & 2 \\ -1 & 3 \end{bmatrix}$

58. **(b)** $(bA)^T = \left(-2\begin{bmatrix} 1 & 2 \\ -1 & 3 \end{bmatrix}\right)^T = \begin{bmatrix} -2 & -4 \\ 2 & -6 \end{bmatrix}^T = \begin{bmatrix} -2 & 2 \\ -4 & -6 \end{bmatrix}$

59. **(c)** $\begin{bmatrix} -4 & -4 \\ -6 & 4 \end{bmatrix}$

60. **(c)** $(a + b)B = (4 - 2)\,B = 2\begin{bmatrix} 4 & 0 \\ 1 & 5 \end{bmatrix} = \begin{bmatrix} 8 & 0 \\ 2 & 10 \end{bmatrix}$

61. **(b)** $\begin{bmatrix} 40 & 50 & 20 \end{bmatrix} \begin{bmatrix} 25 \\ 100 \\ 50 \end{bmatrix} = ₹\,7000$

62. **(a)** Total amount of money
= Amount collected by CVC + Amount collected by KVS

$$= \begin{bmatrix} 25 & 40 & 30 \end{bmatrix} \begin{bmatrix} 25 \\ 100 \\ 50 \end{bmatrix} + \begin{bmatrix} 35 & 50 & 40 \end{bmatrix} \begin{bmatrix} 25 \\ 100 \\ 50 \end{bmatrix}$$
$$= 6125 + 7875 = 14000$$

63. **(c)** $₹\,21000$

64. **(c)** Total money collected $= \begin{bmatrix} 20 & 50 & 40 \end{bmatrix} \begin{bmatrix} 25 \\ 100 \\ 50 \end{bmatrix}$

$$+ \begin{bmatrix} 30 & 40 & 25 \end{bmatrix} \begin{bmatrix} 25 \\ 100 \\ 50 \end{bmatrix} + \begin{bmatrix} 40 & 50 & 35 \end{bmatrix} \begin{bmatrix} 25 \\ 100 \\ 50 \end{bmatrix}$$
$$= 7500 + 6000 + 7750 = ₹\,250$$

65. **(d)** 330

66. **(a)** Since, 8 children less, everyone would have got ₹10 more = Total money
$$\Rightarrow (x - 8)(y + 10) = xy$$
$$\Rightarrow 5x - 4y = 40 \qquad\qquad ...(i)$$
And 16 children more, everyone would have got ₹ 10 less = Total money
$$(x + 16)(y - 10) = xy$$
$$\Rightarrow 5x - 8y = -80 \qquad\qquad ...(ii)$$

67. **(c)** $\begin{bmatrix} 5 & -4 \\ 5 & -8 \end{bmatrix}\begin{bmatrix} x \\ y \end{bmatrix} = \begin{bmatrix} 40 \\ -80 \end{bmatrix}$

68. **(d)** From eq^n (i) and (ii), $x = 32$

69. **(b)** From eq^n (i) and (ii), $y = ₹\,30$

70. **(b)** Total distributed amount $= xy = 32 \times 30 = ₹\,960$

71. **(a)** Total sale = Sale in September + Sale in October = A + B

72. **(a)** 10000

73. **(b)** Decrease in sale from September to October = Sale in September − Sale in October = A − B

74. **(a)** ₹ 100, ₹ 200 and ₹ 120

75. **(b)** ₹ 1000, ₹ 600 ₹ 200

Chapter Test 

1. **(d)**   **2.** **(b)**   **3.** **(b)**   **4.** **(c)**

5. $a_{24} = 6,\ a_{34} = -25,\ a_{32} = 15,\ a_{23} = 9$

6. $\begin{bmatrix} 4 & -11 \\ -5 & -1 \end{bmatrix}$

7. **(b)**   **8.** **(c)**

9. **(i)** **(d)**   **(ii)** **(c)**   **(iii)** **(a)**
    (iv) **(a)**   **(v)** **(b)**

10. $a = 3, x = -3, y = -2, z = 4$

11. $n = 2$

12. $2, 2, 3, 4$

13. 198

4 Determinants

DETERMINANTS

Applications of Determinants and Matrices

Solution of System of Linear Equations using Inverse of a Matrix

Consider the system of equations

$a_1x + b_1y + c_1z = d_1$

$a_2x + b_2y + c_2z = d_2$

$a_3x + b_3y + c_3z = d_3$

Let $A = \begin{bmatrix} a_1 & b_1 & c_1 \\ a_2 & b_2 & c_2 \\ a_3 & b_3 & c_3 \end{bmatrix}$, $X = \begin{bmatrix} x \\ y \\ z \end{bmatrix}$ & $B = \begin{bmatrix} d_1 \\ d_2 \\ d_3 \end{bmatrix}$

Then, we can write, $AX = B$ i.e.,

- Unique solution of the equation $AX = B$ is given by $X = A^{-1}B$, when $|A| \neq 0$
- A system of equations is said to be consistent or inconsistent according as its solution exists or not.
- For a square matrix A in the matrix equation $AX = B$
  - (i) If $|A| \neq 0$, there exists a unique solution.
  - (ii) If $|A| = 0$, and $(\text{adj } A)\,B \neq 0$, then there exists no solution.
  - (iii) If $|A| = 0$ and $(\text{adj } A)\,B = 0$, then the system may or may not be consistent according as the system has either infinitely many solutions or no solution.

Determinant

Every square matrix associates to an expression or a number which is known as its determinant. If $A = [a_{ij}]$ is a square matrix of order n, then the determinant of A is denoted by det (A) or $|A|$ or Δ.

Determinant of a Square Matrix of Order Three

Consider $A = [a_{ij}]_{3\times3}$

Then, $|A| = \begin{bmatrix} a_{11} & a_{12} & a_{13} \\ a_{21} & a_{22} & a_{23} \\ a_{31} & a_{32} & a_{33} \end{bmatrix}$,

Expansion along first Row (R_1)

$|A| = a_{11}(a_{22}a_{33} - a_{32}a_{23}) - a_{12}(a_{21}a_{33} - a_{31}a_{23}) + a_{13}(a_{21}a_{32} - a_{31}a_{22})$
$= a_{11}a_{22}a_{33} - a_{11}a_{32}a_{23} - a_{12}a_{21}a_{33} + a_{12}a_{31}a_{23} + a_{13}a_{21}a_{32} - a_{13}a_{31}a_{22}$

Inverse of a Matrix

If A and B are two matrices such that

$AB = I = BA$

then B is called the inverse of A and it is denoted by A^{-1}.

Also, $A^{-1} = \dfrac{\text{adj}A}{|A|}$, if $|A| \neq 0$

Properties of Inverse Matrix

Let A and B are two invertible matrices of the same order, then

(i) $(AB)^{-1} = B^{-1}A^{-1}$
(ii) $(A^{T})^{-1} = (A^{-1})^{T}$
(iii) adj $(A^{-1}) = (\text{adj } A)^{-1}$

Adjoint of a Matrix

If $A = \begin{bmatrix} a_{11} & a_{12} & a_{13} \\ a_{21} & a_{22} & a_{23} \\ a_{31} & a_{32} & a_{33} \end{bmatrix}$, then adj $A = \begin{bmatrix} A_{11} & A_{21} & A_{31} \\ A_{12} & A_{22} & A_{32} \\ A_{13} & A_{23} & A_{33} \end{bmatrix}$,

where A_{ij} is the cofactor of a_{ij}

Area of a Triangle

Area of a triangle with vertices (x_1, y_1), (x_2, y_2) and (x_3, y_3) is given by

$\Delta = \dfrac{1}{2}\begin{vmatrix} x_1 & y_1 & 1 \\ x_2 & y_2 & 1 \\ x_3 & y_3 & 1 \end{vmatrix}$

Minor and Cofactor of an Element of a Determinant

Minor: The determinant that is left by cancelling the row and column intersecting at a particular element of a determinant is called the minor of that element of the determinant. Minor of an element a_{ij} of a determinant is denoted by M_{ij}.

Cofactor: The cofactor of an element a_{ij} of a determinant is denoted by A_{ij} (or C_{ij}) and is equal to $(-1)^{i+j} M_{ij}$.

> **Topic 1** **Determinant**

DETERMINANT

To every square matrix $A = [a_{ij}]$ of order n we can associate a number (real or complex) called determinant of A. It is denoted by det (A) or $|A|$

If $A = \begin{bmatrix} a & b \\ c & d \end{bmatrix}$, then determinant of A is written as $|A| = \begin{vmatrix} a & b \\ c & d \end{vmatrix}$.

Note that only square matrices have determinants.

DETERMINANT OF A MATRIX OF DIFFERENT ORDER

Determinant of a Matrix of Order One : Let $A = [a]$ be the matrix of order 1 then determinant of A is defined to be equal to a.

Determinant of a Matrix of Order Two : Let $A = \begin{bmatrix} a_{11} & a_{12} \\ a_{21} & a_{22} \end{bmatrix}$ be a matrix of order 2×2

Then $|A| = \begin{vmatrix} a_{11} & a_{12} \\ a_{21} & a_{22} \end{vmatrix} = a_{11} \times a_{22} - a_{12} \times a_{21}$.

Determinant of a Matrix of Order Three : Let $A = \begin{bmatrix} a_{11} & a_{12} & a_{13} \\ a_{21} & a_{22} & a_{23} \\ a_{31} & a_{32} & a_{33} \end{bmatrix}$ be a matrix of order 3×3.

Then $|A| = \begin{vmatrix} a_{11} & a_{12} & a_{13} \\ a_{21} & a_{22} & a_{23} \\ a_{31} & a_{32} & a_{33} \end{vmatrix} = a_{11} \begin{vmatrix} a_{22} & a_{23} \\ a_{32} & a_{33} \end{vmatrix} - a_{12} \begin{vmatrix} a_{21} & a_{23} \\ a_{31} & a_{33} \end{vmatrix} + a_{13} \begin{vmatrix} a_{21} & a_{22} \\ a_{31} & a_{32} \end{vmatrix}$ [Expanding along first row]

$= a_{11}(a_{22}a_{33} - a_{32}a_{23}) - a_{12}(a_{21}a_{33} - a_{23}a_{31}) + a_{13}(a_{21}a_{32} - a_{31}a_{22})$

Note that to evaluate a determinant of order three, the determinant can be expended along any row or column.

Illustration :

Evaluate the determinant D $= \begin{vmatrix} 2 & 3 & -2 \\ 1 & 2 & 3 \\ -2 & 1 & -3 \end{vmatrix}$ by expanding it along first column.

Sol. By definition, we have

$$D = \begin{vmatrix} 2 & 3 & -2 \\ 1 & 2 & 3 \\ -2 & 1 & -3 \end{vmatrix}$$

$$\Rightarrow D = (-1)^{1+1} \cdot 2 \cdot \begin{vmatrix} 2 & 3 \\ 1 & -3 \end{vmatrix} + (-1)^{2+1} \cdot 1 \cdot \begin{vmatrix} 3 & -2 \\ 1 & -3 \end{vmatrix} + (-1)^{3+1} \cdot (-2) \begin{vmatrix} 3 & -2 \\ 2 & 3 \end{vmatrix}$$

$$\Rightarrow D = 2 \begin{vmatrix} 2 & 3 \\ 1 & -3 \end{vmatrix} - \begin{vmatrix} 3 & -2 \\ 1 & -3 \end{vmatrix} - 2 \begin{vmatrix} 3 & -2 \\ 2 & 3 \end{vmatrix}$$

$$\Rightarrow D = 2(-6-3) - (-9+2) - 2(9+4) = -18 + 7 - 26 = -37.$$

Practice Exercise-1

Multiple Choice Questions

1. $\begin{vmatrix} a+ib & c+id \\ -c+id & a-ib \end{vmatrix} =$

(a) $(a+b)^2$ (b) $(a+b+c+d)^2$

(c) $(a^2+b^2-c^2-d^2)$ (d) $a^2+b^2+c^2+d^2$

2. $\begin{vmatrix} \cos 15° & \sin 15° \\ \sin 75° & \cos 75° \end{vmatrix} =$

(a) 0   (b) 5   (c) 3   (d) 7

3. If $A = \begin{bmatrix} 3 & 5 \\ 2 & 0 \end{bmatrix}$ and $B = \begin{bmatrix} 1 & 17 \\ 0 & -10 \end{bmatrix}$, then $|AB|$ is equal to :

(a) 80   (b) 100

(c) -110 (d) 92

Assertion & Reason Questions

DIRECTIONS : *Each of these questions contains an assertion followed by reason. Read them carefully and answer the question on the basis of following options. You have to select the one that best describes the two statements.*

(a) If both Assertion and Reason are correct and the Reason is a correct explanation of the Assertion.

(b) If both Assertion and Reason are correct but Reason is not a correct explanation of the Assertion.

(c) If the Assertion is correct but Reason is incorrect.

(d) If the Assertion is incorrect but the Reason is correct.

4. Let $A = \begin{bmatrix} 1 & 0 & a \\ 2 & 3 & b \\ -3 & 1 & c \end{bmatrix}$, $B = \begin{bmatrix} 1 & 0 & x \\ 2 & 3 & y \\ -3 & 1 & z \end{bmatrix}$

and $C = \begin{bmatrix} 1 & 0 & a+x \\ 2 & 3 & b+y \\ -3 & 1 & c+z \end{bmatrix}$

Assertion: $\det A + \det B = \det C$.

Reason: $A + B = C$.

5. Let $A = [a_{ij}]$ be a matrix of order 3×3.

Assertion: Expansion of determinant of A along second row and first column gives the same value.

Reason: Expanding a determinant along any row or column gives the same value.

One Word Answer Questions

6. If A_{ij} denotes the cofactor of the element a_{ij} of the determinant $\begin{vmatrix} 2 & -3 & 5 \\ 6 & 0 & 4 \\ 1 & 5 & -7 \end{vmatrix}$, then find the value of

$a_{11}A_{31} + a_{13}A_{32} + a_{13}A_{33}$

7. If c_{ij} is the cofactor of the element a_{ij} of the determinant $\begin{vmatrix} 2 & -3 & 5 \\ 6 & 0 & 4 \\ 1 & 5 & -7 \end{vmatrix}$, then find the value of $a_{32}.c_{32}$

Very Short Answer Questions

8. If $(x+9) = 0$ is a factor of $\begin{vmatrix} x & 3 & 7 \\ 2 & x & 2 \\ 7 & 6 & x \end{vmatrix} = 0$, then find the other factor.

9. If $A = \begin{bmatrix} 1 & 2 & 3 \\ -4 & -5 & 6 \end{bmatrix}$, then find $|A|$.

10. Find the value of $\begin{vmatrix} \sin 10° & -\cos 10° \\ \sin 80° & \cos 80° \end{vmatrix}$

11. Find the value of the determinant $\Delta = \begin{vmatrix} 1 & 4 & 3 \\ 0 & 12 & 9 \\ 1 & 2 & 2 \end{vmatrix}$

12. Find the minor of the element a_{11} in the determinant $\begin{vmatrix} 2 & 6 & 9 \\ 1 & 7 & 8 \\ 1 & 4 & 5 \end{vmatrix}$

Short Answer Questions

13. Find the roots of the equation $\begin{vmatrix} 0 & x & 16 \\ x & 5 & 7 \\ 0 & 9 & x \end{vmatrix} = 0$.

14. If $1, \omega, \omega^2$ the cube roots of unity, then find the value of $\begin{vmatrix} 1 & \omega^n & \omega^{2n} \\ \omega^{2n} & 1 & \omega^n \\ \omega^n & \omega^{2n} & 1 \end{vmatrix}$.

15. If $A = \begin{bmatrix} \alpha & 2 \\ 2 & \alpha \end{bmatrix}$ and $|A^3| = 125$, then find the value of α

16. If $A = \begin{bmatrix} \cos 20 & \sin 20° \\ \sin 70 & \cos 70° \end{bmatrix}$ find $|A|$.

17. If $\begin{vmatrix} 4 & 1 \\ 2 & 1 \end{vmatrix}^2 = \begin{vmatrix} 3 & 2 \\ 1 & x \end{vmatrix} - \begin{vmatrix} x & 3 \\ -2 & 1 \end{vmatrix}$, then evaluate x.

NCERT Exercise-1

1. Evaluate the following determinant :

$$\begin{vmatrix} 2 & 4 \\ -5 & -1 \end{vmatrix}$$

2. **(i)** $\begin{vmatrix} \cos\theta & -\sin\theta \\ \sin\theta & \cos\theta \end{vmatrix}$ **(ii)** $\begin{vmatrix} x^2 - x + 1 & x - 1 \\ x + 1 & x + 1 \end{vmatrix}$

3. If $A = \begin{bmatrix} 1 & 2 \\ 4 & 2 \end{bmatrix}$, then show that $|2A| = 4\,|A|$.

4. $A = \begin{bmatrix} 1 & 0 & 1 \\ 0 & 1 & 2 \\ 0 & 0 & 4 \end{bmatrix}$, then show that $|3A| = 27\,|A|$

5. Evaluate the determinants :

(i) $\begin{vmatrix} 3 & -1 & -2 \\ 0 & 0 & -1 \\ 3 & -5 & 0 \end{vmatrix}$ **(ii)** $\begin{vmatrix} 3 & -4 & 5 \\ 1 & 1 & -2 \\ 2 & 3 & 1 \end{vmatrix}$

(iii) $\begin{vmatrix} 0 & 1 & 2 \\ -1 & 0 & -3 \\ -2 & 3 & 0 \end{vmatrix}$ **(iv)** $\begin{vmatrix} 2 & -1 & -2 \\ 0 & 2 & -1 \\ 3 & -5 & 0 \end{vmatrix}$

6. If $A = \begin{bmatrix} 1 & 1 & -2 \\ 2 & 1 & -3 \\ 5 & 4 & -9 \end{bmatrix}$, find $|A|$.

7. Find the value of x, if

(i) $\begin{vmatrix} 2 & 4 \\ 5 & 1 \end{vmatrix} = \begin{vmatrix} 2x & 4 \\ 6 & x \end{vmatrix}$ **(ii)** $\begin{vmatrix} 2 & 3 \\ 4 & 5 \end{vmatrix} = \begin{vmatrix} x & 3 \\ 2x & 5 \end{vmatrix}$

8. If $\begin{vmatrix} x & 2 \\ 18 & x \end{vmatrix} = \begin{vmatrix} 6 & 2 \\ 18 & 6 \end{vmatrix}$, then x is equal to

   (a) 6   (b) $\pm\,6$

   (c) $-\,6$ (d) 6, 6.

Topic 2   Area of Triangle

AREA OF A TRIANGLE

The area of the triangle whose vertices are (x_1, y_1), (x_2, y_2) and (x_3, y_3)

$$= \frac{1}{2}\begin{vmatrix} x_1 & y_1 & 1 \\ x_2 & y_2 & 1 \\ x_3 & y_3 & 1 \end{vmatrix}$$

(i) The area is positive, so take only absolute value.

(ii) If the three points are collinear, the area of triangle is zero.

Illustration :

Find the area of the triangle with vertices A(5,4), B(–2,4) and C(2,–6).

Sol. The area Δ of triangle ABC is given by

$$\Delta = \frac{1}{2}\begin{vmatrix} 5 & 4 & 1 \\ -2 & 4 & 1 \\ 2 & -6 & 1 \end{vmatrix}$$

$$\Rightarrow \quad \Delta = \frac{1}{2}\begin{vmatrix} 5 & 4 & 1 \\ -7 & 0 & 0 \\ -3 & -10 & 0 \end{vmatrix} \qquad \text{[Applying } R_2 \to R_2 - R_1 \text{ and } R_3 \to R_3 - R_1\text{]}$$

$$\Rightarrow \quad \Delta = \frac{1}{2} \cdot 1 \begin{vmatrix} -7 & 0 \\ -3 & -10 \end{vmatrix} \qquad \text{[Expanding along } C_3\text{]}$$

$$\Rightarrow \quad \Delta = \frac{1}{2}\,[70 - 0] = 35 \text{ sq. units}$$

Practice Exercise-2

Multiple Choice Questions

1. If the area of a triangle ABC, with vertices A$(1, 3)$, B$(0, 0)$ and C$(k, 0)$ is 3 sq. units, then the value of k is
   (a) 2   (b) 3   (c) 4   (d) 5

2. If area of triangle is 4 sq. units with vertices $(-2, 0)$, $(0, 4)$ and $(0, k)$, then k is equal to
   (a) $0, -8$ (b) 8   (c) -8 (d) $0, 8$

3. Area of the triangle whose vertices are $(a, b + c)$, $(b, c + a)$ and $(c, a + b)$, is
   (a) 2 sq units   (b) 3 sq units
   (c) 0 sq unit   (d) None of these

4. If $\begin{vmatrix} x_1 & y_1 & 1 \\ x_2 & y_2 & 1 \\ x_3 & y_3 & 1 \end{vmatrix} = \begin{vmatrix} a_1 & b_1 & 1 \\ a_2 & b_2 & 1 \\ a_3 & b_3 & 1 \end{vmatrix}$ then two triangles with vertices

   (x_1, y_1), (x_2, y_2), (x_3, y_3) and (a_1, b_1); (a_2, b_2); (a_3, b_3) are
   (a) congruent   (b) similar
   (c) triangles of equal area   (d) none of these

Assertion & Reason Questions

DIRECTIONS : *Each of these questions contains an assertion followed by reason. Read them carefully and answer the question on the basis of following options. You have to select the one that best describes the two statements.*
   (a) If both Assertion and Reason are correct and the Reason is a correct explanation of the Assertion.
   (b) If both Assertion and Reason are correct but Reason is not a correct explanation of the Assertion.
   (c) If the Assertion is correct but Reason is incorrect.
   (d) If the Assertion is incorrect but the Reason is correct.

5. **Assertion :** The area of triangle with vertices P$(0, 4)$, Q$(-1, 4)$ and R $(2, 4)$ is zero.

   Reason : The area of triangle formed by three collinear points is zero.

6. **Assertion :** The points A$(1, 1)$, B$(4, 2)$ and C$(3, 5)$ are not collinear.

   Reason : Points are collinear if area of the triangle formed by the points is not zero.

One Word Answer Questions

7. Let k be an integer such that triangle with vertices $(k, -3k)$, $(5, k)$ and $(-k, 2)$ has area 28 sq. units. Then find the orthocentre of this triangle.

8. Let two points be $A(1, -1)$ and $B(0, 2)$. If a point $P(x', y')$ be such that the area of $\Delta PAB = 5$ sq. units and it lies on the line, $3x + y - 4\lambda = 0$, then find the value of λ.

Very Short Answer Questions

9. Find the area of triangle whose vertices are L $(4, 9)$, M $(-3, 3)$ and N $(6, 2)$

10. Find the value of k if area of the triangle formed by vertices X $(4, 8)$, Y$(-6, 2)$ and Z$(k, 7)$ is 28 units

11. Find out the area of the triangle whose vertices are P$(0, 0)$ Q $(3, 1)$ and R$(2, 4)$.

Short Answer Questions

12. If $(k, 2)$, $(2, 4)$ and $(3, 2)$ are vertices of the triangle of area 4 square units then determine value of k.

13. Find the area of the triangle whose vertices are $(-2, -3)$, $(3, 2)$ and $(-1, -8)$.

NCERT Exercise-2

1. **Find the area of the triangle with vertices at the point given in each of the following :**
   (i) $(1, 0), (6, 0) (4, 3)$
   (ii) $(2, 7), (1, 1), (10, 8)$
   (iii) $(-2, -3), (3, 2), (-1, -8)$

2. **Show that the points A $(a, b + c)$, B $(b, c + a)$ C $(c, a + b)$ are collinear.**

3. **Find the value of k if area of triangle is 4 square units and vertices are**
   (i) $(k, 0), (4, 0), (0, 2)$ (ii) $(-2, 0), (0, 4), (0, k)$.

4. (i) **Find the equation of line joining $(1, 2)$ and $(3, 6)$ using determinants**
   (ii) **Find the equation of line joining $(3, 1)$, $(9, 3)$ using determinants.**

5. **If area of triangle is 35 sq. units with vertices $(2, -6), (5, 4)$ and $(k, 4)$. Then k is**
   (a) 12   (b) -2 (c) $-12, -2$ (d) $12, -2$

Topic 3   Minors, Co-factors, Singular Matrix
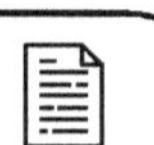

MINORS AND CO-FACTORS

(i) **Minors:** The determinant obtained by deleting the i-the row and j-th column passing through the element a_{ij} is called the minor of element a_{ij} and is denoted by M_{ij}.
   Note that minor of an element of a determinant of order n $(n \geq 2)$ is a determinant of order $n - 1$.

(ii) **Cofactors:** The cofactor of element a_{ij} is $(-1)^{i+j}$ times the determinant obtained by deleting the i-th row and jth column (passed through a_{ij}) and is denoted by C_{ij} i.e. $C_{ij} = (-1)^{i+j} M_{ij}$

SINGULAR MATRIX

A square matrix is a singular matrix if its determinant is zero. Otherwise it is a non-singular matrix.

Practice Exercise-3

Multiple Choice Questions

1. If $\Delta = \begin{vmatrix} 5 & 3 & 8 \\ 2 & 0 & 1 \\ 1 & 2 & 3 \end{vmatrix}$, the minor of the element a_{23} is

(a) 5   (b) 6

(c) 7   (d) 8

2. Find the cofactor of the element a_{32} of the determinant

$$\begin{vmatrix} 2 & 3 & -4 \\ 3 & 6 & 5 \\ 1 & 8 & 9 \end{vmatrix}$$

(a) -2 (b) -4

(c) -6 (d) -9

3. If $\Delta = \begin{vmatrix} 1^2 & 2^2 & 3^2 \\ 2^2 & 3^2 & 4^2 \\ 3^2 & 4^2 & 5^2 \end{vmatrix}$, the minor of a_{22} is

(a) -46 (b) 46

(c) -56 (d) 56

Assertion & Reason Questions

DIRECTIONS : *Each of these questions contains an assertion followed by reason. Read them carefully and answer the question on the basis of following options. You have to select the one that best describes the two statements.*

(a) If both Assertion and Reason are correct and the Reason is a correct explanation of the Assertion.

(b) If both Assertion and Reason are correct but Reason is not a correct explanation of the Assertion.

(c) If the Assertion is correct but Reason is incorrect.

(d) If the Assertion is incorrect but the Reason is correct.

4. **Assertion :** The minor of the element a_{32} of the determinant

$$\begin{vmatrix} 9 & 2 & 3 \\ 2 & 0 & 1 \\ 5 & 3 & 8 \end{vmatrix} \text{ is } 3.$$

Reason : The minor of an element a_{ij} of a determinant is defined as the value of determinant obtained after deleting the ith row and j[th] column.

5. **Assertion :** If $\Delta = \begin{vmatrix} a_{11} & a_{12} & a_{13} \\ a_{21} & a_{22} & a_{23} \\ a_{31} & a_{32} & a_{33} \end{vmatrix}$ and A_{ij} are the co-factors

of a_{ij}, then $a_{11}A_{21} + a_{12}A_{22} + a_{13}A_{23} = 0$

Reason: Determinant is the sum of product of elements of any row (column) with their corresponding co-factors.

Very Short Answer Questions

6. If $\Delta = \begin{vmatrix} 1 & 0 & 0 \\ 0 & 3 & 0 \\ 0 & 0 & 4 \end{vmatrix}$, then find the value of $a_{11}A_{11} + a_{12}A_{12} +$

$a_{13}A_{13}$ where a_{ij} are elements and A_{ij} are cofactors.

7. If $\Delta = \begin{vmatrix} 1 & 2 & 3 \\ 2 & 4 & 5 \\ 3 & 5 & 6 \end{vmatrix}$, then find the value of $a_{11}A_{21} + a_{12}A_{22} +$

$a_{13}A_{23}$ where a_{ij} are elements and A_{ij} are cofactors.

NCERT Exercise-3

1. Write the minors and cofactors of the elements of following determinants :

(i) $\begin{vmatrix} 2 & -4 \\ 0 & 3 \end{vmatrix}$ (ii) $\begin{vmatrix} a & c \\ b & d \end{vmatrix}$

2. Write minors and co-factor of elements of the determinant

(i) $\begin{vmatrix} 1 & 0 & 0 \\ 0 & 1 & 0 \\ 0 & 0 & 1 \end{vmatrix}$ (ii) $\begin{vmatrix} 1 & 0 & 4 \\ 3 & 5 & -1 \\ 0 & 1 & 2 \end{vmatrix}$

3. **Using cofactors of elements of second row, evaluate**

$$\Delta = \begin{vmatrix} 5 & 3 & 8 \\ 2 & 0 & 1 \\ 1 & 2 & 3 \end{vmatrix}.$$

4. **Using cofactors of elements of third column, evaluate**

$$\Delta = \begin{vmatrix} 1 & x & yz \\ 1 & y & zx \\ 1 & z & xy \end{vmatrix}.$$

5. If $\Delta = \begin{vmatrix} a_{11} & a_{12} & a_{13} \\ a_{21} & a_{22} & a_{23} \\ a_{31} & a_{32} & a_{33} \end{vmatrix}$ and A_{ij} is the cofactors of a_{ij}, then value of Δ is given by

(a) $a_{11}A_{31} + a_{12}A_{32} + a_{13}A_{33}$

(b) $a_{11}A_{11} + a_{12}A_{21} + a_{13}A_{31}$

(c) $a_{21}A_{11} + a_{22}A_{12} + a_{23}A_{13}$

(d) $a_{11}A_{11} + a_{21}A_{21} + a_{31}A_{31}$

Topic 4 — Adjoint and Inverse of a Matrix

ADJOINT OF A MATRIX

The adjoint of a square matrix is the transpose of the matrix of cofactors. If A_{ij} is the cofactor of a_{ij} of det A or $|a_{ij}|$, then

$$\text{adj}\, A = \begin{bmatrix} A_{11} & A_{12} & A_{13} \\ A_{21} & A_{22} & A_{23} \\ A_{31} & A_{32} & A_{33} \end{bmatrix}^{T} = \begin{bmatrix} A_{11} & A_{21} & A_{31} \\ A_{12} & A_{22} & A_{32} \\ A_{13} & A_{23} & A_{33} \end{bmatrix}$$

(a) If A be any given square matrix of order n then $A\,[\text{adj}\,(A)] = [\text{adj}\,(A)]\,A = |A|\,I$, where I is the identity matrix of order n.

(b) If A is any non-singular matrix of order n then $|\,\text{adj}\,(A)| = |A|^{n-1}$

(c) $|AB| = |A|\,|B|$, where A and B are square matrces of same order.

(d) A square matrix A is invertible if and only if A is non-singular i.e. $|A| \neq 0$

Properties of Adjoint Matrix

If A, B are square matrices of order n and I_n is corresponding unit matrix, then

(i) $A\,(\text{adj}.\,A) = |A|\,I_n = (\text{adj}\,A)\,A$

(ii) $|\text{adj}\,A| = |A|^{n-1}$

(iii) $\text{adj}\,(\text{adj}\,A) = |A|^{n-2}\,A$

(iv) $|\text{adj}\,(\text{adj}\,A)| = |A|^{(n-1)^2}$

(v) $\text{adj}\,(A^{T}) = (\text{adj}\,A)^{T}$

(vi) $\text{adj}\,(AB) = (\text{adj}\,B)\,(\text{adj}\,A)$

(vii) $\text{adj}\,(A^{m}) = (\text{adj}\,A)^{m}, \; m \in N$

(viii) $\text{adj}\,(kA) = k^{n-1}\,(\text{adj}.\,A), \; k \in R$

(ix) $\text{adj}\,(I_n) = I_n$

(x) $\text{adj}\,O = O$

(xi) A is symmetric $\Rightarrow$ adj A is also symmetric

(xii) A is diagonal matrix $\Rightarrow$ adj A is also diagonal matrix

(xiii) A is triangular matrix $\Rightarrow$ adj A is also triangular matrix

(xiv) A is singular matrix $\Rightarrow |\text{adj}\,A| = O$

INVERSE OF A MATRIX

Inverse of a matrix A, $A^{-1} = \dfrac{1}{|A|}\,\text{adj}\,A$; if $|A| \neq 0$ i.e., matrix A is invertible or non-singular.

(i) $(AB)^{-1} = B^{-1}.\,A^{-1}$

(ii) $|A^{-1}| = |A|^{-1}$

(iii) $(A^{-1})^{-1} = A$

Note that every invertible matrix possesses a unique inverse.

Illustration :

Find the inverse of $A = \begin{bmatrix} 1 & 3 & 3 \\ 1 & 4 & 3 \\ 1 & 3 & 4 \end{bmatrix}$ and verity that $A^{-1}A = I_3$

Sol. We have,

$$|A| = \begin{bmatrix} 1 & 3 & 3 \\ 1 & 4 & 3 \\ 1 & 3 & 4 \end{bmatrix}$$

$$\Rightarrow \; |A| = (-1)^{1+1}\begin{vmatrix}4 & 3 \\ 3 & 4\end{vmatrix} + 3(-1)^{1+2}\begin{vmatrix}1 & 3 \\ 1 & 4\end{vmatrix} + 3(-1)^{1+3}\begin{vmatrix}1 & 4 \\ 1 & 3\end{vmatrix}$$

$$\Rightarrow \; |A| = \begin{vmatrix}4 & 3 \\ 3 & 4\end{vmatrix} - 3\begin{vmatrix}1 & 3 \\ 1 & 4\end{vmatrix} + 3\begin{vmatrix}1 & 4 \\ 1 & 3\end{vmatrix}$$

$$\Rightarrow \; |A| = (16-9) - 3(4-3) + 3(3-4) = 7 - 3 - 3 = 1 \neq 0$$

So, A is invertible.

Let C_{ij} be the cofactor of a_{ij} in $A = [a_{ij}]$. Then,

$$C_{11} = (-1)^{1+1}\begin{vmatrix}4 & 3 \\ 3 & 4\end{vmatrix} = 7, \quad C_{12} = (-1)^{1+2}\begin{vmatrix}1 & 3 \\ 1 & 4\end{vmatrix} = -1,$$

$$C_{13} = (-1)^{1+3}\begin{vmatrix}1 & 4 \\ 1 & 3\end{vmatrix} = -1, \quad C_{21} = (-1)^{2+1}\begin{vmatrix}3 & 3 \\ 3 & 4\end{vmatrix} = -3,$$

$$C_{22} = (-1)^{2+2}\begin{vmatrix}1 & 3 \\ 1 & 4\end{vmatrix} = 1, \quad C_{23} = (-1)^{2+3}\begin{vmatrix}1 & 3 \\ 1 & 3\end{vmatrix} = 0,$$

$$C_{31} = (-1)^{3+1}\begin{vmatrix}3 & 3 \\ 4 & 3\end{vmatrix} = -3, \quad C_{32} = (-1)^{3+2}\begin{vmatrix}1 & 3 \\ 1 & 3\end{vmatrix} = 0,$$

and, $C_{33} = (-1)^{3+3}\begin{vmatrix}1 & 3 \\ 1 & 4\end{vmatrix} = 1$

$$\therefore \; \text{adj } A = \begin{bmatrix}7 & -1 & -1 \\ -3 & 1 & 0 \\ -3 & 0 & 1\end{bmatrix}^T = \begin{bmatrix}7 & -3 & -3 \\ -1 & 1 & 0 \\ -1 & 0 & 1\end{bmatrix}$$

Hence, $\quad A^{-1} = \dfrac{1}{|A|} \text{adj } A$

$$\Rightarrow \; A^{-1} = \frac{1}{1}\begin{bmatrix}7 & -3 & -3 \\ -1 & 1 & 0 \\ -1 & 0 & 1\end{bmatrix} = \begin{bmatrix}7 & -3 & -3 \\ -1 & 1 & 0 \\ -1 & 0 & 1\end{bmatrix}$$

Practice Exercise-4

Multiple Choice Questions

1. If B is a non-singular matrix and A is a square matrix, then det $(B^{-1}AB)$ is equal to
   (a) $\det(A^{-1})$
   (b) $\det(B^{-1})$
   (c) $\det(A)$
   (d) $\det(B)$

2. If $A = \begin{bmatrix}a & 0 & 0 \\ 0 & a & 0 \\ 0 & 0 & a\end{bmatrix}$, then the value of $|\text{adj } A|$ is

   (a) a^{27}
   (b) a^9
   (c) a^6
   (d) a^2

3. If $A = \begin{bmatrix}\alpha & \beta \\ \gamma & \alpha\end{bmatrix}$, then Adj. A is equal to :

   (a) $\begin{bmatrix}\delta & -\gamma \\ -\beta & \alpha\end{bmatrix}$
   (b) $\begin{bmatrix}\delta & -\beta \\ -\gamma & \alpha\end{bmatrix}$
   (c) $\begin{bmatrix}-\delta & \beta \\ \gamma & -\alpha\end{bmatrix}$
   (d) $\begin{bmatrix}-\delta & -\beta \\ \gamma & \alpha\end{bmatrix}$

4. The matrix $\begin{bmatrix} \lambda & -1 & 4 \\ -3 & 0 & 1 \\ -1 & 1 & 2 \end{bmatrix}$ is invertible, if

  (a) $\lambda \neq -17$ (b) $\lambda \neq -18$
  (c) $\lambda \neq -19$ (d) $\lambda \neq -20$

5. If A is a non-singular matrix of order 3, then $|\text{adj } A| = |A|^n$. Here the value of n is
  (a) 2   (b) 4
  (c) 6   (d) 8

Assertion & Reason Questions

DIRECTIONS : *Each of these questions contains an assertion followed by reason. Read them carefully and answer the question on the basis of following options. You have to select the one that best describes the two statements.*
(a) If both Assertion and Reason are correct and the Reason is a correct explanation of the Assertion.
(b) If both Assertion and Reason are correct but Reason is not a correct explanation of the Assertion.
(c) If the Assertion is correct but Reason is incorrect.
(d) If the Assertion is incorrect but the Reason is correct.

6. **Assertion:** If $A = \begin{bmatrix} a & 0 & 0 \\ 0 & b & 0 \\ 0 & 0 & c \end{bmatrix}$ then $A^{-1} = \begin{bmatrix} \frac{1}{a} & 0 & 0 \\ 0 & \frac{1}{b} & 0 \\ 0 & 0 & \frac{1}{c} \end{bmatrix}$

  Reason: The inverse of a diagonal matrix is a diagonal matrix.

7. **Assertion:** The inverse of the matrix $\begin{bmatrix} 1 & 4 & 2 \\ 2 & -2 & 4 \\ -3 & 7 & -6 \end{bmatrix}$ does not exist.

  Reason: The matrix $\begin{bmatrix} 1 & 4 & 2 \\ 2 & -1 & 4 \\ -3 & 7 & -6 \end{bmatrix}$ is singular.

One Word Answer Questions

8. If A and B are square matrices and A^{-1} and B^{-1} of the same order exist, then find $(AB)^{-1}$.
9. If I_3 is the identity matrix of order 3, then find I_3^{-1}.
10. If for $AX = B$, $B = \begin{bmatrix} 9 \\ 52 \\ 0 \end{bmatrix}$ and

  $A^{-1} = \begin{bmatrix} 3 & -1/2 & -1/2 \\ -4 & 3/4 & 5/4 \\ 2 & -3/4 & -3/4 \end{bmatrix}$, then find X.

Very Short Answer Questions

11. Matrix $A = \begin{bmatrix} x & 3 & 2 \\ 1 & y & 4 \\ 2 & 2 & z \end{bmatrix}$, if $x\,y\,z = 60$

  and $8x + 4y + 3z = 20$, then find A (adj A) is equal to

12. If $A = \begin{bmatrix} 0 & -1 & 2 \\ 2 & -2 & 0 \end{bmatrix}$, $B = \begin{bmatrix} 0 & 1 \\ 1 & 0 \\ 1 & 1 \end{bmatrix}$ and $M = AB$, then find the value of M^{-1}.

13. If $A = \begin{bmatrix} 1 & 0 & 3 \\ 2 & 1 & 1 \\ 0 & 0 & 2 \end{bmatrix}$, then find the value of $|\text{adj (adj } A)|$.

14. If $A = \begin{bmatrix} 1 & 0 \\ 1 & 1 \end{bmatrix}$, then find the value of A^{-n}.

Short Answer Questions

15. If matrix $A = \begin{bmatrix} 3 & -2 & 4 \\ 1 & 2 & -1 \\ 0 & 1 & 1 \end{bmatrix}$ and $A^{-1} = \frac{1}{k}(\text{adj } A)$, then k is :

16. If the matrix $\begin{bmatrix} 1 & 3 & \lambda+2 \\ 2 & 4 & 8 \\ 3 & 5 & 10 \end{bmatrix}$ is singular, then $\lambda =$

17. Let $A = \begin{bmatrix} 5 & 5\alpha & \alpha \\ 0 & \alpha & 5\alpha \\ 0 & 0 & 5 \end{bmatrix}$. If $|A^2| = 25$, then $|\alpha|$ equals to

NCERT Exercise-4

Find the adjoint of each of the matrices in Exercises 1 and 2.

1. $\begin{bmatrix} 1 & 2 \\ 3 & 4 \end{bmatrix}$ 2. $\begin{bmatrix} 1 & -1 & 2 \\ 2 & 3 & 5 \\ -2 & 0 & 1 \end{bmatrix}$

Verify A (adj A) = (adj A) · A = |A| I in Qs. 3 and 4.

3. $\begin{bmatrix} 2 & 3 \\ -4 & 6 \end{bmatrix}$ 4. $A = \begin{bmatrix} 1 & -1 & 2 \\ 3 & 0 & -2 \\ 1 & 0 & 3 \end{bmatrix}$

Find the inverse of each of the matrices (if it exists) given in the Exercises 5 to 11 :

5. $\begin{bmatrix} 2 & -2 \\ 4 & 3 \end{bmatrix} = A\,(\text{say})$ 6. $\begin{bmatrix} -1 & 5 \\ -3 & 2 \end{bmatrix} = A\,(\text{say})$

7. $\begin{bmatrix} 1 & 2 & 3 \\ 0 & 2 & 4 \\ 0 & 0 & 5 \end{bmatrix} = A\,(\text{say})$ 8. $\begin{bmatrix} 1 & 0 & 0 \\ 3 & 3 & 0 \\ 5 & 2 & -1 \end{bmatrix} = A\,(\text{say})$

9. $\begin{bmatrix} 2 & 1 & 3 \\ 4 & -1 & 0 \\ -7 & 2 & 1 \end{bmatrix} = A\,(\text{say})$

10. $\begin{bmatrix} 1 & -1 & 2 \\ 0 & 2 & -3 \\ 3 & -2 & 4 \end{bmatrix} = A\,(\text{say})$

11. $\begin{bmatrix} 1 & 0 & 0 \\ 0 & \cos\alpha & \sin\alpha \\ 0 & \sin\alpha & -\cos\alpha \end{bmatrix} = A\,(\text{say})$

12. Let $A = \begin{bmatrix} 3 & 7 \\ 2 & 5 \end{bmatrix}$ and $B = \begin{bmatrix} 6 & 8 \\ 7 & 9 \end{bmatrix}$, verify that

$(AB)^{-1} = B^{-1}A^{-1}$.

13. If $A = \begin{bmatrix} 3 & 1 \\ -1 & 2 \end{bmatrix}$, show that $A^2 - 5A + 7I = 0$. Hence find A^{-1}.

14. For the matrix $A = \begin{bmatrix} 3 & 2 \\ 1 & 1 \end{bmatrix}$, find the numbers a and b such that $A^2 + aA + bI^2 = 0$. Hence, find A^{-1}.

15. For the matrix $A = \begin{bmatrix} 1 & 1 & 1 \\ 1 & 2 & -3 \\ 2 & -1 & 3 \end{bmatrix}$ show that

$A^3 - 6A^2 + 5A + 11I_3 = 0$. Hence find A^{-1}.

16. If $A = \begin{bmatrix} 2 & -1 & 1 \\ -1 & 2 & -1 \\ 1 & -1 & 2 \end{bmatrix}$. Verify that

$A^3 - 6A^2 + 9A - 4I = 0$ and hence, find A^{-1}.

17. Let A be a non-singular square matrix of order 3×3. Then $|\text{Adj } A|$ is equal to:

(a) $|A|$ (b) $|A|^2$

(c) $|A|^3$ (d) $3|A|$

18. If A is an invertible matrix of order 2, then det. (A^{-1}) is equal to:

(a) det. (A)   (b) $\dfrac{1}{\text{det .(A)}}$

(c) 1   (d) 0

Topic 5   Application of Determinant and Matrices 

LINEAR SYSTEM OF EQUATIONS

Consistent System : A system of equations is said to be consistent if it has one or more than one solutions.

Inconsistent System : A system of equation is inconsistent if it has no solution.

SOLUTION OF SYSTEM OF LINEAR EQUATIONS

Consider the system of equation

$a_1x + b_1y + c_1z = d_1$
$a_2x + b_2y + c_2z = d_2$
$a_3x + b_3y + c_3z = d_3$

The given system of equation can be written as

$$\begin{bmatrix} a_1 & b_1 & c_1 \\ a_2 & b_2 & c_2 \\ a_3 & b_3 & c_3 \end{bmatrix} \begin{bmatrix} x \\ y \\ z \end{bmatrix} = \begin{bmatrix} d_1 \\ d_2 \\ d_3 \end{bmatrix}$$

Let $A = \begin{bmatrix} a_1 & b_1 & c_1 \\ a_2 & b_2 & c_2 \\ a_3 & b_3 & c_3 \end{bmatrix}$, $X = \begin{bmatrix} x \\ y \\ z \end{bmatrix}$ and $B = \begin{bmatrix} d_1 \\ d_2 \\ d_3 \end{bmatrix}$

Then $AX = B$

$\therefore$ $X = A^{-1}B$.

(i)   If $|A| \ne 0$, then $AX = B$ has a unique solution.

(ii)   If $|A| = 0$, and $(\text{adj } A)\,B \ne 0$ then the system of equation is inconsistent.

(iii) If $|A| = 0$ and $(\text{adj } A)\, B = 0$, then the system of equation has infinitely many solutions.

In this case, we put one of the variables equal to k. Let $z = k$, then we find the value of x and y in terms of k.

Solution of Homogeneous System of Linear Equations

If in the above given system of equations, constant terms d_1, d_2 and d_3 are zeros, then the given system is called the system of homogeneous linear equations. For the system of homogeneous linear equations

If $|A| \neq 0$, then $x = y = z = 0$. This solution is called trivivial solution.

If $|A| = 0$, then the system has infinite many solutions. This solution is called non-trivivial solution.

Practice Exercise-5

Multiple Choice Questions

1. Given : $2x - y - 4z = 2$, $x - 2y - z = -4$, $x + y + \lambda z = 4$, then the value of λ such that the given system of equation has NO solution, is
   - (a) 3
   - (b) 1
   - (c) 0
   - (d) -3

2. If the equations $x + ay - z = 0$, $2x - y + az = 0$, $ax + y + 2z = 0$ have non-trivial solutions, then $a =$
   - (a) 2
   - (b) -2
   - (c) $\sqrt{3}$
   - (d) $-\sqrt{3}$

3. Consider the system of linear equations;
   $$x_1 + 2x_2 + x_3 = 3$$
   $$2x_1 + 3x_2 + x_3 = 3$$
   $$3x_1 + 5x_2 + 2x_3 = 1$$
   The system has
   - (a) exactly 3 solutions
   - (b) a unique solution
   - (c) no solution
   - (d) infinite solutions

4. The system of linear equations : $x + y + z = 0$, $2x + y - z = 0$, $3x + 2y = 0$ has :
   - (a) no solution
   - (b) a unique solution
   - (c) an infinitely many solution
   - (d) None of these

Case/Passage Based Question

DIRECTIONS (Q. 5) : *has 5 subparts based on case/passage given, attempt any 4 out of 5 questions.*

5. Rohit is a student of class XII, he went to a shop to buy onion, wheat and rice for his family daily needs. Further, the shopkeeper had the price of onion, wheat and rice in combined form. The cost of 4 kg onion, 3 kg wheat and 2 kg ricec is ₹ 60. The cost of 2 kg onion, 4 kg wheat and 6 kg rice is ₹ 90. The cost of 6 kg onion 2 kg wheat and 3 kg rice is ₹ 70.

Now, following questions came to Rohit's mind when he decided to use matrix method of the form $AX = B$ for his problem.

(i) What is the matrix representation of the problem if the cost of onion, wheat and rice by x, y and z respectively.

   (a) $\begin{bmatrix} 60 & 3 & 2 \\ 90 & 4 & 6 \\ 70 & 2 & 3 \end{bmatrix} \begin{bmatrix} x \\ y \\ z \end{bmatrix} = \begin{bmatrix} 4 \\ 2 \\ 6 \end{bmatrix}$

   (b) $\begin{bmatrix} 4 & 3 & 2 \\ 2 & 4 & 6 \\ 6 & 2 & 3 \end{bmatrix} \begin{bmatrix} x \\ y \\ z \end{bmatrix} = \begin{bmatrix} 60 \\ 90 \\ 70 \end{bmatrix}$

   (c) $\begin{bmatrix} 4 & 3 & 60 \\ 2 & 4 & 90 \\ 6 & 2 & 70 \end{bmatrix} \begin{bmatrix} x \\ y \\ z \end{bmatrix} = \begin{bmatrix} 2 \\ 6 \\ 3 \end{bmatrix}$

   (d) $\begin{bmatrix} 2 & 4 & 6 \\ 4 & 3 & 2 \\ 6 & 2 & 3 \end{bmatrix} \begin{bmatrix} x \\ y \\ z \end{bmatrix} = \begin{bmatrix} 60 \\ 90 \\ 70 \end{bmatrix}$

(ii) What is the determinant of coefficient matrix?
   - (a) 30
   - (b) 40
   - (c) 50
   - (d) 60

(iii) What is the adjoint of coefficient matrix?

   (a) $\begin{bmatrix} 0 & -5 & 10 \\ 30 & 0 & -20 \\ -20 & 10 & 10 \end{bmatrix}$

$$\text{(b)} \quad \begin{bmatrix} -20 & 10 & 10 \\ 30 & 0 & -20 \\ 0 & -5 & 10 \end{bmatrix}$$

$$\text{(c)} \quad \begin{bmatrix} -20 & 30 & 0 \\ 10 & 0 & -5 \\ 10 & -20 & 10 \end{bmatrix}$$

$$\text{(d)} \quad \begin{bmatrix} 0 & -5 & 0 \\ 0 & 0 & -20 \\ -20 & 10 & 10 \end{bmatrix}$$

(iv) Determinant of inverse of coefficient matrix is

(a) 50   (b) $\dfrac{1}{50}$

(c) $\dfrac{9}{50}$ (d) 60

(v) Find the cost of each item (x, y, z) per kg.
(a) ₹8, ₹5, ₹8   (b) ₹8, ₹8, ₹5
(c) ₹8, ₹5, ₹5   (d) ₹5, ₹8, ₹8

One Word Answer Questions

6. Does the system of the equations $2x + 3y + 4 = 0$; $3x + 4y + 6 = 0$ and $4x + 5y + 8 = 0$ has unique solution.

7. The system of simultaneous linear equations $kx + 2y - z = 1$, $(k-1)\,y - 2z = 2$ and $(k+2)\,z = 3$ have a unique solution then find the value of k.

8. Represent the following system of linear equations in matrix form
$$a_1 x + b_1 y = c_1$$
$$a_2 x + b_2 y = c_2$$

Very Short Answer Question

9. Find the number of values of k for which the system of equations $(k+1)x + 8y = 4k$; $kx + (k+3)\,y = 3k - 1$ has infinitely many solutions.

Short Answer Questions

10. If the system of linear equations
$$x + 2ay + az = 0$$
$$x + 3by + bz = 0$$
$$x + 4cy + cz = 0$$
has a non‑zero solution, then find the relation among a, b, c

11. If a, b, c are non‑zeros, then the system of equations $(\alpha + a)x + \alpha y + \alpha z = 0$, $\alpha x + (\alpha + b)y + \alpha z = 0$, $\alpha x + \alpha y + (\alpha + c)z = 0$ has a non‑trivial solution then find the relation among α, a, b and c.

NCERT Exercise-5

Examine the consistency of the system of equations in Exercises 1 to 6 :

1.
$$x + 2y = 2$$
$$2x + 3y = 3$$

2.
$$2x - y = 5$$
$$x + y = 4$$

3.
$$x + 3y = 5$$
$$2x + 6y = 8$$

4.
$$x + y + z = 1$$
$$2x + 3y + 2z = 2$$
$$ax + ay + 2az = 4$$

5.
$$3x - y - 2z = 2$$
$$2y - z = -1$$
$$3x - 5y = 3$$

6.
$$5x - y + 4z = 5$$
$$2x + 3y + 5z = 2$$
$$5x - 2y + 6z = -1$$

Solve the following of linear equations using matrix method in Exercises 7 to 14 :

7.
$$5x + 2y = 4$$
$$7x + 3y = 5$$

8.
$$2x - y = -2$$
$$3x + 3y = 3$$

9.
$$4x - 3y = 3$$
$$3x - 5y = 7$$

10.
$$5x + 2y = 3$$
$$3x + 2y = 5$$

11. $\quad 2x + y + z = 1, \quad x - 2y - z = 3/2, \quad 3y - 5z = 9$

12.
$$x - y + z = 4$$
$$2x + y - 3z = 0$$
$$x + y + z = 2.$$

13.
$$2x + 3y + 3z = 5$$
$$x - 2y + z = -4$$
$$3x - y - 2z = 3$$

14.
$$x - y + 2z = 7$$
$$3x + 4y - 5z = -5$$
$$2x - y + 3z = 12.$$

15. If $A = \begin{bmatrix} 2 & -3 & 5 \\ 3 & 2 & -4 \\ 1 & 1 & -2 \end{bmatrix}$. Find A^{-1}. Using A^{-1}.

Solve the following system of linear equations
$$2x - 3y + 5z = 11,\ 3x + 2y - 4z = -5,\ x + y - 2z = -3$$

16. The cost of 4 kg onion, 3 kg wheat and 2 kg rice is ₹ 69. The cost of 2 kg onion, 4 kg wheat and 6 kg rice is ₹ 90. The cost of 6 kg onion, 2 kg wheat and 3 kg rice is ₹ 70. Find the cost of each item per kg by matrix method.

Important Tips & Formulae

- **Symmetric determinant**

  A determinant $|a_{ij}|_{n \times n}$ is called skew symmetric determinant, if $a_{ij} = a_{ji} \ \forall \ i , \ j$

  Skew symmetric determinant

  A determinant $|a_{ij}|_{n \times n}$ is called skew symmetric determinant, if $a_{ij} = - a_{ji} \ \forall \ i, j$

- **Solution of homogeneous system of linear wquations by cramer's rule (or determinant method)**

  Let us now consider a homogeneous system of equations given by

  $$a_1 x + b_1 y + c_1 z = 0$$

  $$a_2 x + b_2 y + c_2 z = 0$$

  $$a_3 x + b_3 y + c_3 z = 0$$

  For this system of equations, we have

  $$D_1 = \begin{vmatrix} 0 & b_1 & c_1 \\ 0 & b_2 & c_2 \\ 0 & b_3 & c_3 \end{vmatrix} = 0, D_2 = \begin{vmatrix} a_1 & 0 & c_1 \\ a_2 & 0 & c_2 \\ a_3 & 0 & c_3 \end{vmatrix} = 0 \text{ and,}$$

  $$D_3 = \begin{vmatrix} a_1 & b_1 & 0 \\ a_2 & b_2 & 0 \\ a_3 & b_3 & 0 \end{vmatrix} = 0$$

  If $D = \begin{vmatrix} a_1 & b_1 & c_1 \\ a_2 & b_2 & c_2 \\ a_3 & b_3 & c_3 \end{vmatrix} \neq 0$, then

  $$x = \frac{D_1}{D} = 0, y = \frac{D_2}{D} = 0 \text{ and } z = \frac{D_3}{D} = 0.$$

  Thus, if $D \neq 0$, then the homogeneous system of equations has unique solution $x = 0, y = 0, z = 0$. This solution is called the trivial solution.

If $D = 0$, then a homogeneous system of equations has infinitely many solutions. This solutions are called non-trivial or non-zero solutions.

- Area of a triangle having vertices (x_1, y_1), (x_2, y_2), (x_3, y_3) can be expressed in determinant form as

  $$\frac{1}{2} \begin{vmatrix} x_1 & y_1 & 1 \\ x_2 & y_2 & 1 \\ x_3 & y_3 & 1 \end{vmatrix}$$

- Three points with coordinates (x_1, y_1), (x_2, y_2) and (x_3, y_3) are collinear if

  $$\begin{vmatrix} x_1 & y_1 & 1 \\ x_2 & y_2 & 1 \\ x_3 & y_3 & 1 \end{vmatrix} = 0$$

- Three straight lines having equations $a_1 x + b_1 y + c_1 = 0$, $a_2 x + b_2 y + c_2 = 0$ and $a_3 x + b_3 y + c_3 = 0$ are concurrent if.

  $$\begin{vmatrix} a_1 & b_1 & c_1 \\ a_2 & b_2 & c_2 \\ a_3 & b_3 & c_3 \end{vmatrix} = 0$$

- $|A|$ exists $\Leftrightarrow$ A is a square matrix
- $|AB| = |A||B|$
- $|A^T| = |A|$
- $|kA| = k^n|A|$, if A is a square matrix of order n.
- If A and B are square matrices of same order then $|AB| = |BA|$
- If A is a skew symmetric matrix of odd order then $|A| = 0$
- If $A = \text{diag}(a_1, a_2, \ldots, a_n)$ then $|A| = a_1 a_2 \ldots a_n$
- $|A|^n = |A^n|$, $n \in N$.
- Every diagonal element of a skew symmetric determinant is always zero.

MISCELLANEOUS NCERT EXERCISE

1. Prove that the determinant

$$\begin{vmatrix} x & \sin \theta & \cos \theta \\ -\sin \theta & -x & 1 \\ \cos \theta & 1 & x \end{vmatrix} \text{ is independent of } \theta.$$

Sol. Let $\Delta = \begin{vmatrix} x & \sin \theta & \cos \theta \\ -\sin \theta & -x & 1 \\ \cos \theta & 1 & x \end{vmatrix}$

Expanding along R_1

$$\Delta = x \begin{vmatrix} -x & 1 \\ 1 & x \end{vmatrix} - \sin \theta \begin{vmatrix} -\sin \theta & 1 \\ \cos \theta & x \end{vmatrix} + \cos \theta \begin{vmatrix} -\sin \theta & -x \\ \cos \theta & 1 \end{vmatrix}$$

$$= x(-x^2 - 1) - \sin \theta (-x \sin \theta - \cos \theta) + \cos \theta (-\sin \theta + \cos \theta)$$

$$= -x^3 - x + x = -x^3$$

which is independent of θ.

2. If $A^{-1} = \begin{bmatrix} 3 & -1 & 1 \\ -15 & 6 & -5 \\ 5 & -2 & 2 \end{bmatrix}$ and $B = \begin{bmatrix} 1 & 2 & -2 \\ -1 & 3 & 0 \\ 0 & -2 & 1 \end{bmatrix}$,

find $(AB)^{-1}$.

Sol. $|B| = \begin{vmatrix} 1 & 2 & -2 \\ -1 & 3 & 0 \\ 0 & -2 & 1 \end{vmatrix} = 1 \neq 0$

$\therefore$ B^{-1} = exists ,

$$B^{-1} = \frac{1}{|B|} \, (\text{adj } B) = \begin{bmatrix} 3 & 2 & 6 \\ 1 & 1 & 2 \\ 2 & 2 & 5 \end{bmatrix}$$

Now $(AB)^{-1} = B^{-1}$

$$A^{-1} = \begin{bmatrix} 3 & 2 & 6 \\ 1 & 1 & 2 \\ 2 & 2 & 5 \end{bmatrix} \begin{bmatrix} 3 & -1 & 1 \\ -15 & 6 & -5 \\ 5 & -2 & 2 \end{bmatrix} = \begin{bmatrix} 9 & -3 & 5 \\ -2 & 1 & 0 \\ 1 & 0 & 2 \end{bmatrix}$$

3. Let $A = \begin{bmatrix} 1 & -2 & 1 \\ -2 & 3 & 1 \\ 1 & 1 & 5 \end{bmatrix}$, verify that

(i) $[\text{Adj } A]^{-1} = \text{Adj}\,(A^{-1})$ (ii) $[A^{-1}]^{-1} = A.$

Sol. (i) To prove $[\text{Adj } A]^{-1} = \text{Adj}\,(A^{-1})$

$$\text{Now } A = \begin{bmatrix} 1 & -2 & 1 \\ -2 & 3 & 1 \\ 1 & 1 & 5 \end{bmatrix}$$

$$|A| = 1\,(15-1) + 2\,(-10-1) + 1(-2-3)$$
$$= 14 - 22 - 5 = -13 \neq 0$$

$\therefore$ A^{-1} exists

$$\text{Adj } A = \begin{bmatrix} 14 & 11 & -5 \\ 11 & 4 & -3 \\ -5 & -5 & -1 \end{bmatrix}$$

$$\therefore A^{-1} = \frac{1}{|A|} \, (\text{Adj } A) = -\frac{1}{13} \begin{bmatrix} 14 & 11 & -5 \\ 11 & 4 & -3 \\ -5 & -5 & -1 \end{bmatrix}$$

Now, let $B = \text{Adj } A$
To find $[\text{Adj } A]^{-1}$, we find B^{-1}

$$\text{Now, } B = \text{Adj } A = \begin{bmatrix} 14 & 11 & -5 \\ 11 & 4 & -3 \\ -5 & -5 & -1 \end{bmatrix}$$

$$|B| = 14\,(-4-9) - 11(-11-15) - 3\,(-33+20)$$
$$= -182 + 286 + 65 = 169$$

$$\text{Adj } B = \begin{bmatrix} -13 & -26 & -13 \\ 26 & -39 & -13 \\ -13 & -13 & -65 \end{bmatrix}$$

$$B^{-1} = \frac{1}{B} \, \text{Adj } B = \frac{1}{169} \begin{bmatrix} -13 & -26 & -13 \\ 26 & -39 & -13 \\ -13 & -13 & -65 \end{bmatrix}$$

$$\text{Thus } (\text{Adj } A)^{-1} = -\frac{1}{13} \begin{bmatrix} 1 & 2 & 1 \\ -2 & 3 & 1 \\ 1 & 1 & 5 \end{bmatrix} = \text{L.H.S.}$$

$$\text{Now } A^{-1} = -\frac{1}{13} \begin{bmatrix} 14 & 11 & -5 \\ 11 & 4 & -3 \\ -5 & -3 & -1 \end{bmatrix}$$

$$\text{Adj}(A^{-1}) = \frac{-1}{169} \begin{bmatrix} -13 & -26 & -13 \\ 26 & -39 & -13 \\ -13 & -13 & -65 \end{bmatrix} = \text{R.H.S.}$$

$$= \frac{1}{-13} \begin{bmatrix} -1 & 2 & -1 \\ 2 & -3 & -1 \\ -1 & -1 & -5 \end{bmatrix}$$

$$\text{Now, let } C = A^{-1} = -\frac{1}{13} \begin{bmatrix} 14 & 11 & -5 \\ 11 & 4 & -3 \\ -5 & -3 & -1 \end{bmatrix}$$

$$= \begin{bmatrix} -\dfrac{14}{13} & -\dfrac{11}{13} & -\dfrac{5}{13} \\ -\dfrac{11}{13} & -\dfrac{4}{13} & \dfrac{3}{13} \\ \dfrac{5}{13} & \dfrac{3}{13} & \dfrac{1}{13} \end{bmatrix}$$

$$\text{Adj }(A^{-1}) = \text{Adj. } C \begin{bmatrix} -\dfrac{1}{13} & \dfrac{2}{13} & -\dfrac{1}{13} \\ \dfrac{2}{13} & -\dfrac{3}{13} & -\dfrac{1}{13} \\ -\dfrac{1}{13} & -\dfrac{1}{13} & \dfrac{5}{13} \end{bmatrix}$$

$$= \frac{1}{13} \begin{bmatrix} -1 & 2 & -1 \\ 2 & -3 & -1 \\ -1 & -1 & -5 \end{bmatrix}$$

Hence $(\text{Adj. } A^{-1}) = (\text{Adj. } A^{-1})$

(ii) Given $A = \begin{bmatrix} 1 & -2 & 1 \\ -2 & 3 & 1 \\ 1 & 1 & 5 \end{bmatrix}$

and $A^{-1} = -\dfrac{1}{13}\begin{bmatrix} 14 & 11 & -5 \\ 11 & 4 & -3 \\ -5 & -3 & -1 \end{bmatrix}$ .... (Proved above)

Let $C = A^{-1} = -\dfrac{1}{13}\begin{bmatrix} 14 & 11 & -5 \\ 11 & 4 & -3 \\ -5 & -3 & -1 \end{bmatrix}$

$= \begin{bmatrix} -\dfrac{14}{13} & -\dfrac{11}{13} & \dfrac{5}{13} \\ -\dfrac{11}{13} & -\dfrac{4}{13} & \dfrac{3}{13} \\ \dfrac{5}{13} & \dfrac{3}{13} & \dfrac{1}{13} \end{bmatrix}$

$|C| = a_{11}A_{11} + a_{21}A_{21} + a_{31}A_{31}$

$= -\dfrac{14}{13}\times-\dfrac{1}{13} + \dfrac{11}{13}\times\dfrac{2}{13} + \dfrac{5}{13}\times\dfrac{-1}{13}$

$= \dfrac{14-22-5}{169} = \dfrac{-13}{169} = \dfrac{-1}{13} \neq 0$

$\therefore$ C^{-1} exists.

$\therefore$ $C^{-1} = \dfrac{1}{|C|}$ Adj. C

$= \dfrac{1}{-\dfrac{1}{13}}\times\dfrac{1}{13}\begin{bmatrix} -1 & 2 & -1 \\ 2 & -3 & -1 \\ -1 & -1 & -5 \end{bmatrix}$

$\Rightarrow (A^{-1})^{-1} = \begin{bmatrix} -1 & 2 & -1 \\ 2 & -3 & -1 \\ -1 & -1 & -5 \end{bmatrix} = \begin{bmatrix} 1 & -2 & 1 \\ -2 & 3 & 1 \\ -1 & 1 & 5 \end{bmatrix}$

Hence, $(A^{-1})^{-1} = A$.

4. **Solve the sysem of the following equations**

$\dfrac{2}{x} + \dfrac{3}{y} + \dfrac{10}{z} = 4$

$\dfrac{4}{x} - \dfrac{6}{y} + \dfrac{5}{z} = 1$

$\dfrac{6}{x} + \dfrac{9}{y} - \dfrac{20}{z} = 2$

Sol. Let $\dfrac{1}{x} = u, \dfrac{1}{y} = v, \dfrac{1}{z} = w$

$\therefore$ System of equations becomes

$2u + 3v + 10w = 4, \qquad 4u - 6v + 5w = 1$

$6u + 9v - 20w = 2$

we have $AX = B$ $\therefore$ $X = A^{-1}B$

where, $A = \begin{bmatrix} 2 & 3 & 10 \\ 4 & -6 & 5 \\ 6 & 9 & -20 \end{bmatrix}, X = \begin{bmatrix} u \\ v \\ w \end{bmatrix}$ & $B = \begin{bmatrix} 4 \\ 1 \\ 2 \end{bmatrix}$

Here adj $A = \begin{bmatrix} 75 & 150 & 75 \\ 110 & -100 & 30 \\ 75 & 0 & -24 \end{bmatrix}$

$|A| = 1200 \neq 0 \Rightarrow A^{-1}$ exist

$\therefore$ $A^{-1} = \dfrac{1}{|A|} = \mathrm{adj}\,(A)$

$= \dfrac{1}{1200}\begin{bmatrix} 75 & 150 & 75 \\ 110 & -100 & 30 \\ 72 & 0 & -24 \end{bmatrix}$

$X = A^{-1}B = \dfrac{1}{1200}\begin{bmatrix} 75 & 110 & 75 \\ 150 & -100 & 30 \\ 72 & 0 & -24 \end{bmatrix}\begin{bmatrix} 4 \\ 1 \\ 2 \end{bmatrix}$

$= \dfrac{1}{1200}\begin{bmatrix} 600 \\ 400 \\ 240 \end{bmatrix} = \begin{bmatrix} \dfrac{1}{2} \\ \dfrac{1}{3} \\ \dfrac{1}{5} \end{bmatrix}$

$\therefore$ $u = \dfrac{1}{2}, v = \dfrac{1}{3}, w = \dfrac{1}{5}$

$\Rightarrow x = \dfrac{1}{u} = 2, y = \dfrac{1}{v} = 3, z = \dfrac{1}{w} = 5$

Hence, $x = 2, y = 3, z = 5$.

5. If x, y, z are nonzero real numbers, then the inverse of

$$\text{matrix } A = \begin{bmatrix} x & 0 & 0 \\ 0 & y & 0 \\ 0 & 0 & z \end{bmatrix} \text{ is}$$

(a) $\begin{bmatrix} x^{-1} & 0 & 0 \\ 0 & y^{-1} & 0 \\ 0 & 0 & z^{-1} \end{bmatrix}$ (b) $xyz \begin{bmatrix} x^{-1} & 0 & 0 \\ 0 & y^{-1} & 0 \\ 0 & 0 & z^{-1} \end{bmatrix}$

(c) $\dfrac{1}{xyz} \begin{bmatrix} x & 0 & 0 \\ 0 & y & 0 \\ 0 & 0 & z \end{bmatrix}$ (d) $\dfrac{1}{xyz} \begin{bmatrix} 1 & 0 & 0 \\ 0 & 1 & 0 \\ 0 & 0 & 1 \end{bmatrix}$

Sol. (a) $A = \begin{bmatrix} x & 0 & 0 \\ 0 & y & 0 \\ 0 & 0 & z \end{bmatrix}$

The cofactors of the elements are

$$A_{11} = yz, \qquad A_{12} = 0$$
$$A_{13} = 0, \qquad A_{21} = 0$$
$$A_{22} = xz, \qquad A_{23} = 0$$
$$A_{31} = 0, \qquad A_{32} = 0$$
$$A_{33} = xy$$
$$|A| = xyz$$

$$\text{adj}(A) = \begin{bmatrix} yz & 0 & 0 \\ 0 & zx & 0 \\ 0 & 0 & xy \end{bmatrix}$$

$$\therefore \ A^{-1} = \frac{1}{xyz} \begin{bmatrix} yz & 0 & 0 \\ 0 & zx & 0 \\ 0 & 0 & xy \end{bmatrix} = \begin{bmatrix} x^{-1} & 0 & 0 \\ 0 & y^{-1} & 0 \\ 0 & 0 & z^{-1} \end{bmatrix}$$

6. Let $A = \begin{bmatrix} 1 & \sin\theta & 1 \\ -\sin\theta & 1 & \sin\theta \\ -1 & -\sin\theta & 1 \end{bmatrix}$, where $0 \le \theta \le 2p$. Then

(a) Det (A) = 0   (b) Det (A) $\in (2, \infty)$

(c) Det (A) $\in (2, 4)$ (d) Det (A) $\in [2, 4]$

Sol. (d) $A = \begin{bmatrix} 1 & \sin\theta & 1 \\ -\sin\theta & 1 & \sin\theta \\ -1 & -\sin\theta & 1 \end{bmatrix}$

$$\text{Det}(A) = \begin{vmatrix} 1 & \sin\theta & 1 \\ -\sin\theta & 1 & \sin\theta \\ -1 & -\sin\theta & 1 \end{vmatrix} = 2(1 + \sin^2\theta)$$

For $\theta = 0, \pi, 2\pi \ \Rightarrow \ \text{Det}(A) = 2$

For $\theta = \dfrac{\pi}{2}, \dfrac{3\pi}{2}$

$$\Rightarrow \ \text{Det}(A) = 2 \cdot (1 + 1) = 4$$

Past year Exercise

Very Short Answer Questions

1. Let A be a square matrix of order 3×3. Write the value of $|2A|$ where, $|A| = 4$.

2. If A_{ij} is the cofactor of the element a_{ij} of the determinant
$$\begin{vmatrix} 2 & -3 & 5 \\ 6 & 0 & 4 \\ 1 & 5 & -7 \end{vmatrix}, \text{ then write the value of } a_{32} \cdot A_{32}.$$

3. If $\begin{vmatrix} 2x & x+3 \\ 2(x+1) & x+1 \end{vmatrix} = \begin{vmatrix} 1 & 5 \\ 3 & 3 \end{vmatrix}$, then write the value of x.

4. If A is an invertible square matrix of order 3 and $|A| = 5$, then find the value of $|\text{adj } A|$.

5. If $\begin{vmatrix} 2x & 5 \\ 8 & x \end{vmatrix} = \begin{vmatrix} 6 & -2 \\ 7 & 3 \end{vmatrix}$, write the value of x.

6. If $A = \begin{bmatrix} 2 & 3 \\ 5 & -2 \end{bmatrix}$, then write A^{-1}.

7. Find the maximum value of $\begin{bmatrix} 1 & 1 & 1 \\ 1 & 1+\sin\theta & 1 \\ 1 & 1 & 1+\cos\theta \end{bmatrix}$

Short Answer Questions

8. The monthly incomes of Aryan and Babban are in the ratio 3 : 4 and their monthly expenditures are in the ratio 5 : 7. If each saves `15,000 per month, find their monthly incomes using matrix method. This problem reflects which value?

9. Given $A = \begin{bmatrix} 2 & -3 \\ -4 & 7 \end{bmatrix}$, compute A^{-1} and show that $2A^{-1} = 9I - A$.

NCERT Exemplar

Multiple Choice Questions

1. If $\begin{vmatrix} 2x & 5 \\ 8 & x \end{vmatrix} = \begin{vmatrix} 6 & -2 \\ 7 & 3 \end{vmatrix}$, then the value of x is

   (a) 3   (b) ± 3

   (c) ± 6 (d) 6

2. If A, B and C are angles of a triangle, then the determinannt
   $$\begin{vmatrix} -1 & \cos C & \cos B \\ \cos C & -1 & \cos A \\ \cos B & \cos A & -1 \end{vmatrix} \text{ is equal to}$$

   (a) 0   (b) -1

   (c) 1   (d) None of these

3. The maximum value of $\begin{vmatrix} 1 & 1 & 1 \\ 1 & 1+\sin\theta & 1 \\ 1+\cos\theta & 1 & 1 \end{vmatrix}$ is (θ is real number)

   (a) $\dfrac{1}{2}$ (b) $\dfrac{\sqrt{3}}{2}$

   (c) $\sqrt{2}$ (d) $\dfrac{2\sqrt{3}}{4}$

4. If $f(x) = \begin{vmatrix} 0 & x-a & x-b \\ x+a & 0 & x-c \\ x+b & x+c & 0 \end{vmatrix}$, then

   (a) $f(a) = 0$ (b) $f(b) = 0$

   (c) $f(0) = 0$ (d) $f(1) = 0$

Short Answer Questions

5. Prove $\begin{vmatrix} y^2 z^2 & yz & y+z \\ z^2 x^2 & zx & z+x \\ x^2 y^2 & xy & x+y \end{vmatrix} = 0$

6. If $\begin{vmatrix} 4-x & 4+x & 4+x \\ 4+x & 4-x & 4+x \\ 4+x & 4+x & 4-x \end{vmatrix} = 0$, then find the value of x.

7. Find the value of $\begin{vmatrix} 0 & xy^2 & xz^2 \\ x^2 y & 0 & yz^2 \\ x^2 z & zy^2 & 0 \end{vmatrix}$

8. If $a+b+c = 0$ then find the value of determinant
   $$\begin{vmatrix} a-b-c & 2a & 2a \\ 2b & b-c-a & 2b \\ 2c & 2c & c-a-b \end{vmatrix}$$

9. Prove that $\begin{vmatrix} a^2+2a & 2a+1 & 1 \\ 2a+1 & a+2 & 1 \\ 3 & 3 & 1 \end{vmatrix} = (a-1)^3$

10. In a triangle ABC, if
    $$\begin{vmatrix} 1 & 1 & 1 \\ 1+\sin A & 1+\sin B & 1+\sin C \\ \sin A+\sin^2 A & \sin B+\sin^2 B & \sin C+\sin^2 C \end{vmatrix} = 0$$
    then prove that $\triangle ABC$ is an isoceles triangle.

11. If $\Delta = \begin{vmatrix} 1 & x & x^2 \\ 1 & y & y^2 \\ 1 & z & z^2 \end{vmatrix}$, $\Delta_1 = \begin{vmatrix} yz & zx & xy \\ x & y & z \\ 1 & 1 & 1 \end{vmatrix}$,

    then prove that $\Delta + \Delta_1 = 0$.

Objective Practice Exercise

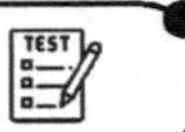

Multiple Choice Questions

DIRECTIONS : *This section contains multiple choice questions. Each question has four choices (a), (b), (c) and (d) out of which only one is correct.*

---

1. If $\begin{vmatrix} x-1 & 5x & 7 \\ x^2-1 & x-1 & 8 \\ 2x & 3x & 0 \end{vmatrix} = ax^3 + bx^2 + cx + d$, then c is equal to

(a) -1 (b) 12 (c) 15 (d) 17

2. If in the determinant $\Delta = \begin{vmatrix} a_1 & b_1 & c_1 \\ a_2 & b_2 & c_2 \\ a_3 & b_3 & c_3 \end{vmatrix}$, A_1, B_1, C_1 etc. be

the co-factors of a_1, b_1, c_1 etc., then which of the following relations is incorrect ?

(a) $a_1 A_1 + b_1 B_1 + c_1 C_1 = \Delta$ (b) $a_2 A_2 + b_2 B_2 + c_2 C_2 = \Delta$

(c) $a_3 A_3 + b_3 B_3 + c_3 C_3 = \Delta$ (d) $a_1 A_2 + b_1 B_2 + c_1 C_2 = \Delta$

3. If $A = \begin{bmatrix} \log x & -1 \\ -\log x & 2 \end{bmatrix}$ and if $\det(A) = 2$, then the value of x is equal to

(a) 2 (b) e^2 (c) -2 (d) e

4. The minors of -4 and 9 and the co-factors of -4 and 9 in

determinant $\begin{vmatrix} -1 & -2 & 3 \\ -4 & -5 & -6 \\ -7 & 8 & 9 \end{vmatrix}$ are respectively.

(a) $42, 3; -42, 3$ (b) $-42, -3; 42, -3$

(c) $42, 3; -42, -3$ (d) $42, 3; 42, 3$

5. The values of x for which the given matrix $\begin{bmatrix} -x & x & 2 \\ 2 & x & -x \\ x & -2 & -x \end{bmatrix}$

will be non-singular are

(a) $-2 \le x \le 2$

(b) For all x other than 2 and -2

(c) $x \ge 2$

(d) $x \le -2$

6. $\begin{vmatrix} \log_3 512 & \log_4 3 \\ \log_3 8 & \log_4 9 \end{vmatrix} \times \begin{vmatrix} \log_2 3 & \log_8 3 \\ \log_3 4 & \log_3 4 \end{vmatrix} =$

(a) 7 (b) 10 (c) 13 (d) 17

7. If $\begin{bmatrix} 2+x & 3 & 4 \\ 1 & -1 & 2 \\ x & 1 & -5 \end{bmatrix}$ is a singular matrix, then x is

(a) $\dfrac{13}{25}$ (b) $-\dfrac{25}{13}$ (c) $\dfrac{5}{13}$ (d) $\dfrac{25}{13}$

8. The sum of the products of the elements of any row of a determinant A with the co-factor of same row is always equal to

(a) 1 (b) 0 (c) $|A|$ (d) $\dfrac{1}{2}|A|$

9. If $f(x) = \begin{vmatrix} x & \lambda \\ 2\lambda & x \end{vmatrix}$, then $f(\lambda x) - f(x)$ is equal to

(a) $x(\lambda^2 - 1)$ (b) $2\lambda(x^2 - 1)$

(c) $\lambda^2(x^2 - 1)$ (d) $x^2(\lambda^2 - 1)$

10. If $A = \begin{vmatrix} 5 & 6 & 3 \\ -4 & 3 & 2 \\ -4 & -7 & 3 \end{vmatrix}$, then co-factors of the elements of 2nd row are,

(a) $39, -3, 11$ (b) $-39, 3, 11$

(c) $-39, 27, 11$ (d) $-39, -3, 11$

11. If $\begin{vmatrix} a & b & 0 \\ 0 & a & b \\ b & 0 & a \end{vmatrix} = 0$, $(a \ne 0)$ then

(a) a is one of cube root of unity

(b) b is one of cube root of unity

(c) (a/b) is one of cube root of unity

(d) (b/a) is one of cube root of -1

12. If $\begin{vmatrix} x^2+x & x+1 & x-2 \\ 2x^2+3x-1 & 3x & 3x-3 \\ x^2+2x+3 & 2x-1 & 2x-1 \end{vmatrix} = Ax - 12$, then the value of A is

(a) 12 (b) 24 (c) -12 (d) -24

13. If $D = \begin{vmatrix} 1 & 1 & 1 \\ 1 & 1+x & 1 \\ 1 & 1 & 1+y \end{vmatrix}$ for $x \ne 0, y \ne 0$, then D is

(a) divisible by x but not y

(b) divisible by y but not x

(c) divisible by neither x nor y

(d) divisible by both x and y

14. If $f(x) = \begin{vmatrix} x-3 & 2x^2-18 & 3x^3-81 \\ x-5 & 2x^2-50 & 4x^3-500 \\ 1 & 2 & 3 \end{vmatrix}$ then

$f(1).f(3)+f(3).f(5)+f(5).f(1) =$

(a) $f(1)$ (b) $f(3)$

(c) $f(1)+f(3)$ (d) $f(1)+f(5)$

15. If $\Delta_1 = \begin{vmatrix} x & \sin\theta & \cos\theta \\ -\sin\theta & -x & 1 \\ \cos\theta & 1 & x \end{vmatrix}$ and

$\Delta_2 = \begin{vmatrix} x & \sin 2\theta & \cos 2\theta \\ -\sin 2\theta & -x & 1 \\ \cos 2\theta & 1 & x \end{vmatrix}, x \neq 0$

then for all $\theta \in \left(0, \dfrac{\pi}{2}\right)$

(a) $\Delta_1 - \Delta_2 = -2x^3$

(b) $\Delta_1 - \Delta_2 = x(\cos 2\theta - \cos 4\theta)$

(c) $\Delta_1 \times \Delta_2 = -2(x^3+x-1)$

(d) $\Delta_1 + \Delta_2 = -2x^3$

16. If $a+b+c=0$, then the solution of the equation

$\begin{vmatrix} a-x & c & b \\ c & b-x & a \\ b & a & c-x \end{vmatrix} = 0$ is

(a) 0 (b) $\pm\dfrac{3}{2}(a^2+b^2+c^2)$

(c) $0, \pm\sqrt{\dfrac{3}{2}(a^2+b^2+c^2)}$ (d) $0, \pm\sqrt{(a^2+b^2+c^2)}$

17. If -9 is a root of the equation $\begin{vmatrix} x & 3 & 7 \\ 2 & x & 2 \\ 7 & 6 & x \end{vmatrix} = 0$ then the

other two roots are

(a) $2,7$ (b) $-2,7$ (c) $2,-7$ (d) $-2,-7$

18. If $A = \begin{bmatrix} 2 & 0 & 0 \\ 0 & 2 & 0 \\ 0 & 0 & 2 \end{bmatrix}$ and $B = \begin{bmatrix} 1 & 2 & 3 \\ 0 & 1 & 3 \\ 0 & 0 & 2 \end{bmatrix}$, then $|AB|$ is equal to

(a) 4 (b) 8 (c) 16 (d) 32

19. Let A be a skew-symmetric matrix of odd order, then $|A|$ is equal to

(a) 0 (b) 1

(c) -1 (d) None of these

20. The roots of the determinant equation (in x) $\begin{vmatrix} a & a & x \\ m & m & m \\ b & x & b \end{vmatrix} = 0$

(a) $x = a, b$ (b) $x = -a, -b$

(c) $x = -a, b$ (d) $x = a, -b$

21. For how many value(s) of x in the closed interval $[-4, -1]$,

is the matrix $\begin{bmatrix} 3 & -1+x & 2 \\ 3 & -1 & x+2 \\ x+3 & -1 & 2 \end{bmatrix}$ singular?

(a) 2 (b) 0 (c) 3 (d) 1

22. $\begin{vmatrix} 11 & 12 & 13 \\ 12 & 13 & 14 \\ 13 & 14 & 15 \end{vmatrix}$ is equal to :

(a) 1 (b) 0 (c) -1 (d) 67

23. The value of $\begin{vmatrix} x+y & y+z & z+x \\ x & y & z \\ x-y & y-z & z-x \end{vmatrix} =$

(a) $2(x+y+z)^2$ (b) $2(x+y+z)^3$

(c) $(x+y+z)^3$ (d) 0

24. A is a square matrix of order 4 and I is a unit matrix, then it is true that

(a) $\det(2A) = 2\det(A)$ (b) $\det(2A) = 16\det(A)$

(c) $\det(-A) = -\det(A)$ (d) $\det(A+I) = \det(A)+I$

25. If $A = \begin{bmatrix} 1 & \tan x \\ -\tan x & 1 \end{bmatrix}$, then the value of $\left|A' A^{-1}\right|$

(a) 2 (b) 1 (c) 4 (d) 3

26. If the adjoint of a 3×3 matrix P is $\begin{bmatrix} 1 & 4 & 4 \\ 2 & 1 & 7 \\ 1 & 1 & 3 \end{bmatrix}$, then the

possible value(s) of the determinant of P is (are)

(a) -2 (b) -1 (c) 1 (d) 0

27. If matrix $A = \begin{bmatrix} 3 & 2 & 4 \\ 1 & 2 & -1 \\ 0 & 1 & 1 \end{bmatrix}$ and $A^{-1} = \dfrac{1}{K} adj(A)$, then K is

(a) 7 (b) -7 (c) $\dfrac{1}{7}$ (d) 11

28. If A and B are invertible square matrices of the same order, then which of the following is not correct

(a) $adj\,(AB) = (adj\,B)(adj\,A)$

(b) $(adj\,A)' = (adj\,A')$

(c) $|adj\,A| = |A|^{2n-1}$, where n is the order of matrix A

(d) $adj\,(adj\,B) = |B|^{n-2}B$, where n is the order of matrix B

29. If $A^{-1} = \begin{bmatrix} 1 & 0 & -2 \\ -2 & 1 & 0 \\ -1 & 1 & 0 \end{bmatrix}$, then

(a) $|A| = 2$

(b) $adj\,A = \begin{bmatrix} \dfrac{1}{2} & 0 & -1 \\ -1 & \dfrac{1}{2} & 0 \\ -\dfrac{1}{2} & \dfrac{1}{2} & 0 \end{bmatrix}$

(c) $|adjA| = 4$

(d) $|A'| = \dfrac{-1}{2}$

30. Let $A = \begin{pmatrix} 0 & 0 & -1 \\ 0 & -1 & 0 \\ -1 & 0 & 0 \end{pmatrix}$, the only correct statement about the matrix A is

(a) $A^2 = I$

(b) $A = (-1)\,I$, where I is a unit matrix

(c) A^{-1} does not exist

(d) A is a zero matrix

31. Inverse of the matrix $\begin{bmatrix} 3 & -2 & -1 \\ -4 & 1 & -1 \\ 2 & 0 & 1 \end{bmatrix}$ is

(a) $\begin{bmatrix} 1 & 2 & 3 \\ 3 & 3 & 7 \\ -2 & -4 & -5 \end{bmatrix}$

(b) $\begin{bmatrix} 1 & -3 & 5 \\ 7 & 4 & 6 \\ 4 & 2 & 7 \end{bmatrix}$

(c) $\begin{bmatrix} 1 & 2 & 3 \\ 2 & 5 & 7 \\ -2 & -4 & -5 \end{bmatrix}$

(d) $\begin{bmatrix} 1 & -3 & 5 \\ 7 & 4 & 6 \\ 4 & 2 & -7 \end{bmatrix}$

32. The matrix $\begin{bmatrix} \lambda & -1 & 4 \\ -3 & 0 & 1 \\ -1 & 1 & 2 \end{bmatrix}$ is invertible, if

(a) $\lambda \neq -15$

(b) $\lambda \neq -17$

(c) $\lambda \neq -16$

(d) $\lambda \neq -18$

33. The multiplicative inverse of matrix $\begin{bmatrix} 2 & 1 \\ 7 & 4 \end{bmatrix}$ is

(a) $\begin{bmatrix} 4 & -1 \\ -7 & -2 \end{bmatrix}$

(b) $\begin{bmatrix} -4 & -1 \\ 7 & -2 \end{bmatrix}$

(c) $\begin{bmatrix} 4 & -7 \\ 7 & 2 \end{bmatrix}$

(d) $\begin{bmatrix} 4 & -1 \\ -7 & 2 \end{bmatrix}$

34. If $A^2 - A + I = 0$, then the inverse of A is

(a) $A + I$ (b) A (c) $A - I$ (d) $I - A$

35. Inverse of the matrix $\begin{bmatrix} \cos 2\theta & -\sin 2\theta \\ \sin 2\theta & \cos 2\theta \end{bmatrix}$ is

(a) $\begin{bmatrix} \cos 2\theta & -\sin 2\theta \\ \sin 2\theta & \cos 2\theta \end{bmatrix}$

(b) $\begin{bmatrix} \cos 2\theta & \sin 2\theta \\ \sin 2\theta & -\cos 2\theta \end{bmatrix}$

(c) $\begin{bmatrix} \cos 2\theta & \sin 2\theta \\ \sin 2\theta & \cos 2\theta \end{bmatrix}$

(d) $\begin{bmatrix} \cos 2\theta & \sin 2\theta \\ -\sin 2\theta & \cos 2\theta \end{bmatrix}$

36. If $A = \begin{bmatrix} 1 & -2 & 2 \\ 0 & 2 & -3 \\ 3 & -2 & 4 \end{bmatrix}$, then A adj(A) is equal to

(a) $\begin{bmatrix} 5 & 1 & 1 \\ 1 & 5 & 1 \\ 1 & 1 & 5 \end{bmatrix}$

(b) $\begin{bmatrix} 5 & 0 & 0 \\ 0 & 5 & 0 \\ 0 & 0 & 5 \end{bmatrix}$

(c) $\begin{bmatrix} 8 & 0 & 0 \\ 0 & 8 & 0 \\ 0 & 0 & 8 \end{bmatrix}$

(d) $\begin{bmatrix} 0 & 0 & 0 \\ 0 & 0 & 0 \\ 0 & 0 & 0 \end{bmatrix}$

37. If A and B are square matrices of the same order and $AB = 3I$, then A^{-1} is equal to

(a) $3B$ (b) $\dfrac{1}{3}B$ (c) $3B^{-1}$ (d) $\dfrac{1}{3}B^{-1}$

38. If $adj\,B = A$, $|P| = |Q| = 1$, then adj $(Q^{-1}BP^{-1})$ is

(a) PQ (b) QAP (c) PAQ (d) $PA^{-1}Q$

39. If for the matrix A, $A^3 = I$, then $A^{-1} =$

(a) A^2

(b) A^3

(c) A

(d) None of these

40. The matrix $\begin{pmatrix} 1 & a & 2 \\ 1 & 2 & 5 \\ 2 & 1 & 1 \end{pmatrix}$ is not invertible, if 'a' has the value

(a) 2 (b) 1 (c) 0 (d) -1

41. If $P = \begin{pmatrix} 2 & 0 & 0 \\ 0 & 2 & 0 \\ 0 & 0 & 2 \end{pmatrix}$ then, det (Adj P) $=$

(a) P^{27}

(b) P^{17}

(c) P^6

(d) None of these

42. If matrix $A = \begin{bmatrix} 3 & -2 & 4 \\ 1 & 2 & -1 \\ 0 & 1 & 1 \end{bmatrix}$ and $A^{-1} = \dfrac{1}{k}adj(A)$, then k is

(a) 7 (b) -7 (c) 15 (d) -11

43. Which one of the following statements is true?
   (a) Non-singular square matrix does not have a unique inverse
   (b) Determinant of a non-singular matrix is zero
   (c) If $A' = A$, then A is a square matrix
   (d) If $|A| \neq 0$, then $|A.\text{adj } A| = |A|^{(n-1)}$, where $A = [a_{ij}]_{n \times n}$

44. If $A = \begin{bmatrix} 0 & 3 \\ 2 & 0 \end{bmatrix}$ and $A^{-1} = \lambda \ (A)$, then λ

   (a) $\dfrac{-1}{6}$ (b) $\dfrac{1}{3}$ (c) $\dfrac{-1}{3}$ (d) $\dfrac{1}{6}$

45. Which of the following
   (i) Adjoint of a symmetric matrix is symmetric
   (ii) Adjoint of a unit matrix is a unit matrix
   (iii) $A(\text{adj } A) = (\text{adj } A) A = |A| I$ and
   (iv) Adjoint of a diagonal matrix is a diagonal matrix, is/are incorrect
   (a) (i)   (b) (ii)
   (c) (iii) and (iv)   (d) None of these

46. If $A = \begin{bmatrix} 2 & 2 \\ -3 & 2 \end{bmatrix}$ and $B = \begin{bmatrix} 0 & -1 \\ 1 & 0 \end{bmatrix}$, then $(B^{-1} A^{-1})^{-1} =$

   (a) $\begin{bmatrix} 2 & -2 \\ 2 & 3 \end{bmatrix}$ (b) $\begin{bmatrix} 3 & -2 \\ 2 & 2 \end{bmatrix}$

   (c) $\dfrac{1}{10}\begin{bmatrix} 2 & 2 \\ -2 & 3 \end{bmatrix}$ (d) $\dfrac{1}{10}\begin{bmatrix} 3 & 2 \\ -2 & 2 \end{bmatrix}$

47. If matrix $A = \begin{bmatrix} 1 & 0 & -1 \\ 3 & 4 & 5 \\ 0 & 6 & 7 \end{bmatrix}$ and its inverse is denoted by

$A^{-1} = \begin{bmatrix} a_{11} & a_{12} & a_{13} \\ a_{21} & a_{22} & a_{23} \\ a_{31} & a_{32} & a_{33} \end{bmatrix}$, then the value of $a_{23} =$

   (a) $\dfrac{21}{20}$ (b) $\dfrac{1}{5}$ (c) $-\dfrac{2}{5}$ (d) $\dfrac{2}{5}$

48. Let A, B and C be $n \times n$ matrices. Which one of the following is a correct statement?
   (a) If $AB = AC$, then $B = C$
   (b) If $A^3 + 2A^2 + 3A + 5I = 0$; then A is invertible.
   (c) If $A^2 = 0$, then $A = 0$
   (d) None of these

DIRECTIONS : *Study the given Case/Passage and answer the following questions.*

Case/Passage

Manjit wants to donate a rectangular plot of land for a school in his village. When he was asked to give dimensions of the plot, he told that if its length is decreased by 50 m and breadth is increased by 50m, then its area will remain same, but if length is decreased by 10m and breadth is decreased by 20m, then its area will decrease by 5300 m^2

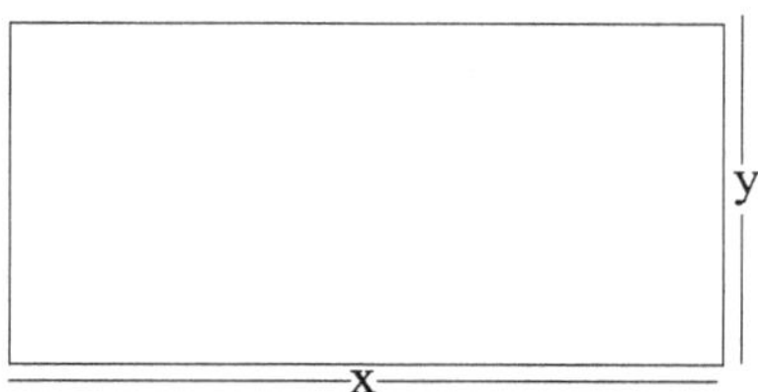

[From CBSE Question Bank-2021]

Based on the information given above, answer the following questions:

49. The equations in terms of x and y are
   (a) $x - y = 50, 2x - y = 550$
   (b) $x - y = 50, 2x + y = 550$
   (c) $x + y = 50, 2x + y = 550$
   (d) $x + y = 50, 2x - y = 550$

50. Which of the following matrix equation is represented by the given information

   (a) $\begin{bmatrix} 1 & -1 \\ 2 & 1 \end{bmatrix}\begin{bmatrix} x \\ y \end{bmatrix} = \begin{bmatrix} 50 \\ 550 \end{bmatrix}$ (b) $\begin{bmatrix} 1 & 1 \\ 2 & 1 \end{bmatrix}\begin{bmatrix} x \\ y \end{bmatrix} = \begin{bmatrix} 50 \\ 550 \end{bmatrix}$

   (c) $\begin{bmatrix} 1 & 1 \\ 2 & -1 \end{bmatrix}\begin{bmatrix} x \\ y \end{bmatrix} = \begin{bmatrix} 50 \\ 550 \end{bmatrix}$ (d) $\begin{bmatrix} 1 & 1 \\ 2 & 1 \end{bmatrix}\begin{bmatrix} x \\ y \end{bmatrix} = \begin{bmatrix} -50 \\ -550 \end{bmatrix}$

51. The value of x (length of rectangular field) is
   (a) 150m   (b) 400m
   (c) 200m   (d) 320m

52. The value of y (breadth of rectangular field) is
   (a) 150m.   (b) 200m.
   (c) 430m.   (d) 350m

53. How much is the area of rectangular field?
   (a) 60000 sq. m.   (b) 30000 sq. m.
   (c) 30000m   (d) 3000m

Chapter Test

Time : *45 Minutes*   **Max. Marks : 20**

(i) Questions number **1-8** carry **1 mark** each.

(ii) Question number **9** carry **4 marks**.

(iii) Questions number **10-13** are **Very Short Answer Questions** and carry **2 marks** each.

Multiple Choice Questions

1. The value of $\begin{vmatrix} a-b & b+c & a \\ b-a & c+a & b \\ c-a & a+b & c \end{vmatrix}$ is

    (a) $a^3 + b^3 + c^3$ (b) $3bc$

    (c) $a^3 + b^3 + c^3 - 3abc$ (d) None of these

2. The value of $\begin{vmatrix} x & x+y & x+2y \\ x+2y & x & x+y \\ x+y & x+2y & x \end{vmatrix}$ is

    (a) $9x^2(x+y)$ (b) $9y^2(x+y)$

    (c) $3y^2(x+y)$ (d) $7x^2(x+y)$

3. If there are two values of a which makes determinant,

$$\Delta = \begin{vmatrix} 1 & -2 & 5 \\ 2 & a & -1 \\ 0 & 4 & 2a \end{vmatrix} = 86 \text{, then the sum of these numbers is}$$

    (a) 4   (b) 5   (c) -4 (d) 9

4. If $A = \begin{bmatrix} \alpha & 2 \\ 2 & \alpha \end{bmatrix}$ and $|A^3| = 125$ then the value of α is

    (a) ± 1 (b) ± 2 (c) ± 3 (d) ± 5

One Word Answer Questions

5. If every element of a third order determinant of value D is multiplied by 5 then find the value of the new determinant.

6. If A is a square matrix of order 3 and $|A| = 5$, then find the value of $|2A'|$.

Assertion & Reason Questions

DIRECTIONS : *Each of these questions contains an assertion followed by reason. Read them carefully and answer the question on the basis of following options. You have to select the one that best describes the two statements.*

(a) If both Assertion and Reason are correct and the Reason is a correct explanation of the Assertion.

(b) If both Assertion and Reason are correct but Reason is not a correct explanation of the Assertion.

(c) If the Assertion is correct but Reason is incorrect.

(d) If the Assertion is incorrect but the Reason is correct.

7. **Assertion:** The determinant of a skew symmetric matrix of even order is perfect square.

    Reason: If A is square matrix of order n, then $|kA| = k^n|A|$ where $k \in R$.

8. **Assertion:** If A is singular matrix, then A^{-1} exists.

    Reason: If A is square matrix, then $A^{-1} = \dfrac{\text{adj } A}{|A|}$, where $|A| \neq 0$.

Case/Passage Based Question

DIRECTIONS (Q. 9) : *has 5 subparts based on case/passage given, attempt any 4 out of 5 questions.*

Case/Passage

9. A school wants to award its students for the values of cleanliness, regularity and good health with a total cash to be awarded is ₹4500. Five times the award money in total for good health and cleanliness is equal to 6 times the award money for regularity. Five times the award money for good health added to two times of regularity is equal to ₹11000. If ₹x be the cash price for cleanliness, ₹y be the cash price for regularity and ₹z be the cash price for good health, then answer the following question.

    (i) Represent the situation in matrix method.

    (a) $\begin{bmatrix} 1 & 1 & 1 \\ 1 & -2 & 1 \\ 0 & 2 & 5 \end{bmatrix} \begin{bmatrix} x \\ y \\ z \end{bmatrix} = \begin{bmatrix} 4500 \\ 0 \\ 11000 \end{bmatrix}$

    (b) $\begin{bmatrix} 1 & -2 & 1 \\ 1 & 1 & 1 \\ 0 & 2 & 5 \end{bmatrix} \begin{bmatrix} x \\ y \\ z \end{bmatrix} = \begin{bmatrix} 4500 \\ 0 \\ 11000 \end{bmatrix}$

(c) $\begin{bmatrix} 0 & 2 & 5 \\ 1 & 1 & 1 \\ 1 & -2 & 1 \end{bmatrix} \begin{bmatrix} x \\ y \\ z \end{bmatrix} = \begin{bmatrix} 4500 \\ 0 \\ 11000 \end{bmatrix}$

(d) $\begin{bmatrix} 0 & 2 & 5 \\ 1 & -2 & 1 \\ 1 & 1 & 1 \end{bmatrix} \begin{bmatrix} x \\ y \\ z \end{bmatrix} = \begin{bmatrix} 4500 \\ 0 \\ 11000 \end{bmatrix}$

(ii) Find the determinant of coefficient matrix of the system.

(a) 10 (b) 15

(c) −15 (d) −20

(iii) Find adjoint matrix of coefficient matrix.

(a) $\begin{bmatrix} -12 & -5 & 2 \\ -3 & 5 & -2 \\ 3 & 0 & -3 \end{bmatrix}$

(b) $\begin{bmatrix} -12 & -3 & 3 \\ -5 & 5 & 0 \\ 2 & -2 & -3 \end{bmatrix}$

(c) $\begin{bmatrix} 3 & 0 & -3 \\ 12 & -5 & -2 \\ 3 & 5 & -2 \end{bmatrix}$

(d) $\begin{bmatrix} 12 & 5 & 2 \\ -3 & 5 & 2 \\ 3 & 0 & -3 \end{bmatrix}$

(iv) Find the inverse of coefficient matrix.

(a) $\dfrac{1}{10} \begin{bmatrix} -12 & -3 & 3 \\ -5 & 5 & 0 \\ 2 & -2 & -3 \end{bmatrix}$

(b) $\dfrac{1}{15} \begin{bmatrix} -12 & -3 & 5 \\ -5 & 5 & 0 \\ 2 & -2 & -3 \end{bmatrix}$

(c) $\dfrac{1}{15} \begin{bmatrix} 12 & 3 & -3 \\ 5 & -5 & 0 \\ -2 & 2 & 3 \end{bmatrix}$

(d) $\dfrac{1}{10} \begin{bmatrix} 12 & 3 & -3 \\ 5 & -5 & 0 \\ -2 & 2 & 3 \end{bmatrix}$

(v) Find the award money for each value using matrix method.

(a) x = ₹1400, y = ₹1500, z = ₹1600

(b) x = ₹1000, y = ₹2000, z = ₹3000

(c) x = ₹1400, y = ₹2000, z = ₹2500

(d) x = ₹1400, y = ₹2000, z = ₹1600

Very Short Answer Questions

10. If $x + y + z = \pi$, then find the value of

$$\Delta = \begin{vmatrix} \sin(x+y+z) & \sin B & \sin C \\ -\sin B & 0 & \tan A \\ \cos(A+B) & -\tan A & 0 \end{vmatrix}$$

11. If $\begin{vmatrix} 2x & 5 \\ 8 & x \end{vmatrix} = \begin{vmatrix} 6 & 5 \\ 8 & 3 \end{vmatrix}$, then find x.

12. Without expanding, show that

$$\Delta = \begin{vmatrix} \operatorname{cosec}^2\theta & \cot^2\theta & 1 \\ \cot^2\theta & \operatorname{cosec}^2\theta & -1 \\ 42 & 40 & 2 \end{vmatrix} = 0$$

13. Evaluate the value of determinant $\begin{vmatrix} x+1 & x+2 & x+4 \\ x+3 & x+5 & x+8 \\ x+7 & x+10 & x+14 \end{vmatrix}$

Solutions 

Practice Exercise-1

1. (d) 2. (a) 3. (b) 4. (c)
5. (a) 6. 0 7. 110
8. $(x-7)(x-2)=0$

9. The given matrix is $A = \begin{bmatrix} 1 & 2 & 3 \\ -4 & -5 & 6 \end{bmatrix}$

   Since, this matrix is not a square matrix.
   Therefore, its determinant does not exist.

10. 1

11. 6

12. minor of $a_{11} = \begin{vmatrix} 7 & 8 \\ 4 & 5 \end{vmatrix} = 35 - 32 = 3$

13. $x = 0, \pm 12$.

14. Let $1, \omega, \omega^2$ be the cube roots of unity.

    $\because \quad \omega^3 = 1, 1 + \omega + \omega^2 = 0$

    Let $A = \begin{vmatrix} 1 & \omega^n & \omega^{2n} \\ \omega^{2n} & 1 & \omega^n \\ \omega^n & \omega^{2n} & 1 \end{vmatrix}$

    $= 1(1 - \omega^{3n}) - \omega^n(\omega^{2n} - \omega^{2n}) + \omega^{2n}(\omega^{4n} - \omega^n)$
    $= 1 - \omega^{3n} + \omega^{6n} - \omega^{3n} = 1 - 2(\omega^3)^n + [\omega^3]^{2n}$
    $= 1 - 2 + 1 = 0 \,(\because \ \omega^3 = 1)$

15. $A = \begin{bmatrix} \alpha & 2 \\ 2 & \alpha \end{bmatrix}$ and $|A^3| = 125 \Rightarrow |A|^3 = 125$

    Now, $|A| = \alpha^2 - 4 \Rightarrow (\alpha^2 - 4)^3 = 125 = 5^3$
    $\Rightarrow \alpha^2 - 4 = 5 \Rightarrow \alpha = \pm 3$

16. $|A| = \begin{vmatrix} \cos 20 & \sin 20 \\ \sin 70 & \cos 70 \end{vmatrix} = \cos(20 + 70) = \cos 90 = 0.$

17. From the given equation, we have
    $4 = (3x - 2) - (x + 6) = 2x - 8 \Rightarrow x = 6.$

NCERT Exercise-1

1. $\begin{vmatrix} 2 & 4 \\ -5 & -1 \end{vmatrix} = 2 \times (-1) - (-5) \times (4) = -2 + 20 = 18$

2. (i) $\begin{vmatrix} \cos\theta & -\sin\theta \\ \sin\theta & \cos\theta \end{vmatrix}$

   $= \cos\theta \cos\theta - (\sin\theta)(-\sin\theta)$
   $= \cos^2\theta + \sin^2\theta = 1.$

(ii) $\begin{vmatrix} x^2 - x + 1 & x - 1 \\ x + 1 & x + 1 \end{vmatrix}$

   $= (x^2 - x + 1)(x + 1) - (x - 1)(x + 1)$
   $\therefore \ (x^3 + 1) - (x^2 - 1) = x^3 - x^2 + 2$

3. $A = \begin{bmatrix} 1 & 2 \\ 4 & 2 \end{bmatrix} \Rightarrow 2A = \begin{bmatrix} 2 & 4 \\ 8 & 4 \end{bmatrix}$

   $|2A| = \begin{bmatrix} 2 & 4 \\ 8 & 4 \end{bmatrix} = -24$ & $4|A| = 4\begin{vmatrix} 1 & 2 \\ 4 & 4 \end{vmatrix} = -24$

   Hence $|2A| = 4|A|$.

4. $3A = 3\begin{bmatrix} 1 & 0 & 1 \\ 0 & 1 & 2 \\ 0 & 0 & 4 \end{bmatrix} = \begin{bmatrix} 3 & 0 & 3 \\ 0 & 3 & 6 \\ 0 & 0 & 12 \end{bmatrix}$

   $\therefore \ |3A| = \begin{vmatrix} 3 & 0 & 3 \\ 0 & 3 & 6 \\ 0 & 0 & 12 \end{vmatrix}$

   Taking common 3 out 3 each from R_1, R_2 and R_3 respectively.

   $|3A| = 3 \times 3 \times 3 \times \begin{vmatrix} 1 & 0 & 1 \\ 0 & 1 & 2 \\ 0 & 0 & 4 \end{vmatrix} = 27\begin{vmatrix} 1 & 0 & 1 \\ 0 & 1 & 2 \\ 0 & 0 & 4 \end{vmatrix}$

   $\Rightarrow |27A| = 27|A|$

5. (i) $\begin{vmatrix} 3 & -1 & -2 \\ 0 & 0 & -1 \\ 3 & -5 & 0 \end{vmatrix} = 3\begin{vmatrix} 0 & -1 \\ -5 & 0 \end{vmatrix} + 1\begin{vmatrix} 0 & -1 \\ 3 & 0 \end{vmatrix} - 2\begin{vmatrix} 0 & 0 \\ 3 & -5 \end{vmatrix}$

   $= 3(0 - 5) + 1(0 + 3) - 2 \times 0$
   $= -15 + 3 = -12.$

(ii) $\begin{vmatrix} 3 & -4 & 5 \\ 1 & 1 & -2 \\ 2 & 3 & 1 \end{vmatrix} = 3\begin{vmatrix} 1 & -2 \\ 3 & 1 \end{vmatrix} + 4\begin{vmatrix} 1 & -2 \\ 2 & 1 \end{vmatrix} + 5\begin{vmatrix} 1 & 1 \\ 2 & 3 \end{vmatrix}$

   $= 3(1 + 6) + 4(1 + 4) + 5(3 - 2) = 21 + 20 + 5 = 46.$

(iii) $\begin{vmatrix} 0 & 1 & 2 \\ -1 & 0 & -3 \\ -2 & 3 & 0 \end{vmatrix} = 0\begin{vmatrix} 0 & -3 \\ 3 & 0 \end{vmatrix} - 1\begin{vmatrix} -1 & -3 \\ -2 & 0 \end{vmatrix} + 2\begin{vmatrix} -1 & 0 \\ -2 & 3 \end{vmatrix}$

   $= 0 - 1(0 - 6) + 2(-3) = 6 - 6 = 0.$

(iv) $\begin{vmatrix} 2 & -1 & -2 \\ 0 & 2 & -1 \\ 3 & -5 & 0 \end{vmatrix} \ 2\begin{vmatrix} 2 & -1 \\ -5 & 0 \end{vmatrix} + 1\begin{vmatrix} 0 & -1 \\ 3 & 0 \end{vmatrix} - 2\begin{vmatrix} 0 & 2 \\ 3 & -5 \end{vmatrix}$

   $= 2(0 - 5) + 1(0 + 3) - 2(0 - 6) = -10 + 3 + 12 = 5$

6. $|A| = \begin{vmatrix} 1 & 1 & -2 \\ 2 & 1 & -3 \\ 5 & 4 & -9 \end{vmatrix} = 1\begin{vmatrix} 1 & -3 \\ 4 & -9 \end{vmatrix} - 1\begin{vmatrix} 2 & -3 \\ 5 & -9 \end{vmatrix} - 2\begin{vmatrix} 2 & 1 \\ 5 & 4 \end{vmatrix}$

$= 1(-9+12) - 1(-18+15) - 2(8-5) = 3 + 3 - 6 = 0.$

7. (i) $\begin{vmatrix} 2 & 4 \\ 5 & 1 \end{vmatrix} = \begin{vmatrix} 2x & 4 \\ 6 & x \end{vmatrix}$

$\Rightarrow \quad 2 - 20 = 2x^2 - 24 \Rightarrow 2x^2 = 6$

$\Rightarrow \quad x^2 = 3 \Rightarrow x = \pm\sqrt{3}$

(ii) $\begin{vmatrix} 2 & 3 \\ 4 & 5 \end{vmatrix} = \begin{vmatrix} x & 3 \\ 2x & 5 \end{vmatrix}$

or $\quad 2 \times 5 - 4 \times 3 = 5 \times x - 2x \times 3$

or $\quad 10 - 12 = 5x - 6x$

$\Rightarrow -2 = -x \quad$ or $\quad x = 2$

8. (b) $\begin{vmatrix} x & 2 \\ 18 & x \end{vmatrix} = \begin{vmatrix} 6 & 2 \\ 18 & 6 \end{vmatrix}$

$\Rightarrow \quad x^2 - 36 = 36 - 36$

$\Rightarrow \quad x^2 = 36 \Rightarrow x = \pm 6$

Practice Exercise-2

1. (a)   **2.** (d)   **3.** (c)   **4.** (c)
5. (a)   **6.** (c)

7. $\left(2, \dfrac{1}{2}\right)$

8. $\lambda = 3, -2$

9. $\dfrac{61}{2}$

10. $k = 5$

11. 5 units

12. $k = 7$

13. 15 square units.

NCERT Exercise-2

1. (i) Area of $\Delta = \dfrac{1}{2}\begin{vmatrix} 1 & 0 & 1 \\ 6 & 0 & 1 \\ 4 & 3 & 1 \end{vmatrix}$

$= \dfrac{1}{2}\,[1(0-3) + 1(18-0)] = \dfrac{15}{2} = 7.5$ sq. units.

(ii) Area of $\Delta = \dfrac{1}{2}\begin{vmatrix} 2 & 7 & 1 \\ 1 & 1 & 1 \\ 10 & 8 & 1 \end{vmatrix}$

$= \dfrac{1}{2}\left[2\begin{vmatrix} 1 & 1 \\ 8 & 1 \end{vmatrix} - 7\begin{vmatrix} 1 & 1 \\ 10 & 1 \end{vmatrix} + 1\begin{vmatrix} 1 & 1 \\ 10 & 8 \end{vmatrix}\right]$

$= \dfrac{1}{2}\,[2(1-8) - 7(1-10) + 1(8-10)]$

$= \dfrac{1}{2}\,[-14 + 63 - 2] = \dfrac{47}{2} = 23.5$ sq. units

(iii) Area of $\Delta = \dfrac{1}{2}\begin{vmatrix} -2 & -3 & 1 \\ 3 & 2 & 1 \\ -1 & -8 & 1 \end{vmatrix}$

$= \dfrac{1}{2}\left[-2\begin{vmatrix} 2 & 1 \\ -8 & 1 \end{vmatrix} + 3\begin{vmatrix} 3 & 1 \\ -1 & 1 \end{vmatrix} + 1\begin{vmatrix} 3 & 2 \\ -1 & -8 \end{vmatrix}\right]$

$= \dfrac{1}{2}\,\left[-2(2+8) + 3(3+1) + 1(-24+2)\right]$

$= \dfrac{1}{2}\,\left[-20 + 12 - 22\right] = \dfrac{-30}{2} = -15$

$\therefore$ Area $= 15$ square units. (As area > 0)

2. The vertices of ΔABC are A $(a, b+c)$, B $(b, c+a)$ and C $(c, a+b)$

$\Delta = $ The area of $\Delta ABC = \dfrac{1}{2}\begin{vmatrix} x_1 & y_1 & 1 \\ x_2 & y_2 & 1 \\ x_3 & y_3 & 1 \end{vmatrix}$

$= \dfrac{1}{2}\begin{vmatrix} a & b+c & 1 \\ b & c+a & 1 \\ c & a+b & 1 \end{vmatrix}$ Operate $C_1 \to C_1 + C_2$

$\Delta = \dfrac{a+b+c}{2}\begin{vmatrix} 1 & b+c & 1 \\ 1 & c+a & 1 \\ 1 & a+b & 1 \end{vmatrix} = 0$

Hence, the points A, B, C are collinear.

3. (i) Area of $\Delta = 4$ (Given)

Again, $\Delta = \dfrac{1}{2}\begin{vmatrix} k & 0 & 1 \\ 4 & 0 & 1 \\ 0 & 2 & 1 \end{vmatrix}$

$= \dfrac{1}{2}\,[-2k + 8] = -k + 4$

Case (a): $-k + 4 = 4$
$\Rightarrow \qquad k = 0$
Case (b): $-k + 4 = -4$
$\Rightarrow \qquad k = 8$
Hence, $\qquad k = 0, 8$

(ii) The area of the triangle whose vertices are $(-2, 0)$, $(0, 4)$, $(0, k)$

$= \dfrac{1}{2}\begin{vmatrix} -2 & 0 & 1 \\ 0 & 4 & 1 \\ 0 & k & 1 \end{vmatrix}$

$= \dfrac{1}{2} \times (-2)(4-k) = k - 4 = \pm 4$ (given)

Taking $+$ve sign $k - 4 = 4 \qquad \therefore\ k = 8$
Taking $-$ve sign $k - 4 = -4 \qquad \therefore\ k = 0$

4. **(i)** **Given :** Points $(1, 2), (3, 6)$

Equation of the line is

$$\begin{vmatrix} x & y & 1 \\ x_1 & y_1 & 1 \\ x_2 & y_2 & 1 \end{vmatrix} = 0 \Rightarrow \begin{vmatrix} x & y & 1 \\ 1 & 2 & 1 \\ 3 & 6 & 1 \end{vmatrix} = 0$$

$\Rightarrow \quad x(2-6) - y(1-3) + 1(6-6) = 0$

$\Rightarrow \quad -4x + 2y = 0 \quad \Rightarrow \quad 2x - y = 0$

Hence, $y = 2x$ is the required line.

(ii) Equation of the line is

$$\Rightarrow \quad \begin{vmatrix} x & y & 1 \\ 3 & 1 & 1 \\ 9 & 3 & 1 \end{vmatrix} = 0$$

$\Rightarrow \quad x(1-3) - y(3-9) + 1(9-9) = 0$

$\Rightarrow \quad -2x + 6y = 0 \quad \Rightarrow \quad 6y = 2x$

Hence $x - 3y = 0$ which is the required line.

5. **(d)** Area of $\Delta = \dfrac{1}{2} \begin{vmatrix} 2 & -6 & 1 \\ 5 & 4 & 1 \\ k & 4 & 1 \end{vmatrix}$

$= \dfrac{1}{2} [50 - 10k] = 25 - 5k$

$\therefore \quad 25 - 5k = 35 \quad$ or $\quad 25 - 5k = -35$

$\qquad -5k = 10 \quad$ or $\quad 5k = 60$

$\Rightarrow \quad k = -2 \quad\quad$ or $\quad k = 12$

Practice Exercise-3

1. **(c)**   **2.** **(a)**   **3.** **(c)**   **4.** **(a)**
5. **(b)**   **6.** 12   **7.** 0

NCERT Exercise-3

1. **(i)** $\begin{vmatrix} 2 & -4 \\ 0 & 3 \end{vmatrix}$

$\therefore$ Minors;

$M_{11} = 3, \quad M_{12} = 0$

$M_{21} = -4, \quad M_{22} = 2$

For cofactors

As $C_{ij} = (-1)^{i+j} M_{ij}$

$\therefore \quad C_{11} = 3, \quad C_{12} = -0 = 0$

$\qquad C_{12} = 4, \quad C_{22} = 3$

(ii) Let $A = \begin{vmatrix} a & c \\ b & d \end{vmatrix}$

Minors :

$\qquad M_{11} = d, \quad M_{12} = b$

$\qquad M_{21} = c, \quad M_{22} = a$

For cofactors

As;

$\qquad C_{ij} = (-1)^{i+J} \quad M_{ij}$

$\qquad C_{11} = d, \qquad C_{12} = -b$

$\qquad C_{21} = -c, \qquad C_{22} = a$

2. **(i)** $\begin{vmatrix} 1 & 0 & 0 \\ 0 & 1 & 0 \\ 0 & 0 & 1 \end{vmatrix}$

$\therefore$ Minors; $M_{11} = \begin{vmatrix} 1 & 0 \\ 0 & 1 \end{vmatrix} = 1,$

$M_{12} = \begin{vmatrix} 0 & 0 \\ 0 & 1 \end{vmatrix} = 0, \ M_{13} = \begin{vmatrix} 0 & 1 \\ 0 & 0 \end{vmatrix} = 0$

$M_{21} = \begin{vmatrix} 0 & 0 \\ 0 & 1 \end{vmatrix} = 0, \ M_{22} = \begin{vmatrix} 1 & 0 \\ 0 & 1 \end{vmatrix} = 1,$

$M_{23} = \begin{vmatrix} 1 & 0 \\ 0 & 0 \end{vmatrix} = 0, \ M_{31} = \begin{vmatrix} 0 & 0 \\ 1 & 0 \end{vmatrix} = 0,$

$M_{32} = \begin{vmatrix} 1 & 0 \\ 0 & 0 \end{vmatrix} = 0, \ M_{33} = \begin{vmatrix} 1 & 0 \\ 0 & 1 \end{vmatrix} = 1$

Cofactors

$A_{11} = (-1)^{1+1} M_{11} = 1,$

$A_{12} = (-1)^{1+2} M_{12} = 0,$

$A_{13} = (-1)^{1+3} M_{13} = 0, \ A_{21} = (-1)^{2+1} M_{21} = 0$

$A_{22} = (-1)^{2+2} M_{22} = 1, \ A_{23} = (-1)^{2+3} M_{23} = 0$

$A_{31} = (-1)^{3+1} M_{31} = 0, \ A_{32} = (-1)^{3+2} M_{32} = 0$

$A_{33} = (-1)^{3+3} M_{33} = 1$

Thus, $M_{11} = A_{11} = 1, \ M_{12} = A_{12} = 0, \ M_{13} = A_{13} = 0$

$M_{21} = A_{21} = 0, \ M_{22} = A_{22} = 1, \ M_{23} = A_{23} = 0$

$M_{31} = A_{31} = 0, \ M_{32} = A_{32} = 0, \ M_{33} = A_{33} = 1$

(ii) $\begin{vmatrix} 1 & 0 & 4 \\ 3 & 5 & -1 \\ 0 & 1 & 2 \end{vmatrix} \therefore$ Minors; $M_{11} = \begin{vmatrix} 5 & -1 \\ 1 & 2 \end{vmatrix} = 10 + 1 = 11,$

$M_{12} = \begin{vmatrix} 3 & -1 \\ 0 & 2 \end{vmatrix} = 6, \ M_{13} = \begin{vmatrix} 3 & 5 \\ 0 & 1 \end{vmatrix} = 3$

$M_{21} = \begin{vmatrix} 0 & 4 \\ 1 & 2 \end{vmatrix} = -4, \ M_{22} = \begin{vmatrix} 1 & 4 \\ 0 & 2 \end{vmatrix} = 2,$

$M_{23} = \begin{vmatrix} 1 & 0 \\ 0 & 1 \end{vmatrix} = 1, \ M_{31} = \begin{vmatrix} 0 & 4 \\ 5 & -1 \end{vmatrix} = -20,$

$M_{32} = \begin{vmatrix} 1 & 4 \\ 3 & -1 \end{vmatrix} = -13, \ M_{33} = \begin{vmatrix} 1 & 0 \\ 3 & 5 \end{vmatrix} = 5$

For cofactors; $C_{ij} = (-1)^{i+j} M_{ij}$
$C_{11} = 11$, $C_{12} = -6$, $C_{13} = 3$, $C_{21} = 4$, $C_{22} = 2$, $C_{23} = -1$
$C_{31} = -20$, $C_{32} = 13$, $C_{33} = 5$

3.
$$\Delta = \begin{vmatrix} 5 & 3 & 8 \\ 2 & 0 & 1 \\ 1 & 2 & 3 \end{vmatrix}$$

$$C_{21} = (-1)^{2+1} \begin{vmatrix} 3 & 8 \\ 2 & 3 \end{vmatrix} = -(9-16) = 7$$

$$C_{22} = (-1)^{2+2} \begin{vmatrix} 5 & 8 \\ 1 & 3 \end{vmatrix} = 15 - 8 = 7$$

$$C_{23} = (-1)^{2+3} \begin{vmatrix} 5 & 3 \\ 1 & 2 \end{vmatrix} = -(10-3) = -7$$

Now $\Delta = a_{21} C_{21} + a_{22} C_{22} + a_{33} C_{33}$
$= 2 \times 7 + 0 \times 7 + 1 \times (-7) = 14 + 0 - 7 = 7.$

4. Elements of third column are yz, zx, xy

$$A_{13} = (-1)^{1+3} \begin{vmatrix} 1 & y \\ 1 & z \end{vmatrix} = z - y$$

$$A_{23} = (-1)^{2+3} \begin{vmatrix} 1 & x \\ 1 & z \end{vmatrix} = -(z-x) \, ,$$

$$A_{33} = (-1)^{3+3} \begin{vmatrix} 1 & x \\ 1 & y \end{vmatrix} = (y-x)$$

$\therefore \Delta = a_{13} A_{13} + a_{23} A_{23} + a_{33} A_{33}$
$= yz(z-y) + zx(-z+x) + xy(y-x)$
$= yz^2 - y^2z + x^2z - xz^2 + xy^2 - x^2y$
$= (-y^2 z - yz^2) + (xy^2 - xz^2) + (-x^2y - x^2z)$
$= -yz(y-z) + x(y^2 - z^2) - x^2(y\ z) = (y-z)$

$\qquad\qquad [-yz + x(y+z) - x^2]$
$= (y-z)[z(x-y) - x(x-y)]$
$= (y-z)(x-y)(z-x) = (x-y)(y-z)(z-x)$

5. Option (d) is correct.

1. (c) **2.** (c) **3.** (b) **4.** (a)
5. (a) **6.** (b)
7. (a)
8. $(AB)^{-1} = B^{-1} \cdot A^{-1}$.
9. Inverse of an identity matrix is the matrix itself.

10. $X = \begin{bmatrix} 1 \\ 3 \\ -21 \end{bmatrix}_{3\times 1}$.

11. $\begin{bmatrix} 68 & 0 & 0 \\ 0 & 68 & 0 \\ 0 & 0 & 68 \end{bmatrix}$

12. $M^{-1} = \dfrac{1}{6} \begin{bmatrix} 2 & -2 \\ 2 & 1 \end{bmatrix} = \begin{bmatrix} 1/3 & -1/3 \\ 1/3 & 1/6 \end{bmatrix}$

13. $|A| = \begin{vmatrix} 1 & 0 & 3 \\ 2 & 1 & 1 \\ 0 & 0 & 2 \end{vmatrix} = 2$

$\therefore |\text{adj}(\text{adj } A)| = |A|^{(n-1)^2} = |A|^{2^2}$ $\quad [\because \text{Here } n = 3]$
$\qquad\qquad = 2^4 = 16$

14. $A = \begin{bmatrix} 1 & 0 \\ 1 & 1 \end{bmatrix} \Rightarrow A^{-1} = \dfrac{1}{1} \begin{bmatrix} 1 & 0 \\ -1 & 1 \end{bmatrix} = \begin{bmatrix} 1 & 0 \\ -1 & 1 \end{bmatrix}$

$A^{-2} = \begin{bmatrix} 1 & 0 \\ -1 & 1 \end{bmatrix}\begin{bmatrix} 1 & 0 \\ -1 & 1 \end{bmatrix} = \begin{bmatrix} 1 & 0 \\ -2 & 1 \end{bmatrix}, A^{-n} = \begin{bmatrix} 1 & 0 \\ -n & 1 \end{bmatrix}$

15. If $A = \begin{bmatrix} 3 & -2 & 4 \\ 1 & 2 & -1 \\ 0 & 1 & 1 \end{bmatrix}$ and $A^{-1} = \dfrac{1}{k} \text{adj}(A)$ $\qquad$ ......(i)

Also, we know $A^{-1} = \dfrac{\text{adj}(A)}{|A|}$ $\qquad$ ....(ii)

$\therefore$ By comparing (i) and (ii)

$$|A| = k \Rightarrow |A| = \begin{vmatrix} 3 & -2 & 4 \\ 1 & 2 & -1 \\ 0 & 1 & 1 \end{vmatrix}$$

$= 3(2+1) + 2(1+0) + 4(1-0)$
$= 9 + 2 + 4 = 15$

16. $\lambda = 4$
17. $|\alpha| = 1/5$

1. Let $A = \begin{bmatrix} 1 & 2 \\ 3 & 4 \end{bmatrix}$. Let c_{ij} be cofactor of a_{ij} in A. Then, the cofactors of elements of A are given by
$C_{11} = (-1)^{1+1} (4) = 4$
$C_{12} = (-1)^{1+2} (3) = -3$
$C_{21} = (-1)^{2+1} (2) = -2$
$C_{22} = (-1)^{2+2} (1) = -1$

$\therefore$ Adj $A = \begin{bmatrix} 4 & -3 \\ -2 & 1 \end{bmatrix} = \begin{bmatrix} 4 & -2 \\ -3 & 1 \end{bmatrix}$

2. Let $A = \begin{bmatrix} 1 & -1 & 2 \\ 2 & 3 & 5 \\ -2 & 0 & 1 \end{bmatrix}$,

$A_{11} = (-1)^{1+1} M_{11} = \begin{vmatrix} 3 & 5 \\ 0 & 1 \end{vmatrix} = 3$

Similarly,
$A_{12} = -12$, $\quad A_{13} = 6$
$A_{21} = 1$, $\qquad A_{22} = 5$

$A_{23} = 2, \qquad A_{31} = -11$
$A_{32} = -1, \qquad A_{33} = 5$

$$\text{adj } A = \begin{bmatrix} 3 & -12 & 6 \\ 1 & 5 & 2 \\ -11 & -1 & 5 \end{bmatrix}^T = \begin{bmatrix} 3 & 1 & -11 \\ -12 & 5 & -1 \\ 6 & 2 & 5 \end{bmatrix}$$

3. Let $A = \begin{bmatrix} 2 & 3 \\ -4 & 6 \end{bmatrix}$

$|A| = 24$

Let c_{ij} be cofactor of a_{ij} in A. Then, the cofactor of elements of A are given by

$C_{11} = (-1)^{1+1}(-6) = 6$
$C_{12} = (-1)^{1+2}(-4) = 4$
$C_{21} = (-1)^{2+1}(3) = -3$
$C_{22} = (-1)^{2+2}(2) = -2$

$\therefore$ Adj $A = \begin{bmatrix} 6 & -3 \\ 4 & 2 \end{bmatrix}$

$$A \, \text{Adj } A = \begin{bmatrix} 2 & 3 \\ -4 & 6 \end{bmatrix} \begin{bmatrix} 6 & -3 \\ 4 & 2 \end{bmatrix} = \begin{bmatrix} 24 & 0 \\ 0 & 24 \end{bmatrix} = 24\,I$$

Hence $A\,(\text{Adj } A) = (\text{Adj } A).\, A = 24\,I = |A|\,I$

4. Let $A = \begin{bmatrix} 1 & -1 & 2 \\ 3 & 0 & -2 \\ 1 & 0 & 3 \end{bmatrix}$

$\therefore \quad A_{11} = 0$
$A_{12} = -11, \quad A_{13} = 0$
$A_{21} = -3, \qquad A_{22} = 1$
$A_{23} = 1, \qquad A_{31} = -2$
$A_{32} = 8, \qquad A_{33} = -3$

$$\text{adj } A = \begin{bmatrix} 0 & -3 & -2 \\ -11 & 1 & 8 \\ 0 & 1 & -3 \end{bmatrix},$$

$|A| = 1 \times 0 + (+1)(-11) + 2 \times 0 = -11$

$$A \cdot \text{adj } A = \begin{bmatrix} 1 & 1 & 2 \\ 3 & 0 & -2 \\ 1 & 0 & 3 \end{bmatrix} \begin{bmatrix} 0 & -3 & -2 \\ -11 & 1 & 8 \\ 0 & 1 & -3 \end{bmatrix}$$

$$= -11 \times \begin{bmatrix} 1 & 0 & 0 \\ 0 & 1 & 0 \\ 0 & 0 & 1 \end{bmatrix} = |A|\,I$$

$$(\text{adj } A)\, A = \begin{bmatrix} 0 & -3 & -2 \\ -11 & 1 & 8 \\ 0 & 1 & -3 \end{bmatrix} \begin{bmatrix} 1 & 1 & 2 \\ 3 & 0 & -2 \\ 1 & 0 & 3 \end{bmatrix}$$

$$= -11 \begin{bmatrix} 1 & 0 & 0 \\ 0 & 1 & 0 \\ 0 & 0 & 1 \end{bmatrix} = |A|\,I$$

$\Rightarrow A\,(\text{adj } A) = (\text{adj } A)\, A = |A|\,I$

5. $|A| = \begin{vmatrix} 2 & -2 \\ 4 & 3 \end{vmatrix} = 6 + 8 = 14 \neq 0.$

So, A is a non-singular matrix and therefore it is invertible. Let c_{ij} be cofactor of a_{ij} in A. Then, the cofactors of elements of A are given by

$C_{11} = (-1)^{1+1}(3) = 3$
$C_{12} = (-1)^{1+2}(4) = -4$
$C_{21} = (-1)^{2+1}(-2) = 2$
$C_{22} = (-1)^{2+2}(2) = 2$

$\therefore$ Adj $A = \begin{bmatrix} 3 & -4 \\ 2 & 2 \end{bmatrix} = \begin{bmatrix} 3 & 2 \\ -4 & 2 \end{bmatrix}$

Hence, $A^{-1} = \dfrac{1}{|A|} \text{Adj}. A = \dfrac{1}{14} \begin{bmatrix} 3 & 2 \\ -4 & 2 \end{bmatrix} = \begin{bmatrix} \dfrac{3}{14} & \dfrac{1}{7} \\ \dfrac{-2}{7} & \dfrac{1}{7} \end{bmatrix}$

6. $\therefore |A| = \begin{vmatrix} -1 & 5 \\ -3 & 2 \end{vmatrix} = -2 + 15 = 13 \neq 0.$

So, A is a non-singular matrix and therefore it is invertible. Let c_{ij} be cofactor of a_{ij} in A. Then, the cofactors of elements of A are given by the cofactors of elements of A are given by

$C_{11} = (-1)^{1+1}(2) = 2; \quad C_{12} = (-1)^{1+2}(-3) = 3$
$C_{21} = (-1)^{2+1}(5) = -5; \quad C_{22} = (-1)^{2+2}(-1) = -1.$

$\therefore$ Adj $A = \begin{bmatrix} 2 & 3 \\ -5 & -1 \end{bmatrix}^T = \begin{bmatrix} 2 & -5 \\ 3 & -1 \end{bmatrix}$

Hence, $A^{-1} = \dfrac{1}{|A|} \text{Adj}. A$

$$= \dfrac{1}{13} \begin{bmatrix} 2 & -5 \\ 3 & -1 \end{bmatrix} = \begin{bmatrix} \dfrac{2}{13} & \dfrac{-5}{13} \\ \dfrac{3}{13} & \dfrac{-1}{13} \end{bmatrix}$$

7. Let $A = \begin{bmatrix} 1 & 2 & 3 \\ 0 & 2 & 4 \\ 0 & 0 & 5 \end{bmatrix}$

$\therefore |A| = 10$

Now for cofactor $C_{ij} = (-1)^{i+j} M_{ij}$

$$\therefore \quad \text{Adj } A = \begin{bmatrix} 10 & 0 & 0 \\ -10 & 5 & 0 \\ 2 & -4 & 2 \end{bmatrix} = \begin{bmatrix} 10 & -10 & 2 \\ 0 & 5 & -4 \\ 0 & 0 & 2 \end{bmatrix}$$

Hence, $A^{-1} = \dfrac{1}{|A|}$ Adj. A

$$= \frac{1}{10} \begin{bmatrix} 10 & -10 & 2 \\ 0 & 5 & -4 \\ 0 & 0 & 2 \end{bmatrix} = \begin{bmatrix} 1 & -1 & \frac{1}{5} \\ 0 & \frac{1}{2} & \frac{-2}{5} \\ 0 & 0 & \frac{1}{5} \end{bmatrix}$$

8. $\quad \therefore \ |A| = \begin{vmatrix} 1 & 0 & 0 \\ 3 & 3 & 0 \\ 5 & 2 & -1 \end{vmatrix} = 1 \begin{vmatrix} 3 & 0 \\ 2 & -1 \end{vmatrix}$

$= -3 - 0 = -3 \neq 0$

So, A is non singular therefore it is invertible.

Let C_{ij} be co-factors of a_{ij} in A.

Then cofactor of elements of A are given by

$\quad C_{11} = -3, C_{12} = 3, C_{13} = -9, C_{21} = 0$

$\quad C_{22} = -1, C_{23} = -2, C_{31} = 0, \ C_{32} = 0, C_{33} = 3$

$$\therefore \quad \text{Adj } A = \begin{bmatrix} -3 & 0 & 0 \\ 3 & -1 & 0 \\ -9 & -2 & 3 \end{bmatrix} A^{-1} = \frac{-1}{3} \begin{bmatrix} -3 & 0 & 0 \\ 3 & -1 & 0 \\ -9 & -2 & 3 \end{bmatrix}$$

9. $\quad A = \begin{bmatrix} 2 & 1 & 3 \\ 4 & -1 & 0 \\ -7 & 2 & 1 \end{bmatrix}.$

$\quad = 2(-1-0) - 1(4-0) + 3(8-3)$

So, A is non-singular matrix and therefore, it is invertible.

$$\therefore \text{Adj } A = \begin{bmatrix} -1 & 5 & 3 \\ -4 & 23 & 12 \\ 1 & -11 & -6 \end{bmatrix}$$

Hence $A^{-1} = \dfrac{1}{|A|} \text{Adj } A$

$$= -\frac{1}{13} \begin{bmatrix} -1 & 5 & 3 \\ -4 & 23 & 12 \\ 1 & -11 & -6 \end{bmatrix}$$

10. $\quad \therefore \ |A| = \begin{vmatrix} 1 & -1 & 2 \\ 0 & 2 & -3 \\ 3 & -2 & 4 \end{vmatrix}$

$= 1(8-6) + 1(0+9) + 2(0-6)$

$= 2 + 9 - 12 = -1 \neq 0$

$\therefore \quad$ A is invertible and $A^{-1} = \dfrac{\text{Adj } A}{|A|}$

$$\therefore \quad \text{Adj } A = \begin{bmatrix} 2 & -9 & -6 \\ 0 & -2 & -1 \\ -1 & 3 & 2 \end{bmatrix}^{T} = \begin{bmatrix} 2 & 0 & -1 \\ -9 & -2 & 3 \\ -6 & -1 & 2 \end{bmatrix}$$

$$\therefore \quad A^{-1} = \begin{bmatrix} -2 & 0 & 1 \\ 9 & 2 & -3 \\ 6 & 1 & -2 \end{bmatrix}$$

11. $\quad \text{adj } A = \begin{bmatrix} -1 & 0 & 0 \\ 0 & -\cos\alpha & -\sin\alpha \\ 0 & -\sin\alpha & \cos\alpha \end{bmatrix}$

First find $|A| = -\cos^2\alpha - \sin^2\alpha = -1 \neq 0$

$$A^{-1} = \frac{1}{|A|} \text{ adj } A = \begin{bmatrix} 1 & 0 & 0 \\ 0 & \cos\alpha & \sin\alpha \\ 0 & \sin\alpha & -\cos\alpha \end{bmatrix}$$

12. $\quad$ Here $|A| = \begin{vmatrix} 3 & 7 \\ 2 & 5 \end{vmatrix} = 15 - 14 = 1 \neq 0.$

$$\therefore \quad \text{Adj } A = \begin{bmatrix} 5 & -7 \\ -2 & 3 \end{bmatrix}$$

Hence, $A^{-1} = \dfrac{1}{|A|} \text{Adj. } A = \begin{bmatrix} 5 & -7 \\ -2 & 3 \end{bmatrix} \quad [\because |A| = 1]$

Also, $|B| = \begin{vmatrix} 6 & 8 \\ 7 & 9 \end{vmatrix} = 54 - 56 = -2 \neq 0.$

$$\therefore \quad \text{Adj } B = \begin{bmatrix} 9 & -8 \\ -7 & 6 \end{bmatrix}$$

Hence, $B^{-1} = \dfrac{1}{|B|} \text{Adj. } B = -\dfrac{1}{2} \begin{bmatrix} 9 & -8 \\ -7 & 6 \end{bmatrix}$

$B^{-1}A^{-1}$

$$= -\frac{1}{2} \begin{bmatrix} 9 & -8 \\ -7 & 6 \end{bmatrix} \begin{bmatrix} 5 & -7 \\ -2 & 3 \end{bmatrix} = -\frac{1}{2} \begin{bmatrix} 61 & -87 \\ -47 & 67 \end{bmatrix}$$

Now, $|AB| = |A||B| = 1 \times (-2) = -2 \neq 0$

$\quad \text{Adj } AB = (\text{Adj } B)(\text{Adj } A)$

$$= \begin{bmatrix} 9 & -8 \\ -7 & 6 \end{bmatrix} \begin{bmatrix} 5 & -7 \\ -2 & 3 \end{bmatrix} = \begin{bmatrix} 61 & -87 \\ -47 & 67 \end{bmatrix}$$

$$AB^{-1} = \frac{1}{-2} \begin{bmatrix} 61 & -87 \\ -47 & 67 \end{bmatrix}$$

Hence, $(AB)^{-1} = B^{-1}A^{-1}.$

13. $\quad A = \begin{bmatrix} 3 & 1 \\ -1 & 2 \end{bmatrix}, A^2 = \begin{bmatrix} 8 & 5 \\ -5 & 3 \end{bmatrix}$

$$\therefore A^2 - 5A + 7I = \begin{bmatrix} 8 & 5 \\ -5 & 3 \end{bmatrix} - 5 \begin{bmatrix} 3 & 1 \\ -1 & 2 \end{bmatrix} + 7 \begin{bmatrix} 1 & 0 \\ 0 & 1 \end{bmatrix}$$

$$= \begin{bmatrix} 0 & 0 \\ 0 & 0 \end{bmatrix} = 0 \qquad \therefore\ A^2 - 5A + 7I = 0$$

Multiplying by A^{-1}

$$(A^{-1}A)A - 5A^{-1}A + 7A^{-1}I = 0$$
$$IA - 5I + 7A^{-1} = 0$$
$$7A^{-1} = 5I - IA = 5I - A$$

$$= 5\begin{bmatrix} 1 & 0 \\ 0 & 1 \end{bmatrix} - \begin{bmatrix} 3 & 1 \\ -1 & 2 \end{bmatrix} = \begin{bmatrix} 2 & -1 \\ 1 & 3 \end{bmatrix}$$

$$\Rightarrow A^{-1} = \frac{1}{7}\begin{bmatrix} 2 & -1 \\ 1 & 3 \end{bmatrix}$$

14. $A = \begin{bmatrix} 3 & 2 \\ 1 & 1 \end{bmatrix}$

Now $A^2 + aA + bI^2 = 0$

$$\begin{bmatrix} 3 & 2 \\ 1 & 1 \end{bmatrix}\begin{bmatrix} 3 & 2 \\ 1 & 1 \end{bmatrix} + a\begin{bmatrix} 3 & 2 \\ 1 & 1 \end{bmatrix} + b\begin{bmatrix} 1 & 0 \\ 0 & 1 \end{bmatrix} = 0$$

$$\Rightarrow \begin{bmatrix} 11 + 3a + b & 8 + 2a \\ 4 + a & 3 + a + b \end{bmatrix} = \begin{bmatrix} 0 & 0 \\ 0 & 0 \end{bmatrix}$$

$$\Rightarrow\ 4 + a = 0 \Rightarrow a = -4$$

Also $3 + a + b = 0$

$$\Rightarrow\ 3 - 4 + b = 0 \ \Rightarrow\ b = 1$$
$$\therefore\ A^2 - 4A + 1 = 0$$
$$\Rightarrow\ (A^{-1}A) - 4AA^{-1} + IA^{-1} = 0$$
$$\Rightarrow\ A - 4I + A^{-1} = 0$$
$$\Rightarrow\ A^{-1} = 4I - A$$

$$\Rightarrow\ A^{-1} = 4\begin{bmatrix} 1 & 0 \\ 0 & 1 \end{bmatrix} - \begin{bmatrix} 3 & 2 \\ 1 & 1 \end{bmatrix}$$

$$\Rightarrow\ A^{-1} = \begin{bmatrix} 4 & 0 \\ 0 & 4 \end{bmatrix} - \begin{bmatrix} 3 & 2 \\ 1 & 1 \end{bmatrix}$$

$$A^{-1} = \begin{bmatrix} 1 & -2 \\ -1 & 3 \end{bmatrix}$$

15. $A^2 = \begin{bmatrix} 4 & 2 & 1 \\ -3 & 8 & -14 \\ 7 & -3 & 14 \end{bmatrix}$

$$A^3 = A^2 \times A = \begin{bmatrix} 4 & 2 & 1 \\ -3 & 8 & -14 \\ 7 & -3 & 14 \end{bmatrix}\begin{bmatrix} 1 & 1 & 1 \\ 1 & 2 & -3 \\ 2 & -1 & 3 \end{bmatrix}$$

$$= \begin{bmatrix} 8 & 7 & 1 \\ -23 & 27 & -69 \\ 32 & -13 & 58 \end{bmatrix}$$

Now, $A^3 - 6A^2 + 5A + 11\,I_3$

$$= \begin{bmatrix} 8 & 7 & 1 \\ -23 & 27 & -69 \\ 32 & -13 & 58 \end{bmatrix} - 6\begin{bmatrix} 4 & 2 & 1 \\ -3 & 8 & -14 \\ 7 & -3 & 14 \end{bmatrix}$$

$$+ 5\begin{bmatrix} 1 & 1 & 1 \\ 1 & 2 & -3 \\ 2 & -1 & 3 \end{bmatrix} + 11\begin{bmatrix} 1 & 0 & 0 \\ 0 & 1 & 0 \\ 0 & 0 & 1 \end{bmatrix}$$

$$= \begin{bmatrix} 0 & 0 & 0 \\ 0 & 0 & 0 \\ 0 & 0 & 0 \end{bmatrix} = 0$$

$$\therefore\ A^3 - 6A^2 + 5A + 11\,I_3 = 0 \ ;$$

Multiplying by A^{-1}

$$(A^{-1}A)A^2 - 6\,(A^{-1}A)A + 5A^{-1}A + 11\,A^{-1}I_3 = 0$$

or $\qquad IA^2 - 6IA + 5I + 11A^{-1} = 0$

$\therefore \qquad 11\,A^{-1} = -A^2 + 6A - 5I$

$$= \begin{bmatrix} 4 & 2 & 1 \\ -3 & 8 & -14 \\ 7 & -3 & 14 \end{bmatrix} + 6\begin{bmatrix} 1 & 1 & 1 \\ 1 & 2 & -3 \\ 2 & -1 & 3 \end{bmatrix}$$

$$+ \begin{bmatrix} -5 & 0 & 0 \\ 0 & -5 & 0 \\ 0 & 0 & -5 \end{bmatrix} = \begin{bmatrix} -3 & 4 & 5 \\ 9 & -1 & -4 \\ 5 & -3 & -1 \end{bmatrix}$$

$$A^{-1} = \frac{1}{11}\begin{bmatrix} -3 & 4 & 5 \\ 9 & -1 & -4 \\ 5 & -3 & -1 \end{bmatrix} = \begin{bmatrix} -3/11 & 4/11 & 5/11 \\ 9/11 & -1/11 & -4/11 \\ 5/11 & -3/11 & -1/11 \end{bmatrix}$$

16.   We have $A = \begin{bmatrix} 2 & -1 & 1 \\ -1 & 2 & -1 \\ 1 & -1 & 2 \end{bmatrix}$

$$= \begin{bmatrix} 6 & -5 & 5 \\ -5 & 6 & -5 \\ 5 & -5 & 6 \end{bmatrix}$$

$$= \begin{bmatrix} 22 & -21 & 21 \\ -21 & 22 & -21 \\ 21 & -21 & 22 \end{bmatrix}$$

Now, $A^3 - 6A^2 + 9A - 4\,I$

$$= \begin{bmatrix} 22 & -21 & 21 \\ -21 & 22 & -21 \\ 21 & -21 & 22 \end{bmatrix} - 6\begin{bmatrix} 6 & -5 & 5 \\ -5 & 6 & -5 \\ 5 & -5 & 6 \end{bmatrix}$$

$$+ 9\begin{bmatrix} 2 & -1 & 1 \\ -1 & 2 & -1 \\ 1 & -1 & 2 \end{bmatrix} - 4\begin{bmatrix} 1 & 0 & 0 \\ 0 & 1 & 0 \\ 0 & 0 & 1 \end{bmatrix} = \begin{bmatrix} 0 & 0 & 0 \\ 0 & 0 & 0 \\ 0 & 0 & 0 \end{bmatrix} = 0$$

Hence, $A^3 - 6A^2 + 9A - 4I = 0$

$$\Rightarrow\ 4I = A^3 - 6A^2 + 9A$$

$$\Rightarrow\ A^{-1} = \frac{1}{4}A^2 - \frac{6}{4}A + \frac{9}{4}I$$

$$= \frac{1}{4}\begin{bmatrix} 6 & -5 & 5 \\ -5 & 6 & -5 \\ 5 & -5 & 6 \end{bmatrix} - \frac{6}{4}\begin{bmatrix} 2 & -1 & 1 \\ -1 & 2 & -1 \\ 1 & -1 & 2 \end{bmatrix}$$

$$+ \frac{9}{4}\begin{bmatrix} 1 & 0 & 0 \\ 0 & 1 & 0 \\ 0 & 0 & 1 \end{bmatrix} = \frac{1}{4}\begin{bmatrix} 3 & 1 & -1 \\ 1 & 3 & 1 \\ -1 & 1 & 3 \end{bmatrix}$$

17. Let $A = \begin{bmatrix} a_{11} & a_{12} & a_{13} \\ a_{21} & a_{22} & a_{23} \\ a_{31} & a_{32} & a_{33} \end{bmatrix}$

Let Adj. $A = \begin{bmatrix} A_{11} & A_{21} & A_{31} \\ A_{12} & A_{22} & A_{32} \\ A_{13} & A_{23} & A_{33} \end{bmatrix}$

A. Adj. $A = \begin{bmatrix} a_{11} & a_{12} & a_{12} \\ a_{21} & a_{22} & a_{23} \\ a_{31} & a_{32} & a_{33} \end{bmatrix} \begin{bmatrix} A_{11} & A_{21} & A_{31} \\ A_{12} & A_{22} & A_{32} \\ A_{13} & A_{23} & A_{33} \end{bmatrix}$

$$= \begin{bmatrix} |A| & 0 & 0 \\ 0 & |A| & 0 \\ 0 & 0 & |A| \end{bmatrix} = [|A|]^3$$

Dividing by $|A|$, $|Adj. A| = |A|^2$
Hence, part (b) is the correct answer.

18. $|A| \neq 0$

$\Rightarrow \quad A^{-1}$ exists $\Rightarrow AA^{-1} = I \quad \Rightarrow \quad |AA^{-1}| = |I| = 1$

$\Rightarrow \quad |A||A^{-1}| = 1 \quad |A^{-1}| = \dfrac{1}{|A|}$

Hence option (b) is correct.

Practice Exercise-5 

1. (d) **2.** (b) **3.** (c) **4.** (c)
5. (i) (b) (ii) (c) (iii) (a) (iv) (b)
(v) (d)
6. The system of equations is consistent with unique solution.

7. $k \neq 0, k \neq 1, k \neq \sqrt{-2}$

8. $\begin{bmatrix} a_1 & b_1 \\ a_2 & b_2 \end{bmatrix}\begin{bmatrix} x \\ y \end{bmatrix} = \begin{bmatrix} c_1 \\ c_2 \end{bmatrix}$

9. $k = 1$

10. a, b, c are in Harmonic Progression.

11. $\dfrac{1}{\alpha} = -\left(\dfrac{1}{a} + \dfrac{1}{b} + \dfrac{1}{c}\right)$

NCERT Exercise-5

1. $x + 2y = 2,\ 2x + 3y = 3$

$$\Rightarrow \begin{bmatrix} 1 & 2 \\ 2 & 3 \end{bmatrix}\begin{bmatrix} x \\ y \end{bmatrix} = \begin{bmatrix} 2 \\ 3 \end{bmatrix} \Rightarrow AX = B$$

Now $|A| = \begin{vmatrix} 1 & 2 \\ 2 & 3 \end{vmatrix} = 3 - 4$

$= -1 \neq 0$. Hence, equations are consistent.

2. $2x - y = 5,\ x + y = 4$

$$\Rightarrow \begin{bmatrix} 2 & -1 \\ 1 & 1 \end{bmatrix}\begin{bmatrix} x \\ y \end{bmatrix} = \begin{bmatrix} 5 \\ 4 \end{bmatrix}$$

$\Rightarrow \quad AX = B$

Now $|A| = \begin{vmatrix} 2 & -1 \\ 1 & 1 \end{vmatrix} = 2 + 1 = 3 \neq 0$

Hence, equations are consistent.

3. $x + 3y = 5,\ 2x + 6y = 8$

$$\Rightarrow \begin{bmatrix} 1 & 3 \\ 2 & 6 \end{bmatrix}\begin{bmatrix} x \\ y \end{bmatrix} = \begin{bmatrix} 5 \\ 8 \end{bmatrix}$$

$\Rightarrow \quad AX = B$

Now $|A| = \begin{vmatrix} 1 & 3 \\ 2 & 6 \end{vmatrix} = 6 - 6 = 0$

A^{-1} does not exists.

$$Adj\,A = \begin{bmatrix} 6 & -3 \\ -2 & 1 \end{bmatrix}$$

Now, Adj $A.\ B = \begin{bmatrix} 6 & -3 \\ -2 & 1 \end{bmatrix}\begin{bmatrix} 5 \\ 8 \end{bmatrix}$

$$= \begin{bmatrix} 6 \\ -2 \end{bmatrix} \neq \begin{bmatrix} 0 \\ 0 \end{bmatrix}$$

Hence, equations are inconsistent with no solution.

4. $x + y + z = 1$
$2x + 3y + 2z = 2$

$$x + y + z = \frac{4}{a}$$

$$\Rightarrow \begin{bmatrix} 1 & 1 & 1 \\ 2 & 3 & 2 \\ 1 & 1 & 2 \end{bmatrix}\begin{bmatrix} x \\ y \\ z \end{bmatrix} = \begin{bmatrix} 1 \\ 2 \\ \dfrac{4}{a} \end{bmatrix}$$

$\Rightarrow \quad AX = B$

$$\therefore \quad |A| = \begin{vmatrix} 1 & 1 & 1 \\ 2 & 3 & 2 \\ 1 & 1 & \dfrac{4}{a} \end{vmatrix} = 3 \neq 0$$

5. $\begin{bmatrix} 3 & -1 & -2 \\ 0 & 2 & -1 \\ 3 & -5 & 0 \end{bmatrix}\begin{bmatrix} x \\ y \\ z \end{bmatrix} = \begin{bmatrix} 2 \\ -1 \\ 3 \end{bmatrix}$

$\Rightarrow \quad AX = B$

$$\therefore \quad |A| = \begin{vmatrix} 3 & -1 & -2 \\ 0 & 2 & -1 \\ 3 & -5 & 0 \end{vmatrix}$$

$$= 3(0-5) + 1(0+3) - 2(0-6)$$
$$= -15 + 3 + 12 = 0$$
$\therefore$ A^{-1} does not exist.

$$\text{Adj. } A = \begin{bmatrix} -5 & 10 & 5 \\ -3 & 6 & 3 \\ -6 & 12 & 6 \end{bmatrix}$$

$$\text{Now, Adj } A . B = \begin{bmatrix} -5 & 10 & 5 \\ -3 & 6 & 3 \\ -6 & 12 & 6 \end{bmatrix} \begin{bmatrix} 2 \\ -1 \\ 3 \end{bmatrix}$$

$$= \begin{bmatrix} -10-10+15 \\ -6-6+9 \\ -12-12+18 \end{bmatrix} = \begin{bmatrix} -5 \\ -3 \\ -6 \end{bmatrix} \neq 0$$

Hence equations are inconsistent with no solution.

6. $5x - y + 4z = 5$
      $2x + 3y + 5z = 2$
      $5x - 2y + 6z = -1$

$$\Rightarrow \begin{bmatrix} 5 & -1 & 4 \\ 2 & 3 & 5 \\ 5 & -2 & 6 \end{bmatrix} \begin{bmatrix} x \\ y \\ z \end{bmatrix} = \begin{bmatrix} 5 \\ 2 \\ -1 \end{bmatrix} \Rightarrow AX = B$$

$$|A| = \begin{vmatrix} 5 & -1 & 4 \\ 2 & 3 & 5 \\ 5 & -2 & 6 \end{vmatrix} = 5(18+10) + 1(12-25) + 4(-4-15)$$

$$= 140 - 13 - 76 = 51 \neq 0$$

Hence equations are consistent with a unique solution.

7.   The given system of equations can be written as

$$\begin{bmatrix} 5 & 2 \\ 7 & 3 \end{bmatrix} \begin{bmatrix} x \\ y \end{bmatrix} = \begin{bmatrix} 4 \\ 5 \end{bmatrix} \text{ i.e., } AX = B$$

$$\text{where } A = \begin{bmatrix} 5 & 2 \\ 7 & 3 \end{bmatrix}, X = \begin{bmatrix} x \\ y \end{bmatrix} \text{ and } B = \begin{bmatrix} 4 \\ 5 \end{bmatrix}$$

$$\text{Now, } |A| = \begin{bmatrix} 5 & 2 \\ 7 & 3 \end{bmatrix} = 15 - 14 = 1 \neq 0$$

$\Rightarrow A^{-1}$ exists and hence the given equation has a unique solution.

$$\therefore \quad \text{Adj } A = \begin{bmatrix} 3 & -7 \\ -2 & 5 \end{bmatrix} = \begin{bmatrix} 3 & -2 \\ -7 & 5 \end{bmatrix}$$

$$\text{and } A^{-1} = \frac{1}{|A|} \text{ (Adj } A)$$

$$= \frac{1}{1} \begin{bmatrix} 3 & -2 \\ -7 & 5 \end{bmatrix} = \begin{bmatrix} 3 & -2 \\ -7 & 5 \end{bmatrix}$$

Solution of given system is given $X = A^{-1}B$

$$\Rightarrow \begin{bmatrix} x \\ y \end{bmatrix} = \begin{bmatrix} 3 & -2 \\ -7 & 5 \end{bmatrix} \begin{bmatrix} 4 \\ 5 \end{bmatrix}$$

$$= \begin{bmatrix} 12 & -10 \\ -28 & +25 \end{bmatrix} = \begin{bmatrix} 2 \\ -3 \end{bmatrix}$$

Hence $x = 2, y = -3$

8.   The given system of equations can be written as

$$\begin{bmatrix} 2 & -1 \\ 3 & 4 \end{bmatrix} \begin{bmatrix} x \\ y \end{bmatrix} = \begin{bmatrix} -2 \\ 3 \end{bmatrix} \text{ i.e., } AX = B$$

$$\text{where } A = \begin{bmatrix} 2 & -1 \\ 3 & 4 \end{bmatrix}$$

$$X = \begin{bmatrix} x \\ y \end{bmatrix} \text{ and } B = \begin{bmatrix} -2 \\ 3 \end{bmatrix}$$

Now $|A| = 8 + 3 = 11 \neq 0$

$\Rightarrow A^{-1}$ exists and hence the given equation has a unique solution.

$$\therefore \quad \text{Adj } A = \begin{bmatrix} 4 & -3 \\ 1 & 2 \end{bmatrix} = \begin{bmatrix} 4 & 1 \\ -3 & 2 \end{bmatrix}$$

$$\text{and } A^{-1} = \frac{1}{|A|} \text{ (Adj } A) = \frac{1}{11} \begin{bmatrix} 4 & 1 \\ -3 & 2 \end{bmatrix}$$

Solution of given system is given by $X = A^{-1}B$

$$\Rightarrow \begin{bmatrix} x \\ y \end{bmatrix} = \frac{1}{11} \begin{bmatrix} 4 & 1 \\ -3 & 2 \end{bmatrix} \begin{bmatrix} -2 \\ 3 \end{bmatrix} = \frac{1}{11} \begin{bmatrix} -8+3 \\ 6+6 \end{bmatrix}$$

$$= \frac{1}{11} \begin{bmatrix} -5 \\ 12 \end{bmatrix} = \begin{bmatrix} \frac{-5}{11} \\ \frac{12}{11} \end{bmatrix}. \text{ Thus } x = -\frac{5}{11}, y = \frac{12}{11}$$

9.   The given system of equations can be written as

$$\begin{bmatrix} 4 & -3 \\ 3 & -5 \end{bmatrix} \begin{bmatrix} x \\ y \end{bmatrix} = \begin{bmatrix} 3 \\ 7 \end{bmatrix} \text{ i.e., } AX = B$$

$$\text{where } A = \begin{bmatrix} 4 & -3 \\ 3 & -5 \end{bmatrix}$$

$$X = \begin{bmatrix} x \\ y \end{bmatrix} \text{ and } B = \begin{bmatrix} 3 \\ 7 \end{bmatrix}$$

$$\text{Now } |A| = \begin{vmatrix} 4 & -3 \\ 3 & -5 \end{vmatrix} = -20 + 9 = -11 \neq 0$$

$\Rightarrow A^{-1}$ exists and hence the given equation has a unique solution.

$\therefore \quad \text{Adj A} = \begin{bmatrix} -5 & -3 \\ 3 & 4 \end{bmatrix}^{T} = \begin{bmatrix} -5 & 3 \\ -3 & 4 \end{bmatrix}$

and $A^{-1} = \dfrac{1}{|A|}(\text{Adj A}) = \dfrac{1}{-11}\begin{bmatrix} -5 & 3 \\ -3 & 4 \end{bmatrix}$

Solution of given system is given by $X = A^{-1}B$

$\Rightarrow \begin{bmatrix} x \\ y \end{bmatrix} = -\dfrac{1}{11}\begin{bmatrix} -5 & 3 \\ -3 & 4 \end{bmatrix}\begin{bmatrix} 3 \\ 7 \end{bmatrix} = \begin{bmatrix} \dfrac{-6}{19} \\ \dfrac{-19}{11} \end{bmatrix}$

Hence, $x = -\dfrac{6}{19}, y = -\dfrac{19}{11}$

10. The given system of equations can be written as

$\begin{bmatrix} 5 & 2 \\ 3 & 2 \end{bmatrix}\begin{bmatrix} x \\ y \end{bmatrix} = \begin{bmatrix} 3 \\ 5 \end{bmatrix}$ i.e., $AX = B$

where $A = \begin{bmatrix} 5 & 2 \\ 3 & 2 \end{bmatrix}$

$X = \begin{bmatrix} x \\ y \end{bmatrix}$ and $B = \begin{bmatrix} 3 \\ 5 \end{bmatrix}$

Now $|A| = \begin{vmatrix} 5 & 2 \\ 3 & 2 \end{vmatrix} = 10 - 6 = 4 \neq 0$

$\Rightarrow A^{-1}$ exists and hence the given equation has a unique solution.

$\therefore \quad \text{Adj A} = \begin{bmatrix} 2 & -3 \\ -2 & 5 \end{bmatrix}^{T} = \begin{bmatrix} 2 & -2 \\ -3 & 5 \end{bmatrix}$

and $A^{-1} = \dfrac{1}{|A|}(\text{Adj A}) = \dfrac{1}{4}\begin{bmatrix} 2 & -2 \\ -3 & 5 \end{bmatrix}$

Solution of given system is given by $X = A^{-1}B$

$\Rightarrow \begin{bmatrix} x \\ y \end{bmatrix} = \dfrac{1}{4}\begin{bmatrix} 2 & -2 \\ -3 & 5 \end{bmatrix}\begin{bmatrix} 3 \\ 5 \end{bmatrix} = \begin{bmatrix} -1 \\ 4 \end{bmatrix}$

Hence, $x = -1, y = 4$.

11. The given system of equations are

$2x + y + z = 1,\ x - 2y - z = 3/2,\ 3y - 5z = 9$

We know $AX = B \Rightarrow X = A^{-1}B$

where, $A = \begin{bmatrix} 2 & 1 & 1 \\ 1 & -2 & -1 \\ 0 & 3 & 5 \end{bmatrix}$,

$X = \begin{bmatrix} x \\ y \\ z \end{bmatrix}$ & $B = \begin{bmatrix} 1 \\ 3/2 \\ 9 \end{bmatrix}$ ...(i)

$\text{adj}(A) = \begin{bmatrix} 13 & 8 & 1 \\ 5 & -10 & 3 \\ 3 & -6 & -5 \end{bmatrix}$

$+$ or $-$ signs are put according as $(-1)^{i+j}$ is $+$ ve or $-$ ve.
Minors of corresponding elements are written in $|A|$
$= 2 \times 13 + 1 \times 5 + 1 \times 3 = 26 + 5 + 3 = 34 \neq 0 \Rightarrow A^{-1}$ exists.

$\therefore A^{-1} = \dfrac{1}{|A|}\text{adj}(A) = \dfrac{1}{34}\begin{bmatrix} 13 & 8 & 1 \\ 5 & -10 & 3 \\ 3 & -6 & -5 \end{bmatrix}$

From (i)

$\therefore X = A^{-1}B = \dfrac{1}{34}\begin{bmatrix} 13 & 8 & 1 \\ 5 & -10 & 3 \\ 3 & -6 & -5 \end{bmatrix}\begin{bmatrix} 1 \\ 3/2 \\ 9 \end{bmatrix} = \begin{bmatrix} 1 \\ 1/2 \\ -3/2 \end{bmatrix}$

$\Rightarrow x = 1,\ y = 1/2,\ z = -3/2$.

12. The given system of equations can be written as

$\begin{bmatrix} 1 & -1 & 1 \\ 2 & 1 & -3 \\ 1 & 1 & 1 \end{bmatrix}\begin{bmatrix} x \\ y \\ z \end{bmatrix} = \begin{bmatrix} 4 \\ 0 \\ 2 \end{bmatrix}$ i.e., $AX = B$

where $A = \begin{bmatrix} 1 & -1 & 1 \\ 2 & 1 & -3 \\ 1 & 1 & 1 \end{bmatrix}$, $X = \begin{bmatrix} x \\ y \\ z \end{bmatrix}$ and $B = \begin{bmatrix} 4 \\ 0 \\ 2 \end{bmatrix}$

Now, $|A| = \begin{vmatrix} 1 & -1 & 1 \\ 2 & 1 & -3 \\ 1 & 1 & 1 \end{vmatrix}$

$= 1(1+3) + 1(2+3) + 1(2-1)$
$= 4 + 5 + 1 = 10 \neq 0$
$\Rightarrow A^{-1}$ exists and hence the given equations have a unique solution.

$\text{Adj A} = \begin{bmatrix} 4 & -5 & 1 \\ 2 & 0 & -2 \\ 2 & 5 & 3 \end{bmatrix}^{T} = \begin{bmatrix} 4 & 2 & 2 \\ -5 & 0 & 5 \\ 1 & -2 & 3 \end{bmatrix}$

and $A^{-1} = \dfrac{1}{|A|}(\text{Adj A}) = \dfrac{1}{10}\begin{bmatrix} 4 & 2 & 2 \\ -5 & 0 & 5 \\ 1 & -2 & 3 \end{bmatrix}$

Solution of given system is given by $X = A^{-1}B$

$\Rightarrow \begin{bmatrix} x \\ y \\ z \end{bmatrix} = \dfrac{1}{10}\begin{bmatrix} 4 & 2 & 2 \\ -5 & 0 & 5 \\ 1 & -2 & 3 \end{bmatrix}\begin{bmatrix} 4 \\ 0 \\ 2 \end{bmatrix} = \begin{bmatrix} 2 \\ -1 \\ 1 \end{bmatrix}$

$\Rightarrow x = 2, y = -1$ and $z = 1$.

13. The given system of equations can be written as :

$$\begin{bmatrix} 2 & 3 & 3 \\ 1 & -2 & 1 \\ 3 & -1 & -2 \end{bmatrix} \begin{bmatrix} x \\ y \\ z \end{bmatrix} = \begin{bmatrix} 5 \\ -4 \\ 3 \end{bmatrix} \text{ i.e., } AX = B$$

where $A = \begin{bmatrix} 2 & 3 & 3 \\ 1 & -2 & 1 \\ 3 & -1 & -2 \end{bmatrix}, X = \begin{bmatrix} x \\ y \\ z \end{bmatrix}$ and $B = \begin{bmatrix} 5 \\ -4 \\ 3 \end{bmatrix}$

Now, $|A| = \begin{vmatrix} 2 & 3 & 3 \\ 1 & -2 & 1 \\ 3 & -1 & -2 \end{vmatrix}$

$= 2(4+1) - 3(-2-3) + 3(-1+6)$
$= 10 + 15 + 15 = 40 \neq 0$

$\therefore \quad A^{-1}$ exists and hence the given equations have a unique solution.

$$\therefore \quad A^{-1} = \frac{1}{|A|} \text{ (Adj A)}$$

$$= \frac{1}{40} \begin{bmatrix} 5 & 5 & 5 \\ 3 & -13 & 11 \\ 9 & 1 & -7 \end{bmatrix} = \frac{1}{40} \begin{bmatrix} 5 & 3 & 9 \\ 5 & -13 & 1 \\ 5 & 11 & -7 \end{bmatrix}$$

Solution of given system is given by $X = A^{-1}B$

$$\Rightarrow \begin{bmatrix} x \\ y \\ z \end{bmatrix} = \frac{1}{40} \begin{bmatrix} 5 & 3 & 9 \\ 5 & -13 & 1 \\ 5 & 11 & -7 \end{bmatrix} \begin{bmatrix} 5 \\ -4 \\ 3 \end{bmatrix}$$

$$= \frac{1}{40} \begin{bmatrix} 25-12+27 \\ 25+52+3 \\ 25-44-21 \end{bmatrix} = \frac{1}{40} \begin{bmatrix} 40 \\ 80 \\ -40 \end{bmatrix} = \begin{bmatrix} 1 \\ 2 \\ -1 \end{bmatrix}$$

Hence, $x = 1, y = 2$ and $z = -1$.

14. The given system of eqeuations can be written as :

$$\begin{bmatrix} 1 & -1 & 2 \\ 3 & 4 & -5 \\ 2 & -1 & 3 \end{bmatrix} \begin{bmatrix} x \\ y \\ z \end{bmatrix} = \begin{bmatrix} 7 \\ -5 \\ 12 \end{bmatrix} \text{ i.e., } AX = B$$

where $A = \begin{bmatrix} 1 & -1 & 2 \\ 3 & 4 & -5 \\ 2 & -1 & 3 \end{bmatrix}, X = \begin{bmatrix} x \\ y \\ z \end{bmatrix}$

and $B = \begin{bmatrix} 7 \\ -5 \\ 12 \end{bmatrix}$

Now, $|A| = \begin{vmatrix} 1 & -1 & 2 \\ 3 & 4 & -5 \\ 2 & -1 & 3 \end{vmatrix}$

$= 1(12-5) + 1(9+10) + 2(-3-8)$
$= 7 + 19 - 22 = 4 \neq 0$

$\therefore \quad A^{-1}$ exists and hence the given equations have a unique solution.

$$\therefore \quad A^{-1} = \frac{1}{|A|} \text{ (Adj A)}$$

$$= \frac{1}{4} \begin{bmatrix} 7 & -19 & -11 \\ 1 & 1 & -1 \\ -3 & 11 & 7 \end{bmatrix}$$

$$= \frac{1}{4} \begin{bmatrix} 7 & 1 & -3 \\ -19 & -1 & 11 \\ -11 & -1 & 7 \end{bmatrix}$$

Solution of given system is given by $X = A^{-1}B$

$$\Rightarrow \begin{bmatrix} x \\ y \\ z \end{bmatrix} = \frac{1}{4} \begin{bmatrix} 7 & 1 & -3 \\ -19 & -1 & 11 \\ -11 & -1 & 7 \end{bmatrix} \begin{bmatrix} 7 \\ -5 \\ 12 \end{bmatrix}$$

$$= \frac{1}{4} \begin{bmatrix} 49-5-36 \\ -133+5+132 \\ -77+5+84 \end{bmatrix} = \frac{1}{4} \begin{bmatrix} 8 \\ 4 \\ 12 \end{bmatrix} = \begin{bmatrix} 2 \\ 1 \\ 3 \end{bmatrix}$$

Hence, $x = 2, y = 1$ and $z = 3$.

15. We have $AX = B$

Where, $A = \begin{bmatrix} 2 & -3 & 5 \\ 3 & 2 & -4 \\ 1 & 1 & -2 \end{bmatrix}, X = \begin{bmatrix} x \\ y \\ z \end{bmatrix}$ and $B = \begin{bmatrix} 11 \\ -5 \\ -3 \end{bmatrix}$

$X = A^{-1}B$ ...(i)

Now, $|A| = \begin{vmatrix} 2 & -3 & 5 \\ 3 & 2 & -4 \\ 1 & 1 & -2 \end{vmatrix} = -1 \neq 0$

$\therefore \quad A^{-1}$ non-cofactory case and hence the given equations have a unique solution.

$$A^{-1} = \frac{1}{|A|} \text{ (adj A)} = \frac{1}{-1} \begin{bmatrix} 0 & 2 & 1 \\ -1 & -9 & -5 \\ 2 & 23 & 13 \end{bmatrix}$$

$$= \frac{1}{-1}\begin{bmatrix} 0 & -1 & 2 \\ 2 & -9 & 23 \\ 1 & -5 & 13 \end{bmatrix} = \begin{bmatrix} 0 & 1 & -2 \\ -2 & 9 & -23 \\ -1 & 5 & -13 \end{bmatrix}$$

From (i)

$$\Rightarrow \begin{bmatrix} x \\ y \\ z \end{bmatrix} = \begin{bmatrix} 0 & 1 & -2 \\ -2 & 9 & -23 \\ -1 & 5 & -13 \end{bmatrix} \begin{bmatrix} 11 \\ -5 \\ -3 \end{bmatrix} = \begin{bmatrix} 1 \\ 2 \\ 3 \end{bmatrix}$$

$\Rightarrow x = 1, y = 2$ and $z = 3$.

16. Let cost of 1 kg onion = ₹ x
and cost of 1 kg wheat = ₹ y
and cost of 1 kg rice = ₹ z

$\therefore \quad 4x + 3y + 2z = 60$
$2x + 4y + 6z = 90$
$6x + 2y + 3z = 70$

$$\Rightarrow \begin{bmatrix} 4 & 3 & 2 \\ 2 & 4 & 6 \\ 6 & 2 & 3 \end{bmatrix} \begin{bmatrix} x \\ y \\ z \end{bmatrix} = \begin{bmatrix} 60 \\ 90 \\ 70 \end{bmatrix}$$

$\Rightarrow \quad AX = B$

Now $\quad |A| = \begin{vmatrix} 4 & 3 & 2 \\ 2 & 4 & 6 \\ 6 & 2 & 3 \end{vmatrix}$

$\qquad = 4(12-12) - 3(6-36) + 2(4-24)$
$\qquad = 90 - 40 = 50 \neq 0$

$\therefore \quad A^{-1}$ exists.

$$\text{Adj } A = \begin{bmatrix} 0 & -5 & 10 \\ 30 & 0 & -20 \\ -20 & 10 & 10 \end{bmatrix}$$

$$A^{-1} = \frac{1}{|A|}\text{Adj } A = \frac{1}{80}\begin{bmatrix} 0 & -5 & 10 \\ 30 & 0 & -20 \\ -20 & 10 & 10 \end{bmatrix}$$

As, $AX = B \Rightarrow X = A^{-1}B$

$$\begin{bmatrix} x \\ y \\ z \end{bmatrix} = \frac{1}{50}\begin{bmatrix} 0 & -5 & 10 \\ 30 & 0 & -20 \\ -20 & 10 & 10 \end{bmatrix}\begin{bmatrix} 60 \\ 90 \\ 70 \end{bmatrix}$$

$$= \frac{1}{5}\begin{bmatrix} 0 & -5 & 10 \\ 30 & 0 & -20 \\ -20 & 10 & 10 \end{bmatrix}\begin{bmatrix} 6 \\ 9 \\ 7 \end{bmatrix} = \begin{bmatrix} 5 \\ 8 \\ 8 \end{bmatrix}$$

$\therefore \quad x = 5, y = 8, z = 8$

Hence, cost of 1 kg of onion = ₹ 5
and cost of 1 kg of wheat = ₹ 8
and cost of 1 kg of rice = ₹ 8

Past year Exercise 

1. For a matrix A of order n × n,
$|kA| = k^n. |A|$. So, here
$|2A| = 2^3 |A| = 2^3 \times 4 = 8 \times 4 = 32$

2. $\Delta = \begin{vmatrix} 2 & -3 & 5 \\ 6 & 0 & 4 \\ 1 & 5 & -7 \end{vmatrix}$

$A_{32} = $ Cofactor of element a_{32}

$= -\begin{vmatrix} 2 & 5 \\ 6 & 4 \end{vmatrix} = -(8-30) = 22$

$\therefore a_{32}.A_{32} = 5(22) = 110 \qquad [\because a_{32} = 5]$

3. Let $\begin{vmatrix} 2x & x+3 \\ 2(x+1) & x+1 \end{vmatrix} = \begin{vmatrix} 1 & 5 \\ 3 & 3 \end{vmatrix}$

$\Rightarrow \quad 2x(x+1) - (2x+2)(x+3) = 3 - 15$
$\Rightarrow \quad 2x^2 + 2x - 2x^2 - 6x - 2x - 6 = -12$
$\Rightarrow \quad -6x = -6 \Rightarrow x = 1$

4. If A is an invertible square matrix of order 3, then
$|\text{adj } A| = |A|^2 = (5)^2 = 25$

5. Let $\begin{vmatrix} 2x & 5 \\ 8 & x \end{vmatrix} = \begin{vmatrix} 6 & -2 \\ 7 & 3 \end{vmatrix}$

$\Rightarrow \quad 2x(x) - 5(8) = 18 + 14 \Rightarrow 2x^2 - 40 = 32$
$\Rightarrow \quad 2x^2 = 72 \Rightarrow x^2 = 36 \Rightarrow x = \pm 6$

6. $A = \begin{bmatrix} 2 & 3 \\ 5 & -2 \end{bmatrix}$

$\therefore |A| = \begin{vmatrix} 2 & 3 \\ 5 & -2 \end{vmatrix} = -4 - 15 = -19 \neq 0$

So, A is a non-singular matrix. Therefore, it is invertible.
Now,

$\therefore \text{adj} A = \begin{bmatrix} -2 & -5 \\ -3 & 2 \end{bmatrix}^T = \begin{bmatrix} -2 & -3 \\ -5 & 2 \end{bmatrix}$

We know

$A^{-1} = \frac{1}{|A|}\text{adj } A$

$\therefore A^{-1} = \frac{1}{(-19)}\begin{bmatrix} -2 & -3 \\ -5 & 2 \end{bmatrix} = \begin{bmatrix} \frac{2}{19} & \frac{3}{19} \\ \frac{5}{19} & \frac{-2}{19} \end{bmatrix}$

7. $\begin{vmatrix} 1 & 1 & 1 \\ 1 & 1+\sin\theta & 1 \\ 1 & 1 & 1+\cos\theta \end{vmatrix} \Rightarrow \begin{vmatrix} 1 & 1 & 1 \\ 0 & \sin\theta & 0 \\ 0 & 0 & \cos\theta \end{vmatrix}$

[Applying $R_2 \to R_2 - R_1$ and $R_3 \to R_3 - R_1$]

$$= \sin\theta\cos\theta = \frac{\sin 2\theta}{2}$$

We know that, $-1 \le \sin 2\theta \le 1$

Therefore, required maximum value $= \dfrac{1}{2} \times 1 = \dfrac{1}{2}$

8. Let the monthly incomes of Aryan and Babban be $3x$ and $4x$, respectively. Suppose their monthly expenditures are $5y$ and $7y$, respectively. Since each saves ₹ 15,000 per month,

Monthly savings of Aryan : $3x - 5y = 15000$
Monthly savings of Babban : $4x - 7y = 15000$
The above system of equations can be written in the matrix form as follows:

$$\begin{bmatrix} 3 & -5 \\ 4 & -7 \end{bmatrix}\begin{bmatrix} x \\ y \end{bmatrix} = \begin{bmatrix} 15000 \\ 15000 \end{bmatrix}$$

or $AX = B$, where

$$A = \begin{bmatrix} 3 & -5 \\ 4 & -7 \end{bmatrix},\ X = \begin{bmatrix} x \\ y \end{bmatrix}\ \text{and}\ B = \begin{bmatrix} 15000 \\ 15000 \end{bmatrix}$$

So, $A^{-1} = \dfrac{1}{|A|}\,\text{Adj}\ A = -1\begin{bmatrix} -7 & 5 \\ -4 & 3 \end{bmatrix} = \begin{bmatrix} 7 & -5 \\ 4 & -3 \end{bmatrix}$

$\therefore\ X = A^{-1}B$

$$\Rightarrow \begin{bmatrix} x \\ y \end{bmatrix} = \begin{bmatrix} 7 & -5 \\ 4 & -3 \end{bmatrix}\begin{bmatrix} 15000 \\ 15000 \end{bmatrix} \Rightarrow \begin{bmatrix} x \\ y \end{bmatrix} = \begin{bmatrix} 105000 - 75000 \\ 60000 - 45000 \end{bmatrix}$$

$$\Rightarrow \begin{bmatrix} x \\ y \end{bmatrix} = \begin{bmatrix} 30000 \\ 15000 \end{bmatrix} \Rightarrow x = 30,000\ \text{and}\ y = 15,000$$

Therefore,
Monthly income of Aryan $= 3 \times ₹\,30,000 = ₹\,90,000$
Monthly income of Babban $= 4 \times ₹\,30,000 = ₹\,1,20,000$
Here, we are encouraged to understand the importance of savings. We should save certain part of our monthly income for the future.

9. $A = \begin{bmatrix} 2 & -3 \\ -4 & 7 \end{bmatrix}$

$C_{11} = (-1)^{1+1}\,(7) = 7,$
$C_{12} = (-1)^{1+2}\,(-4) = 4,$
$C_{21} = (-1)^{2+1}\,(-3) = 3,$
$C_{22} = (-1)^{2+2}\,2 = 2$

$\text{Adj}\ A = \begin{bmatrix} 7 & 4 \\ 3 & 2 \end{bmatrix}' = \begin{bmatrix} 7 & 3 \\ 4 & 2 \end{bmatrix}$

$|A| = 2 \times 7 - (-3) \times (-4) = 14 - 12 = 2 \ne 0$

$\therefore\ A^{-1} = \dfrac{1}{|A|}\,\text{adj}\ A = \dfrac{1}{2}\begin{bmatrix} 7 & 3 \\ 4 & 2 \end{bmatrix} = \begin{bmatrix} 7/2 & 3/2 \\ 2 & 1 \end{bmatrix}$

$\text{L.H.S.} = 2A^{-1} = 2\begin{bmatrix} 7/2 & 3/2 \\ 2 & 1 \end{bmatrix} = \begin{bmatrix} 7 & 3 \\ 4 & 2 \end{bmatrix}$

$\text{R.H.S.} = 9I - A = 9\begin{bmatrix} 1 & 0 \\ 0 & 1 \end{bmatrix} - \begin{bmatrix} 2 & -3 \\ -4 & 7 \end{bmatrix}$

$$= \begin{bmatrix} 9 & 0 \\ 0 & 9 \end{bmatrix} - \begin{bmatrix} 2 & -3 \\ -4 & 7 \end{bmatrix}$$

$$= \begin{bmatrix} 9-2 & 3 \\ 4 & 9-7 \end{bmatrix} = \begin{bmatrix} 7 & 3 \\ 4 & 2 \end{bmatrix}$$

$\therefore\quad \text{L.H.S.} = \text{R.H.S.}$
Hence verified that $2A^{-1} = 9I - A$.

NCERT Exemplar

1. (c)   **2.** (a)   **3.** (a)   **4.** (c)

5. $\text{LHS} = \begin{vmatrix} y^2 z^2 & yz & y+z \\ z^2 x^2 & zx & z+x \\ x^2 y^2 & xy & x+y \end{vmatrix}$

$$= \frac{1}{xyz}\begin{vmatrix} xy^2 z^2 & x\,yz & xy+xz \\ x^2 yz^2 & x\,yz & yz+xy \\ x^2 y^2 z & x\,yz & xz+yz \end{vmatrix}$$

$$[\because\ R_1 \to x\,R_1,\ R_2 \to y\,R_2,\ R_3 \to z\,R_3]$$

$$= \frac{1}{xyz}(x\,yz)^2\begin{vmatrix} yz & 1 & xy+xz \\ xz & 1 & yz+xy \\ xy & 1 & xz+yz \end{vmatrix}$$

$$[\text{taking } (xyz)\text{ common from } C_1 \text{ and } C_2]$$

$$= xyz\begin{vmatrix} yz & 1 & xy+yz+zx \\ xz & 1 & xy+yz+zx \\ xy & 1 & xy+yz+zx \end{vmatrix}\ [C_3 \to C_3 + C_1]$$

$$= xyz\,(xy+yz+zx)\begin{vmatrix} yz & 1 & 1 \\ xz & 1 & 1 \\ xy & 1 & 1 \end{vmatrix}$$

$[\text{taking } (xy+yz+zx)\text{ common from } C_3] = 0$
$[\text{since, } C_2 \text{ and } C_3 \text{ are identicals}]$
$= \text{RHS}$ Hence proved.

6. Given, $\begin{vmatrix} 4-x & 4+x & 4+x \\ 4+x & 4-x & 4+x \\ 4+x & 4+x & 4-x \end{vmatrix} = 0$

$$\Rightarrow \begin{vmatrix} 12+x & 12+x & 12+x \\ 4+x & 4-x & 4+x \\ 4+x & 4+x & 4-x \end{vmatrix} = 0\ \ [\because\ R_1 \to R_1 + R_2 + R_3]$$

$$\Rightarrow (12+x)\begin{vmatrix} 1 & 1 & 1 \\ 4+x & 4-x & 4+x \\ 4+x & 4+x & 4-x \end{vmatrix} = 0$$

$\Rightarrow (12+x)\begin{vmatrix} 0 & 0 & 1 \\ 0 & 8 & 4+x \\ 2x & 8 & 4-x \end{vmatrix}=0$

$$[\because C_1 \to C_1 - C_3 \text{ and } C_2 \to C_2 + C_3]$$

$\Rightarrow \quad (12+x)[1\cdot(-16x)]=0$

$\therefore \quad x=-12, 0$

7. We have,

$$\begin{vmatrix} 0 & xy^2 & xz^2 \\ x^2y & 0 & yz^2 \\ x^2z & zy^2 & 0 \end{vmatrix} = x^2 y^2 z^2 \begin{vmatrix} 0 & x & x \\ y & 0 & y \\ z & z & 0 \end{vmatrix}$$

[taking x^2, y^2 and z^2 common from C_1, C_2 and C_3, respectively]

$$= x^2 y^2 z^2 \begin{vmatrix} 0 & 0 & x \\ y & -y & y \\ z & z & 0 \end{vmatrix} \quad [\because C_2 \to C_2 - C_3]$$

$$= x^2 y^2 z^2 [x(yz+yz)]$$
$$= x^2 y^2 z^2 \times 2xyz = 2x^3 y^3 z^3$$

8. We have

$$\begin{vmatrix} a-b-c & 2a & 2a \\ 2b & b-c-a & 2b \\ 2c & 2c & c-a-b \end{vmatrix} \text{ and } (a+b+c)=0$$

Applying $R_1 \to R_1 + R_2 + R_3$

$$= \begin{vmatrix} a+b+c & a+b+c & a+b+c \\ 2b & b-c-a & 2b \\ 2c & 2c & c-a-b \end{vmatrix}$$

Take $(a+b+c)$ common from R_1

$$= (a+b+c)\begin{vmatrix} 1 & 1 & 1 \\ 2b & b-c-a & 2b \\ 2c & 2c & c-a-b \end{vmatrix}$$

$$= 0 \qquad (\because a+b+c=0)$$

9. Let $\Delta = \begin{vmatrix} a^2+2a & 2a+1 & 1 \\ 2a+1 & a+2 & 1 \\ 3 & 3 & 1 \end{vmatrix}$

$$= \begin{vmatrix} a^2+2a-3 & 2a-2 & 0 \\ 2a-2 & a-1 & 0 \\ 3 & 3 & 1 \end{vmatrix}$$

[Applying $R_1 \to R_1 - R_3$ and $R_2 \to R_2 - R_3$]

$$= \begin{vmatrix} a^2+2a-3 & 2a-2 \\ 2a-2 & a-1 \end{vmatrix} \quad \text{[Expanding along } C_3\text{]}$$

$$= \begin{vmatrix} (a+3)(a-1) & 2(a-1) \\ 2(a-1) & a-1 \end{vmatrix} = (a-1)^2 \begin{vmatrix} a+3 & 2 \\ 2 & 1 \end{vmatrix}$$

$$= (a-1)^2 \cdot (a+3-4) = (a-1)^3$$

10. Let $\Delta = \begin{vmatrix} 1 & 1 & 1 \\ 1+\sin A & 1+\sin B & 1+\sin C \\ \sin A+\sin^2 A & \sin B+\sin^2 B & \sin C+\sin^2 C \end{vmatrix}$

$$= \begin{vmatrix} 1 & 1 & 1 \\ 1+\sin A & 1+\sin B & 1+\sin C \\ -\cos^2 A & -\cos^2 B & -\cos^2 C \end{vmatrix} R_3 \to R_3 - R_2$$

$$= \begin{vmatrix} 1 & 0 & 0 \\ 1+\sin A & \sin B-\sin A & \sin C-\sin B \\ -\cos^2 A & \cos^2 A-\cos^2 B & \cos^2 B-\cos^2 C \end{vmatrix},$$

$$(C_3 \to C_3 - C_2 \text{ and } C_2 \to C_2 - C_1)$$

Expanding along R_1, we get

$\Delta = (\sin B - \sin A)(\sin^2 C - \sin^2 B) - (\sin C - \sin B)(\sin^2 B - \sin^2 A)$

$= (\sin B - \sin A)(\sin C - \sin B)(\sin C - \sin A) = 0$

$\Rightarrow$ either $\sin B - \sin A = 0$ or $\sin C - \sin B$ or $\sin C - \sin A = 0$

$\Rightarrow A = B$ or $B = C$ or $C = A$

i.e. triangle ABC is isoceles.

11. We have $\Delta_1 = \begin{vmatrix} 1 & 1 & 1 \\ yz & zx & xy \\ x & y & z \end{vmatrix}$

Interchanging rows and columns, we get

$$\Delta_1 = \begin{vmatrix} 1 & yz & x \\ 1 & zx & y \\ 1 & xy & z \end{vmatrix} = \frac{1}{xyz}\begin{vmatrix} x & xyz & x^2 \\ y & xyz & y^2 \\ z & xyz & z^2 \end{vmatrix}$$

$$= \frac{xyz}{xyz}\begin{vmatrix} x & 1 & x^2 \\ y & 1 & y^2 \\ z & 1 & z^2 \end{vmatrix} \text{ interchanging } C_1 \text{ and } C_2$$

$$= (-1)\begin{vmatrix} 1 & x & x^2 \\ 1 & y & y^2 \\ 1 & z & z^2 \end{vmatrix} = -\Delta$$

$$\Rightarrow \Delta_1 + \Delta = 0$$

Objective Practice Exercise

1. (d)

2. (d) It is a fundamental concept.

3. (b) $A = \begin{bmatrix} \log x & -1 \\ -\log x & 2 \end{bmatrix}$, det $(A) = 2\log x - \log x$

$$\Rightarrow 2 = \log x^2 - \log x \Rightarrow 2 = \log\left(\frac{x^2}{x}\right) \Rightarrow 2 = \log x$$

$$\Rightarrow x = e^2.$$

4. (b) **5.** (b)

6. (b) $\begin{vmatrix} \log_3 512 & \log_4 3 \\ \log_3 8 & \log_4 9 \end{vmatrix} \times \begin{vmatrix} \log_2 3 & \log_8 3 \\ \log_3 4 & \log_3 4 \end{vmatrix}$

$$= \left(\frac{\log 512}{\log 3} \times \frac{\log 9}{\log 4} - \frac{\log 3}{\log 4} \times \frac{\log 8}{\log 3} \right)$$

$$\times \left(\frac{\log 3}{\log 2} \times \frac{\log 4}{\log 3} - \frac{\log 3}{\log 8} \times \frac{\log 4}{\log 3} \right)$$

$$= \left(\frac{\log 2^9}{\log 3} \times \frac{\log 3^2}{\log 2^2} - \frac{\log 2^3}{\log 2^2} \right) \times \left(\frac{\log 2^2}{\log 2} - \frac{\log 2^2}{\log 2^3} \right)$$

$$= \left(\frac{9 \times 2}{2} - \frac{3}{2} \right) \left(2 - \frac{2}{3} \right) = \frac{15}{2} \times \frac{4}{3} = 10.$$

7. (b)

8. (c) We know that the row to row multiplication of a determinant is always equal to the value of the determinant *i.e.,* |A|.

9. (d)

10. (c)

11. (d) $a^3 + b^3 = 0 \Rightarrow b^3 = -a^3$

$$\frac{b^3}{a^3} = -1 \Rightarrow \frac{b}{a} = (-1)^{1/3} \quad (\because \ a \neq 0)$$

12. (b)

13. (d) Given, $D = \begin{vmatrix} 1 & 1 & 1 \\ 1 & 1+x & 1 \\ 1 & 1 & 1+y \end{vmatrix} = xy$

Hence, D is divisible by both x and y.

14. (b)

15. (d) $\Delta_1 = \begin{vmatrix} x & \sin\theta & \cos\theta \\ -\sin\theta & -x & 1 \\ \cos\theta & 1 & x \end{vmatrix}$

$$= (x - x^2 - 1) - \sin\theta\,(-x\sin\theta - \cos\theta)$$
$$\qquad\qquad\qquad + \cos\theta\,(-\sin\theta + x\cos\theta)$$
$$= -x^3 - x + x\sin^2\theta + \sin\theta\cos\theta - \cos\theta\sin\theta + x\cos^2\theta$$
$$= -x^3 - x + x = -x^3$$

Similarly, $\Delta_2 = -x^3$. Then, $\Delta_1 + \Delta_2 = -2x^3$

16. (c) 17. (a)

18. (c) $|A| = 2 \times 2 \times 2 = 8, |B| = 1 \times 1 \times 2 = 2$
$\therefore |AB| = |A||B| = 2 \times 8 = 16$

19. (a) Let A be a skew-symmetric matrix of odd order, say $(2n + 1)$. Since A is skew-symmetric, therefore $A^T = -A$.
$$\Rightarrow |A^T| = |-A| \Rightarrow |A^T| = (-1)^{2n+1}|A|$$
$$\Rightarrow |A^T| = -|A| \Rightarrow |A| = -|A|$$
$$\Rightarrow 2|A| = 0 \Rightarrow |A| = 0.$$

20. (a) Obviously, the determinant is satisfied for $x = a, b$.

21. (d)

22. (b) Given $\begin{vmatrix} 11 & 12 & 13 \\ 12 & 13 & 14 \\ 13 & 14 & 15 \end{vmatrix} = 0$

23. (d) $\begin{vmatrix} x+y & y+z & z+x \\ x & y & z \\ x-y & y-z & z-x \end{vmatrix} = 0.$

24. (b) A is square matrix of order 4
$\therefore |kA| = k^n |A|$, where n is order of matrix A.
$$\Rightarrow |2A| = 2^4 |A| \Rightarrow |2A| = 16|A|$$

25. (b) $A' = \begin{bmatrix} 1 & -\tan x \\ \tan x & 1 \end{bmatrix}$

$$A^{-1} = \frac{1}{1 + \tan^2 x} \begin{bmatrix} 1 & -\tan x \\ \tan x & 1 \end{bmatrix}$$

$$A'A^{-1} = \begin{bmatrix} \cos 2x & -\sin 2x \\ \sin 2x & \cos 2x \end{bmatrix} \Rightarrow |A'A^{-1}| = 1$$

26. (a) Let $P = [a_{ij}]_{3 \times 3}$

$$adj\,P = \begin{bmatrix} 1 & 4 & 4 \\ 2 & 1 & 7 \\ 1 & 1 & 3 \end{bmatrix}$$

$|adj\,P| = 1(3-7) - 4(6-7) + 4(2-1) = 4$
$\because |adj\,(P)| = |P|^{n-1}$
$\Rightarrow |P|^{3-1} = |adj\,P| = 4 \Rightarrow |P|^2 = 4 \Rightarrow |P| = \pm 2.$

27. (d) $K = |A|; |A| = \begin{vmatrix} 3 & 2 & 4 \\ 1 & 2 & -1 \\ 0 & 1 & 1 \end{vmatrix} = 11.$

28. (c) 29. (b) 30. (a) 31. (c)

32. (b) $\begin{vmatrix} \lambda & -1 & 4 \\ -3 & 0 & 1 \\ -1 & 1 & 2 \end{vmatrix} \neq 0 \Rightarrow \lambda \neq -17.$

33. (d) From option, check $AA^{-1} = I$.

34. (d) Given $A^2 - A + I = 0$
$$A^{-1}A^2 - A^{-1}A + A^{-1}.I = A^{-1}.0$$
(Multiplying A^{-1} on both sides)
$$\Rightarrow A - I + A^{-1} = 0 \text{ or } A^{-1} = I - A.$$

35. (d) Let $A = \begin{bmatrix} \cos 2\theta & -\sin 2\theta \\ \sin 2\theta & \cos 2\theta \end{bmatrix}, |A| = 1$

$$adj\,(A) = \begin{bmatrix} \cos 2\theta & \sin 2\theta \\ -\sin 2\theta & \cos 2\theta \end{bmatrix}$$

$$A^{-1} = \frac{adj(A)}{|A|} = \begin{bmatrix} \cos 2\theta & \sin 2\theta \\ -\sin 2\theta & \cos 2\theta \end{bmatrix}.$$

36. (c) $A(Adj\,A) = |A|\,I = 8I = \begin{bmatrix} 8 & 0 & 0 \\ 0 & 8 & 0 \\ 0 & 0 & 8 \end{bmatrix}.$

37. **(b)** Given, $AB = 3I$

$\Rightarrow A^{-1}(AB) = A^{-1}(3I)$ [Premultiplication by A^{-1}]

$\Rightarrow A^{-1}AB = 3A^{-1}\,I \Rightarrow IB = 3A^{-1}$ $[\because A^{-1}A = 1]$

$\Rightarrow B = 3A^{-1} \Rightarrow A^{-1} = \dfrac{1}{3}B.$

38. **(c)** Given adj $B = A$, $|P| = |Q| = 1$

Consider , adj $(Q^{-1}BP^{-1}) = (\text{adj } P^{-1})(\text{adj } B)(\text{adj } Q^{-1})$

$= (\text{adj } P)^{-1} A.(\text{adj } Q)^{-1}$

$= (P^{-1})^{-1} A(Q^{-1})^{-1}$ $\left(\because P^{-1} = \dfrac{1}{|P|}.\text{adj } P\right) = PAQ.$

39. **(a)** $A^{-1} = A^2$, because $A^3 = I.$

40. **(b)** The matrix is not invertible if $\begin{vmatrix} 1 & a & 2 \\ 1 & 2 & 5 \\ 2 & 1 & 1 \end{vmatrix} = 0$

$\Rightarrow 1(2-5) - a(1-10) + 2(1-4) = 0$

$\Rightarrow -3 + 9a - 6 = 0 \Rightarrow a = 1$

41. **(d)** We know that det $(\text{adj } P) = (\det P)^{n-1}$ if $|P| \neq 0$

Here, $n = 3$

$\therefore$ det $(\text{adj } P) = (\det P)^{3-1} = (\det P)^2$

42. **(c)**

43. **(c)** If $A' = A$, then order of A' will be same to order of A. So it is a square matrix.

44. **(d)** Let $A = \begin{bmatrix} 0 & 3 \\ 2 & 0 \end{bmatrix}$, $|A| = 0 - 6 = -6$

adj $A = \begin{bmatrix} 0 & -3 \\ -2 & 0 \end{bmatrix} = -\begin{bmatrix} 0 & 3 \\ 2 & 0 \end{bmatrix} = -A$

We know that $A^{-1} = \dfrac{\text{adj} A}{|A|} = \lambda(A)$ (given)

$\therefore \lambda(A) = \dfrac{-A}{|A|} \Rightarrow \lambda = \dfrac{1}{-|A|} = \dfrac{1}{6}$

45. **(d)** All the given statements are true.

46. **(a)** $(B^{-1} A^{-1})^{-1} = (A^{-1})^{-1}(B^{-1})^{-1} = AB$

[Reversal law of inverses]

$= \begin{bmatrix} 2 & 2 \\ -3 & 2 \end{bmatrix}\begin{bmatrix} 0 & -1 \\ 1 & 0 \end{bmatrix} = \begin{bmatrix} 2 & -2 \\ 2 & 3 \end{bmatrix}.$

47. **(d)** $|A| = -20$

$\therefore a_{23} = \dfrac{\text{Co-factor of } 6}{-20} = \dfrac{-8}{-20} = \dfrac{2}{5}.$

48. **(b)** We have a theorem that if a square matrix A satisfies the equation

$a_0 + a_1 x + a_2 x^2 + \dots\dots + a_n x^n = 0,$

where $a_0 \neq 0$ then A is invertible.

Since A, B and C are $n \times n$ matrices and A satisfies the equation $x^3 + 2x^2 + 3x + 5 = 0$ as $A^3 + 2A^2 + 3A + 5I = 0$, therefore, A is invertible.

49. **(b)** $(\text{Length} - 50)(\text{Breadth} + 50)$

$= \text{Area} (x - 50)(y + 50) = xy$

$x - y = 50$ ...(i)

$(\text{Length} - 10)(\text{Breadth} - 20) = \text{Area} - 5300$

$(x - 10)(y - 20) = xy - 5300$

$2x + y = 550$ ...(ii)

50. **(a)** $\begin{bmatrix} 1 & -1 \\ 2 & 1 \end{bmatrix}\begin{bmatrix} x \\ y \end{bmatrix} = \begin{bmatrix} 50 \\ 550 \end{bmatrix}$

51. **(c)** From (i) + (ii), $x = 200$ m

52. **(a)** Put the value of x in eqn. (i), $y = 150$ m

53. **(b)** Area of rectangular field

$= xy = 200 \times 150 = 30000$ sq. m

Chapter Test

1. **(d)**   **2.** **(b)**   **3.** **(c)**   **4.** **(c)**

5. $125\,\Delta$ **6.** 40   **7.** **(d)**   **8.** **(d)**

9. **(i)** **(a)**

    (ii) **(c)**

    (iii) **(b)** $A_{11} = -12, A_{12} = -5, A_{13} = 2$

$A_{21} = -3, A_{22} = 5, A_{23} = -2,$

$A_{31} = 3, A_{32} = 0, A_{33} = -3$

$\text{adj } A = \begin{bmatrix} -12 & -3 & 3 \\ -5 & 5 & 0 \\ 2 & -2 & -3 \end{bmatrix}$

    (iv) **(c)** $A^{-1} = \dfrac{1}{|A|} \text{ adj } (A)$

$= \dfrac{1}{-15}\begin{bmatrix} -12 & -3 & 3 \\ -5 & 5 & 0 \\ 2 & -2 & -3 \end{bmatrix} = \dfrac{1}{15}\begin{bmatrix} 12 & 3 & -3 \\ 5 & -5 & 0 \\ -2 & 2 & 3 \end{bmatrix}$

    (v) **(a)** $\because AX = B \Rightarrow X = A^{-1}B$

$\Rightarrow \begin{bmatrix} x \\ y \\ z \end{bmatrix} = \dfrac{1}{15}\begin{bmatrix} 12 & 3 & -3 \\ 5 & -5 & 0 \\ -2 & 2 & 3 \end{bmatrix}\begin{bmatrix} 4500 \\ 0 \\ 11000 \end{bmatrix}$

$\Rightarrow \begin{bmatrix} x \\ y \\ z \end{bmatrix} = \begin{bmatrix} 1400 \\ 1500 \\ 1600 \end{bmatrix}$

$\therefore x = ₹1400, y = ₹1500, z = ₹1600$

10. $\Delta = 0$ **11.** $x = \pm 3$

13. -2

5 Continuity and Differentiability

CONTINUITY AND DIFFERENTIABILITY

① Continuity

Continuity of a Function at a Point
Suppose f is a real function on a subset of the real numbers & let c be a point in the domain of f.
Then f is continuous at c if
$$L.H.L = R.H.L = f(C)$$
i.e. $\lim\limits_{x \to C^-} f(x) = \lim\limits_{x \to C^+} f(x) = f(c)$

② Algebra of Continuous Functions

Theorem 1: Suppose f & g be two real functions continuous at a real number c, Then
(1) $f \pm g$ is continuous at $x = c$
(2) $f \cdot g$ is continuous at $x = c$
(3) f/g is continuous at $x = c$, (provided $g(c) \neq 0$)
Theorem 2: Suppose f & g are real valued functions such that (fog) is defined at c. If g is continuous at c & if f is continuous at g(c), then (fog) is continuous at c.

③ Differentiability

A function f is said to be differentiable at a point c in its domain, if its left hand & right hand derivatives exist at c & are equal.
Here at $x = c$,

Left Hand Derivative,
$$L.H.D. = \lim\limits_{h \to 0} \frac{f(c-h)-f(c)}{-h} = L f'(c)$$

Right Hand Derivative,
$$R.H.D. = \lim\limits_{h \to 0} \frac{f(c+h)-f(c)}{h} = R f'(c)$$

Theorem: If a function f is differentiable at a point c, then it is also continuous at that point. Therefore, every differentiable function is continuous, but the converse is not true.

④ Chain Rule

If y is a function of u, u is a function of v & v is a function of x.
$$\text{Then, } \frac{dy}{dx} = \frac{dy}{du} \times \frac{du}{dv} \times \frac{dv}{dx}$$

⑤ Implicit Functions

An equation in the form f(x, y) = 0 in which y is not expressible in terms of x is called an implicit function of x & y.
Derivative of Implicit Functions
Let y = f(x, y), where f(x, y) be an implicit function of x.
- Firstly differentiate both sides of equation w.r.t x
- Then take all terms involving $\frac{dy}{dx}$ on L.H.S. & remaining terms on R.H.S. to get the required value.

⑥ Logarithmic Differentiation

Logarithmic Differentiation is a very useful technique to differentiate functions of the form
$$f(x) = [u(x)]^{v(x)},$$
where f(x) & u(x) are positive.

⑦ Derivatives of Functions in Parametric Form

The set of equations x = f(t), y = g(t) is called the parametric form of an equation.
$$\text{Here, } \frac{dy}{dx} = \frac{dy/dt}{dx/dt} \text{ or } \frac{g'(t)}{f'(t)}$$

⑧ Second Order Derivative

Let y = f(x), then $\frac{dy}{dx} = f'(x)$
If f'(x) is differentiable, then we may differentiate it again w.r.t. x & get the second order derivative represented by:
$$\frac{d^2y}{dx^2} \text{ or } f''(x) \text{ or } D^2y \text{ or } y'' \text{ or } y_2$$

Topic 1 — Continuity

CONTINUITY AT A POINT

A function is said to be continuous at a point $x = a$ in its domain, iff $\lim\limits_{x \to a} f(x) = f(a)$

Thus, $f(x)$ is continuous at $(x = a)$ $\Rightarrow$ $\lim\limits_{x \to a} f(x) = f(a)$ $\Rightarrow$ $\boxed{\lim\limits_{x \to a^-} f(x) = \lim\limits_{x \to a^+} f(x) = f(a)}$

$$\downarrow \qquad\qquad \downarrow$$

called as Left   called as Right

Hand limit   Hand limit

If $f(x)$ is not continuous at a point $x = a$, then it is said to be discontinuous at $x = a$.

Continuous Function: A function $f(x)$ is said to be continuous if it is continuous at each point of its domain.

Every Where Continuous Function: A function $f(x)$ is said to be everywhere continuous if it is continuous for all real numbers.

ALGEBRA OF CONTINUOUS FUNCTIONS

Suppose f and g be two real functions continuous at a real number c, then

(i) $f + g$ is continuous at $x = c$

(ii) $f - g$ is continuous at $x = c$

(iii) $f \cdot g$ is continuous at $x = c$

(iv) $\dfrac{f}{g}$ is continuous at $x = c$, (provided that $g\,(c) \neq 0$)

(v)   If $g\,(x)$ is a continuous function, then $\dfrac{1}{g(x)}$ is also continuous, at $x = c$ (provided that $g(c) \neq 0$)

(vi)   Suppose f and g are real valued functions such that fog is defined at c. If f and g is continuous at c then fog is also continuous at c.

Important Points to Remember

(i)   The composition of two continuous functions is a continuous function.

(ii)   A constant function is everywhere continuous.

(iii)   The identity function is everywhere continuous.

(iv)   A polynomial function is everywhere continuous.

(v)   Every rational function is continuous at every point in its domain.

(vi)   The modulus function is everywhere continuous.

(vii)   The exponential function is everywhere continuous.

(viii)   The logarithmic function is continuous in its domain.

(ix)   The sine function is everywhere continuous.

(x)   The cosine function is everywhere continuous.

(xi)   The tangent function is continuous in its domain.

(xii) $\sin^{-1} x$ and $\cos^{-1} x$ are continuous on $[-1, 1]$

Illustration :

Find the value of a and b if $f(x) = \begin{cases} \dfrac{a e^{1/(|x+2|)} - 1}{2 - e^{1/(|x+2|)}}; & -3 < x < -2 \\[3mm] b; & x = -2 \\[3mm] \sin\left(\dfrac{x^4 - 16}{x^5 + 32}\right); & -2 < x < 0 \end{cases}$ **is continuous at $x = -2$.**

Sol. At $x = -2$, $f(-2) = b$ ... (i)

$$\text{R.H.L.} = \lim_{x \to -2+} f(x) = \lim_{h \to 0} f(-2+h) = \lim_{h \to 0} \sin\left(\frac{(-2+h)^4 - 16}{(-2+h)^5 + 32}\right) = \sin\left\{\lim_{h \to 0} \frac{(h-2)^4 - 2^4}{2^5 + (-2+h)^5}\right\}$$

$$= \sin\left\{\lim_{h \to 0} \frac{(h-2)^4 - (-2)^4}{(h-2)^5 - (-2)^5}\right\} = \sin\left\{\lim_{h \to 0} \frac{\dfrac{(h-2)^4 - (-2)^4}{(h-2) - (-2)}}{\dfrac{(h-2)^5 - (-2)^5}{(h-2) - (-2)}}\right\} = \sin\left\{\frac{4(-2)^{4-1}}{5(-2)^{5-1}}\right\} = \sin\left\{\frac{4(-8)}{5(16)}\right\} = \sin\left(-\frac{2}{5}\right) \quad ...(ii)$$

$$\text{L.H.L.} = \lim_{x \to -2-} f(x) = \lim_{h \to 0} f(-2-h) = \lim_{h \to 0} \frac{ae^{1/(|-2-h+2|)} - 1}{2 - e^{1/(|-2-h+2|)}} = \lim_{h \to 0} \frac{ae^{1/h} - 1}{2 - e^{1/h}} = \lim_{h \to 0} \frac{a - e^{-1/h}}{2e^{-1/h} - 1} = \frac{a - 0}{0 - 1} = -a \quad ...(iii)$$

From equations (i), (ii), and (iii), we get $a = \sin\left(\dfrac{2}{5}\right)$ and $b = -\sin\left(\dfrac{2}{5}\right)$

Practice Exercise-1

Multiple Choice Questions

1. If $f(x) = \begin{cases} -x^2, & \text{when } x \leq 0 \\ 5x - 4, & \text{when } 0 < x \leq 1 \\ 4x^2 - 3x, & \text{when } 1 < x < 2 \\ 3x + 4, & \text{when } x \geq 2 \end{cases}$, then

   (a) $f(x)$ is continuous at $x = 0$
   (b) $f(x)$ is continuous at $x = 2$
   (c) $f(x)$ is discontinuous at $x = 1$
   (d) None of these

2. If $f(x) = \begin{cases} \dfrac{1 - \sqrt{2}\sin x}{\pi - 4x}, & \text{if } x \neq \dfrac{\pi}{4} \\ a, & \text{if } x = \dfrac{\pi}{4} \end{cases}$ is continuous at $\dfrac{\pi}{4}$,

   then a is equal to

   (a) 4   (b) 2   (c) 1   (d) $\dfrac{1}{4}$

3. Let $f(x) = \begin{cases} \dfrac{x^3 + x^2 - 16x + 20}{(x-2)^2}, & x \neq 2 \\ k, & x = 2 \end{cases}$

   If f(x) is continuous for all x, then k =
   (a) 3   (b) 5   (c) 7   (d) 9

4. In the interval [7, 9] the function f(x) = [x] is discontinuous at _______, where [x] denotes the greatest integer function
   (a) 2   (b) 4   (c) 6   (d) 8

5. The point of discontinuity of $f(x) = \tan\left(\dfrac{\pi x}{x+1}\right)$ other than

   x = −1 are :

   (a) $x = 0$ (b) $x = \pi$

   (c) $x = \dfrac{2m+1}{1-2m}$ (d) $x = \dfrac{2m-1}{2m+1}$

Assertion & Reason Questions

DIRECTIONS : *Each of these questions contains an assertion followed by reason. Read them carefully and answer the question on the basis of following options. You have to select the one that best describes the two statements.*

  (a) If both Assertion and Reason are correct and the Reason is the correct explanation of the Assertion.
  (b) If both Assertion and Reason are correct but Reason is not the correct explanation of the Assertion.
  (c) If the Assertion is correct but Reason is incorrect.
  (d) If the Assertion is incorrect but the Reason is correct.

6. **Assertion :** The function $f(x) = \dfrac{|x|}{x}$ is continuous at x = 0.

   Reason : The left hand limit and right hand limit of the function $f(x) = \dfrac{|x|}{x}$ are not equal at x = 0.

7. **Assertion:** Let f(x) = $\begin{cases} 3x - 4, & 0 \leq x \leq 2 \\ 2x + k, & 2 < x \leq 9 \end{cases}$

   If f is continuous at x = 2, then value of k is −2.

   Reason: A function is said to be continuous at x = a if L.H.L = R.H.L = f(a).

8. **Assertion:** The number of points of discontinuity of the function f(x) = x − [x] in the interval (0, 7) are 6.

   Reason: The greatest integer function [x] is continuous at all integral points.

Case/Passage Based Question

DIRECTIONS (Q. 9) : *has 5 subparts based on case/passage given, attempt any 4 out of 5 questions.*

Case/Passage

9. A teacher prepared a performance grade criteria for +2 students on the basis of the numbers of x hours devoted by the students.

$$f(x) = \begin{cases} 1 & , \text{ if } \quad x \leq 3 \\ ax + b, & \text{ if } \quad 3 < x < 5 \\ 7 & , \text{ if } \quad x \geq 5 \end{cases}$$

$$\Rightarrow \begin{cases} \text{Grade 1, unsatisfactory } x \leq 3 \\ \text{Grade } (ax + b), \text{ satisfactory } x = 4 \\ \text{Grade 7, Average } x \geq 5 \end{cases}$$

Based on the above information answer the following :

(i) If f(x) is continuous at x = 3 then relation between a and b is

(a) $5a + b = 7$ (b) $3a + b = 1$

(c) $5a + b = 1$ (d) $3a + b = 7$

(ii) If f(x) is continuous at x = 5 then relation between a and b is

(a) $5a + b = 7$ (b) $5a + b = 1$

(c) $3a + b = 7$ (d) $3a + b = 1$

(iii) The value of a and b are

(a) 2, 5 (b) 3, 8

(c) 3, –8 (d) 8, 3

(iv) If satisfactory level is x = 4 then grade is

(a) 4 (b) 1

(c) 7 (d) 0

(v) If satisfactory level is x = 10 then grade is

(a) 4 (b) 1 (c) 0 (d) 7

One Word Answer Questions

10. Find $f(0)$, so that $f(x) = \dfrac{x}{1 - \sqrt{1-x}}$ becomes continuous at x = 0.

11. If $f(x) = \begin{cases} \dfrac{x}{\sin 3x}, & x \neq 0 \\ k & , \quad x = 0 \end{cases}$ is continuous at x = 0, then write the value of k.

12. Find the value of k which makes

$$f(x) = \begin{cases} \sin(1/x), & x \neq 0 \\ k & , x = 0 \end{cases} \text{ continuous at } x = 0.$$

13. Find the value of k if the function

$$f(x) = \begin{cases} kx^2, & x \geq 1, \\ 4 & , \quad x < 1 \end{cases} \text{ is continuous at } x = 1$$

Very Short Answer Questions

14. For what values of λ, is the function

$$f(x) = \begin{cases} \lambda(x^2 - 2x), & \text{ if } x \leq 0 \\ 4x + 1, & \text{ if } x > 0 \end{cases} \text{ continuous at }$$

x = 0?

15. If $f(x) = \begin{cases} \dfrac{8^x - 4^x - 2^x + 1}{x^2}, & x > 0 \\ e^x \sin x + \pi x + \lambda \ln 4, & x \leq 0 \end{cases}$ is continuous at

$x = 0$. Then, find the value of λ

16. If $f : R \to R$ is defined by

$$f(x) = \begin{cases} \dfrac{2\sin x - \sin 2x}{2x \cos x}, & \text{ if } x \neq 0 \\ a, & \text{ if } x = 0 \end{cases} \text{ then find the value of}$$

a, so that f is continuous at 0

Short Answer Questions

17. If $f(x) = \begin{cases} \dfrac{1 - \cos x}{x^2}, & x \neq 0 \\ k & , \quad x = 0 \end{cases}$ is continuous at x = 0, find k.

18. Let $f(x) = \begin{cases} \dfrac{x-4}{|x-4|} + a, & x < 4 \\ a + b, & x = 4. \\ \dfrac{x-4}{|x-4|} + b, & x > 4 \end{cases}$ If $f(x)$ is continuous at

x = 4 then, find the value of a and b

19. If $f(x) = \begin{cases} \dfrac{\sin 5x}{x^2 + 2x}, & x \neq 0 \\ k + \dfrac{1}{2}, & x = 0 \end{cases}$ is continuous at x = 0, then

find the value of k

NCERT Exercise-1

1. **Prove that the function $f(x) = 5x - 3$ is continuous at x = 0, at x = –3 and at x = 5.**

2. **Examine the continuity of the function $f(x) = 2x^2 - 1$ at x = 3.**

3. **Examine the following functions for continuity.**

(a) $f(x) = x - 5$ (b) $f(x) = \dfrac{1}{x - 5}$

(c) $f(x) = \dfrac{x^2 - 25}{x + 5}$ (d) $f(x) = |x - 5|$

4. **Prove that the function $f(x) = x^n$ is continuous at x = n, where n is a positive integer.**

5. Is the function f defined by $f(x) = \begin{cases} x, & \text{if } x \le 1 \\ 5, & \text{if } x > 1 \end{cases}$ continuous at $x = 0$? At $x = 1$? At $x = 2$?

Find all points of discontinuity of f, where f is defined by

6. $f(x) = \begin{cases} 2x + 3, & \text{if } x \le 2 \\ 2x - 3, & \text{if } x > 2 \end{cases}$

7. $f(x) = \begin{cases} |x| + 3, & \text{if } x \le -3 \\ -2x, & \text{if } -3 < x < 3 \\ 6x + 2, & \text{if } x \ge 3 \end{cases}$

8. Test the continuity of the function f (x) at the origin

$$f(x) = \begin{cases} \dfrac{|x|}{x}; & x \ne 0 \\ 1 & ; \ x = 0 \end{cases}$$

9. $f(x) = \begin{cases} \dfrac{x}{|x|}, & \text{if } x < 0 \\ -1, & \text{if } x \ge 0 \end{cases}$

10. $f(x) = \begin{cases} x + 1, & \text{if } x \ge 1 \\ x^2 + 1, & \text{if } x < 1 \end{cases}$

11. $f(x) = \begin{cases} x^3 - 3, & \text{if } x \le 2 \\ x^2 + 1, & \text{if } x > 2 \end{cases}$

12. $f(x) = \begin{cases} x^{10} - 1, & \text{if } x \le 1 \\ x^2, & \text{if } x > 1 \end{cases}$

13. Is the function defined by $f(x) = \begin{cases} x + 5, & \text{if } x \le 1 \\ x - 5, & \text{if } x > 1 \end{cases}$ a continuous function?

Discuss the continuity of the function f, where f is defined by

14. $f(x) = \begin{cases} 3, & \text{if } 0 \le x \le 1 \\ 4, & \text{if } 1 < x < 3 \\ 5, & \text{if } 3 \le x \le 10 \end{cases}$

15. $f(x) = \begin{cases} 2x, & \text{if } x < 0 \\ 0, & \text{if } 0 \le x \le 1 \\ 4x, & \text{if } x > 1 \end{cases}$

16. $f(x) = \begin{cases} -2, & \text{if } x \le -1 \\ 2x, & \text{if } -1 < x \le 1 \\ 2, & \text{if } x > 1 \end{cases}$

17. Find the relationship between a and b so that the function f defined by

$$f(x) = \begin{cases} ax + 1, & \text{if } x \le 3 \\ bx + 3, & \text{if } x > 3 \end{cases}$$ is continuous at $x = 3$.

18. For what value of λ is the function defined by

$$f(x) = \begin{cases} \lambda (x^2 - 2x), & \text{if } x \le 0 \\ 4x + 1, & \text{if } x > 0 \end{cases}$$ continuous at $x = 0$? What about continuity at $x = 1$?

19. Show that the function defined by $g(x) = x - [x]$ is discontinuous at all integral points. Here $[x]$ denotes the greatest integer less than or equal to x.

20. Is the function defined by $f(x) = x^2 - \sin x + 5$ continuous at $x = \pi$?

21. Discuss the continuity of the following functions:

   (a) $f(x) = \sin x + \cos x$

   (b) $f(x) = \sin x - \cos x$

   (c) $f(x) = \sin x \cdot \cos x$

22. Discuss the continuity of the cosine, cosecant, secant and cotangent functions.

23. Find all points of discontinuity of f, where

$$f(x) = \begin{cases} \dfrac{\sin x}{x}, & \text{if } x < 0 \\ x + 1, & \text{if } x \ge 0 \end{cases}$$

24. Determine if f defined by

$$f(x) = \begin{cases} x^2 \sin \dfrac{1}{x}, & \text{if } x \ne 0 \\ 0, & \text{if } x = 0 \end{cases}$$ is a continuous function?

25. Examine the continuity of f, where f is defined by $f(x) = \begin{cases} \sin x - \cos x, & \text{if } x \ne 0 \\ -1, & \text{if } x = 0 \end{cases}$

Find the values of k so that the function f is continuous at the indicated point in Exercises 26 to 29.

26. $f(x) = \begin{cases} \dfrac{k \cos x}{\pi - 2x}, & \text{if } x \ne \dfrac{\pi}{2} \\ 3, & \text{if } x = \dfrac{\pi}{2} \end{cases}$ at $x = \dfrac{\pi}{2}$

27. $f(x) = \begin{cases} kx^2, & \text{if } x \le 2 \\ 3, & \text{if } x > 2 \end{cases}$ at $x = 2$

28. $f(x) = \begin{cases} kx + 1, & \text{if } x \le \pi \\ \cos x, & \text{if } x > \pi \end{cases}$ at $x = \pi$

29. $f(x) = \begin{cases} kx + 1, & \text{if } x \le 5 \\ 3x - 5, & \text{if } x > 5 \end{cases}$ at $x = 5$

30. Find the values of a and b such that the function defined by

$f(x) = \begin{cases} 5, & \text{if } x \le 2 \\ ax + b, & \text{if } 2 < x < 10 \\ 21, & \text{if } x \ge 10 \end{cases}$ is a continuous function.

31. Show that the function defined by $f(x) = \cos(x^2)$ is a continuous function.

32. Show that the function defined by $f(x) = |\cos x|$ is a continuous function.

33. Examine that $\sin |x|$ is a continuous function.

34. Find all the points of discontinuity of f defined by $f(x) = |x| - |x + 1|$.

Topic 2 — Differentiablility

DIFFERENTIABILITY AT A POINT

Let f(x) be a real valued function defined in an open interval (a, b) and let $c \in (a, b)$ then f(x) is said to be differentiable or derivable at $x = c$ iff

$$\lim_{x \to c} \frac{f(x) - f(c)}{x - c} \text{ exists finitely}$$

This limit is called the derivative or differential coefficient of the function f(x) at $x = c$ and is denoted by

$f'(c)$ or $\left(\dfrac{df(x)}{dx} \right)$ at $x = c$ $\therefore$ $f'(c) = \lim\limits_{x \to c} \dfrac{f(x) - f(c)}{x - c}$

Thus f(x) is differentiable at $(x = c)$ $\Rightarrow$ $\lim\limits_{x \to c} \dfrac{f(x) - f(c)}{x - c}$ exists finitely

$\Rightarrow$ $\lim\limits_{x \to c^-} \dfrac{f(x) - f(c)}{x - c} = \lim\limits_{x \to c^+} \dfrac{f(x) - f(c)}{x - c}$ $\Rightarrow$ $\underset{\downarrow}{\lim\limits_{h \to o} \dfrac{f(c - h) - f(c)}{-h}} = \underset{\downarrow}{\lim\limits_{h \to o} \dfrac{f(c + h) - f(c)}{h}}$

Called L.H.D   Called R.H.D

(Left hand Derivative)   (Right hand Derivative)

Thus f(x) is differentiable at $(x = c)$ if $Lf'(c) = Rf'(c)$

If $Lf'(c) \ne Rf'(c)$ we say that f(x) is not differentiable at $x = c$

Note that if a function is differentiable at a point, it is necessarily continuous at that point.

i.e. f(x) is differentiable at $x = c \Rightarrow f(x)$ is continuous at $x = c$

The converse of the above statement is not necessarily true i.e., a function may be continuous at a point but may not be differentiable at that point.

For Example: The function $f(x) = |x|$ is continuous at $x = 0$ but it is not differentiable at $x = 0$.

All differentiable functions are continuous also.

DIFFERENTIABILITY OF A FUNCTION IN A SET OR INTERVAL

Differentiability in an Open Interval

A function f (x) defined on an open interval (a, b) is said to be differentiable or derivable in open interval (a, b) if it is differentiable at each point of (a, b).

Differentiability on a Closed Interval

A function f (x) defined on [a, b] is said to be differentiable or derivable at the end points a and b if it is differentiable from the right at a and from the left at b.

In other words $\lim\limits_{x \to a^+} \dfrac{f(x)-f(a)}{x-a}$ and $\lim\limits_{x \to b^-} \dfrac{f(x)-f(b)}{x-b}$ both exist.

If f is derivable in the open interval (a, b) and also at the end points a and b, then f is said to be derivable in the closed interval [a, b]

In other word's f(x) is said to be differentiable in the closed interval [a, b]

(i)   if f(x) is differentiable at every point of interval (a, b)

(ii) right derivative of f(x) exists at x = a

(iii) left derivative of f(x) exists at x = b.

DIFFERENTIABLE FUNCTION

A function f is said to be a differentiable function if it is differentiable at every point of its domain.

Every Where Differentiable Function

If a function is differentiable at each $x \in R$, then it is said to be every where differentiable.

Some Useful Results on Differentiability

(i)   Every polynomial function is differentiable at each $x \in R$.

(ii)   The exponential function a^x, $a > 0$, is differentiable at each $x \in R$

(iii) Every constant function is differentiable at each $x \in R$.

(iv)   The logarithmic function is differentiable at each point in its domain.

(v)   Trigonometric and inverse-trigonometric functions are differentiable in their domains.

(vi)   The sum, difference, product and quotient of two differentiable functions is differentiable.

(vii) The composition of differentiable function is differentiable function.

ALGEBRA OF DERIVATIVES

Let u, v be the function of x.

(i)   Sum and difference rule $(u \pm v)' = u' \pm v'$ 　　　　　(ii)   Product rule $(uv)' = u'v + uv'$

(iii) Quotient rule $\left(\dfrac{u}{v}\right)' = \dfrac{u'v - uv'}{v^2}$, wherever $v \neq 0$.

CHAIN RULE

If y is a function of u, u is a function of v and v is a function of x then $\dfrac{dy}{dx} = \dfrac{dy}{du} \times \dfrac{du}{dv} \times \dfrac{dv}{dx}$.

Illustration :

Discuss the differentiability of $f(x) = x\,|x|$ at $x = 0$.

Sol. $f(x) = x\,|x|$ at $x = \begin{cases} x^2, & x \geq 0 \\ -x^2 & x < 0 \end{cases}$

$$\text{L.H.D} = \lim\limits_{h \to 0^-} \frac{f(0-h)-f(0)}{-h} = \lim\limits_{h \to 0} \frac{-h^2}{-h} = 0$$

$$\text{R.H.D} = \lim\limits_{h \to 0^+} \frac{f(0+h)-f(0)}{h} = \lim\limits_{h \to 0} \frac{h^2}{h} = 0$$

$\therefore$ L.H.D. = R.H.D

So, f(x) is differentiable at $x = 0$

Practice Exercise-2

Multiple Choice Questions

1. If a function f(x) is defined as

$$f(x) = \begin{cases} \dfrac{x}{\sqrt{x^2}}, & x \neq 0 \\ 0, & x = 0 \end{cases} \quad \text{then :}$$

(a) f(x) is continuous at x = 0 but not differentiable at x = 0
(b) f(x) is continuous as well as differentiable at x = 0
(c) f(x) is discontinuous at x = 0
(d) None of these.

2. If $f(x) = \begin{cases} xe^{-\left(\frac{1}{|x|}+\frac{1}{x}\right)}, & x \neq 0 \\ 0, & x = 0 \end{cases}$ then f(x) is

(a) discontinuous every where
(b) continuous as well as differentiable for all x
(c) continuous for all x but not differentiable at $x = 0$
(d) neither differentiable nor continuous at $x = 0$

3. $f(x) = $ maximum $\{2 \sin x, 1 - \cos x\}$ is not differentiable when x is equal to
(a) 1   (b) –1

(c) 0   (d) $\pi - \cos^{-1}\left(\dfrac{3}{5}\right)$

4. If $f(x) = \begin{cases} \dfrac{[x]-1}{x-1}, & x \neq 1 \\ 0, & x = 1 \end{cases}$ then f(x) is

(a) continuous as well as differentiable at x = 1
(b) differentiable but not continuous at x = 1
(c) continuous but not differentiable at x = 1
(d) neither continuous nor differentiable at x = 1

5. At how many points between the interval (–∞, ∞) is the function f (x) = sin x is not differentiable.
(a) 0   (b) 7   (c) 9   (d) 3

Assertion & Reason Questions

DIRECTIONS : *Each of these questions contains an assertion followed by reason. Read them carefully and answer the question on the basis of following options. You have to select the one that best describes the two statements.*

(a) If both Assertion and Reason are correct and the Reason is the correct explanation of the Assertion.
(b) If both Assertion and Reason are correct but Reason is not the correct explanation of the Assertion.
(c) If the Assertion is correct but Reason is incorrect.
(d) If the Assertion is incorrect but the Reason is correct.

6. **Assertion :** $f(x) = x^n \sin\left(\dfrac{1}{x}\right)$ is differentiable for all real values of x ($n \geq 2$).

Reason : For $n \geq 2$, $\lim\limits_{x \to 0} f(x) = 0$

7. **Assertion :** f(x) = | x | sin x, is differentiable at x = 0.

Reason : If f(x) is not differentiable and g (x) is differentiable at x = a, then f(x) . g (x) can still be differentiable at x = a.

One Word Answer Questions

8. Give an example of a function which is continuous but not differentiable at a point.

9. If f(x) = |x – 2| write whether f′ (2) exists or not.

10. Write the points where $f(x) = |\log_e x|$ is not differentiable.

11. Write the number of points where f (x) = |x| + |x – 1| is continuous but not differentiable.

12. If y = sec x°, then $\dfrac{dy}{dx}$ is equal to :

Very Short Answer Questions

13. Differentiate sin [cos (x²)] w.r.t. x.

14. If $y = \sqrt{\dfrac{(1 + \cos 2\theta)}{(1 - \cos 2\theta)}}$, then find $\dfrac{dy}{d\theta}$ at $\theta = \dfrac{3\pi}{4}$

15. If $y = \left(\dfrac{2 - 3\cos x}{\sin x}\right)$, find $\dfrac{dy}{dx}$ at $x = \dfrac{\pi}{4}$.

16. If $y = (\cos x^2)^2$, then $\dfrac{dy}{dx}$ is equal to :

Short Answer Questions

17. If $f(x) = \begin{cases} ax^2 + b, & x \leq 0 \\ x^2, & x > 0 \end{cases}$ possesses derivative at x = 0, then. Find the value of a and b.

18. If f(x) = |cos x |, find $f'\left(\dfrac{3\pi}{4}\right)$.

19. If f(x) = |cos x – sin x |, find $f'\left(\dfrac{\pi}{6}\right)$.

20. If $f(x) = \sqrt{1 + \cos^2(x^2)}$, then find the value of f′$\left(\dfrac{\sqrt{\pi}}{2}\right)$

Differentiate the functions with respect to x in Exercise 1 to 8.

1. $\sin(x^2 + 5)$

2. $\cos(\sin x)$

3. $\sin(ax + b)$

4. $\sec\left(\tan\left(\sqrt{x}\right)\right)$

5. $\dfrac{\sin(ax + b)}{\cos(cx + d)}$

6. $\cos x^3 \cdot \sin^2(x^5)$

7. $2\sqrt{\cot\left(x^2\right)}$

8. $\cos\left(\sqrt{x}\right)$

9. Prove that the function f given by f (x) = |x − 1|, x ∈ R is not differentiable at x = 1.

10. Prove that the greatest integer function defined by f (x) = [x], 0 < x < 3 is not differentiable at x = 1 and x = 2.

Topic 3 — Derivatives of Implicit Functions and Inverse Trignometric Functions

IMPLICIT FUNCTIONS

An equation in the form $f(x, y) = 0$ in which y is not expressible in terms of x is called an implicit function of x and y.

e.g. $x^2 + y^2 = xy$

Algorithm : Both sides of equations are differentiated term wise with respect to x then from this equation $\dfrac{dy}{dx}$ is obtained. It may be noted that when a function of y occurs, then differentiate it w.r.t. y and multiply it by $\dfrac{dy}{dx}$. Collect the terms containing $\dfrac{dy}{dx}$ at one side and find $\dfrac{dy}{dx}$.

DERIVATIVES OF INVERSE TRIGONOMETRIC FUNCTIONS.

Functions	Domain	Derivative
$\sin^{-1} x$	$[-1, 1]$	$\dfrac{1}{\sqrt{1-x^2}}$
$\cos^{-1} x$	$[-1, 1]$	$\dfrac{-1}{\sqrt{1-x^2}}$
$\tan^{-1} x$	R	$\dfrac{1}{1+x^2}$
$\cot^{-1} x$	R	$\dfrac{-1}{1+x^2}$
$\sec^{-1} x$	$(-\infty, -1] \cup [1, \infty)$	$\dfrac{1}{x\sqrt{x^2-1}}$
$\operatorname{cosec}^{-1} x$	$(-\infty, -1] \cup [1, \infty)$	$\dfrac{-1}{x\sqrt{x^2-1}}$

Some Important Substitutions Uses in Finding the Derivatives of Inverse Trigonometric Functions.

S.No.	Expression	Substitutions
(i)	$a^2 - x^2$	$x = a\cos\theta$ or $x = a\sin\theta$
(ii)	$a^2 + x^2$	$x = a\tan\theta$ or $x = a\cot\theta$
(iii)	$x^2 - a^2$	$x = a\sec\theta$ or $x = a\,\text{cosec}\,\theta$
(iv)	$a \pm x$	$x = a\cos\theta$
(v)	$\sqrt{\dfrac{a+x}{a-x}}$ or $\sqrt{\dfrac{a-x}{a+x}}$	$x = a\cos\theta$

Illustration :

Differentiate $\tan^{-1}\left(\dfrac{\sqrt{1+x^2}-1}{x}\right)$, $n \neq 0$ with respect to n.

Sol. Put $x = \tan\theta \Rightarrow \theta = \tan^{-1}x$

$$\therefore \quad y = \tan^{-1}\left(\frac{\sqrt{1+\tan^2\theta}-1}{\tan\theta}\right) = \tan^{-1}\left(\frac{1-\cos\theta}{\sin\theta}\right) = \tan^{-1}\left(\tan\frac{\theta}{2}\right) = \frac{\theta}{2}$$

$$y = \frac{1}{2}\tan^{-1}x$$

$$\therefore \quad \frac{dy}{dn} = \frac{1}{2(1+x^2)}$$

Practice Exercise-3

Multiple Choice Questions

1. $\dfrac{d}{dx}\left[\sin^2\cot^{-1}\left\{\sqrt{\dfrac{1-x}{1+x}}\right\}\right]$ equals

(a) -1 (b) $\dfrac{1}{2}$ (c) $-\dfrac{1}{2}$ (d) 1

2. $\dfrac{d}{dx}\left(\tan^{-1}\sqrt{\dfrac{1+\cos\dfrac{x}{2}}{1-\cos\dfrac{x}{2}}}\right)$ is equal to

(a) $-1/4$ (b) $1/4$ (c) $-1/2$ (d) $1/2$

3. If $y = \cos^{-1}(\cos x)$, then $y'(x)$ is equal to

(a) 1 for all x

(b) -1 for all x

(c) 1 in 2nd and 3rd quadrant

(d) -1 in 3rd and 4th quadrant

4. If $\sin y = x\sin(a+y)$, then $\dfrac{dy}{dx}$ is equal to :

(a) $\dfrac{\sin\sqrt{a}}{\sin(a+y)}$ (b) $\dfrac{\sin^2(a+y)}{\sin a}$

(c) $\sin(a+y)$ (d) None of these

5. $\dfrac{d}{dx}\left(\tan^{-1}\dfrac{\sqrt{1+x^2}-1}{x}\right)$ is equal to :

(a) $\dfrac{1}{1+x^2}$ (b) $\dfrac{x^2}{2\sqrt{1+x^2}\,(\sqrt{1+x^2}-1)}$

(c) $\dfrac{2}{1+x^2}$ (d) $\dfrac{1}{2(1+x^2)}$

One Word Answer Questions

6. Find the derivative of $\sin(\tan^{-1}x)$ w.r.t. x.

7. If $y = \sin^{-1}\left(\dfrac{1}{2}x\right) + \cos^{-1}\left(\dfrac{1}{2}x\right)$, then find $\dfrac{dy}{dx}$

8. Find the value of $\dfrac{d}{dx}\left[\tan^{-1}\left(\dfrac{a-x}{1+ax}\right)\right]$

Very Short Answer Questions

9. If $y = \tan^{-1}\left[\dfrac{1-x^2}{1+x^2}\right]$ then find $= \dfrac{dy}{dx}$

10. If $\dfrac{x^2}{a^2} + \dfrac{y^2}{b^2} = 1$, then find $\dfrac{dy}{dx}$

11. If $y = \cot^{-1}(x^2)$, then the value of $\dfrac{dy}{dx}$ is equal to:

12. If $y = \tan^{-1}\left(\dfrac{\sqrt{x} - x}{1 + x^{3/2}}\right)$, then $y'(1)$ is equal to

Short Answer Questions

13. Differentiate with respect to x,

$$\sin^{-1}\left[\frac{2^{x+1} \cdot 3^x}{1 + (36)^x}\right]$$

[Hint: Put $\tan\theta = 6^x \;\Rightarrow\; \theta = \tan^{-1}(6^x)$]

14. Find $\dfrac{dy}{dx}$ if $y = \sin^{-1}\left(\dfrac{5x + 12\sqrt{1 - x^2}}{13}\right)$

15. Evaluate $\dfrac{d}{dx}\left(x\sqrt{a^2 - x^2} + a^2 \sin^{-1}\left(\dfrac{x}{a}\right)\right)$

NCERT Exercise-3

Find $\dfrac{dy}{dx}$ in the following :

1. $2x + 3y = \sin x$
2. $2x + 3y = \sin y$
3. $ax + by^2 = \cos y$

4. $xy + y^2 = \tan x + y$
5. $x^2 + xy + y^2 = 100$
6. $x^3 + x^2y + xy^2 + y^3 = 81$
7. $\sin^2 y + \cos xy = \pi$
8. $\sin^2 x + \cos^2 y = 1$
9. $y = \sin^{-1}\left(\dfrac{2x}{1 + x^2}\right)$
10. $y = \tan^{-1}\left(\dfrac{3x - x^3}{1 - 3x^2}\right), -\dfrac{1}{\sqrt{3}} < x < \dfrac{1}{\sqrt{3}}$
11. $y = \cos^{-1}\left(\dfrac{1 - x^2}{1 + x^2}\right), 0 < x < 1$
12. $y = \sin^{-1}\left(\dfrac{1 - x^2}{1 + x^2}\right), 0 < x < 1$
13. $y = \cos^{-1}\left(\dfrac{2x}{1 + x^2}\right), -1 < x < 1$
14. $y = \sin^{-1}\left(2x\sqrt{1 - x^2}\right), -\dfrac{1}{\sqrt{2}} < x < \dfrac{1}{\sqrt{2}}$
15. $y = \sec^{-1}\left(\dfrac{1}{2x^2 - 1}\right), 0 < x < \dfrac{1}{\sqrt{2}}$

Topic 4 — Derivatives of Exponental and Logarithmic Functions 

EXPONENTIAL FUNCTION

The exponential function with positive base $b > 1$, is the function $y = b^x$.

(i) The graph of $y = 10^x$ is given as

(ii) Domain $= R$

(iii) Range $= R^+$

(iv) The point $(0, 1)$ always lies on the graph.

(v) It is an increasing function

(vi) As $x \to -\infty, y \to 0$

(vii) $\dfrac{d}{dx}\, a^x = a^x \log_e a, \quad \dfrac{d}{dx}\, e^x = e^x.$

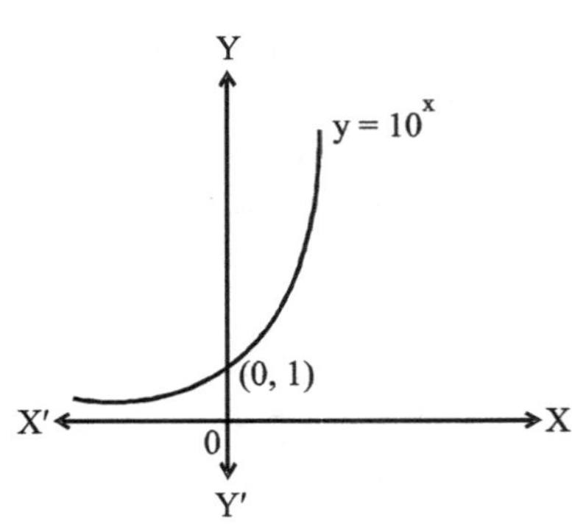

LOGARITHMIC FUNCTION

Let $b > 1$ be a real number. $b^x = a$ may be written as $\log_b a = x$.

(i) The graph of $y = \log_{10} x$ is given as

(ii) Domain $= R^+$

(iii) Range $= R$

(iv) It is an increasing function.

(v) As $x \to 0$, $y \to -\infty$.

(vi) The function $y = e^x$ and $y = \log_e x$ are the mirror images of each other.

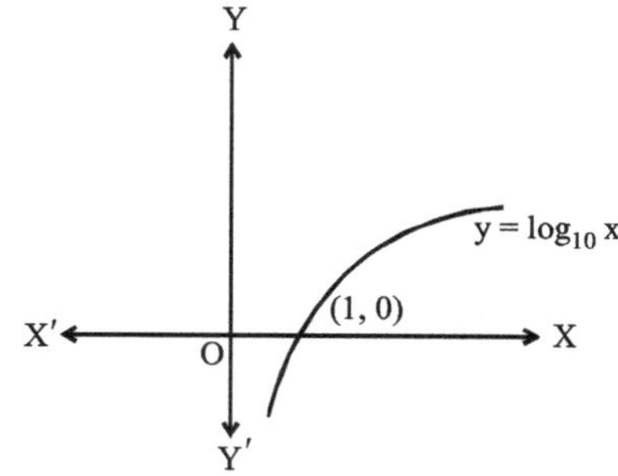

(vii) $\dfrac{d}{dx}(\log_a x) = \dfrac{1}{x}\log_a e$, $\dfrac{d}{dx}\log_e x = \dfrac{1}{x}$

Illustration :

If $y = e^{x^3}\log(1+x^2)$ then find $\dfrac{dy}{dn}$.

Sol. $y = e^{x^3}\log(1+x^2)$

$\Rightarrow \quad \dfrac{dy}{dn} = 3x^2 e^{x^3}.\log(1+x^2) + e^{x^3}.\dfrac{2x}{1+x^2}$

$\qquad = xe^{x^3}\left[3x\log(1+x^2) + \dfrac{2}{1+x^2}\right]$

Practice Exercise-4

Multiple Choice Questions

1. If $y = \log(\log x)$, then the value of $e^y\dfrac{dy}{dx}$ is :

(a) e^y

(b) $\dfrac{1}{x}$

(c) $\dfrac{1}{(\log x)}$

(d) $\dfrac{1}{(x\log x)}$

2. Let $f(x) = \begin{cases} \sin x, & \text{for } x \geq 0 \\ 1 - \cos x, & \text{for } x \leq 0 \end{cases}$ and $g(x) = e^x$. Then the value of $(gof)'(0)$ is

(a) 1

(b) -1

(c) 0

(d) None of these

3. $\dfrac{d}{dx}\left[\log\left\{e^x\left(\dfrac{x-2}{x+2}\right)\right\}^{3/4}\right]$ is equal to

(a) 1

(b) $\dfrac{x^2+1}{x^2-4}$

(c) $\dfrac{x^2-1}{x^2-4}$

(d) $e^x\dfrac{x^2-1}{x^2-4}$

One Word Answer Questions

4. Differentiate $e^{\sqrt{x}}$ w.r.t. x.

5. Find the differential coefficient of $f(\log x)$ w.r.t. x where $f(x) = \log x$

6. If $y = 2^{-x}$, then find $\dfrac{dy}{dx}$

7. If $y = e^{(1+\log_e x)}$, then find $\dfrac{dy}{dx}$

Very Short Answer Questions

8. If $f(x) = e^x$ and $g(x) = \ln x$, then find the value of $(gof)'(x)$.

9. If, $y = e^{3x+7}$, then find the value of $\left.\dfrac{dy}{dx}\right|_{x=0}$

10. If $y = e^{\frac{1}{2}\log\left(1+\tan^2 x\right)}$, then find $\dfrac{dy}{dx}$

Short Answer Questions

11. Differentiate the following functions w.r.t. x

$f(x) = x\sin x\log x$.

12. If $y = \log x \cdot e^{\left(\tan x + x^2\right)}$, then find $\dfrac{dy}{dx}$

13. Let $f(x) = e^x$, $g(x) = \sin^{-1}x$ and $h(x) = f(g(x))$, then find $h'(x)/h(x)$

NCERT Exercise-4

Differentiate the following w.r.t.x :

1. $\dfrac{e^x}{\sin x}$

2. $e^{\sin^{-1} x}$

3. e^{x^3}

4. $\sin(\tan^{-1} e^{-x})$

5. $\log(\cos e^x)$

6. $e^x + e^{x^2} + \cdots + e^{x^5}$

7. $\sqrt{e^{\sqrt{x}}}$, $x > 0$

8. $\log(\log x)$, $x > 1$

9. $\dfrac{\cos x}{\log x}$, $x > 0$

10. $\cos(\log x + e^x)$, $x > 0$

Topic 5   Logarithmic Differentiation 

LOGARITHMIC DIFFERENTIATION

That logarithmic differentiation is a very useful technique to differentiate functions of the form $f(x) = [u(x)]^{v(x)}$ where $f(x)$ and $u(x)$ are positive.

By taking logarithm (to base e) both side we get

$$\log y = v(x) \cdot \log[u(x)]$$

Using chain rule differentiate w.r. to x, we get

$$\frac{1}{y}\frac{dy}{dx} = v(x) \cdot \frac{1}{u(x)} \cdot u'(x) + v'(x) \cdot \log[u(x)]$$

Note: (i) $\log_b pq = \log_b p + \log_b q$ (ii) $\log_b \dfrac{p}{q} = \log_b p - \log_b q$

      (iii) $\log_b p^x = x \log_b p$ (iv) $\log_a p = \dfrac{\log_b p}{\log_b a}$

Illustration :

If $y = e^{x^x}$ then find $\dfrac{dy}{dx}$.

Sol. $y = e^{x^x}$

Taking log two times

$$\log(\log y) = x \log x + \log(\log x)$$

$$\frac{1}{\log y} \times \frac{1}{y}\frac{dy}{dx} = x \cdot \frac{1}{x} + \frac{1}{\log x} \times \frac{1}{x}$$

$$\frac{dy}{dx} = y \log y \left[1 + \frac{1}{x \log x}\right] = x^{x^x} x^x \log x \left(1 + \frac{1}{x \log x}\right)$$

Practice Exercise-5

Multiple Choice Questions

1. If $y = e^{x^x}$, then $\cdot \dfrac{dy}{dx} =$

   (a) $y(1 + \log_e x)$ (b) $yx^x(1 + \log_e x)$

   (c) $ye^x(1 + \log_e x)$ (d) None of these

2. If $y^x = e^{y-x}$, then $\dfrac{dy}{dx}$ is equal to

   (a) $\dfrac{1 + \log y}{y \log y}$ (b) $\dfrac{(1 + \log y)^2}{y \log y}$

   (c) $\dfrac{1 + \log y}{(\log y)^2}$ (d) $\dfrac{(1 + \log y)^2}{\log y}$

3. If $y = \left|\sin x\right|^{|x|}$, then the value of $\dfrac{dy}{dx}$ at $x = -\dfrac{\pi}{6}$ is

   (a) $\dfrac{2^{-\frac{\pi}{6}}}{6}\left[6\log 2 - \sqrt{3}\pi\right]$ (b) $\dfrac{2^{\frac{\pi}{6}}}{6}\left[6\log 2 + \sqrt{3}\pi\right]$

   (c) $\dfrac{2^{-\frac{\pi}{6}}}{6}\left[6\log 2 + \sqrt{3}\pi\right]$ (d) None of these

One Word Answer Question

4. If $y = (\tan x)^{\sin x}$, then find $\dfrac{dy}{dx}$

Very Short Answer Question

5. Differentiate $x^{\sin^{-1}x}$ w.r.t. x

Short Answer Questions

6. If $f(x) = (\log_{\cot x} \tan x)(\log_{\tan x}\cot x)^{-1} + \tan^{-1}\dfrac{4x}{4 - x^2}$,

   then find $f'(2)$

7. If $y = \log_a x + \log_x a + \log_x x + \log_a a$, then find $\dfrac{dy}{dx}$

NCERT Exercise-5

Differentiate the functions given in Exercises 1 to 11 w.r.to x.

1. $\cos x \cdot \cos 2x \cdot \cos 3x$

2. $\sqrt{\dfrac{(x-1)(x-2)}{(x-3)(x-4)(x-5)}}$

3. $(\log x)^{\cos x}$

4. $x^x - 2^{\sin x}$

5. $(x+3)^2 \cdot (x+4)^3 \cdot (x+5)^4$

6. $\left(x + \dfrac{1}{x}\right)^x + x^{\left(1 + \frac{1}{x}\right)}$

7. $(\log x)^x + x^{\log x}$

8. $(\sin x)^x + \sin^{-1}\sqrt{x}$

9. $x^{\sin x} + (\sin x)^{\cos x}$

10. $x^{x\cos x} + \dfrac{x^2 + 1}{x^2 - 1}$

11. $(x\cos x)^x + (x\sin x)^{\frac{1}{x}}$

Find $\dfrac{dy}{dx}$ of the functions given in Exercises 12 to 15.

12. $x^y + y^x = 1$

13. $y^x = x^y$

14. $(\cos x)^y = (\cos y)^x$

15. $xy = e^{(x-y)}$

16. Find the derivative of the function given by $f(x) = (1+x)(1+x^2)(1+x^4)(1+x^8)$ and hence find $f'(1)$.

17. Differentiate $(x^2 - 5x + 8)(x^3 + 7x + 9)$ in three ways mentioned below :

   (i) by using product rule

   (ii) by expanding the product to obtain a single polynomial.

   (iii) by logarithmic differentiation.

   Do they all give the same answer?

18. If u, v and w are functions of w then show that

$$\dfrac{d}{dx}(u.v.w) = \dfrac{du}{dx}\,v.w + u.\dfrac{dv}{dx}.w + u.v\dfrac{dw}{dx}$$

in two ways - first by repeated application of product rule, second by logarithmic differentiation.

Topic 6   Derivatives of Functions in Parametric From 

DERIVATIVES OF FUNCTIONS IN PARAMETRIC FORM

The set of equations $x = f(t)$, $y = g(t)$ is called the parametric form of an equation.

Now, $\quad \dfrac{dx}{dt} = f'(t), \dfrac{dy}{dt} = g'(t), \quad \therefore \quad \dfrac{dy}{dx} = \dfrac{dy/dt}{dx/dt}$ or $\dfrac{g'(t)}{f'(t)}$

Illustration :

If $x = a\sin^2\theta$ and $y = b\cos^2\theta$, find $\dfrac{dy}{dx}$

Sol. $x = a\sin^2\theta$

$\Rightarrow \quad \dfrac{dx}{d\theta} = 2a\sin\theta.\cos\theta \qquad$ and $y = b\cos^2 \Rightarrow \dfrac{dy}{d\theta} = -2b\cos\theta.\sin\theta$

So, $\quad \dfrac{dy}{d\theta} = \dfrac{\dfrac{dy}{d\theta}}{\dfrac{dx}{d\theta}} = \dfrac{-2b\cos\theta.\sin\theta}{2a\sin\theta.\cos\theta} = -\dfrac{b}{a}$

Practice Exercise-6 

Multiple Choice Questions

1. If $x = \sqrt{a^{\sin^{-1}t}}$ and $y = \sqrt{a^{\cos^{-1}t}}$, then

(a) $\quad x\dfrac{dy}{dx} + y = 0$ (b) $\quad x\dfrac{dy}{dx} = y$

(c) $\quad y\dfrac{dy}{dx} = x$ (d) None of these

2. The derivative of $\sin^{-1}\left(\dfrac{2x}{1+x^2}\right)$ with respect to $\cos^{-1}\left[\dfrac{1-x^2}{1+x^2}\right]$ is equal to :

(a) 1   (b) -1

(c) 2   (d) None of these

Assertion & Reason Questions

DIRECTIONS : *Each of these questions contains an assertion followed by reason. Read them carefully and answer the question on the basis of following options. You have to select the one that best describes the two statements.*

(a) If both Assertion and Reason are correct and the Reason is the correct explanation of the Assertion.

(b) If both Assertion and Reason are correct but Reason is not the correct explanation of the Assertion.

(c) If the Assertion is correct but Reason is incorrect.

(d) If the Assertion is incorrect but the Reason is correct.

3. **Assertion :** If $x = a\,(\theta - \sin\theta)$, $y = a(1 + \cos\theta)$, then $\dfrac{dy}{dx} = -\cot\dfrac{\theta}{2}$.

Reason : If $x = \dfrac{\sin^3 t}{\sqrt{\cos 2t}}$, $y = \dfrac{\cos^3 t}{\sqrt{\cos 2t}}$, then derivative of y with respect to x is $-\cot 3t$.

4. **Assertion :** If $u = f(\tan x)$, $v = g(\sec x)$ and $f'(1) = 2$, $g\left(\sqrt{2}\right) = 4$, then $\left(\dfrac{du}{dv}\right)_{x = \pi/4} = \dfrac{1}{\sqrt{2}}$

Reason : If $u = f(x)$, $v = g(x)$, then the derivative of f with respect to g is $\dfrac{du}{dv} = \dfrac{du/dx}{dv/dx}$

Very Short Answer Questions

5. Differantiate $\log(1 + \theta)$ with respect to $\sin^{-1}\theta$.

6. Find the derivative of e^{x^3} with respect to $\log x$

7. If $y = x - x^2$, then find the derivative of y^2 with respect to x^2

Short Answer Questions

8. If $x = a\left(\dfrac{1+t^2}{1-t^2}\right)$ and $y = \dfrac{2t}{1-t^2}$, find $\dfrac{dy}{dx}$.

9. If $x = \sin t\cos 2t$ and $y = \cos t\sin 2t$, then at $t = \dfrac{\pi}{4}$, find the value of $\dfrac{dy}{dx}$ is equal to :

NCERT Exercise-6

If x and y are connected parametrically by the equations given in Exercises 1 to 10, without eliminating the parameter.

Find $\dfrac{dy}{dx}$.

1. $x = 2at^2$, $y = at^4$

2. $x = a \cos \theta$, $y = b \cos \theta$

3. $x = \sin t$, $y = \cos 2t$

4. $x = 4t$, $y = \dfrac{4}{t}$

5. $x = \cos \theta - \cos 2\theta$, $y = \sin \theta - \sin 2\theta$

6. $x = a\,(\theta - \sin \theta)$, $y = a\,(1 + \cos \theta)$

7. $x = \dfrac{\sin^3 t}{\sqrt{\cos 2t}}$ & $y = \dfrac{\cos^3 t}{\sqrt{\cos 2t}}$

8. $x = a\left(\cos t + \log \tan \dfrac{t}{2}\right)$, $y = a \sin t$

9. $x = a \sec \theta$, $y = b \tan \theta$

10. $x = a\,(\cos \theta + \theta \sin \theta)$, $y = a\,(\sin \theta - \theta \cos \theta)$

11. If $x = \sqrt{a^{\sin^{-1} t}}$, $y = \sqrt{a^{\cos^{-1} t}}$, show that $\dfrac{dy}{dx} = -\dfrac{y}{x}$

Topic 7 — Second Order Derivative

SECOND ORDER DERIVATIVE

Let $y = f(x)$ then $\dfrac{dy}{dx} = f'(x)$. If $f'(x)$ is differentiable, then it is again differentiated and get $\dfrac{d}{dx}\left(\dfrac{dy}{dx}\right)$ or $\dfrac{d^2y}{dx^2} = f''(x)$

$\dfrac{d^2y}{dx^2}$ or $f''(x)$ is called the second derivative of y or $f(x)$ with respect to x.

Illustration :

If $y = e^{\tan^{-1} x}$ prove that $(1 + x^2)y_2 + (2x - 1)y_1 = 0$

Sol. $y = e^{\tan^{-1} x}$

Differentiate with respect to x.

$\Rightarrow \quad \dfrac{dy}{dx} = e^{\tan^{-1} x} \cdot \dfrac{1}{1 + x^2} \quad \Rightarrow \quad (1 + x^2)\dfrac{dy}{dx} = y$

Differentiate with respect to x.

$\Rightarrow \quad (1 + x^2)\dfrac{d^2y}{dx^2} + 2x\dfrac{dy}{dx} = \dfrac{dy}{dx} \quad \Rightarrow \quad (1 + x^2)\dfrac{d^2y}{dx^2} + (2x - 1)\dfrac{dy}{dx} = 0$

Practice Exercise-7

Multiple Choice Questions

1. If $x = f(t)$ and $y = g(t)$, then $\dfrac{d^2y}{dx^2}$ is equal to

    (a) $\dfrac{g''(t)}{f''(t)}$

    (b) $\dfrac{g''(t)f'(t) - g'(t)f''(t)}{\left(f'(t)\right)^3}$

    (c) $\dfrac{g''(t)f'(t) - g'(t)f''(t)}{\left(f'(t)\right)^2}$

    (d) None of these

2. Let $f(x) = \sin x$, $g(x) = x^2$ and $h(x) = \log_e x$.

   If $F(x) = (h o g o f)(x)$, then $F''(x)$ is equal to

   (a) $a \csc^3 x$

   (b) $2 \cot x^2 - 4x^2 \csc^2 x^2$

   (c) $2x \cot x^2$

   (d) $-2 \csc^2 x$

3. If $x^2 + y^2 = 1$, then

   (a) $yy'' - (2y')^2 + 1 = 0$

   (b) $yy'' - (y')^2 + 1 = 0$

   (c) $yy'' - (y')^2 - 1 = 0$

   (d) $yy'' - 2(y')^2 + 1 = 0$

One Word Answer Questions

4. Let $y = t^{10} + 1$ and $x = t^8 + 1$, then find $\dfrac{d^2y}{dx^2}$

5. Find the 2nd derivative of $a \sin^3 t$ with respect to $a \cos^3 t$ at

   $t = \dfrac{\pi}{4}$

Very Short Answer Questions

6. Find $\dfrac{d^2y}{dx^2}$ when $y = \log\left(\dfrac{x^2}{e^x}\right)$

7. If $x = a(\theta + \sin\theta)$, $y = a(1 - \cos\theta)$, find $\dfrac{d^2y}{dx^2}$ at $\theta = \dfrac{\pi}{2}$.

Short Answer Questions

8. If $x = 3\sin t - \sin 3t$, $y = 3\cos t - \cos 3t$, find $\dfrac{d^2y}{dx^2}$ at $t = \dfrac{\pi}{3}$.

9. If $y = \tan^{-1}\left(\dfrac{\log_e(e/x^2)}{\log_e(ex^2)}\right) + \tan^{-1}\left(\dfrac{3 + 2\log_e x}{1 - 6\log_e x}\right)$,

   then find $\dfrac{d^2y}{dx^2}$

10. If $y = a^x \cdot b^{2x-1}$, then find $\dfrac{d^2y}{dx^2}$

Find the second order derivatives of the functions given in exercises 1 to 10.

1. $x^2 + 3x + 2$

2. x^{20}

3. $x \cdot \cos x$

4. $\log x$

5. $x^3 \log x$

6. $e^x \sin 5x$

7. $e^{6x} \cos 3x$

8. $\tan^{-1} x$

9. $\log(\log x)$

10. $\sin(\log x)$

11. If $y = 5\cos x - 3\sin x$, prove that $\dfrac{d^2y}{dx^2} + y = 0$

12. If $y = \cos^{-1} x$, Find $\dfrac{d^2y}{dx^2}$ in terms of y alone.

13. If $y = 3\cos(\log x) + 4\sin(\log x)$, show that

    $x^2 y_2 + xy_1 + y = 0$

14. If $y = Ae^{mx} + Be^{nx}$, show that

    $$\dfrac{d^2y}{dx^2} - (m+n)\dfrac{dy}{dx} + mny = 0$$

15. If $y = 500e^{7x} + 600e^{-7x}$, show that $\dfrac{d^2y}{dx^2} = 49y$.

16. If $e^y(x+1) = 1$, show that $\dfrac{d^2y}{dx^2} = \left(\dfrac{dy}{dx}\right)^2$

17. If $y = (\tan^{-1} x)^2$, show that

    $(x^2 + 1)^2 y_2 + 2x(x^2 + 1) y_1 = 2$

Important Tips & Formulae

- **Some standard results on differentiability**

  (a) Every polynomial function is differentiable at each $x \in R$.

  (b) The exponential function a^x, $a > 0$ is differentiable at each $x \in R$.

  (c) Every constant function is differentiable at each $x \in R$.

  (d) The logarithmic function is differentiable at each point in its domain.

  (e) Trigonometric and inverse-trigonometric functions are differentiable in their domains.

  (f) The sum, difference, product and quotient of two differentiable functions is differentiable.

  (g) The composition of differentiable functions is a differentiable function.

  (h) If a function is not differentiable but is continuous at a point, it geometrically implies there is a sharp corner or a kink at that point.

  (i) If $f(x)$ and $g(x)$ both are not differentiable at a point, then the sum function $f(x) + g(x)$ and the product function $f(x) \cdot g(x)$ can still be differentiable at that point.

- $\dfrac{d}{dx}(e^{ax} \sin bx) = e^{ax}(a \sin bx + b \cos bx)$

- $\dfrac{d}{dx}(e^{ax} \cos bx) = e^{ax}(a \cos b x - b \sin b x)$

- The composition of two continuous functions is a continuous function.

- If f is continuous on its domain D_f, then $|f|$ is also continuous on D_f.

- The product of one continuous and one discontinuous function may or may not be continuous.

  Examples :

  (a) $f(x) = x$ is continuous and $g(x) = \cos 1/x$ is discontinuous, whereas their product $x \cos 1/x$ is continuous

  (b) $f(x) = C$ is continuous and $g(x) = \sin 1/x$ is discontinuous, whereas their product $C \sin 1/x$ is discontinuous

- **Relation between continuity and differentiability**

  (a) If a function $f(x)$ is differentiable at a point $(x = a)$ then it is continuous at $(x = a)$.

  (b) If $f(x)$ is continuous at a point $x = a$, there is no guarantee that $f(x)$ is differentiable there.

  (c) If $f(x)$ is not differentiable at $x = a$ then it may or may not be continuous at $x = a$.

  (d) If $f(x)$ is not continuous at $x = a$, then it is not differentiable at $x = a$.

  (e) If left hand derivative and right hand derivative of $f(x)$ at

  $(x = a)$ are finite (they may or may not be equal) then $f(x)$ is continuous at $x = a$.

- The chain rule can also be restated as follows

  If $z = f(y)$ and $y = g(x)$, then $\dfrac{dz}{dx} = \dfrac{dz}{dy} \cdot \dfrac{dy}{dx}$

  Derivative of z w.r.t. x = (Derivative of z w.r.t. y)

  $\times$ (Derivative of y w.r.t. x)

  This chain rule can be extended further

  Derivative of z w.r.t. x = (Derivative of z w.r.t. u)

  $\times$ (Derivative of u w.r.t v) $\times$ (Derivative of v w.r.t x)

MISCELLANEOUS NCERT EXERCISE

Differentiate w.r.t x the functin in exercises 1 to 11

1. $(3x^2 - 9x + 5)^9$

Sol. Let $y = (3x^2 - 9x + 5)^9$

and $y = t^9$, $t = 3x^2 - 9x + 5$

$\therefore \dfrac{dy}{dt} = 9t^8$, $\dfrac{dt}{dx} = 6x = 9$

$\therefore \dfrac{dy}{dx} = 27(3x^2 - 9x + 5)(2x - 3)$

2. $\sin^3 x + \cos^6 x$

Sol. Let $y = \sin^3 x + \cos^6 x$, $y = u + v$, $u = \sin^3 x$,

$v = \cos^6 x$,

Now $u = \sin^3 x$, $t = \sin x$

$u = t^3$, $t = \sin x$, $\quad \dfrac{du}{dt} = 3t^2$, $\dfrac{dt}{dx} = \cos x$

$\dfrac{du}{dx} = 3\sin^2 x \cos x$ and $\dfrac{dv}{dt} = 6t^5$, $\dfrac{dt}{dx} = -\sin x$

$\therefore \dfrac{dv}{dx} = -6\cos^5 x \sin x$,

Now $y = u + v$

$\dfrac{dy}{dx} = \dfrac{du}{dx} + \dfrac{dv}{dx} = 3\sin^2 x \cos x - 6\cos^5 x \sin x$

$\therefore \dfrac{dy}{dx} = 3\sin x \cos x(\sin x - 2\cos^4 x)$

3. $(5x)^{3\cos 2x}$

Sol. Let $y = (5x)^{3\cos 2x}$. Taking log on both sides,

$\log y = 3\cos 2x \log 5x$

Differentiating w.r.t. x,

$\dfrac{1}{y} \dfrac{dy}{dx} = -3 \cdot 2\sin 2x \log 5x + 3\cos 2x \cdot \dfrac{1}{x}$

$= 3\left(\dfrac{\cos 2x}{x} - 2\sin 2x \log 5x\right)$,

$\dfrac{dy}{dx} = (5x)^{3\cos 2x}\left(\dfrac{3\cos 2x}{x} - 6\sin 2x \log 5x\right)$

4. $\sin^{-1}\left(x\sqrt{x}\right)$, $0 \le x \le 1$

Sol. Let $y = \sin^{-1}\left(x\sqrt{x}\right)$, $y = \sin^{-1} x^{3/2}$,

put $t = x^{3/2}$, $y = \sin^{-1} t$

$\dfrac{dt}{dx} = \dfrac{3}{2}x^{1/2}$, $\quad \dfrac{dy}{dt} = \dfrac{1}{\sqrt{1 - t^2}}$

$\therefore \dfrac{dy}{dx} = \dfrac{3\sqrt{x}}{2\sqrt{1 - x^3}}$

5. $\dfrac{\cos^{-1} x/2}{\sqrt{2x + 7}}$, $-2 < x < 2$

Sol. $y = \dfrac{\cos^{-1} x/2}{\sqrt{2x + 7}}$, $-2 < x < 2$, Let $u = \cos^{-1}\dfrac{x}{2}$,

$\dfrac{du}{dx} = \dfrac{-1}{\sqrt{4 - x^2}}$ and $v = \sqrt{2x + 7}$,

$\dfrac{dv}{dx} = \dfrac{1}{\sqrt{2x + 7}}$

Now, $y = \dfrac{u}{v}$

$\therefore \dfrac{dy}{dx} = -\dfrac{(2x + 7) + \sqrt{4 - x^2}\,\cos^{-1} x/2}{(2x + 7)^{3/2}\sqrt{4 - x^2}}$

6. $\cot^{-1}\left[\dfrac{\sqrt{1 + \sin x} + \sqrt{1 - \sin x}}{\sqrt{1 + \sin x} - \sqrt{1 - \sin x}}\right]$, $0 < x < \dfrac{\pi}{2}$

Sol. $y = \cot^{-1}\left[\dfrac{\sqrt{1 + \sin x} + \sqrt{1 - \sin x}}{\sqrt{1 + \sin x} - \sqrt{1 - \sin x}}\right]$, $0 < x < \dfrac{\pi}{2}$

Now $1 + \sin x = \cos^2 x/2 + \sin^2 x/2 + 2\cos x/2 \sin x/2$

$= \left(\cos\dfrac{x}{2} + \sin\dfrac{x}{2}\right)^2$

Similarly, $1 - \sin x = \left(\cos\dfrac{x}{2} - \sin\dfrac{x}{2}\right)^2$,

$y = \cot^{-1}\left[\dfrac{2\cos x/2}{2\sin x/2}\right] = \cot^{-1}(\cot x/2) = \dfrac{x}{2}$, $y = \dfrac{x}{2}$

$\therefore \dfrac{dy}{dx} = \dfrac{1}{2}$

7. $(\log x)^{\log x}$, $x > 1$

Sol. Let $y = (\log x)^{\log x}$, $x > 1$

Taking log on both sides, $\log y = \log x \log(\log x)$

$u = \log x, \quad v = \log \log x, \quad \dfrac{du}{dx} = \dfrac{1}{x}, \quad v = \log t, \ t = \log x,$

$\dfrac{dv}{dt} = \dfrac{1}{t}, \ \dfrac{dt}{dx} = \dfrac{1}{x}$

$\therefore \ \dfrac{dv}{dx} = \dfrac{1}{x \log x}$

Also $(uv)' = u'v + uv'$

$\therefore \ \dfrac{1}{y}\dfrac{dy}{dx} = \dfrac{1}{x}\log(\log x) + \log x \ \dfrac{1}{\log x}\cdot\dfrac{1}{x}$

$\therefore \ \dfrac{dy}{dx} = \dfrac{1}{x}(\log x)^{\log x}(1 + \log \log x)$

8. $\cos(a \cos x + b \sin x)$, **for some constant a and b.**

Sol. Let $y = \cos(a \cos x + b \sin x)$

Put $t = a \cos x + b \sin x, \quad y = \cos t,$

$\dfrac{dy}{dt} = -\sin t, \ \dfrac{dt}{dx} = -a \sin x + b \cos x$

$\therefore \ \dfrac{dy}{dx} = (a \sin x - b \cos x)\sin(a \cos x + b \sin x)$

9. $(\sin x - \cos x)^{\sin x - \cos x}, \ \dfrac{\pi}{4} < x < \dfrac{3\pi}{4}$

Sol. Let $y = (\sin x - \cos x)^{\sin x - \cos x}$

Taking log on both sides, we get

$\log y = (\sin x - \cos x)\log(\sin x - \cos x)$

Differentiating w.r.t. x , we get

$\dfrac{1}{y}\dfrac{dy}{dx} = (\cos x + \sin x)\log(\sin x - \cos x) + (\cos x + \sin x)$

$= (\cos x + \sin x)[\log(\sin x - \cos x) + 1]$

$\therefore \ \dfrac{dy}{dx} = (\sin x - \cos x)^{(\sin x - \cos x)}(\sin x + \cos x)$

$$[1 + \log(\sin x - \cos x)]$$

10. $x^x + x^a + a^x + a^a$, **for some fixed a > 0 and x > 0**

Sol. Let $y = x^x + x^a + a^x + a^a$

Differentiating w.r.t. x ,

$\dfrac{dy}{dx} = \dfrac{d}{dx}x^x + ax^{a-1} + a^x \log a + 0$

Put $u = x^x$

Taking log on both sides

$\log u = x \log x, \quad \dfrac{1}{u}\dfrac{du}{dx} = 1\cdot\log x + x\cdot\dfrac{1}{x}$

$\Rightarrow \ \dfrac{du}{dx} = u(1 + \log x) = x^x(1 + \log x)$

$\therefore \ \dfrac{dy}{dx} = x^x(1 + \log x) + ax^{a-1} + a^x \log a$

11. $x^{x^2-3} + (x-3)^{x^2}$, **for x > 3**

Sol. Let $y = x^{x^2-3} + (x-3)^{x^2}$,

Put $y = u + v, \quad \dfrac{dy}{dx} = \dfrac{du}{dx} + \dfrac{dv}{dx}$,

where $u = x^{x^2-3}$ & $v = (x-3)^{x^2}$

Now $u = x^2 - 3$

Taking log on both sides, $\log u = (x^2 - 3)\log x$,

$\dfrac{1}{u}\dfrac{du}{dx} = 2x \log x + (x^2 - 3)\cdot\dfrac{1}{x}$

$\dfrac{du}{dx} = x^{x^2-3}\left(2x \log x + \dfrac{x^2-3}{3}\right)$

and $v = (x-3)^{x^2}$

Taking log on both side

$\log v = x^2 \log(x-3), \ \dfrac{1}{v}\dfrac{dv}{dx} = 2x \log(x-3) + \dfrac{x^2}{x-3}$,

$\dfrac{dv}{dx} = (x-3)^{x^2}\left[2x \log(x-3) + \dfrac{x^2}{x-3}\right]$

$\therefore \ \dfrac{dy}{dx} = x^{x^2-3}\left(2x \log x + \dfrac{x^2-3}{x}\right) + (x-3)^{x^2}$

$$\left[2x \log(x-3) + \dfrac{x^2}{x-3}\right]$$

12. **Find** $\dfrac{dy}{dx}$, **if** $y = 12(1 - \cos t), \ x = 10(t - \sin t),$

$-\dfrac{\pi}{2} < t < \dfrac{\pi}{2}$

Sol. $y = 12(1 - \cos t)$

$\therefore \ \dfrac{dy}{dt} = 12 \sin t, \ x = 10(t - \sin t), \ \dfrac{dx}{dt} = 10(1 - \cos t)$

$\therefore \ \dfrac{dy}{dx} = \dfrac{3}{5}\cot\dfrac{t}{2}$

13. **Find** $\dfrac{dy}{dx}$, **if** $y = \sin^{-1} x + \sin^{-1}\sqrt{1 - x^2}, -1 \le x \le 1.$

Sol. $y = \sin^{-1} x + \sin^{-1} \sqrt{1 - x^2}$

Put $x = \sin \theta$, $\quad y = \theta + \sin^{-1} \sqrt{1 - \sin^2 \theta}$

$= \theta + \sin^{-1} (\cos \theta) = \theta + \sin^{-1} \sin \left(\dfrac{\pi}{2} - \theta \right)$

$= \theta + \dfrac{\pi}{2} - \theta = \dfrac{\pi}{2} \quad \therefore \ \dfrac{dy}{dx} = 0$

14. If $x \sqrt{1+y} + y \sqrt{1+x} = 0$, for $, -1 < x < 1$, prove that

$$\frac{dy}{dx} = \frac{-1}{(1 + x)^2}.$$

Sol. The given equation may be written as

$$x\sqrt{1 + y} = -y\sqrt{1 + x}$$

Squaring both sides, $x^2 (1 + y) = y^2 (1 + x)$

$\Rightarrow x^2 - y^2 = y^2 x - x^2 y$

$\Rightarrow (x + y)(x - y) = -xy(x - y)$

$\Rightarrow y = \dfrac{-x}{1 + x}$

$$\therefore \ \frac{dy}{dx} = -\left\{ \frac{(1 + x) \cdot 1 - x \cdot (0 + 1)}{(1 + x)^2} \right\} = \frac{-1}{(1 + x)^2}$$

15. If $(x - a)^2 + (y - b)^2 = c^2$, for some $c > 0$, prove that

$$\frac{\left[1 + \left(\dfrac{dy}{dx} \right)^2 \right]^{\frac{3}{2}}}{\dfrac{d^2 y}{dx^2}} \ \text{is a constant independent of a and b.}$$

Sol. Given $(x - a)^2 + (y - b)^2 = c^2 \qquad$ ...(i)

Differentiating w.r.t. x, we get

$$\Rightarrow (x - a) + (y - b)\frac{dy}{dx} = 0 \qquad \text{...(ii)}$$

Again differentiating w.r.t. x ,

$$\Rightarrow (y - b) = -\left\{ \frac{1 + \left(\dfrac{dy}{dx} \right)^2}{\dfrac{d^2 y}{dx^2}} \right\} \qquad \text{...(iii)}$$

Substitute this value of $(y - b)$ in (ii)

$$(x - a) = \left\{ \frac{1 + \left(\dfrac{dy}{dx} \right)^2}{\dfrac{d^2 y}{dx^2}} \right\} \left(\frac{dy}{dx} \right) \qquad \text{...(iv)}$$

Putting these values of $(y-b)$ and $(x-a)$ from (iii) & (iv) in (i)

$$\Rightarrow \frac{\left\{ 1 + \left(\dfrac{dy}{dx} \right)^2 \right\}^{3/2}}{\dfrac{d^2 y}{dx^2}} = c$$

which is a constant, independent of a and b.

16. If $\cos y = x \cos (a + y)$, with $\cos a \neq \pm 1$, prove that

$$\frac{dy}{dx} = \frac{\cos^2 (a + y)}{\sin a}.$$

Sol. $\cos y = x \cos (a + y)$

$$\therefore \ \frac{dy}{dx} = \frac{\sin (a + y - y)}{\cos^2 (a + y)} = \frac{\sin a}{\cos^2 (a + y)}$$

$$\therefore \ \frac{dy}{dx} = \frac{\cos^2 (a + y)}{\sin a}$$

17. If $x = a (\cos t + t \sin t)$ and $y = a (\sin t - t \cos t)$, find $\dfrac{d^2 y}{dx^2}$.

Sol. $x = a (\cos t + t \sin t)$

$$\therefore \ \frac{dx}{dt} = a (-\sin t + \sin t + t \cos t) = a \, t \cos t$$

and $y = a (\sin t - t \cos t)$

$$\frac{dy}{dt} = a (\cos t - \cos t + t \sin t) = a \, t \sin t$$

$$\therefore \ \frac{dy}{dx} = \tan t$$

It is valid $t \neq 0$, $t \neq (2n + 1) \, \pi/2$,

$$\frac{d^2 y}{dx^2} = \frac{d}{dt} \left(\frac{dy}{dx} \right) \times \frac{dt}{dx} = \frac{1}{at} \sec^3 t$$

18. If $f(x) = |x|^3$, show that $f''(x)$ exists for all real x and find it.

Sol. When $x \geq 0$, then $f(x) = |x|^3 = x^3$

$\therefore \ f'(x) = 3x^2$ and $f''(x) = 6x$

which exists for all real values of x.

When $x < 0$, then $f'(x) = |x|^2 = (-x)^3 = -x^3$

$\therefore \ f'(x) = -3x^2$ and $f''(x) = -6x$ which exists for all real values of x.

Hence $f''(x) = \begin{cases} 6x & , \text{if } x \geq 0 \\ -6x, & \text{if } x < 0 \end{cases}$

19. Using mathematical induction prove that $\dfrac{dy}{dx} (x^n) = nx^{n-1}$ for all positive integers n.

Sol. Let P(n) be the given statement in the problem

$$P(x) : \frac{d}{dx}(x^n) = nx^{n-1} \qquad ....(i)$$

The verify that for $n = I$

Put $n = 1$ in (i), we get

$$P(1) : \frac{d}{dx}(x') = (1)x^{1-1} = 1$$

which is true as $\frac{d}{dx}(x) = 1$

We suppose P(m) is true

$$P(m) : \frac{d}{dx}(x^m) = mx^{m-1} \qquad ....(ii)$$

To establish the truth of P($m + 1$), we prove

$$P(m+1) : \frac{d}{dx}(x^{m+1}) = (m+1)x^m$$

$$x^{m+1} = x^1 . x^m$$

$$\frac{d}{dx}(x^{m+1})$$

$\Rightarrow \quad mx^m + x^m = x^m(m+1)$

$\Rightarrow \quad (m+1)x^{(m+1)-1}$

$\therefore \quad$ P($m +1$) is true if P(m) is true but P(1) is true.

$\therefore \quad$ By Principle of Induction P(n) is true for all $n \in N$.

20. Using the fact that sin (A + B) = sin A cos B + cos A sin B and the differentiation, obtain the sum formula for cosines.

Sol. Sin (A + B) = sin A cos B + cos A sin B   ...(i)

Consider A and B as functions of t and differentiating w.r.t. t, we have

$$\cos(A+B)\left(\frac{dA}{dt} + \frac{dB}{dt}\right)$$

$$= \left[\sin A (-\sin B)\frac{dB}{dt} + \cos B \cos A \frac{dA}{dt}\right]$$

$$+ \left[\cos A \cos B \frac{dB}{dt} + \sin B (-\sin A)\frac{dA}{dt}\right]$$

$$\Rightarrow \cos(A+B)\left(\frac{dA}{dt} + \frac{dB}{dt}\right)$$

$$= (\cos A \cos B - \sin A \sin B)\left(\frac{dA}{dt} + \frac{dB}{dt}\right)$$

$$\Rightarrow \cos(A+B) = \cos A \cos B - \sin A \sin B$$

21. Does there exist a function which is continuous everywhere but not differentiable at exactly two points? Justify your answer.

Sol. Consider the function $f(x) = |x| + |x - 1|$

f is continuous every where But it is not differentiable at $x = 0$ and $x = 1$

22. If $y = \begin{vmatrix} \mathbf{f(x)} & \mathbf{g(x)} & \mathbf{h(x)} \\ \ell & \mathbf{m} & \mathbf{n} \\ \mathbf{a} & \mathbf{b} & \mathbf{c} \end{vmatrix}$, **prove that**

$$\frac{dy}{dx} = \begin{vmatrix} \mathbf{f'(x)} & \mathbf{g'(x)} & \mathbf{h'(x)} \\ \ell & \mathbf{m} & \mathbf{n} \\ \mathbf{a} & \mathbf{b} & \mathbf{c} \end{vmatrix}$$

Sol. To differentiate a determinant if

$$y = \begin{vmatrix} f(x) & g(x) & h(x) \\ \ell & m & n \\ a & b & c \end{vmatrix}$$

then $\dfrac{dy}{dx} = \begin{vmatrix} f'(x) & g'(x) & h'(x) \\ \ell & m & n \\ a & b & c \end{vmatrix}$

$$+ \begin{vmatrix} f(x) & g(x) & h(x) \\ 0 & 0 & 0 \\ a & b & c \end{vmatrix} + \begin{vmatrix} f(x) & g(x) & h(x) \\ \ell & m & n \\ 0 & 0 & 0 \end{vmatrix}$$

$$\therefore \quad \frac{dy}{dx} = \begin{vmatrix} f'(x) & g'(x) & h'(x) \\ \ell & m & n \\ a & b & c \end{vmatrix}$$

23. If $y = e^{a\cos^{-1}x}, -1 \le x \le 1$, **show that** $(1 - x^2)$

$$\frac{d^2y}{dx^2} - x\frac{dy}{dx} - a^2 y = 0.$$

Sol. We have $y = e^{a\cos^{-1}x}$

Differentiate w.r.t. x ,

$$\frac{dy}{dx} = y_1 = e^{a\cos^{-1}x}\frac{-a}{\sqrt{1-x^2}}$$

$$\Rightarrow \sqrt{1-x^2}\, y_1 = -ae^{a\cos^{-1}x} , \text{ again differentiate w.r.t. x,}$$

we get

$$\Rightarrow \sqrt{1-x^2}\, y_2 + y_1 \cdot \frac{1}{2}\frac{1}{\sqrt{1-x^2}}(-2x)$$

$$= \frac{a^2 e^{a\cos^{-1}x}}{\sqrt{1-x^2}}$$

$$\Rightarrow (1-x^2)y_2 - xy_1 - a^2 y = 0.$$

Past year Exercise

Short Answer Questions

1. Differentiate $\tan^{-1}\left[\sqrt{\dfrac{1+x^2}{x}}-1\right]$ wrt x.

2. Show that the function
$$f(x)=|x-3|, x \in R,$$
is continuous but not differentiable at $x = 3$.

Or

If $x = a\sin t$ and $y = a\left(\cos t + \log\tan\dfrac{t}{2}\right)$, find $\dfrac{d^2y}{dx^2}$

3. Differentiate the following with respect to x:
$$\sin^{-1}\left(\frac{2^{x+1}.3^x}{1+(36)^x}\right)$$

4. If $y = \log\left[x+\sqrt{x^2+a^2}\right]$, show that
$$\left(x^2+a^2\right)\frac{d^2y}{dx^2}+x\frac{dy}{dx}=0$$

5. If $x\sin(a+y)+\sin a\cos(a+y)=0$, prove that
$$\frac{dy}{dx}=\frac{\sin^2(a+y)}{\sin a}$$

6. Find the value of k, for which
$$f(x)=\begin{cases}\dfrac{\sqrt{1+kx}-\sqrt{1-kx}}{x}, & \text{if } -1\le x<0 \\[2mm] \dfrac{2x+1}{x-1}, & \text{if } 0\le x<1\end{cases}$$
is continuous at $x = 0$

OR

If $x = a\cos^3\theta$ and $y = a\sin^3\theta$, then find the value of $\dfrac{d^2y}{dx^2}$ at $\theta=\dfrac{\pi}{6}$.

7. If $y=\left\{x+\sqrt{x^2+1}\right\}^m$, then show that
$$\left(x^2+1\right)\frac{d^2y}{dx^2}+x\frac{dy}{dx}-m^2y=0$$

8. Differentiate $\tan^{-1}\left(\dfrac{\sqrt{1+x^2}-1}{x}\right)$ with respect to $\sin^{-1}\left(\dfrac{2x}{1+x^2}\right)$, when $x\ne0$

9. If $y=x^x$, prove that $\dfrac{d^2y}{dx^2}-\dfrac{1}{y}\left(\dfrac{dy}{dx}\right)^2-\dfrac{y}{x}=0$

10. If $x=\cos t\,(3-2\cos^2 t)$ and $y=\sin t\,(3-2\sin^2 t)$, find the value of $\dfrac{dy}{dx}$ at $t=\dfrac{\pi}{4}$.

11. If $x=a\sin 2t\,(1+\cos 2t)$ and $y=b\cos 2t\,(1-\cos 2t)$, show that at $t=\dfrac{\pi}{4}$, $\left(\dfrac{dy}{dx}\right)=\dfrac{b}{a}$.

12. If $y=Pe^{ax}+Qe^{bx}$, show that $\dfrac{d^2y}{dx^2}-(a+b)\dfrac{dy}{dx}+aby=0$.

13. Find the value of $\dfrac{dy}{dx}$ at $\theta=\dfrac{\pi}{4}$, if $x=ae^\theta\,(\sin\theta-\cos\theta)$ and $y=ae^\theta\,(\sin\theta+\cos\theta)$

14. Find: $\dfrac{d}{dz}\cos^{-1}\left(\dfrac{z-z^{-1}}{z+z^{-1}}\right)$

15. Find the derivative of the following function $f(x)$
$$=\cos^{-1}\left[\sin\sqrt{\frac{1+x}{2}}\right]+x^x \quad \text{w.r.t. } x, \text{ at } x=1$$

16. If $x=a\cos\theta+b\sin\theta$, $y=a\sin\theta-b\cos\theta$, show that $y^2\dfrac{d^2y}{dx^2}-x\dfrac{dy}{dx}+y=0$.

17. Find the values of p and q for which
$$f(x)=\begin{cases}\dfrac{1-\sin^3 x}{3\cos^2 x}, & \text{if } x<\dfrac{\pi}{2} \\[2mm] p, & \text{if } x=\pi/2 \\[2mm] \dfrac{q(1-\sin x)}{(\pi-2x)^2}, & \text{if } x>\pi/2\end{cases}$$
is continuous at $x=\pi/2$.

18. If $x=\sin t$, $y=\sin pt$, prove that
$$(1-x^2)\frac{d^2y}{dx^2}-x\frac{dy}{dx}+p^2y=0.$$

19. If $y=\sin(\sin x)$, prove that
$$\frac{d^2y}{dx^2}+\tan x\,\frac{dy}{dx}+y\cos^2 x=0.$$

NCERT Exemplar

Multiple Choice Questions

1. If $f(x) = 2x$ and $g(x) = \dfrac{x^2}{2} + 1$, then which of the following can be a discontinuous function?

(a) $f(x) + g(x)$

(b) $f(x) - g(x)$

(c) $f(x).g(x)$

(d) $\dfrac{g(x)}{f(x)}$

2. The function $f(x) = \cot x$ is discontinuous on the set

(a) $\{x = n\pi, n \in Z\}$

(b) $\{x = 2n\pi, n \in Z\}$

(c) $\left\{x = (2n+1)\dfrac{\pi}{2}; n \in Z\right\}$

(d) $\left\{x = \dfrac{n\pi}{2}; n \in Z\right\}$

3. If $f(x) = \begin{cases} mx + 1, & \text{if } x \le \dfrac{\pi}{2} \\ \sin x + n, & \text{if } x > \dfrac{\pi}{2} \end{cases}$ is continuous at $x = \dfrac{\pi}{2}$, then

(a) $m = 1, n = 0$

(b) $m = \dfrac{n\pi}{2} + 1$

(c) $n = \dfrac{m\pi}{2}$

(d) $m = n = \dfrac{\pi}{2}$

4. If $x = t^2$ and $y = t^3$, then $\dfrac{d^2 y}{dx^2}$ is equal to

(a) $\dfrac{3}{2}$

(b) $\dfrac{3}{4t}$

(c) $\dfrac{3}{2t}$

(d) $\dfrac{3}{2t}$

Short Answer Questions

5. Find the differentiability of the function

$$f(x) = \begin{cases} 1 + x, & \text{if } x \le 2 \\ 5 - x, & \text{if } x > 2 \end{cases} \text{ at } x = 2.$$

6. If $y = \log(x + \sqrt{x^2 + a})$, then find $\dfrac{dy}{dx}$.

7. If $y = \tan^{-1}(\sec x + \tan x)$, $\dfrac{-\pi}{2} < x < \dfrac{\pi}{2}$, then find $\dfrac{dy}{dx}$.

8. If, $x = e^{\theta}\left(\theta + \dfrac{1}{\theta}\right)$, $y = e^{-\theta}\left(\theta - \dfrac{1}{\theta}\right)$, then find $\dfrac{dy}{dx}$.

Objective Practice Exercise

Multiple Choice Questions

DIRECTIONS : *This section contains multiple choice questions. Each question has four choices (a), (b), (c) and (d) out of which only one is correct.*

1. If $f(x) = \begin{cases} x + \lambda, & x < 3 \\ 4, & x = 3 \\ 3x - 5, & x > 3 \end{cases}$ is continuous at $x = 3$, then $\lambda =$

(a) 4

(b) 3

(c) 2

(d) 1

2. The value of k so that the function

$$f(x) = \begin{cases} k(2x - x)^2, & \text{when } x < 0 \\ \cos x, & \text{when } x \ge 0 \end{cases} \text{ is continuous at } x = 0,$$
is

(a) 1

(b) 2

(c) 4

(d) None of these

3. Let $f(x) = \begin{cases} \dfrac{x - 4}{|x - 4|} + a, & x < 4 \\ a + b, & x = 4 \\ \dfrac{x - 4}{|x - 4|} + b, & x > 4 \end{cases}$. Then $f(x)$ is continuous at $x = 4$ when

(a) $a = 0, b = 0$

(b) $a = 1, b = 1$

(c) $a = -1, b = 1$

(d) $a = 1, b = -1$

4. If $f(x) = \begin{cases} \dfrac{x}{e^{1/x} + 1}, & \text{when } x \ne 0 \\ 0, & \text{when } x = 0 \end{cases}$, then

(a) $\lim_{x \to 0^+} f(x) = 1$

(b) $\lim_{x \to 0^-} f(x) = 1$

(c) $f(x)$ is continuous at $x = 0$

(d) None of these

5. If $f(x) = \begin{cases} \sin^{-1}|x|, & \text{when } x \neq 0 \\ 0, & \text{when } x = 0 \end{cases}$ then

   (a) $\lim\limits_{x \to 0^+} f(x) \neq 0$

   (b) $\lim\limits_{x \to 0^-} f(x) \neq 0$

   (c) $f(x)$ is continuous at $x = 0$

   (d) None of these

6. If the function $f(x) = \begin{cases} 1 + \sin\dfrac{\pi x}{2}, & \text{for } -\infty < x \leq 1 \\ ax + b, & \text{for } 1 < x < 3 \\ 6\tan\dfrac{x\pi}{12}, & \text{for } 3 \leq x < 6 \end{cases}$ is

   continuous in the interval $(-\infty, 6)$, then the values of a and b are respectively

   (a) $0, 2$ (b) $1, 1$ (c) $2, 0$ (d) $2, 1$

7. Let $f(x) \begin{cases} \dfrac{x^4 - 5x^2 + 4}{|(x-1)(x-2)|}, & x \neq 1, 2 \\ 6, & x = 1 \\ 12, & x = 2 \end{cases}$

   Then $f(x)$ is continuous on the set

   (a) R (b) $R - \{1\}$

   (c) $R - \{2\}$ (d) $R - \{1, 2\}$

8. If $f(x) = \begin{cases} \dfrac{\sqrt{1+kx} - \sqrt{1-kx}}{x} & \text{for } -1 \leq x < 0 \\ 2x^2 + 3x - 2, & \text{for } 0 \leq x \leq 1 \end{cases}$ is

   continuous at $x = 0$, then $k =$

   (a) -4 (b) -3 (c) -2 (d) -1

9. The value of $f(0)$, so that the function

   $$f(x) = \frac{(27 - 2x)^{1/3} - 3}{9 - 3(243 + 5x)^{1/5}}, \ (x \neq 0) \text{ is continuous, at}$$

   $x = 0$ is given by

   (a) $\dfrac{2}{3}$ (b) 6 (c) 2 (d) 4

10. If $f(x) = \begin{cases} \dfrac{x^2 - 4x + 3}{x^2 - 1}, & \text{for } x \neq 1 \\ 2, & \text{for } x = 1 \end{cases}$, then

    (a) $\lim\limits_{x \to 1^+} f(x) = 2$

    (b) $\lim\limits_{x \to 1^-} f(x) = 3$

    (c) $f(x)$ is discontinuous at $x = 1$

    (d) None of these

11. If $f(x) = \begin{cases} \dfrac{|x - a|}{x - a}, & \text{when } x \neq a \\ 1, & \text{when } x = a \end{cases}$, then

    (a) $f(x)$ is continuous at $x = a$

    (b) $f(x)$ is discontinuous at $x = a$

    (c) $\lim\limits_{x \to a} f(x) = 1$

    (d) None of these

12. The function $f(x) = [x]^2 - [x^2]$ (where $[y]$ is the greatest integer less than or equal to y), is discontinuous at

    (a) All integers

    (b) All integers except 0 and 1

    (c) All integers except 0

    (d) All integers except 1

13. $f(x) = \begin{cases} 2x, & x < 0 \\ 2x + 1, & x \geq 0 \end{cases}$. Then

    (a) $f(|x|)$ is continuous at $x = 0$

    (b) $f(x)$ is continuous at $x = 0$

    (c) $f(x)$ is discontinuous at $x = 0$

    (d) None of these

14. $f(x) = x + |x|$ is continuous for

    (a) $x \in (-\infty, \infty)$ (b) $x \in (-\infty, \infty) - \{0\}$

    (c) Only $x > 0$ (d) No value of x

15. At which points the function $f(x) = \dfrac{x}{[x]}$, where $[.]$ is greatest integer function, is discontinuous

    (a) Only positive integers

    (b) All positive and negative integers and $(0, 1)$

    (c) All rational numbers

    (d) None of these

16. If $f(x) = \begin{cases} 1 + x^2, & \text{when } 0 \leq x \leq 1 \\ 1 - x, & \text{when } x > 1 \end{cases}$, then

    (a) $\lim\limits_{x \to 1^+} f(x) \neq 0$

    (b) $\lim\limits_{x \to 1^-} f(x) \neq 2$

    (c) $f(x)$ is discontinuous at $x = 1$

    (d) None of these

17. If $f(x) = \dfrac{1}{2}x - 1$, then on the interval $[0, \pi]$

    (a) $\tan[f(x)]$ and $1/f(x)$ are both continuous

    (b) $\tan[f(x)]$ and $1/f(x)$ are both discontinuous

    (c) $\tan[f(x)]$ and $f^{-1}(x)$ are both continuous

    (d) $\tan[f(x)]$ is continuous but $1/f(x)$ is not

18. If $f(x) = \begin{cases} -x^2, \text{when } x \le 0 \\ 5x-4, \text{when } 0 < x \le 1 \\ 4x^2 - 3x, \text{when } 1 < x < 2 \\ 3x+4, \text{when } x \ge 2 \end{cases}$, then

    (a) $f(x)$ is continuous at $x = 0$

    (b) $f(x)$ is continuous at $x = 2$

    (c) $f(x)$ is discontinuous at $x = 1$

    (d) None of these

19. If $f(x) = \begin{cases} x \sin x, \text{when } 0 < x \le \dfrac{\pi}{2} \\ \dfrac{\pi}{2} \sin(\pi + x), \text{when } \dfrac{\pi}{2} < x < \pi \end{cases}$, then

    (a) $f(x)$ is discontinuous at $x = \dfrac{\pi}{2}$

    (b) $f(x)$ is continuous at $x = \dfrac{\pi}{2}$

    (c) $f(x)$ is continuous at $x = 0$

    (d) None of these

20. The function $f(x) = x - |x - x^2|$ is

    (a) Continuous at $x = 1$ (b) Discontinuous at $x = 1$

    (c) Not defined at $x = 1$ (d) None of these

21. The function $f(x) = \dfrac{2x^2 + 7}{x^3 + 3x^2 - x - 3}$ is discontinuous for

    (a) $x = 1$ only

    (b) $x = 1$ and $x = -1$ only

    (c) $x = 1, x = -1, x = -3$ only

    (d) $x = 1, x = -1, x = -3$ and other values of x

22. If $f(x) = \begin{cases} x, \text{when } 0 < x < 1/2 \\ 1, \text{when } x = 1/2 \\ 1-x, \text{when } 1/2 < x < 1 \end{cases}$, then

    (a) $\lim\limits_{x \to 1/2^+} f(x) = 2$

    (b) $\lim\limits_{x \to 1/2^-} f(x) = 2$

    (c) $f(x)$ is continuous at $x = 1/2$

    (d) $f(x)$ is discontinous at $x = 1/2$

23. If $f(x) = \begin{cases} 1, \text{when } 0 < x \le \dfrac{3\pi}{4} \\ 2 \sin \dfrac{2}{9} x, \text{when } \dfrac{3\pi}{4} < x < \pi \end{cases}$

    (a) $f(x)$ is continuous at $x = 0$

    (b) $f(x)$ is continuous at $x = \pi$

    (c) $f(x)$ is continuous at $x = \dfrac{3\pi}{4}$

    (d) $f(x)$ is discontinuous at $x = \dfrac{3\pi}{4}$

24. For the function $f(x) = \begin{cases} \dfrac{\sin^2 ax}{x^2}, \text{when } x \ne 0 \\ 1, \text{when } x = 0 \end{cases}$ which one is a true statement

    (a) $f(x)$ is continuous at $x = 0$

    (b) $f(x)$ is discontinuous at $x = 0$, when $a \ne \pm 1$

    (c) $f(x)$ is continuous at $x = a$

    (d) None of these

25. If $f(x) = \begin{cases} \dfrac{5}{2} - x, \text{when } x < 2 \\ 1, \text{when } x = 2 \\ x - \dfrac{3}{2}, \text{when } x > 2 \end{cases}$, then

    (a) $f(x)$ is continuous at $x = 2$

    (b) $f(x)$ is discontinuous at $x = 2$

    (c) $\lim\limits_{x \to 2} f(x) = 1$

    (d) None of these

26. If $f(x) = \begin{cases} e^{1/x}, \text{when } x \ne 0 \\ 0, \text{when } x = 0 \end{cases}$, then

    (a) $\lim\limits_{x \to 0+} f(x) = e$

    (b) $\lim\limits_{x \to 0+} f(x) = 0$

    (c) $f(x)$ is discontinuous at $x = 0$

    (d) None of these

27. If $f(x) = \begin{cases} e^x; x \le 0 \\ |1 - x|; x > 0 \end{cases}$, then

    (a) $f(x)$ is differentiable at $x = 0$

    (b) $f(x)$ is continuous at $x = 0$

    (c) $f(x)$ is differentiable at $x = 1$

    (d) $f(x)$ is not continuous at $x = 1$

28. Consider $f(x) = \begin{cases} \dfrac{x^2}{|x|}, x \ne 0 \\ 0, x = 0 \end{cases}$

    (a) $f(x)$ is discontinuous everywhere

    (b) $f(x)$ is continuous everywhere

    (c) $f(x)$ exists in $(-1, 1)$

    (d) $f(x)$ exists in $(-2, 2)$

29. A function f(x) is defined as follows for real x

$$f(x) = \begin{cases} 1-x^2, & \text{for } x < 1 \\ 0, & \text{for } x = 1 \\ 1+x^2, & \text{for } x > 1 \end{cases}, \text{ then}$$

(a) f(x) is not continuous at x = 1
(b) f(x) is continuous but not differentiable at x = 1
(c) f(x) is both continuous and differentiable at x = 1
(d) f(x) is continuous everywhere but differentiable no where

30. If $f(x) = x\,[\sqrt{x} - \sqrt{x+1}]$, then :

(a) f(x) is continuous but not differentiable at x = 0
(b) f(x) is not differentiable at x = 0
(c) f(x) is differentiable at x = 0
(d) None of these

31. At the point x = 1, the given function

$$f(x) = \begin{cases} x^3 - 1; & 1 < x < \infty \\ x - 1; & -\infty < x \le 1 \end{cases} \text{ is}$$

(a) Continuous and differentiable
(b) Continuous and not differentiable
(c) Discontinuous and differentiable
(d) Discontinuous and nor differentiable

32. If $f(x) = \begin{cases} e^x + ax, & x < 0 \\ b(x-1)^2, & x \ge 0 \end{cases}$ is differentiable at x = 0, then (a, b) is

(a) (–3, –1)   (b) (–3, 1)   (c) (3, 1)   (d) (3, –1)

33. The function $y = e^{-|x|}$ is

(a) Continuous and differentiable at x = 0
(b) Neither continuous nor differentiable at x = 0
(c) Continuous but not differentiable at x = 0
(d) Not continuous but differentiable at x = 0

34. If $u = f(x^3)$, $v = g(x^2)$, $f'(x) = \cos x$ and $g'(x) = \sin x$, then $\dfrac{du}{dv} =$

(a) $\dfrac{1}{2} x \cos x^3 \cosec x^2$ (b) $\dfrac{3}{2} x \cos x^3 \cosec x^2$

(c) $\dfrac{1}{2} x \sec x^3 \sin x^2$ (d) $\dfrac{3}{2} x \sec x^3 \cosec x^2$

35. A differentiable function f(x) is defined for all x > 0 and satisfies $f(x^3) = 4x^4$ for all x > 0. The value of $f'(8)$ is

(a) $\dfrac{16}{3}$ (b) $\dfrac{32}{3}$

(c) $\dfrac{16\sqrt{2}}{3}$ (d) $\dfrac{32\sqrt{2}}{3}$

36. If $y = \cot^{-1}(\cos 2x)^{1/2}$, then the value of $\dfrac{dy}{dx}$ at $x = \dfrac{\pi}{6}$ will be

(a) $\left(\dfrac{2}{3}\right)^{1/2}$ (b) $\left(\dfrac{1}{3}\right)^{1/2}$

(c) $(3)^{1/2}$ (d) $(6)^{1/2}$

37. If $y = e^{(1+\log_e x)}$, then $\dfrac{dy}{dx}$ is equal to

(a) e   (b) 1   (c) 0   (d) $\log_e x \cdot x$

38. If $xe^{xy} = y + \sin^2 x$, then at x = 0, $\dfrac{dy}{dx} =$

(a) –1   (b) –2   (c) 1   (d) 2

39. The value of the derivative of $|x-1| + |x-3|$ at $x = 2$ is :

(a) 2   (b) 1   (c) 0   (d) –2

40. If $y = \cot^{-1}(x^2)$, then $\dfrac{dy}{dx}$ is equal to :

(a) $\dfrac{2x}{1+x^4}$ (b) $\dfrac{2x}{\sqrt{1+4x}}$

(c) $\dfrac{-2x}{1+x^4}$ (d) $\dfrac{-2x}{\sqrt{1+x^2}}$

41. If $y = (\cos x^2)^2$ then $\dfrac{dy}{dx}$ is equal to :

(a) $-4x \sin 2x^2$ (b) $-x \sin x^2$
(c) $-2x \sin 2x^2$ (d) $-x \cos 2x^2$

42. If $x = \dfrac{1-t^2}{1+t^2}$ and $y = \dfrac{2t}{1+t^2}$, then $\dfrac{dy}{dx}$ is equal to :

(a) $-\dfrac{y}{x}$ (b) $\dfrac{y}{x}$ (c) $-\dfrac{x}{y}$ (d) $\dfrac{x}{y}$

43. If $y = \log x.e^{(\tan x + x^2)}$, then $\dfrac{dy}{dx} =$

(a) $e^{(\tan x + x^2)}\left[\dfrac{1}{x} + \left(\sec^2 x + x\right)\log x\right]$

(b) $e^{(\tan x + x^2)}\left[\dfrac{1}{x} + \left(\sec^2 x - x\right)\log x\right]$

(c) $e^{(\tan x + x^2)}\left[\dfrac{1}{x} + \left(\sec^2 x + 2x\right)\log x\right]$

(d) $e^{(\tan x + x^2)}\left[\dfrac{1}{x} + \left(\sec^2 x - 2x\right)\log x\right]$

44. If $y = f\left(\dfrac{2x-1}{x^2+1}\right)$ and $f'(x) = \sin x^2$, then $\dfrac{dy}{dx} =$

(a) $\dfrac{6x^2 - 2x + 2}{(x^2+1)^2} \sin\left(\dfrac{2x-1}{x^2+1}\right)^2$

(b) $\dfrac{6x^2 - 2x + 2}{(x^2+1)^2} \sin^2\left(\dfrac{2x-1}{x^2+1}\right)$

(c) $\dfrac{-2x^2 + 2x + 2}{(x^2+1)^2} \sin^2\left(\dfrac{2x-1}{x^2+1}\right)$

(d) $\dfrac{-2x^2 + 2x + 2}{(x^2+1)^2} \sin\left(\dfrac{2x-1}{x^2+1}\right)^2$

45. If $f(x) = \log_x (\ln x)$, then at $x = e$, $f'(x)$ equals-

(a) 0   (b) 1

(c) e (d) $1/e$

46. If $\sqrt{1-x^{2n}} + \sqrt{1-y^{2n}} = a(x^n - y^n)$, then $\sqrt{\dfrac{1-x^{2n}}{1-y^{2n}}}\dfrac{dy}{dx}$ is equal to

(a) 1   (b) x/y

(c) $\dfrac{x^{n-1}}{y^{n-1}}$ (d) None of these

47. If $y = \cos^{-1}(\cos x)$, then $y'(x)$ is equal to

(a) 1 for all x

(b) -1 for all x

(c) 1 in 2nd and 3rd quadrant

(d) -1 in 3rd and 4th quadrant

48. If $x = \exp\left\{\tan^{-1}\left(\dfrac{y-x^2}{x^2}\right)\right\}$, then $\dfrac{dy}{dx}$ equals

(a) $2x\,[1 + \tan(\log x)] + x\sec^2(\log x)$

(b) $x\,[1 + \tan(\log x)] + \sec^2(\log x)$

(c) $2x\,[1 + \tan(\log x)] + x^2\sec^2(\log x)$

(d) $2x\,[1 + \tan(\log x)] + \sec^2(\log x)$

49. If $y = \sin x + e^x$, then $\dfrac{d^2x}{dy^2}$ is equal to

(a) $\dfrac{\sin x - e^x}{(\cos x + e^x)^2}$ (b) $\dfrac{\sin x - e^x}{(\cos x + e^x)^3}$

(c) $\dfrac{\sin x + e^x}{(\cos x - e^x)^2}$ (d) $(-\sin x + e^x)^{-1}$

50. If $x = a\sin\theta$ and $y = b\cos\theta$, then $\dfrac{d^2y}{dx^2}$ is

(a) $\dfrac{a}{b^2}\sec^2\theta$ (b) $\dfrac{-b}{a}\sec^2\theta$

(c) $\dfrac{-b}{a^2}\sec^3\theta$ (d) $\dfrac{b}{a^2}\sec^3\theta$

Case/Passage Based Questions

DIRECTIONS : *Study the given Case/Passage and answer the following questions.*

Case/Passage

A potter made a mud vessel, where the shape of the pot is based on $f(x) = |x-3| + |x-2|$, where $f(x)$ represents the height of the pot. **[From CBSE Question Bank-2021]**

51. When $x > 4$. What will be the height in terms of x ?

(a) $x - 2$ (b) $x - 3$

(c) $2x - 5$ (d) $5 - 2x$

52. Will the slope vary with x value?

(a) Yes   (b) No

53. What is $\dfrac{dy}{dx}$ at $x = 3$

(a) 2

(b) -2

(c) Function is not differentiable

(d) 1

54. When the x value lies between $(2,3)$ then the function is

(a) $2x - 5$ (b) $5 - 2x$

(c) 1   (d) 5

55. If the potter is trying to make a pot using the function $f(x) = [x]$, will he get a pot or not? Why?

(a) Yes, because it is a continuous function

(b) Yes, because it is not continuous

(c) No, because it is a continuous function

(d) No, because it is not continuous

Chapter Test

Time : 45 Minutes   **Max. Marks : 20**

Directions :

(i)   Questions number **1-8** carry **1 mark** each.

(ii)   Question number **9** carry **4 marks.**

(iii)   Questions number **10-13** are **Very Short Answer Questions** and carry **2 marks** each.

Multiple Choice Questions

1. The function $f(x) = \dfrac{4-x^2}{4x-x^3}$ is

   (a)   discontinuous at only one point

   (b)   discontinuous at exactly two points

   (c)   discontinuous at exactly three points

   (d)   None of the above

2. If $y = \sqrt{\sin x + y}$, then $\dfrac{dy}{dx}$ is equal to

   (a) $\dfrac{\cos x}{2y-1}$ (b) $\dfrac{\cos x}{1-2y}$

   (c) $\dfrac{\sin x}{1-2y}$ (d) $\dfrac{\sin x}{2y-1}$

3. The derivative of $\cos^{-1}(2x^2 - 1)$ w.r.t. $\cos^{-1}x$ is

   (a)   2   (b) $\dfrac{-1}{2\sqrt{1-x^2}}$

   (c) $\dfrac{2}{x}$ (d) $1 - x^2$

4. If $f(x) = \begin{cases} mx+1, & \text{if } x \le \dfrac{\pi}{2} \\ \sin x + n, & \text{if } x > \dfrac{\pi}{2} \end{cases}$ is continuous at $x = \dfrac{\pi}{2}$,

   then

   (a) $m=1, n=0$ (b) $m=\dfrac{n\pi}{2}+1$

   (c) $n=\dfrac{m\pi}{2}$ (d) $m=n=\dfrac{\pi}{2}$

One Word Answer Questions

5. Differentiate $\cos^2(x^2)$ w.r.t. x^2.

6. If $f(x) = x^2 + 1$, find $\dfrac{d}{dx}[\text{fof}(x)]$

Assertion & Reason Questions

   (a)   If both Assertion and Reason are correct and the Reason is the correct explanation of the Assertion.

   (b)   If both Assertion and Reason are correct but Reason is not the correct explanation of the Assertion.

   (c)   If the Assertion is correct but Reason is incorrect.

   (d)   If the Assertion is incorrect but the Reason is correct.

7. **Assertion:** $f(x) = \dfrac{x^2+5x+6}{x^2-4x+4}$ is continuous for R.

   Reason: A polynomial function is everywhere continuous.

8. **Assertion:** The function $f(x) = |2x - 1|\sin x$ is differentiable on the set $R - \left\{\dfrac{1}{2}\right\}$.

   Reason: The function $f(x) = |2x - 1|$ is discontinuous at $x = \dfrac{1}{2}$.

Case/Passage Based Questions

DIRECTIONS (Q. 9) : *has 5 subparts based on case/passage given, attempt any 4 out of 5 questions.*

9. A pilot while driving his plane along with path given by $f(y) = \dfrac{1}{y^2+y-2}$, where $y = \dfrac{1}{t-1}$ and all the points of discontinuity are considered dangerous points on the path.

Based on the above information answer the following:

(i)   The value of f at which y is not define is

   (a)   1   (b)   0

   (c)   2   (d)   None

(ii) The value of y at which f(y) is not define are

    (a) 1, 2   (b) –2, 1

    (c) –1, 2   (d) –2, –1

(iii) The dangerous points are

    (a) 1, 2   (b) –1, 2

    (c) $1, \dfrac{1}{2}$ (d) $\dfrac{1}{2}, 1, 2$

(iv) The value of f(y) is

    (a) $\dfrac{-14}{9}$ (b) $\dfrac{1}{18}$

    (c) $\dfrac{5}{9}$ (d) $\dfrac{1}{9}$

(v) The value of f ′(5) is

    (a) $\dfrac{-11}{784}$ (b) $\dfrac{1}{784}$

    (c) $\dfrac{-11}{28}$ (d) None

10. Find $\dfrac{dy}{dx}$, if $y = \tan^{-1}\left(\dfrac{3x - x^3}{1 - 3x^2}\right)$, $-\dfrac{1}{\sqrt{3}} < x < \dfrac{1}{\sqrt{3}}$

11. Let $f(x) = \begin{cases} \left[\tan\left(\dfrac{\pi}{4} + x\right)\right]^{1/x} & , x \neq 0 \\ k & , x = 0 \end{cases}$

For what value of k is f (x) continuous at x = 0

12. Let f (x) be a continuous function and g (x) be a discontinuous function. Prove that f (x) + g (x) is a discontinuous function.

13. Discuss the continuity of the function f(x) = sin x. cos x.

Solutions

Practice Exercise-1

1. (b) 2. (d) 3. (c) 4. (d) 5. (c)

6. (d) 7. (a) 8. (c)

9. (i) (b) (ii) (a) (ii) (c) (iv) (a) (v) (d)

10. 2

11. $\dfrac{1}{3}$

12. The given function is not continuous for any value of k.

13. $k = 4$

14. No value of λ

15. $f(0) = 0 + 0 + \lambda \ln 4 = \lambda \ln 4$ ...(i)

$$\text{R.H.L.} = \lim_{x \to 0^+} f(x) = \lim_{h \to 0} f(0+h)$$

$$= \lim_{h \to 0} \frac{8^h - 4^h - 2^h + 1^h}{h^2} = \lim_{h \to 0} \frac{(4^h - 1)(2^h - 1)}{h \cdot h}$$

$$= \lim_{h \to 0} \left(\frac{4^h - 1}{h}\right) \lim_{h \to 0} \left(\frac{2^h - 1}{h}\right) = \ln 4 \cdot \ln 2 \quad \text{...(ii)}$$

$$\therefore f(0) = \text{R.H.L.} \Rightarrow \lambda = \ln 2.$$

16. Given $f(x) = \begin{cases} \dfrac{2\sin x - \sin 2x}{2x \cos x}, & \text{if } x \neq 0 \\ a, & \text{if } x = 0 \end{cases}$

Now, $\lim\limits_{x \to 0} f(x) = \lim\limits_{x \to 0} \dfrac{2\sin x - \sin 2x}{2x \cos x} \left(\dfrac{0}{0} \text{form}\right)$

$$= \lim_{x \to 0} \frac{2\sin x (1 - \cos x)}{2x \cos x} = \lim_{x \to 0} \frac{\tan x}{x} \cdot \lim_{x \to 0} (1 - \cos x)$$

$$= 1.0 = 0$$

17. $\dfrac{1}{2}$

18. $\lim\limits_{x \to 4^-} f(x) = \lim\limits_{h \to 0} f(4-h) = \lim\limits_{h \to 0} \dfrac{4-h-4}{|4-h-4|} + a$

$$= \lim_{h \to 0} -\frac{h}{h} + a = a - 1. = \lim_{x \to 4^+} f(x) = \lim_{h \to 0} f(4+h)$$

$$= \lim_{h \to 0} \frac{4+h-4}{|4+h-4|} + b = b + 1 \text{ and } f(4) = a+b$$

Since $f(x)$ is continuous at $x = 4$

Therefore $\lim\limits_{x \to 4^-} f(x) = f(4) = \lim\limits_{x \to 4^+} f(x)$

$\Rightarrow a - 1 = a + b = b + 1 \Rightarrow b = -1 \text{ and } a = 1.$

19. $\text{LHL} = \lim\limits_{h \to 0} f(0-h) = \lim\limits_{h \to 0} \dfrac{\sin 5(0-h)}{(0-h)^2 + 2(0-h)}$

$$= -\lim_{h \to 0} \frac{\dfrac{\sin 5h}{5h}}{\dfrac{1}{5}(h-2)} = \frac{5}{2}$$

$$\text{RHL} = \lim_{x \to 0^+} \frac{\sin 5x}{x^2 + 2x} = \lim_{x \to 0^+} \frac{\sin 5x}{5x} \cdot \lim_{x \to 0^+} \frac{1}{(x+2)} = \frac{5}{2}$$

$$f(0) = k + \frac{1}{2}$$

Since, it is continuous at $x = 0$ $\therefore$ LHL = RHL = f(0)

$$\Rightarrow \frac{5}{2} = k + \frac{1}{2} \Rightarrow k = 2$$

NCERT Exercise-1

1. (i) At $x = 0$, $\lim\limits_{x \to 0} f(x) = \lim\limits_{x \to 0} (5x - 3) = -3$ and

$f(0) = -3$

$\therefore$ f is continuous at $x = 0$

(ii) At $x = -3$, $\lim\limits_{x \to -3} f(x) = \lim\limits_{x \to -3} (5x - 3) = -18$ and

$f(-3) = -18$

$\therefore$ f is continuous at $x = -3$

(iii) At $x = 5$, $\lim\limits_{x \to 5} f(x) = \lim\limits_{x \to 5} (5x - 3) = 22$ and

$f(5) = 22$

$\therefore$ f is continuous at $x = 5$

2. $\lim\limits_{x \to 3} f(x) = \lim\limits_{x \to 3} (2x^2 - 1) = 17$ and $f(3) = 17$

$\therefore$ f is continuous at $x = 3$

3. (a) $f(x) = (x - 5) \Rightarrow (x - 5)$ is a polynomial

$\therefore$ it is continuous at each $x \in R$.

(b) $f(x) = \dfrac{1}{x-5}$ at $x = 5$, $f(x)$ is not defined.

$\therefore$ f is not continuous at $x = 5$ when $x \neq 5$,

$$\lim_{x \to c} \frac{1}{x-5} = \frac{1}{c-5}$$

Also $f(c) = \dfrac{1}{c-5}$ $\therefore$ f is continuous at

$x \in R - \{5\}$.

(c) $f(x) = \dfrac{x^2-25}{x+5}$ at $x = -5$, function f is not defined.

  $\therefore$ f is discontinuous at $x = -5$

  $\therefore$ f is continuous for all $x \in R - \{-5\}$.

(d) $f(x) = |x-5|$ at $x = 5$, $f(5) = |5-5| = 0$

  $$\lim_{x \to 5} |x-5| = 0$$

  $\therefore$ f is continuous at $x = 5$

  at $x = c > 5$, $\lim\limits_{x \to c} |x-5| = c-5 \ [c > 5]$

  also $f(c) = c-5$ f is continuous at $x = c > 5$

  Similarly at $x = c < 5$

  $$\lim_{x \to c} |x-5| = 5-c, \ f(c) = 5-c$$

  $\therefore$ f is continuous at $x = c < 5$

  Thus f is continuous for all $x \in R$.

4. $f(x) = x^n$ is a polynomial which is continuous for all $x \in$ R. Hence f is continuous at $x = n$, $n \in N$.

5. (i) At $x = 0$

  $$\lim_{x \to 0^-} f(x) = \lim_{x \to 0^-} x = 0 \text{ and}$$

  $$\lim_{x \to 0^+} f(x) = \lim_{x \to 0^+} x = 0 \ \Rightarrow \ f(0) = 0$$

  $\therefore$ f is continuous at $x = 0$

  (ii) At $x = 1$

  $$\lim_{x \to 1^-} f(x) = \lim_{x \to 1^-} (x) = 1 \text{ and}$$

  $$\lim_{x \to 1^+} f(x) = \lim_{x \to 1^+} (x) = 5$$

  $\therefore \ \lim\limits_{x \to 1^-} f(x) \neq \lim\limits_{x \to 1^+} f(x)$

  $\therefore$ f is discontinuous at $x = 1$

  (iii) At $x = 2$

  $$\lim_{x \to 2} f(x) = 5, \ f(2) = 5$$

  $\therefore$ f is continuous at $x = 2$

6. $f(x) = \begin{cases} 2x+3, & x \leq 2 \\ 2x-3, & x > 2 \end{cases}$ at $x \neq 2$

  L.H.L. $= \lim\limits_{x \to 2^-} (2x+3) = 7$, $f(2) = 2 \times 2 + 3 = 7$

  R.H.L. $= \lim\limits_{x \to 2^+} (2x-3) = 2 \times 2 - 3 = 1$

  $\Rightarrow$ L.H.L. $\neq$ R.H.L.

  $\therefore$ f is discontinuous at $x = 2$

  at $x = c < 2$

  $$\lim_{x \to c} (2x+3) = 2c+3 = f(c)$$

  $\therefore$ f is continuous at $x = c < 2$

  at $x = c > 2$, $\lim\limits_{x \to c} (2x-3) = 2c-3 = f(c)$

  $\therefore$ f is continuous at $x = c > 2$ $\Rightarrow$ Point of discontinuity is $x = 2$

7. $f(x) = \begin{cases} |x|+3, & \text{if } x \leq -3 \\ -2x, & \text{if } -3 < x < 3 \\ 6x+2, & \text{if } x > 3 \end{cases}$

  at $x = -3$, L.H.L. $= \lim\limits_{x \to -3^-} (|x|+3) = \lim\limits_{x \to -3^-} (-x+3)$

  $= 3+3 = 6$, $f(-3) = |-3|+3 = 6$

  R.H.L. $= \lim\limits_{x \to -3^+} f(x) = \lim\limits_{x \to -3^+} = (-2x) = 6$

  L.H.L. $=$ R.H.L. $= f(-3)$ $\Rightarrow$ f is continuous at $x = -3$

  at $x = 3$ L.H.L. $= \lim\limits_{x \to 3^-} f(x) = \lim\limits_{x \to 3^-} (-2x) = -6$, R.H.L.

  $= \lim\limits_{x \to 3^+} f(x) = \lim\limits_{x \to 3^+} (6x+2) = 20$

  $f(3)$ is not defined. L.H.L. $\neq$ R.H.L. $\neq f(3)$

  $\therefore$ f is discontinuous at $x = 3$

  at $x = c < -3$ $\lim\limits_{x \to -c} (|x|+3) = -c+3 = f(c)$

  $\Rightarrow$ $\lim\limits_{x \to -c} f(x) = f(c)$

  $\Rightarrow$ f is continuous at $x = c < -3$ at $x = c$, when $-3 < x < 3$

  $\lim\limits_{x \to c} (-2x) = -2c = f(c) \Rightarrow \lim\limits_{x \to c} f(x) = f(c)$

  $\therefore$ f is continuous at $x = c$, where $-3 < c < 3$

  at $x = c > 3$, $\lim\limits_{x \to c} (6x+2) = 6c+2 = f(c)$

  $\Rightarrow$ $\lim\limits_{x \to c} f(x) = f(c)$

  $\Rightarrow$ f is continuous at $x = c > 3$

8. We have,

$$(\text{LHL at } x = 0) = \lim_{x \to 0^-} f(x) = \lim_{h \to 0} f(0-h) = \lim_{h \to 0} f(-h)$$

$$= \lim_{h \to 0} \frac{|-h|}{-h} = \lim_{h \to 0} \frac{h}{-h} = \lim_{h \to 0} -1 = -1$$

and, $(\text{RHL at } x = 0) = \lim_{x \to 0^+} f(x) = \lim_{h \to 0} f(0+h) = \lim_{h \to 0} f(h)$

$$= \lim_{h \to 0} \frac{|h|}{h} = \lim_{h \to 0} \frac{h}{h} = \lim_{h \to 0} 1 = 1$$

Thus, we have $\lim_{x \to 0^-} f(x) \neq \lim_{x \to 0^+} f(x)$

Hence, $f(x)$ is not continuous at the origin.

9. We have $f(x) = \begin{cases} \dfrac{x}{|x|}; & \text{if } x < 0 \\ -1; & \text{if } x \geq 0 \end{cases}$

$$\text{L.H.L (at } x = 0) = \lim_{x \to 0^-} f(x) = \lim_{h \to 0} f(0-h)$$

$$= \lim_{h \to 0} f(-h) = \lim_{h \to 0} \frac{-h}{|-h|} = -1$$

and R.H.L (at $x = 0$)

$$= \lim_{x \to 0^+} f(x) = \lim_{h \to 0}(f(0+h)) = \lim_{h \to 0} f(h) = \lim_{h \to 0}(-1) = -1$$

Also $f(0) = -1$

Thus, we have $\lim_{x \to 0^-} f(x) = \lim_{x \to 0^+} f(x) = f(0)$

Hence $f(x)$ is continuous at $x = 0$.

10. $f(x) = \begin{cases} x+1 & ,\text{if } x \geq 1 \\ x^2+1 & ,\text{if } x < 1 \end{cases}$

At $x = 1$, L.H.L. $= \lim_{x \to 1^-} f(x) = \lim_{x \to 1^-}(x^2+1) = 2$

R.H.L. $= \lim_{x \to 1^+} f(x) = \lim_{x \to 1^+}(x+1) = 2$,

$f(1) = 1 + 1 = 2$

$\Rightarrow f$ is continuous at $x = 1$

At $x = c > 1$, $\lim_{x \to c} f(x) = \lim_{x \to c}(x+1) = c + 1 = f(c)$

$\Rightarrow f$ is continuous at $x = c > 1$, At $x = c < 1$,

$\lim_{x \to c} f(x) = \lim_{x \to c}(x^2+1) = c^2 + 1 = f(c)$

$\Rightarrow f$ is continuous at $x = c < 1$, there is no point of discontinuity at any point $x \in R$

11. $f(x) = \begin{cases} x^3-3, & \text{if } x \leq 2 \\ x^2+1, & \text{if } x > 2 \end{cases}$

At $x = 2$, L.H.L. $= \lim_{x \to 2^-}(x^3-3) = 8 - 3 = 5$

R.H.L. $= \lim_{x \to 2^+}(x^2+1) = 4 + 1 = 5$

$f(2) = 2^3 - 3 = 8 - 3 = 5 \Rightarrow f$ is continuous at $x = 2$

At $x = c < 2$, $\lim_{x \to c}(x^3-3) = c^3 - 3 = f(c)$,

At $x = c > 2$, $\lim_{x \to c}(x^2+1) = c^2 + 1 = f(c)$

$\Rightarrow f$ is continuous for all $x \in R$.

$\therefore$ There is no point of discontinuity.

12. $f(x) = \begin{cases} x^{10}-1 & ,\text{if } x \leq 1 \\ x^2 & ,\text{if } x < 1 \end{cases}$,

At $x = 1$, L.H.L. $= \lim_{x \to 1^-} f(x) = x^{10}-1 = \lim_{h \to 0}(1-h)^{10} - 1$

$$= \lim_{h \to 0}\left[1 - 10h + \frac{10.9}{2}h^2 + ...\right] - 1 = 0$$

R.H.L. $= \lim_{x \to 1^+} f(x) = \lim_{x \to 1^+} x^2$

$$= \lim_{x \to 0}(1+h)^2 = \lim_{x \to 0} 1^2 + h^2 + 2h = 1$$

$f(1) = 1^{10} - 1 = 0$

$\therefore$ L.H.L. $\neq$ R.H.L. $\neq f(1)$

$\Rightarrow f$ is not continuous at $x = 1$, At $x = c < 1$,

$\lim_{x \to c} x^{10} - 1 = c^{10} - 1 = f(c)$

At $x = c > 1$, $\lim_{x \to c} x^2 = c^2 = f(c)$

$\Rightarrow f$ is continuous at all points $x \in R - \{1\}$

$\therefore$ Point of discontinuity is $x = 1$.

13. At $x = 1$, L.H.L. $= \lim_{x \to 1^-} f(x) = \lim_{x \to 1^-}(x+5) = 6$,

R.H.L. $= \lim_{x \to 1^+} f(x) = \lim_{x \to 1^+}(x-5) = -4$

$$f(1) = 1 + 5 = 6,$$

$f(1) = $ L.H.L. $\neq$ R.H.L.

$\Rightarrow f$ is not continuous at $x = 1$

At $x = c < 1$, $\underset{x \to c}{\text{Lim}}\ (x+5) = c+5 = f(c)$

At $x = c > 1$, $\underset{x \to c}{\text{Lim}}\ (x-5) = c-5 = f(c)$

$\therefore$ f is continuous at all points $x \in R$ except $x = 1$.

14. $f(x) = \begin{cases} 3, & \text{if } 0 \le x \le 1 \\ 4, & \text{if } 1 < x < 3 \\ 5, & \text{if } 3 \le x \le 10 \end{cases}$

In the interval $0 \le x \le 1$, $f(x) = 3$; f is continuous in this interval.

At $x = 1$, L.H.L. $= \underset{x \to 1^-}{\text{Lim}}\ f(x) = 3$,

R.H.L. $= \underset{x \to 1^+}{\text{Lim}}\ f(x) = 4\ \Rightarrow$ f is discontinuous at $x = 1$

At $x = 3$, L.H.L. $= \underset{x \to 3^-}{\text{Lim}}\ f(x) = 4$,

R.H.L. $= \underset{x \to 3^+}{\text{Lim}}\ f(x) = 5\ \Rightarrow$ f is discontinuous at $x = 3$

$\Rightarrow$ f is not continuous at $x = 1$ and $x = 3$.

15. $f(x) = \begin{cases} 2x & ,\text{if } x < 0 \\ 0 & ,\text{if } 0 \le x \le 1 \\ 4x & ,\text{if } x > 1 \end{cases}$

At $x = 0$, L.H.L. $= \underset{x \to 0^-}{\text{Lim}}\ 2x = 0$,

R.H.L. $= \underset{x \to 0^+}{\text{Lim}}\ (0) = 0$, $f(0) = 0$

$\Rightarrow$ f is continuous at $x = 0$

At $x = 1$, L.H.L. $= \underset{x \to 1^-}{\text{Lim}}(0) = 0$,

R.H.L. $= \underset{x \to 1^+}{\text{Lim}}\ 4x = 4$

$f(1) = 0$, $f(1) = $ L.H.L. $\ne$ R.H.L.

$\therefore$ f is not continuous at $x = 1$

when $x < 0$ $f(x) = 2x$, being a polynomial, it is continuous at all points $x < 0$.

when $x > 1$. $f(x) = 4x$ being a polynomial, it is continuous at all points $x > 1$.

when $0 \le x \le 1$, $f(x) = 0$ is a continuous function the point of discontinuity is $x = 1$.

16. $f(x) = \begin{cases} -2, & \text{if } x \le -1 \\ 2x, & \text{if } -1 < x \le 1; \\ 2, & \text{if } x > 1 \end{cases}$

At $x = -1$, L.H.L. $= \underset{x \to 1^-}{\text{Lim}}\ f(x) = -2$, $f(-1) = -2$,

R.H.L. $= \underset{x \to 1^+}{\text{Lim}}\ f(x) = -2$

$\Rightarrow$ f is continuous at $x = -1$

At $x = 1$, L.H.L. $= \underset{x \to 1^-}{\text{Lim}}\ f(x) = 2$, $f(1) = 2$

$\therefore$ f is continuous at $x = 1$,

R.H.L. $= \underset{x \to 1^+}{\text{Lim}}\ f(x) = 2$

Hence, f is continuous function.

17. At $x = 3$, L.H.L. $= \underset{x \to 3^-}{\text{Lim}}\ (ax+1) = 3a+1$,

$f(3) = 3a+1$, R.H.L. $= \underset{x \to 3^+}{\text{Lim}}\ (bx+3) = 3b+3$

f is continuous if L.H.L. $=$ R.H.L. $= f(3)$

$\therefore\ 3a+1 = 3b+3\quad$ or $3(a-b) = 2$

$\therefore\quad a-b = \dfrac{2}{3}\quad$ or $\quad a = b + \dfrac{2}{3}$, for any arbitrary value of b.

Therefore the value of a correeponding to the value of b.

18. At $x = 0$, L.H.L. $= \underset{x \to 0^-}{\text{Lim}}\ \lambda\,(x^2 - 2x) = 0$,

R.H.L. $= \underset{x \to 0^+}{\text{Lim}}\ (4x+1) = 1$, $\quad f(0) = 0$

$f(0) = $ L.H.L. $\ne$ R.H.L. $\Rightarrow$ f is not continuous at $x = 0$, whatever value of $\lambda \in R$ may be

At $x = 1$, $\underset{x \to 1}{\text{Lim}}\ f(x) = \underset{x \to 1}{\text{Lim}}\ (4x+1) = f(1)$

$\Rightarrow$ f is not continuous at $x = 0$ for any value of λ but f is continuous at $x = 1$ for all values of λ.

19. Let c be an integer, $\quad [c-h] = c-1$, $[c+h] = c$,

$[c] = c$, $\ g(x) = x - [x]$.

At $x = c$, $\underset{x \to c^-}{\text{Lim}}\ (x - [x]) = \underset{h \to 0}{\text{Lim}}\ [(c-h) - (c-1)]$

$= \underset{h \to 0}{\text{Lim}}\ (c - h - (c-1)) = 1\ [\because\ [c-h] = c-1]$

R.H.L. $= \underset{x \to c^+}{\text{Lim}}\ (x - [x]) = \underset{h \to 0}{\text{Lim}}\ (c + h - [c+h])$

$= \underset{h \to 0}{\text{Lim}}\ [c + h - c] = 0$

$f(c) = c - [c] = 0$,

Thus L.H.L. $\ne$ R.H.L. $= f(c)\ \Rightarrow$ f is not continuous at integral points.

20. Let $f(x) = x^2 - \sin x + 5$,

At $x = \pi$, L.H.L. $= \displaystyle\lim_{x \to \pi^-} (x^2 - \sin x + 5)$, put $x = \pi - h$,

$\therefore$ L.H.L. $= \displaystyle\lim_{h \to 0} [(\pi - h)^2 - \sin(\pi - h) + 5]$

$\qquad = \displaystyle\lim_{h \to 0} [\pi^2 - 2\pi h + h^2 - \sin h + 5] = \pi^2 + 5$

R.H.L. $= \displaystyle\lim_{x \to \pi^+} (x^2 - \sin x + 5)$, Put $x = \pi + h$,

$\therefore$ L.H.L. $= \displaystyle\lim_{h \to 0} [(\pi + h)^2 - \sin(\pi + h) + 5]$

$\qquad = \displaystyle\lim_{h \to 0} [\pi^2 + 2\pi h + h^2 + \sin h + 5] = \pi^2 + 5$,

$f(\pi) = \pi^2 + 5$, $\quad \therefore$ L.H.L. $=$ R.H.L. $= f(\pi)$

Hence, f is continuous at $x = \pi$

21. (a) $f(x) = \sin x + \cos x = \sqrt{2} \left(\dfrac{1}{\sqrt{2}} \sin x + \dfrac{1}{\sqrt{2}} \cos x \right)$

$\qquad = \sqrt{2} \left(\sin x \cos \dfrac{\pi}{4} + \cos x \sin \dfrac{\pi}{4} \right) = \sqrt{2} \sin \left(x + \dfrac{\pi}{4} \right)$,

At $x = c$, L.H.L.

$\qquad = \displaystyle\lim_{x \to c^-} \sqrt{2} \sin \left(x + \dfrac{\pi}{4} \right) = \sqrt{2} \sin \left(c + \dfrac{\pi}{4} \right)$

R.H.L. $= \displaystyle\lim_{x \to c^+} \sqrt{2} \sin \left(x + \dfrac{\pi}{4} \right) = \sqrt{2} \sin \left(c + \dfrac{\pi}{4} \right) = f(c)$

$\therefore$ f is continuous for all $x \in$ R.

(b) $f(x) = \sin x - \cos x = \sqrt{2} \left(\dfrac{1}{\sqrt{2}} \sin x - \dfrac{1}{\sqrt{2}} \cos x \right)$

$\qquad = \sqrt{2} \left(\sin x \cos \dfrac{\pi}{4} - \cos x \sin \dfrac{\pi}{4} \right) = \sqrt{2} \sin \left(x - \dfrac{\pi}{4} \right)$,

At $x = c$, L.H.L.

$\qquad = \displaystyle\lim_{x \to c^-} \sqrt{2} \sin \left(x - \dfrac{\pi}{4} \right) = \sqrt{2} \sin \left(c - \dfrac{\pi}{4} \right)$

R.H.L. $= \displaystyle\lim_{x \to c^+} \sqrt{2} \sin \left(x - \dfrac{\pi}{4} \right) = \sqrt{2} \sin \left(c - \dfrac{\pi}{4} \right) = f(c)$

$\therefore$ f is continuous for all $x \in$ R.

(c) $f(x) = \sin x \cos x = \dfrac{1}{2} (2 \sin x \cos x)$

$\qquad = \dfrac{1}{2} \sin 2x$. Again f is continuous for all $x \in$ R.

22. (a) Let $f(x) = \cos x$

At $x = c$, $c \in$ R, $\displaystyle\lim_{x \to c} \cos x = \cos c = f(c)$

$\therefore$ f is continuous for all values of $x \in$ R.

(b) Let $f(x) = \sec x$,

$\sec x$ is undefined at $x = (2n + 1) \dfrac{\pi}{2}$, $n \in$ Z.

Also at $x = \dfrac{\pi}{2}$,

L.H.L. $= \displaystyle\lim_{x \to \frac{\pi}{2}^-} \sec x = \displaystyle\lim_{h \to 0} \sec \left(\dfrac{\pi}{2} - h \right)$

$\qquad = \displaystyle\lim_{h \to 0} \operatorname{cosec} h = \infty$

R.H.L. $= \displaystyle\lim_{x \to \frac{\pi}{2}^+} \sec x = \displaystyle\lim_{h \to 0} \sec \left(\dfrac{\pi}{2} + h \right)$

$\qquad = - \displaystyle\lim_{h \to 0} \operatorname{cosec} h = - \infty$

R.H.L. $\neq$ L.H.L.

$\therefore$ f is not continuous at $x = \dfrac{\pi}{2}$

or at $x = (2n + 1) \dfrac{\pi}{2}$

At $x = c \neq (2n + 1) \dfrac{\pi}{2}$

$\displaystyle\lim_{x \to c} \sec x^2 = \sec c = f(c)$

Hence f is continuous at $x \in$ R except

at $x = (2n + 1) \dfrac{\pi}{2}$, where $n \in$ Z.

(c) $f(x) = \operatorname{cosec} x$, f is not defined at $x = n\pi$

$\qquad \Rightarrow$ f is not continuous at $x = n\pi$.

(d) $f(x) = \cot x$, f is not defined at $x = n\pi$, At $x = \pi$, L.H.L.

$= \displaystyle\lim_{x \to \pi^-} \cot x = \displaystyle\lim_{h \to 0} \cot(\pi - h) = \displaystyle\lim_{h \to 0} (-\cot h) = -\infty$,

R.H.L. $= \displaystyle\lim_{x \to \pi^+} \cot x = \displaystyle\lim_{h \to 0} \cot(\pi + h) = \displaystyle\lim_{h \to 0} \cot h = \infty$

Thus this $f(x)$ does not exist at $x = n\pi$

At $x = c \neq n\pi,\ \lim\limits_{x \to c} \cot x = \cot c = f(c)$

Thus f is continuous at all points $x \in R$ except $x = n\pi$, where $n \in Z$.

23. At $x = 0$, L.H.L. $= \lim\limits_{x \to 0^-} f(x) = \dfrac{\sin(-h)}{-h} = 1$,

$\therefore\ f(0) = 1$, R.H.L. $= \lim\limits_{x \to 0^+} f(x) = \dfrac{\sin(-h)}{-h} = 1$

$\therefore\ f$ is continuous at $x = 0$ when $x < 0$, $\sin x$ and x both are continuous

$\therefore\ \dfrac{\sin x}{x}$ is also continuous

when $x > 0$, $f(x) = x + 1$ is a polynomial

Thus f is continuous $\Rightarrow f$ is not discontinuous at any point.

24. At $x = 0$,

L.H.L. $= \lim\limits_{x \to 0^-} \left(x^2 \sin \dfrac{1}{x} \right) = \lim\limits_{h \to 0} (-h)^2 \sin \dfrac{1}{-h}$

$= -\lim\limits_{h \to 0} h^2 \left(\sin \dfrac{1}{h} \right)$

$\sin \dfrac{1}{h}$ lies between -1 and 1, a finite quantity

$\therefore\ h^2 \sin \dfrac{1}{h} \to 0$ as $h \to 0$

$\therefore\ $ L.H.L. $= 0$. Similarly $\lim\limits_{x \to 0^+} \left(x^2 \sin \dfrac{1}{x} \right) = 0$

Also $f(0) = 0$ (given)

$\therefore\ $ L.H.L. $=$ R.H.L. $= f(0)$

Hence f is continuous for all $x \in R$.

25. L.H.L. $= \lim\limits_{x \to 0^-} (\sin x - \cos x)$

$= \lim\limits_{h \to 0} [\sin(-h) - \cos(-h)]$

$= \lim\limits_{h \to 0} (-\sin h - \cos h) = -1$

R.H.L. $= \lim\limits_{x \to 0^+} (\sin x - \cos x)$

$= \lim\limits_{h \to 0} (\sin h - \cos h) = -1$, $f(0) = -1$

$\therefore\ $ L.H.L. $=$ R.H.L. $= f(0)$

Thus, f is continuous at $x = 0$

26. At $x = \pi/2$, L.H.L. $= \lim\limits_{x \to \left(\frac{\pi}{2}\right)^-} \dfrac{k \cos x}{\pi - 2x} = \lim\limits_{h \to 0} \dfrac{k \cos\left(\dfrac{\pi}{2} - h\right)}{\pi - 2\left(\dfrac{\pi}{2} - h\right)}$

$\left(\text{Putting } x = \dfrac{\pi}{2} - h\right)$

$= \lim\limits_{h \to 0} \dfrac{k \sin h}{\pi - \pi + 2h} = \lim\limits_{h \to 0} \dfrac{k}{2} \cdot \dfrac{\sin h}{h} = \dfrac{k}{2}$

R.H.L. $= \lim\limits_{x \to \left(\frac{\pi}{2}\right)^+} \dfrac{k \cos x}{\pi - 2x} = \lim\limits_{h \to 0} \dfrac{k \cos\left(\dfrac{\pi}{2} + h\right)}{\pi - 2\left(\dfrac{\pi}{2} + h\right)}$

$\left(\text{Putting } x = \dfrac{\pi}{2} + h\right)$

$= \lim\limits_{h \to 0} \dfrac{-k \sin h}{-2h} = \lim\limits_{h \to 0} \dfrac{k}{2} \dfrac{\sin h}{h} = \dfrac{k}{2}$, $f\left(\dfrac{\pi}{2}\right) = 3$ (given)

Hence f is continuous if $\dfrac{k}{2} = 3$ or $k = 6$.

27. L.H.L. $= \lim\limits_{x \to 2^-} (kx^2)$,

Put $x = 2 - h$, L.H.L. $= \lim\limits_{h \to 0} k(2-h)^2 = 4k$,

$f(2) = k \cdot 2^2 = 4k$

R.H.L. $= \lim\limits_{x \to 2^+} f(x) = 3$

f is continuous if L.H.L. $=$ R.H.L. $= f(2)$

$\therefore\ 4k = 3\ \Rightarrow\ k = \dfrac{3}{4}$

28. At $x = \pi$, L.H.L. $= \lim\limits_{x \to \pi^-} f(x) = \lim\limits_{x \to \pi^-} -(kx + 1)$

$= k\pi + 1$, $f(x) = k\pi + 1$

R.H.L. $= \lim\limits_{x \to \pi^+} \cos x = -1$,

for continuity at $x = \pi$, L.H.S. $=$ R.H.S. $= f(\pi)$

$\therefore\ k\pi + 1 = -1\ \Rightarrow\ k = \dfrac{-2}{\pi}$

29. At $x = 5$, L.H.L. $= \lim\limits_{x \to 5^-} (kx + 1) = 5k + 1$, $f(5) = k.5 + 1$

$= 5k + 1$, R.H.L. $= \lim\limits_{x \to 5^+} (3x - 5) = 10$

f is continuous if L.H.L. $=$ R.H.L. $= f(5)$

$\therefore \ 5k + 1 = 10 \ \Rightarrow \ k = \dfrac{9}{5}$

30. At $x = 2$, L.H.L. $= \lim\limits_{x \to 2^-} (5) = 5$, $f(2) = 5$,

R.H.L. $= \lim\limits_{x \to 2^+} (ax + b) = 2a + b$

f is continuous at $x = 2$, if $2a + b = 5$ ... (i)

At $x = 10$, L.H.L. $= \lim\limits_{x \to 10^-} f(x) = \lim\limits_{x \to 10^-} (ax + b)$

$= 10a + b$ and R.H.L. $= \lim\limits_{x \to 10^+} f(x) = \lim\limits_{x \to 10^+} (21) = 21$

f is continuous at $x = 10$ if $10a + b = 21$ ... (ii)

Subtracting (i) from (ii)

$8a = 21 - 5 = 16 \Rightarrow \ a = 2$

from (i) $b = 1$ Hence, $a = 2$, $b = 1$

31. Now, $f(x) = \cos x^2$, let $g(x) = \cos x$ and $h(x) = x^2$

$\therefore \ goh(x) = g(h(x)) = \cos x^2$

Now g and h both are continuous $\forall \, x \in R$.

$f(x) = goh(x) = \cos x^2$ is also continuous at all $x \in R$.

32. Let $g(x) = |x|$ and $h(x) = \cos x$, $f(x) = goh(x) = g(h(x))$
$= g(\cos x) = |\cos x|$

Now $g(x) = |x|$ and $h(x) = \cos x$ both are continuous for all values of $x \in R$.

$\therefore \ (goh)(x)$ is also continuous.

Hence, $f(x) = goh(x) = |\cos x|$ is continuous for all values of $x \in R$.

33. Let $g(x) = \sin x$, $h(x) = |x|$, $goh(x) = g(h(x))$

$= g(|x|) = \sin |x| = f(x)$

Now $g(x) = \sin x$ and $h(x) = |x|$ both are continuous for all $x \in R$.

$\therefore \ f(x) = goh(x) = \sin |x|$ is continuous at all $x \in R$.

34. $f(x) = |x| - |x + 1|$, when $x < -1$,

$f(x) = -x - [-(x + 1)] = -x + x + 1 = 1$

when $-1 \le x < 0$, $f(x) = -x - (x + 1) = -2x - 1$,

when $x \ge 0$, $f(x) = x - (x + 1) = -1$

$\therefore \quad f(x) = \begin{cases} 1 & \text{, if } x < -1 \\ -2x - 1 & \text{, if } -1 \le x < 0 \\ -1 & \text{, if } x \ge 0 \end{cases}$

At $x = -1$, L.H.L. $= \lim\limits_{x \to 1^-} f(x) = \lim\limits_{x \to 1^-} (1) = 1$

R.H.L. $= \lim\limits_{x \to 1^+} f(x) = \lim\limits_{x \to 1^+} (-x - 1) = 1$

$\therefore \ f(-1) = -2(-1) - 1 = 2 - 1 = 1$

$\therefore \ $ L.H.L. $=$ R.H.L. $= f(-1)$

$\Rightarrow f$ is continuous at $x = -1$

At $x = 0$, L.H.L. $= \lim\limits_{x \to 0^-} (-2x - 1) = -1$

$f(0) = -1$ (given)

R.H.L. $= \lim\limits_{x \to 0^+} f(x) = \lim\limits_{x \to 0^+} (-1) = -1$

$\therefore \ $ L.H.L. $=$ R.H.L. $= f(0)$

$\therefore \quad f$ is continuous at $x = 0 \Rightarrow$ There is no point of discontinuous. Hence f is continuous for all $x \in R$.

Practice Exercise-2 

1. (c)   **2.** (c)   **3.** (d)   **4.** (d)   **5.** (a)

6. (d)   **7.** (a)

8. $f(x) = |x|$ at $x = 0$

9. Does not exist

10. 1

11. $x = 0, 1$

12. $\dfrac{dy}{dx} = \dfrac{\pi}{180} \sec x°. \tan x°$

13. $-2x \cos (\cos x^2) \sin x^2$

14. $y = \sqrt{\dfrac{2\cos^2 \theta}{2 \sin^2 \theta}} = \sqrt{\cot^2 \theta} = -\cot \theta$

$\qquad \left[\because \cot \theta \text{ is } -ve \text{ in the nbd of } \dfrac{3\pi}{4} \text{ i.e. in } Q_2 \right]$

$\Rightarrow \left(\dfrac{dy}{d\theta} \right)_{\theta = 3\pi/4} (\text{cosec}^2 \theta)_{3\pi/4} = 2.$

15. $6 - 2\sqrt{2}$

16. As given : $y = (\cos x^2)^2$

Diff both side w.r.t 'x'

$\dfrac{dy}{dx} = 2 \cos x^2 (-\sin x^2) 2x = -4x \cos x^2 \sin x^2$

$= -2x (2 \sin x^2 \cos x^2) = -2x \sin 2x^2$

17. $f(x)$ possesses derivative at $x = 0$ so it is both continuous and differentiable at $x = 0$

$\because$ L.H.L $= 0$, R.H.L $= b$

$\therefore$ $b = 0$

also $R f'(0) = 0$, $L f'(0) = 0$ $\forall a \in R$

$f'(0) = 0$ if $b = 0$.

18. When $\dfrac{\pi}{2} < x < \pi$, $\cos x < 0$ so that

$|\cos x| = -\cos x$, i.e. $f(x) = -\cos x$

$\Rightarrow$ $f'(x) = \sin x$.

Hence, $f'\left(\dfrac{3\pi}{4}\right) = \sin\left(\dfrac{3\pi}{4}\right) = \dfrac{1}{\sqrt{2}}$

19. When $0 < x < \dfrac{\pi}{4}$, $\cos x > \sin x$, so that

$\cos x - \sin x > 0$, i.e.,

$f(x) = \cos x - \sin x \Rightarrow f'(x) = -\sin x - \cos x$

Hence $f'\left(\dfrac{\pi}{6}\right) = -\sin\dfrac{\pi}{6} - \cos\dfrac{\pi}{6} = -\dfrac{1}{2}(1 + \sqrt{3})$.

20. We have, $f(x) = \sqrt{1 + \cos^2\left(x^2\right)}$ ...(i)

On differentiating (i) w.r.t.x, we get

$f'(x) = \dfrac{-2\sin x^2 \cos x^2}{\sqrt{1 + \cos^2 x^2}}(x)$

$\Rightarrow f'(x) = \dfrac{-\sin 2x^2}{\sqrt{1 + \cos^2 x^2}}(x)$ ...(ii)

Put, $x = \dfrac{\sqrt{\pi}}{2}$ in (ii), we get

$f'\left(\dfrac{\sqrt{\pi}}{2}\right) = -\dfrac{\sqrt{\pi}}{2} \cdot \dfrac{\sin 2\left(\dfrac{\pi}{4}\right)}{\sqrt{1 + \dfrac{1}{2}}} = -\dfrac{\sqrt{\pi}}{2} \cdot \dfrac{\sin\dfrac{\pi}{2}}{\sqrt{\dfrac{3}{2}}} = -\sqrt{\dfrac{\pi}{6}}$

NCERT Exercise-2

1. Let $y = \sin(x^2 + 5)$, put $x^2 + 5 = t$,

$y = \sin t$, $t = x^2 + 5$, $\dfrac{dy}{dx} = \dfrac{dy}{dt} \cdot \dfrac{dt}{dx}$

$\dfrac{dy}{dx} = \cos t \cdot \dfrac{dt}{dx} = \cos(x^2 + 5)\dfrac{d}{dx}(x^2 + 5)$

$= \cos(x^2 + 5) \times 2x = 2x\cos(x^2 + 5)$

2. Let $y = \cos(\sin x)$, put $\sin x = t$

$\therefore$ $y = \cos t$, $t = \sin x$ $\therefore$ $\dfrac{dy}{dt} = -\sin t$, $\dfrac{dt}{dx} = \cos x$

$\dfrac{dy}{dx} = \dfrac{dy}{dt} \cdot \dfrac{dt}{dx} = (-\sin t) \times \cos x$

Putting the value of t, $\dfrac{dy}{dx} = -\sin(\sin x) \times \cos x$

$\dfrac{dy}{dx} = -[\sin(\sin x)]\cos x$

3. Let $y = \sin(ax + b)$ Put $ax + b = t$ $\therefore$ $y = \sin t$,

$t = ax + b$, $\dfrac{dy}{dt} = \cos t$, $\dfrac{dt}{dx} = \dfrac{d}{dx}(ax + b) = a$

Now $\dfrac{dy}{dx} = \dfrac{dy}{dt} \cdot \dfrac{dt}{dx} = \cos t \times a = a\cos t$,

$\dfrac{dy}{dx} = a\cos(ax + b)$

4. Let $y = \sec\left(\tan\left(\sqrt{x}\right)\right)$

By chain-rule,

$\dfrac{dy}{dx} = \sec\left(\tan\sqrt{x}\right)\tan\left(\tan\sqrt{x}\right)\dfrac{d}{dx}\left(\tan\sqrt{x}\right)$

$\dfrac{dy}{dx} = \sec\left(\tan\sqrt{x}\right).\tan\left(\tan\sqrt{x}\right)\sec^2\sqrt{x}.\dfrac{1}{2.\sqrt{x}}$

5. $y = \dfrac{\sin(ax + b)}{\cos(cx + d)} = \left(\dfrac{u}{v}\right)$, $u = \sin(ax + b)$

$\therefore$ $\dfrac{du}{dx} = \cos(ax + b)\dfrac{d}{dx}(ax + b)$

$= a\cos(ax + b)$, $v = \cos(cx + d)$,

$\dfrac{dv}{dx} = -\sin(cx + d)\dfrac{d}{dx}(cx + d) = -\sin(cx + d) \times c$

$\dfrac{dy}{dx} = -c(\sin(cx + d)$

Now, $y = \dfrac{u}{v}$, $\dfrac{dy}{dx} = \dfrac{v\dfrac{du}{dx} - u\dfrac{dv}{dx}}{v^2}$

$\Rightarrow \dfrac{dy}{dx} = \dfrac{a\cos(ax + b)\cos(cx + d) + c\sin(ax + b)\sin(cx + d)}{\cos^2(cx + d)}$

6. $y = \cos x^3 \sin^2 x^5$, $y = uv$

Let $u = \cos x^3$ and $v = \sin^2 x^5$ for $\dfrac{du}{dx}$, put $x^3 = t$

$\therefore\ u = \cos t$, $t = x^3$, $\dfrac{du}{dt} = -\sin t$, $\dfrac{dt}{dx} = 3x^2$

$\therefore\ \dfrac{du}{dx} = \dfrac{du}{dt} \times \dfrac{dt}{dx} = -\sin t \times 3x^2 = -\sin x^3 \times 3x^2$,

$\dfrac{du}{dx} = -3x^2 \sin x^3$,

for $\dfrac{dv}{dx}$ put $x^5 = t$,

$\sin t = s\ \ \therefore\ v = s^2$

$\dfrac{dv}{ds} = 2s$, $\dfrac{dt}{dx} = 5x^4$, $\dfrac{ds}{dt} = \cos t$,

Now by chain rule $\dfrac{dv}{dx} = \dfrac{dv}{ds} \times \dfrac{ds}{dt} \times \dfrac{dt}{dx}$

$= 2 \sin x^5 \times \cos x^5 \times 5x^4 = 10x^4 \sin x^5 \cos x^5$

Now $y = uv$, $\dfrac{dy}{dx} = \dfrac{du}{dx} \times v + u \times \dfrac{dv}{dx}$

$= -3x^2 \sin x^3 \sin^2 x^5 + 10x^4 \cos x^3 \sin x^5 \cos x^5$

$\therefore\ \dfrac{dy}{dx} = x^2 \sin x^5 (-3 \sin x^3 \sin x^5 + 10x^2 \cos x^3 \cos x^5)$

7. Do it yourself.

8. Do it yourself

9. The given function may be written as,

$$f(x) = \begin{cases} x-1 & , \text{if } x \geq 1 \\ 1-x & , \text{if } x < 1 \end{cases}$$

R.H.D. at $x = 1$ $= \lim_{h\to 0} \dfrac{f(1+h) - f(1)}{h}$

$= \lim_{h\to 0} \dfrac{[(1+h) - 1] - (1-1)}{h} = \lim_{h\to 0} \dfrac{h}{h} = 1$

L.H.D., at $x = 1$ $= \lim_{h\to 0} \dfrac{f(1-h) - f(1)}{-h}$

$= \lim_{h\to 0} \dfrac{1 - (1-h) - (1-1)}{-h} = \lim_{h\to 0} \dfrac{h}{-h} = -1$

R.H.D. $\neq$ L.H.D. $\Rightarrow$ f is not differentiable at $x = 1$.

10. (i) At $x = 1$ R.H.D. $= \lim_{h\to 0} \dfrac{f(1+h) - f(1)}{h}$

$= \lim_{h\to 0} \dfrac{1-1}{h} = 0\ \ \ \ \because [1+h] = 1$

L.H.D. $= \lim_{h\to 0} \dfrac{f(1-h) - f(1)}{-h}$

$= \lim_{h\to 0} \dfrac{0-1}{-h} = $ not defined $\because [1-h] = 1$

$\therefore\ $ f is not differentiable at $x = 1$.

(ii) At $x = 3$ R.H.D. $= \lim_{h\to 0} \dfrac{f(3+h) - f(3)}{h}$

$= \lim_{h\to 0} \dfrac{3-3}{h} = 0$

L.H.D. $= \lim_{h\to 0} \dfrac{f(3-h) - f(3)}{-h}$

$= \lim_{h\to 0} \dfrac{2-3}{h} = \lim_{h\to 0} \dfrac{-1}{h} = $ Not defined.

R.H.D. $\neq$ L.H.D.

$\Rightarrow$ f is not differentiable at $x = 3$.

Practice Exercise-3

1. (b) **2.** (a) **3.** (a) **4.** (b) **5.** (d)

6. $\dfrac{\cos(\tan^{-1} x)}{1+x^2}$

7. $y = \sin^{-1}\left(\dfrac{x}{2}\right) + \cos^{-1}\left(\dfrac{x}{2}\right) = \dfrac{\pi}{2} \Rightarrow \dfrac{dy}{dx} = 0$

8. $-\dfrac{1}{1+x^2}$

9. Putting $x^2 = \tan\theta$, $y = \tan^{-1}\left(\dfrac{1-\tan\theta}{1+\tan\theta}\right)$

$= \tan^{-1}\tan\left(\dfrac{\pi}{4} - \theta\right)$

$y = \dfrac{\pi}{4} - \theta = \dfrac{\pi}{4} - \tan^{-1} x^2\ \ \ \therefore\ \dfrac{dy}{dx} = \dfrac{-2x}{1+x^4}$

10. $\dfrac{dy}{dx} = -\dfrac{b^2 x}{a^2 y}$

11. $\dfrac{-2x}{(x^4+1)}$

12. $y = \tan^{-1}\left(\dfrac{\sqrt{x}-x}{1+x^{3/2}}\right) = \tan^{-1}\left(\dfrac{\sqrt{x}-x}{1+\sqrt{x}.x}\right)$

$\qquad = \tan^{-1}\left(\sqrt{x}\right) - \tan^{-1}\left(x\right)$

On differentiating w.r.t. x, we get

$y' = \dfrac{1}{1+x} \cdot \dfrac{1}{2\sqrt{x}} - \dfrac{1}{1+x^2} \Rightarrow y'(1) = \dfrac{1}{2}.\dfrac{1}{2} - \dfrac{1}{2} = -\dfrac{1}{4}$

13. $\left[\dfrac{2^{x+1} \cdot 3^x}{1+(36)^x}\right] \log 6$

14. $\dfrac{-1}{\sqrt{1-x^2}}$; **Hint :** Put $x = \cos\theta$

15. $2\sqrt{a^2 - x^2}$

<hr>

NCERT Exercise-3

1. Differentiating w.r.t. x , $2 + 3\dfrac{dy}{dx} = \cos x$

$\qquad \therefore \dfrac{dy}{dx} = \dfrac{1}{3}\,(\cos x - 2)$

2. Do it yourself.

3. Differentiating w.r.t. x , $a + 2$ by $\dfrac{dy}{dx} = -\sin y\,\dfrac{dy}{dx}$

$\qquad$ or $\quad (2b + \sin y)\dfrac{dy}{dx} = -a \quad \Rightarrow \quad \dfrac{dy}{dx} = -\dfrac{a}{2b + \sin y}$

4. Differentiating w.r.t. x ,

$\qquad \left(1 \cdot y + x\dfrac{dy}{dx}\right) + \left(2y\dfrac{dy}{dx}\right) = \sec^2 x + \dfrac{dy}{dx}$

$\qquad$ or $\quad (x + 2y - 1)\dfrac{dy}{dx} = \sec^2 x - y \quad \Rightarrow \quad \dfrac{dy}{dx} = \dfrac{\sec^2 x - y}{x + 2y - 1}$

5. $x^2 + xy + xy = 100$

$\qquad$ Differentiating w.r.t. x , $2x + \left(1 \cdot y + x\dfrac{dy}{dx}\right) + 2y\dfrac{dy}{dx} = 0$

$\qquad$ or $\quad (x + 2y)\dfrac{dy}{dx} = -2x - y \quad \Rightarrow \quad \dfrac{dy}{dx} = -\dfrac{2x + y}{x + 2y}$

6. Given that $x^3 + x^2 y + xy^2 + y^3 = 81$

Differentiating both sides we get

$3x^2 + x^2\dfrac{dy}{dx} + y(2x) + y^2 + x\left(2y\dfrac{dy}{dx}\right) + 3y^2\dfrac{dy}{dx} = 0$

$\Rightarrow \dfrac{dy}{dx}[x^2 + 2xy + 3y^2] = -\left(3x^2 + 2xy + y^2\right)$

$\Rightarrow \dfrac{dy}{dx} = \dfrac{-(3x^2 + 2xy + y^2)}{x^2 + 2xy + 3y^2}$

7. Given that $\sin^2 y + \cos xy = \pi$

Differentiating both sides we get

$2\sin y\dfrac{d \sin y}{dx} + (-\sin xy)\dfrac{d(xy)}{dx} = 0$

$\Rightarrow 2\sin y\cos y\dfrac{dy}{dx} + (-\sin xy)\left[x\dfrac{dy}{dx} + y\right] = 0$

$\Rightarrow \dfrac{dy}{dx}\,[2\sin y \cos y - x \sin xy] = y \sin xy$

$\Rightarrow \dfrac{dy}{dx} = \dfrac{y\sin xy}{2\sin y\cos y - x\sin xy} = \dfrac{y\sin xy}{\sin 2y - x\sin xy}$

8. Given that $\sin^2 x + \cos^2 y = 1$

Differentiating both sides, we get

$2\sin x\dfrac{d \sin x}{dx} + 2\cos y\dfrac{d \cos y}{dx} = 0$

$\Rightarrow 2\sin x\cos x + 2\cos y(-\sin y)\dfrac{dy}{dx} = 0$

$\Rightarrow \sin 2x - \sin 2y\dfrac{dy}{dx} = 0$

$\Rightarrow \dfrac{dy}{dx} = \dfrac{\sin 2x}{\sin 2y}$

9. $y = \sin^{-1}\left(\dfrac{2x}{1+x^2}\right)$, put $x = \tan\theta$,

$y = \sin^{-1}\left(\dfrac{2\tan\theta}{1+\tan^2\theta}\right) = \sin^{-1}(\sin 2\theta) = 2\theta$

$y = 2\tan^{-1} x \quad \therefore \quad \dfrac{dy}{dx} = \dfrac{2}{1+x^2}$

10. $y = \tan^{-1}\left(\dfrac{3x - x^3}{1 - 3x^2}\right)$, put $x = \tan\theta$,

$$y = \tan^{-1}\left(\frac{3\tan\theta - \tan^3\theta}{1 - 3\tan^2\theta}\right) = \tan^{-1}(\tan 3\theta) = 3\theta,$$

$$y = 3\tan^{-1}x \quad \therefore \quad \frac{dy}{dx} = \frac{3}{1 + x^2}$$

11. $y = \cos^{-1}\left(\dfrac{1 - x^2}{1 + x^2}\right)$, put $x = \tan\theta$,

$$y = \cos^{-1}\left(\frac{1 - \tan^2\theta}{1 + \tan^2\theta}\right) = \cos^{-1}(\cos 2\theta) = 2\theta$$

$$y = 2\tan^{-1}x \quad \therefore \quad \frac{dy}{dx} = \frac{2}{1 + x^2}$$

12. Putting $x = \tan\theta$, we get

$$y = \sin^{-1}\left(\frac{1 - \tan^2\theta}{1 + \tan^2\theta}\right)$$

$$y = \sin^{-1}(\cos 2\theta)$$

$$y = \sin^{-1}\left\{\sin\left(\frac{\pi}{2} - 2\theta\right)\right\}$$

$$y = \frac{\pi}{2} - 2\theta \quad \left[\begin{array}{l} \because\ 0 < x < 1 \Rightarrow 0 < \tan\theta < 1 \Rightarrow 0 < \theta < \dfrac{\pi}{4} \\[2mm] \Rightarrow 0 < 2\theta < \dfrac{\pi}{2} \Rightarrow 0 < \dfrac{\pi}{2} - 2\theta < \pi \end{array}\right]$$

$$y = \frac{\pi}{2} - 2\tan^{-1}x \quad \left[\because\ x = \tan\theta \Rightarrow \theta = \tan^{-1}x\right]$$

$$\frac{dy}{dx} = -\frac{2}{1 + x^2}$$

13. Putting $x = \tan\theta$, we have

$$y = \cos^{-1}\left(\frac{2\tan\theta}{1 + \tan^2\theta}\right)$$

$$y = \cos^{-1}(\sin 2\theta)$$

$$y = \cos^{-1}\left\{\cos\left(\frac{\pi}{2} - 2\theta\right)\right\}$$

$$y = \frac{\pi}{2} - 2\theta \quad \left[\begin{array}{l} \because\ -1 < x < 1 \Rightarrow -1 < \tan\theta < 1 \\[2mm] \Rightarrow -\dfrac{\pi}{4} < \theta < \dfrac{\pi}{4} \end{array}\right]$$

$$y = \frac{\pi}{2} - 2\tan^{-1}x \quad \left[\begin{array}{l} \Rightarrow -\dfrac{\pi}{2} < 2\theta < \dfrac{\pi}{2} \\[2mm] \Rightarrow 0 < \dfrac{\pi}{2} - 2\theta < \pi \end{array}\right]$$

$$\frac{dy}{dx} = -\frac{2}{1 + x^2}$$

14. $y = \sin^{-1}\left(2x\sqrt{1 - x^2}\right)$, put $x = \sin\theta$,

$$y = \sin^{-1}\left(2\sin\theta\sqrt{1 - \sin^2\theta}\right)$$

$$= \sin^{-1}(2\sin\theta\cos\theta) = \sin^{-1}(\sin 2\theta) = 2\theta,$$

$$y = 2\sin^{-1}x \quad \therefore \quad \frac{dy}{dx} = \frac{2}{\sqrt{1 - x^2}}$$

15. $y = \sec^{-1}\left(\dfrac{1}{2x^2 - 1}\right)$, put $x = \cos\theta$,

$$y = \sec^{-1}\left(\frac{1}{2\cos^2\theta - 1}\right) = \sec^{-1}\left(\frac{1}{\cos 2\theta}\right)$$

$$= \sec^{-1}(\sec 2\theta) = 2\theta, \quad y = 2\cos^{-1}x$$

$$\therefore \quad \frac{dy}{dx} = \frac{-2}{\sqrt{1 - x^2}}$$

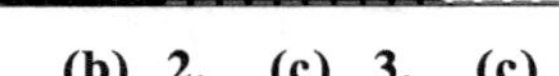
Practice Exercise-4

1. (b)   **2.** (c)   **3.** (c)

4. $\dfrac{e^{\sqrt{x}}}{2\sqrt{x}}$

5. $y = f(\log x) = \log\log x$

$$\therefore \quad \frac{dy}{dx} = \frac{1}{x\log x} = (x\log x)^{-1}$$

6. $\dfrac{\log\dfrac{1}{2}}{2^x}$

7. $\dfrac{dy}{dx} = e$

8. $\dfrac{dy}{dx} = 1$

9. $3e^7$

10. $\dfrac{dy}{dx} = \sec x \tan x$

11. $\sin x \log x + x \cos x \cdot \log x + \sin x.$

Hint: $\dfrac{d}{dx}(uvw) = uv\dfrac{dw}{dx} + uw\dfrac{dv}{dx} + vw\dfrac{du}{dx}.$

12. Given, $y = \log x . e^{\left(\tan x + x^2\right)}$

$\therefore \dfrac{dy}{dx} = e^{\left(\tan x + x^2\right)} . \dfrac{1}{x} + \log x . e^{\left(\tan x + x^2\right)}\left(\sec^2 x + 2x\right)$

$= e^{\left(\tan x + x^2\right)}\left[\dfrac{1}{x} + \left(\sec^2 x + 2x\right)\log x\right]$

13. $f(x) = e^x$ and $g(x) = \sin^{-1}x$ and $h(x) = f(g(x))$

$\Rightarrow \quad h(x) = f(\sin^{-1} x) = e^{\sin^{-1} x}$

$\Rightarrow h'(x) = \dfrac{e^{\sin^{-1} x}}{\sqrt{1 - x^2}} \Rightarrow \dfrac{h'(x)}{h(x)} = \dfrac{1}{\sqrt{1 - x^2}}$

NCERT Exercise-4

1. $y = \dfrac{e^x}{\sin x}$, for $y = \dfrac{u}{v}, \dfrac{dy}{dx} = \dfrac{u'v - uv'}{v^2}$

$\therefore \dfrac{dy}{dx} = \dfrac{e^x \sin x - e^x \cos x}{\sin^2 x}$

or $\dfrac{dy}{dx} = \dfrac{e^x (\sin x - \cos x)}{\sin^2 x}$, when $x \neq n\pi, x \in Z.$

2. $y = e^{\sin^{-1}x}$, $x = \sin t$,

$\therefore \quad y = e^t, \quad \dfrac{dt}{dx} = \dfrac{1}{\sqrt{1 - x^2}}, \dfrac{dy}{dt} = e^t$

$\therefore \quad \dfrac{dy}{dx} = \dfrac{dy}{dt} \cdot \dfrac{dt}{dx} = e^t \cdot \dfrac{1}{\sqrt{1 - x^2}} = \dfrac{e^{\sin^{-1}x}}{\sqrt{1 - x^2}}$

3. $y = e^{x^3}$, Put $x^3 = t$

$\therefore \quad y = e^t, \quad \dfrac{dy}{dt} = e^t, \quad \dfrac{dt}{dx} = 3x^2,$

Now $\dfrac{dy}{dx} = \dfrac{dy}{dt} \times \dfrac{dt}{dx} = e^t \times 3x^2 \quad \therefore \quad \dfrac{dy}{dx} = 3x^2 e^{x^3}$

4. Let $y = \sin(\tan^{-1} e^{-x})$, diff. w.r.to x

$\dfrac{dy}{dx} = \cos\left(\tan^{-1}e^{-x}\right)\dfrac{d}{dx}\left(\tan^{-1}e^{-x}\right)$

$= \cos\left(\tan^{-1}e^{-x}\right) . \dfrac{1}{1 + e^{-2x}} . \dfrac{d}{dx}\left(e^{-x}\right)$

$= -\cos\left(\tan^{-1}e^{-x}\right)\dfrac{1}{1 + e^{-2x}} . e^{-x}$

5. Let $y = \log(\cos e^x)$,

$\Rightarrow \dfrac{dy}{dx} = \dfrac{1}{\cos e^x}\left(-\sin e^x\right).e^x = \dfrac{-e^x \sin e^x}{\cos e^x}$

$= -e^x \tan\left(e^x\right)$

6. $y = e^x + e^{x^2} + e^{x^3} + e^{x^4} + e^{x^5}$, let $u = e^{x^n}$,

put $x^n = t$, $u = e^t, t = x^n$

$\dfrac{du}{dt} = e^t, \quad \dfrac{dt}{dx} = nx^{n-1}$

Now, $\dfrac{du}{dx} = \dfrac{du}{dt} \times \dfrac{dt}{dx} = e^t \times nx^{n-1}$

$= e^{x^n} \times nx^{n-1}, \quad \dfrac{du}{dx} = nx^{n-1} e^{x^n}$

for $n = 2$ $\dfrac{d}{dx} e^{x^2} = 2x\, e^{x^2}$, $n = 3$ $\dfrac{d}{dx} e^{x^3} = 3x^2\, e^{x^3}$,

$n = 4$ $\dfrac{d}{dx} e^{x^4} = 4x^3\, e^{x^4}$, $n = 5$ $\dfrac{d}{dx} e^{x^5} = 5x^4\, e^{x^5}$

Now $y = e^x + e^{x^2} + e^{x^3} + e^{x^4} + e^{x^5}$

$\therefore \dfrac{dy}{dx} = \dfrac{d}{dx} e^x + \dfrac{d}{dx} e^{x^2} + \dfrac{d}{dx} e^{x^3} + \dfrac{d}{dx} e^{x^4} + \dfrac{d}{dx} e^{x^5}$

$\therefore \dfrac{dy}{dx} = e^x + 2xe^{x^2} + 3x^2 e^{x^3} + 4x^3 e^{x^4} + 5x^4 e^{x^5}$

7. $y = \sqrt{e^{\sqrt{x}}}$, let $y = \sqrt{s}$, $s = e^t$, $t = \sqrt{x}$,

$\dfrac{dy}{ds} = \dfrac{1}{2} s^{\frac{1}{2}-1} = \dfrac{1}{2\sqrt{s}}, \dfrac{ds}{dt} = e^t, \dfrac{dt}{dx} = \dfrac{1}{2\sqrt{x}}$

Now By chain rule $\dfrac{dy}{dx} = \dfrac{dy}{ds} \times \dfrac{ds}{dt} \times \dfrac{dt}{dx}$

$= \dfrac{1}{2\sqrt{s}} \times e^t \times \dfrac{1}{2\sqrt{x}} = \dfrac{1}{2\sqrt{e^{\sqrt{x}}}} \times e^{\sqrt{x}} \times \dfrac{1}{2\sqrt{x}}$

$\therefore \dfrac{dy}{dx} = \dfrac{\sqrt{e^{\sqrt{x}}}}{4\sqrt{x}}, \; x > 0 .$

8. $y = \log(\log x)$, Put $y = \log t$, $t = \log x$, Differentiating

$$\dfrac{dy}{dt} = \dfrac{1}{t}, \dfrac{dt}{dx} = \dfrac{1}{x}$$

Now $\dfrac{dy}{dx} = \dfrac{dy}{dt} \times \dfrac{dt}{dx} = \dfrac{1}{t} \times \dfrac{1}{x}$

$\therefore \dfrac{dy}{dx} = \dfrac{1}{\log x} \times \dfrac{1}{x} = \dfrac{1}{x \log x}, \; x > 0$

9. Do it yourself.

10. $y = \cos(\log x + e^x)$, Put $y = \cos t$, $t = \log x + e^x$,

$$\dfrac{dy}{dt} = -\sin t, \; \dfrac{dt}{dx} = \dfrac{1}{x} + e^x$$

Now $\dfrac{dy}{dx} = \dfrac{dy}{dt} \times \dfrac{dt}{dx} = -\sin t \left(\dfrac{1}{x} + e^x \right)$

$\therefore \quad \dfrac{dy}{dx} = -\dfrac{1}{x} (1 + x\,e^x) \sin(\log x + e^x)$

Practice Exercise-5

1. (b) **2.** (d) **3.** (a)

4. We have, $y = (\tan x)^{\sin x}$
Taking logarithm on both sides $\log y = \sin x \log(\tan x)$
Differentiating w.r.t. x

5. $x^{\sin^{-1} x} \left[\dfrac{\sin^{-1} x}{x} + \dfrac{\log x}{\sqrt{1-x^2}} \right]$

Hint : Let $y = x^{\sin^{-1} x}$, taking log on both side and differentiate.

6. $f(x) = 1 + \tan^{-1}\left(\dfrac{4x}{4-x^2} \right)$

$\therefore \; f'(x) = \dfrac{1}{1+\left(\dfrac{4x}{4-x^2}\right)^2} \cdot \dfrac{\left(4-x^2\right)4 - 4x(-2x)}{\left(4-x^2\right)^2}$

Hence, $f'(2) = \dfrac{1}{2}$

7. $\dfrac{1}{x \log a} - \dfrac{\log a}{x \left(\log x\right)^2}$

NCERT Exercise-5

1. Let $y = \cos x . \cos 2x . \cos 3x$,

Taking log on both sides,

$\log y = \log(\cos x . \cos 2x . \cos 3x)$

$\log y = \log \cos x + \log \cos 2x + \log \cos 3x$,

Differentiating w.r.t. x, we get

$\dfrac{1}{y} \dfrac{dy}{dx} = \dfrac{1}{\cos x} \dfrac{d}{dx} \cos x + \dfrac{1}{\cos 2x} \dfrac{d}{dx} \cos 2x$

$\qquad\qquad\qquad + \dfrac{1}{\cos 3x} \dfrac{d}{dx} \cos 3x$

$= \dfrac{-\sin x}{\cos x} - \dfrac{2 \sin 2x}{\cos 2x} - \dfrac{3 \sin 3x}{\cos 3x}$

$= -(\tan x + 2 \tan 2x + 3 \tan 3x)$

$\therefore \quad \dfrac{dy}{dx} = -y \,(\tan x + 2\tan 2x + 3 \tan 3x)$

$\therefore \quad \dfrac{dy}{dx} = -\cos x . \cos 2x . \cos 3x$

$\qquad\qquad\qquad (\tan x + 2 \tan 2x + 3 \tan 3x)$

2. Let $y = \sqrt{\dfrac{(x-1)(x-2)}{(x-3)(x-4)(x-5)}}$

Taking log on both sides, we get

$\log y = \log \sqrt{\dfrac{(x-1)(x-2)}{(x-3)(x-4)(x-5)}}$

$\log y = \dfrac{1}{2} [\log(x-1) + \log(x-2)$

$\qquad\qquad - \log(x-3) - \log(x-4) - \log(x-5)]$

Differentiating w.r.t. x ,

$\dfrac{1}{y} \dfrac{dy}{dx} = \dfrac{1}{2} \left[\dfrac{1}{x-1} + \dfrac{1}{x-2} - \dfrac{1}{x-3} - \dfrac{1}{x-4} - \dfrac{1}{x-5} \right]$

$\therefore \quad \dfrac{dy}{dx} = \dfrac{1}{2} \sqrt{\dfrac{(x-1)(x-2)}{(x-3)(x-4)(x-5)}}$

$\qquad\qquad \left[\dfrac{1}{x-1} + \dfrac{1}{x-2} - \dfrac{1}{x-3} - \dfrac{1}{x-4} - \dfrac{1}{x-5} \right]$

3. Let $y = (\log x)^{\cos x}$,

Taking log on both sides, $\log y = \log (\log x)^{\cos x}$

$\log y = \cos x \, \log (\log x)$,

Differentiating w.r.t. x,

$$\frac{1}{y} \frac{dy}{dx} = (-\sin x) \log (\log x) + \cos x \frac{d}{dx} \log (\log x)$$

$$= -\sin x \, \log (\log x) + \frac{\cos x}{x \log x}$$

$$\therefore \frac{dy}{dx} = y \left[\sin x \, \log (\log x) + \frac{\cos x}{x \log x} \right]$$

$$= (\log x)^{\cos x} \left[-\sin \log (\log x) + \frac{\cos x}{x \log x} \right]$$

4. Let $y = x^x - 2^{\sin x}$, $y = u - v$

$$\therefore \frac{dy}{dx} = \frac{du}{dx} - \frac{dv}{dx}, \quad u = x^x,$$

Taking log on both side

$$\log u = x \log x, \quad \frac{1}{u} \frac{du}{dx} = 1 \cdot \log x + x \cdot \frac{1}{x}$$

$$= (1 + \log x)$$

$$\frac{du}{dx} = x^x (1 + \log x) \quad \text{and} \quad v = 2^{\sin x},$$

Taking log on both side

$$\log v = \sin x \log 2, \quad \frac{1}{v} \frac{dv}{dx} = \cos x \log 2 \ ,$$

$$\frac{dv}{dx} = 2^{\sin x} \cos x \log 2$$

$$\therefore \frac{dy}{dx} = \frac{du}{dx} - \frac{dv}{dx}$$

$$\Rightarrow \frac{dy}{dx} = x^x (1 + \log x) - 2^{\sin x} \cos x \log 2.$$

5. Let $y = (x + 3)^2 \cdot (x + 4)^3 \cdot (x + 5)^4$

Taking log on both side.

$\log y = \log [(x + 3)^2 \cdot (x + 4)^3 \cdot (x + 5)^4]$

$= \log (x + 3)^2 + \log (x + 4)^3 + \log (x + 5)^4$

$\log y = 2 \log (x + 3) + 3 \log (x + 4) + 4 \log (x + 5)$

Differentiating w.r.t. x , we get

$$\frac{dy}{dx} = y \left[\frac{2}{x + 3} + \frac{3}{x + 4} + \frac{4}{x + 5} \right]$$

$$= (x + 3)^2 \cdot (x + 4)^2 \cdot (x + 5)^4 \left[\frac{2}{x + 3} + \frac{3}{x + 4} + \frac{4}{x + 5} \right].$$

6. Let $y = \left(x + \dfrac{1}{x} \right)^x + x^{\left(1 + \frac{1}{x}\right)}$,

Let $u = \left(x + \dfrac{1}{x} \right)^x$ and $v = x^{\left(1 + \frac{1}{x}\right)}$

$$\therefore \quad y = u + v \Rightarrow \frac{dy}{dx} = \frac{du}{dx} + \frac{dv}{dx} \qquad ...(i)$$

Now $u = \left(x + \dfrac{1}{x} \right)^x$

Taking log on both side , $\log u = x \log \left(x + \dfrac{1}{x} \right)$

$$\Rightarrow \log u = x \log \left(\frac{x^2 + 1}{x} \right)$$

$\log u = x [\log (x^2 + 1) - \log x]$,

Differentiating w.r.t. x , we get

$$\frac{1}{u} \frac{du}{dx} = 1 \cdot [\log (x^2 + 1) - \log x] + x \left[\frac{1}{x^2 + 1} \cdot 2x - \frac{1}{x} \right]$$

$$= \log \left(x + \frac{1}{x} \right) + \frac{x^2 - 1}{x^2 + 1} \ ,$$

$$\frac{du}{dx} = u \left[\log \left(x + \frac{1}{x} \right) + \frac{x^2 - 1}{x^2 + 1} \right]$$

$$\frac{du}{dx} = \left(x + \frac{1}{x} \right)^x \left[\log \left(x + \frac{1}{x} \right) + \frac{x^2 - 1}{x^2 + 1} \right] ,$$

and $v = x^{\left(1 + \frac{1}{x}\right)}$

Taking log on both sides, we get

$$\log v = \left(1 + \frac{1}{x} \right) \log x \ ,$$

$$\frac{1}{v}\frac{dv}{dx} = -\frac{1}{x^2}\log x + \left(1 + \frac{1}{x}\right)\cdot\frac{1}{x}$$

$$\frac{dv}{dx} = v\frac{(x+1-\log x)}{x^2},$$

$$\frac{dv}{dx} = \frac{x^{\left(1+\frac{1}{x}\right)}(x+1-\log x)}{x^2}$$

Put in (i) $\quad \dfrac{dy}{dx} = \left(x+\dfrac{1}{x}\right)^x \left[\log\left(x+\dfrac{1}{x}\right) + \dfrac{x^2-1}{x^2+1}\right]$

$$+ \frac{x^{\left(1+\frac{1}{x}\right)}(x+1-\log x)}{x^2}$$

7. Let $y = (\log x)^x + x^{\log x} = u + v$

where $\quad u = (\log x)^x$

$\therefore \log u = x\log(\log x)$

$$\frac{1}{u}\cdot\frac{du}{dx} = x\frac{d}{dx}\log(\log x) + \log(\log x)$$

$$= x\cdot\frac{1}{\log x}\cdot\frac{1}{x} + \log(\log x) \quad = \frac{1}{\log x} + \log(\log x)$$

$$\frac{du}{dx} = (\log x)^x\left[\frac{1}{\log x} + \log(\log x)\right] \text{ and } v = x^{\log x}$$

$$\log v = \log x\log x = (\log x)^2$$

$$\frac{1}{v}\frac{dv}{dx} = 2\log x\cdot\frac{1}{x} \quad \frac{dv}{dx} = x^{\log x}\left[\frac{2\log x}{x}\right]$$

$\therefore \quad y = u+v \implies \dfrac{dy}{dx} = \dfrac{du}{dx} + \dfrac{dv}{dx}$

$\therefore \quad \dfrac{dy}{dx} = (\log x)^x\left[\dfrac{1}{\log x} + \log(\log x)\right] + x^{\log x}\left[\dfrac{2\log x}{x}\right]$

8. Let $y = (\sin x)^x + \sin^{-1}\sqrt{x}$ let $u = (\sin)x,\ v = \sin^{-1}\sqrt{x}$,

$\therefore \ y = u+v \implies \dfrac{dy}{dx} = \dfrac{du}{dx} + \dfrac{dv}{dx}, \quad \ldots(i)$

Now $u = (\sin x)^x$

Taking log on both sides, $\log u = x\log(\sin x)$,

$$\frac{1}{u}\frac{du}{dx} = \log(\sin x) + x\cdot\frac{1}{\sin x}\cos x$$

$$= \log(\sin x) + x\frac{\cos x}{\sin x},$$

$$\frac{du}{dx} = (\sin x)^x[\log(\sin x) + x\cot x] \quad \text{and } v = \sin^{-1}\sqrt{x}$$

Taking $t = \sqrt{x},\quad v = \sin^{-1}t,\quad \dfrac{dv}{dt} = \dfrac{1}{\sqrt{1-t^2}}$

and $\dfrac{dt}{dx} = \dfrac{1}{2\sqrt{x}}\quad \therefore\quad \dfrac{dv}{dx} = \dfrac{dv}{dt}\times\dfrac{dt}{dx}$

$$\frac{dv}{dx} = \frac{1}{\sqrt{1-x}}\cdot\frac{1}{2\sqrt{x}} = \frac{1}{2\sqrt{x}\sqrt{1-x}}$$

Put (i) we get $\dfrac{dy}{dx} = \dfrac{du}{dx} + \dfrac{dv}{dx}$

$\therefore \quad \dfrac{dy}{dx} = (\sin x)^x[\log(\sin x) + x\cot x] + \dfrac{1}{2\sqrt{x}\sqrt{1-x}}$

9. Let $y = x^{\sin x} + (\sin x)^{\cos x} = u + v$

where $\quad u = x^{\sin x}$

$\qquad \log u = \sin x\log x$

$\implies \dfrac{1}{u}\dfrac{du}{dx} = \sin x\dfrac{d\log x}{dx} + \log x\dfrac{d\sin x}{dx}$

$$= \sin x\cdot\frac{1}{x} + \log x\cos x$$

$$\frac{du}{dx} = x^{\sin x}\left[\frac{\sin x}{x} + \log x\cos x\right]$$

and $\ v = (\sin x)^{\cos x}$

$\qquad \log v = \cos x\log\sin x$

$$\frac{1}{v}\frac{dv}{dx} = \cos x\frac{d}{dx}\log\sin x + \log\sin x\frac{d}{dx}\cos x$$

$$= \cos x\frac{1}{\sin x}\cdot\cos x + \log\sin x(-\sin x)$$

$$= \cos x\cot x - \sin x\log\sin x$$

$$\frac{dv}{dx} = (\sin x)^{\cos x}\left[\cos x\cot x - \sin x\log\sin x\right]$$

$\therefore \quad y = u + v \Rightarrow \dfrac{dy}{dx} = \dfrac{du}{dx} + \dfrac{dv}{dx}$

$\therefore \quad \dfrac{dy}{dx} = x^{\sin x} \left[\dfrac{\sin x}{x} + \log x \cos x \right]$

$$+ (\sin x)^{\cos x} \left[\cos x \cot x - \sin x \log \sin x \right]$$

10. $y = x^{x \cos x} + \dfrac{x^2 + 1}{x^2 - 1}, \quad y = u + v$

$\therefore \quad \dfrac{dy}{dx} = \dfrac{du}{dx} + \dfrac{dv}{dx} \qquad \ldots(i)$

Now $u = x^{x \cos x}$

Taking log on both sides, $\log u = x \cos x \log x$,

$\dfrac{du}{dx} = x^{x \cos x} [\cos x \log x - x \sin x \log x + \cos x]$

and $v = \dfrac{x^2 + 1}{x^2 - 1}, \quad \dfrac{dv}{dx} = \dfrac{-4x}{(x^2 - 1)^2}$

Put in (i). $\dfrac{dy}{dx} = \dfrac{du}{dx} + \dfrac{dv}{dx}$

$\therefore \quad \dfrac{dy}{dx} = x^{x \cos x} [\cos x \log x - x \sin x \log x + \cos x]$

$$- \dfrac{4x}{(x^2 - 1)^2}$$

11. $y = (x \cos x)^x + (x \sin x)^{1/x}$

Let $u = (x \cos x)^x$

$\log u = x \log (x \cos x)$

$\dfrac{1}{u} \dfrac{du}{dx} = x \dfrac{d}{dx} \log (x \cos x) + \log (x \cos x)$

$= x \left[\dfrac{1}{x \cos x} \dfrac{d(x \cos x)}{dx} \right] + \log (x \cos x)$

$= x \left[\dfrac{1}{x \cos x} \left(x \dfrac{d \cos x}{dx} + \cos x \right) \right] + \log(x \cos x)$

$= x \left[\dfrac{1}{x \cos x} (x(-\sin x) + \cos x) \right] + \log(x \cos x)$

$= 1 - x \tan x + \log (x \cos x)$

$\dfrac{du}{dx} = (x \cos x)^x [1 - x \tan x + \log(x \cos x)]$

Now $v = (x \sin x)^{1/x}$

$\log v = \dfrac{1}{x} \log(x \sin x)$

$\dfrac{1}{v} \dfrac{dv}{dx} = \dfrac{1}{x} \dfrac{d \log(x \sin x)}{dx} + \log(x \sin x) \dfrac{d\left(\frac{1}{x}\right)}{dx}$

$= \dfrac{1}{x} \cdot \dfrac{1}{x \sin x} \cdot \dfrac{d(x \sin x)}{dx} + \log(x \sin x) \cdot \left(\dfrac{-1}{x^2} \right)$

$= \dfrac{1}{x^2 \sin x} [x \cos x + \sin x] - \dfrac{\log(x \sin x)}{x^2}$

$= \dfrac{x \cot x + 1 - \log(x \sin x)}{x^2}$

$\dfrac{dv}{dx} = (x \sin x)^{1/x} \left[\dfrac{x \cot x + 1 - \log(x \sin x)}{x^2} \right]$

$\therefore \quad y = u + v \Rightarrow \dfrac{dy}{dx} = \dfrac{du}{dx} + \dfrac{dv}{dx}$

$\dfrac{dy}{dx} = (x \cos x)^x [1 - x \tan x + \log(x \cos x)]$

$$+ (x \sin x)^{1/x} \left[\dfrac{x \cot x + 1 - \log(x \sin x)}{x^2} \right]$$

12. $x^y + y^x = 1, \quad$ let $u = x^y$ and $v = y^x$

$\therefore \quad u + v = 1, \quad \dfrac{du}{dx} + \dfrac{dv}{dx} = 0 \qquad \ldots(i)$

Now $u = x^y$

Taking log on both sides, $\log u = y \log x$

Differentiating w.r.t. x

$\Rightarrow \quad \dfrac{du}{dx} = x^y \left[(\log x) \dfrac{dy}{dx} + \dfrac{y}{x} \right] \quad$ and $v = y^x$

Taking log on both sides, $\log v = x \log y$

Differentiating w.r.t. x

$\therefore \quad \dfrac{dv}{dx} = y^x \left[(\log y) + \dfrac{x}{y} \dfrac{dy}{dx} \right]$

Put in (i) $\dfrac{du}{dx} + \dfrac{dv}{dx} = 0$

$\Rightarrow x^y \left[(\log x)\dfrac{dy}{dx} + \dfrac{y}{x} \right] + y^x \left[\log y + \dfrac{x}{y}\dfrac{dy}{dx} \right] = 0$

$\therefore \quad \dfrac{dy}{dx} = -\dfrac{yx^{y-1} + y^x \log y}{x^y \log x + x\,y^{x-1}}$

13. $y^x = x^y$

$x \log y = y \log x$

$\Rightarrow x \cdot \dfrac{1}{y} \cdot \dfrac{dy}{dx} + \log y = \dfrac{y}{x} + \log x \cdot \dfrac{dy}{dx}$

$\Rightarrow \dfrac{dy}{dx}\left[\log x - \dfrac{x}{y} \right] = \log y - \dfrac{y}{x}$

$\Rightarrow \dfrac{dy}{dx} = \dfrac{y\left(x \log y - y\right)}{x\left(y \log x - x\right)}$

14. We have, $(\cos x)^y = (\cos y)^x$

$\Rightarrow y \log\left(\cos x\right) = x \log\left(\cos y\right)$

$\Rightarrow y\dfrac{d}{dx}\log\left(\cos x\right) + \log\left(\cos x\right)\dfrac{dy}{dx}$

$= x\dfrac{d}{dx}\left(\log\left(\cos y\right)\right) + \log\left(\cos y\right)$

$\Rightarrow y \cdot \dfrac{1}{\cos x}(-\sin x) + \log\left(\cos x\right)\dfrac{dy}{dx}$

$= x \cdot \dfrac{1}{\cos y}(-\sin y)\dfrac{dy}{dx} + \log\left(\cos y\right)$

$\Rightarrow \dfrac{dy}{dx}\left[\log\left(\cos x\right) + x \tan y\right] = \log\left(\cos y\right) + y \tan x$

$\Rightarrow \dfrac{dy}{dx} = \dfrac{\log\left(\cos y\right) + y \tan x}{\log\left(\cos x\right) + x \tan y}$

15. $xy = e^{(x-y)}$

$\log(xy) = \log e^{(x-y)}$

$\log(xy) = x - y$

$\Rightarrow \log x + \log y = x - y$

$\Rightarrow \dfrac{1}{x} + \dfrac{1}{y}\dfrac{dy}{dx} = 1 - \dfrac{dy}{dx} \Rightarrow \dfrac{dy}{dx} = \dfrac{y(x-1)}{x(y+1)}$

16. Let $f(x) = y$

$y = (1 + x)(1 + x^2)(1 + x^4)(1 + x^8)$

Taking log both sides, we get

$\log y = \log[(1 + x)(1 + x^2)(1 + x^4)(1 + x^8)]$

$\log y = \log(1 + x) + \log(1 + x^2) + \log(1 + x^4) + \log(1 + x^8)$

$\dfrac{1}{y}\dfrac{dy}{dx} = \dfrac{1}{(1+x)} + \dfrac{1}{(1+x^2)}(2x)$

$\qquad\qquad + \dfrac{1}{\left(1+x^4\right)}(4x^3) + \dfrac{1}{\left(1+x^8\right)}(8x^7)$

$\dfrac{dy}{dx} = y\left[\dfrac{1}{1+x} + \dfrac{2x}{1+x^2} + \dfrac{4x^3}{(1+x^4)} + \dfrac{8x^7}{(1+x^8)}\right]$

$f'(x) = \left(1+x\right)\left(1+x^2\right)\left(1+x^4\right)\left(1+x^8\right)$

$\qquad \left[\dfrac{1}{1+x} + \dfrac{2x}{1+x^2} + \dfrac{4x^3}{1+x^4} + \dfrac{8x^7}{1+x^8}\right]$

$f'(1) = \dfrac{16}{2}(15) = 8(15) = 120$

17. (i) By using product rule

$f' = (x^2 - 5x + 8)(x^3 + 7x + 9)' + (x^3 + 7x + 9)(x^2 - 5x + 8)'$

$f' = (x^2 - 5x + 8)(3x^2 + 7) + (x^3 + 7x + 9)(2x - 5)$

$f' = 3x^4 - 15x^3 + 24x^2 + 7x^2 - 35x + 56 +$

$\qquad\qquad 2x^4 + 14x^2 + 18x - 5x^3 - 35x - 45$

$f' = 5x^4 - 20x^3 + 45x^2 - 52x + 11.$

(ii) By expanding the product to obtain a single polynomial

$f(x) = x^5 - 5x^4 + 15x^3 - 26x^2 + 11x + 72$

$f' = 5x^4 - 20x^3 + 45x^2 - 52x + 11$

(iii) By logarithm differentiation

Let $f(x) = y = (x^2 - 5x + 8)(x^3 + 7x + 9)$

Taking log both the sides, we get

$\log y = \log(x^2 - 5x + 8) + \log(x^3 + 7x + 9)$

$\dfrac{1}{y}\dfrac{dy}{dx} = \dfrac{1}{(x^2 - 5x + 8)}(2x - 5) + \dfrac{1}{(x^3 + 7x + 9)}(3x^2 + 7)$

$\dfrac{dy}{dx} = 5x^4 - 20x^3 + 45x^2 - 52x + 11$

in all the three case answer is same.

18. Let $y = u \cdot v \cdot w \implies y = u \cdot (vw)$

(i) $\dfrac{dy}{dx} = u' \cdot (vw) + u \dfrac{d}{dx}(vw)$

$= u' \cdot v.w + u\, v'w + uvw'$

$\therefore \dfrac{dy}{dx} = \dfrac{du}{dx} v.\,w + u.\dfrac{dv}{dx}.w + u.v.\dfrac{dw}{dx}$

(ii) $y = u \cdot v \cdot w$

Taking log of both sides,

$\log y = \log u + \log v + \log w ,$

Differentiating w.r.t. x

$\dfrac{1}{y}\dfrac{dy}{dx} = \dfrac{1}{u}\dfrac{du}{dx} + \dfrac{1}{v}\dfrac{dv}{dx} + \dfrac{1}{w}\dfrac{dw}{dx}$

$\implies \dfrac{dy}{dx} = uvw\left(\dfrac{1}{u}\dfrac{du}{dx} + \dfrac{1}{v}\dfrac{dv}{dx} + \dfrac{1}{w}\dfrac{dw}{dx}\right)$

$\therefore \dfrac{dy}{dx} = \dfrac{du}{dx}.v.\,w + u.\dfrac{dv}{dx}.w + u.v.\dfrac{dw}{dx}$

Practice Exercise-6

1. (a) **2.** (a) **3.** (b) **4.** (a)

5. $\sqrt{\dfrac{1-\theta}{1+\theta}}$

6. $3x^3 e^{x^3}$

7. $1 - 3x + 2x^2$

8. $\dfrac{1+t^2}{2at}$

9. $\dfrac{1}{2}$

NCERT Exercise-6

1. $\dfrac{dx}{dt} = 4at, \dfrac{dy}{dt} = 4at^3 \implies \dfrac{dy}{dx} = \dfrac{\frac{dy}{dt}}{\frac{dx}{dt}} = \dfrac{4at^3}{4at} = t^2$

2. $\dfrac{dx}{d\theta} = -a\sin\theta, \dfrac{dy}{d\theta} = -\sin b \sin\theta$

$\therefore \dfrac{dy}{dx} = \dfrac{\frac{dy}{d\theta}}{\frac{dx}{d\theta}} = \dfrac{b}{a}$

3. Do it yourself.

4. Do it yourself.

5. Do it yourself.

6. Do it yourself.

7. Do it yourself.

8. Do it yourself.

9. Do it yourself.

10. Do it yourself.

11. Let $x = \sqrt{s}, \; s = a^u, u = \sin^{-1} t$

$\dfrac{dx}{ds} = \dfrac{1}{2\sqrt{s}}, \dfrac{ds}{du} = a^4 \log a, \dfrac{du}{dt} = \dfrac{1}{\sqrt{1-t^2}},$

$\dfrac{dx}{dt} = \dfrac{dx}{ds} \times \dfrac{ds}{du} \times \dfrac{du}{dt} = \dfrac{\sqrt{a^{\sin^{-1}t}}\log a}{2\sqrt{1-t^2}}$

Let $y = \sqrt{s}, s = a^u, u = \cos^{-1} t ,$

$\dfrac{dy}{ds} = \dfrac{1}{2\sqrt{s}}, \dfrac{ds}{du} a^4 \log a, \dfrac{du}{dt} = \dfrac{-1}{\sqrt{1-t^2}}$

$\dfrac{dy}{dt} = \dfrac{dy}{ds} \times \dfrac{ds}{du} \times \dfrac{du}{dt} = \dfrac{-\sqrt{a^{\cos^{-1}t}}\log a}{2\sqrt{1-t^2}}$

$\therefore \dfrac{dy}{dx} = \dfrac{\frac{dy}{dt}}{\frac{dx}{dt}} = \dfrac{\sqrt{a^{\cos^{-1}t}}}{\sqrt{a^{\sin^{-1}t}}} = -\dfrac{y}{x}$

Practice Exercise-7

1. (b) **2.** (d) **3.** (b) **4.** $\dfrac{5}{16+6}$ **5.** $\dfrac{4\sqrt{2}}{3a}$

6. $\dfrac{-2}{x^2}$

Hint : $y = \log\left(\dfrac{x^2}{e^x}\right) = \log x^2 - \log e^x.$

7. $\dfrac{1}{a}$

8. $-\dfrac{8}{9}$

9. $\dfrac{d^2 y}{dx^2} = 0$

10. $\dfrac{d^2 y}{dx^2} = \dfrac{dy}{dx} \log ab^2 = y\left(\log ab^2\right)^2$

NCERT Exercise-7

1. Here, $\dfrac{dy}{dx} = 2x + 3$ and $\dfrac{d^2 y}{dx^2} = 2.$

2. Do it yourself.

3. $\dfrac{dy}{dx} = x\,(-\sin x) + \cos x \cdot 1 = -x \sin x + \cos x$

and $\dfrac{d^2 y}{dx^2} = -x \cos x - \sin x - \sin x = -x \cos x - 2 \sin x$

4. Do it yourself.

5. $\dfrac{dy}{dx} = x^3 \cdot \dfrac{1}{x} + \log x \times 3x^2 = x^2 + 3x^2 \log x$

and $\dfrac{d^2 y}{dx^2} = 2x + 3x^2 \cdot \dfrac{1}{x} + \log x \cdot 6x = 5x + 6x \log x$

6. $\dfrac{dy}{dx} = e^x \cdot \cos 5x \cdot 5 + \sin 5x \cdot e^x = e^x\,(5 \cos 5x + \sin 5x)$

$\Rightarrow \dfrac{d^2 y}{dx^2} = e^x\,(-25 \sin 5x + t \cos 5x)$

$+ (5 \cos 5x + \sin 5x) \cdot e^x$

$= 2e^x\,(5 \cos 5x - 12 \sin 5x)$

7. Do it yourself.

8. $\dfrac{dy}{dx} = \dfrac{1}{1 + x^2}$ and $\dfrac{d^2 y}{dx^2} = \dfrac{-2x}{(1 + x^2)^2}$

9. Do it yourself.

10. $\dfrac{dy}{dx} = \cos\,(\log x) \cdot \dfrac{1}{x}$

$\Rightarrow \dfrac{dy}{dx} = \dfrac{\cos\,(\log x)}{x}$

and $\dfrac{d^2 y}{dx^2} = \dfrac{x \cdot [-\sin\,(\log x)] \cdot \dfrac{1}{x} - \cos\,(\log x) \cdot 1}{x^2}$

$= \dfrac{[-\sin\,(\log x) + \cos\,(\log x)]}{x^2}$

11. Here, $\dfrac{dy}{dx} = -5 \sin x - 3 \cos x$

$\dfrac{d^2 y}{dx^2} = -5 \cos x + 3 \sin x = -y$

$\Rightarrow \dfrac{d^2 y}{dx^2} + y = 0.$

12. $y = \cos^{-1} x \Rightarrow \dfrac{dy}{dx} = -(1 - x^2)^{-\frac{1}{2}}$

$\Rightarrow \dfrac{d^2 y}{dx^2} = \dfrac{-\cos y}{(\sin^2 y)^{3/2}} = \dfrac{-\cos y}{\sin^3 y} = -\cot y \,\operatorname{cosec}^2 y.$

13. Here, $\dfrac{dy}{dx} = y_1 = \dfrac{-3 \sin\,(\log x)}{x} + \dfrac{4 \cos\,(\log x)}{x}$

$xy_1 = -3 \sin\,(\log x) + 4 \cos\,(\log x)$

Again $xy_2 + y_1 \cdot 1 = -\dfrac{3 \cos\,(\log x)}{x} - \dfrac{4 \sin\,(\log x)}{x}$

$\Rightarrow xy_2 + y_1 = -\dfrac{y}{x} \Rightarrow x^2 y_2 + xy_1 + y = 0.$ Hence proved.

14. We have $y = A\,e^{mx} + B\,e^{nx},$

$\dfrac{dy}{dx} = A \cdot m\,e^{mx} + B \cdot n e^{nx}$

and $\dfrac{d^2 y}{dx^2} = A \cdot m^2\,e^{mx} + B \cdot n^2\,e^{nx}$

L.H.S. $= \dfrac{d^2 y}{dx^2} - (m + n)\,\dfrac{dy}{dx} + mny$

$= A \cdot m^2\,e^{mx} + B \cdot n^2\,e^{nx} - (m + n)$

$(A \cdot me^{mx} + B \cdot ne^{nx}) + mny$

$= A \cdot m^2\,e^{mx} + B \cdot n^2\,e^{nx} - A \cdot m^2\,e^{mx} - B \cdot mne^{nx}$

$-A \cdot mne^{mx} - B \cdot n^2\,e^{nx} + A \cdot mn\,e^{mx} + B \cdot mne^{nx}$

$= 0 = $ R.H.S. Hence proved.

15. We have $y = 500\,e^{7x} + 600\,e^{-7x}$

$\dfrac{dy}{dx} = 500 \times 7\,e^{7x} + 600 \times (-7)\,e^{-7x}$

and $\dfrac{d^2 y}{dx^2} = 500 \times 49\,e^{7x} + 600 \times (49)\,e^{-7x}$

$= 49\,(500\,e^{7x} + 600\,e^{-7x}) = 49\,y$

$\therefore \quad \dfrac{d^2 y}{dx^2} = 49\,y.$ Hence proved.

16. $e^y (x + 1) = 1 \Rightarrow e^y = \dfrac{1}{x+1}$

$e^y \dfrac{dy}{dx} = \dfrac{-1}{(x+1)^2} \Rightarrow \dfrac{dy}{dx} = \dfrac{-1}{(x+1)^2} \cdot \dfrac{1}{e^y} = \dfrac{-1}{(x+1)}$

$\Rightarrow \dfrac{d^2 y}{dx^2} = \left(\dfrac{-1}{x+1}\right)^2 = \left(\dfrac{dy}{dx}\right)^2 \Rightarrow \dfrac{d^2 y}{dx^2} = \left(\dfrac{dy}{dx}\right)^2$

17. We have $y = (\tan^{-1} x)^2$,

$\dfrac{dy}{dx} = y_1 = 2 \tan^{-1} x \cdot \dfrac{1}{1 + x^2}$

$y_1 = \dfrac{2 \tan^{-1} x}{1 + x^2} \Rightarrow (1 + x^2) y_1 = 2 \tan^{-1} x$

Again $(1 + x^2) y_2 + y_1 \cdot 2x = \dfrac{2}{1 + x^2}$

$\Rightarrow (1 + x^2)^2 y_2 + 2x (1 + x^2) y_1 = 2.$ Hence proved.

Past year Exercise 

1. Let $y = \tan^{-1}\left[\dfrac{\sqrt{1 + x^2} - 1}{x}\right]$

Put $x = \tan \theta \Rightarrow \theta = \tan^{-1} x$

$\therefore$ We get $y = \tan^{-1} \dfrac{\sqrt{1 + \tan^2 \theta} - 1}{\tan \theta}$

$y = \tan^{-1}\left[\dfrac{\sec \theta - 1}{\tan \theta}\right]$

$\Rightarrow y = \tan^{-1}\left[\dfrac{\dfrac{1}{\cos \theta} - 1}{\dfrac{\sin \theta}{\cos \theta}}\right]$

$\Rightarrow y = \tan^{-1}\left[\dfrac{1 - \cos \theta}{\sin \theta}\right]$

$\Rightarrow y = \tan^{-1}\left[\dfrac{2 \sin^2 \dfrac{\theta}{2}}{2 \sin \dfrac{\theta}{2} \cos \dfrac{\theta}{2}}\right]$

$\left(\because 1 - \cos x = 2 \sin^2 \dfrac{x}{2} \text{ and } \sin x = 2 \sin \dfrac{x}{2} \cos \dfrac{x}{2}\right)$

$\Rightarrow y = \tan^{-1}\left(\tan \dfrac{\theta}{2}\right)$

$\Rightarrow y = \dfrac{\theta}{2} \Rightarrow y = \dfrac{\tan^{-1} x}{2}$

Differentiating both sides wrt x, we get

$\dfrac{dy}{dx} = \dfrac{1}{2} \cdot \dfrac{1}{1 + x^2}$

Hence, $\dfrac{dy}{dx} = \dfrac{1}{2(1 + x^2)}$

2. Here, $f(x) = |x - 3|, x \in R$

$f(x) = \begin{cases} -(x - 3), & \text{if } x < 3 \\ x - 3, & \text{if } x \geq 3 \end{cases}$

When $x < 3$, $f(x) = -(x - 3)$, which being a polynomial function, is continuous and differentiable for all $x < 3$.
When $x > 3$, $f(x) = x - 3$, which being a polynomial function, is continuous and differentiable for all $x > 3$.

Check for Differentiability at $x = 3$

L.H.D. (at $x = 3$)

$= \lim_{x \to 3^-}\left(\dfrac{f(x) - f(3)}{x - 3}\right) = \lim_{x \to 3^-} \dfrac{-(x - 3) - 0}{x - 3} = -1$

R.H.D. (at $x = 3$)

$= \lim_{x \to 3^+}\left(\dfrac{f(x) - f(3)}{x - 3}\right) = \lim_{x \to 3^+} \dfrac{x - 3 - 0}{x - 3} = 1$

Since, L.H.D. (at $x = 3$) $\neq$ R.H.D. (at $x = 3$)

$\therefore$ $f(x)$ is not differentiable at $x = 3$

$\lim_{x \to 3^-} f(x) = \lim_{x \to 3^-} -(x - 3) = 0$ and

$\lim_{x \to 3^+} f(x) = \lim_{x \to 3^+} (x - 3) = 0$ and $f(3) = 0$

$\lim_{x \to 3^-} f(x) = \lim_{x \to 3^+} f(x) = f(3)$

Thus, $f(x)$ is continuous at $x = 3$

OR

Here, $x = a \sin t \Rightarrow \dfrac{dx}{dt} = a \cos t$ ...(i)

And $y = a\left(\cos t + \log \tan \dfrac{t}{2}\right)$

$\Rightarrow \dfrac{dy}{dt} = a\left\{-\sin t + \dfrac{1}{\tan \dfrac{t}{2}}.\sec^2 \dfrac{t}{2}.\dfrac{1}{2}\right\}$

$= a\left\{-\sin t + \dfrac{1}{\dfrac{\sin \dfrac{t}{2}}{\cos \dfrac{t}{2}}}.\dfrac{1}{\cos^2 \dfrac{t}{2}}.\dfrac{1}{2}\right\} = a\left\{-\sin t + \dfrac{1}{\sin t}\right\}$

$= a\left(\dfrac{\cos^2 t}{\sin t}\right)$ ...(ii)

From (i) and (ii), we have

$\dfrac{dy}{dx} = \dfrac{a\left(\dfrac{\cos^2 t}{\sin t}\right)}{a\cos t} = \cot t$

$\dfrac{d^2y}{dx^2} = -\cos ec^2 t.\dfrac{dt}{dx}$

$= -\cos ec^2 t.\dfrac{1}{a\cos t} = -\dfrac{1}{a}\cos ec^2 t.\sec t$

3. Let $y = \sin^{-1}\left(\dfrac{2^{x+1}.3^x}{1+(36)^x}\right)$

$= \sin^{-1}\left(\dfrac{2^x.2.3^x}{1+(6)^{2x}}\right) = \sin^{-1}\left(\dfrac{2.6^x}{1+(6)^{2x}}\right)$

Put $6^x = \tan\theta \Rightarrow 1 + (6)^{2x} = 1 + \tan^2\theta = \sec^2\theta$

Now, $y = \sin^{-1}\left(\dfrac{2\tan\theta}{\sec^2\theta}\right)$

$= \sin^{-1}\left(2\dfrac{\sin\theta}{\cos\theta}.\cos^2\theta\right) = \sin^{-1}(\sin 2\theta)$

$y = 2\theta$

$y = 2\tan^{-1}(6^x)$

Differentiate both sides w.r.t. x, we have

$\dfrac{dy}{dx} = 2.\dfrac{1}{1+\left(6^x\right)^2}.6^x \log 6 = \dfrac{2.6^x \log 6}{1+(6)^{2x}}$

4. Let $y = \log\left[x + \sqrt{x^2 + a^2}\right]$

Differentiating w.r.t. x, we have

$\dfrac{dy}{dx} = \dfrac{1}{x + \sqrt{x^2 + a^2}} \times \left(1 + \dfrac{1}{2}.\left(x^2 + a^2\right)^{-\frac{1}{2}}.2x\right)$

$= \dfrac{1}{x + \sqrt{x^2 + a^2}} \times \left(1 + \dfrac{x}{\sqrt{x^2 + a^2}}\right)$

$\dfrac{dy}{dx} = \dfrac{1}{x + \sqrt{x^2 + a^2}} \times \left(\dfrac{\sqrt{x^2 + a^2} + x}{\sqrt{x^2 + a^2}}\right)$

$= \dfrac{1}{\sqrt{x^2 + a^2}} \Rightarrow \left(\sqrt{x^2 + a^2}\right)\dfrac{dy}{dx} = 1$

Again differentiating both sides w.r.t. x, we have

$\left(\sqrt{x^2 + a^2}\right)\dfrac{d^2y}{dx^2} + \dfrac{1}{2}\left(x^2 + a^2\right)^{-\frac{1}{2}}.(2x).\dfrac{dy}{dx} = 0$

$\Rightarrow \left(x^2 + a^2\right)\dfrac{d^2y}{dx^2} + x\dfrac{dy}{dx} = 0$

5. Let, $x \sin(a + y) + \sin a \cos(a + y) = 0$

$\Rightarrow x = -\dfrac{\sin a \cos(a + y)}{\sin(a + y)}$

Differentiating w.r.t. y, we have

$\dfrac{dx}{dy} = \dfrac{-\sin a[\sin(a+y)\{-\sin(a+y)\} - \cos(a+y)\cos(a+y)]}{[\sin(a+y)]^2}$

$= \dfrac{\sin a\left[\sin^2(a+y) + \cos^2(a+y)\right]}{\sin^2(a+y)}$

$\dfrac{dx}{dy} = \dfrac{\sin a}{\sin^2(a+y)} \quad \left(\because \sin^2\theta + \cos^2\theta = 1\right)$

$\Rightarrow \dfrac{dy}{dx} = \dfrac{\sin^2(a+y)}{\sin a}$

6. $\lim\limits_{x\to 0^-} f(x) = \lim\limits_{x\to 0^-}\left(\dfrac{\sqrt{1+kx}-\sqrt{1-kx}}{x}\right)$

$= \lim\limits_{x\to 0^-}\left(\dfrac{\sqrt{1+kx}-\sqrt{1-kx}}{x}\times\dfrac{\sqrt{1+kx}+\sqrt{1-kx}}{\sqrt{1+kx}+\sqrt{1-kx}}\right)$

$= \lim\limits_{x\to 0^-}\left(\dfrac{1+kx-1+kx}{x\left(\sqrt{1+kx}+\sqrt{1-kx}\right)}\right)$

$= \lim\limits_{x\to 0^-}\left(\dfrac{2kx}{x\left(\sqrt{1+kx}+\sqrt{1-kx}\right)}\right)$

$= \lim\limits_{x\to 0^-}\left(\dfrac{2k}{\left(\sqrt{1+kx}+\sqrt{1-kx}\right)}\right) = \dfrac{2k}{2} = k$

$\lim\limits_{x\to 0^+} f(x) = \lim\limits_{x\to 0^+}\dfrac{2x+1}{x-1} = \dfrac{0+1}{0-1} = -1$

Since f(x) is continuous at x = 0

$\Rightarrow \lim\limits_{x\to 0^-} f(x) = \lim\limits_{x\to 0^+} f(x) \Rightarrow k = -1$

OR

Let $x = a\cos^3\theta$

Diff. w.r.t., 'θ'

$\Rightarrow \dfrac{dx}{d\theta} = -3a\cos^2\theta\sin\theta$ ...(i)

and $y = a\sin^3\theta$

Diff. w.r.t., 'θ'

$\Rightarrow \dfrac{dy}{d\theta} = 3a\sin^2\theta\cos\theta$ ...(ii)

From (i) and (ii), we have

$\dfrac{dy}{dx} = \dfrac{3a\sin^2\theta\cos\theta}{-3a\cos^2\theta\sin\theta}$

$\dfrac{dy}{dx} = -\tan\theta \Rightarrow \dfrac{d^2y}{dx^2} = -\sec^2\theta\dfrac{d\theta}{dx}$

$\dfrac{d^2y}{dx^2} = -\sec^2\theta\cdot\dfrac{1}{-3a\cos^2\theta\sin\theta} = \dfrac{1}{3a}\sec^4\theta.\cos ec\theta$

Now, $\dfrac{d^2y}{dx^2}\bigg]_{\theta=\frac{\pi}{6}} = \dfrac{32}{27a}$

7. We have $y = \left(x+\sqrt{x^2+1}\right)^m$ ....(i)

$\therefore \dfrac{dy}{dx} = m\left(x+\sqrt{x^2+1}\right)^{m-1}\dfrac{d}{dx}\left(x+\sqrt{x^2+1}\right)$

$= m\left(x+\sqrt{x^2+1}\right)^{m-1}\left[1+\dfrac{1}{2\sqrt{x^2+1}}(2x-0)\right]$

$= m\left(x+\sqrt{x^2+1}\right)^{m-1}\left(\dfrac{x+\sqrt{x^2+1}}{\sqrt{x^2+1}}\right)$

$\Rightarrow \sqrt{x^2+1}\dfrac{dy}{dx} = m\left(x+\sqrt{x^2+1}\right)^m$

$\Rightarrow \sqrt{x^2+1}\dfrac{dy}{dx} = my$ ...(ii) [using (i)]

Diff. w.r.t. x, $\sqrt{x^2+1}\dfrac{d^2y}{dx^2}+\dfrac{1}{2\sqrt{x^2+1}}(2x+0)\dfrac{dy}{dx}$

$= m\dfrac{dy}{dx}$

$\Rightarrow \sqrt{x^2+1}\dfrac{d^2y}{dx^2}+\dfrac{x}{\sqrt{x^2+1}}\dfrac{dy}{dx} = m\dfrac{dy}{dx}$

$\Rightarrow \left(x^2+1\right)\dfrac{d^2y}{dx^2}+x\dfrac{dy}{dx} = m\sqrt{x^2+1}\dfrac{dy}{dx}$

$\Rightarrow \left(x^2+1\right)\dfrac{d^2y}{dx^2}+x\dfrac{dy}{dx} = m(my)$ [using (ii)]

$\Rightarrow \left(x^2+1\right)\dfrac{d^2y}{dx^2}+x\dfrac{dy}{dx}-m^2y = 0$

8. Let $u = \tan^{-1}\left(\dfrac{\sqrt{1+x^2}-1}{x}\right)$

Let $x = \tan \theta$, $\theta = \tan^{-1} x$

$$= \tan^{-1} \left(\frac{\sqrt{1+\tan^2 \theta} - 1}{\tan \theta} \right)$$

$$= \tan^{-1} \left(\frac{\sqrt{\sec^2 \theta} - 1}{\tan \theta} \right) = \tan^{-1} \left(\frac{\sec \theta - 1}{\tan \theta} \right)$$

$$= \tan^{-1} \left(\frac{\dfrac{1}{\cos \theta} - 1}{\dfrac{\sin \theta}{\cos \theta}} \right) = \tan^{-1} \left(\frac{1 - \cos \theta}{\sin \theta} \right)$$

$$= \tan^{-1} \left(\frac{2\sin^2 \dfrac{\theta}{2}}{2\sin \dfrac{\theta}{2} \cos \dfrac{\theta}{2}} \right) = \tan^{-1} \left(\tan \frac{\theta}{2} \right) = \frac{\theta}{2}$$

$$u = \frac{1}{2} \tan^{-1} x$$

differentiating w.r.t. x

$$\frac{du}{dx} = \frac{1}{2} \left(\frac{1}{1+x^2} \right) \qquad \qquad ...(i)$$

$$v = \sin^{-1} \left(\frac{2x}{1+x^2} \right) = 2 \tan^{-1} x$$

$$\frac{dv}{dx} = 2 \left(\frac{1}{1+x^2} \right) \qquad \qquad ...(ii)$$

dividing (i) and (ii)

$$\frac{du/dx}{dv/dx} = \frac{du}{dv} = \frac{1(1+x^2)}{2(1+x^2).2} = \frac{1}{4}$$

differentiation of $\tan^{-1} \left(\dfrac{\sqrt{1+x^2} - 1}{x} \right)$ w.r.t. $\sin^{-1} \left(\dfrac{2x}{1+x^2} \right)$

is $\dfrac{1}{4}$.

9.   Let $y = x^x$

Taking log on both sides, we get $\log y = x \log x$

Differentiate both side, w.r.t. 'x'

$$\frac{1}{y} . \frac{dy}{dx} = \frac{x}{x} + \log x = 1 + \log x$$

$$\frac{dy}{dx} = x^x (1 + \log x) = x^x + x^x \log x$$

$$\frac{d^2 y}{dx^2} = \frac{d}{dx}(x^x) + \frac{d}{dx}\left(x^x \log x\right)$$

$$= \left[x^x + x^x \log x \right] + \left[\frac{x^x}{x} + \log x \left\{ \frac{d}{dx} x^x \right\} \right]$$

$$= x^x + x^x \log x + x^{x-1} + \log x \left[x^x (1 + \log x) \right]$$

$$= x^x + x^{x-1} + 4x^x \log x$$

Consider

$$\frac{d^2 y}{dx^2} - \frac{1}{y}\left(\frac{dy}{dx} \right)^2 - \frac{y}{x} = x^x + x^{x-1} + 4x^x \log x$$

$$- \frac{1}{x^x}\left[x^{2x} + (x^x \log x)^2 + 2(x^x)^2 \log x \right] - \frac{x^x}{x}$$

$$= x^x + x^{x-1} + 4x^x \log x - x^x - 2x^x \log x - 2x^x \log x - x^{x-1} = 0$$

Hence proved.

10.   Let $x = \cos t (3 - 2 \cos^2 t)$

and $y = \sin t (3 - 2 \sin^2 t)$

Now, $\dfrac{dx}{dt} = \cos t [4 \cos t (\sin t)] + (3 - 2 \cos^2 t)(- \sin t)$

$$\frac{dy}{dt} = \sin t [- 4 \sin t \cos t] + (3 - 2 \sin^2 t)(\cos t)$$

$$\Rightarrow \quad \frac{dx}{dt} = 6 \sin t \cos^2 t - 3 \sin t = 3 \sin t [2 \cos^2 t - 1]$$

$$= 3 \sin t \cos 2t$$

$$\frac{dy}{dt} = - 6 \sin^2 t \cos t + 3 \cos t$$

$$= 3 \cos t (1 - 2 \sin^2 t) = 3 \cos t \cos 2t$$

Now, $\dfrac{dy}{dx} = \dfrac{dy}{dt} \times \dfrac{dt}{dx} = \dfrac{3 \cos t \cos 2t}{3 \sin t \cos 2t} = \cot t$

$$\left. \frac{dy}{dx} \right|_{t=\frac{\pi}{4}} = \cot \frac{\pi}{4} = 1$$

11. $x = a \sin 2t \, (1 + \cos 2t)$, $y = b \cos 2t \, (1 - \cos 2t)$

$$\frac{dx}{dt} = a \sin 2t \, (-2 \sin 2t) + (1 + \cos 2t)(2a \cos 2t)$$

$$= -2a \sin^2 2t + 2a \cos 2t + 2a \cos^2 2t$$

$$= 2a \, [\cos^2 2t - \sin^2 2t + \cos 2t]$$

$$\frac{dx}{dt} = 2a \, [\cos 4t + \cos 2t]$$

$$\frac{dy}{dt} = b \cos 2t \, (2 \sin 2t) + (1 - \cos 2t)(-2b \sin 2t)$$

$$= 2b \sin 2t \cos 2t - 2b \sin 2t + 2b \sin 2t \cos 2t$$

$$= 2b \, [2 \sin 2t \cos 2t - \sin 2t]$$

$$= 2b \, [\sin 4t - \sin 2t]$$

Using $[\sin C - \sin D = 2 \cos \dfrac{C+D}{2} \sin \dfrac{C-D}{2}]$ and

$[\cos C + \cos D = 2 \cos \dfrac{C+D}{2} \cos \dfrac{C-D}{2}]$

$$\frac{dy/dt}{dx/dt} = \frac{dy}{dx} = \frac{2b[\sin 4t - \sin 2t]}{2a[\cos 4t + \cos 2t]}$$

$$\frac{dy}{dx} = \frac{b}{a} \left[\frac{2 \cos 3t \sin t}{2 \cos 3t \cos t} \right] = \frac{b}{a}(\tan t)$$

$$\frac{dy}{dt}\bigg|_{t=\frac{\pi}{4}} = \frac{b}{a} \left[\tan \frac{\pi}{4} \right] = \frac{b}{a}$$

12. Let $y = Pe^{ax} + Qe^{bx}$

$$\frac{dy}{dx} = Pae^{ax} + Qbe^{bx} \qquad .....(i)$$

$$\frac{d^2y}{dx^2} = Pa^2 e^{ax} + Qb^2 e^{bx} \qquad .....(ii)$$

$$aby = ab \, [Pe^{ax} + Q e^{bx}]$$

$$aby = P \, a \, b \, e^{ax} + Q \, a \, b \, e^{bx}] \qquad .....(iii)$$

Consider

$$\frac{d^2y}{dx^2} - (a+b)\frac{dy}{dx} + aby$$

$$= (Pa^2 e^{ax} + Q b^2 e^{bx}) - (a+b)(Pae^{ax} + Q.be^{bx})$$

$$\qquad + Pabe^{ax} + Q \, abe^{bx} \text{ (from (i), (ii) and (iii))}$$

$$= Pa^2 e^{ax} + Q b^2 e^{bx} - Pa^2 e^{ax} - Qb^2 e^{bx} - Pabe^{ax} - Q \, a \, b \, e^{bx} + P \, a \, b \, e^{ax} + Q \, a \, b \, e^{bx} = 0$$

Hence proved.

13. Let $x = ae^{\theta}(\sin \theta - \cos \theta)$

$$\frac{dx}{d\theta} = ae^{\theta}(\cos \theta + \sin \theta) + (\sin \theta - \cos \theta)a.e^{\theta}$$

$$= 2ae^{\theta} \sin \theta$$

$$y = ae^{\theta}(\sin \theta + \cos \theta)$$

$$\frac{dy}{d\theta} = ae^{\theta}[\cos \theta - \sin \theta] + [\sin \theta + \cos \theta]a.e^{\theta} = 2ae^{\theta} \cos \theta$$

Now, $\dfrac{dy}{dx} = \dfrac{dy}{d\theta} \times \dfrac{d\theta}{dx} = \dfrac{2ae^{\theta} \cos \theta}{2ae^{\theta} \sin \theta} = \cot \theta$

Now, $\dfrac{dy}{dx}\bigg|_{\theta = \frac{\pi}{4}} = \cot \dfrac{\pi}{4} = 1$

14. $y = \cos^{-1}\left(\dfrac{z - z^{-1}}{z + z^{-1}} \right) = \cos^{-1}\left(\dfrac{z^2 - 1}{z^2 + 1} \right)$

Let $z = \tan \theta$

$$\therefore y = \cos^{-1}\left(\frac{\tan^2 \theta - 1}{\tan^2 \theta + 1} \right) = \cos^{-1}\left(-\frac{1 - \tan^2 \theta}{1 + \tan^2 \theta} \right)$$

$$= \pi - \cos^{-1}(\cos 2\theta) \qquad [\cos^{-1}(-x) = \pi - \cos^{-1} x]$$

$$= \pi - 2\theta = \pi - 2 \tan^{-1} z$$

Differentiating both sides w.r.t. z, we have

$$\frac{dy}{dz} = 0 - 2 \times \frac{1}{1 + z^2}$$

$$\therefore \frac{d}{dz} \cos^{-1}\left(\frac{z - z^{-1}}{z + z^{-1}} \right) = \frac{-2}{1 + z^2}$$

15. $f(x) = \cos^{-1}\left[\sin \sqrt{\dfrac{1+x}{2}} \right] + x^x$

Let $f_1(x) = \cos^{-1}\left[\sin \sqrt{\dfrac{1+x}{2}} \right]$ and $f_2(x) = x^x$

Now, $f_1(x) = \cos^{-1}\left[\sin\sqrt{\dfrac{1+x}{2}}\right]$

$= \cos^{-1}\left[\cos\left(\dfrac{\pi}{2} - \sqrt{\dfrac{1+x}{2}}\right)\right] = \dfrac{\pi}{2} - \sqrt{\dfrac{1+x}{2}}$

$\Rightarrow f_1'(x) = -\dfrac{1}{2}\sqrt{\dfrac{2}{1+x}} = -\sqrt{\dfrac{1}{2(1+x)}}$ and $f_2(x) = x^x$

Taking log on both sides, we get $\log f_2(x) = x \log x$

$\Rightarrow \dfrac{1}{f_2(x)} f_2'(x) = \log x + x \cdot \dfrac{1}{x}$

$\Rightarrow \dfrac{1}{f_2(x)} f_2'(x) = \log x + 1$

$\Rightarrow f_2'(x) = f_2(x)(\log x + 1) \Rightarrow f_2' = x^x(\log x + 1)$

$\because \ f(x) = f_1(x) + f_2(x)$

$\because \ f'(x) = f_1'(x) + f_2'(x)$

$= -\sqrt{\dfrac{1}{2(1+x)}} + x^x(\log x + 1)$

At $x = 1$

$f'(1) = -\sqrt{\dfrac{1}{2(1+1)}} + 1^1(\log 1 + 1) = -\dfrac{1}{2} + 1 = \dfrac{1}{2}$

16. We have

$x = a\cos\theta + b\sin\theta$ ....(i)

$y = a\sin\theta - b\cos\theta$ ....(ii)

Squaring and adding (i) and (ii), we get

$x^2 + y^2 = (a\cos\theta + b\sin\theta)^2 + (a\sin\theta - b\sin\theta)^2$

$= a^2\cos^2\theta + b^2\sin^2\theta + 2ab\cos\theta\sin\theta + a^2\sin^2\theta + b^2\cos^2\theta - 2ab\cos\theta\sin\theta$

$= a^2(\cos^2\theta + \sin^2\theta) + b^2(\sin^2\theta + \cos^2\theta)$

$\Rightarrow \ x^2 + y^2 = a^2 + b^2$ .... (iii)

Differentiating both sides of (iii) w.r.t x, we get

$2x + 2y\dfrac{dy}{dx} = 0 \ \Rightarrow \ 2y\dfrac{dy}{dx} = -2x$

$\Rightarrow \ \dfrac{dy}{dx} = -\dfrac{x}{y}$ .... (iv)

Differentiating both sides of (iv) w.r.t. x, we get

$\dfrac{d^2y}{dx^2} = -\left(\dfrac{y\times 1 - x\times\dfrac{dy}{dx}}{y^2}\right) = -\left[\dfrac{y - x\left(-\dfrac{x}{y}\right)}{y^2}\right]$ [From (iv)]

$= -\dfrac{x^2 + y^2}{y^3}$ .... (v)

Now, $y^2\dfrac{d^2y}{dx^2} - x\dfrac{dy}{dx} + y$

$= y^2\left(-\dfrac{x^2 + y^2}{y^3}\right) - x\left(-\dfrac{x}{y}\right) + y$ [From (iv) and (v)]

$= -\dfrac{x^2 + y^2}{y} + \dfrac{x^2}{y} + y = \dfrac{-x^2 - y^2 + x^2 + y^2}{y} = 0$

17. $f(x) = \begin{cases} \dfrac{1 - \sin^3 x}{3\cos^2 x} &, \ \text{if } x < \dfrac{\pi}{2} \\[2ex] p &, \ \text{if } x = \dfrac{\pi}{2} \\[2ex] \dfrac{q(1 - \sin x)}{(\pi - 2x)^2} &, \ \text{if } x > \dfrac{\pi}{2} \end{cases}$

For f(x) to be continuous at $x = \dfrac{\pi}{2}$,

$\lim\limits_{x\to\frac{\pi}{2}^-} f(x) = \lim\limits_{x\to\frac{\pi}{2}^+} f(x) = f\left(\dfrac{\pi}{2}\right)$

L.H.L: $\lim\limits_{x\to\frac{\pi}{2}^-} f(x) = \lim\limits_{x\to\frac{\pi}{2}^-}\left(\dfrac{1 - \sin^3 x}{3\cos^2 x}\right)$

$= \lim\limits_{x\to\frac{\pi}{2}^-} \dfrac{(1 - \sin x)(1 + \sin^2 x + \sin x)}{3\left[1 - \sin^2 x\right]}$

$= \lim\limits_{x\to\frac{\pi}{2}^-} \dfrac{1 + \sin^2 x + \sin x}{3(1 + \sin x)} = \dfrac{1 + 1 + 1}{3(2)} = \dfrac{1}{2}$

R.H.L. $\displaystyle\lim_{x\to\frac{\pi^+}{2}} f(x) = \lim_{x\to\frac{\pi^+}{2}} \frac{q(1-\sin x)}{(\pi-2x)^2}$

As the above form is a $\dfrac{0}{0}$ indeterminate form, we can use L hospital's rule.

$$\lim_{x\to\frac{\pi^+}{2}} f(x) = \lim_{x\to\frac{\pi^+}{2}} \frac{q\sin x}{8} = \frac{q}{8}$$

Now, $\displaystyle\lim_{x\to\frac{\pi^-}{2}} f(x) = \lim_{x\to\frac{\pi^+}{2}} f(x) = f\left(\frac{\pi}{2}\right)$

$$\Rightarrow \quad \frac{1}{2} = \frac{q}{8} = p$$

Therefore, $p = \dfrac{1}{2}$ and $q = \dfrac{8}{2} = 4$

18. $x = \sin t$ & $y = \sin pt$.

$$\therefore \quad \frac{dx}{dt} = \cos t \ \& \ \frac{dy}{dt} = p\cos pt$$

$$\Rightarrow \quad \frac{dy}{dx} = p\frac{\cos pt}{\cos t}$$

$$\Rightarrow \quad y'\cos t = p\cos pt \quad \left(\frac{dy}{dx} = y'\right)$$

Squaring both sides we get:

$y'^2 \cos^2 t = p^2 \cos^2 pt$

$\Rightarrow \quad y'^2(1-\sin^2 t) = p^2(1-\sin^2 pt)$

$\Rightarrow \quad y'^2(1-x^2) = p^2(1-y^2)$

Differentiate w.r.t. 'x' we get

$2y'y''(1-x^2) + (-2x)y'^2 = p^2(-2yy')$

$\Rightarrow \quad y''(1-x^2) - xy' = -p^2 y$

$$\Rightarrow \quad (1-x^2)\frac{d^2y}{dx^2} - x\frac{dy}{dx} + p^2 y = 0 \quad \text{(Hence proved).}$$

19. As $y = \sin(\sin x)$

$$\Rightarrow \quad \frac{dy}{dx} = \cos(\sin x)\cos x \qquad \dots \text{(i)}$$

and $\dfrac{d^2y}{dx^2} = \cos(\sin x)(-\sin x) - \cos^2 x\,(\sin(\sin x))$

Now $\dfrac{d^2y}{dx^2} + \tan x\,\dfrac{dy}{dx} + y\cos^2 x$

$= -\sin x\cos(\sin x) - \cos^2 x\sin(\sin x)$

$\qquad + \dfrac{\sin x}{\cos x} \times \cos x\cos(\sin x) + \sin(\sin x)\cos^2 x$

$= -\sin x\cos(\sin x) - \cos^2 x\sin(\sin x)$

$\qquad\qquad + \sin x\cos(\sin x) + \cos^2 x\sin(\sin x)$

$= 0 = $ R.H.S.

Hence we have proved that

$$\frac{d^2y}{dx^2} + \tan x\,\frac{dy}{dx} + y\cos^2 x = 0 \text{ for } y = \sin(\sin x)$$

NCERT Exemplar 

1. **(d)** We know that, sum, product and difference of two polynomials is a polynomials, and polynomial function is everywhere continuous.

Now, we check the continuity of $\dfrac{g(x)}{f(x)}$

$$\frac{g(x)}{f(x)} = \frac{\dfrac{x^2}{2}+1}{2x}$$

Clearly, $\dfrac{g(x)}{f(x)}$ is not defined at $x = 0$

$\therefore$ It is discontinuous at $x = 0$

2. **(a)** $f(x) = \cot x$ is discontinuous if $\cot x \to \infty$

$\Rightarrow \cot x = \cot 0 \Rightarrow x = n\pi$ and $\forall n \in Z$

3. **(c)** Since, $f(x) = \begin{cases} mx+1, & \text{if } x \le \dfrac{\pi}{2} \\[2mm] (\sin x + n), & \text{if } x > \dfrac{\pi}{2} \end{cases}$

is continuous at $x = \dfrac{\pi}{2}$

$$\text{RHL} = \lim_{x \to \left(\frac{\pi}{2}\right)^+} (\sin x + n) = \lim_{h \to 0}\left[\sin\left(\frac{\pi}{2} + h\right) + n\right]$$

$$= \lim_{h \to 0}[\cos h + n] = \cos 0 + n = 1 + n$$

$$\text{LHL} = \lim_{x \to \left(\frac{\pi}{2}\right)^-} (mx + 1) = \lim_{h \to 0}\left[m\left(\frac{\pi}{2} - h\right) + 1\right] = \frac{m\pi}{2} + 1$$

As $f(x)$ is continuous at $x = \dfrac{\pi}{2}$. So

$$\text{LHL} = \text{RHL}$$

$$\Rightarrow \quad m\frac{\pi}{2} + 1 = n + 1 \text{ Hence, } n = m\frac{\pi}{2}$$

4.   (b) Since, $x = t^2$ and $y = t^3$

So, $\dfrac{dx}{dt} = 2t$ and $\dfrac{dy}{dt} = 3t^2$ ...(i)

and $\dfrac{dy}{dx} = \dfrac{dy/dt}{dx/dt} = \dfrac{3t^2}{2t} = \dfrac{3}{2}t$

Again differentiating w.r.t. x, we have

$$\frac{d^2 y}{dx^2} = \frac{3}{2}\left(\frac{d}{dt}t\right)\left(\frac{dt}{dx}\right) = \frac{3}{2}\left(\frac{1}{2t}\right) \qquad \text{[From eq. (i)]}$$

$$= \frac{3}{4t}$$

5.   Here $f(x) = \begin{cases} 1 + x, \text{if } x \le 2 \\ 5 - x, \text{if } x > 2 \end{cases}$ at $x = 2$

For differentiability at $x = 2$,

$$\text{LHD} = \lim_{x \to 2^-} \frac{f(x) - f(2)}{x - 2} = \lim_{x \to 2^-} \frac{(1 + x) - (1 + 2)}{x - 2}$$

$$= \lim_{h \to 0} \frac{(1 + 2 - h) - 3}{2 - h - 2} = \lim_{h \to 0} \frac{-h}{-h} = 1$$

$$\text{RHD} = \lim_{x \to 2^+} \frac{f(x) - f(2)}{x - 2} = \lim_{x \to 2^+} \frac{(5 - x) - 3}{x - 2}$$

$$= \lim_{h \to 0} \frac{5 - (2 + h) - 3}{2 + h - 2} = \lim_{h \to 0} \frac{-h}{+h} = -1 \ne \text{LHD}.$$

Therefore, $f(x)$ is not differentiable at $x = 2$.

6. $\therefore \quad \dfrac{dy}{dx} = \dfrac{d}{dx}\log(x + \sqrt{x^2 + a})$

$$= \frac{1}{(x + \sqrt{x^2 + a})} \cdot \frac{d}{dx}[x + \sqrt{x^2 + a}]$$

$$= \frac{1}{(x + \sqrt{x^2 + 1})}\left[1 + \frac{1}{2}(x^2 + a)^{-1/2} \cdot 2x\right]$$

$$= \frac{1}{x + \sqrt{x^2 + a}} \cdot \int 1 + \frac{x}{\sqrt{x^2 + a}}$$

$$= \frac{\left(\sqrt{x^2 + a} + x\right)}{\left(x + \sqrt{x^2 + a}\right)\left(\sqrt{x^2 + a}\right)} = \frac{1}{\left(\sqrt{x^2 + a}\right)}$$

7. $\dfrac{dy}{dx} = \dfrac{d}{dx}\tan^{-1}(\sec x + \tan x)$

$$= \frac{1}{1 + (\sec x + \tan x)^2} \cdot \frac{d}{dx}(\sec x + \tan x)$$

$$\left[\because \frac{d}{dx}(\tan^{-1} x) = \frac{1}{1 + x^2}\right]$$

$$= \frac{1}{1 + \sec^2 x + \tan^2 x + 2\sec x \cdot \tan x}$$

$$\cdot [\sec x \cdot \tan x + \sec^2 x]$$

$$= \frac{1}{2}$$

8. $\because \quad x = e^{\theta}\left(\theta + \dfrac{1}{\theta}\right)$ and $y = e^{-\theta}\left(\theta - \dfrac{1}{\theta}\right)$

$$\therefore \quad \frac{dx}{d\theta} = \frac{d}{d\theta}\left[e^{\theta} \cdot \left(\theta + \frac{1}{\theta}\right)\right]$$

$$= e^{\theta} \cdot \frac{d}{d\theta}\left(\theta + \frac{1}{\theta}\right) + \left(\theta + \frac{1}{\theta}\right) \cdot \frac{d}{d\theta}e^{\theta}$$

$$= e^{\theta}\left(1 - \frac{1}{\theta^2}\right) + \left(\theta + \frac{1}{\theta}\right)e^{\theta}$$

$$= e^{\theta}\left(\frac{\theta^2 - 1 + \theta^3 + \theta}{\theta^2}\right) \qquad \text{...(i)}$$

and $\dfrac{dy}{d\theta} = \dfrac{d}{d\theta}\left[e^{-\theta}\cdot\left(\theta-\dfrac{1}{\theta}\right)\right]$

$= e^{-\theta}\cdot\dfrac{d}{d\theta}\left(\theta-\dfrac{1}{\theta}\right)+\left(\theta-\dfrac{1}{\theta}\right)\dfrac{d}{d\theta}e^{-\theta}$

$= e^{-\theta}\left(1+\dfrac{1}{\theta^2}\right)+\left(\theta-\dfrac{1}{\theta}\right)e^{-\theta}\cdot\dfrac{d}{d\theta}(-\theta)$

$= e^{-\theta}\left[\dfrac{\theta^2+1-\theta^3+\theta}{\theta^2}\right]$　...(ii)

$\therefore \dfrac{dy}{dx} = \dfrac{dy/d\theta}{dx/d\theta} = \dfrac{e^{-\theta}\left(\dfrac{\theta^2+1-\theta^3+\theta}{\theta^2}\right)}{e^{\theta}\left(\dfrac{\theta^2-1+\theta^3+\theta}{\theta^2}\right)}$

$= e^{-2\theta}\left(\dfrac{-\theta^3+\theta^2+\theta+1}{\theta^3+\theta^2+\theta-1}\right)$

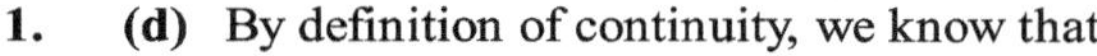

Objective Practice Exercise

1. **(d)** By definition of continuity, we know that

$$\lim_{x\to 3^+} f(x) = f(3) = \lim_{x\to 3^-} f(x)$$

$\Rightarrow \lim_{x\to 3^-} f(x) = 4$　or　$\lim_{h\to 0} 3-h+\lambda = 4$

$\Rightarrow 3 + \lambda = 4 \Rightarrow \lambda = 1$

2. **(d)** $f(0^-) = \lim_{x\to 0^-} k(2x-x^2) = 0$

$f(0^+) = \lim_{x\to 0^+} \cos x = 1$ and $f(0) = \cos x = 1$

Hence no value of k can make $f(0^-) = 1$

3. **(d)**

4. **(c)** $f(0) = 0$;

$$\lim_{h\to 0} f(0-h) = \lim_{h\to 0}\dfrac{-h}{e^{-1/h}+1} = \lim_{h\to 0}\dfrac{-h}{1+\dfrac{1}{e^{1/h}}} = 0$$

$$\lim_{h\to 0} f(0-h) = \lim_{h\to 0}\dfrac{h}{e^{1/h}+1} = 0$$

5. **(c)** $\lim_{x\to 0} f(x) = \sin^{-1}(0) = 0$ and $f(0) = 0$

Hence f(x) is continuous at x = 0.

6. **(c)**

7. **(d)** For any x ≠ 1, 2 we find that f(x) is the quotient of two polynomials and a polynomial is everywhere continuous. Therefore f(x) is continuous for all x ≠ 1, 2. Check continuity at x = 1, 2.

8. **(c)** L.H.L. $= \lim_{x\to 0^-}\dfrac{\sqrt{1+kx}-\sqrt{1-kx}}{x} = k$

R.H.L $= \lim_{x\to 0^+}\left(2x^2+3x-2\right) = -2$

Since it is continuous,

Hence, L.H.L = R. H. L $\Rightarrow$ k = −2

9. **(c)**

10. **(c)**

11. **(b)** $\lim_{x\to a^-} f(x) = -1,\ \lim_{x\to a^+} f(x) = 1$ and $f(a) = 1$

$\therefore$ f(x) is discontinuous at x = a

12. **(c)** $f(x) = [x]^2 - [x^2]$

Check continuity at x = 0

$$\lim_{x\to 0^+} f(x) = \lim_{x\to 0^+} [x]^2 - [x^2] = 0$$

$$\lim_{x\to 0^-} f(x) = \lim_{x\to 0^-} [x]^2 - [x^2] \Rightarrow (-1)^2 - 0 = 1$$

Thus, discontinuous at x = 0

Check continuity at x = 1

$$\lim_{x\to 1^+} f(x) = 1-1 = 0$$

$$\lim_{x\to 1^-} f(x) = 0-0 = 0$$

Also f(1) = 0

Hence continuous at x = 1.

13. **(c)**

14. **(a)**

15. **(b)** (i) When $0 \le x < 1$, f(x) doesn't exist as [x] = 0 here.

(ii) Also $\lim_{x\to 1+} f(x) = 1$ and $\lim_{x\to 1-} f(x)$ does not exist.

Hence f(x) is discontinuous at all integers and also in (0, 1).

16. **(c)** $\lim_{x\to 1^+} f(x) = 0$ and $\lim_{x\to 1^-} f(x) = 1+1 = 2$

Hence f'(x) is discontinuous at x = 1.

17. **(b)**   **18** **(b)**

19. **(a)** $\lim\limits_{x\to\pi/2^-} f(x) = \dfrac{\pi}{2},\ \lim\limits_{x\to\pi/2^+} f(x) = \dfrac{-\pi}{2}$

and $f\left(\dfrac{\pi}{2}\right) = \dfrac{\pi}{2}$

20. **(a)**

21. **(c)** $f(x) = \dfrac{2x^2 + 7}{x^2(x+3) - 1(x+3)} = \dfrac{2x^2 + 7}{(x^2 - 1)(x + 3)}$

$= \dfrac{2x^2 + 7}{(x-1)(x+1)(x+3)}$

Hence points of discontinuity are x = 1, x = –1 and x = –3 only.

22. **(d)**

23. **(c)**

24. **(b)** $\lim\limits_{x\to 0} f(x) = \dfrac{\sin^2 ax}{(ax)^2}a^2 = a^2$ and $f(0) = 1$

Hence f(x) is discontinuous at x = 0, when $a \ne \pm 1$.

25. **(b)** $\lim\limits_{x\to 2^-} f(x) = \dfrac{1}{2}$ and $\lim\limits_{x\to 2^+} f(x) = \dfrac{1}{2}$ and $f(2) = 1$

Hence f(x) is discontinuous at x = 2.

26. **(c)** $f(0) = 0$

$\lim\limits_{x\to 0^-} f(x) = \lim\limits_{h\to 0} e^{-1/h} = 0$

and $\lim\limits_{x\to 0^+} f(x) = \lim\limits_{h\to 0} e^{1/h} = \infty$

Hence function is discontinuous at x = 0.

27. **(b)** $f(x) = \begin{cases} e^x\ ; & x \le 0 \\ 1 - x; & 0 < x \le 1 \\ x - 1; & x > 1 \end{cases}$

Right hand derivative,

$Rf'(0) = \lim\limits_{h\to 0} \dfrac{f(0+h) - f(0)}{h} = \lim\limits_{h\to 0} \dfrac{1 - h - 1}{h} = -1$

Left hand derivative,

$Lf'(0) = \lim\limits_{h\to 0} \dfrac{f(0-h) - f(0)}{-h} = \lim\limits_{h\to 0} \dfrac{e^{-h} - 1}{-h} = 1$

So, it is not diffeentiable at x = 0.

Similarly, it is not differentiable at x = 1.

But it is continous at x = 0,1.

28. **(b)**   **29.** **(a)**   **30.** **(c)**   **31.** **(b)**   **32.** **(b)**

33. **(c)**   **34.** **(b)**

35. **(b)** $f(x^3) = 4x^4 \Rightarrow f'(x^3)\,3x^2 = 16x^3 \Rightarrow f'(x^3) = \dfrac{16x^3}{3x^2}$

$f'(8) = \dfrac{16(2)}{3} = \dfrac{32}{3}$

36. **(a)**

37. **(a)**   We have, $y = e^{(1+\log_e x)} \Rightarrow y = e^1 \cdot e^{\log_e x}$

$\Rightarrow\ y = ex$ $\qquad\qquad [\because e^{\log_e x} = x]$

On differentiating, w. r. to x, we get

$\dfrac{dy}{dx} = \dfrac{d}{dx}(ex) \Rightarrow \dfrac{dy}{dx} = e$.

38. **(c)** $xe^{xy} = y + \sin^2 x$ $\qquad$ ...... (i)

When x = 0, then y = 0

Differentiating (i) both sides with respect to x, we get

$e^{xy} + xe^{xy}\left[x\dfrac{dy}{dx} + y\right] = \dfrac{dy}{dx} + 2\sin x \cos x$

Putting x = 0, y = 0, we get: $\dfrac{dy}{dx} = 1$.

39. **(c)**   Given : $f(x) = |x - 1| + |x - 3|$

At $x = 2, |x - 1| = x - 1$

and $|x - 3| = -x + 3$

$\Rightarrow f(x) = x - 1 - x + 3 = 2$

which is a constant function $\Rightarrow f'(2) = 0$

40. **(c)**   Let $y = \cot^{-1}(x^2)$

Differentiate both side w.r.t 'x', we get

$\dfrac{dy}{dx} = -\dfrac{1}{\left[1 + (x^2)^2\right]} \cdot \dfrac{d}{dx}(x^2)$

$\Rightarrow \dfrac{dy}{dx} = -\dfrac{1}{1 + (x^2)^2} \cdot (2x)s \Rightarrow \dfrac{dy}{dx} = \dfrac{-2x}{1 + x^4}$

41. **(c)**   **42.** **(c)**   **43.** **(c)**

44. (d) Let $t = \dfrac{2x-1}{x^2+1}$ then $\Rightarrow y = f(t) \Rightarrow \dfrac{dy}{dx} = f'(t) \cdot \dfrac{dt}{dx}$

$$= \sin t^2 \dfrac{d}{dx}\left(\dfrac{2x-1}{x^2+1}\right) = \dfrac{2(1+x-x^2)}{(1+x^2)^2} \cdot \sin\left(\dfrac{2x-1}{x^2+1}\right)^2$$

45. (d) $\because \ln x = \log_e x$, so

$$f(x) = \log_x (\log_e x) = \dfrac{\log(\log x)}{\log x}$$

$$\Rightarrow f'(x) = \dfrac{\log x \left(\dfrac{1}{x \log x}\right) - \log(\log x) \cdot \dfrac{1}{x}}{(\log x)^2}$$

$$\therefore f'(e) = \dfrac{1/e - 0}{(1)^2} = \dfrac{1}{e}$$

46. (c)

47. (a) Let $y = \cos^{-1}(\cos x)$

$$y' = \dfrac{dy}{dx} = \dfrac{-1}{\sqrt{1-\cos^2 x}}[-(\sin x)] = \dfrac{\sin x}{\sin x} = 1$$

Thus, $\dfrac{dy}{dx} = 1$ in the whole plane or for all x

48. (a) 49. (b)   50. (b)

51. (c) $f(x) = |x-3| + |x-2| = \begin{cases} 2x-5, & x \geq 3 \\ 1, & 2 < x < 3 \\ -2x+5, & x \leq 2 \end{cases}$

$\therefore f(x) = 2x - 5$, for $x > 4$

52. (a) $f'(x) = \begin{cases} 2, & x \geq 3 \\ 0, & 2 < x < 3 \\ -2, & x \geq 2 \end{cases}$

$\Rightarrow$ Slope varies with x value.

53. (c) Function is not differentiable

54. (c) $f(x) = 1, 2 < x < 3$

55. (d) No, because the function $f(x) = [x]$ is not continuous.

Chapter Test

1. (c)

2. (a)

3. (a)

4. (c)

5. $\sin(2x^2)$

6. $4x(x^2 + 1)$

7. (d)

8. (a)

9. (i) (a) (ii) (b) (iii) (d) (iv) (b) (v) (a)

10. $\dfrac{dy}{dx} = \dfrac{3}{1+x^2}$

11. $k = e^2$

13. $f(x) = \sin x \cdot \cos x$ is a continuous function.

6

Application of Derivatives

APPLICATION OF DERIVATIVES

① Increasing and Decreasing Functions

A function $f(x)$ defined in the interval [a,b] will be

Monotonic increasing $\quad f'(x) \geq x \quad (a,b)$
Monotonic decreasing $\quad f'(x) \leq x \quad (a,b)$
Constant function $\quad f'(x) = 0 \ \forall \ x \quad (a,b)$
Strictly increasing $\quad f'(x) > 0 \ \forall \ x \quad (a,b)$
Strictly decreasing $\quad f'(x) < 0 \ \forall \ x \quad (a,b)$

Properties of Monotonic Functions

(1) If $f(x)$ and $g(x)$ are monotonically (strictly) increasing (decreasing) functions on [a, b], then gof (x) is a monotonically (strictly) increasing function on [a, b].
(2) If one of the two functions $f(x)$ and $g(x)$ is strictly (monotonically) increasing and other a strictly (monotonically) decreasing, then gof (x) is strictly (monotonically) decreasing on [a, b].

② Tangents and Normals

- The equation of the tangent at (x_0, y_0) is given below:

  $y - y_0 = m(x - x_0)$, where m = slope of tangent $= \dfrac{dy}{dx}\Big|_{x_0, y_0}$ or $f'(x_0)$

- The equation of the normal at (x_0, y_0) is given below:

  $y - y_0 = -\dfrac{1}{m}(x - x_0)$, where m = slope of tangent at (x_0, y_0)

③ Test of Local Maxima & Minima

First Derivative Test:

Let $f(x)$ be a function differentiable at $x = a$. Then

(a) $x = a$ is a point of local maximum of $f(x)$, if
(I) $f'(a) = 0$ and
(ii) $f'(x)$ changes sign from positive to negative as x increases through a

(b) $x = a$ is a point of local minimum of $f(x)$, if
(I) $f'(a) = 0$ and
(ii) $f'(x)$ changes sign from negative to positive as x increases through a

(c) If $f'(a) = 0$, but $f'(x)$ does not change sign as x increases through a, that is $f'(a)$ has the same sign in the complete neighourhood of a, then a is neither a point of local maximum nor a point of local minimum. In this case, $x = a$ is a point of inflection.

Second Derivative Test:

Let f be a function defined on an interval I and c ∈ I. Let f be twice differentiable at c. Then

(I) $x = c$ is a point of local maxima if $f'(c) = 0$ and $f''(c) < 0$
The value $f(c)$ is local maximum value of f.
(ii) $x = c$ is a point of local minima if $f'(c) = 0$ and $f''(c) > 0$
In this case, $f(c)$ is local minimum value of f.
(iii) The test fails if $f'(c) = 0$ and $f''(c) = 0$
In this case, we go back to the first derivative test and find whether c is a point of local maxima, local minima or a point of inflection.

④ Steps for Finding Absolute Maxima and/or Absolute Minima

(I) Find all critical points of f in the interval, i.e., find value of x where either $f'(x) = 0$ or f is not differentiable.
(ii) Take the end points of the interval.
(iii) At all the above points (in step (i) and (ii)) calculate the value of f.
(iv) Identify the maximum and minimum values of f out of the values calculated in step (iii). The maximum value will be the absolute maximum value of f and the minimum value will be the absolute minimum value of f.

Topic 1   Increasing and Decreasing Functions

INCREASING AND DECREASING FUNCTIONS

(i) Increasing Function

f is said to be increasing on I, if $x_1 < x_2$ on I, then $f(x_1) \le f(x_2)$. for all $x_1, x_2 \in$ I.
In other words, f is increasing on $[a, b]$, if $f'(x) > 0$ for each $x \in (a, b)$

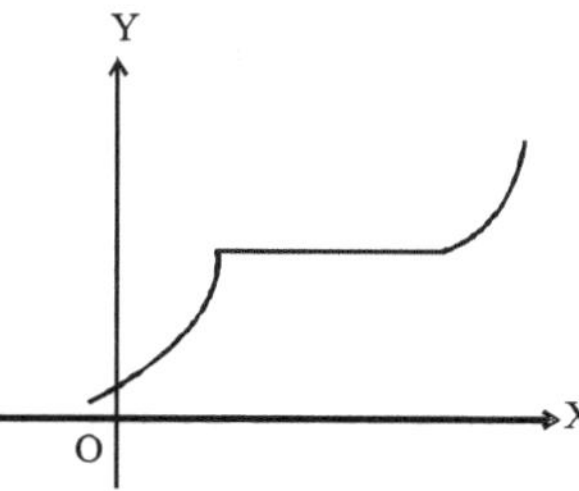

(ii) Strictly Increasing Function

f is said to be strictly increasing on I, if $x_1 < x_2$ in I then $f(x_1) < f(x_2)$ for all $x_1, x_2 \in$ I.
In other words, f is strictly increasing in (a, b) if $f'(x) > 0$ for each $x \in (a, b)$.

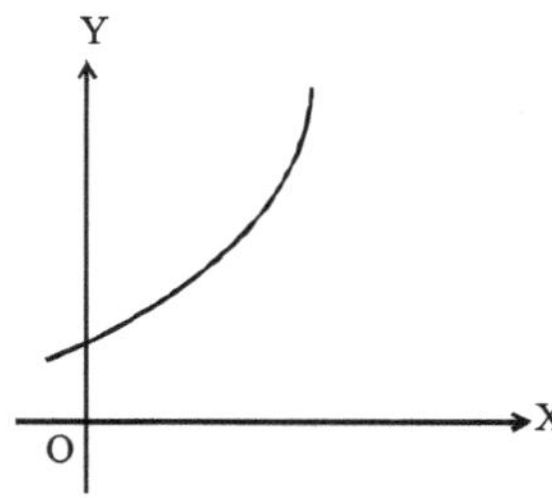

(iii) Decreasing Function

f is said to be decreasing function on I, if $x_1 < x_2$ in I, then $f(x_1) \ge f(x_2)$ for all $x_1, x_2 \in$ I.
In other words, f is decreasing on $[a, b]$, if $f'(x) < 0$ for each $x \in (a, b)$

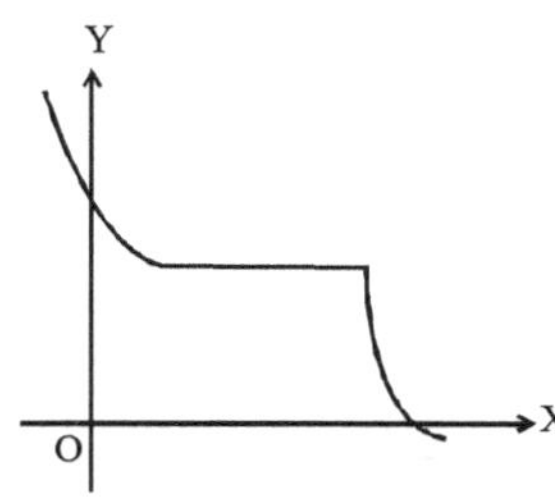

(iv) Strictly Decreasing Function

f is said to be strictly decreasing function on I, if $x_1 > x_2$ in I, then
$f(x_1) > f(x_2)$ for all $x_1, x_2 \in$ I.
In other words, f is strictly decreasing in (a, b) if $f'(x) < 0$ for each $x \in (a, b)$.

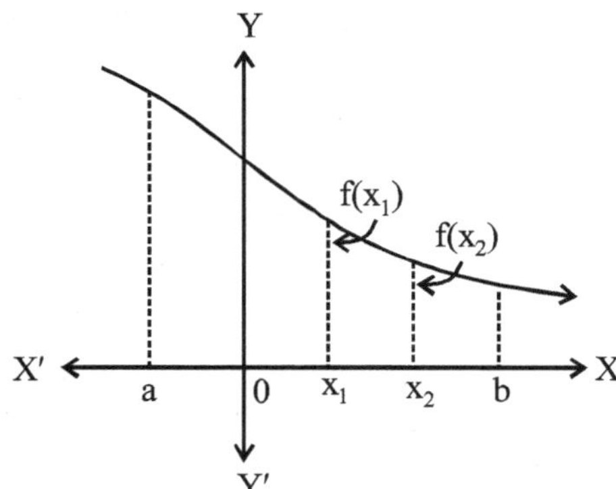

Illustration :

Find the intervals in which the function $f(x)$ is (i) increasing, (ii) decreasing:

$$f(x) = 2x^3 - 9x^2 + 12x + 15$$

Sol. $f(x) = 2x^3 - 9x^2 + 12x + 15$

$f'(x) = 6x^2 - 18x + 12 = 6(x^2 - 3x + 2)$

For increasing and decreasing

$f'(x) = 0$

$\Rightarrow x^2 - 3x + 2 = 0$

$\Rightarrow x = 1, 2$

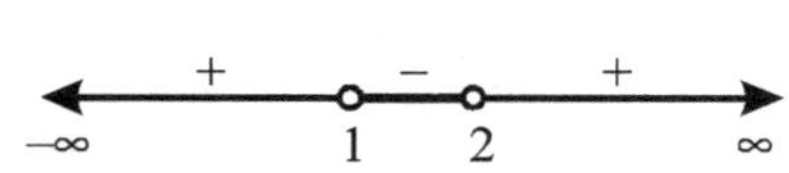

$\therefore$ (i) $f(x)$ is increasing on $(-\infty, 1) \cup (2, \infty)$

     (ii) $f(x)$ is decreasing on $(1, 2)$

Practice Exercise-1

Multiple Choice Questions

1. The function $f(x) = \tan x - 4x$ is strictly decreasing on

(a) $\left(-\dfrac{\pi}{3}, \dfrac{\pi}{3}\right)$ (b) $\left(\dfrac{\pi}{3}, \dfrac{\pi}{2}\right)$

(c) $\left(-\dfrac{\pi}{3}, \dfrac{\pi}{2}\right)$ (d) $\left(\dfrac{\pi}{2}, \pi\right)$

2. If $f(x) = \dfrac{x}{\sin x}$ and $g(x) = \dfrac{x}{\tan x}$, where $0 < x \le 1$, then in this interval,

(a) both $f(x)$ and $g(x)$ are increasing functions
(b) both $f(x)$ and $g(x)$ are decreasing functions
(c) $f(x)$ is an increasing function
(d) $g(x)$ is an increasing function

3. If $f(x) = x + \sin x$, $g(x) = e^{-x}, u = \sqrt{c+1} - \sqrt{c}$,

$v = \sqrt{c} - \sqrt{c-1}, (c > 1)$, then

(a) $fog(u) < fog(v)$ (b) $gof(u) < gof(v)$
(c) $gof(u) > gof(v)$ (d) $fog(u) < fog(v)$

4. $f(x) = \left(\dfrac{e^{2x} - 1}{e^{2x} + 1}\right)$ is

(a) an increasing function   (b) a decreasing function
(c) an even function   (d) None of these

5. If $f(x) = \cos x$, $g(x) = \cos 2x$, $h(x) = \cos 3x$ and $I(x) = \tan x$, then which of the following option is correct?
(a) $f(x)$ and $g(x)$ are strictly decreasing in $(0, \pi/2)$
(b) $h(x)$ is neither increasing nor decreasing in $(0, \pi/2)$
(c) $I(x)$ is strictly increasing in $(0, \pi/2)$
(d) All are correct

Assertion & Reason Questions

DIRECTIONS : *Each of these questions contains an assertion followed by reason. Read them carefully and answer the question on the basis of following options. You have to select the one that best describes the two statements.*

(a) If both Assertion and Reason are correct and the Reason is a correct explanation of the Assertion.
(b) If both Assertion and Reason are correct but Reason is not a correct explanation of the Assertion.
(c) If the Assertion is correct but Reason is incorrect.
(d) If the Assertion is incorrect but the Reason is correct.

6. **Assertion :** Let $f : R \to R$ be a function such that $f(x) = x^3 + x^2 + 3x + \sin x$. Then f is one-one.
Reason : $f(x)$ neither increasing nor decreasing function.

7. **Assertion:** The logarithm function is strictly increasing on $(0, \infty)$.
Reason: The function f given by $f(x) = x^2 - x + 1$ is neither increasing nor decreasing strictly on $(-1, 1)$

Case/Passage Based Question

DIRECTIONS (Q. 8) : *has 5 subparts based on Case/Passage given, attempt any 4 out of 5 questions.*

8. Let f be continuous on $[a, b]$ and differentiable on the open interval (a, b) then :
(a) f is strictly increasing in $[a, b]$ if $f'(x) > 0$ and $f'(x) > 0$ for each $x \in (a, b)$
(b) f is strictly decreasing in $[a, b]$ if $f'(x) < 0$ and $f'(x) < 0$ for each $x \in (a, b)$
(c) f is a constant function in $[a, b]$ if $f'(x) = 0$ and $f'(x) = 0$ for each $x \in (a, b)$
Based on the above information answer the following questions:

(i) The function $f(x) = \sin x$ is strictly increasing in:

(a) $(0, \pi)$ (b) $\left(0, \dfrac{\pi}{2}\right)$ (c) $\left(\dfrac{\pi}{2}, \pi\right)$ (d) $(0, 2\pi)$

(ii) The function $f(x) = x^2 + 3$ is strictly increasing in:
(a) R   (b) R^+ (c) R^- (d) Z

(iii) The function $f(x) = \cos x$ is:

(a) Strictly increasing in $\left(0, \dfrac{\pi}{2}\right)$

(b) Strictly decreasing in $[0, \pi]$
(c) Strictly decreasing in $(0, \pi)$
(d) None of these

(iv) The function $f(x) = e^x$ is strictly increasing on :
(a) R^+ (b) R^- (c) R   (d) N

(v) The function $f(x) = \sin^4 x + \cos^4 x$ is increasing on :

(a) $\left[\dfrac{\pi}{4}, \dfrac{\pi}{2}\right]$ (b) $\left[0, \dfrac{\pi}{4}\right]$

(c) $\left[0, \dfrac{\pi}{2}\right]$ (d) None of these

One Word Questions

9. Find the interval in which the function $f(x) = \dfrac{4x^2 + 1}{x}$ is decreasing.

10. Find the interval in which the function $f(x) = 3x^4 + 4x^3 - 12x^2 + 12$, is increasing.

Very Short Answer Questions

11. Find the values of 'a' for which the function $f(x) = \sin x - ax + b$ increases on R.

12. Find the least value of a such that the function $x^2 + ax + 1$ is increasing on $[1, 2]$.

Short Answer Questions

13. Find the interval in which the function

$f(x) = \dfrac{2x^2 - 1}{x^4}, x > 0$ decreases.

14. Prove that the function $f(x) = x^2 - x + 1$ is neither increasing nor decreasing on $(-1, 1)$.

15. Find the interval in which the function $f(x) = \tan^{-1}(\sin x + \cos x)$ is an increasing function.

NCERT Exercise-1

1. Show that the function given by $f(x) = 3x + 17$ is strictly increasing on R.

2. Show that the function given by $f(x) = e^{2x}$ is strictly increasing on R.

3. Show that the function given by $f(x) = \sin x$ is

(a) strictly increasing in $\left(0, \dfrac{\pi}{2}\right)$

(b) strictly decreasing in $\left(\dfrac{\pi}{2}, \pi\right)$

(c) neither increasing nor decreasing in $(0, \pi)$

4. Find the intervals in which the function f given by $f(x) = 2x^2 - 3x$ is
(a) strictly increasing
(b) strictly decreasing

5. Find the intervals in which the function f given by $f(x) = 2x^3 - 3x^2 - 36x + 7$ is
(a) strictly increasing
(b) strictly decreasing

6. Find the intervals in which the following functions are strictly increasing or decreasing:
(a) $x^2 + 2x - 5$ (b) $10 - 6x - 2x^2$
(c) $-2x^3 - 9x^2 - 12x + 1$ (d) $6 - 9x - x^2$
(e) $(x + 1)^3 (x - 3)^3$

7. Show that $y = \log(1 + x) - \dfrac{2x}{2 + x}$, $x > -1$, is an increasing function of x throughout its domain.

8. Find the values of x for which $y = [x(x - 2)]^2$ is an increasing function.

9. Prove that $y = \dfrac{4\sin\theta}{(2 + \cos\theta)} - \theta$ is an increasing function of θ in $\left[0, \dfrac{\pi}{2}\right]$.

10. Prove that the logarithmic function is strictly increasing on $(0, \infty)$.

11. Prove that the function f given by $f(x) = x^2 - x + 1$ is neither strictly increasing nor strictly decreasing on $(-1, 1)$.

12. Which of the following functions are strictly decreasing on $\left(0, \dfrac{\pi}{2}\right)$?

(a) cos x   (b) cos 2x
(c) cos 3x   (d) tan x

13. On which of the following intervals is the function f given by $f(x) = x^{100} + \sin x - 1$ strictly decreasing ?

(a) $(0, 1)$ (b) $\left(\dfrac{\pi}{2}, \pi\right)$

(c) $\left(0, \dfrac{\pi}{2}\right)$ (d) None of these

14. Find the least value of a such that the function f given by $f(x) = x^2 + ax + 1$ is strictly increasing on $(1, 2)$.

15. Let I be any interval disjoint from $(-1, 1)$. Prove that the function f given by $f(x) = x + \dfrac{1}{x}$ is strictly increasing on I.

16. Prove that the function f given by $f(x) = \log \sin x$ is strictly increasing on $\left(0, \dfrac{\pi}{2}\right)$ and strictly decreasing on $\left(\dfrac{\pi}{2}, \pi\right)$.

17. Prove that the function f given by $f(x) = \log \cos x$ is strictly decreasing on $\left(0, \dfrac{\pi}{2}\right)$ and strictly increasing on $\left(\dfrac{\pi}{2}, \pi\right)$.

18. Prove that the function given by $f(x) = x^3 - 3x^2 + 3x - 100$ is increasing in R.

19. The interval in which $y = x^2 e^{-x}$ is increasing is
(a) $(-\infty, \infty)$ (b) $(-2, 0)$
(c) $(2, \infty)$ (d) $(0, 2)$

Topic 2   Tangents and Normals

TANGENT TO A CURVE

Let $y = f(x)$ be the equation of a curve. The equation of the tangent at (x_0, y_0) is $y - y_0 = m(x - x_0)$, where m = slope of the tangent

$$= \frac{dy}{dx}\bigg]_{(x_0, y_0)} \quad \text{or} \quad f'(x_0)$$

NORMAL TO THE CURVE

Let $y = f(x)$ be the equation of the curve.
Equation of the normal at (x_0, y_0) is

$$y - y_0 = -\frac{1}{m}(x - x_0) \quad \text{where } m = \text{Slope of the tangent at } (x_0, y_0) = \frac{dy}{dx}\bigg]_{(x_0, y_0)} \quad \text{or} \quad f'(x_0)$$

Note : If a tangent line to the curve $y = f(x)$ makes an angle θ with x-axis in the positive direction, then $\dfrac{dy}{dx} = \tan\theta$

Illustration :

Find the condition that the curves $ax^2 + by^2 = 1$ and $a_1x^2 + b_1y^2 = 1$ may cut each other orthogonally

Sol. The given curves are $ax^2 + by^2 = 1$ ....(i)

and $a_1x^2 + b_1y^2 = 1$ ....(ii)

from (1) $2ax + 2by\dfrac{dy}{dx} = 0 \Rightarrow \dfrac{dy}{dx} = -\dfrac{ax}{by} = m_1\,(\text{say})$

from (2)

$2a_1x + 2b_1y\dfrac{dy}{dx} = 0 \Rightarrow \dfrac{dy}{dx} = -\dfrac{a_1x}{b_1y} = m_2\,(\text{say})$

Since the curves are orthogonal, $m_1m_2 = -1$

$\therefore \left(\dfrac{-ax}{by}\right)\left(-\dfrac{a_1x}{b_1y}\right) = -1 \Rightarrow aa_1x^2 = -bb_1y^2$ ..(iii)

Solving (i) and (ii) we get $(a - a_1)x^2 = (b_1 - b)y^2$ ...(iv)

Dividing by (3), $\dfrac{a - a_1}{aa_1} = \dfrac{b - b_1}{bb_1}$.

Illustration :

Find the locus of all the points on the curve $y^2 = 4a\left(x + a\sin\dfrac{x}{a}\right)$ at which the tangent is parallel to x-axis

Sol. We have $y^2 = 4a\left(x + a\sin\dfrac{x}{a}\right)$ ....(i)

Differentiating w.r. to x, $2y\dfrac{dy}{dx} = 4a\left[1 + \cos\dfrac{x}{a}\right]$

Since, the tangent is parallel to $x = axis$, $\dfrac{dy}{dx} = 0$

This gives $4a\left(1 + \cos\dfrac{x}{a}\right) = 0 \Rightarrow \cos\dfrac{x}{a} = -1 \Rightarrow \sin\dfrac{x}{a} = 0$

$\therefore$ From (i) $y^2 = 4a(x + 0) \Rightarrow y^2 = 4ax$, which is the required locus.

Practice Exercise-2

Multiple Choice Questions

1. The two curves $x^3 - 3xy^2 + 2 = 0$ and $3x^2y - y^3 - 2 = 0$ intersect at an angle of

(a) $\dfrac{\pi}{4}$ (b) $\dfrac{\pi}{3}$

(c) $\dfrac{\pi}{2}$ (d) $\dfrac{\pi}{6}$

2. What is the x-coordinate of the point on the curve $f(x) = \sqrt{x}\,(7x - 6)$, where the tangent is parallel to x-axis?

(a) $-\dfrac{1}{3}$ (b) $\dfrac{2}{7}$

(c) $\dfrac{6}{7}$ (d) $\dfrac{1}{2}$

3. The equation of one of the tangents to the curve $y = \cos(x + y)$, $-2\pi \le x \le 2\pi$ that is parallel to the line $x + 2y = 0$, is

(a) $x + 2y = 1$ (b) $x + 2y = \pi/2$

(c) $x + 2y = \pi/4$ (d) None of these

4. Angle formed by the positive Y-axis and the tangent to $y = x^2 + 4x - 17$ at $\left(\dfrac{5}{2}, \dfrac{-3}{4}\right)$ is

(a) $\tan^{-1}9$ (b) $\dfrac{\pi}{2} - \tan^{-1}9$

(c) $\dfrac{\pi}{2} + \tan^{-1}9$ (d) $\dfrac{\pi}{2}$

5. The angle of intersection of the curve $y^2 = x$ and $x^2 = y$ is

(a) $\tan^{-1}\left(\dfrac{3}{2}\right)$ (b) $\tan^{-1}\left(\dfrac{3}{4}\right)$

(c) $\tan^{-1}\left(\dfrac{1}{2}\right)$ (d) $\tan^{-1}\left(\dfrac{1}{5}\right)$

Assertion & Reason Questions

DIRECTIONS : *Each of these questions contains an assertion followed by reason. Read them carefully and answer the question on the basis of following options. You have to select the one that best describes the two statements.*

(a) If both Assertion and Reason are correct and the Reason is a correct explanation of the Assertion.

(b) If both Assertion and Reason are correct but Reason is not a correct explanation of the Assertion.

(c) If the Assertion is correct but Reason is incorrect.

(d) If the Assertion is incorrect but the Reason is correct.

6. The slope of the normal to the curve

Assertion: $x = a \cos^3\theta$, $y = a \sin^3\theta$ at $\theta = \dfrac{\pi}{4}$ is 1

Reason: $x = 1 - a \sin\theta$, $y = b \cos^2\theta$ at $\theta = \dfrac{\pi}{2}$ is $\dfrac{a}{2b}$

7. **Assertion:** The curves $x = y^2$ and $xy = k$ cut at right angle, if $8k^2 = 1$.

Reason: Two curves intersect at right angle, if the tangents to the curves at the point of intersection are perpendicular to each other i.e., product of their slope is -1.

Case/Passage Based Question

DIRECTIONS (Q. 8) : *has 5 subparts based on Case/Passage given, attempt any 4 out of 5 questions.*

8. The equation of a straight line passing through a given point (x_1, y_1) having slope m is given by $y - y_1 = m(x - x_1)$. Slope of the tangent to the curve $y = f(x)$ at the point (x_1, y_1) is given by $\dfrac{dy}{dx} = f(x_1)$.

Based on the above information, answer the following questions:

(i) Slope of the tangent to the curve $y = x^2 - 2$ at the point $x = 5$ is:

(a) 10   (b) 23

(c) 5   (d) None of these

(ii) Slope of the tangent to the curve $y = 4x^2 + 2x - 1$ at the point whose x coordinate is 2

(a) 11   (b) 9   (c) 3   (d) 18

(iii) Slope of the normal to the curve $x = a \sin\theta$ and $y = 1 - b \cos\theta$ at $\theta = \dfrac{\pi}{4}$ is:

(a) $\dfrac{b}{a}$ (b) $\dfrac{a}{b}$ (c) $-\dfrac{a}{b}$ (d) $-\dfrac{b}{a}$

(iv) Slope of the normal to the curve $y = \sqrt{x^2 - 2x}$ at $x = 3$ is:

(a) $\dfrac{4}{\sqrt{3}}$ (b) $-\dfrac{4}{\sqrt{3}}$

(c) $\dfrac{\sqrt{3}}{4}$ (d) $-\dfrac{\sqrt{3}}{4}$

(v) The equation of the normal to the curve $f(x) = \sin x$ at $x = \dfrac{\pi}{2}$ is:

(a) $y = 1$ (b) $x = \dfrac{\pi}{2}$

(c) $x + y = 1$ (d) $x - y = 0$

One Word Questions

9. Find the equation of normal to the curve $y = \tan x$ at $(0, 0)$.

10. At what points on the curve $x^2 + y^2 - 2x - 1y + 1 = 0$, is the tangent parallel to y-axis?

Very Short Answer Questions

11. Find the equation of the tangent to the curve $y = -5x^2 + 6x + 7$ at the point $(1/2, 35/4)$.

12. Prove that the tangents to the curve $y = x^2 - 5x + 6$ at the points $(2, 0)$ and $(3, 0)$ are at right angles.

13. Find the equation of the tangent to the curve $x^2 + 3y = 3$ which is parallel to the line $y - 4x + 5 = 0$.

14. Find the equation of the tangent to the curve $y = \sqrt{3x - 2}$ which is parallel to the line $4x - 2y + 5 = 0$

Short Answer Questions

15. For the curve $y = 4x^3 - 2x^5$, find all points at which the tangent passes through the origin.

16. Find the equations of the tangent and the normal to the curve $y = x^2 + 4x + 1$ at the point whose x-coordinate is 3.

17. Prove that the line $\dfrac{x}{a} + \dfrac{y}{b} = 1$ is a tangent to the curve $y = be^{-x/a}$ at the point where the curve cuts y-axis.

18. Find the intervals in which the function $f(x) = 2x^3 - 15x^2 + 36x + 1$ is strictly increasing or decreasing. Also find the points on which the tangents are parallel to the x-axis.

NCERT Exercise-2

1. Find the slope of the tangent to the curve $y = 3x^4 - 4x$ at $x = 4$.

2. Find the slope of the tangent to the curve $y = \dfrac{x - 1}{x - 2}$, $x \neq 2$ at $x = 10$.

3. Find the slope of the tangent to curve $y = x^3 - x + 1$ at the point whose x-coordinate is 2.

4. Find the slope of the tangent to the curve $y = x^3 - 3x + 2$ at the point whose x-coordinate is 3.

5. Find the slope of the normal to the curve $x = a \cos^3\theta$, $y = a \sin^3\theta$ at $\theta = \dfrac{\pi}{4}$.

6. Find the slope of the normal to the curve $x = 1 - a \sin\theta$, $y = b \cos^2\theta$ at $\theta = \dfrac{\pi}{2}$

7. Find points at which the tangent to the curve $y = x^3 - 3x^2 - 9x + 7$ is parallel to the x-axis.

8. Find a point on the curve $y = (x-2)^2$ at which the tangent is parallel to the chord joining the points $(2, 0)$ and $(4, 4)$.

9. Find the point on the curve $y = x^3 - 11x + 5$ at which the tangent is $y = x - 11$.

10. Find the equation of all lines having slope -1 that are tangents to the curve $y = \dfrac{1}{x-1}$, $x \neq 1$.

11. Find the equation of all lines having slope 2 which are tangents to the curve $y = \dfrac{1}{x-3}$, $x \neq 3$.

12. Find the equations of all lines having slope 0 which are tangent to the curve $y = \dfrac{1}{x^2 - 2x + 3}$.

13. Find points on the curve $\dfrac{x^2}{9} + \dfrac{y^2}{16} = 1$ at which the tangents are
    (a) parallel to x-axis (b) parallel to y-axis

14. Find the equations of the tangent and normal to the given curves at the indicated points:
    (i) $y = x^4 - 6x^3 + 13x^2 - 10x + 5$ at $(0, 5)$
    (ii) $y = x^4 - 6x^3 + 13x^2 - 10x + 5$ at $(1, 3)$
    (iii) $y = x^3$ at $(1, 1)$ (iv) $y = x^2$ at $(0, 0)$
    (v) $x = \cos t$, $y = \sin t$ at $t = \dfrac{\pi}{4}$

15. Find the equation of the tangent line to the curve $y = x^2 - 2x + 7$ which is
    (a) parallel to the line $2x - y + 9 = 0$
    (b) perpendicular to the line $5y - 15x = 13$.

16. Show that the tangents to the curve $y = 7x^3 + 11$ at the points where $x = 2$ and $x = -2$ are parallel.

17. Find the points on the curve $y = x^3$ at which the slope of the tangent is equal to the y-coordinate of the point.

18. For the curve $y = 4x^3 - 2x^5$, find all the points at which the tangent passes through the origin.

19. Find the points on the curve $x^2 + y^2 - 2x - 3 = 0$ at which the tangents are parallel to the x-axis.

20. Find the equation of the normal at the point (am^2, am^3) for the curve $ay^2 = x^3$.

21. Find the equation of the normals to the curve $y = x^3 + 2x + 6$ which are parallel to the line $x + 14y + 4 = 0$.

22. Find the equations of the tangent and normal to the parabola $y^2 = 4ax$ at the point $(at^2, 2at)$.

23. Prove that the curves $x = y^2$ and $xy = k$ cut at right angles* if $8k^2 = 1$.

24. Find the equations of the tangent and normal to the hyperbola $\dfrac{x^2}{a^2} - \dfrac{y^2}{b^2} = 1$ at the point (x_0, y_0).

25. Find the equation of the tangent to the curve $y = \sqrt{3x-2}$ which is parallel to the line $4x - 2y + 5 = 0$.

Choose the correct answer in Exercises 26 and 27.

26. The slope of the normal to the curve $y = 2x^2 + 3 \sin x$ at $x = 0$ is
    (a) 3　　　　　　　(b) $\dfrac{1}{3}$
    (c) -3　　　　　　(d) $-\dfrac{1}{3}$

27. The line $y = x + 1$ is a tangent to the curve $y^2 = 4x$ at the point
    (a) $(1, 2)$　　　　　(b) $(2, 1)$
    (c) $(1, -2)$　　　　(d) $(-1, 2)$

Topic 3　Maxima and Minima 

MAXIMUM VALUE, MINIMUM VALUE, EXTREME VALUE

Let f be a function defined in the interval I, then

(i) **Maximum Value :** If there exists a point c in I such that $f(c) \geq f(x)$, for all $x \in I$ then $f(c)$ is called maximum value of f in I. The point c is known as a point of maximum value of f in I.

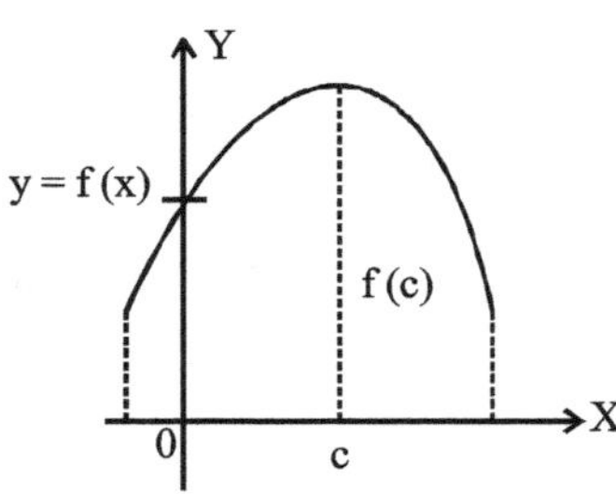

(ii) **Minimum Value:** If there exists a point c in I such that $f(c) \leq f(x)$, $\forall x \in I$, then $f(x)$ is called the minimum value of f in I. The point c is called as a point of minimum value of f in I

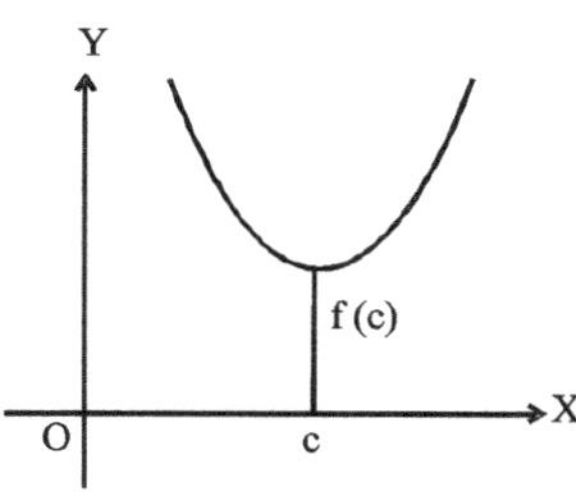

(iii) **Extreme Value:** If there exists a point c in I such that f(c) is either a maximum value or a minimum value of f in I, then f(c) is the extreme value of f(x) in I.

The point c is said to be an extreme point.

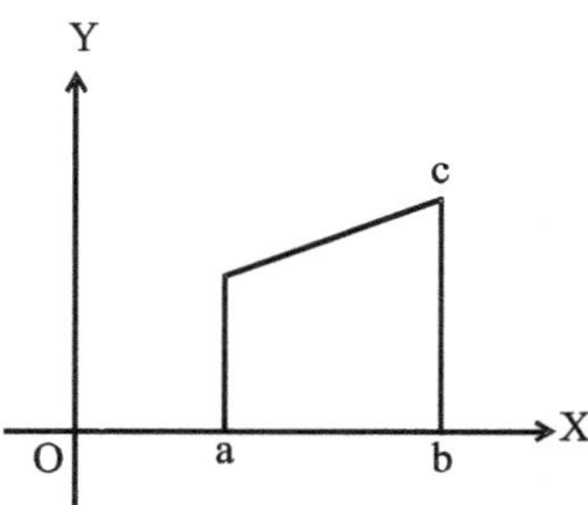

Note that (i) Every continuous function on a closed interval has a maximum and a minimum value.

(ii) Every monotonic function i.e. either increasing or decreasing function assumes its maximum/minimum value at the end points of the domain of the function.

ABSOLUTE MAXIMA AND MINIMA

Let f be a continuous function on an interval I = [a, b]. Then f has the absolute maximum value and f attains it at least once in I. Similarly, f has the absolute minimum value and attains at least once in I

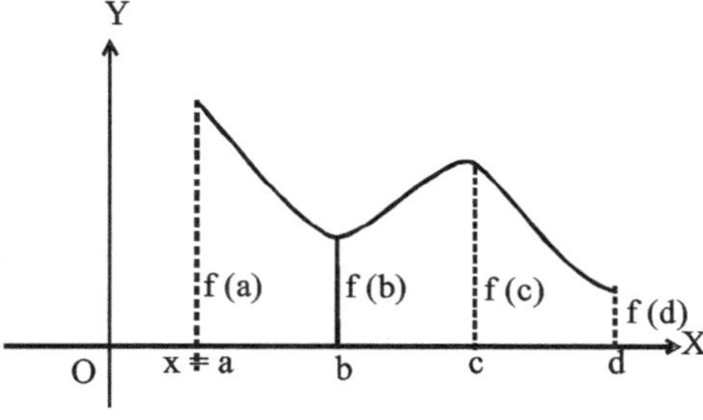

At x = b , there is a local minima

At x = c, there is a local maxima

At x = a, f(a) is the greatest value or absolute max. value.

At x = d, f(d) is the least value or absolute min. value.

Important Theorems

(i) Let f be a continuous function on an interval I = [a, b]. Then f has the absolute maximum value and f attains it atleast once in I. Also f has the absolute minimum value and attains it atleast once in I.

(ii) Let f be a differentiable function on a closed interval I and c be any interior point of I. Then,

(a) f'(c) = 0, if f attains its absolute maximum value at c.

(b) f'(c) = 0, if f attains its absolute minimum value at c.

LOCAL MAXIMA AND MINIMA

Let f be a real valued function and c be an interior point in the domain of f, then

(a) **Local Maxima:** c is a point of local maxima if there is an h > 0, such that $f(c) \geq f(x)$ for all $x \in (c - h, c + h)$

The value f(c) is called local maximum value of f.

(b) **Local Minima:** c is a point of local minima if there is an h > 0, such that $f(c) \leq f(x)$ for all $x \in (c - h, c + h)$

The value f(c) is known as the local minimum value of f.

Geometrically

If x = c is a point of local maxima of f, then

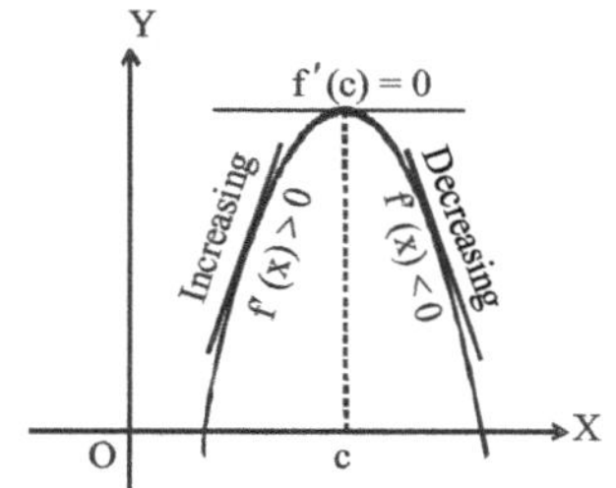

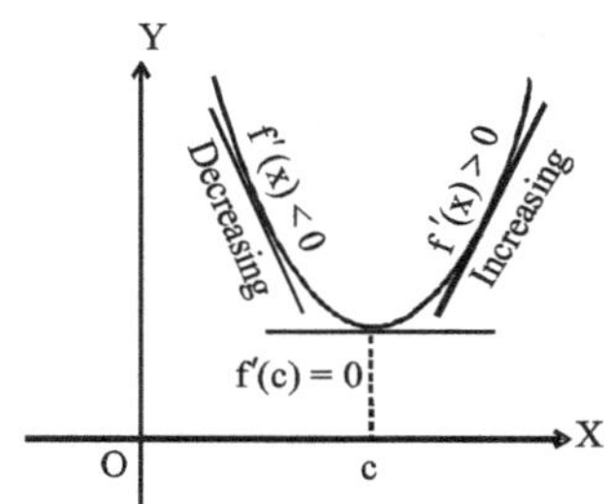

f is increasing (i.e., $f'(x) > 0$) in the interval $(c - h, c)$ and decreasing (i.e., $f'(x) < 0$) in the interval $(c, c + h) \Rightarrow f'(c) = 0$

Similarly, if $x = c$ is a point of local minima of f, then f is decreasing (i.e., $f'(x) < 0$) in the interval $(c - h, c)$ and increasing (i.e., $f'(x) > 0$) in the interval $(c, c + h)$. $\Rightarrow f'(c) = 0$

Important Theorem

Let f be a function defined on an open interval I. Suppose $c \in I$ be any point. If f has a local maxima or a local minima at $x = c$, then either $f'(c) = 0$ or f is not differentiable at c.

Critical Point

A point c in the domain of a function f at which either $f'(c) = 0$ or f is not differentiable is called a critical point of f. If f is continuous at a point c and $f'(c) = 0$ then there exists $h > 0$ such that f is differentiable in the interval $(c - h, c + h)$

TEST OF LOCAL MAXIMA AND MINIMA

First Derivative Test

Let f be a differentiable function defined on an open interval I and $c \in I$ be any point. f has a local maxima or a local minima at $x = c$, $f'(c) = 0$.

The above statement suggests the following working steps to find the points to local maxima or local minima of differentiable functions.

Working Steps:

Step- 1 Put $y = f(x)$, **Step- 2** Find $\dfrac{dy}{dx}$, **Step- 3** Put $\dfrac{dy}{dx} = 0$ and solve this equation for x.

Let $c_1, c_2 - - - c_n$ be the roots of this equation $c_1, c_2 \text{------} c_n$ are stationary value of x and these are the possible points where the function can attains a local $\max^m$ or local minimum.

Step- 4 Consider $x = c_1$

$\Rightarrow$ If $\dfrac{dy}{dx}$ changes sign from +ve to –ve as x increases through c_1 then the function

attains a local $\max^m$ at $x = c_1$

$\Rightarrow$ If $\dfrac{dy}{dx}$ changes its sign from –ve to +ve as x increases through c_1 then the function

attains a local minimum at $x = c_1$

$\Rightarrow$ If $\dfrac{dy}{dx}$ does not changes sign as increases through c_1 then $x = c_1$ is neither a point

of local $\max^m$ nor a point of local $\min^m$. In this case x is a point of inflexion.

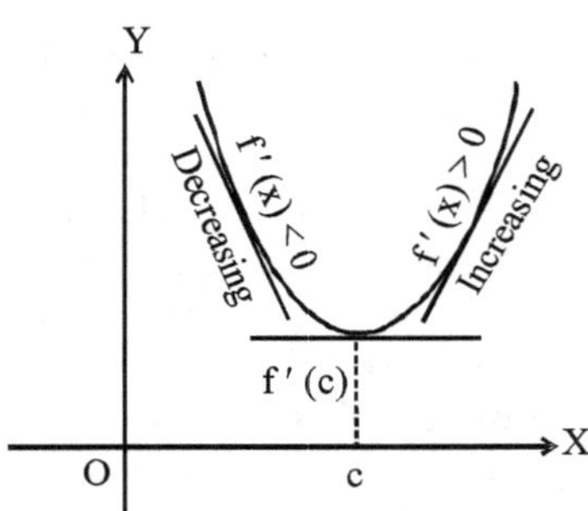

Second Derivative Test

Working Steps:

Step- 1   Find $f'(x)$

Step- 2   Put $f'(x) = 0$ and solve this equation for x

Let $c_1, c_2 - - - c_n$ be the roots of this equation $c_1, c_2 - - - c_n$ are stationary value of x and there are possible points where the function can attain a local maximum or a local minima. So we test the function as each one of these points.

Step-3   Find $f''(x)$ Consider $x = c_1$

If $f''(x)$ at $x = c_1 < o$ then $x = c_1$ is a point of local maxima.

If $f''(x)$ at $x = c_1 > o$ then $x = c_1$ is a point of local minima.

If $f''(x)$ at $x = c_1 = o$ then $x = c_1$ is a point of inflection

and we must find $f'''(x)$ substitute in if c_1 for x.

Illustration :

Show that the rectangle of maximum perimeter which can be inscribed in a circle of radius a is a square of side $\sqrt{2}a$.

Sol. Let $ABCD$ be a rectangle in a given circle of radius a with centre at O.

Let $AB = 2x$ and $AD = 2y$ be the sides of the rectangle. Then,

$$AM^2 + OM^2 = OA^2$$
$$\Rightarrow x^2 + y^2 = a^2$$
$$\Rightarrow y = \sqrt{a^2 - x^2}$$

Let P be the perimeter of the rectangle $ABCD$. Then,

$$P = 4x + 4y$$

$$\Rightarrow P = 4x + 4\sqrt{a^2 - x^2} \qquad \text{[Using (i)]}$$

$$\Rightarrow \frac{dP}{dx} = 4 - \frac{4x}{\sqrt{a^2 - x^2}}$$

For maximum or minimum, values of P, we have

$$\frac{dP}{dx} = 0$$

$$\Rightarrow 4 - \frac{4x}{\sqrt{a^2 - x^2}} = 0 \Rightarrow x = \frac{a}{\sqrt{2}}$$

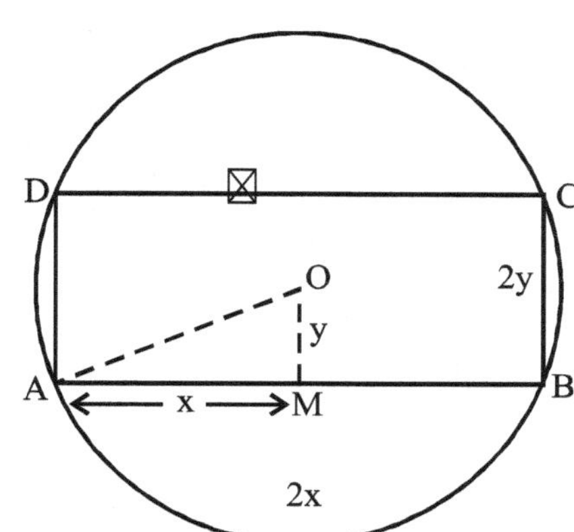

$$\text{Now, } \frac{d^2P}{dx^2} = \frac{-4\left\{\sqrt{a^2 - x^2} \cdot 1 - \dfrac{x(-x)}{\sqrt{a^2 - x^2}}\right\}}{\left(\sqrt{a^2 - x^2}\right)^2} = \frac{-4a^2}{(a^2 - x^2)^{3/2}}$$

$$\therefore \left(\frac{d^2P}{dx^2}\right)_{x = a/\sqrt{2}} = \frac{-4a^2}{\left(a^2 - \dfrac{a^2}{2}\right)^{3/2}} = \frac{-8\sqrt{2}}{a} < 0$$

Thus, P is maximum when $x = \dfrac{a}{\sqrt{2}}$.

Putting $x = \dfrac{a}{\sqrt{2}}$ in (i), we obtain $y = \dfrac{a}{\sqrt{2}}$. Therefore, $x = y = a\sqrt{2} \Rightarrow 2x = 2y$

Hence, P is maximum when the rectangle is square of side

$$2x = \frac{2a}{\sqrt{2}} = \sqrt{2}a.$$

Practice Exercise-3

Multiple Choice Questions

1. The maximum value of $\dfrac{\ln x}{x}$ in $(2, \infty)$ is

  (a) 1   (b) e

  (c) 2/e   (d) 1/e

2. The range of the function $f(x) = 2\sqrt{x - 2} + \sqrt{4 - x}$ is

  (a) $\left(\sqrt{2}, \sqrt{10}\right)$ (b) $\left[\sqrt{2}, \sqrt{10}\right)$

  (c) $\left(\sqrt{2}, \sqrt{10}\right]$ (d) $\left[\sqrt{2}, \sqrt{10}\right]$

3. Find the greatest value of the function

$$f(x) = \frac{\sin 2x}{\sin\left(x + \dfrac{\pi}{4}\right)} \text{ on the interval } \left[0, \frac{\pi}{2}\right]$$

  (a) 1   (b) 2

  (c) 3   (d) None of these

4. If the function f be given by
$f(x) = x^3 - 3x + 3$, then

  I. $x = \pm 2$ are the only critical points for local maxima or local minima.

  II. $x = 1$ is a point of local minima.

  III.   local minimum value is 2.

  IV.   local maximum value is 5.

  (a) Only I and II are true

  (b) Only II and III are true

  (c) Only I, II and III are true

  (d) Only II and IV are true

5. Find the maximum profit that a company can make, if the profit function is given by $P(x) = 41 + 24x - 18x^2$.

  (a) 25   (b) 43   (c) 62   (d) 49

Assertion & Reason Questions

DIRECTIONS: *Each of these questions contains an assertion followed by reason. Read them carefully and answer the* *question on the basis of following options. You have to select the one that best describes the two statements.*

(a) If both Assertion and Reason are correct and the Reason is a correct explanation of the Assertion.

(b) If both Assertion and Reason are correct but Reason is not a correct explanation of the Assertion.

(c) If the Assertion is correct but Reason is incorrect.

(d) If the Assertion is incorrect but the Reason is correct.

6. **Assertion:** If the length of three sides of a trapezium other than base are equal to 10 cm, then the area of trapezium when it is maximum, is $75\sqrt{3}$ cm^2.

    Reason: Area of trapezium is maximum at x = 5.

7. Consider the function

$$f(x) = \begin{cases} |\sin x| & \text{for } 0 < |x| \le \dfrac{\pi}{2} \\ \dfrac{1}{2} & \text{for } x = 0 \end{cases}$$

    Assertion: f has a local maximum value at x = 0.

    Reason: $f'(0) = 0$ and $f''(0) < 0$

Case/Passage Based Question

DIRECTIONS (Q. 8) : *has 5 subparts based on Case/Passage given, attempt any 4 out of 5 questions.*

8. A teacher discussed the shape of window with certain information to get the maximum light and air through it.

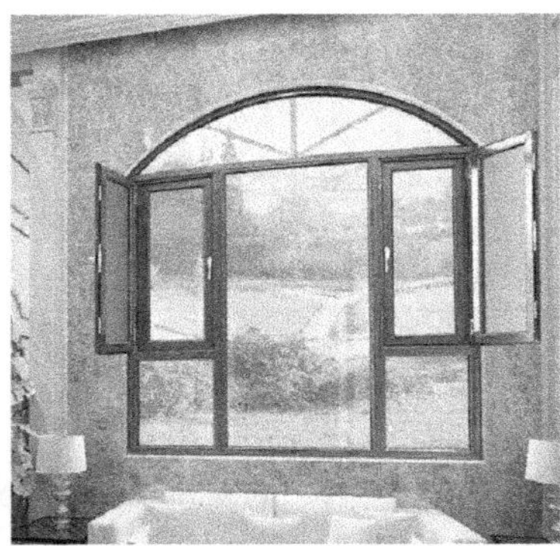

In the figure, a window is in the form of a rectangle surmounted by a semicircular opening. The total perimeter of the window is 10 m.

If x be the width of window and r be the radius of semicircular opening, then students were asked the following questions.

(i) What is the relation between width x and radius r?

(a) $2x + (\pi + 2)r = 10$ (b) $x + (\pi + 2)r = 10$

(c) $2x + 2(\pi + 2)r = 5$ (d) $2x + 2r = 10$

(ii) Find the area (A) of window in terms of radius r only.

(a) $A = r - \left(\dfrac{1}{2}\pi + 2\right)r^2$

(b) $A = 5r - \left(\dfrac{1}{2}\pi + 2\right)r^2$

(c) $A = 10r - \left(\dfrac{1}{2}\pi + 2\right)r^2$

(d) $A = 10r - (\pi + 2)r^2$

(iii) Find the critical points of the area A.

(a) $r = \dfrac{10}{\pi + 2}$ (b) $r = \dfrac{5}{\pi + 4}$

(c) $r = \dfrac{10}{\pi + 4}$ (d) $r = \dfrac{10}{2\pi + 4}$

(iv) Find the dimensions of window to admit the maximum light and air.

(a) $\dfrac{20}{\pi + 4}, \dfrac{10}{\pi + 4}$ (b) $\dfrac{10}{\pi + 4}, \dfrac{10}{\pi + 4}$

(c) $\dfrac{5}{\pi + 4}, \dfrac{5}{\pi + 4}$ (d) $\dfrac{20}{\pi + 4}, \dfrac{20}{\pi + 4}$

(v) Find the maximum area (A) of the window? $\left(\text{Use } \pi = \dfrac{22}{7}\right)$

(a) $4.76 \, \text{m}^2$ (b) $4 \, \text{m}^2$

(c) $4.1 \, \text{m}^2$ (d) $3.08 \, \text{m}^2$

One Word Questions

9. Find the least value of the function

$$f(x) = ax + \frac{b}{x} \quad (a > 0, b > 0, x > 0).$$

10. Find the point in the interval [0, 1] the function $x^{25}(1 - x)^{75}$ takes its maximum value.

11. Find the minimum value of the function $y = x^4 - 2x^2 + 1$ in the interval $\left[\dfrac{1}{2}, 2\right]$.

Very Short Answer Questions

12. Prove that the area of a right angled triangle of given hypotenuse is maximum when the triangle is isosceles.

13. If at x = 1, the function $x^4 - 62x^2 + ax + 9$ attains its maximum value on the interval [0, 2], then find the value of a.

14. The difference between the greatest and least values of the function $f(x) = \sin 2x - x$, on $\left[\dfrac{-\pi}{2}, \dfrac{\pi}{2}\right]$ is

(a) $\dfrac{\pi}{2}$ (b) π (c) $\dfrac{3\pi}{2}$ (d) $\dfrac{\pi}{4}$

Short Answer Questions

15. Prove that the surface area of a solid cuboid, of square base and given volume, is minimum when it is a cube.

16. Find the largest possible area of the right angle triangle whose hypotenuse is 5 cm.

17. Find the shortest distance between two points, one of which lies on the curve $y^2 = 4ax$, and the other on the circle $x^2 + y^2 - 24ay + 128\,a^2 = 0$

18. A student is given card board of area 27 square centimeters. He wishes to form a box with square base to have maximum capacity and no wastage of the board. What are the dimensions of the box so formed?

19. Assuming that petrol burnt per hour in driving a motor boat varies as the cube of its velocity. Show that the most economical speed when going against a current of k km/hour is $\dfrac{3k}{2}$ km/hour. Keeping in mind 'save environment', which boat you prefer to be used.

NCERT Exercise-3

1. Find the maximum and minimum values, if any, of the following functions given by
   (i) $f(x) = (2x-1)^2 + 3$ (ii) $f(x) = 9x^2 + 12x + 2$
   (iii) $f(x) = -(x-1)^2 + 10$ (iv) $g(x) = x^3 + 1$

2. Find the maximum and minimum values, if any, of the following functions given by
   (i) $f(x) = |x+2| - 1$ (ii) $g(x) = -|x+1| + 3$
   (iii) $h(x) = \sin 2x + 5$ (iv) $f(x) = |\sin(4x+3)|$
   (v) $h(x) = x + 1, x \in (-1, 1)$

3. Find the local maxima and local minima, if any, of the following functions. Find also the local maximum and the local minimum values, as the case may be :
   (i) $f(x) = x^2$ (ii) $g(x) = x^3 - 3x$
   (iii) $h(x) = \sin x + \cos x, 0 < x < \dfrac{\pi}{4}$
   (iv) $f(x) = \sin^4 x + \cos^4 x, 0 < x < \pi/2$
   (v) $f(x) = x^3 - 6x^2 + 9x + 15$
   (vi) $g(x) = \dfrac{x}{2} + \dfrac{2}{x}, x > 0$ (vii) $g(x) = \dfrac{1}{x^2 + 2}$
   (viii) $f(x) = x\sqrt{1-x}, x > 0$

4. Prove that the following functions do not have maxima or minima:
   (i) $f(x) = e^x$ (ii) $f(x) = \log x$
   (iii) $h(x) = x^3 + x^2 + x + 1$

5. Find the absolute maximum value and the absolute minimum value of the following functions in the given intervals:
   (i) $f(x) = x^3, x \in [-2, 2]$
   (ii) $f(x) = \sin x + \cos x, x \in [0, \pi]$
   (iii) $f(x) = 4x - \dfrac{1}{2}x^2, x \in \left[-2, \dfrac{9}{2}\right]$
   (iv) $f(x) = (x-1)^2 + 3, x \in [-3, 1]$.

6. Find the maximum profit that a company can make, if the profit function is given by $p(x) = 41 - 24x - 18x^2$

7. Find both the maximum value and the minimum value of $3x^4 - 8x^3 + 12x^2 - 48x + 25$ on the interval $[0, 3]$.

8. At what points in the interval $[0, 2\pi]$, does the function sin $2x$ attain its maximum value?

9. What is the maximum value of the function sin $x + \cos x$?

10. Find the maximum value of $2x^3 - 24x + 107$ in the interval $[1, 3]$. Find the maximum value of the same function in $[-3, -1]$.

11. It is given that at $x = 1$, the function $x^4 - 62x^2 + ax + 9$ attains its maximum value, on the interval $[0, 2]$. Find the value of a.

12. ∵ Find the maximum and minimum values of $x + \sin 2x$ on $[0, 2\pi]$

13. Find two numbers whose sum is 24 and whose product is as large as possible.

14. Find two positive numbers x and y such that $x + y = 60$ and xy^3 is maximum.

15. Find two positive numbers x and y such that their sum is 35 and the product $x^2 y^5$ is a maximum.

16. Find two positive numbers whose sum is 16 and the sum of whose cubes is minimum.

17. A square piece of tin of side 18 cm is to be made into a box without top, by cutting a square from each corner and folding up the flaps to form the box. What should be the side of the square to be cut off so that the volume of the box is the maximum possible.

18. A rectangular sheet of tin 45 cm by 24 cm is to be made into a box without top, by cutting off square from each corner and folding up the flaps. What should be the side of the square to be cut off so that the volume of the box is maximum?

19. Show that of all the rectangles inscribed in a given fixed circle, the square has the maximum area.

20. Show that the right circular cylinder of given surface and maximum volume is such that its height is equal to the diamter of the base.

21. Of all the closed cylindrical cans (right circular), of a given volume of 100 cubic centimetres, find the dimensions of the can which has the minimum surface area ?

22. A wire of length 28 m is to be cut into two pieces. One of the pieces is to be made into a square and the other into a circle. What should be the length of the two pieces so that the combined area of the square and the circle is minimum ?

23. Prove that the volume of the largest cone that can be inscribed in a sphere of radius R is $\dfrac{8}{27}$ of the volume of the sphere.

24. Show that the right circular cone of least curved surface and given volume has an altitude equal to $\sqrt{2}$ time the radius of the base.

25. Show that the semi-vertical angle of the cone of the maximum volume and of given slant height is $\tan^{-1}\sqrt{2}$.

26. Show that semi-vertical angle of right circular cone of given surface area and maximum volume is $\sin^{-1}\left(\dfrac{1}{3}\right)$.

Choose the correct answer in the Exercises 27 and 29.

27. The point on the curve $x^2 = 2y$ which is nearest to the point $(0, 5)$ is
   (a) $(2\sqrt{2}, 4)$ (b) $(2\sqrt{2}, 0)$
   (c) $(0, 0)$ (d) $(2, 2)$

28. For all real values of x, the minimum value of $\dfrac{1 - x + x^2}{1 + x + x^2}$ is
   (a) 0   (b) 1   (c) 3   (d) $\dfrac{1}{3}$

29. The maximum value of $\left[x(x-1)+1\right]^{\frac{1}{3}}, 0 \le x \le 1$ is
   (a) $\left(\dfrac{1}{3}\right)^{\frac{1}{3}}$ (b) $\dfrac{1}{2}$ (c) 1   (d) 0

Important Tips & Formulae

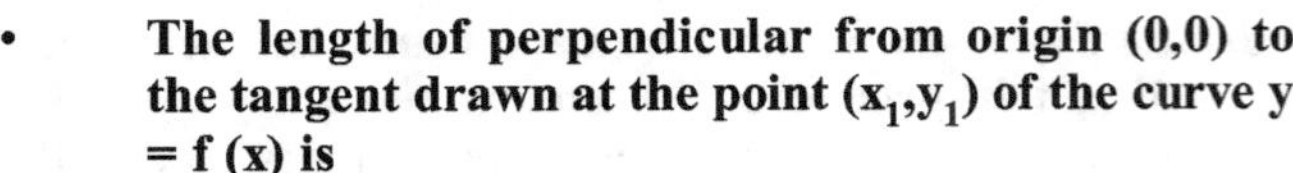

- **The length of perpendicular from origin (0,0) to the tangent drawn at the point (x_1, y_1) of the curve y = f (x) is**

$$\left| \frac{y_1 - x_1 \left(\frac{dy}{dx} \right)_P}{\sqrt{1 + \left(\frac{dy}{dx} \right)^2_P}} \right|$$

The length of perpendicular from origin to normal is

$$\left| \frac{x_1 + y_1 \left(\frac{dy}{dx} \right)_p}{\sqrt{1 + \left(\frac{dy}{dx} \right)^2_p}} \right|$$

- **Angle of interesection of two curves**

Let $y = f_1(x)$ and $y = f_2(x)$ be the two curves, meeting at some point P (x_1, y_1)

∴ The angle of intersection of two curves θ is given by

$$\tan \theta = \pm \frac{m_1 - m_2}{1 + m_1 m_2},$$

where $m_1 = \left(\frac{df_1}{dx} \right)_{(x_1, y_1)}$ and $m_2 = \left(\frac{df_2}{dx} \right)_{(x_1, y_1)}$

(a) If $\theta = \pm \frac{\pi}{2}$, $m_1 m_2 + 1 = 0 \Rightarrow \left(\frac{df_1}{dx} \right)_{(x_1, y_1)} \left(\frac{df_2}{dx} \right)_{(x_1, y_1)} = -1,$

Such curves are called **ORTHOGONAL CURVES.**

(b) If $\theta = 0$, $m_1 = m_2 \Rightarrow \left(\frac{df_1}{dx} \right)_{(x_1, y_1)} = \left(\frac{df_2}{dx} \right)_{(x_1, y_1)}$.

Then the curves are tangential at (x_1, y_1).

- **Consider a curve y = f(x), then for the curve:**

(a) Length of tangent $= y \dfrac{\sqrt{1 + (dy / dx)^2}}{(dy / dx)}$

(b) Length of normal $= y \sqrt{1 + \left(\dfrac{dy}{dx} \right)^2}$

(c) Length of sub tangent $= y / \left(\dfrac{dy}{dx} \right)$

(d) Length of sub normal $= y \left(\dfrac{dy}{dx} \right)$

- **Properties of monotonic functions**

(a) If f (x) is strictly increasing function on an interval [a, b], then f^{-1} exists and it is also a strictly increasing function.

(b) If f (x) is strictly increasing function on an interval [a, b] such that it is continuous, then f^{-1} is continuous on [f (a), f(b)].

- **Some standard geometrical results related to maxima & minima**

The following results can easily be established.

(a) Area of rectangle with given perimeter is greatest when it is a square.

(b) Perimeter of a rectangle with given area is least when it is a square.

(c) Area of a rectangle inscribed in a given circle is greatest, if it is a square.

(d) Area of a triangle inscribed in a given circle is greatest, of it is equilateral.

(e) Semi vertical angle of a cone with given slant height and maximum volume is $\tan^{-1} \sqrt{2}$.

(f) Height of a cylinder of maximum volume inscribed in a sphere of radius a is $2a / \sqrt{3}$.

- If normal makes an angle of θ with positive direction of x-axis, then

$$-\frac{dx}{dy} = \tan \theta \quad \text{or} \quad \frac{dy}{dx} = -\cot \theta$$

- If $\left(\dfrac{dy}{dx} \right)_P = \infty$, then the tangent at $P(x_1, y_1)$ to the given curve is parallel to y-axis and its equation is $x = x_1$.

- If $\left(\dfrac{dy}{dx} \right)_P = 0$, then the tangent at $P(x_1, y_1)$ to the given curve is parallel to x-axis and its equation is $y = y_1$

- If $\left(\dfrac{dy}{dx} \right)_P = 0$, then the normal at $P(x_1, y_1)$ is parallel to y-axis and its equation is $x = x_1$.

- If $\left(\dfrac{dy}{dx} \right)_P = \infty$, then the normal at $P(x_1, y_1)$ is parallel to x-axis and its equation is $y = y_1$.

- If $\dfrac{dy}{dx} > 0$, the tangent makes an acute angle with the x-axis.

- If $\dfrac{dy}{dx} < 0$, the tangent makes an obtuse angle with the x-axis

- If the tangent is equally inclined to the axes, then

$$\frac{dy}{dx} = \pm 1 .$$

MISCELLANEOUS NCERT EXERCISE

1. Show that the function given by $f(x) = \dfrac{\log x}{x}$ has maximum at $x = e$.

Sol. $f(x) = \dfrac{\log x}{x}$ $f'(x) = \dfrac{1 - \log x}{x^2}$ 1

For maxima and minima, $f'(x) = 0$

$\Rightarrow \log x = 0$ or $\log x = 1$ $\therefore$ $x = e' = e$

$f''(k) = \dfrac{d}{dx}\left(\dfrac{1 - \log x}{x^2}\right) = -\dfrac{3 - 2\log x}{x^3}$

$f''(e) = \dfrac{3 - 2\log_e e}{e^3} = -\dfrac{3 - 2}{e^3} = -\dfrac{1}{e^3} = -ve$

$\therefore$ f is maximum at $x = e$.

2. The two equal sides of an isosceles triangle with fixed base b are decreasing at the rate of 3 cm per second. How fast is the area decreasing when the two equal sides are equal to the base?

Sol. Let x be the equal side of isosceles triangle with fixed base b.

i.e. $AB = AC = x$ and $BC = b$

In $\triangle ABL$, $AL = \sqrt{AB^2 - BL^2}$

$\Rightarrow AL = \sqrt{x^2 - \dfrac{b^2}{4}}$

Area of $\triangle ABC$

$= A = \dfrac{1}{2} \times BC \times AL = \dfrac{1}{2} \times b \times \sqrt{x^2 - \dfrac{b^2}{4}}$

$\therefore \dfrac{dx}{dt} = 3$ cm/sec. $\Rightarrow \dfrac{dA}{dt} = \dfrac{bx}{2} \times \dfrac{2}{\sqrt{4b^2 - b^2}} \times \dfrac{dx}{dt}$

When $x = b$, we get $\dfrac{dA}{dt} = \dfrac{3b^2}{b\sqrt{3}} = b\sqrt{3}$

Hence, the area is decreasing at $b\sqrt{3}$ cm²/sec.

3. Find the equation of the normal to curve $y^2 = 4x$ at the point (1, 2).

Sol. The curve is $y^2 = 4x \Rightarrow \dfrac{dy}{dx} = \dfrac{4}{2y} = \dfrac{2}{y}$ At $(1, 2)$, $\dfrac{dy}{dx} = \dfrac{2}{2} = 1$

$\therefore$ Slope of normal $= -1$

Eq. of normal at $(1, 2)$: $y - 2 = -x + 1$ or $x + y - 3 = 0$

4. Show that the normal at any point θ to the curve $x = a\cos\theta + a\theta\sin\theta$, $y = a\sin\theta - a\theta\cos\theta$ is at a constant distance from the origin.

Sol. $\because$ $x = a\cos\theta + a\theta\sin\theta$ and $y = a\sin\theta - a\theta\cos\theta$

$\therefore \dfrac{dx}{d\theta} = a\theta\cos\theta$ and $\dfrac{dy}{d\theta} = a\theta\sin\theta$

Slope of the tangent $= \dfrac{dy}{dx} = \dfrac{dy}{d\theta} \div \dfrac{dx}{d\theta} = \tan\theta$

$\therefore$ Slope of the normal at θ is $\dfrac{-1}{dy/dx} = \dfrac{-1}{\tan\theta} = -\cot\theta$

$\therefore$ The equation of the normal at the point θ is

$[y - (a\sin\theta - a\theta\cos\theta)] = -\cot\theta \cdot [x - (a\cos\theta + a\theta\sin\theta)]$

$\Rightarrow$ $x\cos\theta + y\sin\theta = a$

Which is the equation of the normal. The distance of this

normal from the origin is $\dfrac{a}{\sqrt{\cos^2\theta + \sin^2\theta}} = a = $ constant.

5. Find the intervals in which the function f given by

$f(x) = \dfrac{4\sin x - 2x - x\cos x}{2 + \cos x}$ is

(i) increasing

(ii) decreasing.

Sol. $\because f(x) = \dfrac{4\sin x - 2x - x\cos x}{2 + \cos x} = \dfrac{4\sin x}{2 + \cos x} - x$

$\therefore$ $f'(x) = \dfrac{\cos x\,(4 - \cos x)}{(2 + \cos x)^2}$

$-1 \le \cos x \le 1$ $\Rightarrow$ $4 - \cos x > 0$ and also $(2 + \cos x)^2 > 0$

$\therefore$ $f'(x) > 0$ or < 0 according as $\cos x > 0$

or $\cos x < 0$ respectively

$\therefore$ $f(x)$ is increasing when $0 < x < \dfrac{\pi}{2}$

$\dfrac{3\pi}{2} < x < 2\pi$ and decreasing when $\dfrac{\pi}{2} < x < \dfrac{3\pi}{2}$

6. Find the intervals in which the function f given by

$f(x) = x^3 + \dfrac{1}{x^3}$, $x \ne 0$ is

(i) increasing

(ii) decreasing

Sol. $\therefore$ $f(x) = x^3 + \dfrac{1}{x^3}$, $x \ne 0$, $\therefore$ $f'(x) = 3x^2 - \dfrac{1}{x^4}$,

For $f(x)$ is an increasing function of x.

$f'(x) > 0$ i.e. $3\left(x^2 - \dfrac{1}{x^4}\right) > 0$

$\Rightarrow$ $x^6 - 1 > 0$ $\Rightarrow$ $x^3 > 1$ or $x^3 > -1$

$\Rightarrow$ $x > 1$ or $x > -1$

$\Rightarrow$ $x > 1$ and $x^3 - 1 < 0$ and $x^3 + 1 < 0$

$\Rightarrow$ $x^3 < 1$ or $x^3 < -1$ $\Rightarrow$ $x < 1$ or $x < -1 \Rightarrow x < -1$

Hence, $f(x)$ is increasing, when $x < -1$ and $x > 1$. For f (x) to be decreasing function of x.

$f'(x) < 0$ i.e. $3\left(x^2 - \dfrac{1}{x^4}\right) < 0$ $\Rightarrow x^2 - \dfrac{1}{x^4} < 0$ $\Rightarrow x^6 - 1 < 0$

$\Rightarrow$ $(x^3 - 1)(x^3 + 1) < 0$

(a) $x^3 - 1 > 0$ and $x^3 + 1 < 0$

(b) $x^3 - 1 < 0$ and $x^3 + 1 > 0$

$\Rightarrow$ (a) $x^3 > 1$ and $x^3 < -1$ or $x > 1$ and $x < -1$ not admissible

(b) $x^3 < 1$ and $x^3 > -1$ or $x < 1$ and $x > -1$ i.e. $-1 < x < 1$

Hence, $f(x)$ is decreasing when $-1 < x < 1$.

7. Find the maximum area of an isosceles triangle inscribed in the ellipse $\dfrac{x^2}{a^2} + \dfrac{y^2}{b^2} = 1$ with its vertex at one end of the major axis.

Sol. $A = $ Area of isosceles $\triangle APP' = \dfrac{1}{2}\, PP'.\, AM$

$= \dfrac{1}{2} \cdot ab\, (2b \sin \theta)\, (a - a \cos \theta) = ab\, (\sin \theta - \dfrac{1}{2} \sin 2\theta)$

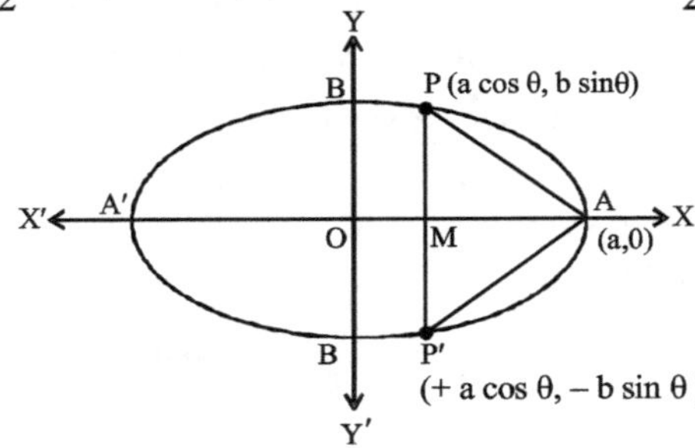

For maxima Area $\dfrac{dA}{d\theta} = 0$

$\Rightarrow \cos 2\theta = \cos \theta \Rightarrow \theta = \dfrac{2\pi}{3}$

Now, $\dfrac{d^2 A}{d\theta^2} = ab\, (-\sin \theta + 2 \sin 2\theta)$

At $\theta = \dfrac{2\pi}{3}$, $\dfrac{d^2 A}{d\theta^2} = \dfrac{-3\sqrt{3}}{2}\, ab < 0$

$\Rightarrow$ A is maximum, when $\theta = \dfrac{2\pi}{3} = 120°$,

Maximum value of $A = ab\left(\sin 120° - \dfrac{1}{2} \sin 240° \right)$

$= ab\left[\dfrac{\sqrt{3}}{2} - \dfrac{1}{2}\left(-\dfrac{\sqrt{3}}{2} \right) \right];$

Max value of $A = \dfrac{3\sqrt{3}}{4}\, ab$

8. A tank with rectangular base and rectangular sides, open at the top is to be constructed so that its depth is 2m and volume is 8 m³. If building of tank costs ₹ 70 per sq metres for the base and ₹ 45 per square metre for sides. What is the cost of least expensive tank?

Sol. Let the length and breadth of the tank be x metre and y metre. The depth of it is 2 metre

$\therefore$ Volume of tank $= 2 \times x \times y = 2xy = 8 \Rightarrow xy = 4$ ...(i)

$\therefore$ Area of base $= xy$, Area of sides $= 4\,(x + y)$

Cost of construction $= ₹\, [70\, xy + 180\, (x + y)]$ ...(ii)

Putting value of y in (ii) from (i), $y = \dfrac{4}{x}$,

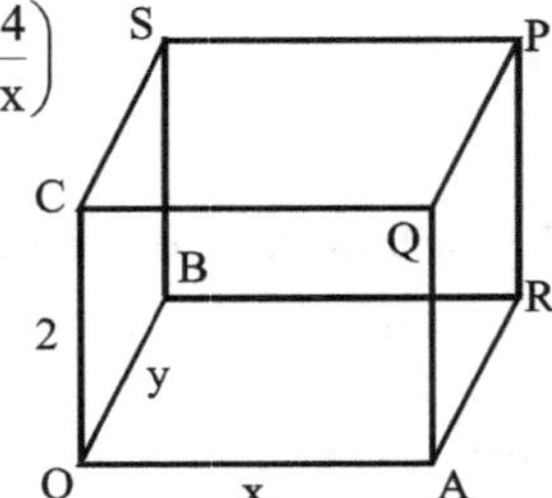

$\therefore$ $C = 70 \times 4 + 180 \left(x + \dfrac{4}{x} \right)$

or $\dfrac{dC}{dx} = 180 \left(\dfrac{x^2 - 4}{x^2} \right)$,

For maximum or minimum

$\dfrac{dC}{dx} = 0 \Rightarrow x = \pm 2$,

$\dfrac{dC}{dx}$ changes sign from $-$ve to $+$ve at $x = 2$

$\therefore$ C is minimum at $x = 2$, $\therefore$ $x = 2$ and $y = 2$,

$\therefore$ Thus tank is a cube of side 2m

$\therefore$ Least cost of construction $= ₹\,1000$.

9. The sum of the perimeter of a circle and square is k, where k is some constant. Prove that the sum of their areas is least when the side of square is double the radius of the circle.

Sol. Let x be the radius of the circle and y be the side of the square

Circumference of the circle $= 2\pi x$; Perimeter of square $= 4y$

Sum of Perimeters $= 2\pi x + 4y = k$ ...(i)

Area of circle $= \pi r^2$, Area of square $= y^2$,

Sum of Areas $= \pi x^2 + y^2$ ...(ii)

from (i) $y = \dfrac{k - 2\pi x}{4}$ ...(iii)

$\therefore A = \pi x^2 + \left(\dfrac{k - 2\pi x}{4} \right)^2 \Rightarrow \dfrac{dA}{dx} = \left(2\pi + \dfrac{\pi^2}{2} \right) x - \dfrac{k\pi}{4}$

$\dfrac{dA}{dx} = 0$ at $x = \dfrac{k\pi}{4} \times \dfrac{2}{4\pi + \pi^2} = \dfrac{k}{2\,(\pi + 4)}$,

$\dfrac{d^2 A}{dx^2} = \left(2\pi + \dfrac{\pi^2}{2} \right) = +$ ve

$\therefore$ A is least when $x = \dfrac{k}{2\,(\pi + 4)}$,   from (iii),

$y = \dfrac{1}{4}\left[k - 2\pi\, \dfrac{k}{2\,(\pi + 4)} \right] = \dfrac{k}{\pi + 4}$, $\Rightarrow y = 2x$ hence proved

10. A window is in the form of a rectangle surmounted by a semicircular opening. The total perimeter of the window is 10m. Find the dimensions of the window to admit maximum light through the whole opening.

Sol. Perimeter of the window when the width of window is x and 2r is the length

$\Rightarrow 10 = (\pi + 2)\, r + 2x$ ...(i)

For maximum light through the opening the area of the window must be maximum

A = sum of areas of rectangle and semi-circle.

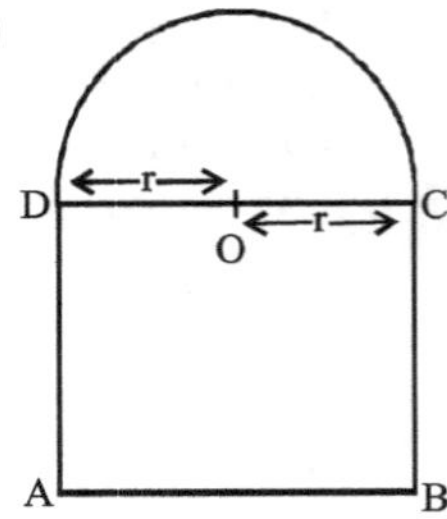

$$= 10\,r - \left(\frac{1}{2}\pi + 2\right) r^2 ,$$

$$\therefore \ \frac{dA}{dr} = 0 \ \Rightarrow \ r = \frac{10}{\pi + 4} \ \text{and} \ \frac{d^2A}{dr^2} = -(\pi + 4) ,$$

i.e. $\dfrac{d^2A}{dr^2}$ is $-$ve for $r = \dfrac{10}{\pi + 4} \Rightarrow$ A is max.

Put the value of r in (i) $\Rightarrow x = 5 - \dfrac{5(\pi + 2)}{\pi + 4} \Rightarrow x = \dfrac{10}{\pi + 4}$

$\therefore$ length of rectangle $= 2r = \dfrac{20}{\pi + 4}$ and breadth $= \dfrac{10}{\pi + 4}$

11. **A point on the hypotenuse of a triangle is at distance a and b from the sides of the triangle. Show that the minimum length of the hypotenuse is $\left(a^{\frac{2}{3}} + b^{\frac{2}{3}}\right)^{\frac{3}{2}}$.**

Sol. Let P be a point on the hypotenuse AC of $\triangle$ABC such that PL ($\perp$AB) = a and PM ($\perp$BC) = b

Let $\angle$APL $= \angle$ACB $= \theta$

AP $= a \sec\theta$, PC $= b \cosec\theta$

let ℓ be the length of the hypotenuse, then

$\ell = AP + PC = a \sec\theta + b \cosec\theta,$

$\therefore \ \dfrac{d\ell}{d\theta} = a \sec\theta \tan\theta - b \cosec\theta \cot\theta$

For maxima or minima, $\dfrac{d\ell}{d\theta} = 0$

$\Rightarrow \dfrac{\sin^3\theta}{\cos^2\theta} = \dfrac{b}{a} \Rightarrow \tan^3\theta = \dfrac{b}{a} \Rightarrow \tan\theta = \left(\dfrac{b}{a}\right)^{1/3}$

$\dfrac{d^2\ell}{d\theta^2} = a \sec\theta(\sec^2\theta + \tan^2\theta) + b \cosec\theta(\cosec^2\theta + \cos^2\theta)$

$\therefore$ Also, $a > 0$, and $b > 0$ $\therefore \left(\dfrac{d^2\ell}{d\theta^2}\right)$ at $\tan\theta = (b/a)^{1/3} > 0$

So it attains for minimum length.

$\Rightarrow \ \ell$ is least when $\tan\theta = \left(\dfrac{b}{a}\right)^{1/3}$,

$\therefore$ Least value of
$\ell = a \sec\theta + b \cosec\theta$

$= (a^{2/3} + b^{2/3})^{3/2}$

Hence least value of
$\ell = (a^{2/3} + b^{2/3})^{3/2}$.

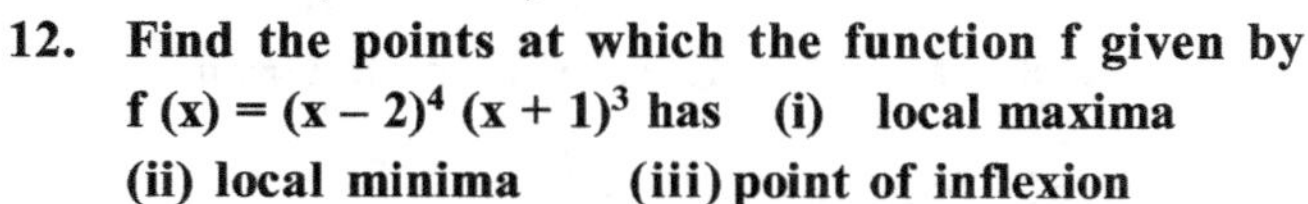

12. **Find the points at which the function f given by $f(x) = (x - 2)^4 (x + 1)^3$ has (i) local maxima (ii) local minima (iii) point of inflexion**

Sol. $f(x) = (x - 2)^4 (x + 1)^3$, $\because f'(x) = 7(x - 2)^3 (x + 1)^2 (x - 2/7)$

For maxima and minima, $f'(x) = 0 \Rightarrow x = 2, -1, 2/7$ At $x = 2$

When x is slightly < 2, $f'(x) = (-)(+)(+) = -$ve

When x is slightly > 2, $f'(x) = (+)(+)(+) = +$ve

$\therefore f'(x)$ changes its sign from $-$ve to $+$ve

While crossing the point $x = 2$,

$\Rightarrow \ f(x)$ is minimum at $x = 2$, At $x = -1$

When x is slightly < -1, $f'(x) = (-)(+)(-) = +$ve,

When x is slightly > -1, $f'(x) = (-)(+)(-) = -$ve

$\Rightarrow \ f'(x)$ does not changes its sign while passing through -1. Thus $x = -1$ is a point of inflexion,

At $x = \dfrac{2}{7} = 0.28$

When x is slightly $< \dfrac{2}{7}$, $f'(x) = (-)(+)(-) = +$ve ,

When x is slightly $> \dfrac{2}{7}$, $f'(x) = (-)(+)(+) + -$ve

$\Rightarrow \ f'(x)$ changes its sign from $+$ve to $-$ve while crossing the point $x = \dfrac{2}{7}$ $\therefore f(x)$ is maximum at $x = 2/7$.

13. **Find the absolute maximum and minimum values of the function f given by $f(x) = \cos^2 x + \sin x$, $x \in [0, \pi]$**

Sol. Let $f(x) = \cos^2 x + \sin x$, $x \in [0, \pi]$

$f'(x) = \cos x(-2\sin x + 1)$

For maximum or minimum, $f'(x) = 0 \therefore -2\sin x + 1 = 0$

$\Rightarrow \quad \cos x = 0 \ \big| \ \Rightarrow \sin x = 1/2$

$\Rightarrow \quad x = \dfrac{\pi}{2} \ \big| \ \Rightarrow \quad x = \dfrac{\pi}{6}$

Now, $f(0) = \cos^2 0 + \sin 0 = 1^2 + 0 = 1$,

$f\left(\dfrac{\pi}{6}\right) = \cos^2\dfrac{\pi}{6} + \sin\dfrac{\pi}{6} = \left(\dfrac{\sqrt{3}}{2}\right)^2 + \dfrac{1}{2} = \dfrac{5}{4}$,

$f\left(\dfrac{\pi}{2}\right) = \cos^2\dfrac{\pi}{2} + \sin\dfrac{\pi}{2} = 0 + 1 = 1$

and $f(\pi) = \cos^2\pi + \sin\pi = 1 + 0 = 1$ of these values, the maximum and minimum values of $f(x)$ are $\dfrac{5}{4}$ and 1

respectively so, absolute max $= \dfrac{5}{4}$ and absolute min $= 1$.

14. **Show that the altitude of the right circular cone of maximum volume that can be inscribed in a sphere of radius r is $\dfrac{4r}{3}$.**

Sol. The radius of sphere is r in which a cone is inscribed. Let O be the centre of the sphere. BC is the diameter of the base of cone.

Let AM = Altitude, $\angle$BOM $= \theta$, Radius of the cone R $= r \sin\theta$,

Altitude of the cone ABC $= AM = AO + OM = r(1 + \cos\theta)$,

Vol. of the cone $v = \dfrac{1}{3}\pi R^2 H$

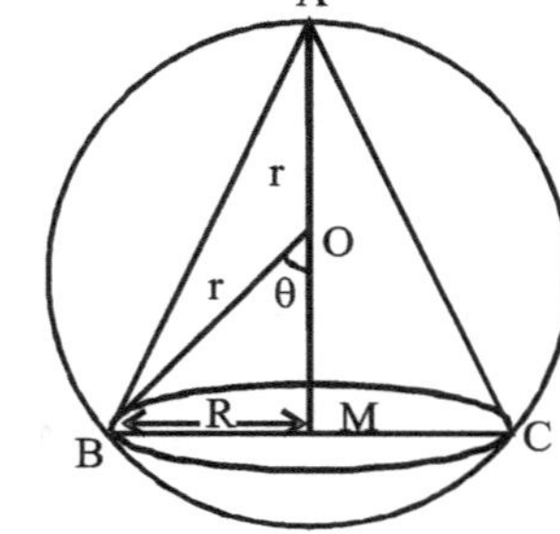

$$= \frac{1}{3}\pi r^3 \sin^2\theta\,(1+\cos\theta)$$

$$\frac{dv}{d\theta} = \frac{1}{3}\pi r^3 \sin\theta\,(\cos\theta+1)\,(3\cos\theta-1),$$

$$\frac{dv}{d\theta} = 0 \text{ at } \cos\theta = \frac{1}{3},\ \cos\theta \neq -1$$

Since, $\theta \neq \pi$, $\dfrac{dv}{d\theta}$ changes sign from $+$ ve to $-$ ve., $\therefore$ v is

max. at $\cos\theta = \dfrac{1}{3}$ $\therefore$ Alt. $= r(1+\cos\theta) = r\left(1+\dfrac{1}{3}\right) = \dfrac{4r}{3}$

15. Let f be a function defined on [a, b] such that f ′ (x) > 0, for all x ∈ (a, b). Then prove that f is an increasing function on (a, b).

Sol. Let $x_1, x_2 \in (a, b)$ such that $x_1 < x_2$,
Consider the sub-interval $[x_1, x_2]$
Since, $f(x)$ is differentiable on (a, b) and $[x_1, x_2] \subset (a, b)$

$\therefore$ $f(x)$ is continuous on $[x_1, x_2]$ and differentiable on (x_1, x_2)
By the lagrange's mean value theorem there exists

$$c \in (c_1\ c_2) \text{ such that } f'(c) = \frac{f(x_2)-f(x_1)}{x_2-x_1} \qquad ...(i),$$

Since, $f'(x) > 0$ for all $x \in (a, b)$
So, in particular, $f'(c) > 0$, Now, $f'(c) > 0$
$\Rightarrow f(x_2) - f(x_1) > 0 \Rightarrow f(x_2) > f(x_1)$
$\Rightarrow f(x_1) < f(x_2)$ if $x_1 < x_2$
$\therefore$ x_1, x_2 are arbitrary points in (a, b) ,
$\therefore$ $x_1 < x_2 \Rightarrow f(x_1) < f(x_2)\ \forall\ x_1\,x_2 \in (a, b)$
Hence, $f(x)$ is increasing on (a, b).

16. Show that the height of the cylinder of maximum volume that can be inscribed in a sphere of radius R is $\dfrac{2R}{\sqrt{3}}$. Also find the maximum volume.

Sol. Radius of the sphere $= R$, let h be the height and x be the diameter of the base of the inscribed cylinder.

$$\Rightarrow\quad h^2 + x^2 = 4R^2 \qquad ...(i)$$

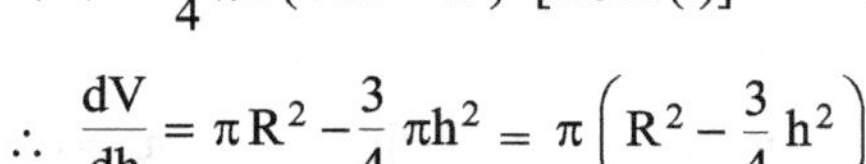

Volume of the cylinder $= \pi\left(\dfrac{x}{2}\right)^2 \times h$

$$\Rightarrow V = \frac{1}{4}\pi h\,(4R^2 - h^2)\ \text{[from (i)]}$$

$$\therefore\quad \frac{dV}{dh} = \pi R^2 - \frac{3}{4}\pi h^2 = \pi\left(R^2 - \frac{3}{4}h^2\right)$$

$$\Rightarrow \frac{dV}{dh} = 0 \Rightarrow R^2 = \frac{3}{4}h^2 \Rightarrow\quad h = \frac{2R}{\sqrt{3}}$$

Also, $\dfrac{d^2V}{dh^2} = -\dfrac{3}{4}\cdot 2\pi h = -\dfrac{3}{2}\pi h$

At $h = \dfrac{2R}{\sqrt{3}}$, $\dfrac{d^2v}{dh^2} = -\dfrac{3}{2}\pi\left(\dfrac{2R}{\sqrt{3}}\right) = -$ ve

$\Rightarrow$ V is maximum at $h = \dfrac{2R}{\sqrt{3}}$,

Maximum volume at $h = \dfrac{2R}{\sqrt{3}}$, is $\dfrac{4\pi R^3}{3\sqrt{3}}$ sq. units

17. Show that height of the cylinder of greatest volume which can be inscribed in a right circular cone of height h and semi vertical angle α is one-third that of the cone and the greatest volume of cylinder is $\dfrac{4}{27}\pi h^3 \tan^2\alpha$.

Sol. Let VAB be the cone of height h, semi-vertical angle α and let x be the radius of the base of the cylinder A′B′DC which is inscribed in the cone VAB. Then OO′ height of the cylinder

$$= VO - VO' = h - x\cot\alpha\ ,$$

volume of the cylinder
$$= \pi x^2\,(h - x\cot\alpha) \qquad ...(i)$$

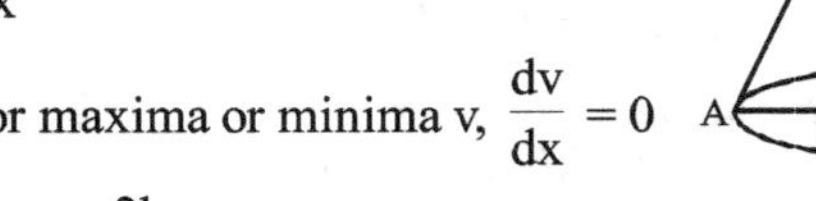

$$\frac{dv}{dx} = 2\pi\,xh - 3\pi\,x^2\cot\alpha\ ,$$

For maxima or minima v, $\dfrac{dv}{dx} = 0$

$$\Rightarrow\quad x = \frac{2h}{3}\tan\alpha$$

Now, $\dfrac{d^2v}{dx^2} = 2\pi h - 6\pi x\cot\alpha$ When $x = \dfrac{2h}{3}\tan\alpha$,

we have $\dfrac{d^2v}{dx^2} = \pi\,(2h - 4h) = -2\pi h < 0$

$\Rightarrow$ v is maximum, when $x = \dfrac{2h}{3}\tan\alpha$, $OO' = h - x\cot\alpha$

$$= h - \frac{2h}{3} = \frac{h}{3}$$

$\therefore$ The maximum volume of the cylinder is, $v = \dfrac{4}{27}\pi h^3 \tan^2\alpha$.

Choose the correct answer in Exercises from 18 to 23.

18. A cylindrical tank of radius 10 m is being filled with wheat at the rate of 314 cubic metre per hour. Then the depth of the wheat is increasing at the rate of

  (a) 1 m³/h   (b) 0.1 m³/h

  (c) 1.1 m³/h   (d) 0.5 m³/h

Sol. **(a)** Let h be the height of the cylindrical tank at any instant.
Volume of cylindrical tank $= V = \pi r^2 h\ = \pi\,(10)^2\,h$,
$= 100\,\pi h$

Rate of change of volume $= \dfrac{dv}{dt} = 100\,\pi\,\dfrac{dh}{dt}$ ...(i)

The tank is filled at the rate of 314 cubic feet per minute i.e.

$$\frac{dv}{dt} = 314 \text{ from (i) } 314 = 100\,\pi\,\frac{dh}{dt} \Rightarrow \frac{dh}{dt} = 1$$

Hence, the depth of the tank changes at 1 cubic ft/min.

19. The slope of the tangent to the curve $x = t^2 + 3t - 8,\ y = 2t^2 - 2t - 5$ at the point $(2, -1)$ is

  (a) $\dfrac{22}{7}$ (b) $\dfrac{6}{7}$ (c) $\dfrac{7}{6}$ (d) $\dfrac{-6}{7}$

Sol. **(b)** The curve is $x = t^2 + 3t - 8$, $y = 2t^2 - 2t - 5$ ...(i)

Put $x = 2, \Rightarrow (t + 5)(t - 2) = 0$

put $t = 2$ in $y = 2t^2 - 2t - 5 = 8 - 4 - 5 = -1$

At $x = 2, y = -1, t = 2$,

Differentiating (i) $\dfrac{dx}{dt} = 2t + 3$, $\dfrac{dy}{dt} = 4t - 2$

$\therefore \dfrac{dy}{dx} = \dfrac{dy}{dt} \times \dfrac{dt}{dx} = \dfrac{4t - 2}{2t + 3}$; At $t = 2$, $\dfrac{dy}{dx} = \dfrac{6}{7}$

20. **The line $y = mx + 1$ is a tangent to the curve $y^2 = 4x$ if the value of m is**

(a) 1   (b) 2   (c) 3   (d) $\dfrac{1}{2}$

Sol. **(a)** The equation of the curve is $y^2 = 4x$,

Differentiating w.r.t. x

$\therefore \dfrac{dy}{dx} = \dfrac{4}{2y} = \dfrac{2}{y}$, Slope of tangent $= \dfrac{2}{y} = m$,

$\therefore \quad y = \dfrac{2}{m}$ ...(i)

(x_1, y_1) lies on $y^2 = 4x$, $y_1^2 = 4x_1$ ...(ii)

Equation of tangent at (x_1, y_1)

or $\quad y = mx + y_1 - mx_1$ ...(iii)

$\quad\quad y = mx + 1$ ...(iv)

Comparing (iii) & (iv) $y_1 - mx_1 = 1$ ...(v)

from (i) & (ii) $m = \dfrac{2}{y_1}$, $x_1 = \dfrac{y_1^2}{4}$

$\therefore$ Put these values in (v) or $y_1 - \dfrac{y_1}{2} = \dfrac{y_1}{2} = 1$

$\therefore y_1 = 2$ $\quad\quad\quad \therefore m = \dfrac{2}{y_1} = \dfrac{2}{2} = 1$

21. **The normal at the point (1, 1) on the curve $2y + x^2 = 3$ is**

(a) $x + y = 0$ (b) $x - y = 0$

(c) $x + y + 1 = 0$ (d) $x - y = 0$

Sol. **(b)** The equation of the curve $2y + x^2 = 3$,

Differentiating $\therefore \dfrac{dy}{dx} = -x$

$\dfrac{dy}{dx}$ at $(1, 1) = -1 =$ Slope of tangent,

Since slope of normal $= \dfrac{-1}{\text{Slope of tangent}} = 1$

$\therefore$ The equation of the normal is

$y - y_1 = $ (slope of normal) $(x - x_1)$ or $y - 1 = 1(x - 1)$

or $\quad x - y = 0$

22. **The normal to the curve $x^2 = 4y$ passing (1, 2) is**

(a) $x + y = 3$ (b) $x - y = 3$

(c) $x + y = 1$ (d) $x - y = 1$

Sol. **(a)** $\therefore \quad x^2 = 4y$

$\dfrac{dy}{dx} = \dfrac{2x}{4} = \dfrac{x}{2} =$ slope of the tangent

$\therefore$ Slope of the normal $= -\dfrac{1}{\text{slope of tangent}}$

$= -\dfrac{2}{x_1}$ at (x_1, y_1)

$\therefore$ Eq. of normal is ; $y - y_1 = -\dfrac{2}{x_1}(x - x_1)$ ..(i)

It passes through $(1, 2)$ $\therefore$ $2 - y_1 = -\dfrac{2}{x_1}(1 - x_1)$

$\Rightarrow y_1 = \dfrac{2}{x_1}$ ...(ii)

The point (x_1, y_1) lies on $x^2 = 4y$ $\therefore x_1^2 = 4y_1$ ...(iii)

From (ii) and (iii) ; $x_1^2 = 4 \cdot \dfrac{2}{x_1}$

$\Rightarrow x_1^3 = 8$ or $x_1 = 2$; From (iii) $4 = 4y_1$ $\therefore y_1 = 1$

Putting these values in (i), equation of normal is

$y - 1 = \dfrac{-2}{2}(x - 2)$ or $y - 1 = -x + 2$ or $x + y = 3$

23. **The points on the curve $9y^2 = x^3$, where the normal to the curve makes equal intercepts with the zxes are**

(a) $\left(4, \pm \dfrac{8}{3}\right)$ (b) $\left(4, \dfrac{-8}{3}\right)$

(c) $\left(4, \pm \dfrac{3}{8}\right)$ (d) $\left(\pm 4, \dfrac{3}{8}\right)$

Sol. **(a)** The equation of the curve is $9y^2 = x^3$,

Differentiating $18y \dfrac{dy}{dx} = 3x^2$ $\therefore \dfrac{dy}{dx} = \dfrac{x^2}{6y}$

Let P (x_1, y_1) be the point where normal is drawn. Slope of

tangent $= \dfrac{x_1^2}{6y_1}$ $\therefore$ Slope of normal $= -6y_1/x_1^2$,

Normal make equal intercepts on the curve

$\therefore$ its slope $= \pm 1 \Rightarrow \dfrac{-6y_1}{x_1} = \pm 1$

or $6y_1 = \pm x_1^2$ ...(i)

(x_1, y_1) lies on the curve $9y^2 = x^3$

or $9y_1^2 = x_1^3$ ...(ii)

Taking $+$ ve sign, eliminating y_1, from (i) & (ii)

$9 \times \left(\dfrac{x_1^2}{6}\right)^2 = x_1^3$ or $9x_1^4 = 36 x_1^3 \Rightarrow x_1 = 4$ from (i)

$y_1 = \pm \dfrac{x_1^2}{6} = \pm \dfrac{16}{6}$ $[x_1 = 4]$, $y_1 = \pm \dfrac{8}{3}$; The point P is

$\left(4, \pm \dfrac{8}{3}\right)$

Past year Exercise

Short Answer Questions

1. Find the equations of the tangent and normal to the curve

   $x = a \sin^3\theta$ and $y = a \cos^3\theta$ at $\theta = \dfrac{\pi}{4}$.

2. Find the equations of the tangent and normal to the curve

   $\dfrac{x^2}{a^2} - \dfrac{y^2}{b^2} = 1$ at the point $(\sqrt{2}\,a, b)$.

3. Show that the equation of normal at any point t on the curve $x = 3\cos t - \cos^3 t$ and $y = 3\sin t - \sin^3 t$ is

   $4\,(y \cos^3 t - x \sin^3 t) = 3 \sin 4t$.

4. Find the points on the curve $y = x^3 - 3x^2 - 4x$ at which the tangent lines are parallel to the line $4x + y - 3 = 0$.

NCERT Exemplar

Multiple Choice Questions

1. If the curve $ay + x^2 = 7$ and $x^3 = y$, cut orthogonally at $(1, 1)$, then the value of a is:

   (a) 1   (b) 0

   (c) −6   (d) .6

2. The interval on which the function $f(x) = 2x^3 + 9x^2 + 12x - 1$ is decreasing is:

   (a) $[-1, \infty)$ (b) $[-2, -1]$

   (c) $(-\infty, -2]$ (d) $[-1, 1]$

3. Let the $f : \mathbf{R} \to \mathbf{R}$ be defined by $f(x) = 2x + \cos x$, then f :

   (a) has a minimum at $x = \pi$

   (b) has a maximum, at $x = 0$

   (c) is a decreasing function

   (d) is an increasing function

4. $f(x) = x^x$ has a stationary point at

   (a) $x = e$

   (b) $x = \dfrac{1}{e}$

   (c) $x = 1$

   (d) $x = \sqrt{e}$

Short Answer Questions

5. Show that the line $\dfrac{x}{a} + \dfrac{y}{b} = 1$, touches the curve $y = b \cdot e^{-x/a}$ at the point, where the curve intersects the axis of Y.

6. If $y = 2x + \cot^{-1} x + \ell n\left[\sqrt{1+x^2} - x\right]$, then show that y increases in R.

7. Show that for $a \geq 1$, $f(x) = \sqrt{3}\,\sin x - \cos x - 2ax + b$ is decreasing in R.

8. At what point, the slope of the curve $y = -x^3 + 3x^2 + 9x - 27$ is maximum? Also, find the maximum slope.

9. Prove that $f(x) = \sin x + \sqrt{3}\,\cos x$ has maximum value at $x = \dfrac{\pi}{6}$.

Objective Practice Exercise

Multiple Choice Questions

DIRECTIONS : *This section contains multiple choice questions. Each question has four choices (a), (b), (c) and (d) out of which only one is correct.*

1. Which of the following function is decreasing on $\left(0,\dfrac{\pi}{2}\right)$?

(a) $\sin 2x$ (b) $\tan x$

(c) $\cos x$ (d) $\cos 3x$

2. The function $f(x) = \tan x - x$

(a) always increases

(b) always decreases

(c) never increases

(d) sometimes increases and sometimes decreases

3. If x is real, then the minimum value of $x^2 - 8x + 17$ is

(a) -1 (b) 0

(c) 1 (d) 2

4. The smallest value of the polynomial $x^3 - 18x^2 + 96x$ in $[0, 9]$ is

(a) 126 (b) 0

(c) 135 (d) 160

5. The function $f(x) = 2x^3 - 3x^2 - 12x + 4$, has

(a) two points of local maximum

(b) two points of local minimum

(c) one maxima and one minima

(d) no maxima or minima

6. The maximum value of $\sin x . \cos x$ is

(a) $\dfrac{1}{4}$ (b) $\dfrac{1}{2}$

(c) $\sqrt{2}$ (d) $2\sqrt{2}$

7. At $x = \dfrac{5\pi}{6}$, $f(x) = 2\sin 3x + 3\cos 3x$ is

(a) maximum 1

(b) minimum

(c) zero

(d) neither maximum nor minimum

8. The function $f(x) = x^x$ has a stationary point at

(a) $x = e$ (b) $x = \dfrac{1}{e}$

(c) $x = 1$ (d) $x = \sqrt{e}$

9. The maximum value of $\left(\dfrac{1}{x}\right)^x$ is

(a) e (b) e^e

(c) $e^{\frac{1}{e}}$ (d) $\left(\dfrac{1}{e}\right)^{\frac{1}{e}}$

10. The normal to the curve $x = a(1 + \cos \theta)$, $y = a \sin\theta$ at 'θ' always passes through the fixed point

(a) (a, a) (b) $(0, a)$

(c) $(0, 0)$ (d) $(a, 0)$

11. The slope of the normal to the curve $y^3 - xy - 8 = 0$ at the point $(0, 2)$ is equal to

(a) -3 (b) -6

(c) 3 (d) 6

12. The curve $y - e^{xy} + x = 0$ has a vertical tangent at

(a) $(1, 1)$ (b) $(0, 1)$

(c) $(1, 0)$ (d) no point

13. The equation of the normal to the curve $y^4 = ax^3$ at (a, a) is

(a) $x + 2y = 3a$ (b) $3x - 4y + a = 0$

(c) $4x + 3y = 7a$ (d) $4x - 3y = 0$

14. The equation of the normal to the curve

$y = (1 + x)^y + \sin^{-1}(\sin^2 x)$ at $x = 0$ is

(a) $x + y = 1$ (b) $x + y + 1 = 0$

(c) $2x - y + 1 = 0$ (d) $x + 2y + 2 = 0$

15. The equation of the tangent to curve $y = be^{-x/a}$ at the point where it crosses y-axis is

(a) $ax + by = 1$ (b) $ax - by = 1$

(c) $\dfrac{x}{a} - \dfrac{y}{b} = 1$ (d) $\dfrac{x}{a} + \dfrac{y}{b} = 1$

16. At which point the line $\dfrac{x}{a} + \dfrac{y}{b} = 1$, touches the curve $y = be^{-x/a}$

(a) $(0, 0)$ (b) $(0, a)$

(c) $(0, b)$ (d) $(b, 0)$

17. If a tangent to the curve $y = 2 + \sqrt{4x + 1}$ has slope $\dfrac{2}{5}$ at a point, then the point is

(a) $(0, 2)$ (b) $\left(\dfrac{3}{4}, 4\right)$

(c) $(2, 5)$ (d) $(6, 7)$

18. The point of the curve $y^2 = 2(x-3)$ at which the normal is parallel to the line $y - 2x + 1 = 0$ is

(a) $(5, 2)$

(b) $\left(-\dfrac{1}{2}, -2\right)$

(c) $(5, -2)$

(d) $\left(\dfrac{3}{2}, 2\right)$

19. If the normal to the curve $y = f(x)$ at the point $(3, 4)$ makes an angle $\dfrac{3\pi}{4}$ with the positive x-axis then $f'(3)$ is equal to

(a) -1

(b) $-\dfrac{3}{4}$

(c) $\dfrac{4}{3}$

(d) 1

20. If $y = 4x - 5$ is tangent to the curve $y^2 = px^3 + q$ at $(2, 3)$, then

(a) $p = 2, q = -7$

(b) $p = -2, q = 7$

(c) $p = -2, q = -7$

(d) $p = 2, q = 7$

21. If the curves $\dfrac{x^2}{a^2} + \dfrac{y^2}{12} = 1$ and $y^3 = 8x$ intersect at right angles, then the value of a^2 is equal to

(a) 16 (b) 12 (c) 8 (d) 4

22. The angle between the curves $y^2 = 4x + 4$ and $y^2 = 36(9 - x)$ is

(a) $30°$

(b) $45°$

(c) $60°$

(d) $90°$

23. The tangent to the curve $y = ax^2 + bx$ at $(2, -8)$ is parallel to x-axis. Then

(a) $a = 2, b = -2$

(b) $a = 2, b = -4$

(c) $a = 2, b = -8$

(d) $a = 4, b = -4$

24. Angle between the tangents to the curve $y = x^2 - 5x + 6$ at the points $(2, 0)$ and $(3, 0)$ in

(a) $\pi/3$

(b) $\pi/2$

(c) $\pi/6$

(d) $\pi/4$

25. If normal to the curve $y = f(x)$ is parallel to x-axis, then correct statement is

(a) $\dfrac{dy}{dx} = 0$

(b) $\dfrac{dy}{dx} = 1$

(c) $\dfrac{dx}{dy} = 0$

(d) None of these

26. The co-ordinates of the point on the curve $y = x^2 - 3x + 2$ where the tangent is perpendicular to the straight line $y = x$ are

(a) $(0, 2)$

(b) $(1, 0)$

(c) $(-1, 6)$

(d) $(2, -2)$

27. The function $f(x) = \cot^{-1} x + x$ increases in the interval

(a) $(1, \infty)$

(b) $(-1, \infty)$

(c) $(-\infty, \infty)$

(d) $(0, \infty)$

28. If $f(x) = \dfrac{1}{x+1} - \log(1 + x), x > 0$, then f is

(a) An increasing function

(b) A decreasing function

(c) Both increasing and decreasing function

(d) None of these

29. The function $f(x) = 1 + x (\sin x) [\cos x], 0 < x \le \dfrac{\pi}{2}$ (where $[\,\cdot\,]$ is G.I.F.)

(a) is continuous on $\left(0, \dfrac{\pi}{2}\right)$

(b) is strictly increasing in $\left(0, \dfrac{\pi}{2}\right)$

(c) is strictly decreasing in $\left(0, \dfrac{\pi}{2}\right)$

(d) has global maximum value 2

30. The least value of k for which the function $x^2 + kx + 1$ is an increasing function in the interval $1 < x < 2$ is

(a) -4

(b) -3

(c) -1

(d) -2

31. For the every value of x the function $f(x) = \dfrac{1}{5^x}$ is

(a) Decreasing

(b) Increasing

(c) Neither increasing nor decreasing

(d) Increasing for $x > 0$ and decreasing for $x < 0$

32. On the interval $(1, 3)$, the function $f(x) = 3x + \dfrac{2}{x}$ is

(a) Strictly decreasing

(b) Strictly increasing

(c) Decreasing in $(2, 3)$ only

(d) Neither increasing nor decreasing

33. The function $f(x) = \tan x - x$:

(a) always increases

(b) always decreases

(c) never decreases

(d) some times increases and some times decreases

34. If $f'(x)$ is zero in the interval (a, b), then in this interval it is

(a) Increasing function

(b) Decreasing function

(c) Only for $a > 0$ and $b > 0$ is increasing function

(d) None of these

35. If $f(x) = x^x$, then $f(x)$ is decreasing in interval :

(a) $]0, e[$

(b) $]0, \dfrac{1}{e}[$

(c) $]0, 1[$

(d) none of these

36. The function f defined by $f(x) = x^3 - 6x^2 - 36x + 7$ is increasing, if

(a) $x > 2$ and also $x > 6$

(b) $x > 2$ and also $x < 6$

(c) $x < -2$ and also $x < 6$

(d) $x < -2$ and also $x > 6$

37. The function $f(x) = x^3 - 3x$ is

(a) increasing on $(-\infty, -1) \cup (1, \infty)$ and decreasing on $(-1, 1)$

(b) decreasing on $(-\infty, -1) \cup (1, \infty)$ and increasing on $(-1, 1)$

(c) increasing on $(0, \infty)$ and decreasing on $(-\infty, 0)$

(d) decreasing on $(0, \infty)$ and increasing on $(-\infty, 0)$

38. The function $f(x) = \log(1+x) - \dfrac{2x}{2+x}$ is increasing on

(a) $(0, \infty)$

(b) $(-\infty, 0)$

(c) $(-\infty, \infty)$

(d) None of these

39. The function $f(x) = e^{ax} + e^{-ax}$, $a > 0$ is monotonically increasing for

(a) $-1 < x < 1$

(b) $x < -1$

(c) $x > -1$

(d) $x > 0$

40. On the interval $\left(0, \dfrac{\pi}{2}\right)$, the function $\log \sin x$ is

(a) Increasing

(b) Decreasing

(c) Neither increasing nor decreasing

(d) None of these

41. The function $\dfrac{1}{1+x^2}$ is decreasing in the interval

(a) $(-\infty, -1]$

(b) $(-\infty, 0]$

(c) $[1, \infty)$

(d) $(0, \infty)$

42. The function $f(x) = x + \cos x$, is

(a) Always increasing

(b) Always decreasing

(c) Increasing for certain range of x

(d) None of these

43. The function $x^4 - 4x$ is decreasing in the interval

(a) $[-1, 1]$

(b) $(-\infty, 1)$

(c) $[1, \infty)$

(d) None of these

44. If $f(x) = \dfrac{a^2 - 1}{a^2 + 1} x^3 - 3x + 5$ is a decreasing function of x in **R** then the set of possible values of a (independent of x) is

(a) $(1, \infty)$

(b) $(-\infty, -1)$

(c) $[-1, 1]$

(d) None of these

DIRECTIONS : *Study the given Case/Passage and answer the following questions.*

Case/Passage-I

The Relation between the height of the plant (y in cm) with respect to exposure to sunlight is governed by the following equation $y = 4x - \dfrac{1}{2}x^2$ where x is the number of days exposed to sunlight.

[From CBSE Question Bank-2021]

45. The rate of growth of the plant with respect to sunlight is

(a) $4x - \dfrac{1}{2}x^2$

(b) $4 - x$

(c) $x - 4$

(d) $x - \dfrac{1}{2}x^2$

46. What is the number of days it will take for the plant to grow to the maximum height?

(a) 4

(b) 6

(c) 7

(d) 10

47. What is the maximum height of the plant?

(a) 12 cm

(b) 10 cm

(c) 8 cm

(d) 6 cm

48. What will be the height of the plant after 2 days?

    (a) 4 cm   (b) 6 cm

    (c) 8 cm   (d) 10 cm

49. If the height of the plant is 7/2 cm, the number of days it has been exposed to the sunlight is.

    (a) 2   (b) 3

    (c) 4   (d) 1

Case/Passage-II

$P(x) = -5x^2 + 125x + 37500$ is the total profit function of a company, where x is the production of the company.

[From CBSE Question Bank-2021]

50. What will be the production when the profit is maximum?

    (a) 37500   (b) 12.5

    (c) −12.5   (d) −37500

51. What will be the maximum profit?

    (a) ₹ 38,28,125

    (b) ₹ 38281.25

    (c) ₹ 39,000   (d) None

52. Check in which interval the profit is strictly increasing.

    (a) $(12.5, \infty)$

    (b) for all real numbers

    (c) for all positive real numbers

    (d) $(0, 12.5)$

53. When the production is 2 units what will be the profit of the company?

    (a) 37500

    (b) 37,730

    (c) 37,770

    (d) None

54. What will be production of the company when the profit is ₹ 38250?

    (a) 15

    (b) 30

    (c) 2

    (d) data is not sufficient to find

Case/Passage-III

The shape of a toy is given as $f(x) = 6(2x^4 - x^2)$. To make the toy beautiful 2 sticks which are perpendicular to each other were placed at a point $(2,3)$, above the toy.

[From CBSE Question Bank-2021]

55. Which value from the following may be abscissa of critical point?

    (a) $\pm\dfrac{1}{4}$ (b) $\pm\dfrac{1}{2}$

    (c) ± 1 (d) None

56. Find the slope of the normal based on the position of the stick.

    (a) 360   (b) −360   (c) $\dfrac{1}{360}$ (d) $\dfrac{-1}{360}$

57. What will be the equation of the tangent at the critical point if it passes through $(2, 3)$?

    (a) $x + 360y = 1082$

    (b) $y = 360x - 717$

    (c) $x = 717y + 360$

    (d) None

58. Find the second order derivative of the function at $x = 5$.

    (a) 598   (b) 1176   (c) 3588   (d) 3312

59. At which of the following intervals will $f(x)$ be increasing?

    (a) $\left(-\infty, -\dfrac{1}{2}\right) \cup \left(\dfrac{1}{2}, \infty\right)$ (b) $\left(-\dfrac{1}{2}, 0\right) \cup \left(\dfrac{1}{2}, \infty\right)$

    (c) $\left(0, \dfrac{1}{2}\right) \cup \left(\dfrac{1}{2}, \infty\right)$ (d) $\left(-\infty, -\dfrac{1}{2}\right) \cup \left(0, \dfrac{1}{2}\right)$

Chapter Test 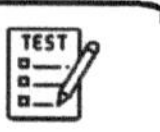

Time : *45 Minutes* Max. Marks : **20**

(i) Questions number **1-8** carry **1 mark** each.

(ii) Question number **9** carry **4 marks.**

(iii) Questions number **10-13** are **Very Short Answer Questions** and carry **2 marks** each.

Multiple Choice Questions

1. The slope of tangent to the curve $x = t^2 + 3t - 8$, $y = 2t^2 - 2t - 5$ at the point $(2, -1)$ is :

(a) $\dfrac{22}{7}$ (b) $\dfrac{6}{7}$

(c) $\dfrac{-6}{7}$ (d) -6

2. The function $f(x) = \tan x - x$

(a) always increases

(b) always decreases

(c) never increases

(d) sometimes increases and sometimes decreases

3. The maximum value of $\sin x . \cos x$ is

(a) $\dfrac{1}{4}$ (b) $\dfrac{1}{2}$ (c) $\sqrt{2}$ (d) $2\sqrt{2}$

4. The function $f(x) = 4\sin^3 x - 6\sin^2 x + 12\sin x + 100$ is strictly

(a) increasing in $\left(\pi, \dfrac{3\pi}{2}\right)$

(b) decreasing in $\left(\dfrac{\pi}{2}, \pi\right)$

(c) decreasing in $\left[\dfrac{-\pi}{2}, \dfrac{\pi}{2}\right]$

(d) decreasing in $\left[0, \dfrac{\pi}{2}\right]$

One Word Answer Questions

5. If $f(x) = x^x$, then find the interval in which $f(x)$ is decreasing.

6. If $f(x) = \dfrac{1}{4x^2 + 2x + 1}$, then find its maximum value.

Assertion & Reason Questions

DIRECTIONS : *Each of these questions contains an assertion followed by reason. Read them carefully and answer the question on the basis of following options. You have to select the one that best describes the two statements.*

(a) If both Assertion and Reason are correct and the Reason is the correct explanation of the Assertion.

(b) If both Assertion and Reason are correct but Reason is not the correct explanation of the Assertion.

(c) If the Assertion is correct but Reason is incorrect.

(d) If the Assertion is incorrect but the Reason is correct.

7. **Assertion :** The tangent to the curve $y = x^3 - x^2 - x + 1$ at $(1, 1)$ is parallel to x-axis.
Reason : The slope of the tangent to the curve at $(1, 1)$ is zero.

8. **Assertion :** Let $f : R \to R$ be a function such that $f(x) = x^3 + 3$. Then f is one-one
Reason : $f(x)$ is neither increasing nor decreasing function on $[-1, 1]$.

Case/Passage Based Question

DIRECTIONS (Q. 9) : *has 5 subparts based on Case/Passage given, attempt any 4 out of 5 questions.*

9. A group of class XII students had to analyse the water in a water tank has the shape of an inverted right circular cone with its axis vertical and vertex lowermost. Its semi-vertical angle is $\tan^{-1}$ (0.5). Water is poured into it at a constant rate of 5 cubic metre per hour. The figure of the water tank is given below.

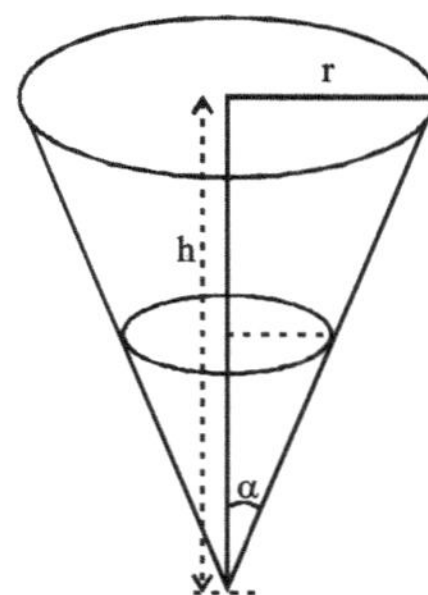

In the class, teacher asked the following questions to the students who analysed the scenario. [Use $\pi = \dfrac{22}{7}$]

(i) The relation between r and h.

(a) $r = 2h$ (b) $h = 2r$

(c) $r^2 = h$ (d) $h^2 = r$

(ii) The rate at which the level of water is rising at instant when the depth of water in the tank is 4 m.

(a) $\dfrac{35}{88}$ m/h

(b) $\dfrac{25}{88}$ m/h

(c) $\dfrac{53}{88}$ m/h

(d) $\dfrac{35}{53}$ m/h

(iii) The relation between volume (V), surface area (S) and radius (r) is

(a) $V^2 = \dfrac{1}{9}Sr^2(S - 2\pi r^2)$

(b) $V^2 = \dfrac{2}{9}Sr^2(S - 2\pi r^2)$

(c) $V^2 = \dfrac{1}{9}Sr(S - 2\pi r)$

(d) $V^2 = \dfrac{1}{9}Sr^2(S - \pi r^2)$

(iv) The surface area for which volume of water tank is maximum

(a) $S = 2\pi r^2$ (b) $S = 4\pi r^2$

(c) $S = \pi r^2$ (d) $S = 8\pi r^2$

(v) What is the maximum volume of the water tank?

(a) $V = \dfrac{\pi}{3}r^2\sqrt{8\pi r^2 - 1}$

(b) $V = \dfrac{2\pi}{3}r^2\sqrt{8\pi r^2 - 1}$

(c) $V = \dfrac{\sqrt{2\pi}}{3}r^2\sqrt{8\pi r^2 - 1}$

(d) $V = \dfrac{2}{9}r^2\sqrt{8\pi r^2 - 1}$

10. Find the minimum value of f if $f(x) = \sin x$ in $\left[\dfrac{-\pi}{2}, \dfrac{\pi}{2}\right]$

11. Find the acute angle between the curves $y = |x^2 - 1|$ and $y = |x^2 - 3|$ at their points of intersection.

12. Find the coordinates of the point on the curve $\sqrt{x} + \sqrt{y} = 4$ at which tangent in equally inclined to the axes.

13. At what points on the curve $x^2 + y^2 - 2x - 4y + 1 = 0$ the tangents are parallel to y-axis?

Solutions

Practice Exercise-1

1. (a)   2. (c)   3. (c)   4. (a)
5. (d)   6. (c)   7. (b)
8. (i) (b) (ii) (b)   (iii) (c)   (iv) (c)
   (v) (a)

9. 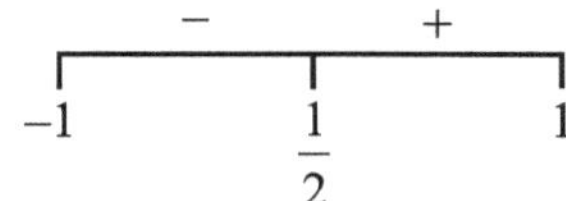

10. $(-2, 0) \cup (1, \infty)$.

11. $a \in (-\infty, -1)$.

12. the least value of a is –2.

13. $(1, \infty)$.

14. We have, $f(x) = x^2 - x + 1$

   $\Rightarrow f'(x) = 2x - 1$

   Thus, $f(x)$ does not have the same sign throughout the interval $(-1, 1)$.

   Hence $f(x)$ is neither increasing nor decreasing on $(-1, 1)$.

15. (b) Since, $f(x) = \tan^{-1}(\sin x + \cos x)$

   $\therefore f'(x) = \dfrac{1}{1 + (\sin x + \cos x)^2}(\cos x - \sin x)$

   $= \dfrac{\sqrt{2}\cos\left(x + \dfrac{\pi}{4}\right)}{1 + (\sin x + \cos x)^2}$

   $f(x)$ is increasing if $f'(x) > 0 \Rightarrow \cos\left(x + \dfrac{\pi}{4}\right) > 0$

   $\Rightarrow -\dfrac{\pi}{2} < x + \dfrac{\pi}{4} < \dfrac{\pi}{2} \Rightarrow -\dfrac{3\pi}{4} < x < \dfrac{\pi}{4}$

NCERT Exercise-1

1. $f(x) = 3x + 17$

   $\therefore f'(x) = 3 > 0 \ \forall \ x \in R$

   $\Rightarrow$ f is strictly increasing on R.

2. We have $f(x) = e^{2x}$

   $\Rightarrow f'(x) = 2e^{2x}$

Case I When $x > 0$, then $f'(x) = 2e^{2x}$

$= 2\left[1 + 2x + \dfrac{(2x)^2}{2!} + \dfrac{(2x)^3}{3!} + \cdots\cdots\right]$

$\Rightarrow f'(x) > 0 \ \forall \ x > 0$

Case II When $x = 0$, then $f'(x) = 2e^{\circ} = 2 > 0$

for $x = 0$

Case III When $x < 0$

Let $x = -y$ where y is a positive quantity

$\therefore f'(x) = 2e^{-2y} = \dfrac{2}{e^{zy}} = \dfrac{2}{+ve \text{ quantity}} > 0$

for $x < 0$

Thus $f'(x) > 0 \ \forall \ x \in R$. Hence, e^{2x} is strictly increasing on R.

3. We have $f(x) = \sin x$

   $\therefore f'(x) = \cos x$

   (a) $f'(x) = \cos x$ is $+$ve in the interval $= \left(0, \dfrac{\pi}{2}\right)$

   $\Rightarrow f(x)$ is strictly increasing on $= \left(0, \dfrac{\pi}{2}\right)$

   (b) $f'(x) = \cos x$ is a $-$ve in the interval $\left(\dfrac{\pi}{2}, \pi\right) \Rightarrow f(x)$ is strictly decreasing in $\left(\dfrac{\pi}{2}, \pi\right)$

   (c) $f'(x) = \cos x$ is $+$ve in the interval $\left(0, \dfrac{\pi}{2}\right)$ while $f'(x)$ is $-$ve in the interval $\left(\dfrac{\pi}{2}, \pi\right)$

   $\Rightarrow f(x)$ does not have the same sign in the interval $(0, \pi)$. Hence $f(x)$ is neither increasing nor decreasing in $(0, \pi)$

4. $f(x) = 2x^2 - 3x$

   $\Rightarrow f'(x) = 4x - 3$

   $\Rightarrow f'(x) = 0$ at $x = \dfrac{3}{4}$

   The point $x = \dfrac{3}{4}$ divides the real

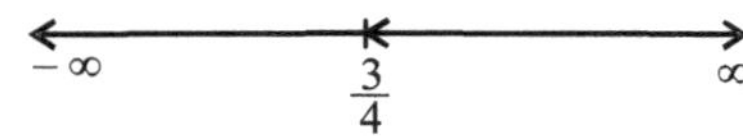

Line into two disjoint intervals viz. $\left(-\infty, \dfrac{3}{4}\right)$ and $\left(\dfrac{3}{4}, \infty\right)$.

In the interval , $\left(-\infty, \dfrac{3}{4}\right)$ f′ (x) is –ve

∴ f is strictly decreasing in $\left(-\infty, \dfrac{3}{4}\right)$

In the interval $\left(\dfrac{3}{4}, \infty\right)$, f′ is + ve.

Hence f is strictly increasing in the interval $\left(\dfrac{3}{4}, \infty\right)$

5. $f(x) = 2x^3 - 3x^2 - 36x + 7$

$f'(x) = 6x^2 - 6x - 36 = 6(x^2 - x - 6)$

$f'(x) = 6(x-3)(x+2)$

$\Rightarrow f'(x) = 0$ at $x = 3$ and $x = -2$

The points $x = 3$, $x = -2$, divide the real line into three disjoint intervals viz. $(-\infty, -2), (-2, 3), (3, \infty)$

Now f′(x) is +ve in the intervals $(-\infty, -2)$ and $(3, \infty)$. Since in the interval $(-\infty, -2)$ each factor $x - 3$, $x + 2$ is –ve.

$\Rightarrow f'(x) = +ve.$

(a) f is strictly increasing in $(-\infty, -2) \cup (3, \infty)$

(b) In the interval $(-2, 3)$, $x + 2$ is +ve and $x - 3$ is –ve.

$\quad f'(x) = 6(x-3)(x+2) = + \times - = -ve$

∴ f is strictly decreasing in the interval $(-2, 3)$.

6. (c) Let $f(x) = -2x^3 - 9x^2 - 12x + 1$

∴ $f'(x) = -6x^2 - 18x - 12 = -6(x^2 + 3x + 2)$

$f'(x) = -6(x+1)(x+2)$, $f'(x) = 0$ gives $x = -1$

or $x = -2$

The points $x = -2$ and $x = -1$ divide the real line into three disjoint intervals namely $(-\infty, -2)$ $(-2, -1)$ and $(-1 \,\infty)$.

In the interval $(-\infty, -2)$ i.e., $-\infty < x < -2$ $(x+1)(x+2)$ are –ve.   ∴ $f'(x) = (-)(-)(-) = -$ ve.

$\Rightarrow$ f (x) is decreasing in $(-\infty, -2)$

In the interval $(-2, -1)$ i.e., $-2 < x < -1$, $(x+1)$ is –ve and $(x+2)$ is + ve.

∴ $f'(x) = (-)(-)(+) = +$ ve.

$\Rightarrow$ f (x) is increasing in $(-2, -1)$

In the interval $(-1, \infty)$ i.e., $-1 < x < \infty$, $(x+1)$ and $(x+2)$ are both positive.

∴ f′ (x) = (–) (+) (+) = –ve.

$\Rightarrow$ f(x) is decreasing in $(-1, \infty)$

Hence, f(x) is increasing for $-2 < x < -1$ and decreasing for $x < -2$ and $x > -1$.

7. Let $f(x) = \log(1+x) - \dfrac{2x}{2+x}$

$\Rightarrow f'(x) = \dfrac{x^2}{(x+1)(x+2)^2}$

For f (x) to be increasing f′ (x) > 0

$\Rightarrow \dfrac{1}{x+1} > 0 \Rightarrow x > -1$

Hence, $y = \log x - \dfrac{2x}{x+2}$ is an increasing function of x

for all values of $x > -1$.

8. Let $y = [x(x-2)]^2 = x^4 - 4x^3 + 4x^2$

∴ $\dfrac{dy}{dx} = 4x^3 - 12x^2 + 8x$

For the function to be increasing $\dfrac{dy}{dx} > 0$

$\Rightarrow 4x^3 - 12x^2 + 8x > 0$

$\Rightarrow 4x(x^2 - 3x + 2) > 0$

$\Rightarrow 4x(x-1)(x-2) > 0$

∴ For $0 < x < 1$, $\dfrac{dy}{dx} = (+)(-)(-) = +ve$

and for $x > 2$, $\dfrac{dy}{dx} = (+)(+)(+) = +ve$

Thus, the function is increasing for $0 < x < 1$ and $x > 2$.

9. ∴ $\dfrac{dy}{dx} = \dfrac{8\cos\theta + 4}{(2+\cos\theta)^2} - 1 = \dfrac{\cos\theta(4-\cos\theta)}{(2+\cos\theta)^2}$

For the function to be increasing $\dfrac{dy}{d\theta} > 0$

$\Rightarrow \dfrac{\cos\theta(4-\cos\theta)}{(2+\cos\theta)^2} > 0$

$\Rightarrow \cos\theta(4-\cos^2\theta) > 0$

$\Rightarrow \cos\theta > 0$

$\qquad [\because (4-\cos^2\theta) > 0]$

$\Rightarrow \theta \in \left(0, \dfrac{\pi}{2}\right) 1$

10. Let $f(x) = \log x$

Now, $f'(x) = \dfrac{1}{x}$

When takes the values $x > 0$, $\dfrac{1}{x} > 0$, when $x > 0$,

$\because f'(x) > 0$

Hence, $f(x)$ is an increasing function for $x > 0$ i.e. $f(x)$ is increasing function whenever is defined.

11. $f'(x) = 2x - 1 = 2\left(x - \dfrac{1}{2}\right)$

Now $-1 < x < \dfrac{1}{2} \Rightarrow \left(x - \dfrac{1}{2}\right) < 0$

$\Rightarrow 2\left(x - \dfrac{1}{2}\right) < 0$

$\Rightarrow f'(x) < 0$ and $\dfrac{1}{2} < x < 1$

$\Rightarrow x - \dfrac{1}{2} > 0$

$\Rightarrow 2\left(x - \dfrac{1}{2}\right) > 0 \Rightarrow f'(x) > 0$

Thus $f'(x)$ does not have the same sign throughout the interval $(-1, 1)$.

Hence, $f(x)$ is neither increasing nor decreasing on $(-1, 1)$.

12. (a) We have $f(x) = \cos x$

$\therefore f'(x) = -\sin x \quad$ for $0 < x < \dfrac{\pi}{2}$, $\sin x > 0$

$\therefore f'(x) = -\sin x < 0$ in $\left(0, \dfrac{\pi}{2}\right)$

$\therefore f'(x)$ is a decreasing function.

(b) We have $f(x) = \cos 2x$

$\therefore f'(x) = -2\sin 2x$

For $0 < x < \dfrac{\pi}{2}$ or $0 < 2x < \pi$, $\sin 2x$ is +ve

$\therefore f'(x)$ is a decreasing function.

(c) We have $f(x) = \cos 3x$

$\therefore f'(x) = -3\sin 3x$

For $0 < x < \dfrac{\pi}{2}$

$\Rightarrow 0 < 3x < \dfrac{3\pi}{2}$, $\sin 3x$ is +ve in $0 < 3x < \pi$

$\therefore f'(x) < 0$

$\Rightarrow f(x)$ is decreasing.

And $\sin 3x$ is $-$ve in $\pi < 3x < \dfrac{3\pi}{2}$

$\therefore f'(x) > 0 \Rightarrow f(x)$ is increasing

$\therefore f'(x)$ is neither increasing nor decreasing in $\left(0, \dfrac{\pi}{2}\right)$

Hence, $f(x)$ is not a decreasing function in $\left(0, \dfrac{\pi}{2}\right)$.

(d) We have $f(x) = \tan x$;

$f'(x) = \sec^2 x > 0 \ \forall \ x \in \left(0, \dfrac{\pi}{2}\right)$

$\therefore f(x)$ is an increasing function. Thus (a) $\cos x$ (b) $\cos 2x$ are strictly decreasing function on $\left(0, \dfrac{\pi}{2}\right)$

13. (d) Let $f(x) = x^{100} + \sin x - 1$

$\therefore f'(x) = 100\, x^{99} + \cos x$

(a) for $(-1, 1)$ i.e., $-1 < x < 1$, $-1 < x^{99} < 1$

$\Rightarrow -100 < 100\, x^{99} < 100$;

Also $0 < \cos x < 1$

$\Rightarrow f'(x)$ can either be +ve or $-$ve on $(-1, 1)$

$\therefore f(x)$ is neither increasing nor decreasing on $(-1, 1)$.

(b) for $(0, 1)$ i.e. $0 < x < 1$ $\quad x^{99}$ and $\cos x$ are both +ve

$\therefore f'(x) > 0$

$\Rightarrow f(x)$ is increasing on $(0, 1)$

(c) For $\left(\dfrac{\pi}{2}, \pi\right)$ i.e. $\dfrac{\pi}{2} < x < \pi$, x^{99} is +ve and $-1 < \cos x < 0$

$\therefore f'(x) > 0$

$\Rightarrow f(x)$ is increasing on $\left(\dfrac{\pi}{2}, \pi\right)$

(d) For $\left(0, \dfrac{\pi}{2}\right)$, i.e. $0 < x < \dfrac{\pi}{2}$, x^{99} and $\cos x$ are both $-$ve.

$\therefore f'(x) < 0$ $f(x)$ is decreasing on $\left(0, \dfrac{\pi}{2}\right)$.

Option (d) is correct.

14. We have $f(x) = x^2 + ax + 1 \qquad f'(x) = 2x + a$.

Since $f(x)$ is an increasing function on $(1, 2)$

$\therefore f'(x) > 0$ for all $1 < x < 2$

Now, $f''(x) = 2$ for all $x \in (1, 2)$

$\Rightarrow f''(x) > 0$ for all $x \in (1, 2)$

$\Rightarrow f'(x)$ is an increasing function on $(1, 2)$

$\Rightarrow f'(x)$ is the least value of $f'(x)$ on $(1, 2)$

But $f'(x) > 0 \ \forall \ x \in (1, 2)$

$\therefore \ f'(1) > 0 \Rightarrow 2 + a > 0 \ \Rightarrow a > -2$

Thus, the least value of a is -2.

15. We have $f(x) = x + \dfrac{1}{x}$

$f'(x) = 1 - \dfrac{1}{x^2} = \dfrac{x^2 - 1}{x^2}$

Now $x \in I \Rightarrow x \notin (-1, 1)$

$\Rightarrow x \le -1$ or $x \ge 1 \Rightarrow x^2 \ge 1 \ \Rightarrow x^2 - 1 \ge 0$

$\Rightarrow \dfrac{x^2 - 1}{x^2} \ge 0 \ \Rightarrow f'(x) \ge 0$

Thus $f'(x) \ge 0 \ \forall \ x \in I$.

Hence, $f'(x)$ is strictly increasing on I.

16. $f'(x) = \dfrac{1}{\sin x} \cdot \cos x \cot x$

When $0 < x < \dfrac{\pi}{2}$, $f'(x)$ is +ve;

i.e. is increasing

When $\dfrac{\pi}{2} < x < \pi$, $f'(x)$ is $-$ve; i.e. decreasing,

$\therefore \ f(x)$ is decreasing.

Hence, f is increasing on $(0, \pi/2)$ and strictly decreasing on $(\pi/2, \pi)$.

17. $f(x) = \log \cos x$, $f'(x) = \dfrac{1}{\cos x}(-\sin x) = -\tan x$

In the interval $\left(0, \dfrac{\pi}{2}\right)$, $f'(x) = -$ve

$\therefore \ f$ is strictly decreasing

In the interval $\left(\dfrac{\pi}{2}, \pi\right)$, $f'(x)$ is $+$ve.

$\therefore \ f$ is strictly increasing in the interval.

18. $f'(x) = 3x^2 - 6x + 3 = 3(x^2 - 2x + 1) = 3(x - 1)^2$

Now $x \in R$, $\ f'(x) = (x - 1)^2 \ge 0$

i.e. $f'(x) \ge 0 \ \forall \ x \in R$.

Hence, $f(x)$ is increasing on **R**.

19. **(d)** $f'(x) = 2xe^{-x} + x^2(-e^{-x}) = xe^{-x}(2 - x) = e^{-x}x(2 - x)$

Now e^{-x} is positive for all $x \in R$

$f'(x) = 0$ at $x = 0, 2$

$x = 0, x = 2$ divide the number line into three disjoint intervals.

viz. $(-\infty, 0), (0, 2), (2, \infty)$

(a) Interval $(-\infty, 0)$ $\quad x$ is $+$ ve and $(2 - x)$ is $+$ve

$\quad \therefore \ f'(x) = e^{-x}x(2 - x) = (+)(-)(+) = -$ve

$\quad \Rightarrow \ f$ is decreasing in $(-\infty, 0)$

(b) Interval $(0, 2)$ $\ f'(x) = e^{-x}x(2 - x)$

$\quad = (+)(+)(+) = +$ve

$\quad \Rightarrow \ f$ is increasing in $(0, 2)$

(c) Interval $(2, \infty)$ $\ f'(x) = e^{-x}x(2 - x)$

$\quad = (+)(+)(-) = -$ve

$\quad \Rightarrow \ f$ is decreasing in the interval $(2, \infty)$

Practice Exercise-2 

1. (c)   **2.** (b)   **3.** (b)   **4.** (b)

5. (b)   **6.** (c)   **7.** (a)

8. (i) (a)   (ii) (d)   (iii) (c)   (iv) (d)

    (v) (a)

9. $x + y = 0$

10. $(3, 2), (-1, 2)$

11. $y = x + \dfrac{33}{4}$

12. $\dfrac{dy}{dx} = 2x - 5$.

$m_1 = 2 \times 2 - 5 = -1$

and, $m_2 = 2 \times 3 - 5 = 1$

Clearly, $m_1 m_2 = -1 \times 1 = -1$.

13. $y = 4x + 13$

14. $y = 2x - \dfrac{23}{24}$

Hint: $\dfrac{dy}{dx} = \dfrac{1}{\sqrt{3x - 2}} \times 3 = 2$

15. $(0, 0), (\pm 1, \pm 2)$

Hint: $-y = 4x^3 - 2x^5$ ...(i)

$\Rightarrow \dfrac{dy}{dx} = 12x^2 - 10x^4$

Equ. of any tangent at $P(\alpha, \beta)$ is $\quad y - \beta = \left(\dfrac{dy}{dx}\right)_p (x - \alpha)$

$\Rightarrow \quad y - (4\alpha^3 - 2\alpha^5) = (12\alpha^2 - 10\alpha^4)(x - \alpha)$

$[\because (\alpha, \beta)$ lies on (i)]

let this tangent passes through the origin $(0, 0)$,

$0 - (4\alpha^3 - 2\alpha^5) = (12\alpha^2 - 10\alpha^4)(x - \alpha)$

$\Rightarrow \alpha = 0, 1, -1, \quad$ As (α, β) lies on (i)

so, $\quad \beta = 4\alpha^3 - 2\alpha^5, \quad$ when $\alpha = 0, \ \beta = 0$

when $\alpha = 1, \ \beta = 2, \quad$ when $\alpha = -1, \beta = -2$

$\therefore \quad$ The reqd. points are $(0, 0), (1, 2),$ and $(-1, -2)$

16. $y = 10x - 8, x + 10y = 223$

Hint: when $x = 3, y = 3^2 + 4 \times 3 + 1 = 22.$

$\dfrac{dy}{dx} = 2x + 4$

$\therefore$ Equ. of the tangent at $P(3, 22)$ is

$y - 22 = 10(x - 3) \Rightarrow y = 10x - 8,$

Equ. of the normal at P is

$x + 10y = 223$

17. Hint $- y = be^{-x/a}$ ...(i),

This meets y-axis, where $x = 0$

$\therefore y = b \times e^0 = b,$ equ (i) meets y-axis is at $(0, b),$

Diff(i) w.r.t. x $\dfrac{dy}{dx} = be^{-x/a}\left(-\dfrac{1}{a}\right)$

$\therefore \quad m = \left(\dfrac{dy}{dx}\right)_{(0,b)} = b.e^0, \left(-\dfrac{1}{a}\right) = -\dfrac{b}{a}$

Equation of the tangent at $(0, b)$ with

slope $= -\dfrac{b}{a}$ is $\dfrac{x}{a} + \dfrac{y}{b} = 1$

18. Do it yourself.

NCERT Exercise-2

1. The curve is $y = 3x^4 - 4x$

$\therefore \quad \dfrac{dy}{dx} = 12x^3 - 4$

$\therefore$ Req. slope $= \left(\dfrac{dy}{dx}\right)_{x=4} = 12 \times 4^3 - 4 = 764.$

2. The curve is $y = \dfrac{x-1}{x-2},$

$\dfrac{dy}{dx} = \dfrac{1(x-2) - (x-1) \cdot 1}{(x-2)^2} = \dfrac{-1}{(x-2)^2}$

$\therefore$ Req. slope $= \left(\dfrac{dy}{dx}\right)_{x=10} = \dfrac{-1}{(10-2)^2} = \dfrac{-1}{8^2} = \dfrac{-1}{64}$

3. The curve is $y = x^3 - x + 1 \quad \therefore \dfrac{dy}{dx} = 3x^2 - 1$

$\therefore$ Slope of the tangent $= \left(\dfrac{dy}{dx}\right)_{x=2} = 3 \times 2^2 - 1 = 11$

4. The curve is $y = x^3 - 3x + 2 \quad \therefore \dfrac{dy}{dx} = 3x^2 - 3$

Slope of the tangent at $x = 3$ is $\left(\dfrac{dy}{dx}\right)_{x=3} = 3 \times 3^2 - 3 = 24.$

5. $\dfrac{dx}{d\theta} = -3a\cos^2\theta\sin\theta, \quad \dfrac{dy}{d\theta} = 3a\sin^2\theta\cos\theta$

$\therefore \dfrac{dy}{dx} = \dfrac{dy/d\theta}{dx/d\theta} = -\dfrac{\sin\theta}{\cos\theta}, \dfrac{dy}{dx} = -\tan\theta$

$\therefore$ Req. slope $\left(\dfrac{dy}{dx}\right)_{\theta=\frac{\pi}{4}} = -\tan\dfrac{\pi}{4} = -1$

Hence slope of normal $= -\dfrac{1}{m} = \dfrac{-1}{-1} = 1$

6. $\dfrac{dx}{d\theta} = -a\cos\theta \ \& \ \dfrac{dy}{d\theta} = 2b\cos\theta(-\sin\theta)$

Now $\dfrac{dy}{dx} = \dfrac{dy/d\theta}{dx/d\theta} = \dfrac{-2b\sin\theta\cos\theta}{-a\cos\theta} = \dfrac{2b}{a}\sin\theta$

At $\theta = \dfrac{\pi}{2}, \dfrac{dy}{dx} = \dfrac{2b}{a}\sin\dfrac{\pi}{2} = \dfrac{2b}{a} \times 1 = \dfrac{2b}{a}$

$\therefore$ slope of normal at $\theta = \dfrac{\pi}{2}$ is $\dfrac{-1}{(dy/dx)_{\theta=\frac{\pi}{2}}} = \dfrac{-a}{2b}$

7. Differentiating w.r.t. x; $\dfrac{dy}{dx} = 3(x-3)(x+1)$

Tangent is parallel to x-axis if the slope of tangent $= 0$

or $\dfrac{dy}{dx} = 0 \Rightarrow 3(x+3)(x+1) = 0$

$\Rightarrow x = -1, 3$

when $x = -1, y = 12$ & When $x = 3, y = -20$

Hence the tangent to the given curve are parallel to x-axis at the points $(-1, -12), (3 - 20)$

8. The equation of the curve is $y = (x-2)^2$

Differentiating w.r.t. x

$\dfrac{dy}{dx} = 2(x-2)$

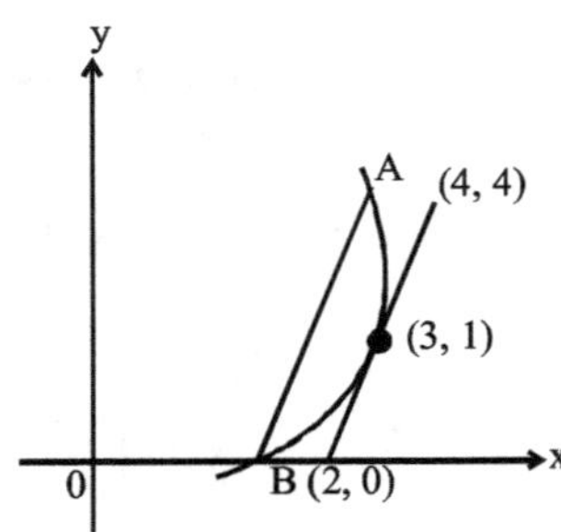

The point A and B are $(2, 0)$ and $(4, 4)$ respectively.

$\therefore$ Slope of $AB = \dfrac{y_2 - y_1}{x_2 - x_1}$

$= \dfrac{4-0}{4-2} = \dfrac{4}{2} = 2$. ...(i)

Slope of the tangent $= 2\,(x - 2)$ ...(ii)

from (i) & (ii) $2\,(x - 2) = 2$

$\therefore$ $x - 2 = 1$ or $x = 3$ when $x = 3, y = (3 - 2)^2 = 1$

Hence the tangent is parallel to the chord AB at $(3, 1)$.

9. Here, $y = x^3 - 11x + 5 \Rightarrow \dfrac{dy}{dx} = 3x^2 - 11$

The slope of tangent line $y = x - 11$ is 1

$\therefore$ $3x^2 - 11 = 1 \quad 3x^2 = 12 \quad x^2 = 4, x = \pm 2$

When $x = 2, \quad y = -9$ & when $x = -2, y = -13$

But $(-2, -13)$ does not lie on the curve

$\therefore$ $y = x - 11$ is the tangent at $(2, -9)$

10. Here, $y = \dfrac{1}{x - 1} \Rightarrow \dfrac{dy}{dx} = \dfrac{-1}{(x - 1)^2}$

Slope of tangent $= -1$ $\therefore$ $\dfrac{-1}{(x - 1)^2} = -1$

or $(x - 1)^2 = 1$

$\therefore$ $x - 1 = \pm 1$ or $x = 2, 0$ when $x = 2, \ y = \dfrac{1}{x - 1} = \dfrac{1}{1} = 1$

when $x = 0, y = \dfrac{1}{0 - 1} = -1$

The point where the tangents to the given curve have the slope -1 are $(2, 1)\,(0, -1)$

$\therefore$ Equation of the tangents at $(2, 1)$

$y - 1 = -1 \times (x - 2)$ or $x + y = 3$

Equation of tangent at $(0, 1), y + 1 = -1 \times (x - 0)$

or $x + y + 1 = 0$

Thus, the required lines are $x + y - 3 = 0, x + y + 1 = 0$.

11. Here $y = \dfrac{1}{x - 3} \Rightarrow \dfrac{dy}{dx} = (-1)\,(x - 3)^{-2} = \dfrac{-1}{(x - 3)^2}$

$\because$ slope of tangent $= 2 \Rightarrow \dfrac{-1}{(x - 3)^2} = 2$

$\Rightarrow (x - 3)^2 = -\dfrac{1}{2}$

Which is not possible as $(x - 3)^2 > 0$

Thus, no tangent to the curve $y = \dfrac{1}{x - 3}$ has slope 2.

12. Let the tangent at the point (x_1, y_1) to the curve

$$y = \dfrac{1}{x^2 - 2x + 3} \qquad \text{...(i)}$$

$\therefore$ $y_1 = \dfrac{1}{x_1^2 - 2x_1 + 3}$ ...(ii)

$\therefore$ $\dfrac{dy}{dx} = \dfrac{-(2x - 2)}{(x^2 - 2x + 3)^2}$

$\Rightarrow \left(\dfrac{dy}{dx}\right) \text{at}\,(x_1\ y_1) = \dfrac{-(2x_1 - 2)}{(x_1^2 - 2x_1 + 3)^2}$

But slope at (x_1, y_1) is 0 $\therefore$ $\dfrac{-(2x_1 - 2)}{(x_1^2 - 2x_1 + 3)^2} = 0$

$\Rightarrow -2\,(x_1 - 1) = 0 \Rightarrow x_1 = 1$

When $x_1 = 1$, then from (ii) $y_1 = \dfrac{1}{1 - 2 + 3} = \dfrac{1}{2}$

The tangent at (x_1, y_1) i.e. $(1, 1/2)$ having slope

0 is $y - \dfrac{1}{2} = 0\,(x - 1) \Rightarrow y - \dfrac{1}{2} = 0 \Rightarrow y = \dfrac{1}{2}$

13. The equation of the curve is $\dfrac{x^2}{9} + \dfrac{y^2}{16} = 1$ ...(i)

Differentiating w.r.t. x; $\dfrac{2x}{9} + \dfrac{2y}{16}\dfrac{dy}{dx} = 0$

$\Rightarrow \dfrac{dy}{dx} = \dfrac{16}{9}, \dfrac{x}{y}$

(a) if the tangent is parallel to x-axis $\dfrac{dy}{dx} = 0$

$\therefore$ $-\dfrac{16}{9} \cdot \dfrac{x}{y} = 0 \Rightarrow x = 0$

in (i) $\dfrac{y^2}{16} = 1, \ \therefore \ y = \pm 4$

$\therefore$ Tangents are parallel to x-axis at $(0, 4)$ & $(0, -4)$

(b) When tangents are parallel to y-axis, then denominator of $\dfrac{dy}{dx}$ is zero. $y = 0$, Putting $y = 0$ in (i)

$$\frac{x^2}{9} = 1, x = \pm 3$$

14. (i) $\dfrac{dy}{dx} = 4x^3 - 18x^2 + 26x - 10$

Putting $x = 0$, $\dfrac{dy}{dx}$ at $(0, 5) = -10$

Thus, the equation of tangent at P $(0, 5)$ is

$$\Rightarrow y - 5 = -10(x - 0) \Rightarrow y + 10x - 5 = 0$$

and the equation of normal at P $(0, 5)$

$$(x - x_1) + \left(\frac{dy}{dx}\right)_{at\,p} (y - y_1) = 0$$

$$\Rightarrow x - 10y + 50 = 0.$$

(ii) $\dfrac{dy}{dx}\bigg]_{(1,3)} = 4(1)^3 - 18(1)^2 + 26(1) - 10 = 2$

∴ Equation of the tangent is

$$y - 3 = 2(x - 1) \Rightarrow 2x - y + 1 = 0$$

Equation of the normal is

$$y - 3 = \frac{-1}{2}(x - 1) \Rightarrow x + 2y - 7 = 0$$

(iii) $y = x^3 \Rightarrow \dfrac{dy}{dx}\bigg]_{(1,1)} = 3x^2 = 3(1)^2 = 3$

∴ The equation of the tangent is

$$y - 1 = 3(x - 1) \Rightarrow 3x - y - 2 = 0$$

The equation of the normal is

$$y - 1 = \frac{-1}{3}(x - 1) \Rightarrow x + 3y - 4 = 0$$

(iv) $y = x^2 \Rightarrow \dfrac{dy}{dx}\bigg]_{(0,0)} = 2x = 2(0) = 0$

∴ The equation of the tangent is

$$y - 0 = 0(x - 0) \Rightarrow y = 0$$

∴ The equation of the normal is

$$y - 0 = \frac{-1}{0}(x - 0) \Rightarrow x = 0$$

(v) $x = \cos t$ and $y = \sin t$

$$\frac{dy}{dt} = \cos t, \quad \frac{dx}{dt} = -\sin t \quad \therefore \quad \frac{dy}{dx} = \frac{\dfrac{dy}{dt}}{\dfrac{dx}{dt}} = -\cot t$$

$$\frac{dy}{dx}\bigg]_{t=\frac{\pi}{4}} = -\cot \frac{\pi}{4} = -1 \quad \text{Now } x = \cos = \cos \frac{\pi}{4} = \frac{1}{\sqrt{2}}$$

and $y = \sin t = \sin \dfrac{\pi}{4} = \dfrac{1}{\sqrt{2}} \therefore x = \dfrac{1}{\sqrt{2}}$ and $y = \dfrac{1}{\sqrt{2}}$

∴ The equation of the tangent at the point $\left(\dfrac{1}{\sqrt{2}}, \dfrac{1}{\sqrt{2}}\right)$ is

$$y - \frac{1}{\sqrt{2}} = -1\left(x - \frac{1}{\sqrt{2}}\right) \Rightarrow \frac{\sqrt{2}y - 1}{\sqrt{2}} = \frac{-\sqrt{2}x + 1}{\sqrt{2}}$$

$$\Rightarrow \quad \sqrt{2} \cdot x + \sqrt{2} \cdot y - 2 = 0 \Rightarrow x + y = \sqrt{2}$$

The equation of the normal at the point $\left(\dfrac{1}{\sqrt{2}}, \dfrac{1}{\sqrt{2}}\right)$ is

$$y - \frac{1}{\sqrt{2}} = 1\left(x - \frac{1}{\sqrt{2}}\right) \Rightarrow \quad x - y = 0.$$

15. Equation of the curve is $y = x^2 - 2x + 7$ ...(i)

$$\frac{dy}{dx} = 2x - 2 = 2(x - 1)$$

(a) Slope of the line $2x - y + 9 = 0$ is 2

$$\Rightarrow \text{ Slope of tangent} = \frac{dy}{dx} = 2(x - 1) = 2$$

$$\Rightarrow x = 2$$

Putting $x = 2$ in (i) $y = 2^2 - 2 \cdot 2 + 7 = 7$

∴ Tangent parallel to $2x - y + 9 = 0$ at $(2, 7)$ is

$$y - 7 = 2(x - 2) \quad \text{or} \quad 2x - y + 3 = 0$$

(b) Tangent is perpendicular to the line $5y - 15x = 13$

$$\Rightarrow \text{ Slope of tangent x slope of line} = -1$$

$$\Rightarrow x = 1 - \frac{1}{6} = \frac{5}{6}; \text{Put } x = \frac{5}{6} \text{ in (i) } y = \frac{217}{36}$$

∴ Equation of the tangent which is perpendicular to

$5y - 15x = 13$ at $\left(\dfrac{5}{6}, \dfrac{217}{36}\right)$ is $y - \dfrac{217}{36} = -\dfrac{1}{3}\left(x - \dfrac{5}{6}\right)$

$$\therefore \quad 12x + 36y - 227 = 0.$$

16. Here, $y = 7x^3 + 11 \Rightarrow x \dfrac{dy}{dx} = 21x^2$

Now $m_1 = $ Slope at $x = 2$ is $\left(\dfrac{dy}{dx}\right)_{x=2} = 21 \times 2^2 = 84$

and $m_2 = $ Slope at $x = -2$ is $\left(\dfrac{dy}{dx}\right)_{x=2} = 21 \times (-2)^2 = 84.$

Hence, $m_1 = m_2$. Thus, the tangents to the given curve at the points where $x = 2$ and $x = -2$ are parallel

17. Let $P(x_1, y_1)$ be the required point. The given curve is

$$y = x^3 \qquad \qquad \text{...(i)}$$

$$\Rightarrow \quad \frac{dy}{dx} = 3x^2 \Rightarrow \left(\frac{dy}{dx}\right)_{(x_1, y_1)} = 3x_1^2$$

Since the slope of the tangent at $(x_1, y_1) = y_1$

$$\therefore \quad 3x_1^2 = y_1 \qquad \qquad \text{...(ii)}$$

Also (x_1, y_1) lies on (i) so $y_1 = x_1^3$ ...(iii)

from (ii) & (iii), we have

$$3x_1^2 = x_1^3 \Rightarrow x_1^2(3 - x_1) = 0$$

$$\Rightarrow x_1 = 0 \text{ or } x_1 = 3$$

When $x_1 = 0$, $y_1 = 0^3 = 0$ when $x_1 = 3$, $y_1 = 3^3 = 27$

$\therefore$ The required points are $(0, 0)$ and $(3, 27)$

18. Let (x_1, y_1) be the required point on the given curve

$$y = 4x^3 - 2x^5, \text{ then } y_1 = 4x_1^3 - 2x_1^5 \qquad \text{...(i)}$$

$$\frac{dy}{dx} = 12x^2 - 10x^4 \Rightarrow \left(\frac{dy}{dx}\right)_{(x_1, y_1)} = 12x_1^2 - 10x_1^4$$

Now, equation of the tangent at (x_1, y_1) is

$$y - y_1 = \left(\frac{dy}{dx}\right)_{(x_1, y_1)} (x - x_1) \text{ or } y - y_1 = (12x_1^2 - 10x_1^4)(x - x_1)$$

This passes through the origin

$$\therefore \quad 0 - y_1 = (12 x_1^2 - 10x_1^4)(0 - x_1^4)$$

$$\Rightarrow y_1 = 12 x_1^3 - 10x_1^5 \qquad \qquad \text{...(ii)}$$

Subtracting (ii) from (i), we get

$$0 = -8x_1^3 + 8x_1^5 \Rightarrow 8x_1^3(x_1^2 - 1) = 0 \Rightarrow x_1 = 0$$

or $x_1 = \pm 1$

When $x_1 = 0$ from (ii) $y_1 = 0$, When $x_1 = 1$, from (ii) $y_1 = 4$.

$1^3 - 2 \cdot 1^5 = 4 - 2 = 2$; when $x_1 = -1$, from (ii) $y_1 = -2$

Hence, the required points are $(0, 0)$, $(1, 2)$, $(-1, -2)$.

19. Here, $x^2 + y^2 - 2x - 3 = 0 \Rightarrow \dfrac{dy}{dx} = \dfrac{1 - x}{y}$

Tangent is parallel to x-axis, if $\dfrac{dy}{dx} = 0$ i.e.

if $1 - x = 0 \Rightarrow x = 1$ Putting $x = 1$ in (i) $\Rightarrow y = \pm 2$

Hence, the required points are $(1, 2)$, $(1, -2)$ i.e. $(1, \pm 2)$.

20. Here, $ay^2 = x^3 \Rightarrow 2ay \dfrac{dy}{dx} = 3x^2 \Rightarrow \dfrac{dy}{dx} = \dfrac{3x^2}{2ay}$

At (am^2, am^3), $\dfrac{dy}{dx} = \dfrac{3m}{2}$

$\Rightarrow$ Slope of the tangent at (am^2, am^3) is $\dfrac{3m}{2}$ and slope of

the normal at (am^2, am^3) is $\dfrac{-2}{3m}$

Equation of normal is; $3my - 3am^4 = -2x + 2am^2$

$\Rightarrow 2x + 3my - am^2(2 + 3m^2) = 0.$

21. Let the required normal be drawn at the point (x_1, y_1)

The equation of the given curve is $y = x^3 + 2x + 6$ ...(i)

Differentiating w.r.t. x $\dfrac{dy}{dx} = 3x^2 + 2$

$$\Rightarrow \left(\frac{dy}{dx}\right)_{(x_1, y_1)} = 3x_1^2 + 2$$

Since the normal at (x_1, y_1) is parallel to the line

$$x + 14y + 4 = 0$$

$\therefore$ Slope of the normal at (x_1, y_1) = Slope of the line

$$x + 14y + 4 = 0$$

$$\Rightarrow \frac{-1}{(dy/dx)_{(x_1, y_1)}} = \frac{-1}{14} \Rightarrow 3x_1^2 = 12 \Rightarrow x_1^2 = 4$$

$$\Rightarrow x_1 = \pm 2 \qquad \qquad \because (x_1, y_1) \text{ lies in (i)}$$

$$\therefore \quad y_1 = x_1^3 + 2x_1 + 6$$

When $x_1 = 2$, $y_1 = 8 + 4 + 6 = 18$

When $x_1 = -2$, $y_1 = -8 - 4 + 6 = -6$

Thus the co-ordinates of the points are $(2, 18)$ and $(-2, -6)$

The equation of the normal at $(2, 18)$ is : $x + 14y - 254 = 0$

The equation of the normal at $(-2, -6)$ is

$$y + 6 = \frac{-1}{14}(x + 2) \Rightarrow x + 14y + 86 = 0$$

22. Here, $y^2 = 4ax \Rightarrow \dfrac{dy}{dx} = \dfrac{2a}{y} \Rightarrow \left(\dfrac{dy}{dx}\right)_{(at^2, 2at)} = \dfrac{2a}{2at} = \dfrac{1}{t}$

The eq. of the tangent at $(at^2, 2at)$ is $y - 2at = \dfrac{1}{t}(x - at^2)$

$ty - 2at^2 = x - at^2 \Rightarrow ty = x + at^2$ and the equation of the

normal at $(at^2, 2at)$ is $y = -tx + 2at + at^3$

23. The given curves are $x = y^2$ ...(i)

and $xy = k$ ...(ii)

Putting $x = y^2$ in (ii), $\Rightarrow y = k^{1/3}$

from (i) $x = y^2 = (k^{1/3})^2 = k^{2/3}$

Thus the point of intersection is $(k^{2/3}, k^{1/3})$ Differentiating
(i) w.r.t. x : $1 = 2y\dfrac{dy}{dx} \Rightarrow \dfrac{dy}{dx} = \dfrac{1}{2y}$ at $(k^{2/3}, k^{1/3})$,

$\dfrac{dy}{dx} = \dfrac{1}{2k^{1/3}} \Rightarrow$ Slope of tangent at $(k^{2/3}, k^{1/3}) = \dfrac{1}{2k^{1/3}}$

Differentiating $xy = k$ w.r.t. x

$x\dfrac{dy}{dx} + y\cdot 1 = 0 \Rightarrow x\dfrac{dy}{dx} = -y \Rightarrow \dfrac{dy}{dx} = -\dfrac{y}{x}$,

At $(k^{2/3}, k^{1/3})$, $\dfrac{dy}{dx} = \dfrac{-k^{1/3}}{k^{2/3}} = \dfrac{-1}{k^{1/3}}$

$\Rightarrow$ Slope of tangent at $(k^{2/3}, k^{1/3}) = \dfrac{-1}{k^{1/3}}$

Now the curves cut at right angles if the product of slopes of tangents to two curves at $(k^{2/3}, k^{1/3})$ is -1.

i.e., if $\left(\dfrac{1}{2k^{1/3}}\right)\left(\dfrac{-1}{k^{1/3}}\right) = -1 \Rightarrow -1 = 2k^{2/3} \Rightarrow 8k^2 = 1$

24. $\therefore \dfrac{x^2}{a^2} - \dfrac{y^2}{b^2} = 1 \Rightarrow \dfrac{dy}{dx} = \dfrac{b^2 x}{a^2 y}; \left(\dfrac{dy}{dx}\right)_{(x_0, y_0)} = \dfrac{b^2 x_0}{a^2 y_0}$

slope of the tangent $= \dfrac{b^2 x_0}{a^2 y_0}$

Since (x_0, y_0) lies on $\dfrac{x^2}{a^2} - \dfrac{y^2}{b^2} = 1$

$\therefore \dfrac{x_0^{\,2}}{a^2} - \dfrac{y_0^{\,2}}{b^2} = 1$ ...(i)

Equation of the tangent is

$\dfrac{xx_0}{a^2} - \dfrac{yy_0}{b^2} = \dfrac{x_0^{\,2}}{a^2} - \dfrac{y_0^{\,2}}{b^2} \Rightarrow \dfrac{xx_0}{a^2} - \dfrac{yy_0}{b^2} = 1$ [from (i)]

Now, Slope of normal $= \dfrac{-1}{(dy/dx)_{(x_0, y_0)}} = \dfrac{-a^2 y_0}{b^2 x_0}$

Equation of the normal is

$y - y_0 = \dfrac{-a^2 y_0}{b^2 x_0}(x - x_0) \Rightarrow \dfrac{y - y_0}{a^2 y_0} + \dfrac{x - x_0}{b^2 x_0} = 0.$

25. Let the point of contact of the tangent line parallel to the given line be P (x_1, y_1). The equation of the curve is $y = \sqrt{3x - 2}$.

$\Rightarrow \dfrac{dy}{dx} = \dfrac{3}{2\sqrt{3x-2}} \Rightarrow \left(\dfrac{dy}{dx}\right)_{(x_1, y_1)} = \dfrac{3}{2\sqrt{3x_1 - 2}}$

Since the tangent at (x_1, y_1) is parallel to the line
$4x - 2y + 5 = 0$

$\therefore \left(\dfrac{dy}{dx}\right)_{(x_1, y_1)} =$ slope of line $4x - 2y + 5 = 0$

$\Rightarrow 4\sqrt{3x_1 - 2} = 3 \Rightarrow 16(3x_1 - 2) = 9 \Rightarrow x_1 = \dfrac{41}{48}$

Since (x_1, y_1) lies on $y = \sqrt{3x - 2}$

$\therefore y_1 = \dfrac{3}{4}$

So, the point of contact is $\left(\dfrac{41}{48}, \dfrac{3}{4}\right)$. Hence, the required equation of the tangent is $48x - 24y = 23$.

26. **(d)** $\because y = 2x^2 + 3\sin x$

$\therefore \dfrac{dy}{dx} = 4x + 3\cos x$ at $x = 0$, $\dfrac{dy}{dx} = 3$,

$\therefore$ Slope $= 3 \Rightarrow$ Slope of normal is $= -\dfrac{1}{3}$

27. **(a)** The curve is $y^2 = 4x$, $2y\dfrac{dy}{dx} = 4$

$\therefore \dfrac{dy}{dx} = \dfrac{4}{2y} = \dfrac{2}{y}$

Slope of the given line $y = x + 1$ is 1. $\therefore \dfrac{2}{y} = 1$

$\therefore$ $y = 2$ Putting $y = 2$ in $y^2 = 4x$ $2^2 = 4x$

$\Rightarrow$ $x = 1$ $\therefore$ Point of contact is $(1, 2)$.

Practice Exercise-3

1. **(d)**   2. **(d)**   3. **(a)**   4. **(d)**

5. **(d)**   6. **(a)**   7. **(c)**

8. **(i)** **(a)** $\because$ Perimeter $= 10$

$2x + \pi r + 2r = 10$

$2x + (\pi + 2)r = 10$

(ii) **(c)** A = sum of areas of rectangle and semicircle

$= 2rx + \dfrac{1}{2}\pi r^2 = r[10 - (\pi + 2)r] + \dfrac{1}{2}\pi r^2$

$= 10r - \left(\dfrac{1}{2}\pi + 2\right)r^2$

(iii) **(c)** $\dfrac{dA}{dr} = 10 - (\pi + 4)r$

For critical point

$\dfrac{dA}{dt} = 0 \Rightarrow 10 - (\pi + 4)r = 0$

$\Rightarrow r = \dfrac{10}{(\pi + 4)}$

(iv) (a) $\dfrac{d^2A}{dt^2} = -(\pi+4)$

$$\Rightarrow \left(\dfrac{d^2A}{dt^2}\right)_{(r)} = -(\pi+4) < 0$$

$$\Rightarrow r = \dfrac{10}{\pi+4} \text{ is point of maxima}$$

$\because\ 2x + (\pi+2)r = 10$

$$\Rightarrow x = \dfrac{10}{\pi+4}$$

$\therefore$ Length of rectangle $= 2r$

$$= \dfrac{20}{\pi+4} \text{ and width} = \dfrac{10}{\pi+4}$$

$\therefore$ Required dimension is

$$\dfrac{20}{\pi+4},\ \dfrac{10}{\pi+4}$$

(v) (d) $\because$ A is maximum for

$$r = \dfrac{10}{\pi+4} = \dfrac{10}{\dfrac{22}{7}+4} = \dfrac{7}{5}$$

$$\therefore A = 10r - \left(\dfrac{1}{2}\pi+4\right)r^2$$

$$= 10 \times \dfrac{7}{5} - \left(\dfrac{1}{2}\times\dfrac{22}{7}+4\right)\times\left(\dfrac{7}{5}\right)^2$$

$$= 14 - 10.92 = 3.08\,\text{m}^2$$

9. $2\sqrt{ab}$.

10. $\dfrac{1}{4}$

11.   (0)

12.   Do it yourself.

13.   120

14. π

15.   **Hint:** Let a be the side of the square base of the cuboid and h its height. let s (v) be its surface area (volume). Then $v = a^2h$ ...(i) ,

$$s = 2a^2 + 4ah = 2a^2 + \dfrac{4v}{a}, \quad \text{Diff w.r.t. a}$$

$$\dfrac{ds}{da} = 4a - \dfrac{4v}{a^2}, \quad \text{for max. or min.} \dfrac{ds}{da} = 0$$

$$\Rightarrow\ v = a^3\ \Rightarrow\ a = v^{1/3}$$

Also $\dfrac{d^2s}{da^2} = 4 + \dfrac{8v}{v} = 12 > 0,$ when $a = v^{1/3}$

$\Rightarrow$ s is minimum.

Now, $h = \dfrac{a^3}{a^2} = a$

$\Rightarrow$ All the sides of the cuboid are equal.

$\Rightarrow$ Cuboid is a cube.)

16. $\dfrac{25}{4}$ sq. units.

17. $4\left(\sqrt{5}-1\right)a$

18. $\dfrac{3\sqrt{2}}{2}$ cm $\times \dfrac{3}{2}\sqrt{2}$ cm $\times \dfrac{3}{2}\sqrt{2}$ cm.

19.   Keeping in mind "save environment" traditional boat should be preferred.

1.   **(i)**   Minimum value of $(2x-1)^2$ is zero.

          Minimum value of $(2x-1)^2 + 3$ is 3

          Clearly it does not have maximum value.

   (ii) $f(x) = 9x^2 + 12x + 2 \Rightarrow f(x) = (3x+2)^2 - 2$

Minimum value of $(3+2)^2$ is zero.

       $\therefore$ Minimum value of $(3x+2)^2 - 2$

       $= 9x^2 + 12x + 2$ is -2

       $f(x)$ does not have finite maximum value.

   (iii) $f(x) = -(x-1)^2 + 10$

          Maximum value of $-(x-1)^2$ is zero

          $\therefore$ Maximum value of $f(x) = -(x-1)^2 + 10$ is 10

          $f(x)$ does not have finite minimum value.

   (iv)   As $x \to \infty,\ g(x) \to \infty;$ Also $x \to -\infty,\ g(x) \to -\infty$

          Thus there is no maximum or minimum value of $f(x)$.

2.   **(i)**   We have : $f(x) = |x+2| - 1\ \forall\ x \in R$

          Now $|x+2| \geq 0\ \forall\ x \in R$ or $|x+2| - 1 \geq 0 - 1\ \forall\ x \in R$

          $|x+2| - 1 \geq -1\ \forall\ x \in R,$ So -1 is the min. value of $f(x)$

          now $f(x) = -1 \Rightarrow |x+2| - 1 \Rightarrow |x+2| = 0 \Rightarrow x = -2$

   (ii)   We have $g(x) = -|x+1| + 3\ \forall\ x \in R$

          Now $|x+1| \geq 0\ \forall\ x \in R$ or $-|x+1| \leq 0\ \forall\ x \in R$

          $-|x+1| + 3 \leq 0 + 3\ \forall\ x \in R$

          $-|x+1| + 3 \leq 3\ \forall\ x \in R$

So 3 is the minimum value of $f(x)$.

Now $f(x) = 3 \Rightarrow -|x+1| + 3 \Rightarrow |x+1| = 0$

$\Rightarrow x = -1$.

(iii) Thus maximum value of $f(x)$ is 6 and minimum value is 4.

(iv) Let $f(x) = |\sin 4x + 3|$

Maximum value of $\sin 4x$ is 1

∴ Maximum value of $|\sin(4x+3)|$ is $|1+3| = 4$

Minimum value of $\sin 4x$ is -1

∴ Minimum value of $f(x)$ is $|-1+3| = |2| = 2$

(v) Greatest value of $f(x)$ is 2 and least value is 0.

3. (i) Let $f(x) = x^2 \Rightarrow f'(x) = 2x$

Now $f'(x) = 0 \Rightarrow 2x = 0$ i.e., $x = 0$

At $x = 0$; When x is slightly < 0, $f'(x)$ is –ve

When x is slightly > 0, $f'(x)$ is +ve

∴ $f'(x)$ changes sign from –ve to +ve as x increases through 0.

$\Rightarrow$ $f'(x)$ has a local minimum at $x = 0$

local minimum value $f(0) = 0$.

(ii) Let $g(x) = x^3 - 3x \Rightarrow g'(x) = 3(x-1)(x+1)$

Now $f'(x) = 0 \Rightarrow$ either $x = 1$ or $x = -1$

At $x = 1$ When x is slightly < 1 $g'(x)$ is $(+)(-1)(+)$ i.e.,–ve.

When x is slightly > 1 $g'(x)$ is $(+)(+)(+)$ i.e., +ve.

Thus $f'(x)$ changes sign from negative to positive as x increases through 1 and hence $x = 1$ is a point of local minimum. At $x = -1$

When x is slightly < -1 $g'(x)$ is $(+)(-)(-)$ i.e., +ve.

When x is slightly > -1 $g'(x)$ is $(+)(-)(+)$ i.e.,–ve.

Thus $g'(x)$ changes sign from positive to negative as x increases through -1 and hence $x = -1$ is a point of local minimum.

Hence local minimum value is $g(x) = g(1) = 1 - 3 = -2$

and local maximum value is $g(x) = g(-1) = -1 + 3 = 2$.

(iii) $h(x) = \sin x + \cos x$ $h'(x) = \cos x - \sin x$

$h'(x) = \cos x (1 - \tan x)$

$h'(x) = 0$

$\Rightarrow \cos x - \sin x = 0$

or $\tan x = 1, x = \dfrac{\pi}{4}$,

$x = \dfrac{\pi}{4} \in \left(0, \dfrac{\pi}{4}\right)$

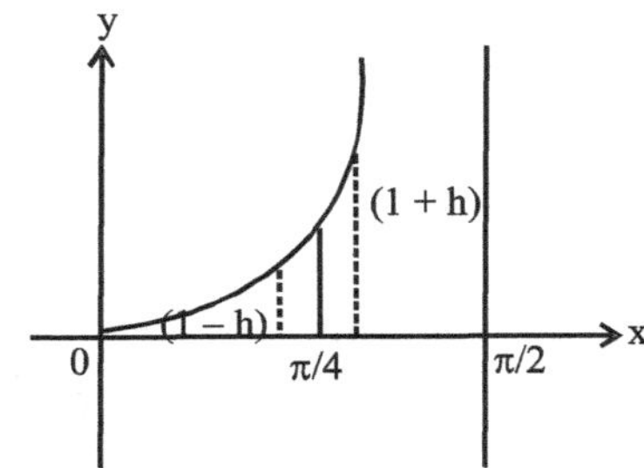

At $\alpha = \dfrac{\pi}{4}$, $h'(x) = \cos x (1 - \tan x)$

when x is slightly $< \dfrac{\pi}{4}$; $\cos x = +ve$, $\tan x = 1 - h$

where h is small :

∴ $1 - \tan x = 1 - (1-h) = +ve$,

$h'(x) = \cos x (1 - \tan x)$, $h'(x) = (+)(+) = +ve$

When x is slightly $> \pi/4$

$\cos x = +ve$ $\tan x = 1 + h$, where h is small

∴ $1 - \tan x = 1 - (1+h) = -h = -ve$

$h'(x) = \cos x (1 - \tan x) \Rightarrow h'(x) = (+)(-) = -ve$

∴ There is a local maxima at $x = \pi/4$

Local maximum value $= h\left(\dfrac{\pi}{4}\right)$

$= \sin \frac{\pi}{4} + \cos \frac{\pi}{4} = \frac{1}{\sqrt{2}} + \frac{1}{\sqrt{2}} = \dfrac{2}{\sqrt{2}} = \sqrt{2}$

(iv) $f'(x) = 4 \sin^3 x \cos x - 4 \cos^3 x \sin x$

$f'(x) = -4 \sin x \cos x (\cos^2 x - \sin^2 x)$

$f'(x) = -2 \sin 2x \cos 2x = -\sin 4x$

For local max. or local minimum, we have

$f'(x) = 0 \Rightarrow -\sin 4x = 0 \Rightarrow 4x = \pi$

$\Rightarrow x = \dfrac{\pi}{4}$: Now $f''(x) = -4 \cos x$

$f''\left(\dfrac{\pi}{4}\right) = -4 \cos \pi = (-4)(-1) = 4 > 0$

So $x = \dfrac{\pi}{4}$ is a point of local minimum and local minimum value is : $f\left(\dfrac{\pi}{4}\right) = \sin^4 x + \cos^4 x$

$$= \sin^4\left(\dfrac{\pi}{4}\right) + \cos^4\left(\dfrac{\pi}{4}\right) = \left(\dfrac{1}{\sqrt{2}}\right)^4 + \left(\dfrac{1}{\sqrt{2}}\right)^4 = \dfrac{1}{2}.$$

(v) Let $f(x) = x^3 - 6x^2 + 9x - 8 \quad f'(x) = 3x^2 - 12x + 9$

$$= 3(x^2 - 4x + 3)$$

Now, $f'(x) = x = 1, 3$

At $x = 1$:

When x is slightly < 1, $f'(x) = (-)(-) = +ve$

When x is slightly > 1, $f'(x) = (+)(-) = -ve$

$\therefore \quad f'(x)$ changes sign from +ve to –ve as x increases through 1.

$\Rightarrow \quad f(x)$ has a local maximum at $x = 1$.

Local maximum value $= f(1) = 1 - 6 + 9 + 15 = 19$

At $x = 3$:

When x is slightly < 3, $f'(x) = (+)(-) = -ve$

When x is slightly > 3, $f'(x) = (+)(+) = +ve$

$\therefore \quad f'(x)$ changes sign from –ve to +ve as x increases through 3.

$\Rightarrow \quad f(x)$ has a local minimum at $x = 3$.

Local minimum value $= f(3) = (3)^3 - 6(3)^2 + 9(3) + 15$

$= 27 - 54 + 27 + 15 = 15$

Note : How to determine the change of sign of $f(x)$ as x increases through a particular point?

Let $f'(x) = (x - a)(x - b)(x - c)$

At $x = a$, $x - a = a - a = 0$, $x - b = a - b$,

$x - c = a - c$

Sign corresponding to $x - a$ changes from –ve to +ve, sign corresponding to $x - c$ is that of $a - c$ and remains to be the same.

Let $f'(x) = (x - 1)(x - 3)$

At $x = 1$, $x - 1 = 1 - 1 = 0$; $x - 3 = 1 - 3 = -2 = -ve$

Factor $(x - 1)(x - 3)$

Signs when x is slightly < 1, $(-)(-) = +ve$

Signs when x is slightly > 1 $(+)(-) = -ve$

$\therefore \quad f'(x)$ changes from +ve to –ve

At $x = 3$, $x - 1 = 3 - 1 = 2 = +ve$; $x - 3 = 3 - 3 = 0$

Factor $(x - 1)(x - 3)$

Sign when x is slightly < 3, $(+)(-) = -ve$

Sign when x is slightly > 3, $(+)(+) = +ve$

$\therefore \quad f'(x)$ changes sign from –ve to **+ve**

(vi) Let $g(x) = \dfrac{x}{2} + \dfrac{2}{x}$, $x > 0$; $\quad g'(x) = \dfrac{x^2 - 4}{2x^2}$

Now $g'(x) = 0 \Rightarrow x = \pm 2$

Since it is given that $x > 0$ hence $x = -2$ is rejected.

At $x = 2$

For x slightly < 2, $g'(x) = \dfrac{-}{+} = -ve$

For x slightly > 2, $g'(x) = \dfrac{+}{+} = +ve$

Thus $g'(x)$ changes sign from –ve to +ve as x increases through 2.

Hence $f(x)$ has a local minimum at $x = 2$.

Hence local minimum value $= g(x) = 2$

(vii) Let $g(x) = \dfrac{1}{x^2 + 2}$

$\therefore g'(x) = -\dfrac{2x}{(x^2 + 2)^2}$

Now $g'(x) = 0 \Rightarrow x = 0$

At $x = 0$

When x is slightly < 0, $g'(x) = \dfrac{(-)(-)}{+} = +ve$

When x is slightly > 0, $g'(x) = \dfrac{(-)(+)}{+} = -ve$

$\therefore \quad g'(x)$ changes sign from +ve to –ve as x increases through 0

$\therefore \quad f(x)$ has a local maximum at $x = 0$.

$\therefore \quad$ Local maximum value $f(0) = \dfrac{1}{2}$.

(viii) Let $f(x) = x\sqrt{1 - x}$, $x > 0$

$$f'(x) = 1 = \dfrac{-3(x - 2/3)}{2\sqrt{1 - x}}$$

Now, $f'(x) = 0 \Rightarrow 2 - 3x = 0 \Rightarrow x = 2/3$

At $x = \dfrac{2}{3}$, $1 - x = 1 - \dfrac{2}{3} = \dfrac{1}{3} = +\,ve$

When x is slightly $< 2/3$: $f'(x) = \dfrac{(-)\,(-)}{(+)} = +\,ve$

When x is slightly $> \dfrac{2}{3}$; $f'(x) = \dfrac{(-)\,(+)}{(+)} = -\,ve$

$\therefore$ $f'(x)$ changes sign from $(+ve)$ to $(-)ve$ as x increases through $x = \dfrac{2}{3}$

$\therefore$ $f(x)$ has a local maxima at $x = \dfrac{2}{3}$ local maximum

value $= f\left(\dfrac{2}{3}\right) = \dfrac{2\sqrt{3}}{9}$

4. (i) $f'(x) = e^x$; Since $f'(x) \neq 0$ for any value of x.

So $f(x) = e^x$ does not have a maximum or minimum.

(ii) $f'(x) = \dfrac{1}{x}$; Clearly $f'(x) \neq 0$ for any value of x.

So, $f(x) = \log x$ does not have a maximum or a minimum.

(iii) We have $f(x) = x^3 + x^2 + x + 1 \Rightarrow f'(x) = 3x^2 + 2x + 1$

Now, $f'(x) = 0 \Rightarrow 3x^2 + 2x + 1 = 0$

$\Rightarrow x = \dfrac{-2 \pm \sqrt{4 - 12}}{6} = \dfrac{-1 + \sqrt{-2}}{3}$

i.e. $f'(x) = 0$ at imaginary points

i.e. $f'(x) \neq 0$ for any real value of x

Hence, there is neither maximum nor minimum.

5. (i) We have $f'(x) = x^3$ in $[-2, 2]$

$\therefore$ $f'(x) = 3x^2$; Now, $f'(x) = 0$ at $x = 0$, $f(0) = 0$

Now, $f(-2) = (-2)^3 = -8; f(0) = (0)^2 = 0$

and $f(0) = (2) = 8$

Hence, the absolute maximum value of $f(x)$ is 8 which it attained at $x = 2$ and absolute minimum value of $f(x) = -8$ which is attained at $x = -2$.

(ii) We have $f(x) = \sin x + \cos x$ in $[0, \pi]$
$f'(x) = \cos x - \sin x$ for extreme values $f'(x) = 0$

$\Rightarrow \cos x - \sin x = 0 \Rightarrow 1 - \tan x = 0$

$\Rightarrow \tan x = 1 \Rightarrow x = \dfrac{\pi}{4}$

Now, we find $f(x)$ at $x = 0, \dfrac{\pi}{4}, \pi$;

$f(0) = \sin 0 + \cos 0 = 1$

$f(\pi/4) = \sin \pi/4 + \cos \pi/4 = \dfrac{2}{\sqrt{2}} = \sqrt{2}$

and $f(\pi) = \sin \pi + \cos \pi = 0 - 1 = -1$

$\therefore$ Absolute maximum value $= \sqrt{2}$

at $x = \pi/4$ and Absolute minimum value $= -1$ at $x = \pi$.

(iii) We have $f(x) = 4x - \dfrac{x^2}{2}$ in $\left[-2, \dfrac{9}{2}\right]$

$\therefore f'(x) = 4 - \dfrac{1}{2} \cdot 2x = 4 - x$

For extreme values, $f'(x) = 0 \Rightarrow x = 4$

Now we find the values of $f(x)$ at $x = -2, 4, \dfrac{9}{2}$

$f(-2) = -10$, $f(4) = 8$, $f\left(\dfrac{9}{2}\right) = 7.875$

At $x = 4$, absolute maximum value $= 8$

At $x = 2$, absolute minimum value $= -10$.

(iv) Let $f(x) = (x - 1)^2 + 3 \Rightarrow f'(x) = 2(x - 1)$

For external values $f(x) = 0$

$2(x - 1) = 0 \Rightarrow x - 1 = 0 \Rightarrow x = 1$

Now find $f(x)$ at $x = 1, -1, 0$

$f(1) = 3 = f(-3) = 19$ and $f(0) = 4$

$\therefore$ Absolute max. value 19 at $x = -3$ and absolute minimum value 3 at $x = 1$.

6. Profit function in p $(x) = 41 - 24x - 18x^2$

$\therefore$ p$'(x) = -24 - 36x = -12(2 + 3x)$

for maxima and minima, p$'(x) = 0$

Now, p$'(x) = 0 \Rightarrow -12(2 + 3x) = 0 \Rightarrow x = -2/3$,

p$'(x)$ changes sign from $+ve$ to $-ve$.

$\Rightarrow$ p (x) has maximum value at $x = -\dfrac{2}{3}$

Maximum Profit $= 41 + 16 - 8 = 49$.

7. Let f $(x) = 3x^4 - 8x^3 + 12x^2 - 48x + 25$

$\therefore$ f$'(x) = 12x^3 - 24x^2 + 24x - 48 = 12(x^2 + 2)(x - 2)$

For maxima and minima, f$'(x) = 0$

$\Rightarrow 12(x^2 + 2)(x - 2) = 0 \Rightarrow x = 2$

Now, we find f (x) at $x = 0, 2$ and 3, f $(0) = 25$,

$f(2) = 3(2^4) - 8(2^3) + 12(2^2) - 48(2) + 25 = -39$

and f $(3) = (3^4) - 8(3^3) + 12(3^2) - 48(3) + 25$

$= 243 - 216 + 108 - 144 + 25 = 16$

Hence at $x=0$, Maximum value $=25$

at $x=2$, Minimum value $=-39$.

8. We have $f(x)=\sin 2x$ in $[0, 2\pi]$, $f'(x)=2\cos 2x$

For maxima and minima $f'(x)=0 \Rightarrow \cos 2x=0$

$$\Rightarrow \quad 2x=\frac{\pi}{2},\frac{3\pi}{2},\frac{5\pi}{2},\frac{7\pi}{2} \Rightarrow x=\frac{\pi}{4},\frac{3\pi}{4},\frac{5\pi}{4},\frac{7\pi}{4}$$

Now, we find $f(x)$ at $x=0,\dfrac{\pi}{4},\dfrac{3\pi}{4},\dfrac{5\pi}{4},\dfrac{7\pi}{4}, 2\pi$, $f(0)=0$,

$f(\pi/4)=\sin \pi/2=1$ $f(3\pi/4)=\sin 3\pi/2=-1$, $f(5\pi/4)$

$=\sin 5\pi/2=1$, $f(7\pi/4)=\sin 7\pi/2=-1$

and $f(2\pi)=\sin 2\pi=0$

Hence maxima value of $f(x)=1$ at $x=\pi/4, 5\pi/4$

9. Consider the interval $[0, 2\pi]$,

Let $f(x)=\sin x+\cos x$, $\quad f'(x)=\cos x-\sin x$

For maxima and minima, $f'(x)=0$
$\Rightarrow \cos x-\sin x=0 \Rightarrow \tan x=1$

$$\Rightarrow x=\frac{\pi}{4},\frac{5\pi}{4}$$

Now, we find $f(x)$ at $x=0,\dfrac{\pi}{4},\dfrac{5\pi}{4},2\pi$

$f(0)=\sin 0+\cos 0=1;\quad f(\pi/4)=\sin \pi/4+\cos \pi/4=\sqrt{2}$,

$$f(5\pi/4)=\sin 5\pi/4+\cos 5\pi/4=\frac{-1}{\sqrt{2}}-\frac{1}{\sqrt{2}}=\frac{-2}{\sqrt{2}}=-\sqrt{2}$$

$f(2\pi)=\sin 2\pi+\cos 2\pi=1$ Hence, maximum value of $f(x)$
$=\sqrt{2}$

10. $\because f(x)=2x^3-24x+107$ in $[1, 3]$

$\therefore f'(x)=6x^2-24,$

For maxima and minima $f'(x)=0 \Rightarrow 6x^2-24=0$

$\Rightarrow x=\pm 2$

For the interval $[1, 3]$, we find the values of $f(x)$ at $x=1, 2, 3$

$\qquad f(1)=85$, $f(2)=75$, $f(3)=89$

Hence, maximum $f(x)=89$ at $x=3$

For the interval $[-3, -1]$, we find the values of
$f(x)$ at $x=-3, -2, -1$

$\qquad f(-3)=125 \quad f(-2)=139 \quad f(-1)=129$

Hence, maximum $f(x)=139$ at $x=-2$.

11. $\because f(x)=x^4-62x^2+ax+9$

$\therefore f'(x)=4x^3-124x+a$

Now $f'(x)=0$ at $x=1$

$\Rightarrow \quad 4-124+a=0 \Rightarrow a=120$

Now $f''(x)=12x^2-124$: At $x=1$ $f''(1)$

$=12-124=-112<0$

$\Rightarrow f(x)$ has a maximum at $x=1$ when $a=120$.

12. $\therefore f(x)=x+\sin 2x$ on $[0, 2\pi]$

$\therefore f'(x)=1+2\cos 2x$

For maxima and minima $f'(x)=0$

$$\Rightarrow \cos 2x=-\frac{1}{2}$$

$$\Rightarrow 2x=\frac{2\pi}{3},\frac{4\pi}{3},\frac{8\pi}{3},\frac{10\pi}{3}$$

$$\Rightarrow x=\frac{\pi}{3},\frac{2\pi}{3},\frac{4\pi}{3},\frac{5\pi}{3}$$

Now, $f(x)$ at $x=0,\dfrac{\pi}{3},\dfrac{2\pi}{3},\dfrac{4\pi}{3},\dfrac{5\pi}{3},2\pi$

$f(0)=0+\sin 0=0$, $f(\pi/3)=\pi/3+\sin 2\pi/3=\pi/3+\dfrac{\sqrt{3}}{2}$

$f(2\pi/3)=2\pi/3-\dfrac{\sqrt{3}}{2}$, $f(4\pi/3)=4\pi/3+\dfrac{\sqrt{3}}{2}$

$f(5\pi/3)=5\pi/3-\dfrac{\sqrt{3}}{2}$ and $f(2\pi)=2\pi$

Hence, maximum $f(x)=2\pi$ and minimum $f(x)=0$.

13. Let the required numbers be x and $(24-x)$

$\therefore$ Their product, $p=x(24-x)=24x-x^2$

Now $\dfrac{dp}{dx}=0 \Rightarrow 24-2x=0 \Rightarrow x=12$

Also $\dfrac{d^2p}{dx^2}=-2<0 \Rightarrow P$ is maximum at $x=12$

Hence, the required numbers are 12 and $(24-12)$ i.e. 12.

14. We have $x+y=60 \Rightarrow y=60-x \qquad$ ...(i)

Let $p=xy^3=x(60-x)^3$ $\quad$ Now $\dfrac{dp}{dx}=(60-x)^2(60-4x)$

$\therefore \dfrac{dp}{dx}=0 \Rightarrow (60-x)^2(60-4x)=0 \Rightarrow x=60$ or 15

The value $x=60$ is rejected as it makes $y=0$

At $x=15$; When x is slightly <15, $\dfrac{dp}{dx}=(+)(+)=+ve$,

When x is slightly >15 $\dfrac{dp}{dx}=(+)(-)=-ve$

$\Rightarrow \dfrac{dp}{dx}$ changes sign from $(+)$ve to $(-)$ve as x increases

through 15.

$\therefore$ p is maximum at x = 15

Hence, the required numbers are 15 and (60 – 15) i.e. 15 and 45.

15. We have $x + y = 35 \Rightarrow y = 35 - x$

Product $p = x^2 y^5 = x^2 (35 - x)^5$

$\therefore \dfrac{dp}{dx} = x(35-x)^4[-5x+2(35-x)] = x(35-x)^4(70-7x)$

Now, $\dfrac{dp}{dx} = 0 \Rightarrow x = 0, 35, 10$

Only admissible value is x = 10, as x = 0 and 35 are rejected

At x = 10

When x is slightly < 10, $\dfrac{dp}{dx} = (+)(+)(+) = (+)$ ve When x

is slightly > 10, $\dfrac{dp}{dx} = (+)(+)(-) = (-)$ ve

$\Rightarrow \dfrac{dp}{dx}$ changes sign from (+) ve to (–) ve as x increases

through 10 $\Rightarrow$ p is maximum at x = 10, y = 35 – 10 = 25

Hence, the required numbers are 10 and 25.

16. Let two numbers be x and 16 – x

$\therefore$ Sum of cubes, $s = x^3 + (16 - x)^3$

$\therefore \dfrac{ds}{dx} = 3(32x - 256)$

Now $\dfrac{ds}{dx} = 0$

$\Rightarrow 3(32x - 256) = 0$

$\Rightarrow x = \dfrac{256}{32} = 8$

Also $\dfrac{d^2s}{dx^2} = 96 > 0$

$\Rightarrow$ s is minimum at 8

Hence, the required numbers are 8 and (16 – 8) i.e. 8 and 8.

17. Let each side of the square to be cut off be x cm.

$\therefore$ for the box length = 18 – 2x breadth = 18 – 2x

and height = x

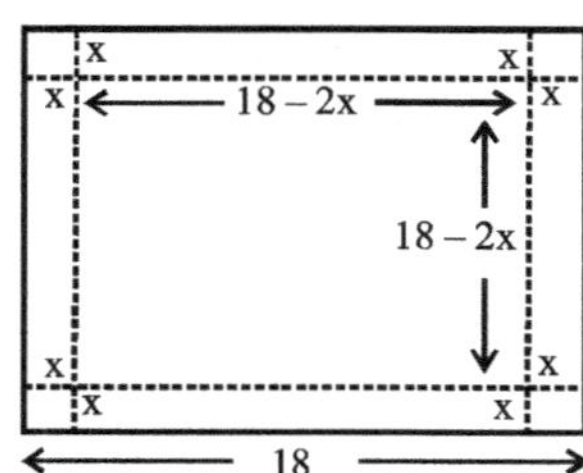

$\therefore$ Volume = x (18 – 2x)^2

$\dfrac{dv}{dx} = (18 - 2x)(-4x + 18 - 20)$

$\dfrac{dv}{dx} = (18 - 2x)(18 - 6x)$

For maxima and minima,

$\dfrac{dv}{dx} = 0 \Rightarrow (18 - 2x)(18 - 6x) = 0 \Rightarrow x = 3, 9$

But x = 9 cm is not possible

Also $\dfrac{d^2v}{dx^2} = (18 - 2x)(-6) + (18 - 6x)(-2)$

At x = 3, $\dfrac{d^2v}{dx^2} = (18 - 6)(-6) + (18 - 18)(-2) = -72 < 0$

$\therefore$ x = 3 attains for max^m volume

i.e. Square of side = 3 cm is cut from each corner.

18. Let each side of the square cut off from each corner be x cm.

$\therefore$ Sides of the rectangular box are (45 – 2x), (24 – 2x) and x cm.

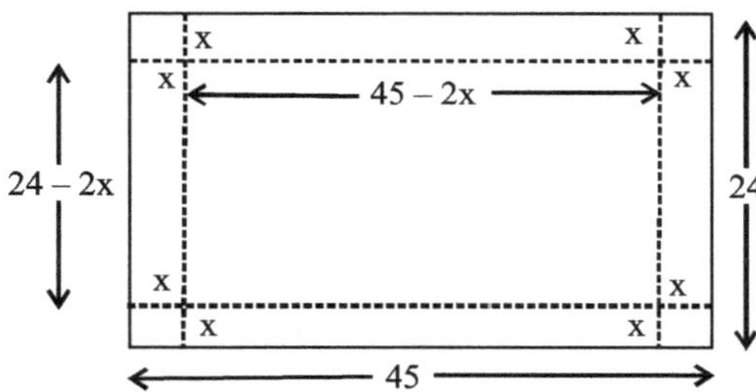

Then, volume of the box

$V = (45 - 2x)(24 - 2x)(x) = 2(2x^3 - 69x^2 + 540x)$

$\Rightarrow \dfrac{dV}{dx} = 12(x^2 - 23x + 90)$

For maxima and minima $\dfrac{dV}{dx} = 0 \Rightarrow x = 5, 18$

But x cannot be greater than 12

$\therefore$ x = 5, $\dfrac{d^2V}{dx^2} = 12(10 - 23) = -$ ve $[\because x = 5]$

$\therefore$ V is maximum at x = 5 i.e. square of side 5 cm is cut off from each corner.

19. Let the length and breadth of the rectangle inscribed in a circle of radius a be x and y respectively.

$\therefore x^2 + y^2 = (2a)^2 \Rightarrow x^2 + y^2 = 4a^2$ ...(i)

$\therefore$ Perimeter $= 2(x+y)$

$$\Rightarrow P(x) = 2\left[x + \sqrt{4a^2 - x^2}\right]$$

$$\therefore P'(x) = 2\left[1 - \frac{x}{\sqrt{4a^2 - x^2}}\right] \qquad ..(ii)$$

and $P''(x) = \dfrac{-8a^2}{(4a^2 - x^2)^{3/2}}$ \qquad ...(iii)

For P (x) to be minimum $P'(x) = 0$ and $P''(x) < 0$

$\therefore$ from (i), $P'(x) = 0 \Rightarrow 4a^2 - x^2 = x^2 \Rightarrow x = a\sqrt{2}$

from (iii) $P''(x) = \dfrac{-8a^2}{(2a^2)^{3/2}}$

$\Rightarrow P(x)$ is maximum at $x = a\sqrt{2}$

from (i) $y = \sqrt{2}\,a = x$;

Thus, $x = y$

Hence rectangle becomes square hence found.

20. Let S be the given surface area of the closed cylinder whose radius is r and height h let v be the its Volume. Then

Surface area $S = 2\pi r^2 + 2\pi rh$, $h = \dfrac{S - 2\pi r^2}{2\pi r}$ \qquad ...(i)

$\therefore$ Volume $V = \pi r^2 h = \pi r^2 \left(\dfrac{S - 2\pi r^2}{2\pi r}\right) = \dfrac{1}{2}[Sr - 2\pi r^3]$

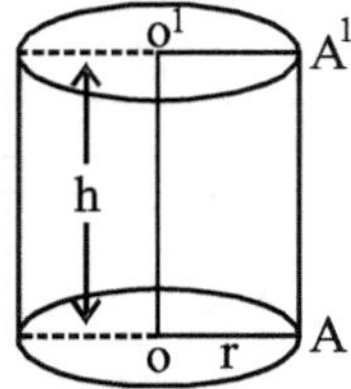

$\therefore \dfrac{dV}{dx} = \dfrac{1}{2} \times [S - 6\pi r^2]$ \qquad ...(ii)

For maxima and minima $\dfrac{dV}{dx} = 0$

$\therefore S = 6\pi r^2 \Rightarrow r = \sqrt{\dfrac{S}{6\pi}}$

from (i), $h = \dfrac{S - 2\pi r^2}{2\pi r}$ \qquad (Putting values of S)

Now, $\dfrac{d^2 v}{dr^2} = -6\pi r < o$ at $r = \sqrt{\dfrac{s}{6\pi}}$

$\therefore$ V is maximum. Thus, volume is maximum when $h = 2r$ i.e. when height of cylinder = diameter of the base.

21. Let r be the radius and h be the height of cylindrical can.

Volume $= \pi r^2 h = 100$ cc.

$\therefore h = \dfrac{100}{\pi r^2}$

Total surface area of the can.

$S = \dfrac{200}{r} + 2\pi r^2$, $\dfrac{dS}{dr} = \dfrac{-200 + 4\pi r^3}{r^2}$

Now, $\dfrac{dS}{dr} = 0 \Rightarrow r = \left(\dfrac{50}{\pi}\right)^{1/3}$ Also, $\dfrac{d^2 S}{dr^2} = \dfrac{400}{r^3} + 4\pi$

At $r = \left(\dfrac{50}{\pi}\right)^{1/3}$, $\dfrac{d^2 S}{dr^2} = \dfrac{400}{50/\pi} + 4\pi = 12\pi = +\text{ve}$

$\Rightarrow$ S is minimum or least when $r = \left(\dfrac{50}{\pi}\right)^{1/3}$

Hence, the total surface area is least when radius of base

is $\left(\dfrac{50}{\pi}\right)^{1/3}$ cm and $h = \dfrac{100}{\pi r^2}$, $h = \dfrac{100}{\pi}\left(\dfrac{\pi}{50}\right)^{2/3}$ cm.

22. Let one part be of length x, then the other part $= 28 - x$

Let the part of the length x be converted into a circle of radius r.

$\therefore 2\pi r = x \Rightarrow r = \dfrac{x}{2\pi}$

$\therefore$ Area of circle $= \pi r^2 = \dfrac{x^2}{4\pi}$

Now, second part of length $28 - x$ is converted into a square.

$P = 4 \times \text{side}$ $\therefore$ side $= \dfrac{28 - x}{4}$, $2\pi r = x$ $\therefore r = \dfrac{x}{2\pi}$

$\therefore$ Side of square $= \dfrac{28 - x}{4}$, Area of square $= \left(\dfrac{28 - x}{4}\right)^2$

Total Area $A = \dfrac{x^2}{4\pi} + \left(\dfrac{28 - x}{4}\right)^2$

$\therefore \dfrac{dA}{dx} = \dfrac{x}{2\pi} - \dfrac{28 - x}{8}$ \qquad ...(i)

$\dfrac{dA}{dx} = 0 \Rightarrow x = \dfrac{28\pi}{4 + \pi}$

Other part $= 28 - x = 28 - \dfrac{28\pi}{4 + \pi} = \dfrac{112}{4 + \pi}$

Differentiating (i),

we get $\dfrac{d^2A}{dx^2} = \dfrac{1}{2\pi} + \dfrac{1}{8} = +\,ve$

$\Rightarrow$ A is minimum

When $x = \dfrac{28\pi}{4 + \pi}$ and $28 - x = \dfrac{112}{4 + \pi}$

23. Let a cone. VAB of greatest volume be inscribed in the sphere let AOC = θ

$\therefore$ AC, radius of the base of the cone = R sin θ

and VC = VO + OC

$= R(1 + \cos\theta) = R + R\cos\theta$

= height of the cone.,

V, the volume of the cone.

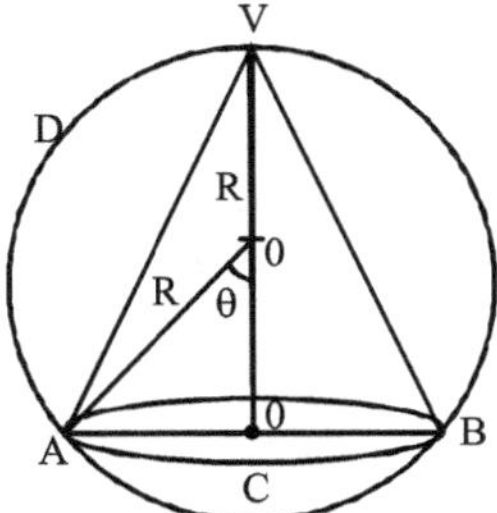

$V = \dfrac{1}{3}\pi\,(AC)^2\,(VC)$

$\Rightarrow \quad V = \dfrac{1}{3}\pi R^3 \sin^2\theta\,(1 + \cos\theta)$

$\therefore \quad \dfrac{dV}{d\theta} = \dfrac{1}{3}\pi R^3(-3\sin^3\theta + 2\sin\theta + 2\sin\theta\cos\theta)$

For maximum and minimum, we have

$\dfrac{dV}{d\theta} = 0 \Rightarrow \quad \cos\theta = \dfrac{1}{3} \quad \text{or } \cos\theta = -1$

But $\cos\theta \neq -1$ as $\cos\theta = -1 \Rightarrow \theta = \pi$,

which is not possible $\quad \therefore \quad \cos\theta = \dfrac{1}{3}$

When $\cos\theta = \dfrac{1}{3}$, $\sin\theta = \sqrt{1 - \cos^2\theta} = \dfrac{2\sqrt{2}}{3}$

$\left(\dfrac{d^2V}{d\theta^2}\right)$ at $\theta = \cos^{-1}\left(\dfrac{1}{3}\right) < 0$

Hence V is maximum at $\theta = \cos^{-1}\left(\dfrac{1}{3}\right)$

Now, $\cos\theta = \dfrac{1}{3}$, $\sin\theta = \dfrac{2\sqrt{2}}{3}$

$\therefore$ Maximum volume of cone. $= \dfrac{8}{27}\left(\dfrac{4}{3}\pi R^3\right)$

Max. volume $= \dfrac{8}{27} \times$ volume of the sphere of cone.

24. Let r and h be the radius and height of the cone.

Volume $V = \dfrac{1}{3}\pi r^2 h = \dfrac{\pi k}{3} \Rightarrow h = \dfrac{k}{r^2}$ ...(i)

Surface $S = \pi r\,\ell = \pi r\sqrt{h^2 + r^2}$

Put $h = \dfrac{k}{r^2}$ $\quad \therefore S = \dfrac{\pi\sqrt{k^2 + r^6}}{r}$

$\Rightarrow \dfrac{dS}{dr} = \dfrac{2r^6 - k^2}{r^2\sqrt{r^6 + k^2}}$

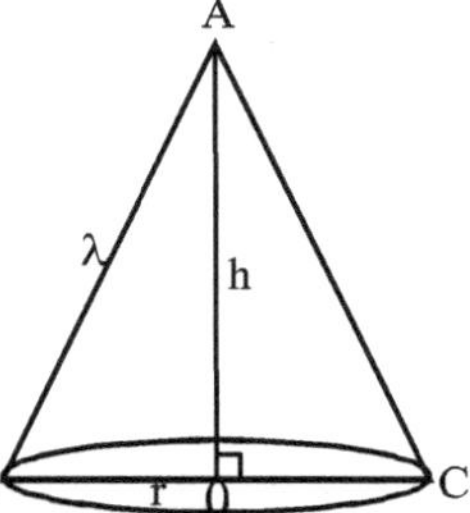

for minimum curved surface area

$\Rightarrow \dfrac{dS}{dr} = 0 \Rightarrow k^2 = 2r^6 \Rightarrow r^3 = \dfrac{k}{\sqrt{2}}$ ...(ii)

$\dfrac{d^2S}{dr^2} = \dfrac{r^2\sqrt{r^6 + k^2}\,(12r^5) - \left(2r^6 - k^2\right)\left[\dfrac{r^2 \times 5r^5}{2\sqrt{r^6 + k^2}} + 2r\sqrt{r^6 + k^2}\right]}{r^4(r^6 + k^2)}$

At $r^3 = \dfrac{k}{\sqrt{2}}$, $\dfrac{d^2S}{dr^2} > 0$

So it attains minimum curved surface area.

25. Let v be the volume, ℓ be the slant height and θ be the semi vertical angle of a cone.

$v = \dfrac{1}{3}\pi r^2 h$, Vertical height h = $\ell \cos\theta$

and radius = $\ell \sin\theta$

$\therefore v = \dfrac{1}{3}\pi\,(\ell\sin\theta)^2\,(\ell\cos\theta)$

$\dfrac{dv}{d\theta} = \dfrac{1}{3}\pi\ell^3\sin\theta\,(2\cos^2\theta - \sin^2\theta)$,

$= 0$ at $\tan\theta = \sqrt{2}$

Further $\dfrac{dv}{d\theta} = -\dfrac{1}{3}\pi\ell^3\sin\theta\cos^2\theta\left(\tan\theta - \sqrt{2}\right)\left(\tan\theta + \sqrt{2}\right)$

When θ is slightly $< \tan^{-1}\sqrt{2}$ $\sin\theta\cos^2\theta = +\mathrm{ve}$,

$\tan\theta - \sqrt{2} = -\mathrm{ve}$; $\tan\theta + \sqrt{2} = +\mathrm{ve}$

$\therefore \dfrac{dv}{d\theta} = (-)(+)(-)(+) = +\mathrm{ve}$,

when θ is slightly $> \tan^{-1}\sqrt{2}$

$\sin\theta\cos^2\theta = +\mathrm{ve}$, $\tan\theta - \sqrt{2} = +\mathrm{ve}$

$\tan\theta + \sqrt{2} = +\mathrm{ve}$, $\therefore \dfrac{dv}{d\theta} = (-)(+)(+)(+) = -\mathrm{ve}$

$\therefore \dfrac{dv}{d\theta}$ changes sign $+$ ve to $-$ ve

$\therefore$ v is maximum at $\theta = \tan^{-1} \sqrt{2}$.

26. Let r be radius, l be the slant height and h be the height of the cone of given surface area s. Then

$$s = \pi r^2 + \pi r l$$

$$\Rightarrow \quad l = \dfrac{s - \pi r^2}{\pi r} \qquad \qquad \text{...(i)}$$

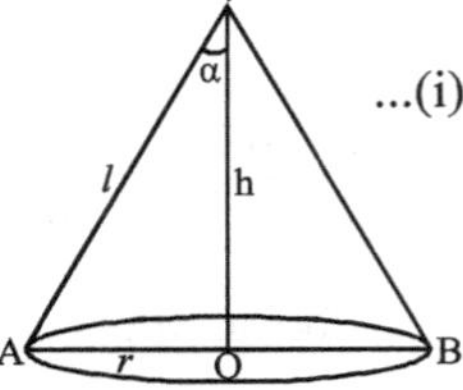

Let V be the volume of cone, then

$$V = \dfrac{1}{3} \pi r^2 h$$

$$\therefore V^2 = \dfrac{1}{9} \pi^2 r^4 h^2 = \dfrac{1}{9} \pi^2 r^4 (l^2 - r^2) \text{ Using (i)}$$

$$\Rightarrow V^2 = \dfrac{\pi^2 r^4}{9} \left[\left(\dfrac{s - \pi r^2}{\pi r} \right)^2 - r^2 \right] = \dfrac{1}{9} s(sr^2 - 2\pi r^4)$$

Let $z = V^2$. Then V is maximum or minimum according as z is maximum or minimum.

$$z = \dfrac{1}{9} s(sr^2 - 2\pi r^4) \Rightarrow \dfrac{dz}{dr} = \dfrac{1}{9} s(2sr - 8\pi r^3) \qquad \text{...(ii)}$$

For maximum or minimum, we must have $\dfrac{dz}{dr} = 0$

$$\Rightarrow \quad 2sr - 8\pi r^3 = 0 \quad \Rightarrow \quad s = 4\pi r^2 \qquad \qquad \text{...(iii)}$$

Diff. (ii) w.r.t. r, we get $\dfrac{d^2 z}{dr^2} = \dfrac{s}{9}(2s - 24\pi r^2)$

$$\dfrac{d^2 z}{dr^2} = \dfrac{s}{9} \left[2s - 24\pi \dfrac{s}{4\pi} \right] = -\dfrac{4s^2}{9} < 0$$

So z is maximum when $s = 4\pi r^2$

Now $s = 4\pi r^2 \Rightarrow s = \pi r l + \pi r^2 \Rightarrow 4\pi r^2 = \pi r l + \pi r^2$

$$3\pi r^2 = \pi r l \Rightarrow l = 3r \therefore \sin \alpha = \dfrac{r}{l} = \dfrac{r}{3r} = \dfrac{1}{3}$$

Hence V is maximum when $\alpha = \sin^{-1} \dfrac{1}{3}$.

27. (a) Let P (x, y) be a point on the curve The other point is A $(0, 5)$

$$Z = PA^2 = x^2 + y^2 + 25 - 10y \qquad \qquad [\because x^2 = 2y]$$

$$z = y^2 - 8y + 25 \therefore \dfrac{dz}{dy} = 2y - 8, \dfrac{d^2 z}{dy^2} = 2 = + \text{ve}$$

$$\dfrac{dz}{dy} = 0 \Rightarrow y = 4 \quad \dfrac{d^2 z}{dy^2} = + \text{ve, z is minimum}$$

$$\therefore x^2 = 2y = 2 \times 4 = 8,$$

$$\therefore x = 2\sqrt{2}$$

$$\Rightarrow z \text{ is minimum at } \left(2\sqrt{2}, 4 \right)$$

$$\Rightarrow \sqrt{z} \text{ is minimum at } \left(2\sqrt{2}, 4 \right)$$

28. (d) Let $y = \dfrac{1 - x + x^2}{1 + x + x^2}$

$$\dfrac{dy}{dx} = \dfrac{(-1 + 2x)(1 + x + x^2) - (1 - x + x^2)(1 + 2x)}{(1 + x + x^2)}$$

Numerator of $\dfrac{dy}{dx} = 2(x - 1)(x + 1)$,

$$\therefore \dfrac{dy}{dx} = \dfrac{2(x - 1)(x + 1)}{(x^2 + x + 1)^2}, \dfrac{dy}{dx} = 0 \text{ at } x = 1, -1$$

At $x = 1$, $\dfrac{dy}{dx}$ changes sign from $-$ ve to $+$ ve

$\therefore \quad$ y is minimum at $x = 1$

Minimum value of $\dfrac{1 - x + x^2}{1 + x + x^2} = \dfrac{1 - 1 + 1}{1 + 1 + 1} = \dfrac{1}{3}$

29. (c) Let $y = [x(x - 1) + 1]^{1/3}$

$$\therefore \dfrac{dy}{dx} = \dfrac{(2x - 1)}{3[x(x - 1) + 1]^{2/3}}, \dfrac{dy}{dx} = 0 \text{ at } x = \dfrac{1}{2}$$

$\dfrac{dy}{dx}$ Changes sign from $-$ve to $+$ ve at $x = \dfrac{1}{2}$

$\therefore \quad$ y is minimum at $x = \dfrac{1}{2}$

Value of y at $x = 0$, $(0 + 1)^{1/3} = 1^{1/3} = 1$

Value of y at $x = 1$, $(0 + 1)^{1/3} = 1^{1/3} = 1$

$\therefore \quad$ The maximum value of y is 1.

Past year Exercise

1. $x = a \sin^3 \theta, \quad y = a \cos^3 \theta$

$$\dfrac{dx}{d\theta} = 3a \sin^2 \theta (\cos \theta), \dfrac{dy}{d\theta} = 3a \cos^2 \theta (-\sin \theta)$$

$$\dfrac{dy}{dx} = \dfrac{dy}{d\theta} \times \dfrac{d\theta}{dx}$$

$$= \dfrac{-3a \cos^2 \theta \sin \theta}{3a \sin^2 \theta \cos \theta} = -\cot \theta$$

Now, slope of tangent, $m = \dfrac{dy}{dx}\bigg]_{\theta = \frac{\pi}{4}} = -\cot\dfrac{\pi}{4} = -1$

Now, at $\theta = \dfrac{\pi}{4}$

$$x_1 = a\sin^3\left(\dfrac{\pi}{4}\right) = \dfrac{a}{2\sqrt{2}}$$

$$y_1 = a\cos^3\left(\dfrac{\pi}{4}\right) = \dfrac{a}{2\sqrt{2}}$$

So, equation of tangent is $(y - y_1) = m\,(x - x_1)$

$$\left(y - \dfrac{a}{2\sqrt{2}}\right) = (-1)\left(x - \dfrac{a}{2\sqrt{2}}\right)$$

$$\Rightarrow \quad y - \dfrac{a}{2\sqrt{2}} = \left(\dfrac{a}{2\sqrt{2}} - x\right)$$

Equation of normal is

$$y - \dfrac{a}{2\sqrt{2}} = 1\left(x - \dfrac{a}{2\sqrt{2}}\right)$$

$$\Rightarrow \quad y - \dfrac{a}{2\sqrt{2}} = x - \dfrac{a}{2\sqrt{2}}$$

$$\Rightarrow \quad y = x.$$

2. We have $\dfrac{x^2}{a^2} - \dfrac{y^2}{b^2} = 1$

Differentiating *w.r.t.* x, we get

$$\dfrac{dy}{dx} = \dfrac{b^2 x}{a^2 y}$$

Now $\left(\dfrac{dy}{dx}\right)_{(x_0, y_0) = (\sqrt{2}\,a,\,b)} = \dfrac{b^2\sqrt{2}\,a}{a^2 b}$

slope of the tangent $= \dfrac{\sqrt{2}\,b}{a}$

Since (x_0, y_0) lies on $\dfrac{x^2}{a^2} - \dfrac{y^2}{b^2} = 1$

$$\therefore \quad \dfrac{x_0^2}{a^2} - \dfrac{y_0^2}{b^2} = 1 \qquad\qquad .....(i)$$

Equation of the tangent is

$$\dfrac{x x_0}{a^2} - \dfrac{y y_0}{b^2} = \dfrac{x_0^2}{a^2} - \dfrac{y_0^2}{b^2}$$

i.e. $\dfrac{x\sqrt{2}\,a}{a^2} - \dfrac{yb}{b^2} = \dfrac{(\sqrt{2}\,a)^2}{a^2} - \dfrac{b^2}{b^2}$

$$\dfrac{\sqrt{2}\,x}{a} - \dfrac{y}{b} = 1 \qquad\qquad \text{(from (i))}$$

Now, slope of the normal is

$$\dfrac{-1}{\left(\dfrac{dy}{dx}\right)_{(x_0, y_0) = (\sqrt{2}\,a,\,b)}} = -\dfrac{a}{\sqrt{2}\,b}$$

Equation of the normal is

$$y - y_0 = \dfrac{-a^2 y_0}{b^2 x_0}(x - x_0)$$

$$\dfrac{y - y_0}{a^2 y_0} + \dfrac{x - x_0}{b^2 x_0} = 0$$

$$\dfrac{y - b}{a^2 b} + \dfrac{x - \sqrt{2}\,a}{\sqrt{2}\,ab} = 0$$

$$(y - b)\sqrt{2} + a(x - \sqrt{2}\,a) = 0$$

$$\sqrt{2}\,y - \sqrt{2}\,b + ax - \sqrt{2}\,a^2 = 0$$

$$ax + \sqrt{2}\,y - \sqrt{2}(a^2 + b) = 0$$

3. Given:

$$x = 3\cos t - \cos^3 t$$

$$y = 3\sin t - \sin^3 t$$

Slope of the tangent,

$$\dfrac{dy}{dx} = \dfrac{\dfrac{dy}{dt}}{\dfrac{dx}{dt}} = \dfrac{3\cos t - 3\sin^2 t\,\cos t}{-3\sin t + 3\cos^2 t\,\sin t} = \dfrac{3\cos t\left[\cos^2 t\right]}{-3\sin t\left[\sin^2 t\right]}$$

$$\dfrac{dy}{dx} = \dfrac{-\cos^3 t}{\sin^3 t}$$

$$\therefore \text{ Slope of the normal} = \dfrac{-1}{\dfrac{dy}{dx}} = \dfrac{\sin^3 t}{\cos^3 t}$$

The equation of the normal is given by

$$\dfrac{y - (3\sin t - \sin^3 t)}{x - (3\cos t - \cos^3 t)} = \dfrac{\sin^3 t}{\cos^3 t}$$

$$\Rightarrow \quad y\cos^3 t - 3\sin t\,\cos^3 t + \sin^3 t\,\cos^3 t$$

$$= x\sin^3 t - 3\cos t\,\sin^3 t + \sin^3 t\,\cos^3 t$$

$\Rightarrow y\cos^3 t - x\sin^3 t = 3(\sin t \cos^3 t - \cos t \sin^3 t)$

$\Rightarrow y\cos^3 t - x\sin^3 t = 3\sin t \cos t(\cos^2 t - \sin^2 t)$

$\Rightarrow y\cos^3 t - x\sin^3 t = \dfrac{3}{2}\sin^2 t \cos^2 t$

$\Rightarrow y\cos^3 t - x\sin^3 t = \dfrac{3}{4}\times 2\sin^2 t \cos^2 t$

$\Rightarrow 4(y\cos^3 t - x\sin^3 t) = 3\sin 4t$

Hence, proved.

4. $y = x^3 - 3x^2 - 4x$

$\dfrac{dy}{dx} = 3x^2 - 6x - 4$

Slope of tangent $= \dfrac{dy}{dx} = 3x^2 - 6x - 4$ ...(1)

Given that tangent is parallel to $4x + y - 3 = 0$

$\qquad 4x + y - 3 = 0$

$\qquad y = -4x + 3$

Slope, $m = -4$ ....(2)

$\qquad [\because y = mx + C]$

From (1) and (2),

$\qquad 3x^2 - 6x - 4 = -4$

(Slope of parallel lines are equal)

$\qquad 3x^2 - 6x = 0$

$\qquad 3x(x - 2) = 0$

$\qquad x = 0, 2$

$\qquad y = x^3 - 3x^2 - 4x$

when $x = 0, y = 0$ $\qquad\qquad$ $(0, 0)$

when $x = 2, y = 2^3 - 3(2)^2 - 4(2) = -12$ $\quad (2, -12)$

$\therefore$ Required points are $(0, 0)$ and $(2, -12)$

NCERT Exemplar

1. (d) $\qquad$ **2.** (b)

3. (d) $\qquad$ **4.** (b)

5. Since, the curve $y = b \cdot e^{-x/a}$ intersects the Y-axis i.e., $x = 0$.

$\therefore y = b \cdot e^{-0/a} = b \qquad [\because e^0 = 1]$

Since, So, the point of intersection of the curve with Y-axis is $(0, b)$.

Now, slope of the given line $\dfrac{x}{a} + \dfrac{y}{b} = 1$ at $(0, b)$ is given by

$\dfrac{1}{a}\cdot 1 + \dfrac{1}{b}\cdot\dfrac{dy}{dx} = 0$

$\Rightarrow \dfrac{dy}{dx} = \dfrac{-b}{a} = m_1$ [say]

Also, the slope of the curve at $(0, b)$ is given as:

$\dfrac{dy}{dx} = \dfrac{-b}{a}e^{-x/a}$

$\Rightarrow \left(\dfrac{dy}{dx}\right)_{(0,b)} = \dfrac{-b}{a}e^{-0} = \dfrac{-b}{a} = m_2$ [say]

Therefore, $m_1 = m_2 = \dfrac{-b}{a}$

Hence, the line touches the curve at the point, where the curve intersects the axis of Y.

6. We have

$y = 2x + \cot^{-1} x + \log[\sqrt{1+x^2} - x]$

$\Rightarrow \dfrac{dy}{dx} = 2 - \dfrac{1}{1+x^2} + \dfrac{1}{\sqrt{1+x^2} - x}\times\left[\dfrac{x}{\sqrt{1+x^2}} - 1\right]$

$= \dfrac{2x^2 + 1}{1+x^2} - \dfrac{1}{\sqrt{1+x^2}} = \dfrac{(2x^2 + 1) - \sqrt{1+x^2}}{1+x^2}$

Now, $\dfrac{dy}{dx} \geq 0$

$\Rightarrow (2x^2 + 1) - \sqrt{1+x^2} \geq 0$

$\Rightarrow (2x^2 + 1)^2 \geq 1 + x^2$

$\Rightarrow 4x^4 + 3x^2 \geq 0$

Which is true for all real values of x.

$\therefore y$ increases for all real values of x.

7. We have, $a \geq 1$,

$f(x) = \sqrt{3}\,\sin x - \cos x - 2ax + b$

$\therefore f'(x) = \sqrt{3}\,\cos x - (-\sin x) - 2a$

$= \sqrt{3}\,\cos x + \sin x - 2a$

$= 2\left[\dfrac{\sqrt{3}}{2}\cdot\cos x + \dfrac{1}{2}\cdot\sin x\right] - 2a$

$= 2\left[\cos\dfrac{\pi}{6}\cdot\cos x + \sin\dfrac{\pi}{6}\cdot\sin x\right] - 2a$

$= 2\cos\left(\dfrac{\pi}{6} - x\right) - 2a$

$[\because \cos(A - B) = \cos A \cdot \cos B + \sin A \cdot \sin B]$

$= 2\left[\cos\left(\dfrac{\pi}{6} - x\right) - a\right]$

Since, $\cos x \in [-1, 1]$

and $a \geq 1$ (given)

$$\therefore \quad 2\left[\cos\left(\frac{\pi}{6} - x\right) - a\right] \leq 0$$

$$\Rightarrow f'(x) \leq 0$$

Hence, $f(x)$ is a decreasing function in R.

8. We have, $y = -x^3 + 3x^2 + 9x - 27$

$$\therefore \quad \frac{dy}{dx} = -3x^2 + 6x + 9$$

$$= \text{Slope of tangent to the curve}$$

Now, $\dfrac{d^2y}{dx^2} = -6x + 6$

For maxzimum $\dfrac{dy}{dx}\left(\dfrac{dy}{dx}\right) = 0$

$$\Rightarrow x = \frac{-6}{-6} = 1$$

$$\therefore \quad \frac{d}{dx}\left(\frac{d^2y}{dx^2}\right) = -6 < 0$$

So, the slope of tangent to the curve is maximum, when x = 1,

For x = 1,

$$\left(\frac{dy}{dx}\right)_{(x=1)} = -3.1^2 + 6.1 + 9 = 12,$$

which is maximum slope.

Also, for x = 1,

$$y = -1^3 + 3.1^2 + 9.1 - 27 = -16$$

So, the required point is $(1, -16)$.

9. Since, $f(x) = \sin x + \sqrt{3} \cos x$

$$\therefore \quad f'(x) = \cos x - \sqrt{3} \sin x$$

For $f'(x) = 0$; $\cos x - \sqrt{3}\sin x = 0$

$$\Rightarrow \tan x = \frac{1}{\sqrt{3}} = \tan\frac{\pi}{6}$$

$$\Rightarrow x = \frac{\pi}{6}$$

Again, differentiating $f'(x)$, we get

$$f''(x) = -\sin x - \sqrt{3}\cos x$$

At $x = \dfrac{\pi}{6}$, $f''(x) = -\sin\dfrac{\pi}{6} - \sqrt{3}\cos\dfrac{\pi}{6} = -\dfrac{1}{2} - \sqrt{3}\cdot\dfrac{\sqrt{3}}{2}$

$$= -2 < 0$$

Hence, at $x = \dfrac{\pi}{6}$, $f(x)$ has maximum value at $\dfrac{\pi}{6}$ is the point of local maxima.

Objective Practice Exercise

1. **(c)** $\because f(x) = \cos x$

$$\Rightarrow f'(x) = -\sin x < 0 \text{ for all } x \in \left(0, \frac{\pi}{2}\right)$$

So, $f(x) = \cos x$ is decreasing in $\left(0, \dfrac{\pi}{2}\right)$

2. **(a)** Since, $f(x) = \tan x - x$

After differentiating w.r.t. x, we get

$f'(x) = \sec^2 x - 1$ So, $f'(x) > 0$, $\forall x \in R$

Hence, $f(x)$ is always increases

3. **(c)** Since, $f(x) = x^2 - 8x + 17$

After differentiating w.r.t. x, we get

$f'(x) = 2x - 8$ As $f'(x) = 0 \Rightarrow x = 4$

Here, $f''(x) = 2 > 0$, $\forall x$

Hence, $x = 4$ is point of local minnima

and minimum value of $f(x)$

$$f(4) = (4 \times 4) - (8 \times 4) + 17 = 1$$

4. **(b)** $f(x) = x^3 - 18x^2 + 96x \Rightarrow f'(x) = 3x^2 - 36x + 96$

$\therefore$ $f'(x) = 0 \Rightarrow x^2 - 12x + 32 = 0 \Rightarrow x = 8, 4$

Now, $f(0) = 0$, $f(4) = 160$, $f(8) = 128$, $f(9) = 135$

So, smallest value of $f(x)$ is 0 at $x = 0$.

5. **(c)** **6.** **(b)** **7.** **(d)**

8. **(b)** Since, $f(x) = x^x$

Suppose $y = x^x$ $\therefore$ $\log y = x \log x$

After differentiating w.r.t. x, we get

$\dfrac{1}{y}\dfrac{dy}{dx} = x\left(\dfrac{1}{x}\right) + \log x$ So, $\dfrac{dy}{dx} = (1 + \log x)x^x$

Now, $\dfrac{dy}{dx} = 0$

$\Rightarrow (1 + \log x) \cdot x^x = 0$

$\Rightarrow$ $\log x = -1 \Rightarrow x = e^{-1} = \dfrac{1}{e}$

Hence, $f(x)$ has a stationary point at $x = \dfrac{1}{e}$

9. **(c)**

10. **(d)** $\dfrac{dx}{d\theta} = -a\sin\theta$ and $\dfrac{dy}{d\theta} = a\cos\theta$

$\therefore \dfrac{dy}{dx} = -\cot\theta.$

$\therefore$ the slope of the normal at $\theta = \tan\theta$

$\therefore$ the equation of the normal at θ is

$y - a\sin\theta = \tan\theta(x - a - a\cos\theta)$

$\Rightarrow y\cos\theta - a\sin\theta\cos\theta = x\sin\theta - a\sin\theta - a\sin\theta\cos\theta$

$\Rightarrow x\sin\theta - y\cos\theta = a\sin\theta$
$\Rightarrow y = (x - a)\tan\theta$

which always passes through $(a, 0)$

11. **(b)** **12.** **(c)** **13.** **(c)** **14.** **(a)**

15. **(d)** Curve is $y = be^{-x/a}$

Since the curve crosses y-axis (*i.e.*, $x = 0$)
$\therefore y = b$

Now $\dfrac{dy}{dx} = \dfrac{-b}{a}e^{-x/a}$. At point $(0, b)$, $\left(\dfrac{dy}{dx}\right)_{(0,b)} = \dfrac{-b}{a}$

$\therefore$ equation of tangent is, $y - b = \dfrac{-b}{a}(x - 0)$

$\Rightarrow \dfrac{x}{a} + \dfrac{y}{b} = 1.$

16. **(c)** Slope of line is $m = \dfrac{-b}{a}$ *i.e.*, $m_{Tangent} = -\dfrac{b}{a}$

also, $y = be^{-x/a}$

$\therefore \dfrac{dy}{dx} = \dfrac{-b}{a}e^{-x/a}$ $\quad \therefore \dfrac{-b}{a} = \dfrac{-b}{a}e^{-x/a}$

$e^{-x/a} = 1 \Rightarrow -\dfrac{x}{a} = 0 \Rightarrow x = 0.$

If $x = 0$ then $0 + \dfrac{y}{b} = 1 \Rightarrow y = b$

So point is $(0, b)$.

17. **(d)**

18. **(c)**

19. **(d)**

20. **(a)**

21. **(d)** $\because y^3 = 8x \Rightarrow 3y^2\dfrac{dy}{dx} = 8 \Rightarrow \dfrac{dy}{dx} = \dfrac{8}{3y^2}$ ...(i)

Also, $y^2 = 12 - \dfrac{12x^2}{a^2} \Rightarrow 2y\dfrac{dy}{dx} = \dfrac{-24x}{a^2}$

$\Rightarrow \dfrac{dy}{dx} = \dfrac{-12x}{a^2 y}$ ...(ii)

$\therefore \left(\dfrac{-12x}{a^2 y}\right)\left(\dfrac{8}{3y^2}\right) = -1$ [$\because$ Intersect at right angles]

$\Rightarrow a^2 y^3 = 32x \Rightarrow a^2 = 4$ [$\because y^3 = 8x$]

22. (d)

23. (c) $y = ax^2 + bx$

$\dfrac{dy}{dx} = 2ax + b \Rightarrow \left(\dfrac{dy}{dx}\right)_{(2,-8)} = 4a + b$

$\because$ tangent is parallel to x-axis

$\therefore \dfrac{dy}{dx} = 0 \Rightarrow b = -4a$ ... (i)

Now, point (2, –8) is on the curve $y = ax^2 + bx$

$\therefore -8 = 4a + 2b$ ... (ii)

From (i) and (ii), we get $a = 2$, $b = -8$.

24. (b)

25. (c)

26. (b) $y = x^2 - 3x + 2 \Rightarrow \dfrac{dy}{dx} = 2x - 3 = -1 \Rightarrow x = 1$

At $x = 1$, $y = 0$

$\therefore$ point is (1, 0).

27. (c) $f'(x) = -\dfrac{1}{1+x^2} + 1$

$f'(x) = \dfrac{x^2}{1+x^2} \Rightarrow f'(x) \geq 0$

$\Rightarrow$ Always increasing

28. (b)

29. (a)   For $0 < x \leq \dfrac{\pi}{2}$; $[\cos x] = 0$

Hence, $f(x) = 1$ for all $\left(0, \dfrac{\pi}{2}\right]$

Trivially $f(x)$ is continuous on $\left(0, \dfrac{\pi}{2}\right)$

This function is neither strictly increasing nor strictly decreasing and its global maximum is 1.

30. (d)   To be increasing, $\dfrac{d}{dx}\left(x^2 + kx + 1\right) > 0 \Rightarrow 2x + k > 0$.

For $x \in (1, 2)$, the least value of k is –2.

31. (a) $f(x) = 5^{-x} \Rightarrow f'(x) = -5^{-x} \log_e 5 = -\dfrac{\log_e 5}{5^x}$

$\Rightarrow f'(x) < 0$ for all x

i.e., f(x) is decreasing for all x.

32. (b) $f(x) = 3x + \dfrac{2}{x} \Rightarrow f'(x) = 3 - \dfrac{2}{x^2}$

Clearly $f'(x) > 0$ on the interval (1, 3)

$\therefore$ f(x) is strictly increasing.

33. (a)   Given function : f(x) = tan x – x   ...(i)

Differentiating the eq. (i), we get

f'(x) = sec²x – 1 at x = 0

f'(0) = sec²0 – 1 = (1)² – 1 = 1 – 1

f(0) = 0 i.e. f(x) is always increase.

34. (d)   If the function is monotonic, then its value must change according to its monotonocity.

35. (b)   **36. (d)**

37. (a)

38. (a)   Given $f(x) = \log(1+x) - \dfrac{2x}{2+x}$

$f'(x) = \dfrac{1}{1+x} - \dfrac{(2+x)(2) - 2x}{(2+x)^2}$

$= \dfrac{1}{1+x} - \dfrac{4}{(2+x)^2} = \dfrac{(2+x)^2 - 4 - 4x}{(1+x)(2+x)^2}$

$$= \frac{x^2}{(1+x)(2+x)^2} > 0 \text{ for all } x \in (0, \infty)$$

Thus, given function f(x) is increasing on $(0, \infty)$.

39. (d) $f(x) = e^{ax} + e^{-ax}, a > 0$

$$\Rightarrow f'(x) = ae^{ax} - ae^{-ax} = a\left(e^{ax} - e^{-ax}\right) = a\left(\frac{e^{2ax} - 1}{e^{ax}}\right)$$

$\Rightarrow$ Increasing if $x > 0$.

40. (a) Let $f(x) = \log \sin x \Rightarrow f'(x) = \cot x$.

Hence function is increasing on the interval $\left(0, \dfrac{\pi}{2}\right)$.

41. (d) $y = \dfrac{1}{1+x^2} \Rightarrow \dfrac{dy}{dx} = -\dfrac{2x}{\left(1+x^2\right)^2}$

To be decreasing,

$$-\frac{2x}{\left(1+x^2\right)^2} < 0 \Rightarrow x > 0 \Rightarrow x \in (0, \infty).$$

42. (a) $f(x) = x + \cos x \Rightarrow f'(x) = 1 - \sin x$

$f'(x) > 0$ for all values of x.

$\therefore f(x)$ is always increasing.

43. (b) Let $f(x) = x^4 - 4x \Rightarrow f'(x) = 4x^3 - 4$

So, $4x^3 - 4 < 0$ or $x^3 < 1$

Hence function is decreasing in $(-\infty, 1)$.

44. (c) $f'(x) = 3\left(\dfrac{a^2 - 1}{a^2 + 1}\right)x^2 - 3$

$f'(x) < 0$ for all x if $a^2 - 1 \le 0 \Rightarrow -1 \le a \le 1$

45. (b) Rate of growth of the plant $= \dfrac{dy}{dx} = \dfrac{d}{dx}\left(4x - \dfrac{1}{2}x^2\right)$

$= 4 - x.$

46. (a) For maximum height, $\dfrac{dy}{dx} = 0 \Rightarrow x = 4$

So, required number of days $= 4$.

47. (c) Since $\left(\dfrac{d^2 y}{dx^2}\right)_{x=4} = -1 < 0$

$\Rightarrow$ x = 4 is point of maximum

So, maximum height of the plant

$$= 4(4) - \frac{1}{2}(4)^2 = 8 \text{ cm}$$

48. (b) Height of the plant after 2 days, $y = 4(2) - \dfrac{1}{2}(2)^2$

$= 8 - 2 = 6 \text{ cm}$

49. (d) Height of the plant $= \dfrac{7}{2}$ cm

$$4x - \frac{1}{2}x^2 = \frac{7}{2}$$

$\Rightarrow (x-1)(x-7) = 0$

$\Rightarrow x = 1, 7$

50. (b) For maximum profit $P'(x) = 0 \Rightarrow -10x + 125 = 0$

$\Rightarrow x = 12.5$

So, when profit is maximum, the production is 12.5.

51. (b) Since, $[P''(x)]_{x=12.5} = -10 < 0$

So, $x = 12.5$ is point of maxima.

Then, maximum profit $= P(12.5) = ₹38281.25$

52. (d) Since the profit is strictly increasing

$\Rightarrow P'(x) > 0$

$\Rightarrow -10x + 125 > 0$

$\Rightarrow x > 12.5$

So, the required interval is (0, 12.5)

53. (b) Since, production $x = 2$ units

So, profit $= P(2) = ₹ 37730.$

54. (a) Since, profit $= 38250$

$\Rightarrow$ $P(x) = 38250$

$\Rightarrow$ $-5x^2 + 125x + 37500 = 38250$

$\Rightarrow$ $(x - 10)(x - 15) = 0$

$\Rightarrow$ $x = 10, 15$

So, production is 15 unit.

55. (b) For critical point, $f'(x) = 0$

$\Rightarrow$ $12(4x^3 - x) = 0$

$\Rightarrow$ $x = 0, x = \pm\dfrac{1}{2}$

So, abscissa of critical point, $x = \pm\dfrac{1}{2}$.

56. (d) Slope of tangent on the position $(2, 3)$ of the stick $= f'(2) = 360$

$\therefore$ Required slope of normal $= \dfrac{-1}{\text{Slope of tangent}}$

$= -\dfrac{1}{360}$

57. (b) Equation of tangent passing through the point $(2, 3)$

$y - 3 = 360(x - 2)$

$\Rightarrow$ $y = 360x - 717$.

58. (c) $\because f'(x) = 12(x^2 - 1)$

$\therefore$ $f''(5) = 3588$.

59. (b) $f'(x) > 0$

$12x(4x^2 - 1) > 0$

$\Rightarrow$ $x \in \left(-\dfrac{1}{2}, 0\right) \cup \left(\dfrac{1}{2}, \infty\right)$

Chapter Test

1. (b)   **2.** (a)   **3.** (b)   **4.** (b)

5. $\left(0, \dfrac{1}{e}\right)$ **6.** $\dfrac{4}{3}$ **7.** (a)

8. (b)

9. (i) (b)   (ii) (a)   (iii) (a)   (iv) (b)

   (v) (c)

10. -1 **11.** $\theta = \tan^{-1}\dfrac{4\sqrt{2}}{7}$ **12.** $(4, 4)$

13. $(-1, 2), (3, 2)$

7 Linear Programming

Linear Programming Problems

A linear programming problem is concerned with finding the minimum or maximum value of a linear function Z (called objective function) of several variables (say x & y), subject to certain conditions that the variables are non-negative & satisfy a set of linear inequalities (called linear constraints).

LINEAR PROGRAMMING

Some Important Terms Related to LPP

(1) **Objective Function :** A linear function $Z = ax + by$, where a & b are constants, which has to be maximized or minimized according to a set of given conditions, is called a linear objective function.

(2) **Decision Variables :** In the objective function $Z = ax + by$, the variables x, y are said to be decision variables.

(3) **Constraints :** The restrictions in the form of inequalities on the variables of a linear programming problem are called constraints. The condition $x \geq 0$, $y \geq 0$ are known as non-negative restrictions. In the constraints given in the general form of a LPP there may be anyone of the 3 signs $\leq, =, \geq$.

(4) **Feasible Region :** The common region determined by all the constraints including non-negative constraints x, $y \geq 0$ of linear programming problem is known as feasible region (or solution region). If we shade the region according to the given constraints, then the shaded area is the feasible region which is the common area of the regions drawn under the given constraints.

(5) **Feasible Solution :** Each point within & on the boundary of the feasible region represents feasible solution of constraints. Note that in the feasible region there are infinitely many points which satisfy the given condition.

(6) **Optimal Solution :** Any point in the feasible region that gives the optimal value (maximum or minimum) of the objective function is called an optimal solution.

Corner Point Method of Solving LPP

Steps Involved :

(1) Find the feasible region of the LPP & determine its corner points (vertices) either by inspection or by solving the two equations of the lines intersecting at that point.

(2) Evaluate the objective function $Z = ax + by$ at each corner point. Let M & m, respectively be the largest & smallest values of these points.

(3) (i) When the feasible region is bounded, M & m are the maximum & minimum values of Z.

(ii) In case the feasible region is unbounded, we have:

(4) (a) M is the maximum value of Z, if the open half plane determined by $ax + by > M$ has no point in common with the feasible region. Otherwise, Z has no maximum value.

(b) Similarly, m is the minimum value of Z, if the open half plane determined by $ax + by < m$ has no point in common with the feasible region. Otherwise, Z has no minimum value.

 **Topic 1** Linear Programming Problem and its Solution 

LINEAR PROGRAMMING PROBLEMS

Problems which concern with finding the minimum or maximum value of a linear function Z (called objective function) of several variables (say x and y), subject to certain conditions that the variables are non-negative and satisfy a set of linear inequalities (called linear constraints) are known as linear programming problems.

MATHEMATICAL FORM OF LPP

The general mathematical form of a linear programming problem may be written as follow.

Objective Function : $Z = C_1 x + C_2 y$

Subject to constraints are:

$a_1 x + b_1 y \leq d_1$

$a_2 x + b_2 y \leq d_2$ etc

and non-negative restrictions are $x \geq 0, y \geq 0$

(i) **Objective Function:** A linear function $z = ax + by$, where a and b are constants, which has to be maximised or minimised according to a set of given conditions, is called a linear objective function.

(ii) **Decision Variables:** In the objective function $z = ax + by$, the variables x, y are said to be decision variables.

(iii) **Constraints:** The restrictions in the form of inequalities on the variables of a linear programming problem are called constraints. The condition $x \geq 0, y \geq 0$ are known as non-negative restrictions.

In the constraints given in the general form of a LPP there may be any one of the three signs $\leq, =, \geq$.

FEASIBLE REGION

The common region determined by all the constraints including non–negative constraints $x, y \geq 0$ of linear programming problem is known as feasible region (or solution region). If we shade the region according to the given constraints, then the shaded areas is the feasible region which is the common area of the regions drawn under the given constraints.

FEASIBLE SOLUTION

Each points within and on the boundary of the feasible region represents feasible solution of constraints.

Note that in the feasible region there are infinitely many points which satisfy the given condition.

OPTIMAL SOLUTION

Any point in the feasible region that gives the optimal value (maximum or minimum) of the objective function is called an optimal solution.

CORNER POINT

A corner point of a feasible region is a point of intersection of two boundary lines in the region.

THEOREM 1

Let R be the feasible region (convex polygon) for a linear programming problem and let $Z = ax + by$ be the objective function. When Z has an optimal value (maximum or minimum), where the variables x and y are subject to constraints described by linear inequalities, the optimal value must occur at a corner point of the feasible region.

THEOREM 2

Let R be the feasible region for a linear programming problem, and let $Z = ax + by$ be the objective function. If R is bounded then the objective function Z has both maximum and minimum value on R and each of these occurs at a corner point of R.

SOLUTION OF THE LPP

(i) First of all formulate the given problem in terms of mathematical constraints and an objective function.

(ii) The constraints would be inequations which shall be plotted and relevant area shall be shaded and check that feasible region is bounded or unbounded.

(iii) The corner points of common shaded area shall be identified and the coordinates corresponding to these points shall be substitued in the objective function.

(iv)   The coordinates of one corner point which maximize or minimize the objective function shall be optimal solution of the given problem.

   Note that if feasible region is unbounded, then a maximum or a minimum value of the objective function may not exist. However, if it exists, it must occur at a corner point of feasible region.

Illustration :

Solve : Maximize $Z = -50x + 20y$

Subject to constraints:

$2x - y \geq -5$

$3x + y \geq 3$

$2x - 3y \leq 12$

$x \geq 0, y \geq 0$

Sol.

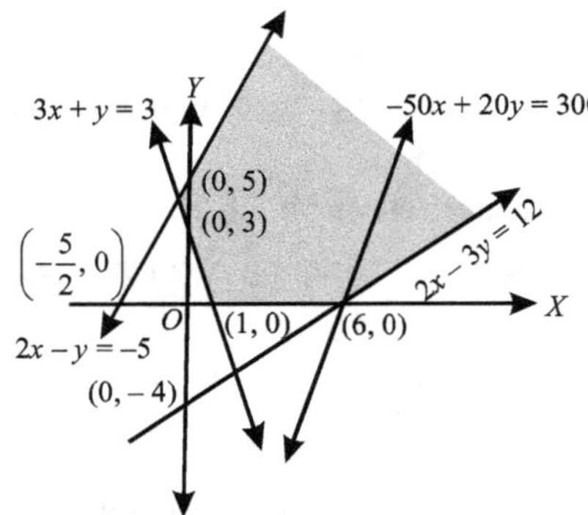

Corner point (x, y)	Value of the objective function $Z = -50x + 20y$
$(0, 5)$	$Z = -50 \times 0 + 20 \times 5 = 100$
$(0, 3)$	$Z = -50 \times 0 + 20 \times 3 = 60$
$(1, 0)$	$Z = -50 \times 1 + 20 \times 0 = -50$
$(6, 0)$	$Z = -50 \times 6 + 20 \times 0 = -300$

Clearly -300 is the smallest value of Z at the corner point $(6, 0)$. Since the feasible region is unbounded. We draw the line $-300 = -50x + 20y$, we find that the open half plane represented by $-50x + 20y < -300$ has points in common with the feasible region. Therefore, $Z = -50x + 20y$ has no minimum value subject to the given constraints.

Practice Exercise-1

Multiple Choice Questions

1.   The constraints
   $-x_1 + x_2 \leq 1,\ -x_1 + 3x_2 \leq 9,\ x_1, x_2 \geq 0$ define on
   (a)   Bounded feasible space
   (b)   Unbounded feasible space
   (c)   Both bounded and unbounded feasible space
   (d)   None of these

2.   A vertex of bounded region of inequalities $x \geq 0\ \ x + 2y \geq 0$ and $2x + y \leq 4$ is
   (a) $(1, 1)$ (b) $(0, 1)$
   (c) $(3, 0)$ (d) $(0, 4)$

3.   The inequalities $5x + 4y \geq 20,\ x \leq 6,\ y \leq 4$ form
   (a)   A square   (b)   A rhombus
   (c)   A triangle   (d)   A quadrilateral

4.   The maximum vale of $P = x + 3y$ such that $2x + y \leq 20$, $x + 2y \leq 20\ \ x \geq 0, y \geq 0$ is
   (a)   10   (b)   60
   (c)   30   (d)   None

5.   Which of the following is not a vertex of the positive region bounded by the inqualities $2x + 3y \leq 6,\ 5x + 3y \leq 15$ and $x, y \geq 0$
   (a) $(0, 2)$ (b) $(0, 0)$
   (c) $(3, 0)$ (d)   None

Short Answer Questions

6.   Maximise $Z = x + y$, subject to the constraints are $x - y \leq -1$, $-x + y \leq 0$ and $x, y \geq 0$.

7.   Define below given terms.
   (a)   Objective function
   (b)   Feasible region
   (c)   Optimal feasible solution.

8.   Find the point at which the maximum value of $z = 3x + 2y$, subject to the constraints $x + y \leq 2, x \geq 0, y \geq 0$, occurs.

NCERT Exercise-1

Solve the following linear programming problems graphically:

1. Maximize $Z = 3x + 4y$

   subject to the constraints:

   $x + y \leq 4, x \geq 0, y \geq 0$.

2. Minimise $Z = -3x + 4y$

   subject to $x + 2y \leq 8, 3x + 2y \leq 12, x \geq 0, y \geq 0$

3. Maximize $Z = 5x + 3y$

   subject to $3x + 5y \leq 15, 5x + 2y \leq 10, x \geq 0, y \geq 0$

4. Minimize $Z = 3x + 5y$ such that $x + 3y \geq 3$,

   $x + y \geq 2, x, y \geq 0$.

5. Maximize $Z = 3x + 2y$ subject to $x + 2y \leq 10$,

   $3x + y \leq 15, x, y \geq 0$.

6. Minimize $Z = x + 2y$ subject to $2x + y \geq 3$,

   $x + 2y \geq 6, x, y \geq 0$.

7. Minimise and Maximise $Z = 5x + 10y$

   subject to $x + 2y \leq 120, x + y \geq 60, x - 2y \geq 0$,

   $x, y \geq 0$

8. Minimize and maximize $Z = x + 2y$ subject to $x + 2y$

   $\geq 100, 2x - y \leq 0, 2x + y \leq 200 ; x, y \geq 0$.

9. Maximise $Z = -x + 2y$, subject to the constraints: $x \geq 3$,

   $x + y \geq 5, x + 2y \geq 6, y \geq 0$

10. Maximise $Z = x + y$ subject to $x - y \leq -1$,

    $-x + y \leq 0, x, y \geq 0$

Important Tips & Formulae

- The term linear implies that all the mathematical relations used in the problem are linear relations.

- The term programming refers to the method of determining a particular programme or plan of action.

- A corner point of a feasible region is the point of intersection of two boundary lines, which form the region.

- A feasible region of a given system of linear inequalities is said to be bounded if it can be enclosed. Otherwise, it is unbounded. Unbounded means that the feasible region may extend indefinitely in any direction.

- The feasible region is always a convex region.

- Basic Feasible Solution A BFS is a basic solution which also satisfies the non-negativity restrictions.

- Optimum Basis Feasible Solution A BFS is said to be optimum, if it also optimizes (Max or min) the objective function.

- The maximum (or minimum) solution of the objective function occurs at the vertex (corner) of the feasible region.

- If two corner points produce the same maximum (or minimum) value of the objective function, then every point on the line segemnt joiningb these points will also give the same maximum (or minimum) value.

Past year Exercise

Very Short Answer Question

1. The corner points of the feasible region determined by the system of linear inequalities are $(0, 0)$, $(4, 0)$, $(2, 4)$ and $(0, 5)$. If the maximum value of $z = ax + by$, where $a, b > 0$ occurs at both $(2, 4)$ and $(4, 0)$, then

   (a) $a = 2b$ (b) $2a = b$

   (c) $a = b$ (d) $3a = b$

2. Maximise $Z = x + 2y$

   subject to the constraints

   $x + 2y \geq 100$

   $2x - y \leq 0$

   $2x + y \leq 200$

   $x, y \geq 0$

   Solve the above LPP graphically.

2. Solve the following LPP graphically.

   Minimise $Z = 5x + 10\,y$

   Subject to $x + 2y \leq 120$

   Constraint $x + y \geq 60$

   $x - 2y \geq 0$

   and $x, y \geq 0$ **[Delhi 2017]**

4. Find graphically, the maximum value of

   $z = 2x + 5y$, subject to constraints given below:

                            [Delhi 2015]

   $2x + 4y \leq 8$

   $3x + y \leq 6$

   $x + y \leq 4$

   $x \geq 0, y \geq 0$

NCERT Exemplar

Short Answer Question

1. Determine the maximum value of $Z = 11x + 7y$ subject to the constraints $2x + y \leq 6$, $x \leq 2$, $x \geq 0, y \geq 0$.

2. Maximise $Z = 3x + 4y$, subject to the constraints $x + y \leq 1$, $x \geq 0, y \geq 0$.

3. Maximise the function $Z = 11x + 7y$, subject to the constraints $x \leq 3$, $y \leq 2$, $x \geq 0$ and $y \geq 0$.

4. Minimise $Z = 13x - 15y$ subject to the constraints $x + y \leq 7$, $2x - 3y + 6 \geq 0$, $x \geq 0$ and $y \geq 0$.

5. Determine the maximum value of $Z = 3x + 4y$, if the feasible region (shaded) for a LPP is shown in following figure.

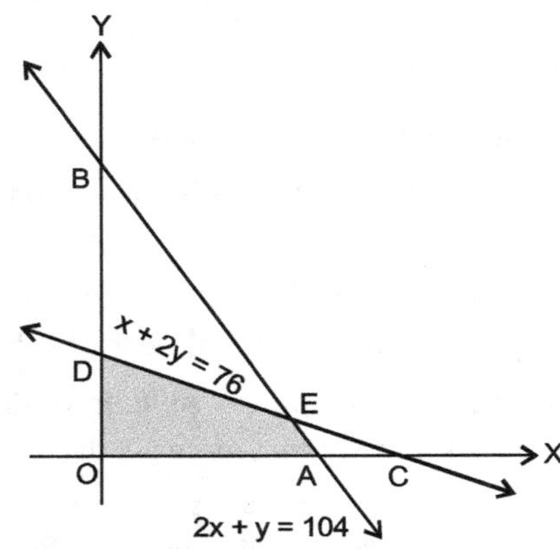

6. Feasible region (shaded) for a LPP is shown in following figure. Maximise $Z = 5x + 7y$.

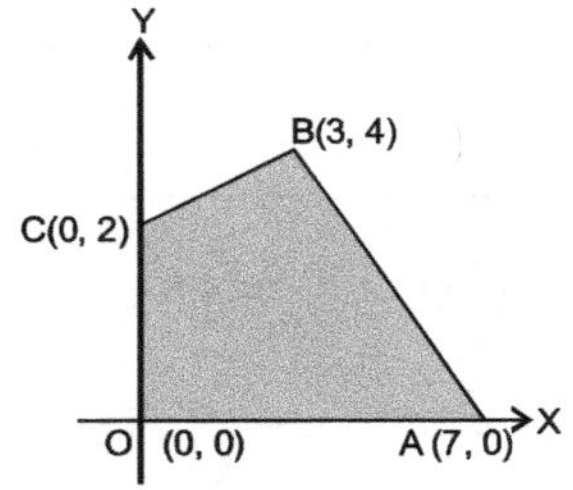

7. The feasible region for a LPP is shown in following figure. Find the minimum value of $Z = 11x + 7y$.

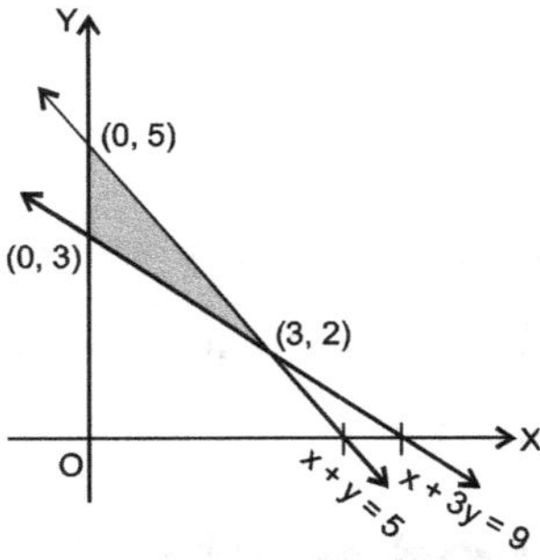

8. The feasible region for a LPP is shown in the following figure. Evaluate $Z = 4x + y$ at each of the corner points of this region. Find the minimum value of Z, if it exists.

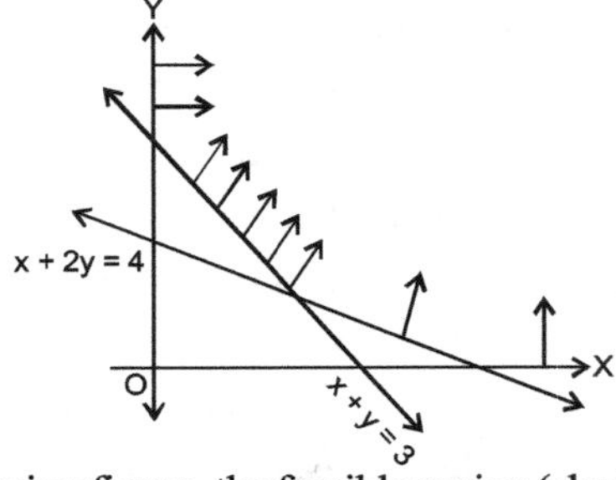

9. In following figure, the feasible region (shaded) for a LPP is shown. Determine the maximum and minimum value of $Z = x + 2y$.

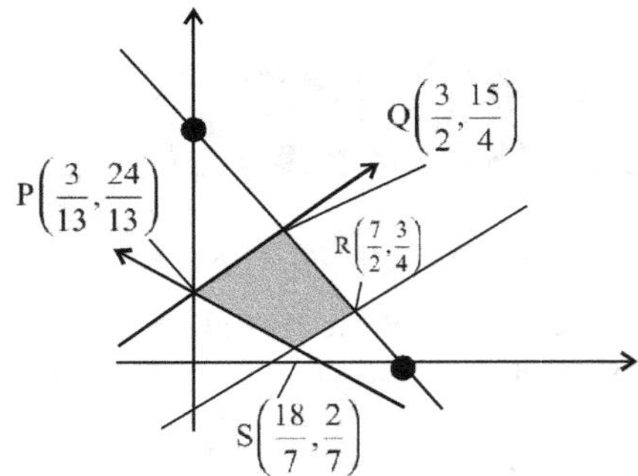

Objective Practice Exercise

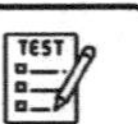

Multiple Choice Questions

DIRECTIONS : *This section contains multiple choice questions. Each question has four choices (a), (b), (c) and (d) out of which only one is correct.*

1. x and b are real numbers. If $b > 0$ and $|x| > b$, then
   (a) $x \in (-b, \infty)$ (b) $x \in (-\infty, b)$
   (c) $x \in (-b, b)$ (d) $x \in (-\infty, -b) \cup (b, \infty)$

2. If $|x - 1| > 5$, then
   (a) $x \in (-4, 6)$
   (b) $x \in [-4, 6]$
   (c) $x \in (-\infty, -4) \cup (6, \infty)$
   (d) $x \in (-\infty, -4) \cup (6, \infty)$

3. If $|x + 2| \le 9$, then

(a) $x \in (-7, 11)$

(b) $x \in [-11, 7]$

(c) $x \in (-\infty, -7) \cup (11, \infty)$

(d) $x \in (-\infty, -7) \cup [11, \infty)$

4. The inequality representing the following graphs is

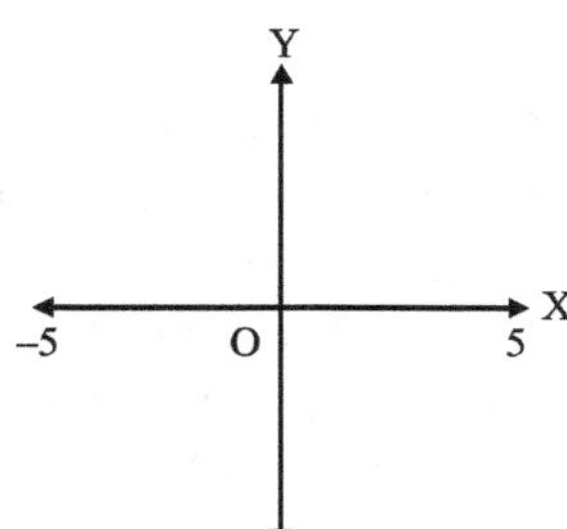

(a) $|x| < 5$ (b) $|x| \le 5$

(c) $|x| > 5$ (d) $|x| \ge 5$

5. Solution of a linear inequality in variable x is represented on number line is

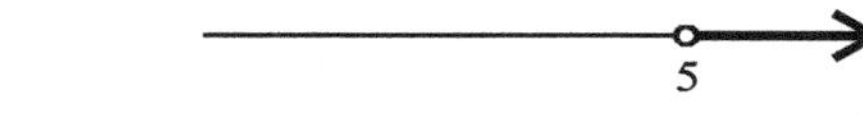

(a) $x \in (-\infty, 5)$ (b) $x \in (-\infty, 5]$

(c) $x \in [5, \infty)$ (d) $x \in (5, \infty)$

6. If the constraints in a linear programming problem are changed

(a) The problem is to be re-evaluated

(b) Solution is not defined

(c) The objective function has to be modified

(d) The change in constraints is ignored

7. If the number of available constraints is 3 and the number of parameters to be optimized is 4, then

(a) The objective function can be optimized

(b) The constraint are short in number

(c) The solution is problem oriented

(d) None of these

8. The maximum value of $z = 5x + 2y$ subject to constraints $x + y \le 7, x + 2y \le 10, x, y \ge 0$

(a) 10   (b) 26   (c) 35   (d) 70

9. Minimum value of $Z = 3x + 5y$ subject to constraints $x + y \ge 2, x + 3y \ge 3, x, y \ge 0$

(a) 6   (b) 7   (c) 8   (d) 9

10. Maximize $Z = 8x + 7y$

subject to constraints $3x + y \le 66$,

$x + y \le 45, x \le 20, , y \le 40, x, y \ge 0$

(a) 305.5   (b) 315.5   (c) 325.5   (d) 335.5

11. Inequations $3x - y \ge 3$ and $4x - y \ge 4$

(a) Have solution for positive x and y

(b) Have no solution for positive x and y

(c) Have solution for all x

(d) Have solution for all y

12. The constraints

$-x_1 + x_2 \le 1, -x_1 + 3x_2 \le 9, x_1, x_2 \ge 0$ define on

(a) Bounded feasible space

(b) Unbounded feasible space

(c) Both bounded and unbounded feasible space

(d) None of these

13. The maximum vale of $P = x + 3y$ such that $2x + y \le 20, x + 2y \le 20, x \ge 0, y \ge 0$ is

(a) 10   (b) 60

(c) 30   (d) None of these

14. Shaded region is represented by

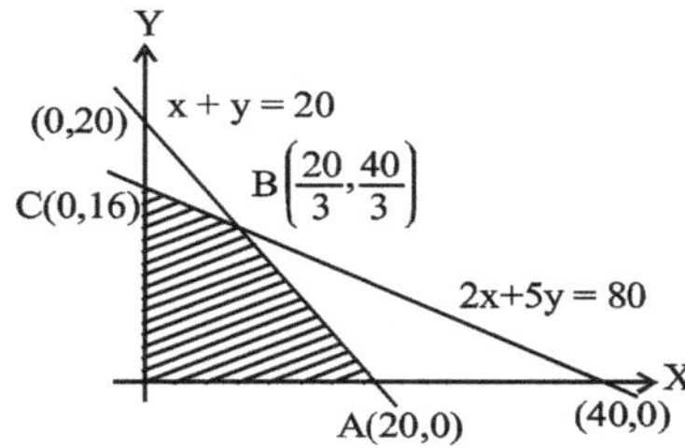

(a) $2x + 5y \ge 80, x + y \le 20, x \ge 0, y \le 0$

(b) $2x + 5y \ge 80, x + y \ge 20, x \ge 0, y \ge 0$

(c) $2x + 5y \le 80, x + y \le 20, x \ge 0, y \ge 0$

(d) $2x + 5y \le 80, x + y \le 20, x \le 0, y \le 0$

15. Minimize $z = \sum\limits_{j=1}^{n} \sum\limits_{i=1}^{m} c_{ij} x_{ij}$

Subject To: $\sum\limits_{j=1}^{n} x_{ij} \le a_i, i = 1, \ldots\ldots m$

$\sum\limits_{i=1}^{m} x_{ij} = b_j, j = 1, \ldots\ldots n$

is a (L.P.P.) with number of constraints

(a) $m + n$ (b) $m - n$ (c) mn (d) $\dfrac{m}{n}$

16. For the constraints of a L.P. problem given by $x_1 + 2x_2 \le 2000, x_1 + x_2 \le 1500$ and $x_2 \le 600$ and $x_1, x_2 \ge 0$, which one of the following points does not lie in the positive bounded region?

(a) $(1000, 0)$ (b) $(0, 500)$

(c) $(2, 0)$ (d) $(2000, 0)$

17. The maximum value of $z = 2x + 5y$ subject to the constraints $2x + 5y \le 10, x + 2y \ge 1, x - y \le 4, x \ge y \ge 0$, occurs at

(a) exactly one point   (b) exactly two points

(c) infinitely many points   (d) None of these

Chapter Test

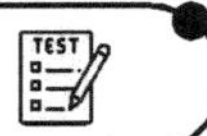

Time : 45 Minutes   **Max. Marks : 20**

Directions :

(i)   Questions number **1-12** carry **1 mark** each.

(ii)   Questions number **13-16** are **Very Short Answer Questions** and carry **2 marks** each.

Multiple Choice Questions

1. Corner points of feasible region of inequalities gives
(a) optimal solution of L.P.P.   (b) objective function
(c) constraints.   (d) linear assumption

2. The solution set of constraints $x + 2y \geq 11$, $3x + 4y \leq 30$, $2x + 5y \leq 30$ and $x \geq 0$, $y \geq 0$, includes the point
(a) $(2, 3)$ (b) $(3, 2)$ (c) $(3, 4)$ (d) $(4, 3)$.

3. For the following feasible region, the linear constraints are

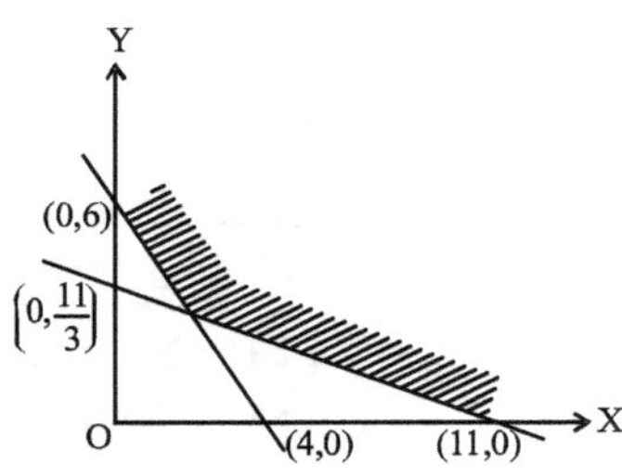

(a) $x \geq 0$, $y \geq 0$, $3x + 2y \geq 12$, $x + 3y \geq 11$
(b) $x \geq 0$, $y \geq 0$, $3x + 2y \leq 12$, $x + 3y \geq 11$
(c) $x \geq 0$, $y \geq 0$, $3x + 2y \leq 12$, $x + 3y \leq 11$
(d) None of these

4. The maximum value of xy subject to $x + y = 8$ is:
(a) 8   (b) 16   (c) 20   (d) 24

5 Shaded region is represented by

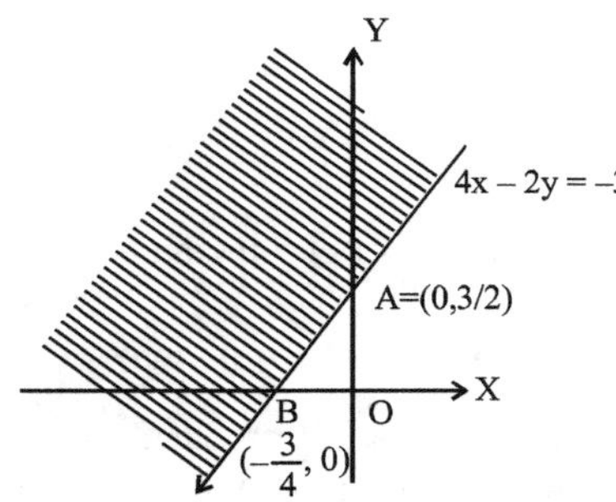

(a) $4x - 2y \leq 3$ (b) $4x - 2y \leq -3$
(c) $4x - 2y \geq 3$ (d) $4x - 2y \geq -3$

6. The optimal value of the objective function is attained at the points
(a) Given by intersection of inequations with axes only
(b) Given by intersection of inequations with x- axis only
(c) Given by corner points of the feasible region
(d) None of these

7. Which of the following statements is correct?
(a) Every L.P.P. admits an optimal solution
(b) A L.P.P. admits a unique optimal solution
(c) If a L.P.P. admits two optimal solutions, it has an infinite number of optimal solutions
(d) The set of all feasible solutions of a L.P.P. is not a convex set.

8. Inequation $y - x \leq 0$ represents
(a) The half plane that contains the positive x-axis
(b) Closed half plane above the line $y = x$ which contains positive y-axis
(c) Half plane that contains the negative x-axis
(d) None of these

9. The true statement for the graph of inequations $3x + 2y \leq 6$ and $6x + 4y \geq 20$, is
(a) Both graph are disjoint
(b) Both do not contain origin
(c) Both contain point $(1, 1)$
(d) None of these

10. The coordinates of the point for minimum value of $z = 7x - 8y$, subject to the condition $x + y \leq 20$, $y \geq 5$, $x \geq 0$, $y \geq 0$ is
(a) $(20, 0)$ (b) $(15, 5)$ (c) $(0, 5)$ (d) $(0, 20)$

One word Answer Questions

11. In first quadrant, what is the nature of the region represented by $2x + 3y - 5 \leq 0$ and $4x - 3y + 2 \leq 0$?

12. Find the point at which the maximum value of $z = 3x - 2y$, subject to the constraints $x + y \leq 5$, $x \geq 0$, $y \geq 0$, occurs.

Very Short Answer Questions

13. If (h, k) satisfies an equation $ax + by \geq 4$ then find the inequation that represent the half plane.

14. What is optimal feasible solution?

15. In which quadrants, the solution set of $2x + 3y > 0$, $x + 2y \leq 2$ lies?

16. Solve the following graphically
Maximise $Z = 4x + 3y$
Subject to constraints are: $x + 2y \leq 45$, $x \leq 20$, $y \leq 15$

Solutions

Practice Exercise-1

1. (b) 2. (d) 3. (d) 4. (d)
5. (d)
6. There is no feasible region, so no maximum value exist.
7. (a) **Objective function** : Linear function

   $Z = ax + by$, where a and b are constants, which has to be maximised or minimised is called a linear objective function.

   (b) **Feasible region :** The common region determined by all the constraints including non-negative constraints $x \geq 0$, $y \geq 0$ of an LPP is called the feasible region for the problem.

   (c) **Optimal feasible solution :** A feasible solution of a LPP is said to be an optimal feasible solution, if it also optimizes (maximizes or minimizes) the objective function.

8. Equation corresponding to $x + y \leq 2$ is $x + y = 2$ and the inequation $x + y \leq 2$ represents the shaded region (since $(0, 0)$ satisfies $x + y \leq 2$).

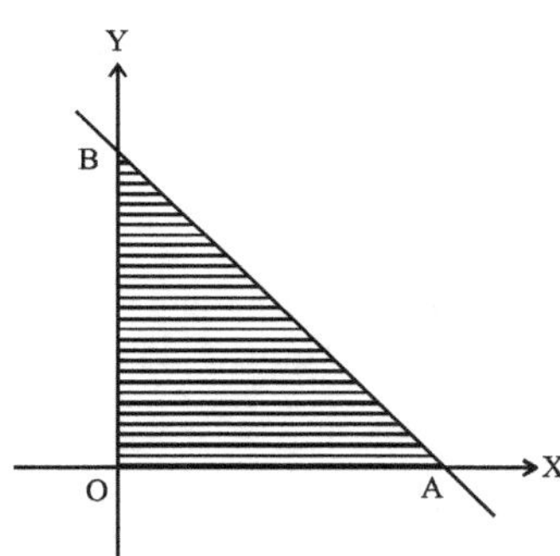

   Hence $z = 3x + 2y$ will have maximum value at O, A or B.
   $z]_A = 3x + 2y]_{(2,0)} = 6$, $z]_B = 3x + 2y]_{(0,2)} = 4$, $z]_O = 0$.
   Maximum value of $3x + 2y$ is, thus, 6 which occurs at $(2, 0)$.

NCERT Exercise-1

1. As $x \geq 0$, $y \geq 0$, therefore we shall shade the other inequalities in the first quadrant only. Now consider $x + y \leq 4$.

   Let $x + y = 4 \Rightarrow \dfrac{x}{4} + \dfrac{y}{4} = 1$

   Thus the line has 4 and 4 as intercepts along the axes. Now $(0, 0)$ satisfies the inequation i.e., $0 + 0 \leq 4$. Now shaded region OAB is the feasible solution.

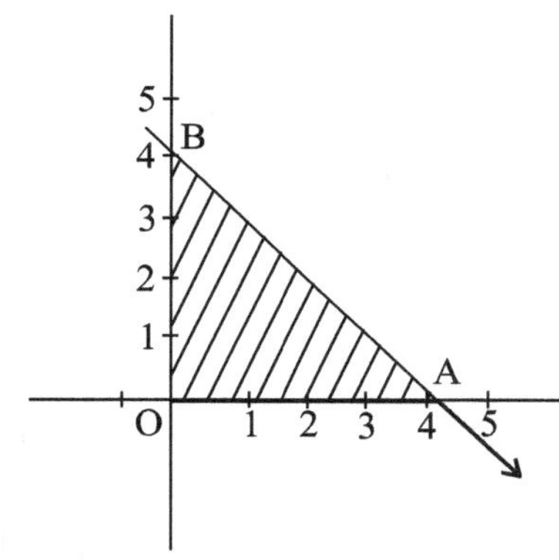

   Now its corners are O $(0,0)$, A $(4, 0)$, B $(0,4)$.
   At O $(0, 0)$ $Z = 0$
   At A $(4, 0)$, $Z = 3 \times 4 = 12$
   At B $(0, 4)$, $Z = 4 \times 4 = 16$
   Now max $Z = 16$ at $x = 0$, $y = 4$.

2. Objective function $Z = -3x + 4y$
   constraints are $x + 2y \leq 8$,
   $3x + 2y \leq 12$, $x \geq 0$, $y \geq 0$

   (i) Consider the line $x + 2y = 8$. It pass through A $(8, 0)$ and B $(0, 4)$, putting $x = 0$, $y = 0$ in $x + 2y \leq 8$, $0 \leq 8$ which is true.

   $\Rightarrow$ region $x + 2y \leq 8$ lies on and below AB.

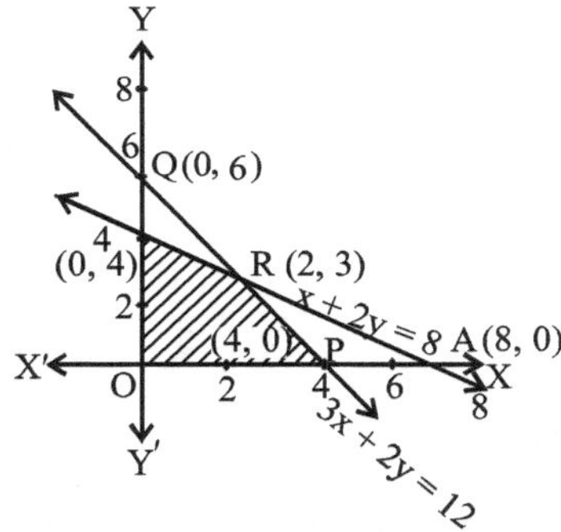

   (ii) The line $3x + 2y = 12$ passes through P $(4, 0)$, Q $(0, 6)$ putting $x = 0$, $y = 0$ in
   $3x + 2y \leq 12$
   $\Rightarrow$ $0 \leq 12$, which is true.
   $\therefore$ Region $3x + 2y \leq 12$ lies on and below PQ.

   (iii) $x \geq 0$ the region lies on and to the right of y-axis.

   (iv) $y \geq 0$ lies on and above x-axis.

   (v) Solving the equations $x + 2y = 8$ and $3x + 2y = 12$ we get $x = 2$, $y = 3$ $\Rightarrow$ R is $(2,3)$ where AB and PQ. intersect. The shaded region OPRB is the feasible region.

   At P $(4,0)$ $Z = -3x + 4y = -12 + 0 = -12$
   At R $(2,3)$ $Z = -6 + 12 = 6$
   At B $(0,4)$ $Z = 0 + 16 = 16$
   At Q $(0,0)$ $Z = 0$
   Thus minimum value of Z is -12 at P $(4, 0)$

3. The objective function is $Z = 5x + 3y$ constraints are
$3x + 5y \le 15,\ 5x + 2y \le 10,\ x \ge 0,\ y \ge 0$

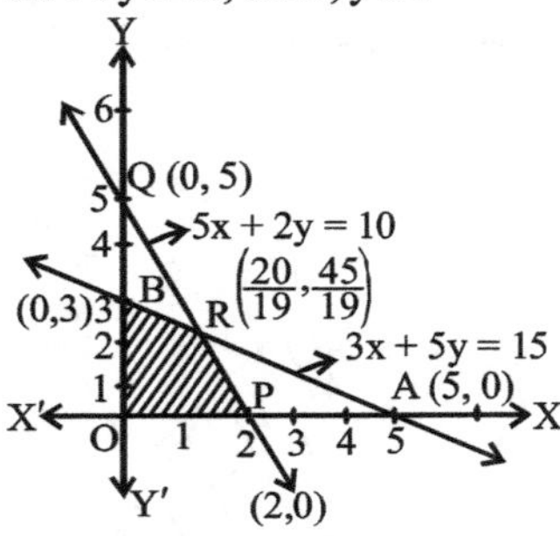

(i) Consider the line $3x + 5y = 15$ which passes through A $(5,0)$ and B $(0,3)$ putting $x = 0, y = 0$ in $3x + 5y \le 15$

$\Rightarrow \quad 0 \le 15$ which is true.

$\therefore$ Region $3x + 5y \le 15$ lies on and below AB.

(ii) The line $5x + 2y = 10$ passes through P $(2, 0)$ and Q $(0, 5)$, Put $x = 0, y = 0$ in $5x + 2y \le 10$

$\therefore \quad 0 \le 10$ which is true.

$\therefore$ Region $5x + 2y \le 10$ lies on and below PQ.

(iii) $x \ge 0$ Region lies on and to the right of y-axis.

(iv) $y \ge 0$ lies on the above x-axis.

(v) The feasible region is the shaded area OPRB. Solving the equation $3x + 5y = 15$ and $5x + 2y = 10$

$\Rightarrow \quad x = \dfrac{20}{19}$ and $y = \dfrac{45}{19}$

$\Rightarrow$ AB and PQ intersect at R $\left(\dfrac{20}{19}, \dfrac{45}{19}\right)$

At P $(2, 0)$ $Z = 5x + 3y = 10 + 0 = 10$, At R $\left(\dfrac{20}{19}, \dfrac{45}{19}\right)$,

$Z = \dfrac{100}{19} + \dfrac{135}{19} = \dfrac{235}{19} = 12\dfrac{7}{19}$

At B $(0, 3)$ $Z = 9$, AT O $(0, 0)$ $Z = 0$,

$\therefore$ Maximum value of $Z = \dfrac{235}{19}$ at $\left(\dfrac{20}{19}, \dfrac{45}{19}\right)$

4. For plotting the graph of $x + 3y = 3$, we have the following table:

x	0	3
y	1	0

Plot the points $(0, 1)$ and $(3, 0)$ on a graph paper and join them to get a line which represents the equation $x + 3y = 3$. For equation $x + y = 2$, we have the following table:

x	1	0
y	1	2

Plot the points $(1,1)$ and $(0,2)$ on the graph paper and join them to get the line representing the equation $x + y = 2$.

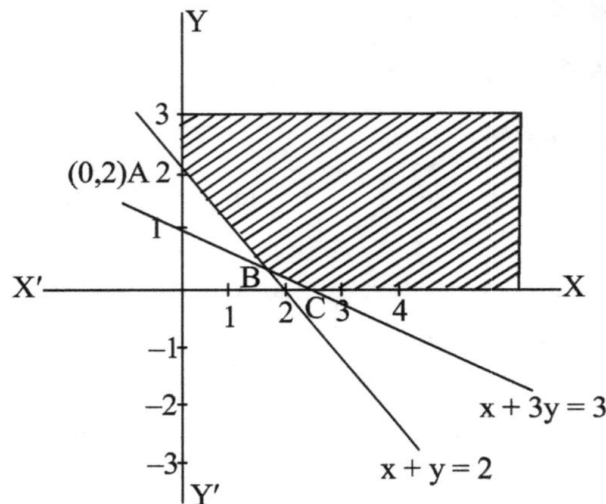

The feasible portion represented by the inequalities $x + 3y \ge 3, x + y \ge 2$ and $x, y \ge 0$ is ABC which is shaded in the figure. The co-ordinates of point B are $\left(\dfrac{3}{2}, \dfrac{1}{2}\right)$ which can be obtained by solving $x + y = 2$ and $x + 3y = 3$.

$$Z = 3x + 5y$$

At $(0, 2)$, $\qquad Z = 3 \times 0 + 5 \times 2 = 10$

At $B\left(\dfrac{3}{2}, \dfrac{1}{2}\right)$, $\quad Z = 3 \times \dfrac{3}{2} + 5 \times \dfrac{1}{2} = 7$

At C $(3, 0)$, $\qquad Z = 3 \times 3 + 5 \times 0 = 9$

So, Z is minimum is $= 7$ when

$$x = \dfrac{3}{2} \text{ and } y = \dfrac{1}{2}.$$

5. Consider $x + 2y \le 10$

Let $x + 2y = 10 \quad \Rightarrow \quad \dfrac{x}{10} + \dfrac{y}{5} = 1$

Now $(0,0)$ satisfies the inequation, therefore the half plane containing $(0,0)$ is the required plane.

Again $\quad 3x + 2y \le 15$

Let $3x + y = 15 \Rightarrow \dfrac{x}{5} + \dfrac{y}{15} = 1$

It is also satisfies by $(0,0)$ and its required half plane contains $(0,0)$.

Now double shaded region in the first quadrant contains the solution.

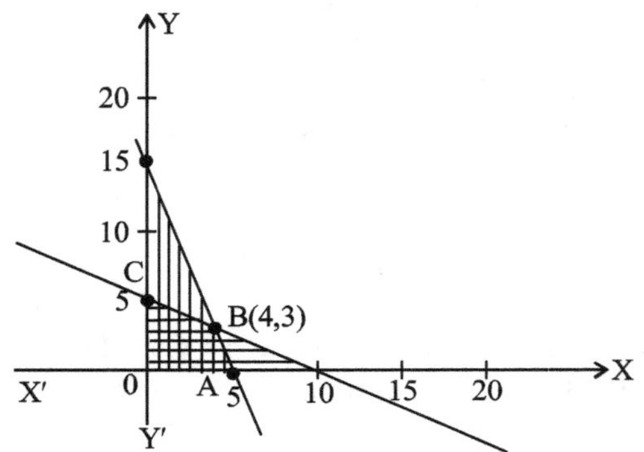

Now OABC, represents the feasible region

$$Z = 3x + 2y$$

At O $(0, 0)$, $\quad Z = 0 + 0 = 0$
At A $(5, 0)$, $\quad Z = 15$
At B $(4, 3)$, $\quad Z = 18$
At C $(0, 5)$, $\quad Z = 10$
Now Max $Z = 18$ at $x = 4, y = 3$.

6. Consider $2x + y \geq 3$
Let $2x + y = 3 \Rightarrow y = 3 - 2x$

	A	B	C
x	0	2	–1
y	3	–1	5

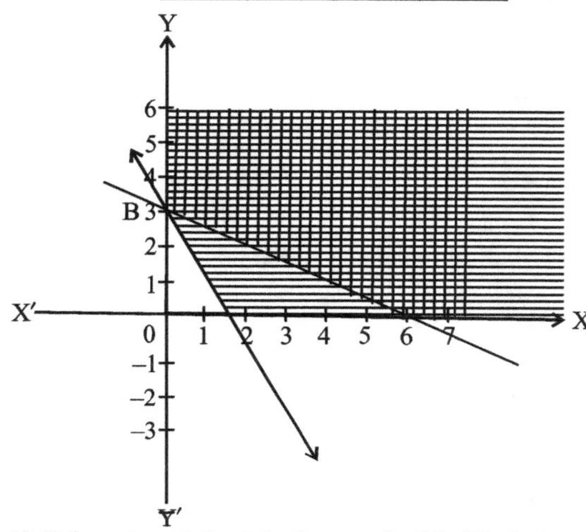

$(0, 0)$ is not contained in the required half plane as $(0, 0)$ does not satisfy the inequation $2x + y \geq 3$.

Again consider $x + 2y \geq 6$

Let $x + 2y = 6 \Rightarrow \dfrac{x}{6} + \dfrac{y}{3} = 1$

Here also $(0, 0)$ does not contain the required half plane. The double-shaded region XABY′ is the solution set. Its corners are A $(6, 0)$ and B $(0, 3)$.
At A, $Z = 6 + 0 = 6$
At B, $Z = 0 + 2 \times 3 = 6$
We see that at both points the value of $Z = 6$ which is minimum. In fact at every point on the line AB makes $Z = 6$ which is also minimum.

7. The objective function is $Z = 5x + 10y$ contraints are $x + 2y \leq 120, x + y \geq 60, x - 2y \geq 0, x, y \geq 0$

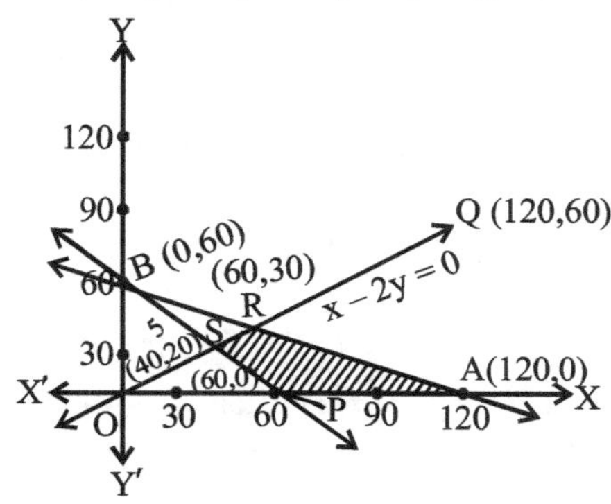

(i) The line $x + 2y = 120$ passes through A $(120, 0)$ and B $(0, 60)$ putting $x = 0, y = 0$ is $x + 2y \leq 120$ we get $0 \leq 12$ which is true.
$\Rightarrow \quad x + 2y \leq 120$ lies on AB and below AB.

(ii) The line $x + y = 60$ passes through P $(60, 0)$ and B $(0, 60)$ putting $x = 0$ and $y = 0$ in $x + y \geq 60$, We get $0 \geq 60$ which is not true.
$\Rightarrow \quad x + y \geq 60$ lies on PB.

(iii) The line $x - 2y = 0$ passes through O $(0, 0)$ and Q $(120, 60)$ putting $x = 60, y = 0$ is $x - 2y \geq 0, 60 \geq 0$ which is true.
$\Rightarrow \quad x - 2y \geq 0$ region is on OQ

(iv) $x \geq 0$ lies on y-axis and on its right.

(v) $y \geq 0$ lies on x-axis $\Rightarrow$ feasible region is PARS which has been shaded.

(a) Sloving OQ : $x - 2y = 0$ and AB : $x + 2y = 120$
$\Rightarrow x = 60, y = 30 \Rightarrow$ R is $(60, 30)$

(b) Solving OQ : $x - 2y = 0$ and PB : $x + y = 60$, $x = 40$, $y = 20 \Rightarrow$ S is $(40, 20)$

At A $(120, 0)$, $\quad Z = 5x + 10y = 600 \quad$ max^m
At R $(60, 30)$, $\quad Z = 300 + 300 = 600 \quad$ max^m
At S $(40, 20)$, $\quad Z = 200 + 200 = 400$
At P $(60, 0)$, $\quad Z = 300 + 0 = 300 \quad$ min^m.
$\Rightarrow$ Minimum value of Z at P is 300 at P$(60, 0)$ and maximum value of Z is 600 at all points joining A $(120, 0)$ and R $(60, 30)$.

8. Consider $x + 2y \geq 100$

Let $x + 2y = 100 \Rightarrow \dfrac{x}{100} + \dfrac{y}{50} = 1$

Now $x + 2y \geq 100$ represents which does not include $(0, 0)$ as it does not made it true.

Again consider $\quad 2x - y \leq 0$
Let $2x - y = 0$ or $y = 2x$

x	0	25	50	100
y	0	50	100	200

Now let the test point be $(10, 0)$
$\therefore \quad 2 \times 10 - 0 \leq 0$ which is false.
$\therefore \quad$ The required half does not contain $(10, 0)$.

Again consider $2x + y \leq 200$

Let $\quad 2x + y = 200 \Rightarrow \dfrac{x}{100} + \dfrac{y}{100} = 1$

Now $(0, 0)$ satisfies $2x + y \leq 200$
$\therefore \quad$ The required half plane contains $(0, 0)$.

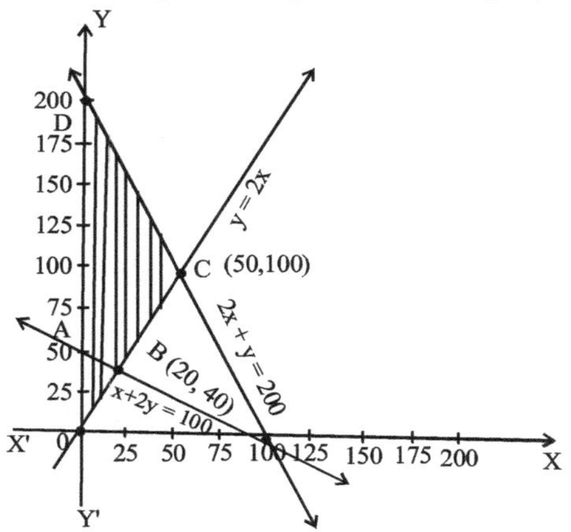

Now triple shaded region is ABCDA which is the required feasible region.

At A (0, 50), $Z = x + 2y = 0 + 2 \times 50 = 100$

At B (20 , 40), $Z = 20 + 2 \times 40 = 100$

At C (50, 100), $Z = 50 + 2 \times 100 = 250$

At D(0, 200), $Z = 0 + 2 \times 200 = 400$

Thus maximum $Z = 400$ at $x = 0$, $y = 200$ and minimum $Z = 100$ at $x = 0$, $y = 50$ or $x = 20$, $y = 40$

9. The objective function is $Z = -x + 2y$. The constraints are $x \geq 3$, $x + y \geq 5$, $x + 2y \geq 6$, $y \geq 0$

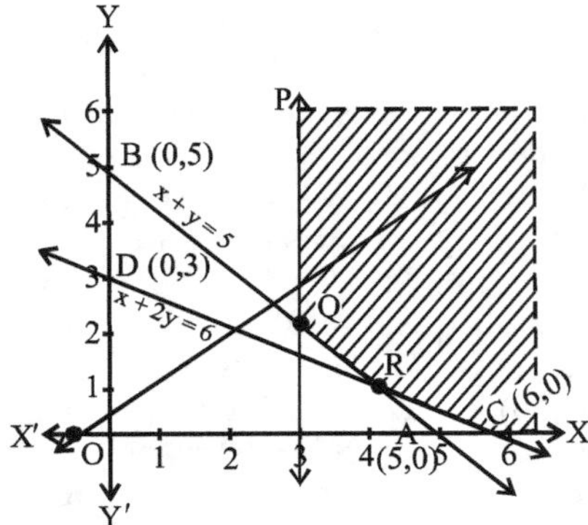

(i)   The line $x + y = 5$ passes through A (5, 0), B (0, 5) putting $x = 0$, $y = 0$ in $x + y \geq 5$, we get $0 \geq 5$ which is not true

$\Rightarrow$ $x + y \geq 5$ liles on and above AB.

(ii)   The line $x + 2y = 6$ passes through C (6, 0), D (0, 3) putting $x = 0$, $y = 0$ in $x + 2y \geq 6$. we get $0 \geq 6$ which is not true. $\Rightarrow x + 2y \geq 6$ lies on and above CD.

(iii) $x \geq 3$ lies on PQ or on the right of it.

(iv) $y \geq 0$ lies on and above x-axis.

(v)   The feasible region is PQRCX.

(a)   Solving $x = 3$ and $x + y = 5$, we get $x = 3$, $y = 2$

    $\therefore$ these lines meet at Q (3, 2)

(b) $x + y = 5$ and $x + 2y = 6$ meet at R *i.e.,* the point R is (4, 1)

At Q (3, 2) $Z = -x + 2y = -3 + 4 = 1$ max^m

At R (4, 1) $Z = -4 + 2 = -2$

At C (6, 0) $Z = -6 + 0 = -6$ min^m

The maximum value of Z is 1 is but the feasible region is unbounded. Consider the inequality $-x + 2y > 1$.

The line $-x + 2y = 1$ passes through $(-1, 0)$ and $(0, 1/2)$ putting $x = 0$, $y = 0$ in $-x + 2y > 1$, we get $0 > 1$ which is not true.

$\Rightarrow$ $-x + 2y > 1$ lies above the line $-x + 2y = 1$ feasible region of $-x + 2y > 1$ have many points in common.

Therefore, there is no maximum value.

10. Objective function $Z = x + y$, constraints $x - y \leq -1$, $-x + y \leq 0$ x , $y \geq 0$

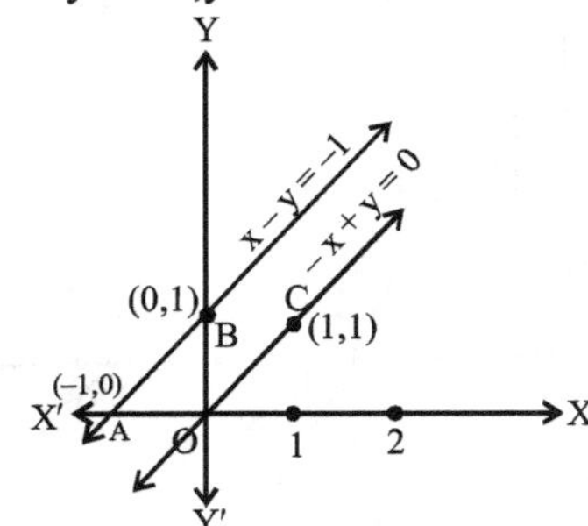

(i)   The line $x - y = -1$ passes through $(-1, 0)$ and $(0, 1)$ putting $x = 0$, $y = 0$ in $x - y \leq -1$ we get $0 \leq -1$ which is not true.

$\Rightarrow$ $x - y \leq -1$ lies on and above AB, $x - y = -1$

(ii)   The line $-x + y = 0$ passes through O $(0, 0)$ and C (1, 1) putting $x = 0$, $y = 1$ in $-x + y \leq 0$ we get $1 \leq 0$ which is not true.

$\Rightarrow$ $-x + y \leq 0$ lies on and below OC.

(iii) $x \geq 0$ lies on and on the right of y-axis.

(iv) $y \geq 0$ lies on and above x-axis. There is no common region *i.e.,* there is no feasible region.

There is no maximum value of Z.

1.   **(a)** $Z = ax + by$

      Maximum value at (2, 4) is

      $Z = a(2) + b(4) = 2a + 4b$ ...(1)

      Maximum value at (4, 0)

      $Z = a(4) + b(0)$

      $Z = 4a$ ...(2)

      Maximum value occur at both points.

      So it should have equal value

      $2a + 4b = 4a$ [from (1) and (2)]

      $4b = 4a - 2a$

      $4b = 2a$

      $2b = a$

      $\Rightarrow$ $a = 2b$

2.   Since $x + 2y \geq 100, 2x + y \leq 200, 2x - y \leq 0, x \geq 0, y \geq 0$.

Converting the given inequations into equation, we have

$x + 2y = 100, 2x + y = 200, 2x - y = 0, x = 0, y = 0$

The line $x + 2y = 100$ meets the x- axis at $A_1 (100, 0)$ and y-axis $B_1 (0, 50)$. Join these points to obtain the line. $x + 2y = 100$. It is clear that $(0, 0)$ does not satisfy the inequation $x + 2y \geq 100$. Thus, the region not containing the origin represents the solution set of the inequation $x - 2y \geq 100$.

The line $2x + y = 200$ meets the X-axis at $A_1 (100, 0)$ and Y-axis $B_2 (0, 200)$. Join these points to obtain the line $2x + y = 200$. It is clear that $(0, 0)$ satisfies the inequation $2x + y \leq 200$. Thus, the region containing the origin represents the solution set of the inequation $2x + y \leq 200$.

The line $2x - y = 0$ is the line that passes through the origin.

Point of intersection of line $2x - y = 0$ with line $2x + y = 200$ is R (50, 100)

Point of intersection of line $2x - y = 0$ with line $x + 2y = 100$ is Q (20, 40)

For $x \geq 0$ and $y \geq 0$, the first quadrant is the region represented by the inequations $x \geq 0$ and $y \geq 0$.

The feasible region determined by the system of constraints is shown below.

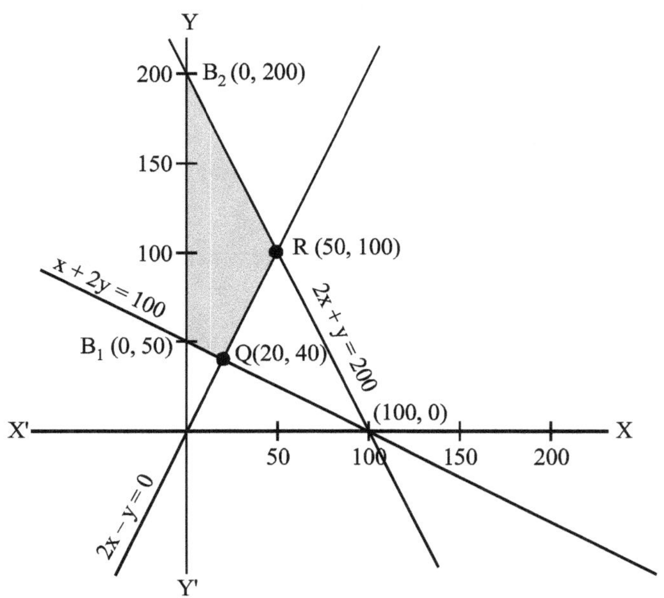

The corner points of the feasible region are $B_1(0,50), B_2(0,200), R(50,100)$ and $Q(20,40)$.

The values of Z at these corner points are as follows.

Corner points	Value of the objective function $Z = x + 2y$
$B_1(0,50)$	$Z = 0 + 2 \times 50 = 100$
$B_2(0.200)$	$Z = 0 + 2 \times 200 = 400$ (maximum)
$R(50, 100)$	$Z = 50 + 2 \times 100 = 250$
$Q(20.40)$	$Z = 20 + 2 \times 40 = 100$

Thus the maximum value of the objective function Z is 400 which is obtained at $x = 0$ and $y = 200$.

3. The feasible region determined by the constraints,

$x + 2y \le 120, x + y \ge 60, x - 2y \ge 0, x \ge 0$, and $y \ge 0$ is as follow.

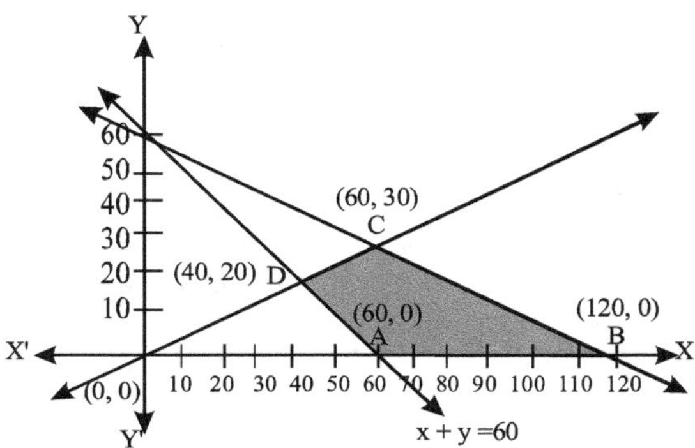

The corner points of the feasible region are A (60, 0), B (120, 0), C (60, 30) and D (40, 20).

The values of Z at these corner points are as follows.

Corner points	$Z = 5x + 10y$	
$A(60,0)$	300	$\rightarrow$ Minimum
$B(120,0)$	600	$\rightarrow$ Maximum
$C(60,30)$	600	$\rightarrow$ Maximum
$D(40,20)$	400	

$\therefore$ The minimum value of Z is 300 at (60, 0).

4. The given constraints are

$$2x + 4y \le 8 \qquad \text{..... (1)}$$
$$3x + y \le 6 \qquad \text{.... (2)}$$
$$x + y \le 4 \qquad \text{..... (3)}$$
$$x \ge 0, y \ge 0$$

We need to maximise the objective function $z = 2x + 5y$.

Converting the inequations into equations, we obtain the line

$2x + 4y = 8, 3x + y = 6, x + y = 4, x = 0$ and $y = 0$.

These lines are drawn and the feasible region of the LPP is shaded.

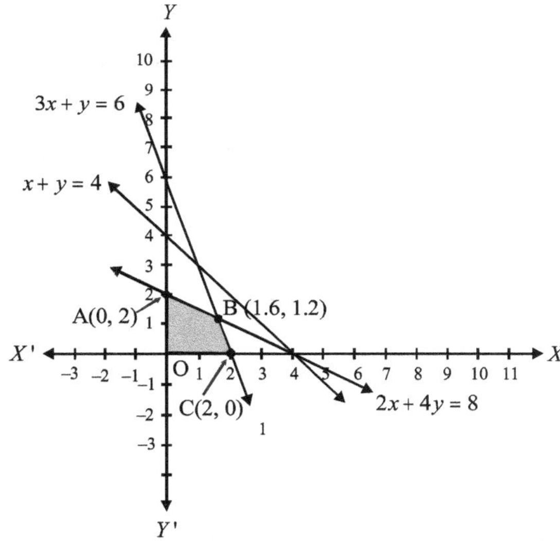

The coordinates of the corner points of the feasible region are 0 (0, 0), A (0, 2) B (1. 6, 1.2) and C (2, 0). The value of the objective function at these points are given in the following table.

Points	Value of the objective function $z = 2x + 5y$
$O(0,0)$	$2 \times 0 + 5 \times 0 = 0$
$A(0,2)$	$2 \times 0 + 5 \times 2 = 10$
$B(1.6,1.2)$	$2 \times 1.6 + 5 \times 1.2 = 9.2$
$C(2,0)$	$2 \times 2 + 5 \times 0 = 4$

Out of these value of z, the maximum value of z is 10 which is attained at the point (0, 2). Thus, the maximum value of z is 10

1. Maximise $Z = 11x + 7y$ ...(i)
$2x + y \leq 6$ ...(ii)
$x \leq 2$ ...(iii)
$x \geq 0, y \geq 0$ ...(iv)
The graph is as follows

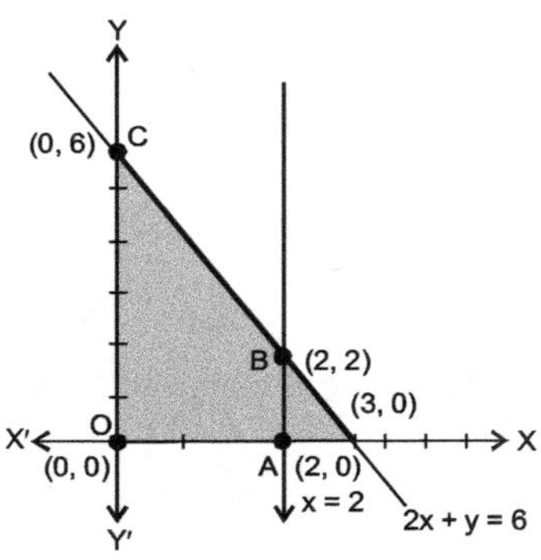

Corner points	Value of Z
(0, 0)	0
(2, 0)	22
(2, 2)	36
(0, 6)	42 ← Maximum

Hence, the maximum value of Z is 42 at (0, 6)

2. Maximise $Z = 3x + 4y$, subject to the constraints
$x + y \leq 1, x \geq 0, y \geq 0$
The co-ordinates of corner points O, A and B are (0, 0), (1, 0) and (0, 1), respectively.

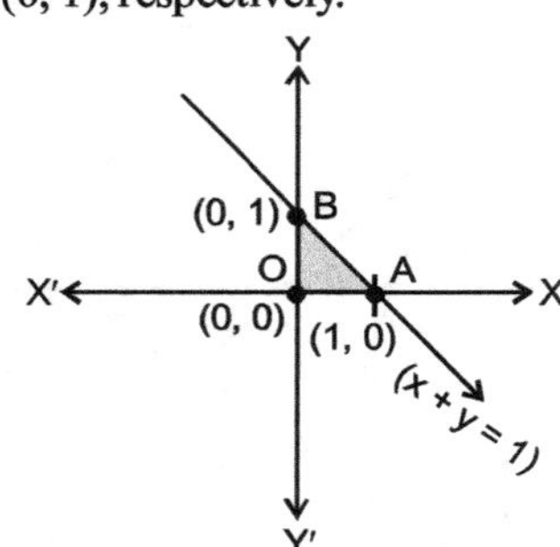

Corner points	Value of Z
(0, 0)	0
(1, 0)	3
(0, 1)	4 ← Maximum

Hence, the maximum value of Z is 4 at (0, 1)

3. Maximise $Z = 11x + 7y$, subject to the constraints $x \leq 3, y \leq 2, x \geq 0$ and $y \geq 0$.

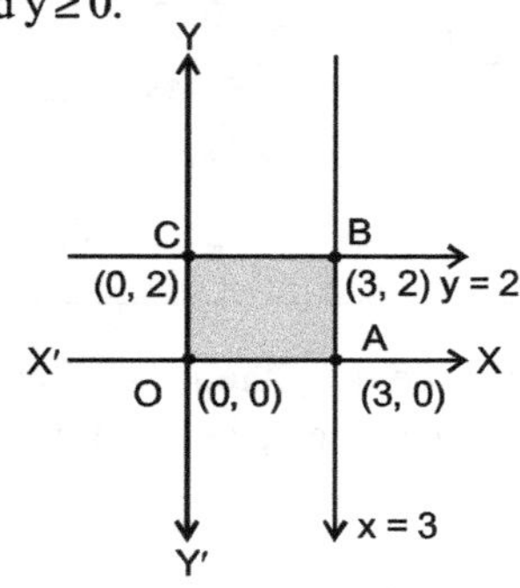

The coordinates of corner points are (0, 0), (3, 0), (3, 2) and (0, 2), respectively.

Corner points	Value of Z
(0, 0)	0
(3, 0)	33
(3, 2)	47 ← Maximum
(0, 2)	14

Maximum value is 47 at $x = 3, y = 2$.

4. Objective function is $Z = 13x - 15y$ constraints are $x + y \leq 7, 2x - 3y + 6 \geq 0, x \geq 0, y \geq 0$.

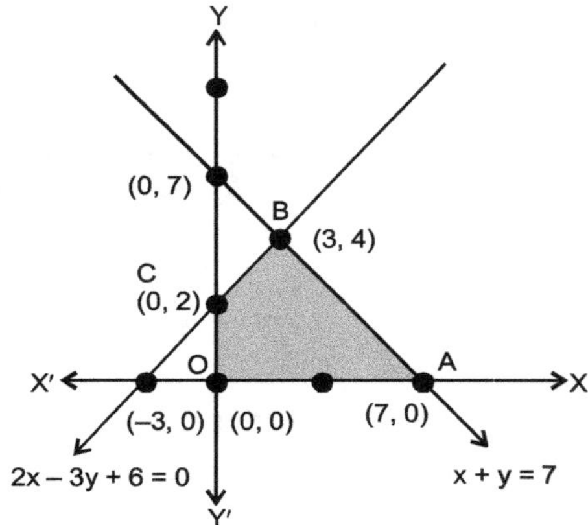

Coordinates of corner points of shaded region are O (0, 0), A(7, 0) B(3, 4) and C(0, 2), respectively.

Corner points	Value of Z
(0, 0)	0
(7, 0)	91
(3, 4)	–21
(0, 2)	–30 ← Minimum

Hence, the minimum value of Z is (– 30) at (0, 2).

5. points O, A, E and D are (0, 0), (52, 0), (44, 16) and (0, 38), respectively

Here, $Z = 3x + 4y$

∵ $2x + y = 104$ and $2x + 4y = 152$

⇒ $-3y = -48$

⇒ $y = 16$ and $x = 44$

Corner points	Z = 3x + 4y
(0, 0)	0
(52, 0)	156
(44, 16)	196 Maximum
(0, 38)	152

Maximum value of Z is 196 at $x = 44, y = 16$.

6. Corner points are (0, 0), (7, 0), (3, 4) and (0, 2), $Z = 5x + 7y$.

Corner points	Value of Z
(0, 0)	0
(7, 0)	35
(3, 4)	43 ← Maximum
(0, 2)	14

Hence, the maximum value of Z is 43 at (3, 4).

7. $Z = 11x + 7y$

$\because \quad x + 3y = 9 \text{ and } x + y = 5$

$\Rightarrow \quad 2y = 4$

$\therefore \quad y = 2 \text{ and } x = 3$

Point of intersection of $x + y = 5$ and $x + 3y = 9$ is $(3, 2)$

Corner points	Value of Z
$(0, 3)$	$21 \leftarrow$ Minimum
$(3, 2)$	47
$(0, 5)$	35

Hence, the minimum value of Z is 21 at $(0, 3)$.

8. Corner points are A $(4, 0)$, B $(2, 1)$ and C $(0, 3)$.

We have $\quad Z = 4x + y$

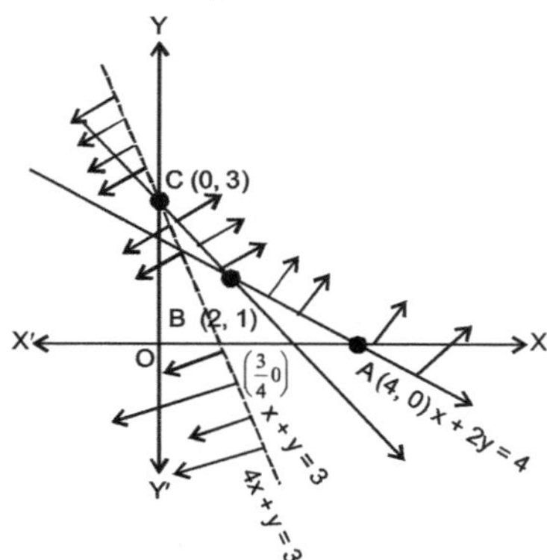

Corner points	Value of Z
$(4, 0)$	16
$(2, 1)$	9
$(0, 3)$	$3 \leftarrow$ Minimum

From the shown graph above, its is clear that there is no point in common with feasible region and hence Z has minimum value 3 at $(0, 3)$.

9. It is clear that the coordinates of corner points are P, Q, R, S

$\left(\dfrac{3}{13}, \dfrac{24}{13}\right), \left(\dfrac{18}{7}, \dfrac{2}{7}\right), \left(\dfrac{7}{2}, \dfrac{3}{4}\right)$ and $\left(\dfrac{3}{2}, \dfrac{15}{4}\right)$.

Putting these values in objective function $Z = x + 2y$.

Corner points	Value of Z
$\left(\dfrac{3}{13}, \dfrac{24}{13}\right)$	$\dfrac{3}{13} + \dfrac{48}{13} = \dfrac{51}{13} = 3\dfrac{12}{13}$
$\left(\dfrac{18}{7}, \dfrac{2}{7}\right)$	$\dfrac{18}{7} + \dfrac{4}{7} = \dfrac{22}{7} = 3\dfrac{1}{7}$ Minimum
$\left(\dfrac{7}{2}, \dfrac{3}{4}\right)$	$\dfrac{7}{2} + \dfrac{6}{4} = \dfrac{20}{4} = 5$
$\left(\dfrac{3}{2}, \dfrac{15}{4}\right)$	$\dfrac{3}{2} + \dfrac{30}{4} = \dfrac{36}{4} = 9$ Maximum

Hence, the maximum and minimum values of Z are 9 and $3\dfrac{1}{7}$, respectively.

1. **(d)** We have, $|x| > b, \, b > 0$

$\Rightarrow x < -b \text{ and } x > b \Rightarrow x \in (-\infty, -b) \cup (b, \infty)$

2. **(c)** Since, $|x - 1| > 5$ So, $(x - 1) < -5$ or $(x - 1) > 5$

$\qquad\qquad [\, |x| > a \Rightarrow x < -a \text{ or } x > a \,]$

Therefore, $x < -4$ or $x > 6$

Hence, $x \in (-\infty, -4) \cup (6, \infty)$

3. **(b)** Given, $|x + 2| \le 9$

$\Rightarrow -9 \le x + 2 \le 9$

$\Rightarrow -11 \le x \le 7$

4. **(a)** The graph represents $x > -5$ and $x < 5$. So, $|x| < 5$.

5. **(d)**   **6.** **(a)**   **7.** **(b)**

8. **(c)** Change the inequalities into equations and draw the graph of lines, thus we get the required feasible region as shown below.

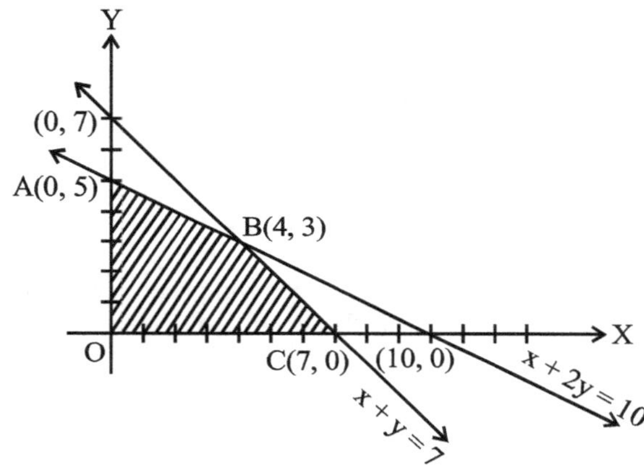

The region bounded by the vertices
$\qquad$ A$(0, 5)$, B$(4, 3)$, C$(7, 0)$.

The objective function is maximum at C$(7, 0)$ and

Max $z = 5 \times 7 + 2 \times 0 = 35$.

9. **(b)** Z is 7 minimum at $\left(\dfrac{3}{2}, \dfrac{1}{2}\right)$

10. **(c)** Z is 325·5 maximum at $\left(\dfrac{21}{2}, \dfrac{69}{2}\right)$

11. **(a)** Following figure will be obtained on drawing the graphs of given inequations.

From $3x - y \ge 3$,

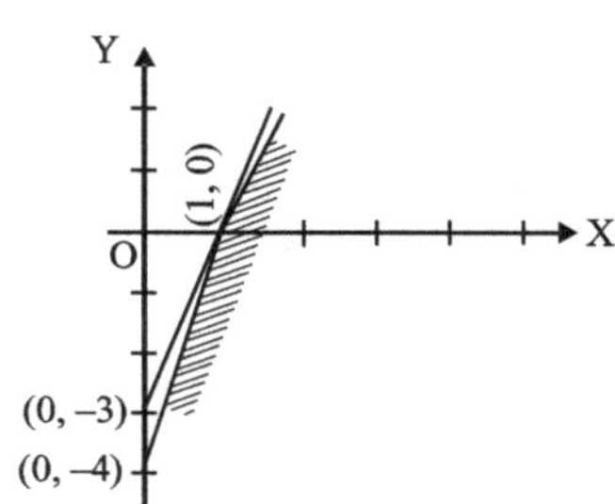

$\Rightarrow \dfrac{x}{1} + \dfrac{y}{-3} = 1$

From $4x - y > 4$,

$$\Rightarrow \frac{x}{1} + \frac{y}{-4} = 1$$

Clearly the common region of both is true for positive value of (x, y).

12. **(b)** It is clear from the graph, the constraints define the unbounded feasible space.

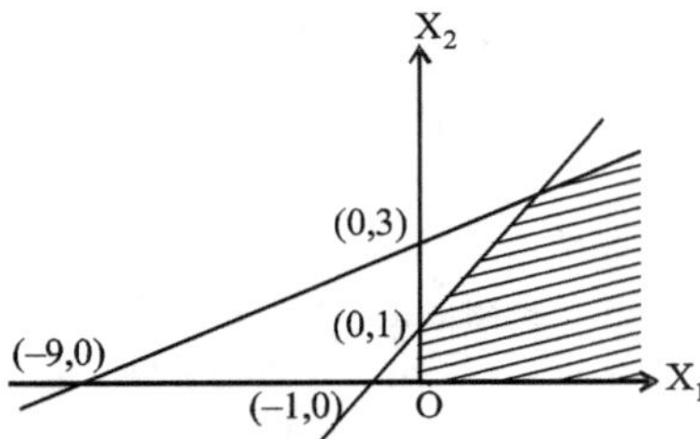

13. **(c)** Obviously, $P = x + 3y$ will be maximm at $(0, 10)$.

$\therefore P = 0 + 3 \times 10 = 30$.

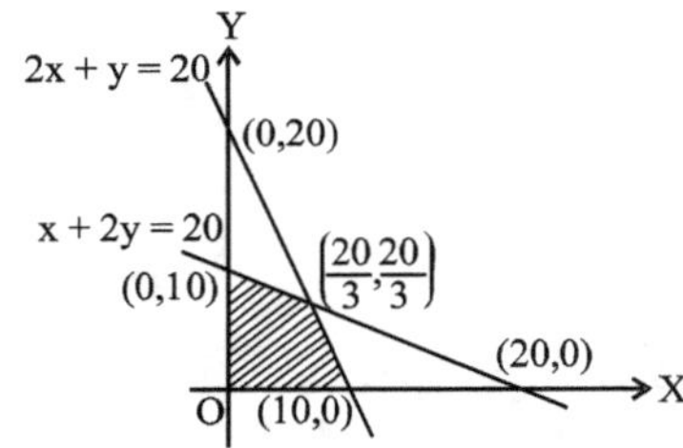

14. **(c)** In given all equations, the origin is present in shaded area, option (c) satisfy this condition.

15. **(a)** Condition (i)

$i = 1, x_{11} + x_{12} + x_{13} + \ldots\ldots\ldots + x_{1n}$

$i = 2, x_{21} + x_{22} + x_{23} + \ldots\ldots\ldots + x_{2n}$

$i = 3, x_{31} + x_{32} + x_{33} + \ldots\ldots\ldots + x_{3n}$

$\ldots\ldots\ldots\ldots\ldots\ldots\ldots$

$i = m, x_{m1} + x_{m2} + x_{m3} + \ldots\ldots\ldots + x_{mn} \rightarrow m$ constraints

Condition (ii)

$j = 1, x_{11} + x_{21} + x_{31} + \ldots\ldots\ldots + x_{m1}$

$j = 2, x_{12} + x_{22} + x_{32} + \ldots\ldots\ldots + x_{m2}$

$\ldots\ldots\ldots\ldots$

$j = n, x_{1n} + x_{2n} + x_{3n} + \ldots\ldots + x_{mn} \rightarrow n$ constraints

$\therefore$ total constraints $= m + n$.

16. **(d)** Clearly point $(2000, 0)$ is outside.

17. **(c)** We find that the feasible region is on the same side of the line $2x + 5y = 10$ as the origin, on the same side of the line $x - y = 4$ as the origin and on the opposite side of the line $x + 2y = 1$ from the origin. Moreover, the lines meet the coordinate axes at $(5, 0)$, $(0, 2)$; $(1, 0)$, $(0, 1/2)$ and $(4, 0)$. The lines $x - y = 4$ and $2x + 5y = 10$ intersect at $\left(\frac{30}{7}, \frac{2}{7}\right)$.

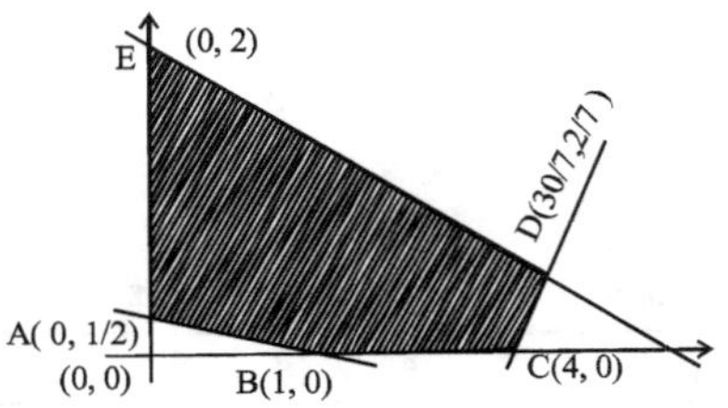

The values of the objective function at the vertices of the pentagon are:

(i) $Z = 0 + \dfrac{5}{2} = \dfrac{5}{2}$ 　　(ii) $Z = 2 + 0 = 2$

(iii) $Z = 8 + 0 = 8$ 　　(iv) $Z = \dfrac{60}{7} + \dfrac{10}{7} = 10$

(v) $Z = 0 + 10 = 10$

The maximum value 10 occurs at the points $D(30/7, 2/7)$ and $E(0, 2)$. Since D and E are adjacent vertices, the objective function has the same maximum value 10 at all the points on the lines DE.

Chapter Test 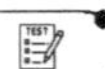

1. **(a)**

2. **(c)** Obviously, solution set of constraints included the point $(3, 4)$.

3. **(a)**

4. **(b)** (xy) will be maximum at $\dfrac{x}{1} = \dfrac{y}{1} = \dfrac{8}{1+1}$

$\Rightarrow x = 4, y = 4$

$\therefore$ Maximum value of $xy = 4 \times 4 = 16$

5 **(d)**

6. **(c)**

7. **(c)**

8. **(a)**

9. **(a)** The equations, corresponding to inequalities $3x + 2y \leq 6$ and $6x + 4y \geq 20$, are $3x + 2y = 6$ and $6x + 4y = 20$, So the lines represented by these equation are parallel. Hence the graphs are disjoint.

10. **(d)**

11. Bounded in first quadrant.

12. $(5, 0)$

13. $ax + by = 4$

15. First, second and third quadrants.

16. $Z = 117.5$ at $(20, 12.5)$ is the maximum value of Z.

www.ingramcontent.com/pod-product-compliance
Lightning Source LLC
LaVergne TN
LVHW080540200726
843508LV00008B/1484